Managerial Motivation

and

Compensation

Managerial Motivation
and
Compensation

A Selection of Readings

edited by

HENRY L. TOSI

ROBERT J. HOUSE

MARVIN D. DUNNETTE

1972
MSU Business Studies

Division of Research
Graduate School of Business Administration
Michigan State University, East Lansing

ISBN: 0-87744-101-4
Library of Congress Catalog Card Number: 72-619500
Copyright © 1972   ʀ ⅼⱨ
By the Board of Trustees of Michigan State University
East Lansing, Michigan

PRINTED IN THE UNITED STATES OF AMERICA

Contents

Preface

Although managerial motivation and compensation have long been of primary concern to students and practitioners of management, only recently have these topics been subjected to systematic, theoretical analysis and empirical research. There are several books and numerous articles available on these two subjects. However, most of the available literature is either polemic or prescriptive and provides only a meager scientific basis for explaining how compensation affects motivation. We believe this is unfortunate. We believe that if management practices are to accomplish what they are intended to accomplish, with a minimum of unintended and undesirable consequences, then the effects of such practices must be predictable.

Consistent predictability is aided by an understanding of the phenomenon in question. Thus it is helpful, and perhaps even necessary, to have a theory to explain such phenomena. Theory, however, should be subjected to empirical tests both under controlled and field conditions before being accepted as practical.

At present, there are several theories of motivation that have relevance for managerial compensation. We have selected for inclusion in this book those theories which we believe to have both managerial implications and some empirical support. In an attempt to bridge the gap between theory and practice, four kinds of articles have been included: statements of theories, illustrations of empirical tests of theories, illustrations of managerial applications of theories, and state of the art papers which summarize and present critical commentary on the empirical research relevant to theories.

This book grew out of a seminar sponsored by the McKinsey

1

Foundation for Management Research. Several of the papers originally written for that seminar are included here. In addition, several
previously published papers and several papers specifically prepared
for this book are included. We wish to thank all of the authors for
their contributions and acknowledge both authors and publishers
whose previously published articles are included here. Such ac-
knowledgment is indicated on the title page of each article.

We are grateful to the McKinsey Foundation for the financial support which made this book possible, and to Warren M. Cannon for his
personal interest and helpfulness in this endeavor.

It is hoped that this book will be useful to both students and
practitioners of management.

Henry L. Tosi
Robert J. House
Marvin D. Dunnette

PART ONE

Introduction

In 1967, the McKinsey Foundation for Management Research sponsored a Seminar on Managerial Motivation and Compensation at Tarrytown, New York. A number of people—theorists, researchers, and practicing managers—attended to discuss the problems of linking compensation and performance. Some of the papers presented at that seminar form the core of this collection. Other relevant work has been added; for example, the article by Opsahl and Dunnette, which has been selected to serve as an introduction to the volume.

Opsahl and Dunnette review theoretical and empirical efforts dealing with motivation and compensation. Their article is meant to provide an overview of what follows, since many of the theories and research studies they cite are examined in later sections.

The plan of this book is a simple one. Following the introductory section, Part Two contains a set of theoretical formulations which are widely used by practitioners and researchers in examining the problems of motivation and compensation.

Part Three presents a set of criticisms of each theory discussed in Part Two. These criticisms generally attempt to focus on the weaker elements of the particular theory under consideration.

Part Four includes a set of research studies in compensation. The coverage of the studies is not meant to be exhaustive, certainly, but with them we try to illustrate how theory can be researched in both a field setting and in the laboratory.

The subject of performance appraisal is considered in Part Five. Performance appraisal methods typically are intended to do at least three things. First, they are supposed to be used in assessing the level

3

of an individual's performance, that is, how good or bad it is. Second, they are often used as a basis for compensation decisions. Third, they are used for purposes of developmental feedback to the appraisee.

The final section points to some of the many problems that need to be resolved. A number of important issues are raised which are of extreme interest to both the theorist and the practicing manager.

1

The Role of Financial Compensation
in Industrial Motivation

ROBERT L. OPSAHL

AND

MARVIN D. DUNNETTE

Widespread interest in money as a motivational tool for spurring production was first stimulated in this country by Frederick Taylor. Some years before the turn of the century, Taylor observed an energetic steelworker, who, after putting in a 12-hour day of lifting pigs of iron, would run 12 miles up a mountainside to work on his cabin. If this excess energy could be used to produce more on the job, thought Taylor, higher profits from lower fixed costs could be used to pay the worker significantly more for his increased efforts. Such was the beginning of *scientific management,* which is based essentially on the assumption that workers will put forth extra effort on the job to maximize their economic gains. This became a guiding principle in pay practices until the late 1920s when the *human relations movement* in industrial psychology was ushered in with the Western Electric studies directed by Elton Mayo. As a result of these studies, recognition of man's ego and social needs became widespread, and job factors other than pay came to be emphasized as the major reasons why men work. To a large extent, these later ideas are still with us. Yet, few would disagree that money has been and continues to be the primary means of rewarding and modifying human behavior in industry.

Strangely, in spite of the large amounts of money spent and the obvious relevance of behavioral theory for industrial compensation practices, there is probably less solid research in this area than in any other field related to worker performance. We know amazingly little

Reprinted by permission of the authors and publisher from *Psychological Bulletin* 66 no. 2 (1966): 94-118.

about how money either interacts with other factors or how it acts individually to affect job behavior. Although the relevant literature is voluminous, much more has been written about the subject than is actually known. Speculation, accompanied by compensation fads and fashions, abounds; research studies designed to answer fundamental questions about the role of money in human motivation are all too rare.

In this review, we have attempted to identify and summarize research studies designed to show how opportunities to get money affect the way people actually do their work. It was decided to focus attention on the role of money in motivating behavior *on the job*. The large body of literature on manpower economics relevant to relationships between wage and salary practices and manpower mobility has been largely ignored. Thus, we review here those theories and studies designed to illuminate possible effects of financial compensation for inducing greater effort in the job setting, and we ignore those theories and studies related to money's effects in inducing employees to take jobs, persist in them, or to leave them. First, several theories offered to explain how money affects behavior and research studies relevant to these theories are considered. Second, the behavioral consequences of compensation are examined by stressing and analyzing the variables relevant to the money-motivation relationship. Throughout, our purpose is to pinpoint the role of financial compensation in industrial job motivation. We seek to summarize and to evaluate critically what is already known and to suggest directions for future research.

THEORIES OF THE ROLE OF MONEY

Does money serve to stimulate job effort? If so, why does it do so? How does it take on value in our industrial society? There are at least five theories or interpretations of the role of money in affecting the job behavior of employees.

Money as a Generalized Conditioned Reinforcer

One widely held hypothesis is that money acts as a generalized conditioned reinforcer because of its repeated pairings with primary reinforcers (Holland & Skinner, 1961; Kelleher & Gollub, 1962; Skinner, 1953). Skinner (1953) has stated that such a generalized reinforcer should be extremely effective because some deprivation will usually exist for which the conditioned reinforcer is appropriate. Unfortunately, solid evidence of the behavioral effectiveness of such reinforcers is lacking, and what evidence there is has been based almost entirely on animal studies.

In a series of experiments conducted by Wike and Barrientos (1958), a goal box (containing wet mash) paired with both food and water deprivation proved to be a more effective reinforcer for rats than different goal boxes paired with food or water deprivation alone. The implications of these results are that money ought to be more potent when its attainment is paired with many, rather than only single, needs. Unfortunately, the magnitude of the difference in preferences in the above study, though statistically significant, was extremely small. In 15 test trials in a T-maze, rats turned to the goal box previously paired with both deprivations an average of only .62 trials more often than to the goal box paired only with food deprivation.

Moreover, this and most other studies on generalized conditioned reinforcers can be criticized because of the nonindependence of food and water as primary reinforcers (Grice & Davis, 1957; Verplanck & Hayes, 1953). A water-deprived rat eats less than his normal intake of food. What is needed are studies with human subjects in which a stimulus has been paired with many independent reinforcers. In one such study (Ferster & DeMyer, 1962), coins paired with games and candy were used successfully with autistic children to develop and maintain complex operant behaviors. Although the effectiveness of the coins was well-demonstrated by the increased frequencies of responding contingent on their presentation, their effectiveness under different conditions of deprivation was not studied, nor was their relative effectiveness compared with that of coins operating as simple conditioned reinforcers.

Some theorists (e.g., Brown, 1961; Dollard & Miller, 1950) have referred to the token-reward studies of Wolfe (1936) and Cowles (1937) as examples of how money acquires value. In these studies, initially neutral poker chips apparently acquired reinforcement value because they could be exchanged for various foods. The analogy between the poker chips and the industrial use of money as wages is incomplete, however, because the reinforcement value of the poker chips came about because of the association with removing deprivation in a single primary area, whereas the theory of money's generalized reinforcing role would hypothesize that it is valued quite aside from and independent of any particular state of deprivation. It should be apparent that evidence in support of money as a generalized conditioned reinforcer is, at best, limited and inconclusive.

Money as a Conditioned Incentive

According to this hypothesis, repeated pairings of money with primary incentives[2] establish a learned drive for money (Dollard & Miller, 1950). For example, in Wolfe's (1936) study, the sight of a poker chip out of reach served as an incentive to motivate the chimpanzee to pull it in. The fact that chimpanzees refused to work if given a free supply of poker chips suggests that the act of obtaining the chips served a drive-reducing function (Dollard & Miller, 1950). Presumably, money could become a generalized conditioned incentive in the same manner that it is presumed by some to become a generalized conditioned reinforcer—that is, by many pairings with many different types of incentives. Perhaps the main difference between the conditioned reinforcer and conditioned incentive interpretations is the introduction of drive reduction in the incentive hypothesis. In contrast, no such drive need be hypothesized under empirical reinforcement principles.

Money as an Anxiety Reducer

Brown (1953, 1961) also utilized the concept of drive in an effort to explain how money affects behavior. He suggested that one learns to become anxious in the presence of a variety of cues signifying the absence of money. Presumably, anxiety related to the absence of money is acquired in childhood through a process of higher-order conditioning. The first stage consists of pairings of pain with cues of warning or alarm provided by adults. For example, before a child actually touches a hot stove, a nearby adult may provide facial gestures of alarm and warnings such as "Look out, you'll get hurt!" These cues eventually elicit anxiety without the unconditioned stimulus. In the second stage, anxiety-arousing warnings are conditioned to a wide variety of cues indicating lack of money. After such learning, the child becomes anxious upon hearing phrases such as "That costs too much money," or "We can't afford to buy you that." The actual presence of money produces cues for the cessation of anxiety. This concept of anxiety as a learned motivating agent for money-seeking responses in no way contradicts the possible action of money according to the two previous hypotheses; money as an anxiety-reducer could operate jointly with them as an additional explanatory device.

Harlow (1953), however, has taken issue with Brown's thesis, stating: "It is hard to believe that parental expression at the time a child suffers injury is identical with or highly similar to a parent's expression when he says 'we have no money' [p. 22]." Harlow pointed out further that an infant's ability to recognize emotional expression when suffering pain has not been reliably demonstrated. Unfortunately, Brown presented no experimental evidence bearing on his theory.

Money as a "Hygiene Factor"

Herzberg, Mausner, and Snyderman (1959) postulated that money is a so-called "hygiene factor" serving as a potential dissatisfier if it is not present in appropriate amounts, but not as a potential satisfier or positive motivator. According to them, improvements in salary may only remove impediments to job satisfaction but do not actually generate job satisfaction. The main value of money, according to them, is that it leads to both the avoidance of economic deprivation and the avoidance of feelings of being treated unfairly. Thus, its hygienic role is one of avoiding pain and dissatisfaction ("disease") but not one of promoting heightened motivation ("health"). These notions were originally derived from content analyses of anecdotal accounts of unusually satisfying and unusually dissatisfying job events elicited from 200 engineers and accountants. Fifteen percent of their description of satisfying events involved the mention of salary and 17% of their descriptions of dissatisfying events involved salary. Moreover, Herzberg et al. suggested that salary may be viewed as a "dissatisfier" because its impact on favorable job feelings was largely short-term while its impact on unfavorable feelings was long-term—extending over periods of several months. Herzberg et al.'s use of this finding to argue that money acts only as a potential dissatisfier is mystifying. It becomes even more so when their data are examined more carefully. In all of the descriptions of unusually good job feelings, salary was mentioned as a major reason for the feelings 19% of the time. Of the unusually good job feelings that lasted several months, salary was reported as a causal factor 22% of the time; of the short-term feelings, it was a factor 5% of the time. In contrast, salary was named as a major cause of unusually bad job feelings only 13% of the time. Of the unusually bad job feelings lasting several months, it was mentioned

only 18% of the time (in contrast with the 22% of long-term good feelings, mentioned above).

These data seem inconsistent with the interpretations and lend no
substantial support to hypotheses of a so-called differential role for
money in leading to job satisfaction or job dissatisfaction.

Money as an Instrument for Gaining Desired Outcomes

Vroom's (1964) cognitive model of motivation has implications for
understanding how money functions in affecting behavior. According
to Vroom's interpretation, money acquires valence as a result of its
perceived instrumentality for obtaining other desired outcomes. The
concept of valence refers simply to affective orientations toward particular outcomes and has no direct implications for behavioral consequences. However, the "force" impelling a person toward action was
postulated to be the product of the valence of an outcome and the
person's expectancy that a certain action will lead to attainment of the
outcome. Thus, for example, if money is perceived by a given person
as instrumental to obtaining security, and if security is desired, money
itself acquires positive valence. The probability, then, of his making
money-seeking responses depends on the degree of his desire for
security *multiplied* by his expectancy that certain designated job behaviors lead to attaining money. Although Vroom summarized studies
giving general support to his theory, the specific role of money in his
theory was not dealt with in any detail.

Gellerman's (1963) statement of how money functions in industry
also stressed its instrumental role. According to him, money in itself
has no intrinsic meaning and acquires significant motivating power
only when it comes to symbolize intangible goals. Money acts as a
symbol in different ways for different persons, and for the same person at different times. Gellerman presented the interesting notion
that money can be interpreted as a projective device—a man's reaction
to money "summarizes his biography to date: his early economic environment, his competence training, the various nonfinancial motives
he has acquired, and his current financial status [p. 166]." Gellerman's evidence was largely anecdotal, but nonetheless rather convincing.

Summary of Theoretical Speculations

Much remains to be learned before we will understand very well what meaning money has for different persons, how it affects their job behaviors, which motives it serves, and how its effectiveness may come about. It is probably doubtful that there will ever be a "theory of money" in the sense that money will be given a unique or special status as a psychological variable. It is true that money functions in many ways, depending upon the setting, the antecedent conditions, and the particular person involved. According to Brown, money must be present to avoid anxiety. For Herzberg et al., it serves to avoid feelings of being unfairly treated or economically deprived. Reinforcement theories, on the other hand, seem to treat money either as a generalized entity, functioning independently of specific deprivations, or as a general incentive that has been coupled with variously valued goals during a person's total learning history. Obviously, the answers are not yet available, and it is probably best to view the money symbolically, as Vroom and Gellerman do, and to begin to learn and measure the personal, situational, and job parameters that may define more fully what it is the symbol of and what its attainment is instrumental to. Only by mapping the domain in this way will we come to know the relevant factors associated with money as a "motivator" of behavior in industry.

BEHAVIORAL CONSEQUENCES OF COMPENSATION

The major research problem in industrial compensation is to determine exactly what effects monetary rewards have for motivating various behaviors. More specifically, we need to understand more precisely how money can be used to induce employees to perform at high levels. Relevant research centers around two major groupings: studies related to the job or the job content and studies related to personal characteristics—preferences, perceptions, opinions, and other responses—made by the job incumbent. The first of these, the job or task variables, include primarily the policies and practices constituting the "compensation package" for any given job or job setting. The personal or subject variables influence not only the way a job holder responds to the specific policies and practices in any given situation, but they also vary as a function of these task or job variables. Thus, it is necessary to give careful attention to the interaction between job and personal variables which is frequently overlooked in research designs and has an important bearing on the interpretations to be attached to the results of such research studies.

JOB AND TASK VARIABLES

Compensation Policies

Our assumption is that the manner in which financial compensation is administered may account for a large amount of the variation in job behavior. The particular schedule of payment, the degree of secrecy surrounding the amount of pay one receives, how the level of salary or pay is determined, and the individual's long-term or career pay history all have important potential effects on how the employee responds to any specific amount of money.

Schedules of pay. In this review we shall be concerned solely with "incentive" payment systems[3] which are based on behavioral criteria (usually amount of output) rather than biographical factors such as education, seniority, and experience. Incentive pay schemes of various sorts are believed to function primarily to "increase or maintain some already initiated activity or . . . to encourage some new form of activity . . . [Marriott, 1957, p. 12]."

There is considerable evidence that installation of such plans usually results in greater output per man hour, lower unit costs, and higher wages in comparison with outcomes associated with straight payment systems (e.g., Dale, 1959; Rath, 1960; Viteles, 1953). However, the installation of an incentive plan is not and can never be an isolated event. Frequently, changes in work methods, management policies, and organization accompany the changeover, and it is difficult to determine the amount of behavioral variance that each of these other events may contribute. This would seem to constitute a persuasive argument for placing workers in a controlled laboratory situation and analyzing the effectiveness of different methods of payment, isolated from the usual changes accompanying their installation. Unfortunately, there have been few studies of this nature.[4]

Incentive plans can be based on either the worker's own output or on the total output of his working group. The relative efficiency of the two methods are dependent upon such factors as the nature of the task performed (Babchuk & Goode, 1951; Marriott, 1957), the size of the working group (Campbell, 1952; Marriott, 1949, 1951; Marriott & Denerley, 1955; Shimmin, Williams, & Buck, 1956), the social environment (Selekman, 1941), and the particular group or individual plan employed. The chief disadvantage with group incentives is the likelihood of a low correlation between a worker's own individual performance and his pay in larger groups. There is also evidence (Campbell, 1952) that individual output decreases as the size of the work group increases, and this is apparently due to workers' perceiving a decreased probability that their efforts will yield increased outcomes (i.e., the workers have less knowledge of the relationships between effort and earnings). Both of these effects run counter to the main principle of incentive plans—immediate reward for desired job behaviors.

Not only do financial incentives operate with different efficacy in different situations, but often they do not even lead to increased production. Group standards and social pressures frequently induce workers to perform considerably below their potential. Most of the data on such rate restriction are either observational (e.g., Dalton, 1948; Dalton, Collins, & Roy, 1946; Dyson, 1956; Mathewson, 1951; Myers, 1920; Roethlisberger & Dickson, 1939; Roy, 1952; Whyte, 1955) or in the form of verbal responses to surveys (Opinion Research Corporation, 1949; Viteles, 1953). The results of these studies suggest that changes in the monetary consequences of performance are usually accompanied by changes in other expected consequences of performance. Thus, instituting an incentive plan may alter not only the expected consequences in terms of amount of money received, but also expected consequences related to possible loss of esteem in the eyes of one's co-workers or the presumed bad connotations of "selling out" or accepting the goals of management.

Hickson (1961) has divided the causes of rate restriction into five categories. Three of the causes are essentially negative or avoidance reasons: uncertainty about the continuance of the existing "effort-bargain" between the workers and management, uncertainty about the continuance of employment, and uncertainty about the continuance of existing social relationships. The other two causes are positive or approach-type factors: the desire to continue social satisfactions derived from the practice of restriction, and a desire for at least a minimal area of external control over one's own behavior. Hickson stated that we haven't studied sufficiently the positive reasons or advantages of rate restriction. We shall go a step further and state that the main method of studying rate restriction—on the job observation—is essentially a loose and ineffective way of determining any causative linkages. Just as schedules of pay can best be assessed by experimental manipulations under controlled conditions, so should rate restriction be studied by laboratory investigations characterized by controlled and objective observations.

The most intensive analysis of rate restriction was undertaken by Whyte (1952, 1955). It was the thesis of Whyte and his co-workers that many piece-rate incentive situations actually resemble the conditions of experimentally induced neurosis. He reasoned that most incentive "packages" do not provide the employee with sufficient cues to allow him to discriminate effectively between stimuli signaling the onset of punishing circumstances (loss of co-worker respect, etc.) and stimuli signaling the onset of rewarding circumstances (more pay, higher job success, etc.) (Whyte, 1955). Thus, money itself is only *one* of many possible rewards and punishments that invariably accompany any incentive situation.

Whyte's effort to show similarity between piece-rate incentive systems and the conditions accompanying experimental neurosis is misleading. The discriminative stimuli for the rewards and punishments administered by the work group and by management seem to be clearly differentiable. A double approach-avoidance conflict between the rewards and punishments of management and the work group is more descriptive of the situation. If this is the case, the conditions necessary for maintaining the group as an effective reinforcing agent even in the face of an incentive piece-rate plan should be studied more thoroughly. Variables for study would include group cohesiveness; interaction patterns within the group; amount of intergroup competition; identification of individuals within the group; uniformity of group opinion; group control over the environment; and the extent to which group pressures support rather than subvert organizational goals and demands (March & Simon, 1958, pp. 59-61).

Thus, although "everyone knows" that incentive pay schemes work very effectively some of the time, it is painfully apparent that they are far from uniformly effective. The emphasis in research should now turn to more controlled observations of the effects of money in the context of the many other sources of reward and punishment in the work setting. So far, we have only a wealth of field observations. It is necessary now to learn more exactly just what employees will or will not give up for money or, more importantly, to learn how incentive payments may be made without engendering the painful and onerous circumstances which so often seem to accompany such payments.

Secret pay policies. In addition to the particular kind of pay plan, the secrecy surrounding the amount of money given an employee may have motivational implications. Lawler's (1965) recent study indicates that secret pay policies may contribute to dissatisfaction with pay and to the possibility of lowered job performance. He found that managers overestimated the pay of subordinates and peers, and underestimated their superiors' pay; they saw their own pay as being too low by comparison with all three groups. Moreover, they also underestimated the financial rewards associated with promotion. Lawler argued that these two results of pay secrecy probably reduce the motivation of managers both to perform well on their present jobs and to seek higher level jobs. Another disadvantage of secrecy is that it lowers money's effectiveness as a knowledge-of-results device to let the manager know how well he is doing in comparison to others. Lawler advocated the abandonment of secrecy policies—"there is no reason why organizations cannot make salaries public information [p. 8]."

Lawler's assertion seems to have a good deal of merit; his results are impressive and his arguments sound. It would be very useful, at this stage, to conduct "before-after" studies of the effects of instituting policies of openness concerning wage and salary payments on employees' perceptions of relationships between pay and job performance. At the very least, Lawler's data suggest that useful effects would be produced by informing employees (particularly managers) about how their salaries are derived; the next logical step would be to provide normative data (e.g., percentile distributions of employee pay levels); and, finally, salary administrators might even publicize actual salary levels of persons in the firm.

This is not to say, of course, that there might not be negative outcomes from the sudden implementation of such policies. For example, one obvious possibility is that such action might crystallize present hierarchical "pecking orders"; group cohesiveness could be disrupted by the sudden awareness of substantial intra-work-group differences. Most such fears stem from the prevalence of actual pay inequities related to inadequate job-performance appraisal systems and current weaknesses in administering salary payments in such a way as to reflect valid relationship with job performance. We believe, with Lawler, that present policies of secrecy are undoubtedly due, in part, to fear on the part of salary administrators that they would have a difficult time mustering convincing arguments in favor of many of their present practices. Thus, it is true that until salaries are determined more rationally and until money becomes more firmly accepted as a way of rewarding outstanding job behavior, public disclosure of salary arrangements may probably not have the desirable consequences suggested by Lawler. Perhaps his results are merely symptomatic of present unsuccessful efforts to use pay effectively for motivating employees. If this is true, it seems all the more important and timely to undertake thorough studies of the effects of relaxing present policies of pay secrecy.

Pay curves. An employee's periodic pay increases, as he progresses in his career with a company, constitute another job or task variable with the potential for differentially motivating effects. Wittingly or not, every company "assigns" each employee a "pay curve" which is the result of successive alterations in compensation and compensation policies through the years. One way of doing this (the usual way) is with little or no advanced planning; increments are given haphazardly on a year-to-year basis and the resulting career pay curve simply "grows" somewhat akin to Topsy. Another alternative is to plan the future compensation program shortly after the individual enters the organization and then to modify it subsequently on the basis of his job behavior as his career unfolds. No matter which pay policy is adopted, the results will most likely affect the employee's job behavior, his aspirations and anticipations of future earnings, and his feelings of fairness with respect to his career-pay "program."

Most companies administer pay increments on a periodic (e.g., year-to-year) basis.[5] The rationale for this is quite simple, the usual idea being that differential pay increments may be given for differential results produced by employees on their jobs. Over a span of many years, then, we might expect a consistent pattern of positive correlations for the salary increments received by the individuals comprising any particular group of employees. This expectation would be based on two rather reasonable and closely related assumptions—first, that the acquisition of job skills is a predictable process; and, second, that the effectiveness of a person's job performance in any given period is predictable from his own patterns of job performance.

In fact, however, career pay histories for employee groups do *not* usually show such patterns of consistently positive relationships between year-to-year salary gains. Haire (1965) mapped the correlations between salary levels at the end of each year and raises over 5- and 10-year periods in two large national companies. In one company, the correlations decreased over the 5-year span from .38 to -.06 for one executive group (median salary $41,600), and from .36 to -.25 for a second group (median salary $18,000). In the second firm, the correlations between salaries and raises for adjacent years over the 10-year period varied between -.33 and .83 with no consistent pattern discernible. Haire believed that his results constituted damning evidence that these two companies had no consistent policies with respect to the incentive use of salary increases; he suggested that the trend in the first company reflected a shift from a policy of distributing raises under the assumption that good performance is related to past excellence to the assumption that it is either not related at all or that it is negatively related. He also asserted that a pattern showing extremely low correlations between present salary levels and salary increments indicates that wage increases might just as well be distributed by lottery—that the incentive character of a raise is thereby nullified and that consistent striving for job excellence would seem futile under such circumstances. Haire's assertions are provocative and they may indeed follow from his results, but we believe that other explanations may be equally compatible with his findings. For example, low correlations could just as reasonably be viewed as reflecting a successfully administered wage policy allowing for greater rather than less flexibility in using money to reward top job performance. Such a policy might suggest, in effect, that an employee who has done well in the past cannot rest on his laurels in expectation of future "rewards" and that a lower salaried employee (with presumably a history of less effective performance) still has rich opportunities to be recognized and appropriately rewarded for improved job performance in the future. It is true that a finding of consistently low correlations would tend to refute our earlier stated assumptions about the acquisition of job skills and the consistency of job performance over time.

Be that as it may, future analyses of historical pay patterns such as these provided by Haire will probably yield more explicit insights about company wage policies if they focus more closely on individual employee pay and job performance histories rather than rely solely on coarse within-group comparisons and correlations such as those reported by Haire. The idea of inspecting historical patterns in the relationships between job performance, salaries, and raises is a good one and should be utilized more broadly.

The idea of specifying individual career pay curves has received extensive attention by Jaques (1961), through his "standard payment and progression method." By analyzing the pay histories of 250 male workers, he derived a family of negatively accelerated pay curves extending from ages 20 to 65. It should be noted, however, that his curves were plotted with a log scale for the ordinate (salary). If actual dollar values were plotted, the data would very likely yield positively rather than negatively accelerated curves. However, as plotted by Jaques, the curves rise rapidly in the younger age groups, slow down at older ages, and show a greater rate of progression at the higher earning levels. According to Jaques, these smoothed curves (called standard earning progressions), follow "the sigmoidal progression characteristic of biological growth [1961, p. 185]," and are the basis for his payment theory. Jaques believed that the standard earning progression curves represent a close approximation to the lines of growth of "time-span of discretion" in individuals. This time-span of discretion is the maximum period of time during which the work assigned by a manager requires his subordinate to exercise discretion, judgment, or initiative in his job without that discretion being subject to review by the manager. This objective yardstick can supposedly be used for direct comparison of work levels between any two jobs, regardless of content. The major significance of the time-span, according to Jaques, is that workers in jobs having different contents but the same time-span of discretion privately perceive the same wage or salary bracket to be equitable for the work they are doing.

Assuming that individuals seek an equitable level of payment for the level of work consistent with their capacity, an employee's future pay curve can be determined by: (a) determining the employee's present time-span of discretion along with the equitable payment ɪor that time-span; (b) plotting the employee's achieved earning progression to date; (c) allowing the manager once-removed to determine the employee's potential progress assessment (i.e., the manager's assessment of the level of work a person is likely to achieve—this can be expressed in terms of the earning progression that the employee would likely achieve given that he receives equitable payment for his work); (d) letting the immediate manager assess the employee's performance, and altering the employee's wage or salary according to this assessment; (e) having the once-removed manager revise the potential progress assessment if performance continues above or below the original potential progress assessment.

The above is only a brief sketch of Jaques' theory of payment. It is a highly interesting one, but until further data concerning its motivational consequences are compiled, it must be regarded as highly tentative.

The "sigmoidal biological growth" pay curves that Jaques described are not the only possible ones; Ghiselli (1965) has pointed out other possibilities and has attempted to provide the rationale behind them. For instance, one suggested possibility was having average increments in pay increase from year to year. The result would be a positively accelerated pay curve consonant with the philosophy of paying an employee a substantial amount only after he becomes highly effective in the organization instead of when he is in the early stages of his career and easily tempted to move to another organization. If the organization wished to budget a fixed amount for pay increases each year, linear pay curves would result. If, on the other hand, it is assumed that an employee is unlikely to leave a firm after he has been with it a long time and has a huge personal investment in it (such as retirement benefits, stock options, etc.), it might be advantageous to reward him generously when he first starts his job to help insure that he will not go to another firm (i.e., assign him a negatively accelerated curve). To our knowledge, no empirical studies on the relative effectiveness of different possible pay curves have been undertaken.

Although it would appear that pay curves have a significant influence on job behavior, parametric experiments in this area are practically non-existent. Several aspects of pay curves need to be studied before these curves can be constructed or used with even a moderate degree of effectiveness.

First and most important, it must be determined how a given pay curve differentially affects employees' motivation and job behaviors. It is not plausible to assume that one best curve can be found for *all* employees, or even for a subgroup of employees at a given job level or with common job duties. Some evidence of this was revealed by Festinger (1965) who found that promotions (with related pay increases, presumably *increased* the aspired-to job level and perceived importance of pay for about 30% of a sample of employees within one company but *decreased* the job level-of-aspiration and perceived importance of pay in another 30% of the cases. It is not known why these groups reacted so differently to promotions. The overall level-of-aspiration of the employees certainly would be a prime variable; need Achievement might be another. Little is known about the stability of these two variables; therefore, assessment of them early in an employee's career may not be a valid index of later expectations or the effectiveness of career pay-curve policies. It is necessary to conduct longitudinal studies over extended periods of time—studies which are all too infrequent in the area of compensation. Some of the data necessary for this type of study are already on file in computer memory banks in the larger companies and need only to be retrieved and analyzed.

Since pay curves do not operate within a vacuum, the effect of one employee's pay curve on another employee must not be overlooked. Ghiselli's (1965) rationale for positively and negatively accelerated curves, for instance, may not prove effective in the context of the total industrial situation. Since pay is on a competitive basis across companies, a negatively accelerated curve in one company might lead to feelings of inequity and possible job termination for a young employee if other companies offered linear or positively accelerated pay increments in a similar situation. It is not implied that the effectiveness of the different curves should not be studied. However, the concept of equity applies to pay-curve comparisons as well as to wage comparisons, and this is an important potential area for investigation.

Several methods of deriving pay curves deserve further investigation. One option would be to inform the employee of the tentative curve agreed upon for him. This could be done piecemeal, by setting monetary goals for him to shoot at within a specific time period. An interesting variation of this procedure that, to our knowledge, has not been studied, would be to include pay goals in the goal-setting interviews given high level managers in some companies. The behavioral goals set in these interviews could have monetary rewards attached to them, thereby providing further incentive for their attainment. Informing an employee of his progress along his proposed pay curve might also serve a valuable feedback function, helping him evaluate his progress to date.

Other relevant research problems are numerous. Important ones include determining how to alter an employee's subsequent curve on the basis of under- or over-achievement, discovering valid criteria for constructing a tentative curve, and determining which variables influence the perception of pay increments and *how* they influence it. With expanded knowledge in these areas, pay curves and their determination may come to play a central role in industrial compensation practices of the future.

Industrial psychologists have too often turned prematurely to the study of employee characteristics without giving sufficient attention to the job context. The significant research reviewed here and the questions suggested testify to the potential importance of task and job content variables. Certainly the complexities of the interaction between task and job variables and subject (employee) variables, discussed in the following section, demand research evidence bearing on both. The failure to place research emphasis in either area will very likely impede progress and understanding in the other.

SUBJECT VARIABLES

Perceived Relations between Performance and Pay

According to Vroom's (1964) theory of work motivation, the valence of effective performance increases as the instrumentality of effective performance for the attainment of money increases, assuming that the valence of money is positive. Vroom cited supporting evidence from experiments by Atkinson and Reitman (1956), Atkinson (1958), and Kaufman (1962) showing a higher level of performance by subjects who were told that their earnings were contingent on the effectiveness of their performance. Georgopoulos, Mahoney, and Jones' (1957) Path-Goal Approach theory similarly states that if a worker has a desire for a given goal and perceives a given path leading to that goal, he will utilize that path if he has freedom to do so. Georgopoulos et al. found that workers who perceived higher personal productivity as a means to increased earnings performed more effectively than workers who did not perceive this relationship.

The effectiveness of incentive plans in general depends upon the worker's knowledge of the relation between performance and earnings. The lack of this knowledge is one cause of failure in incentive schemes. As already mentioned, Campbell's (1952) study showed that one of the major reasons for lower productivity in large groups under group incentive plans is that the workers often do not perceive the relation between pay and productivity as well as they do in smaller groups. In the Georgopoulos et al.'s (1957) study, only 38% of the workers perceived increased performance as leading to increased earnings. More amazingly, 35% perceived *low* productivity as an aid to higher earnings in the long run. Lawler (1964) recently found that 600 managers perceived their training and experience to be the most important factors in determining their pay—not how well or how poorly they performed their jobs. Since Lawler found that the relation between their pay and their rated job performance also was low, their perceptions were probably quite accurate. A separate analysis of the most highly motivated managers, however, indicated that they attached greater importance to pay and felt that good job performance would lead to higher pay.

These studies confirm the importance of knowing how job performance and pay are related. The relation between performing certain desired behaviors and attainment of the pay-incentive must be explicitly specified. The foregoing statement seems so obvious as hardly to warrant mentioning. Unfortunately, as we have seen, the number of times in industry that the above *rule* is ignored is surprising. Future research must determine how goals or incentives may best be presented in association with desired behaviors. Practically nothing has been done in this area—especially for managers. In fact, programs for the recognition of individual merit are notoriously poor. Methods for tying financial compensation in with management-by-results (Schleh, 1961) or with systematic efforts to set job goals and methods of unambiguously outlining what the end result of various job behaviors will be should be developed and studied.

Personality-Task Interactions

Under some conditions, it appears that even specifying the relation between performance and pay is not sufficient. Early studies (Wyatt & Fraser, 1929; Wyatt, Fraser, & Stock, 1929; Wyatt & Langdon, 1937) conducted on British factory workers showed that feelings of boredom are associated with reduced output even under a carefully developed program of incentive pay. More recent studies have failed to reproduce the daily output curve found by the British investigators, and, moreover, indicate that boredom is not *necessarily* accompanied by reduced output (Cain, 1942; Smith, 1953; Ryan & Smith, 1954). Thus, boredom *may* lead to a decrease in performance; but, as in most other areas of investigation, a ceteris paribus clause must be included. Little is known of the factors which may outweigh the effects of boredom in a particular situation.

It is obvious that repetitiveness and uniformity in job tasks are likely to contribute to feelings of boredom, but personality variables are also important determinants. Smith (1955) found that susceptibility to boredom is associated with such factors as youth, restlessness in daily habits and leisure-time activities, and dissatisfaction with personal, home, and plant situations not directly concerned with uniformity or repetitiveness. The commonly held assumption that workers of higher intelligence are more easily bored with repetitive work, however, is based on meager and conflicting data (Ryan & Smith, 1954).

One possible method of alleviating feelings of boredom is suggested by Wyatt and Fraser's (1929) finding that piece-rate systems lead to fewer symptoms of boredom than does straight hourly pay. This is in keeping with Whyte's (1955) contention that, in addition to money, there are three other sources of reward in a piece-rate situation: escape from fatigue, because the worker has a meaningful goal to shoot at; escape from management pressure and gain of control over one's own time; and "playing the game" of trying to attain quota.

Even if piece-rate systems relieve boredom, output under such plans may still suffer if the task is disliked. This was Wyatt's (1934) finding when he compared the levels of performance of 10 female workers in a British candy factory under hourly, bonus, and piece-rate payment methods. He observed a strong positive relation between an incentive plan's effectiveness (defined as increased productivity) and liking for the job. The best liked job was wrapping the candy and employees increased their output on it 200% when payment was changed from straight pay to a group bonus and finally to piece-rate payment. In contrast, unwrapping damaged packages was viewed as most onerous—"an aimless and destructive process"—and output on this task showed no change under different conditions of pay.

The net conclusion from these studies is that repetitive tasks, destructive tasks, boring tasks, and disliked tasks are apparently much less susceptible to monetary incentives. Little has been done, however, to explore other possible interactions in this area. What little data we do have suggest that nonmonetary incentives are more effective for subjects who have high ability on the task being measured. Thus, Fleishman (1958) found that subjects high in ability on a complex coordination task increased their performance under incentive conditions significantly more than did low ability subjects. However, we do not know if such findings would generalize to situations in which monetary incentives are used or how the effectiveness of incentives varies as a function of other important variables such as the type of task, the amount of physical effort demanded, or the degree of interpersonal interaction involved, to mention but a few examples. Without knowledge of the range of behaviors susceptible to incentives or the degree to which they are susceptible, we cannot make optimal use of them in any specific situation. Should we use incentives for maintaining or improving leadership behavior? And how about jobs which are highly challenging and intrinsically rewarding? Are incentives in this situation a cause of mercenary feelings which detract from the main source of reinforcement—the job itself—and ultimately lower job effectiveness? Or do they spur the employees on to yet greater heights? Of course, we do not know; and, even more unfortunately, little research seems to be under way to test assumptions implicitly made by many firms' present compensation policies.

Perceived Importance of Pay

It seems obvious that employees must regard money as a highly desirable commodity before increased amounts of it motivate increased behavior. Results of studies in this area are extremely confusing because of the almost exclusive dependence on self-reports to estimate the relative importance of pay. For example, when Wilkins (1949, 1950) asked 18- and 19-year-old males at the British Army Reception Center to rank various job incentives on importance, "pay" was placed second only to "friendly workmates." Only 8% ranked pay as most important. "Friendly workmates," "security," and "future prospects" all received more first-place rankings than pay. Factor analysis of the responses revealed two broad factors: One was of long-term appeal and included "security," "future prospects," "variety," and "efficient organization." The other factor included "pay," "workmates," "working hours," and "leave." The second factor was interpreted as consisting of items incidental to the job and mainly of short-term appeal. When Wilkins divided the group into high and low intelligence, he found that both "pay" and "workmates" were relatively more important for the low intelligence group—41% of the youths in this group gave "workmates" top ranking. He concluded that "a large proportion of such workers would be prepared to accept lower wages if they could be with workmates they liked [1950, p. 562]."

In a study by Watson (1939), employees ranked pay third in importance on a list of eight "morale" factors. However, when their employers were asked to rank the eight factors according to how they thought the employees would respond, pay was selected as the most important factor. This differential perception of the importance of money by employees and higher management has been confirmed in a survey conducted by the National Industrial Conference Board (1947), showing that executives ranking 71 morale factors in terms of overall importance gave top rank to compensation, while fewer than 30% of the rank-and-file employees included this among the five most important factors.

Worthy's (1950) analysis of surveys conducted by Sears, Roebuck, and Company over a 12-year period showed that pay ranked eighth among factors related to high morale, whereas rates of pay ranked fourteenth. Over a span of nearly 20 years, Jurgensen[6] has asked applicants for employment with the Minneapolis Gas Company to rank 10 job factors in order of their importance. Now with a total accumulation of over 42,000 cases, he finds that pay has consistently ended up in sixth place. On the other hand, when Ganuli (1954) asked employees in a Calcutta, India, engineering factory to rank eight items relating to working conditions in order of importance, he found that "adequate earnings" was ranked first, above such factors as "job security," "opportunity for promotion," and "personal benefits." Graham and Sluckin (1954) also found pay the most important job factor in a survey of skilled and semi-skilled workers in England.

The discrepancies in the above-mentioned studies can be partially explained by the different samples of employees used. One would not expect executives to have the same values and goals as blue-collar workers (nor, for that matter, should it be assumed that executives or blue-collar workers are homogeneous groups in themselves). Another cause of the discrepant findings is the variety in the dimensions of job incentives used. Seldom are the same variables ranked in any two studies. Also, it is probable that many of the factors are not independent. Bendig and Stillman (1958) have criticized the bulk of studies for these last two reasons. They further contended that the factors used were not selected within any theoretical framework of hypothesized dimensions of job incentives. In an attempt to isolate the fundamental dimensions of job incentives, Bendig and Stillman (1958) factor-analyzed eight incentive statements given to college students. They found three orthogonal bipolar factors that they tentatively named "need achievement vs. fear of failure," "interest in the job vs. the job as an opportunity of acquiring status," and "job autonomy of supervision vs. supervisor dependency." Salary loaded highest on "the job as an opportunity for acquiring status," and had small loadings on "fear of failure" and "job autonomy." Still another possible reason for discrepancies in the above studies is that they have failed to assess the degree to which various respondents' job circumstances are or are not providing sufficient rewards in each job area. For example, a respondent who perceives his present pay as adequate may rate pay as relatively less important than he would if he perceived his present pay level to be low. It is probably impossible for respondents to detach themselves sufficiently from their present circumstances to be able to give completely accurate self-report estimates of the relative importance of different job aspects.

While most self-report surveys place salary in a position of only moderate importance, it is easy to find people in industry who *behave* as if they value money highly. Executives strive mightily to advance to high-paying jobs; entertainers work toward more and more lucrative arrangements; bankers embezzle; robbers rob; university professors publish to win increased salary and to enjoy royalty checks. Why is it then that money or pay seldom is ranked commensurate with these behaviors? The answer is not simple, but it may include at least the following possibilities: (*a*) There is probably a social desirability response set pervading the self-reports. The Protestant Ethic is still with us; one may not readily admit that he is running after the almighty dollar without feeling some twinge of conscience which can be dissipated by relegating pay to a relatively low position on the value hierarchy and giving lip service to other more acceptable factors such as "job autonomy" or "intrinsic job satisfaction." (*b*) The reinforcement contingencies present in filling out a self-report questionnaire are quite different from those in the real life situation. It is apparent that an individual is reinforced generously for actually obtaining money, but it is much less evident what the reinforcement contingencies are when he simply *admits* in a self-report checklist that attaining money may be a prime goal. Certainly one is reinforced for engaging in a bit of rationalization while filling out such self-reports. (c) Finally, as implied above, people are poor judges (and therefore poor reporters) of what they really want in a job. They do not know with certainty which job factors really attract and hold them; hence they cannot validly describe or rank these job factors.

Thus, research on the valence of money must move beyond the dependency on self-report measures and strive to establish the actual linkages between money and behavior by more sophisticated observational techniques. It is not implied that bankers embezzle *only* for money or that university professors publish *only* for money or that executives strive *only* for money. Money plays a role in all these—a role probably far greater than that suggested by the self-report studies. The self-report studies are based on oversimplified notions tending to ignore the complexities and multidetermined aspects of human behavior. Further accumulation of such rankings or ratings will add little to our understanding of the behavioral effects of compensation. Laboratory studies and experimental observations of the behavioral effects of money are needed here just as in the many other areas we have discussed.

These may, in part, be supplemented with more sophisticated techniques of scaling. Some modification of the paired-comparison technique used by Jones and Jeffrey (1964) in which a more inclusive domain of job incentive aspects are compared against some monetary standard would be a promising start. We should also heed Bendig and Stillman's (1958) plea for the isolation of basic independent job incentive dimensions in future research in order to unify research and allow for cross-study comparisons. In sum, the question, "How do people value money?" will not be answered accurately simply by asking them.

Pay Preferences

Although money *per se* is usually accorded a middle position in any ranking of job factors, different ways of making salary payments are differentially preferred. Mahoney (1964) found that managers prefer straight salary over various types of management incentive payments (such as stock options, deferred compensation, etc.). This is in keeping with the results of other surveys. Jaques, Rice, and Hill (1951), for example, reported that the majority of both workers and management in an English factory were in favor of a change from individual piece-rates to hourly wages. Likewise, Davis (1948) found that 60% of a sample of building operatives were opposed to incentive schemes, with only 21% expressing definite or conditional approval. The main arguments against incentive systems, as reported by Davis, include the fear that the incentive would inhibit other strong and pleasurable motives for working, such as the pleasure of work for its own sake and the solidarity and good fellowship of the working group.

A study conducted by the Michigan Survey Research Center (Larke, 1953) revealed that group incentive payments were favored by fewer than 50% of the employees who already were under such plans. Similarly, Mahoney (1964) found that his sample of managers also preferred individual to group pay plans. On the other hand, Wyatt and Marriott (1956) found more approval than disapproval of group incentives by 62% of the workers sampled in three factories. With respect to particular types of incentives, Spriegal and Dale (1953) found individual piecework much more popular than group piecework.

Using paired-comparison techniques, Nealey (1963) found that a large sample ($N = 1,333$) of electrical workers accorded direct pay increases a lower position than such fringe benefits as sick leave, extra vacation time, or hospital insurance. He also discovered that such preferences do not follow a simple dollar value. For example, dental insurance cost the company less than life insurance but was preferred by more workers. Jones and Jeffrey (1964) asked employees in two electrical equipment plants to make paired comparisons among 16 alternative compensation plans, each characterized by a combination of four features and having identical overall costs to the company. The unique aspect of this study is the possibility of directly comparing the average value of each compensation characteristic with that of a pay raise and, thus, attaching a monetary equivalent to each preferred characteristic. Results showed that the average value of a change from hourly wage to weekly salary is judged to be equivalent to a pay increase of between 1 and 2 cents an hour. A piece-rate incentive plan was perceived as equivalent to a 5- to 10-cent hourly pay increase and was preferred mainly by the skilled workers who already had experience with such a plan. At the nonunion plant, a supervisory merit-rating incentive was considered equal to a 4-cent pay raise. At the union plant, however, the scheme was so disliked that the absence of the plan was considered worth more than a 6-cent hourly raise.

Jones and Jeffrey believed that their approach may have direct bearing upon administrative decisions concerning changes in compensation plans. If the monetary value equivalent of the change, perceived by the worker, substantially exceeds the actual cost to the company of a change in benefits, then it may be considered—if it does not hinder other compensation goals. Basing company compensation policies directly on the measured perceptions of employees regarding the policies also has the additional advantage of designing the pay schemes directly to fit the motive (or preference) systems of the employees being compensated under the plans. The Nealey study and the Jones and Jeffrey study provide rare examples of the analysis of employees' preferences by sophisticated scaling techniques. They well deserve to be emulated by other researchers in this area.

Mahoney (1964, p. 144) concluded that preferences for alternative forms of compensation are relatively uniform and that "fine distinctions among alternative forms of compensation probably are considerably less important in managerial motivation than is often suggested." Such preferences should not be the sole criterion for assessing the effects of compensation on motivation if we are mainly interested in actual job behavior, not satisfaction,[7] since the relation between the two is complex and, in many instances, unknown. From stated preferences one cannot easily infer that the compensation program is optimally motivating.

Although there has been a fair amount of research done in determining the pay preferences of managers and other employees, no work has been done on the relation between preference for a particular plan and the actual incentive value of that plan. The implicit, but unwarranted, assumption in all the above-mentioned studies is that if a person has a pay plan he likes, this plan will motivate behavior more than one that he does not like. Although this is an appealing assumption, future studies, in addition to determining employees' pay-plan preferences, should seek to map the relation between such preferences and the incentive value of different plans. The motivation of behavior, *not* the preference for compensation policies, is the prime goal of company pay plans, and research strategies should be directed toward this end.

Concept of Equitable Payment

Several theories have been independently advanced proposing that employees seek a just or equitable return for what they have contributed to the job (Adams, 1963a, 1965; Homans, 1961; Jaques, 1961; Patchen, 1961; Sayles, 1958; Zaleznik, Christenson, & Roethlisberger, 1958). A common feature of these theories is the assumption that compensation either above or below that which is perceived by the employee to be "equitable" results in tension and dissatisfaction due to dissonant cognitions. The tension, in turn, causes the employee to attempt to restore consonance by a variety of behavioral or cognitive methods.

One of the earlier theorists in this area was Homans, who suggested the concept of distributive justice—that is, justice in the way the rewards and costs of activities are distributed among men. He postulated that:

A man in an exchange relation with another will expect that the rewards of each man be proportional to his costs—the greater the rewards, the greater the costs—and that the net rewards, or profits, of each man be proportional to his investments—the greater the investments, the greater the profits [Homans, 1961, p. 232].

Schematically, then, there is distributive justice when

Person A's rewards minus his costs = A's investments

Person B's rewards minus his costs = B's investments

(after Adams, 1965). If the two ratios are unequal, the members of the exchange experience feelings of injustice, one or the other perceiving that he is on the short end in terms of profits. Either member sensing injustice will attempt to bring his profits and investments into line through various behaviors or, perhaps, by changing his perception of the situation.

Homans briefly treated the relation between distributive justice and satisfaction. He proposed that if there is a state of injustice, the person at a disadvantage will "display the emotional behavior we call anger [1961, p. 75]." If, on the other hand, the injustice is in his favor, the person will feel guilty. He implied that the threshold for guilt is higher than that for anger.

Zaleznik et al. (1958) applied Homans' theory to compensation and tested the postulates on 50 production workers. They constructed a reward-investment index to determine whether a worker was receiving an equitable return for his services. When the index was related to worker satisfaction, however, a completely random distribution of high- and low-satisfied workers was found, no matter how favorable the reward-investment index. Since the index was crude and nonempirical, the lack of any relation between satisfaction and distributive justice is not particularly surprising.

Jaques' (1961) theory of equitable payment differs from Homans' mainly in its psychoanalytic orientation. His theory is based on the assumptions that (*a*) there exists "an unrecognized system of norms of fair payment for any given level of work, unconscious knowledge of these norms being shared among the population engaged in employment work [1961, p. 124]"; and that (b) and individual is "unconsciously aware" of his own potential capacity for work, as well as the equitable pay level for that work. Jaques claimed that this optimal level of payment is that which allows an optimal consumption of goods and services consistent with "dynamic psychological equilibrium." He stated that equitable payments are accompanied by feelings of satisfaction, but that deviations in payment below or above the equitable level are usually accompanied by feelings of dissatisfaction or uneasiness.

As Vroom (1964) has pointed out, however, Jaques did a rather poor job of scientific reporting. He failed to specify the methods employed in measuring dissatisfaction, the means and variances in his dependent variable, and, frequently, the number of workers on whom various observations were made. Until these and other aspects of Jaques' research are adequately reported, his conclusions, as Vroom indicated, must be regarded with caution.

A third formulation of a theory of equity is found in the work of Patchen (1961). He postulated that equitable payment is achieved when the following two ratios are congruent:

$$\frac{\text{My pay}}{\text{His (their) pay}} \quad \text{compared to} \quad \frac{\text{My position on dimensions related to pay}}{\text{His (their) position on dimensions related to pay}}$$

A unique aspect of this theory is the concept of potential, or future, perceived equitable payment. This results from the congruence of these ratios:

$$\frac{\text{My pay now}}{\text{His (their) pay now}} \quad \text{compared to} \quad \frac{\text{My future position on dimensions related to pay}}{\text{His (their) present position on dimensions related to pay}}$$

Thus, although a person perceives a wage comparison as presently equitable, he may still perceive future inequity. This would occur, for example, if the comparison person(s) is someone more skilled, but the person feels he should receive gradual pay increases as his own skill improves—that is, as he becomes more like his comparison person(s) on dimensions related to pay. Such dissonant comparisons may provide a basis for mobility (promotional) aspirations for the person; he may feel that a higher status would be more appropriate for him. Under these circumstances, it is quite possible that dissatisfaction from future perceived inequity may be tolerated.

Substantiation of Patchen's theory comes from interviews with 489 employees in a Canadian oil refinery (Patchen, 1961). The employees were asked to name two persons whose yearly earnings were different from theirs. Those who chose objectively dissonant comparisons (e.g., comparison persons who were of similar status but whose earnings were greater) judged the comparison unsatisfactory. They explained their feelings in terms of dissonance between the wage difference and other related differences. For example, 75% of the employees justified their feelings by pointing out their own equality or superiority with respect to the comparison person on factors directly relevant to pay—such as education, seniority, and skill. Those employees who were satisfied with their comparisons based their feelings of satisfaction on a perceived consonance between the wage difference and other related differences between the workers. Other interesting findings were that men relatively low in pay were less satisfied than others in the comparisons they chose; and, as a worker's mobility chances improved, these men would more frequently choose potentially dissonant comparisons and be more dissatisfied with the idea of remaining below their comparison persons in wages. However, workers who had the best mobility chances *within* the company chose fewer *presently* dissonant comparisons than workers who had the best mobility chances *outside* the company. Since those with good mobility chances within the company were virtually assured of rapid advancement in rank and wages, Patchen believed that the difference between the two groups depended largely upon whether advancement had to be fought for or was largely assured. If it was assured, as typified by the high within-company mobility group, presently dissonant comparisons need not have been chosen as justification for advancement or as a protest against one's present status. These reasons, however, become highly salient when advancement must be earned the hard way.

Further effects of within and outside company wage comparisons are found in Andrews and Henry's (1963) study of 228 managers in five companies. They found that, at a given level of management, overall satisfaction with pay was more highly related to the similarity between the pay of the managers in one company and the average pay of managers in the other four companies than to the similarity between their pay and the average pay of other managers in their own company. Together, these two studies suggest that both mobility aspirations and wage comparisons, particularly comparisons outside of one's own company, are important determinants of wage satisfaction. Further studies along these lines should increase our meager knowledge concerning the factors influencing wage comparisons.

The most rigorous and best researched theory of equity is that of Adams (1963a), 1965). His theory is derived mostly from the postulates of Festinger's cognitive dissonance theory (1957) but was influenced also by Stouffer et al.'s (1949) earlier work on relative deprivation and by Homans' (1961) research on distributive justice. Adams' most recent definition of inequity stated that

inequity exists for Person[8] whenever he perceives that the ratio of his outcomes to inputs and the ratio of Other's outcomes to Other's inputs are unequal, either (a) when he and Other are in a direct exchange or (b) when both are in an exchange relationship with a third party and Person compares himself to Other [1965, p. 22].

This implies, as do all the above-mentioned theories, that an inequitable relation occurs not only when the exchange is not in Person's favor, but when it is to his advantage as well. Adams like Homans hypothesized that the thresholds for underreward and overreward differ. Thus, a certain amount of overreward may be written off as "good luck," whereas similar deviations in the direction of underreward will not be so easily tolerated.

Inputs mentioned in the definition are anything a worker perceives as constituting his contribution to the job—age, skill, education, experience, and amount of effort expended on the job. Outcomes, or rewards from the job, are also dependent upon the worker's perception and would normally include pay, status symbols, intrinsic job satisfaction, and fringe benefits, to mention a few examples.

The existence of equity or inequity is not an all-or-none phenomenon. Many degrees of inequity can be distinguished, and the magnitude of the inequity is assumed to be some increasing monotonic function of the size of the difference between the ratios of outcomes to inputs. Thus, it is not the absolute magnitudes of perceived inputs and outcomes that are important, but rather the discrepancy between the two ratios. Inequity may exist for both Person and Other, so long as each perceives discrepant ratios. The greatest inequity exists when both inputs and outcomes are discrepant.

The presence of inequity creates tension within a person in an amount proportional to the magnitude of the inequity. This tension creates a drive to reduce the inequity feelings, the strength of the drive being proportional to the tension created. Adams (1963a, 1965) suggested several possible avenues of achieving an equitable state. A person may increase or decrease his inputs (e.g., by increasing or decreasing either the quality or quantity of his work); he may increase or decrease his outcomes (by asking for a raise, or by giving part of his pay to charity, for example); he may change his comparison group or cognitively alter its inputs or outcomes, or force it out of the field; he may leave the field himself (by quitting, transferring, or being absent); or he may cognitively distort his own inputs and outcomes. It is not yet clear what principles govern the choice of method for inequity reduction, although Lawler and O'Gara (in press) have recently obtained evidence that the choice is related to such personality "traits" as self-esteem and responsibility.

A series of experiments to test this theory have been undertaken (Adams, 1963a, 1963b, 1965; Adams & Jacobsen, 1964; Adams & Rosenbaum, 1962; Arrowood, 1961). These studies have all been directed toward the effects of overcompensation on behavior. In the first of these (Adams & Rosenbaum, 1962), the hypothesis that workers who felt they were overpaid would reduce their feelings of inequity by increasing the amount of work performed was tested. Twenty-two college students were hired to conduct interviews at $3.50 per hour; half of them were made to feel qualified and equitably paid, and the other half were made to feel unqualified and thus overpaid. As predicted, the overpaid group conducted significantly more interviews within the allotted time than did the control group.

It could reasonably be hypothesized that the group made to feel overpaid for the job worked harder because they felt insecure and were afraid of being fired. Another experiment was performed by Arrowood (1961, reported in Adams, 1963a, 1965) with the same design—but with the addition of a "private" group that was under the impression that their employer would never see their work. Within this private group, the students who felt overcompensated also conducted significantly more interviews than the students who felt equitably compensated, thus showing the predicted effect is still obtained when pains are taken to remove the insecurity motive.

Although it is predicted from the theory that workers overpaid on an hourly basis will increase the quantity of their work, workers overpaid on a piecework basis would actually increase feelings of inequity if they produced more since they would be increasing the amount of their overpayment. Therefore, it was hypothesized that these workers would reduce inequity by reducing the quantity of their output—a procedure which increases inputs and decreases outcomes. Adams and Jacobsen (1964) tested this hypothesis on students hired for a proofreading task.

Persons in the overpaid, experimental group were told they were not qualified but would be paid the usual rate of 30 cents per page anyway. Persons in one equitably paid control group were made to feel qualified and were also paid 30 cents per page. Persons in a second equitably paid control group were made to feel unqualified but were paid the more equitable rate of only 20 cents per page. Adams also sought to assess any possible effects due to differing feelings of job security by manipulating the perceived possibility of future employment. This was done because it was reasoned that subjects made to feel overpaid and unqualified might perceive an implication that their tenure was in jeopardy unless they showed they were good workers. Thus, for half the subjects in each group, Adams created a condition in which they perceived that there was something to lose (i.e., insecurity) and for the other half a condition in which they perceived that there was nothing to lose (i.e., relative security). Adams reasoned that if job security were important, the overpaid secure subjects would work fast but carelessly whereas the overpaid insecure subjects ought to work with much greater care.

The index of quantity was the number of pages proofread, and the index of quality was the number of implanted errors detected (each page, averaging 450 words, had an average of 12 errors implanted in the text, such as misspellings or grammatical, punctuational, and typographical errors).

At first glance, the results substantiate the hypothesis. They show that the overpaid, experimental group proofed significantly fewer pages and detected significantly more implanted errors per page than the two equitably paid groups. The job security manipulation had no significant effect, which was in keeping with the hypothesis that quality and productivity should vary with feelings of equity and not as a function of perceived job security.

It should be noted, however, that quality was not entirely adequately measured in the experiment. Detecting implanted errors is only one possible evidence of quality in proofreading. Another aspect of quality not included in Adams' quality score is the number of words detected as errors, but which were actually correctly spelled or punctuated. If a proofreader detected all of the real errors in a text, but also claimed several words or punctuation marks to be in error when they actually were correct, his stay on the job probably would be short-lived. Yet, in the experiment just described, he would get a perfect quality score because the specification of detecting nonerrors as errors was ignored. Significantly more of these nonerrors were falsely called errors by the overpaid group. If these "errors" had been taken into account, their quality scores would have been considerably lower. It can be argued, of course, that such nonerror detection simply illustrates the increased effort and conscientiousness that these subjects were devoting to the task, and this would then be further evidence in favor of the theory and of the effectiveness of the experimental manipulation. Even so, the net effect of "correcting" nonerrors is to reduce the job effectiveness of a proof-reader; and it is not entirely clear whether this aspect of ineffectiveness was due to the equity manipulation, the different emphasis on detecting errors in two sets of directions,[9] or some interaction of the two.

Recent research (e.g., Freedman, 1963; Leventhal, 1964; Weick & Penner, 1965—all mentioned in Weick, 1965; Linder, 1965) indicates that predictions derived from equity theory in cases of underreward may require modification. All of the above studies showed that underpaid persons work harder, and also like the task more than persons who are overpaid or equitably paid.

Weick (1965) hypothesized that high effort for insufficient pay represents an attempt to raise outcomes, and suggested that proponents of equity theory give greater consideration to the proposition that persons may control their outcomes to reduce inequity. Thus, in the above-mentioned studies, increased satisfaction gained from performing the task may heighten outcomes and bring them more in line with the person's inputs. So far, with the exception of the recent paper by Lawler and O'Gara (in press), research directed toward testing equity theory has dealt only with overpayment, but the effects of insufficient reward are equally important in industry. We hope that more attention is devoted to this area in future research on equity theory.

Several additions to the theory may help to increase its efficiency of prediction. First and most important, there is need for specifying the conditions governing the choice of one mode of resolution over another. The theory itself does not specify any priority of different methods, and, since there are so many potential methods of reducing inequity, the mere prediction that some one of them will occur is not a very useful or meaningful one. Several propositions about the choice of a method have been advanced tentatively by Adams (1965). These include the following hypotheses:

1. Person will maximize positively valent outcomes and the valence of outcomes.
2. He will minimize increasing inputs that are effortful and costly to change.
3. He will resist real and cognitive changes in inputs that are central to his self-concept and to his self-esteem.
4. He will be more resistant to changing cognitions about his own outcomes and inputs than to changing his cognitions about Other's outcomes and inputs.

5. Leaving the field will be resorted to only when the magnitude of inequity is high and other means of reducing it are unavailable [p. 46].

However, the above hypotheses have not yet been tightly incorporated into equity theory. Since so many modes for resolving inequity are possible, the difficulty of specifying exactly when any specific mode may or may not be used renders the theory more "hazy" and less directly testable than we would like to see it. For example if an overcompensated group failed to show increased input (in the form of higher quantity or quality), might this be regarded as disconfirmation of the theory or merely an instance of the subjects' choosing another mode (e.g., altering their perceptions of their own or others' inputs or of the nature of the job being performed) for reducing feelings of inequity? Because the principles specifying the choice of mode have not yet been specified, tightly reasoned deductions cannot yet be derived from the theory.

As implied above, it is quite likely that people differ substantially from one another in the mode they might choose for resolving feelings of inequity; moreover, these differences are undoubtedly a function of individual motive configurations and ability, interest, and personality variables. Lawler and O'Gara (in press) have shown, for example, that persons scoring higher on the Responsibility scale of the California Psychological Inventory (CPI) were less likely to sacrifice quality of work for quantity, when underpaid, than were persons scoring low on the scale. In a similar fashion, underpaid persons scoring high on CPI scales of Dominance and Self Assurance were less likely to react with high productivity than those scoring low. Apparently, there are distinct differences in the way different kinds of people respond to feelings of inequity. The incorporation of such variables into the theory may increase its explanatory power. As it stands, the theory ignores individual differences.

Not only may motivational variables determine methods of resolution, but it has been hypothesized that the number and kinds of similarities on which Person compares himself to Other may also affect his choice of how he resolves inequity (Weick, 1965). For example, if a person compares himself with someone who is similar only with respect to education, perhaps education inputs will be the only salient means for resolving inequity when it occurs. Similarly, as Weick pointed out, as comparability increases and Person compares himself to Other with respect to many variables, it is plausible to expect that the intensity of discomfort associated with inequity will change. These two hypotheses, unfortunately, have not yet been investigated.

As it stands, the theory fails to specify methods of resolution relating to various kinds of perceptual alteration. Weick (1965) has pointed out that the theory overlooks such possibilities as denial, differentiation, toleration of the discrepancy, alteration of the object of judgment, bolstering, and task enhancement. This last method seems particularly important. If a person had proportionately low outcomes, task enhancement would be a relatively easy way to increase his outcomes without alienating his co-workers in the process.

One of the major problems with which equity theory must cope, therefore, is the obvious fact of the large number of variables, the complexities of their interaction, and the inadequacy of the operational definitions. Vroom (1964) pointed out that, according to the theory, a worker's satisfaction with his pay is a function of:

1. His beliefs concerning the degree to which he possesses various characteristics;
2. His convictions concerning the degree to which these characteristics should result in the attainment of rewarding outcomes from his job, i.e., their value as inputs;
3. His beliefs concerning the degree to which he receives these rewarding outcomes from his job;
4. His beliefs concerning the degree to which others possess these characteristics;
5. His beliefs concerning the degree to which others receive rewarding outcomes from their jobs; and
6. The extent to which he compares himself with these others [p. 171].

We agree with Vroom's conclusion that the complexity of equity theory makes conclusive tests difficult, and that "a great deal of theoretical and methodological refinement remains to be carried out before this approach can be properly evaluated [1964, p. 172]."

Nonetheless, Adams is to be commended for beginning the difficult task of trying to work through some of the complexities related to an understanding of how pay and employees' perceptions of pay affect the way they work on the job. These early studies on equity, though subject to some criticism, certainly bear the stamp of careful thought and careful experimentation, and we hope that Adams and others will continue in their efforts to explicate more fully some of the questions which have been raised here.

FUTURE RESEARCH

Although it is generally agreed that money is the major mechanism for rewarding and modifying behavior in industry, we have seen that very little is known about how it works. Haire remarked at a recent symposium on managerial compensation that, in spite of the tremendous amount of money spent and the obvious relevance of behavioral theory for compensation practices, there is less research and theory in this area than in almost any other field related to management (Haire, 1965). Similarly, Dunnette and Bass (1963), in a critique of current personnel management practices, pointed out that personnel men have relied on faddish and assumptive practices in administering pay which lack empirical support. One reason for this is the dearth of sound research upon which to base practices. The following are some suggested directions for research which may help to remedy these current deficiencies.

The principal research problem is to discover in what way money motivates employees and how this, in turn, affects their behavior. For this, we must know more about the motives of employees—which motives are dominant, and how employees differ from one another in the configuration of their motives. We must also determine which of these motives can be linked to money as an incentive. Can money be linked with insatiable needs so goal attainment does not cause cessation of behavior? Can money act as an incentive for the "higher order" needs? The two main hypotheses here—that money can serve only "lower order" needs, and that it can serve essentially all needs—have very different implications for compensation practices. Investigation of this question requires not only the discovery of the motives for which money has instrumental value but also the extent to which money can serve to fulfill or satisfy these needs. Quite obviously, money serves to satisfy needs for food, clothing, and shelter, but it is much less obvious how money may be related to such other areas as need Achievement or need Power. It seems obvious that money serves these needs too, but solid evidence of a relationship is lacking. To what extent may money be a primary way of dispensing feelings of achievement, competence, power, and the like? In other words, what needs are currently served by money, and what needs, not now perceived as associated with money, may it be called upon to serve? Moreover, we believe that future studies of the effects of money on behavior will prove more fruitful if they are conducted in laboratory or in tightly controlled field settings rather than continuing to depend on survey and self-report instruments as is characteristic of so much of the research now available.

As this review shows, very little is known about the behavioral laws regulating the effectiveness of incentives. We continue to dole out large sums of money under the guise of "incentive pay" without really knowing much about its incentive character. We do not know, for instance, the nature of the effect of a pay raise or the length of time before that effect occurs; or, for that matter, how long the raise may be effective. Nor do we know the optimal reinforcement schedule to be used in giving salary increases for obtaining desired changes in job behavior. A simple monitoring of work outputs on jobs where amount of production is under the direct control of the employee and where it is easily assessed, may provide valuable information here. Such knowledge would have important implications for how often and in what amounts incentive raises should be built into the compensation package.

We also need to investigate the relation between amount of money and the amount of behavior money motivates. Is there some point beyond which increases in compensation are no longer related to increases in relevant behavior? That is, do humans show the same negatively accelerated relation between amount of reward and number of responses that lower organisms display? Or do increases in money "whet the appetite" and lead to behavior that follows some exponential or positively accelerated function?

If we are to effectively manipulate incentives, more information is needed about how they function. Money's incentive character, to be fully understood, must also take account of the perceptions of money by the recipient. For example, if it is assumed that the amount of extra pay needed in a raise before it assumes incentive character is partly determined by the value of a sum of money, recent evidence (Haire, 1965) shows that not only the amount of money but also how a person perceives his work role are vital factors. Presidents apparently need a larger percentage increase than vice-presidents before they see it as constituting an incentive raise. Is this difference a function of the work role alone? Or do anticipations of future earnings, differences in abilities and dominant motives, and past earning history account for a good share of the variance? So far, these research questions are virtually untapped.

We have seen from Wyatt (1934) that money can be cheapened or lowered in value by the behavior demanded to attain it. To understand more about this relationship, it would be helpful to scale money values against behaviors demanded for money's attainment. This could best be done in a laboratory setting and by using actual workers. Such controlled laboratory experiments have been utilized *almost not at all* with actual employees as subjects. So far, we have depended heavily on rats and psychology sophomores to build a psychology of motivation. We sorely need studies in which real workers are brought into the laboratory and the effects of incentives under different conditions studied.

A very important variable influencing money's effectiveness is the schedule by which it is administered. Of the simple reinforcement schedules, the fixed interval—reinforcement following a fixed period of time after the last reinforced response—leads to notoriously poor performance in lower organisms (Ferster & Skinner, 1957). Yet this is the present pay schedule of most industrial employees. Lower organisms on this schedule tend not to respond very rapidly until just before their "payday." The notable exception to this type of pay schedule in industry occurs for commission salesmen (e.g., life insurance selling) and for entrepreneurs. It is probably worth noting that these two groups contain "workers" who must certainly be viewed as being among the most highly motivated persons in our industrial society.

Although more is known about the simple schedules of reinforcement, the complex schedules—composed of both interval and ratio elements—may be applicable in an industrial setting. In particular, the effects of alternative, conjunctive, and interlocking schedules are worth investigating. With these schedules, it would be possible to follow the suggestion of Haire, Ghiselli, and Porter (1963); that is, divide the paycheck into several parts: so much for tenure, so much for minimum services rendered, so much for excellent performance, etc. For example, about 70% of the total available might be given on a fixed interval for minimum services. The rest of the potential pay could be divided and incorporated into different variable ratio schedules, made contingent on outstanding performance.

Finally, evidence seems to indicate that, at various times, employees seek to maximize the amount of their reward, the fairness of their reward, and their acceptance by the group in which they work. The research question is: in which situations, and in what ways is behavior directed toward maximizing one or more of these goals? Which goals are maximized at the expense of others? What are the relative saliencies of each goal in differing situations? What are the functional relationships between goals? Which goals account for most of the variance in productivity, and under what conditions? These are vital questions that must be answered before we can effectively utilize incentives.

As research on the role of financial compensation in industrial motivation becomes more and more prevalent, answers to many of the questions posed above should be forthcoming. Increased knowledge should be accompanied by more effective use of money in industry. It is hoped that the firm of the future will be able to establish compensation policies and practices based on empirical evidence about the behavioral effects of money as an incentive rather than on the nontested assumptions, hunches, and time worn "rules-of-thumb" so common in industry today.

NOTES

[1] This investigation was supported in part by a Public Health Service Fellowship (5-Fl-MH-21, 814-03 PS) from the National Institute of Mental Health, United States Public Health Service, and in part by a behavioral science research grant to Marvin D. Dunnette from the General Electric Foundation.

[2] Incentive: "an object or external condition, perceived as capable of satisfying an aroused motive, that tends to elicit action to obtain the object or condition [English & English, 1958]."

[3] We will not attempt to evaluate all the evidence on incentive plans. For an excellent review and evaluation of these, see Marriott (1957).

[4] Marriott (1957) mentioned only three experimental studies, all in an industrial setting and all conducted at least 30 years ago: Burnett (1925); Roethlisberger and Dickson (1939), and Wyatt (1934).

[5] Since there are innumerable ways to administer pay on a periodic basis, and since these methods are largely administrative and have little interest of a psychological nature, we will not attempt to review them.

[6] Personal communication, 1965.

[7] There is correlational evidence that amount of pay is positively associated with satisfaction with pay (Andrews & Henry, 1963; Lawler & Porter, 1963), job satisfaction (Barnett, Handelsman, Stewart, & Super, 1952; Centers & Cantril, 1946; Marriott & Denerley, 1955; Miller, 1951; Smith & Kendall, 1963; Thompson, 1939; all as reported in Vroom, 1964), and with need satisfaction (Lawler & Porter, 1963; Porter, 1962). However, it is not known to what degree the satisfaction is a result of the level of pay or the changes in job status, duties, and privileges that so often accompany higher pay.

[8] Person is anyone for whom equity or inequity exists. Other is any individual or group used by Person as a referent in social comparisons of what he contributes to and what he receives from an exchange.

[9] The two sets of instructions used in the experiment are as follows: First, the overpaid group and the "reduced rate" equitable group were told about their qualifications in the following manner:

Well, you don't have nearly enough experience of the type we're looking for. We were hoping to find someone who had previously had actual job experience correcting publishers' proofs of a manuscript. It's really important that this be done by someone who is experienced in this sort of work. It takes special training to have the skill necessary to catch all the sorts of errors that can creep into the proofs. They will have to be returned to the publishers soon, and we can't afford to have any mistakes slip by. (Pause) Your score on this proofreading test isn't really satisfactory either. Would you wait here just a moment? (Brief exit).

After a brief exit by the experimenter, the persons in the overpaid group were told they would be paid the usual rate anyway, whereas the persons in the "reduced rate" equitable group were informed that they would be paid at a lower, more equitable, rate. The other group, the qualified equitable group, was instructed as follows:

This is fine; you're just what we were looking for. You meet all the qualifications that were required, and your score on this proofreaders' test looks very good. So far as pay is concerned, you probably are aware that we pay 30 cents per page. This rate is standard for work of this kind done by qualified people. [Adams & Jacobsen, 1964, p. 21].

The different emphases on quality in the two sets of instructions are obvious; thus, it appears that the first two groups were given very different sets concerning the expectations of the employer about the quality demands of the work to be done. It can still be argued, of course, that the reduced-rate group should then have shown an increase in quality of about the same magnitude as that shown by the overpaid group. We do not believe this would necessarily obtain. It is likely, for example, that the pay reduction would be sufficient to suggest to an "unqualified" subject that his expected poor performance was already being taken into account, and he might then work in accordance with his employer's implied expectation. The confounding of the differing emphases on quality with the equity manipulation in this study seems to us to confuse seriously the interpretation of the results obtained by Adams and Jacobsen.

REFERENCES

ADAMS, J.S. Toward an understanding of inequity. *Journal of Abnormal and Social Psychology*, 1963, **67**, 422-436. (a)

ADAMS, J.S. Wage inequities, productivity, and work quality. *Industrial Relations*, 1963, **3**, 9-16. (b)

ADAMS, J. S. Injustice in social change. In L. Berkowitz (Ed.), *Advances in experimental social psychology*. Vol. 2. New York: Academic Press, 1965, Pp. 267-299.

ADAMS, J. S., & JACOBSEN, P. Effects of wage inequities on work quality. *Journal of Abnormal and Social Psychology*, 1964, **69**, 19-25.

ADAMS, J.S., & ROSENBAUM, W.B. The relationship of worker productivity to cognitive dissonance about wage inequities. *Journal of Applied Psychology*, 1962, **46**, 161-164.

ANDREWS, I. R. & HENRY, M. M. Management attitudes toward pay. *Industrial Relations*, 1963, **3**, 29-39.

ARROWOOD, A.J. Some effects of productivity of justified and unjustified levels of reward under public and private conditions. Unpublished doctoral dissertation, University of Minnesota, 1961.

ATKINSON, J.W. (Ed.) *Motives in fantasy, action, and society.* Princeton: Van Nostrand, 1958.

ATKINSON, J.W., & REITMAN, W.R. Performance as a function of motive strength and expectancy of goal attainment. *Journal of Abnormal and Social Psychology*, 1956, **53**, 361-366.

BABCHUK, N., & GOODE, W.J. Work incentives in a self-determined group. *American Social Review*, 1951, **16**, 679-687.

BARNETT, G.J., HANDELSMAN, I., STEWART, L.H., & SUPER, D.E. The Occupational Level scale as a measure of drive. *Psychological Monographs*, 1952, **66** (10, Whole No. 342).

BENDIG, A. W., & STILLMAN, E. L. Dimensions of job incentives among college students. *Journal of Applied Psychology*, 1958, **42**, 367-371.

BROWN, J.S. Problems presented by the concept of acquired drives. In, *Current theory and research in motivation: A symposium.* Lincoln: University of Nebraska Press, 1953. Pp. 1-21.

BROWN, J.S. *The motivation of behavior.* New York: McGraw-Hill, 1961.

BURNETT F. *An experimental investigation into repetitive work.* (Industrial Fatigue Research Board Report No. 30) London: His Majesty's Stationery Office, 1925.

CAIN, P.A. Individual differences in susceptibility to monotony. Unpublished doctoral dissertation, Cornell University, 1942.

CAMPBELL, H. Group incentive payment schemes: The effects of lack of understanding and group size. *Occupational Psychology*, 1952, **26**, 15-21.

CENTERS, R., & CANTRIL, H. Income satisfaction and income aspiration. *Journal of Abnormal and Social Psychology*, 1946, **41**, 64-69.

COWLES, J.T. Food-tokens as incentives for learning by chimpanzees. *Comparative Psychology Monographs*, 1937, **14**, 1-96.

DALE, J. Increase productivity 50% in one year with sound wage incentives. *Management Methods*, 1959, **16**, 38-42.

DALTON, M. The industrial "rate-buster": A characterization. *Applied Anthropology*, 1948, **7**, 5-18.

DALTON, M., COLLINS, O., & ROY, D. Restriction of output and social cleavage in industry. *Applied Anthropology*, 1946, **5**(3), 1-14.

DAVIS, N.M. Attitudes to work among building operatives. *Occupational Psychology*, 1948, **22**, 56-62.

DOLLARD, J., & MILLER, N. E. *Personality and psychotherapy.* New York: McGraw-Hill, 1950.

DUNNETTE, M. D., & BASS, B. M. Behavioral scientists and personnel management. *Industrial Relations*, 1963, **2**, 115-130.

DYSON, B.H. Whether direct individual incentive systems based on time-study, however accurately computed, tend over a period to limitation of output. Paper read at Spring Conference, British Institute of Management, London, 1956.

ENGLISH, H.B., & ENGLISH, C.A. *A comprehensive dictionary of psychological and psychoanalytical terms.* New York: McKay, 1958.

FERSTER, C.B., & DEMYER, M.K. A method for the experimental analysis of the behavior of autistic children. *American Journal of Orthopsychiatry*, 1962, **32**, 89-98

FERSTER, C.B., & SKINNER, B.F. *Schedules of reinforcement.* New York: Appleton-Century-Crofts, 1957.

FESTINGER, L. *A theory of cognitive dissonance.* Evanston, Ill.: Row, Peterson, 1957.

FESTINGER, L. How attitudes toward compensation change with promotion. In R. Andrews (Ed.), *Managerial compensation.* Ann Arbor: Foundation for Research on Human Behavior, 1965. Pp. 19-20.

FLEISHMAN, E.A. A relationship between incentive motivation and ability level in psychomotor performance. *Journal of Experimental Psychology*, 1958, **56**, 78-81.

FREEDMAN, J.L. Attitudinal effects of inadequate justification. *Journal of Personality*, 1963, **31**, 371-385.

GANULI, H.C. An inquiry into incentives for workers in an engineering factory. *Indian Journal of Social Work*, 1954, **15**, 30-40.

GELLERMAN, S.W. *Motivation and productivity.* New York: American Management Association, 1963.

GEORGOPOULOS, B. S., MAHONEY, G. M., & JONES, N. W. A path-goal approach to productivity. *Journal of Applied Psychology*, 1957, **41**, 345-353.

GHISELLI, E.E. The effects on career pay of policies with respect to increases in pay. In R. Andrews (Ed.), *Managerial compensation.* Ann Arbor: Foundation for Research on Human Behavior, 1965. Pp. 21-34.

GRAHAM, D., & SLUCKIN, W. Different kinds of reward as industrial incentives. *Research Review, Durham,* 1954, **5**, 54-56.

GRICE, G.R., & DAVIS, J.D. Effect of irrelevant thirst motivation on a response learned with food reward. *Journal of Experimental Psychology,* 1957, **53**, 347-352.

HAIRE, M. The incentive character of pay. In R. Andrews (Ed)., *Managerial compensation.* Ann Arbor: Foundation for Research on Human Behavior, 1965. Pp. 13-17.

HAIRE, M., GHISELLI, E. E., & PORTER, L. W. Psychological research on pay: An overview. *Industrial Relations,* 1963, **3**, 3-8.

HARLOW, H.F. Comments on Professor Brown's paper. In, *Current theory and research in motivation.* Lincoln: University of Nebraska Press, 1953. Pp. 22-23.

HERZBERG, F., MAUSNER, B., & SNYDERMAN B., *The motivation to work.* (2nd ed.) New York: Wiley, 1959.

HICKSON, D. J. Motives of work people who restrict their output. *Occupational Psychology,* 1961, **35**, 110-121.

HOLLAND, J.G., & SKINNER B.F. *The analysis of behavior.* New York: McGraw-Hill, 1961.

HOMANS, G.C. *Social behavior: Its elementary forms.* New York: Harcourt, Brace & World, 1961.

JAQUES, E. *Equitable payment.* New York: Wiley, 1961.

JAQUES, E., RICE, A.K., & HILL, J.M. The social and psychological impact of a change in method of wage payment. *Human Relations,* 1951, **4**, 315-340.

JONES, L. V., & JEFFREY, T. E. A quantitative analysis of expressed preferences for compensation plans. *Journal of Applied Psychology,* 1964, **49**, 201-210.

KAUFMAN, H. Task performance, expected performance, and responses to failure as functions of imbalance in the self-concept. Unpublished doctoral dissertation, University of Pennsylvania, 1962.

KELLEHER, R.T., & GOLLUB, L.R. A review of positive conditioned reinforcement. *Journal of the Experimental Analysis of Behavior,* 1962, **5**, 543-597.

LARKE, A.G. Workers' attitudes on incentives. *Dun's Review and Modern Industry,* Dec. 1953, 61-63.

LAWLER, E.E., III. Managers' job performance and their attitudes toward their pay. Unpublished doctoral dissertation, University of California, Berkeley, 1964.

LAWLER, E.E., III. Managerial perceptions of compensation. Paper read at Midwestern Psychological Association convention, Chicago, April 1965.

LAWLER, E.E., III, & O'GARA, P.W. The effects of inequity produced by underpayment on work output, work quality, and attitudes toward the work. *Journal of Personality and Social Psychology,* in press.

LAWLER, E.E., III, & PORTER L.W. Perceptions regarding management compensation. *Industrial Relations,* 1963, **3**, 41-49.

LEVENTHAL, G.S. Reward magnitude and liking for instrumental activity: Further test of a two-process model. Unpublished manuscript, Yale University, 1964.

LINDER, D.E. Some psychological processes which mediate task liking. Unpublished doctoral dissertation, University of Minnesota, 1965.

MAHONEY, T. Compensation preferences of managers. *Industrial Relations,* 1964, **3**, 135-144.

MARCH, J.G., & SIMON, H.A. *Organizations.* New York: Wiley, 1958.

MARRIOTT, R. Size of working group and output. *Occupational Psychology,* 1949, **23**, 47-57.

MARRIOTT, R. Socio-psychological factors in productivity. *Occupational Psychology,* 1951, **25**, 15-24.

MARRIOTT, R. *Incentive payment systems: A review of research and opinion.* London: Staples Press, 1957.

MARRIOTT, R., & DENERLEY, R.A. A method of interviewing used in studies of workers' attitudes: II. Validity of the method and discussion of the results. *Occupational Psychology,* 1955, **29**, 69-81.

MATHEWSON, S.B. *Restriction of output among unorganized workers.* New York: Viking Press, 1951.

MILLER, D.C., & FORM, W.H. *Industrial sociology.* New York: Harper, 1951.

MYERS, C.S. *Mind and work.* London: University of London Press, 1920.

NATIONAL INDUSTRIAL CONFERENCE BOARD. Factors affecting employee morale. (Studies in Personnel Policy No. 85) New York: Author, 1947.

NEALEY, S. Pay and benefit preferences. *Industrial Relations,* 1963, **1**, 17-28.

OPINION RESEARCH CORPORATION. *Productivity from the worker's standpoint.* Princeton: Author, 1949.

PATCHEN, M. *The choice of wage comparisons.* Englewood Cliffs, N.J.: Prentice-Hall, 1961.

PORTER, L.W. Job attitudes in management: I. Perceived deficiencies in need fulfillment as a function of job level. *Journal of Applied Psychology,* 1962, **46**, 375-384.

RATH, A.A. The case for individual incentives. *Personnel Journal,* 1960, **39**, 172-175.

ROETHLISBERGER, F.J., & DICKSON, W.J. *Management and the worker.* Cambridge: Harvard University Press, 1939.

ROY, D. Quota restriction and gold bricking in a machine shop. *American Journal of Sociology,* 1952, **57**, 427-442.

RYAN, R.A., & SMITH, P.C. *Principles of industrial psychology.* New York: Ronald Press, 1954.

SAYLES, L.R. *Behavior of industrial work groups: Prediction and control.* New York: Wiley, 1958.

SCHLEH, E.C. *Management by results: The dynamics of profitable management.* New York: McGraw-Hill, 1961.

SELEKMAN, B.M. Living with collective bargaining. *Harvard Business Review,* 1941, **22**, 21-23.

SHIMMIN, S., WILLIAMS, J., & BUCK, L. Studies of some factors in incentive payment systems. Report to the Medical Research Council. London: Industrial Psychology Research Group, 1956. (Mimeo)

SKINNER, B. F. *Science and human behavior.* New York: Macmillan, 1953.

SMITH, P.C. The curve of output as a criterion of boredom. *Journal of Applied Psychology,* 1953, **37**, 69-47.

SMITH, P. C. The prediction of individual differences in susceptibility to industrial monotony. *Journal of Applied Psychology,* 1955, **39**, 322-329.

SMITH, P.C., & KENDALL, L.M. Cornell Studies of job satisfaction: VI: Implications for the future. Unpublished manuscript, Cornell University, 1963.

SPRIEGEL W.R., & DALE, A.G. Trends in personnel selection and induction. *Personnel,* 1953, **30**, 169-175.

STOUFFER, S.A., SUCHMAN,E.A., DeVINNEY, L.C., STAR, S.A., & WILLIAMS, R.M. *The American Soldier: Adjustment during army life.* Vol. 1. Princeton, N.J.: Princeton University Press, 1949.

Thompson, W.A. Eleven years after graduation. *Occupations,* 1939, **17**, 709-714.

Verplanck, W.S., & Hayes, J.R. Eating and drinking as a function of maintenance schedule. *Journal of Comparative and Physiological Psychology,* 1953, **46**, 327-333.

Viteles, M.S. *Motivations and morale in industry.* New York: Norton, 1953.

Vroom, V.H. *Work and motivation.* New York: Wiley, 1964.

Watson, G. Work satisfaction. In G. W. Hartmann & T. Newcomb (Eds.), *Industrial conflict.* New York: The Cordon Co., 1939. Pp. 114-124.

Weick, K.E. The concept of equity in the perception of pay. Paper read at Midwestern Psychological Association, April 1965.

Weick, K.E., & Penner, D.D. Comparison of two sources of inadequate and excessive justification. Unpublished manuscript, Purdue University, 1965.

Whyte, W.F. Economic incentives and human relations. *Harvard Business Review,* 1952, **30**, 73-80.

Whyte, W.F. *Money and motivation: An analysis of incentives in industry.* New York: Harper, 1955.

Wike, E.L., & Barrientos, G. Secondary reinforcement and multiple drive reduction. *Journal of Comparative and Physiological Psychology,* 1958, **51**, 640-643.

Wilkins, L.T. Incentives and the young male worker in England. *International Journal of Opinion and Attitude Research,* 1950, **4**, 541-562.

Wilkins, L. T. Incentives and the young worker. *Occupational Psychology,* 1949, **23**, 235-247.

Wolfe, J. B. Effectiveness of token-rewards for chimpanzees. *Comparative Psychology Monographs,* 1936, **12**, No. 60, 1-72.

Worthy, J.C. Factors influencing employee morale. *Harvard Business Review,* 1950, **28**, 61-73.

Wyatt, S. *Incentives in repetitive work: A practical experiment in a factory.* (Industrial Health Research Board Report No. 69) London: His Majesty's Stationery Office, 1934.

Wyatt, S., and Fraser, J. *The comparative effects of variety and uniformity in work* (Industrial Fatigue Research Board Report No. 52). London: His Majesty's Stationery Office, 1929.

Wyatt, S., Fraser, J., and Stock, F. G. L. *The effects of monotony in work.* (Industrial Fatigue Research Board Report No. 56) London: His Majesty's Stationery Office, 1929.

Wyatt, S., & Langston, J. N. *Fatigue and boredom in repetitive work.* (Industrial Health Research Board Report No. 77) London: His Majesty's Stationery Office, 1937.

Wyatt, S., & Marriott, R. *A study of attitudes to factory work.* London: Her Majesty's Stationery Office, 1956.

Zaleznik, A., Christenson, C.R. & Roethlisberger, F.J. *The motivation, productivity, and satisfaction of workers: A prediction study.* Boston: Harvard University, Graduate School of Business Administration, 1958.

PART TWO

Theories

In this section, formulations are presented which are intended to deal with theoretical constructs in both compensation and motivation. The classical motivational positions are stated. Filley and House outline the basic elements of the orientation toward motivation by the "Scientific Management School." Schein follows this with a description of the implications that such a set of assumptions about behavior have for the practice of management. The burden for performance, Schein says, "falls upon management" and the organization has the "obligation of protecting itself *and the employee* from the irrational side of his (the employee's) nature by a system of authority and controls."

However, the narrow view of the Scientific Management School has been broadened considerably by the work of Roethlisberger and Dickson in the Western Electric Plant at Hawthorne. Their research has led them to conclude that the effects of wages are dependent upon other factors. They cite cases from their studies which make evident the fact that the worker is motivated by substantially more factors than simply economic interest.

The needs approach, generally associated with and described here by Maslow, offers a tentative explanation for the failure of financial incentives. Man has a more complex set of needs than is generally assumed. Satisfied needs are not motivators, for once a basic need is satisfied, a higher level need becomes activated. The need structure of the human is indeed complex and, more importantly, variable within the population so that financial incentives in fact may not have the impact presumably attributed to them by the Scientific Management Theory.

The question of motivation of organizational members generally

47

resolves itself into one of behavior. "Why is it that someone does what he does?" The classical management theorists propose a "rational man" concept. Maslow emphasizes need satisfaction. Atkinson, in his paper, uses a more complex set of concepts to examine motivation to "perform some act." Motive, expectancy, and incentive are concepts central to this formulation. The approach here revolves heavily around achievement needs, or, in Atkinson's terms, *motivation to succeed* or *motivation to avoid failure.*

Atkinson's conclusions are partially based on his assertion that motivation strength and the relative attractiveness of tasks are both related in a curvilinear fashion to the probabilities of success. Locke takes issue with Atkinson's assumption about the relationship between performance and intentions, or goals. He argues that the more difficult the goal, the higher the performance. His findings lead him to conclude that goals as well as the intentions of the individual mediate the relationship between incentives and performance.

House and Wahba state the concepts relevant in instrumentality theory. The theory has been used to attempt explanation of many variables, one of which is performance.

The major thrust of the formulations to this point, for the most part, has emphasized the relationship between performance and incentives. The last two pieces are directed more toward the reactions of individuals to their compensation levels. Using a set of "equity" concepts, Adams and Jaques attempt to relate the satisfaction of an individual with the rewards he receives relative to his own assessment of the contribution/reward ratios of others. Essentially, both these writers focus on situations and conditions which lead the worker to conclude that his contribution is inequitably rewarded. There are, of course, some behavioral consequences to these kinds of evaluations, and these are discussed by Adams.

2

Classical Theory

ALAN C. FILLEY

AND

ROBERT J. HOUSE

Classical theory is an outgrowth of the principles of scientific management proposed by Frederick Taylor (1919). As a machine-shop foreman, Taylor found his men producing far less than they were capable of producing with the equipment available; he was sure of this because he had worked as a machinist himself. In explaining it, Taylor's reasoning was simple: If the energetic man who is naturally disposed to high productivity finds that he earns no more than the lazy man who does as little as possible, he will soon lose interest in producing as much as he can. Therefore, the solution is to make it possible for the men to earn more by producing more.

One of the troubles, Taylor decided, was that no one knew exactly how much it was reasonable to expect men to produce. To set the standard, he broke jobs down into their various elements and measured with a stopwatch the time needed to perform each one. In this way, he was able to set what he considered a "scientific" standard.

Piece rates, which were already used in many plants, enabled a man to earn more by producing more, but Taylor's plan was unique in that it greatly increased the reward for high productivity. Men were paid at one rate for each piece produced up to the point where they met the standard, but once they surpassed it, they received a higher rate not only for each additional piece but for all the pieces produced that day. Many men could even double their wages under this system.

Reprinted by permission of the authors and publisher from *Managerial Process and Organizational Behavior*, by A. C. Filley and R. J. House, pp. 356-57. Chicago, Illinois: Scott, Foresman and Company, © 1969.

The classical theory of motivation is frequently used in the business world of today, on the premise that money is the best motivator. Based on the "economic man" theory of decision making, it assumes that men rationally choose the course which is most profitable financially, and that there is no real conflict between the organizational goal of productivity and efficiency, and individual goals. Thus classical theory predicts that, if sufficient financial reward is offered for productivity, workers will choose productivity as a means to financial gain.

3

Implications of Classical Theory
for Managerial Strategy

Implied Managerial Strategy

The kinds of assumptions a manager makes about the nature of people will determine his managerial strategy and his concept of the psychological contract between the organization and the employee. The above assumptions, for example, imply essentially a *calculative* involvement, in Etzioni's terms. The organization is buying the services and obedience of the employee for economic rewards, and the organization assumes the obligation of protecting itself *and the employee* from the irrational side of his nature by a system of authority and controls. Authority rests essentially in designated offices or positions and the employee is expected to obey whoever occupies a position of authority regardless of his expertise or personality.

Primary emphasis is on efficient task performance. Management's responsibility for the feelings and morale of people is secondary. The managerial strategy which emerges is well summarized by Koontz and O'Donnell in their four principal functions which the manager must perform—(1) plan; (2) organize; (3) motivate; and (4) control.[1]

If people are not producing or morale is low, the solution is to be sought either in the redesign of jobs and organizational relationships, or in changing the incentive and control system to insure adequate moti-

---

[1]H. Koontz and C. O'Donnell. *Principles of management.* 3rd ed. New York: McGraw-Hill, 1964.

Reprinted by permission of the author and publisher from *Organizational Psychology,* by E. Schein, pp. 49-50. Englewood Cliffs, New Jersey: Prentice-Hall, Inc., ©1965.

vation and production levels. Thus an industrial organization operating by these principles will seek to improve its over-all effectiveness by worrying first about the organization itself—who reports to whom, who does what job, are the jobs designed properly in terms of efficiency and economy, and so on? Secondly, it will re-examine its incentive plans, the system by which it tries to motivate and reward performance. If productivity is low, the company may well try an individual bonus scheme which rewards the high producer, or it may stimulate competition among workers and give special rewards to the winners. Thirdly, it will re-examine its control structure. Are supervisors putting enough pressure on the men to produce? Does the system adequately identify and punish the man who fails to produce, who shirks on the job? Are there adequate information-gathering mechanisms to enable management to identify which part of the organization is failing to carry its proper share of the load?

The burden for organizational performance falls entirely on management. Employees are expected to do no more than the incentive and control systems encourage and allow; hence, even if an employee did not fit the assumptions made about him, it is unlikely that he could express alternative behavior. Consequently, the greatest danger for an organization operating by these assumptions is that they tend to be self-fulfilling. If employees are expected to be indifferent, hostile, motivated only by economic incentives, and the like, the managerial strategies used to deal with them are very likely to train them to behave in precisely this fashion.

Evidence for Rational-Economic Man

The best evidence for this image of man comes from our own day-to-day experience and most of the history of industry. The assumptions about man and the management principles which follow from them *work* in many different kinds of situations. For example, the concept of the assembly line as an efficient way to produce has proven itself over and over again. Money and individual incentives have proven to be successful motivators of human effort in many kinds of organizations. The fact that the employee's emotional needs were not fulfilled on the job was of little consequence because he often did not expect them to be fulfilled. He had learned from his parents what life in organizations was like and behaved accordingly.

Yet, in spite of the dramatic success of management strategies based on the rational-economic image of man, there were problems and instances of failure. If pay was the only thing workers could expect from the organization, then they wanted more of it. As the standard of living in industrial society rose, employees changed their expectations of what should be provided in the way of pay and privileges. Large industrial organizations initially found it easy to exploit workers; the exploitation led ultimately to the development of unions, however, which gave workers a more powerful tool for influencing management if their expectations were not met.

Jobs became more complex, and competition among organizations became more severe, which meant that management had to depend increasingly on the judgment, creative capacity, and loyalty of the worker. As organizations came to expect more of employees, they also had to reexamine their assumptions about them. And as organizations came to expect more, employees came to expect more as well. Thus, the nature of the psychological contract has tended to shift as organizations have become more complex and more dependent on their human resources.

At the same time, industrial psychologists and industrial sociologists began to study more carefully what the motivations and behavior patterns of organizational members actually were. As studies such as the Hawthorne series were conducted, it became clear that workers brought with them many motives, needs, and expectations which did not fit the rational-economic-man assumptions, yet which influenced the quality and quantity of their work and their relationship to the organization. These studies led to another set of assumptions which characterized what we may call the *social* man.

4

The Hawthorne Approach

F. J. ROETHLISBERGER

AND

W. J. DICKSON

Wage Incentives and Wage Incentive Systems

The results from the different inquiries provided considerable material for the study of financial incentive. None of the results, however, gave the slightest substantiation to the theory that the worker is primarily motivated by economic interest. The evidence indicated that the efficacy of a wage incentive is so dependent on its relation to other factors that it is impossible to separate it out as a thing in itself having an independent effect. The studies provided examples of a number of situations in which the wage incentive had either lost its power to motivate or functioned differently than is frequently assumed.

1) In the interviews, for example, most of the dissatisfaction with wages implied that the employee is just as much concerned with wage differentials, that is, the relation of his wages to the wages of other workmen, as with the absolute amount of his wages. Complaints arise when wage differentials do not express appropriately the differences in social significance which the different jobs have to the employees themselves. Many workers who expressed a grievance about wages went on to say that the reason for their complaint was not that they were dissatisfied with their own wages but that "it isn't fair."

2) In the Bank Wiring Observation room a wage plan particularly designed to appeal to the employees' monetary interests failed to

work as it should because it was not in line with the dominant social values of the situation.

3) In the Mica Splitting Test Room output dropped in the last year of the experiment when the operators first began to fear that the business depression would lead to a reduction of available work. Logically it might have been expected that in this situation the monetary incentive would have been at the peak of its efficacy. The operators should have wanted to earn as much money as they could before they were laid off. However, output dropped. The wage incentive in the face of these doubts and fears had lost its power to motivate.

In this connection there was no more interesting experiment than the Second Relay Assembly Group. This experiment, it will be remembered, was designed to test the effect of a wage incentive. In the Second Relay Assembly Group, unlike the Relay Assembly Test Room, the only change made was in the direction of an increased financial incentive. This was done in the same way that it had been accomplished in the Relay Assembly Test Room, not by changing the wage incentive system in itself, the system still remaining group piecework, but by reducing the size of the group. The operators were not segregated in a separate room but remained in the regular department. They were supposed to be a "group" in name only. A closer scrutiny, however, revealed a new element, which had not been considered important at the time. Actually the operators had not been left in their respective positions at different benches; they had been moved to one common bench in the regular department in order to facilitate the keeping of records.

When the change was made, the investigators were not alert to its social consequences. It seemed of minor importance inasmuch as supervision had not been altered by the move, but the investigators failed to take into account the competitive attitude which existed in the regular department toward the Relay Assembly Test Room operators. When the girls were moved together to form the Second Relay Assembly Group this rivalry was brought to a focus. Their output rose rapidly. This in turn jeopardized the security of their fellow workers in the regular department, and processes were set in motion which ultimately led to the discontinuance of the study. This experiment, designed to test the effect of a single variable, succeeded only in exposing a most complex social situation. Conclusions about the efficacy of a wage incentive drawn from it, unrelated to the basic social situation, would have been entirely misleading.

5

A Theory of Human Motivation

A. H. MASLOW

I. INTRODUCTION

In a previous paper[1] various propositions were presented which would have to be included in any theory of human motivation that could lay claim to being definitive. These conclusions may be briefly summarized as follows:

1) The integrated wholeness of the organism must be one of the foundation stones of motivation theory.

2) The hunger drive (or any other physiological drive) was rejected as a centering point or model for a definitive theory of motivation. Any drive that is somatically based and localizable was shown to be atypical rather than typical in human motivation.

3) Such a theory should stress and center itself upon ultimate or basic goals rather than partial or superficial ones, upon ends rather than means to these ends. Such a stress would imply a more central place for unconscious than for conscious motivations.

4) There are usually available various cultural paths to the same goal. Therefore conscious, specific local-cultural desires are not as fundamental in motivation theory as the more basic, unconscious goals.

5) Any motivated behavior, either preparatory or consummatory, must be understood to be a channel through which many basic needs may be simultaneously expressed or satisfied. Typically an act has *more* than one motivation.

6) Practically all organismic states are to be understood as motivated and as motivating.

Reprinted by permission of the publisher from *Psychological Review* 50 (1943):370-96.

7) Human needs arrange themselves in hierarchies of prepotency. That is to say, the appearance of one need usually rests on the prior satisfaction of another, more pre-potent need. Man is a perpetually wanting animal. Also no need or drive can be treated as if it were isolated or discrete; every drive is related to the state of satisfaction or dissatisfaction of other drives.

8) *Lists* of drives will get us nowhere for various theoretical and practical reasons. Furthermore any classification of motivations must deal with the problem of levels of specificity or generalization of the motives to be classified.

9) Classifications of motivations must be based upon goals rather than upon instigating drives or motivated behavior.

10) Motivation theory should be human-centered rather than animal-centered.

11) The situation or the field in which the organism reacts must be taken into account but the field alone can rarely serve as an exclusive explanation for behavior. Furthermore the field itself must be interpreted in terms of the organism. Field theory cannot be a substitute for motivation theory.

12) Not only the integration of the organism must be taken into account, but also the possibility of isolated, specific, partial or segmental reactions.

It has since become necessary to add to these another affirmation.

13) Motivation theory is not synonymous with behavior theory. The motivations are only one class of determinants of behavior. While behavior is almost always motivated, it is also almost always biologically, culturally and situationally determined as well.

The present paper is an attempt to formulate a positive theory of motivation which will satisfy these theoretical demands and at the same time conform to the known facts, clinical and observational as well as experimental. It derives most directly, however, from clinical experience. This theory is, I think, in the functionalist tradition of James and Dewey, and is fused with the holism of Wertheimer,[2] Goldstein,[3] and Gestalt Psychology, and with the dynamicism of Freud,[4] and Adler.[5] This fusion or synthesis may arbitrarily be called a "general-dynamic" theory.

It is far easier to perceive and to criticize the aspects in motivation theory than to remedy them. Mostly this is because of the very serious lack of sound data in this area. I conceive this lack of sound facts to be due primarily to the absence of a valid theory of motivation. The present theory then must be considered to be a suggested program or framework for future research and must stand or fall, not so much on facts available or evidence presented, as upon researches yet to be done, researches suggested perhaps, by the questions raised in this paper.

II. THE BASIC NEEDS

The *"physiological"* needs.—The needs that are usually taken as the starting point for motivation theory are the so-called physiological drives. Two recent lines of research make it necessary to revise our customary notions about these needs, first, the development of the concept of homeostasis, and second, the finding that appetites (preferential choices among foods) are a fairly efficient indication of actual needs or lacks in the body.

Homeostasis refers to the body's automatic efforts to maintain a constant, normal state of the blood stream. Cannon[6] has described this process for (1) the water content of the blood, (2) salt content, (3) sugar content, (4) protein content, (5) fat content, (6) calcium content, (7) oxygen content, (8) constant hydrogen-ion level (acid-base balance) and (9) constant temperature of the blood. Obviously this list can be extended to include other minerals, the hormones, vitamins, etc.

Young in a recent article[7] has summarized the work on appetite in its relation to body needs. If the body lacks some chemical, the individual will tend to develop a specific appetite or partial hunger for that food element.

Thus it seems impossible as well as useless to make any list of fundamental physiological needs for they can come to almost any number one might wish, depending on the degree of specificity of description. We can not identify all physiological needs as homeostatic. That sexual desire, sleepiness, sheer activity and maternal behavior in animals, are homeostatic, has not yet been demonstrated. Furthermore, this list would not include the various sensory pleasures (tastes, smells, tickling, stroking) which are probably physiological and which may become the goals of motivated behavior.

In a previous paper[8] it has been pointed out that these physiological drives or needs are to be considered unusual rather than typical because they are isolable, and because they are localized somatically. That is to say, they are relatively independent of each other, or other motivations and of the organism as a whole, and secondly, in many cases, it is possible to demonstrate a localized, underlying somatic base for the drive. This is true less generally than has been thought (exceptions are fatigue, sleepiness, maternal responses) but it is still true in the classic instances of hunger, sex, and thirst.

It should be pointed out again that any of the physiological needs and the consummatory behavior involved with them serve as channels for all sorts of other needs as well. That is to say, the person who thinks he is hungry may actually be seeking more for comfort, or dependence, than for vitamins or proteins. Conversely, it is possible to satisfy the hunger need in part by other activities such as drinking water or smoking cigarettes. In other words, relatively isolable as these physiological needs are, they are not completely so.

Undoubtedly these physiological needs are the most prepotent of all needs. What this means specifically is, that in the human being who is missing everything in life in an extreme fashion, it is most likely that the major motivation would be the physiological needs rather than any others. A person who is lacking food, safety, love, and esteem would most probably hunger for food more strongly than for anything else.

If all the needs are unsatisfied, and the organism is then dominated by the physiological needs, all other needs may become simply nonexistent or be pushed into the background. It is then fair to characterize the whole organism by saying simply that it is hungry, for consciousness is almost completely preempted by hunger. All capacities are put into the service of hunger-satisfaction, and the organization of these capacities is almost entirely determined by the one purpose of satisfying hunger. The receptors and effectors, the intelligence, memory, habits, all may now be defined simply as hunger-gratifying tools. Capacities that are not useful for this purpose lie dormant, or are pushed into the background. The urge to write poetry, the desire to acquire an automobile, the interest in American history, the desire for a new pair of shoes are, in the extreme case, forgotten or become of secondary importance. For the man who is extremely and dangerously hungry, no other interests exist but food. He dreams food, he remembers food, he thinks about food, he emotes only about food, he perceives only food and he wants only food. The more subtle determinants that ordinarily fuse with the physiological drives in organizing even feeding, drinking or sexual behavior, may now be so completely overwhelmed as to allow us to speak at this time (but *only* at this time) of pure hunger drive and behavior, with the one unqualified aim of relief.

Another peculiar characteristic of the human organism when it is dominated by a certain need is that the whole philosophy of the future tends also to change. For our chronically and extremely hungry man, Utopia can be defined very simply as a place where there is plenty of food. He tends to think that, if only he is guaranteed food for the rest of his life, he will be perfectly happy and will never want anything more. Life itself tends to be defined in terms of eating. Anything else will be definded as unimportant. Freedom, love, community feeling, respect, philosophy, may all be waved aside as fripperies which are useless since they fail to fill the stomach. Such a man may fairly be said to live by bread alone.

It cannot possibly be denied that such things are true but their *generality* can be denied. Emergency conditions are, almost by definition, rare in the normally functioning peaceful society. That this truism can be forgotten is due mainly to two reasons. First, rats have few motivations other than physiological ones, and since so much of the research upon motivation has been made with these animals, it is easy to carry the rat-picture over to the human being. Secondly, it is too often not realized that culture itself is an adaptive tool, one of whose main functions is to make the physiological emergencies come less and less often. In most of the known societies, chronic extreme hunger of the emergency type is rare, rather than common. In any case, this is still true in the United States. The average American citizen is experiencing appetite rather than hunger when he says "I am hungry." He is apt to experience sheer life-and-death hunger only by accident and then only a few times through his entire life.

Obviously a good way to obscure the "higher" motivations, and to get a lopsided view of human capacities and human nature, is to make the organism extremely and chronically hungry or thirsty. Anyone who attempts to make an emergency picture into a typical one, and who will measure all of man's goals and desires by his behavior during extreme physiological deprivation is certainly being blind to many things. It is quite true that man lives by bread alone—when there is no bread. But what happens to man's desires when there *is* plenty of bread and when his belly is chronically filled?

At once other (and "higher") needs emerge and these, rather than physiological hungers, dominate the organism. And when these in turn are satisfied, again new (and still "higher") needs emerge and so on. This is what we mean by saying that the basic human needs are organized into a hierarchy of relative prepotency.

One main implication of this phrasing is that gratification becomes as important a concept as deprivation in motivation theory, for it releases the organism from the domination of a relatively more physiological need, permitting thereby the emergence of other more social goals. The physiological needs, along with their partial goals, when chronically gratified cease to exist as active determinants or organizers of behavior. They now exist only in a potential fashion in the sense that they may emerge again to dominate the organism if they are thwarted. But a want that is satisfied is no longer a want. The organism is dominated and its behavior organized only by unsatisfied needs. If hunger is satisfied, it becomes unimportant in the current dynamics of the individual.

This statement is somewhat qualified by a hypothesis to be discussed more fully later, namely that it is precisely those individuals in whom a certain need has always been satisfied who are best equipped to tolerate deprivation of that need in the future, and that furthermore, those who have been deprived in the past will react differently to current satisfactions than the one who has never been deprived.

The safety needs.—If the physiological needs are relatively well gratified, there then emerges a new set of needs, which we may categorize roughly as the safety needs. All that has been said of the physiological needs is equally true, although in lesser degree, of these desires. The organism may equally well be wholly dominated by them. They may serve as the almost exclusive organizers of behavior, recruiting all the capacities of the organism in their service, and we may then fairly describe the whole organism as a safety-seeking mechanism. Again we may say of the receptors, the effectors, of the intellect and the other capacities that they are primarily safety-seeking tools. Again, as in the hungry man, we find that the dominating goal is a strong determinant not only of his current world-outlook and philosophy but also of his philosophy of the future. Practically everything looks less important than safety, (even sometimes the physiological needs which being satisfied, are now underestimated). A man, in this state, if it is extreme enough and chronic enough, may be characterized as living almost for safety alone.

Although in this paper we are interested primarily in the needs of the adult, we can approach an understanding of his safety needs perhaps more efficiently by observation of infants and children, in whom these needs are much more simple and obvious. One reason for the clearer appearance of the threat or danger reaction in infants, is that they do not inhibit this reaction at all, whereas adults in our society have been taught to inhibit it at all costs. Thus even when adults do feel their safety to be threatened we may not be able to see this on the surface. Infants will react in a total fashion and as if they were endangered, if they are disturbed or dropped suddenly, startled by loud noises, flashing light, or other unusual sensory stimulation, by rough handling, by general loss of support in the mother's arms, or by inadequate support.[9]

In infants we can also see a much more direct reaction to bodily illnesses of various kinds. Sometimes these illnesses seem to be immediately and *per se* threatening and seem to make the child feel unsafe. For instance, vomiting, colic or other sharp pains seem to make the child look at the whole world in a different way. At such a moment of pain, it may be postulated that, for the child, the appearance of the whole world suddenly changes from sunniness to darkness, so to speak, and becomes a place in which anything at all might happen, in which previously stable things have suddenly become unstable. Thus a child who because of some bad food is taken ill may, for a day or two, develop fear, nightmares, and a need for protection and reassurance never seen in him before his illness.

Another indication of the child's need for safety is his preference for some kind of undisrupted routine or rhythm. He seems to want a predictable, orderly world. For instance, injustice, unfairness, or inconsistency in the parents seems to make a child feel anxious and unsafe. This attitude may be not so much because of the injustice *per se* or any particular pains involved, but rather because this treatment threatens to make the world look unreliable, or unsafe, or unpredictable. Young children seem to thrive better under a system which has at least a skeletal outline of rigidity, in which there is a schedule of a kind, some sort of routine, something that can be counted upon, not only for the present but also far into the future. Perhaps one could express this more accurately by saying that the child needs an organized world rather than an unorganized or unstructured one.

The central role of the parents and the normal family setup are indisputable. Quarreling, physical assault, separation, divorce or death within the family may be particularly terrifying. Also parental outbursts of rage or threats of punishment directed to the child, calling him names, speaking to him harshly, shaking him, handling him roughly, or actual physical punishment sometimes elicit such total panic and terror in the child that we must assume more is involved than the physical pain alone. While it is true that in some children this terror may represent also a fear of loss of parental love, it can also occur in completely rejected children, who seem to cling to the hating parents more for sheer safety and protection than because of hope of love.

Confronting the average child with new, unfamiliar, strange unmanageable stimuli or situations will too frequently elicit the danger or terror reaction, as for example, getting lost or even being separated from the parents for a short time, being confronted with new faces, new situations or new tasks, the sight of strange, unfamiliar or uncontrollable objects, illness or death. Particularly at such times, the child's frantic clinging to his parents is eloquent testimony to their role as protectors (quite apart from their roles as food-givers and love-givers).

From these and similar observations, we may generalize and say that the average child in our society generally prefers a safe, orderly, predictable, organized world, which he can count on, and in which unexpected, unmanageable or other dangerous things do not happen, and in which, in any case, he has all-powerful parents who protect and shield him from harm.

That these reactions may so easily be observed in children is in a way a proof of the fact that children in our society, feel too unsafe (or, in a word, are badly brought up). Children who are reared in an unthreatening, loving family do *not* ordinarily react as we have described above.[10] In such children the danger reactions are apt to come mostly to objects or situations that adults too would consider dangerous.[11]

The healthy, normal, fortunate adult in our culture is largely satisfied in his safety needs. The peaceful, smoothly running, "good" society ordinarily makes its members feel safe enough from wild animals, extremes of temperature, criminals, assault and murder, tyranny, etc. Therefore, in a very real sense, he no longer has any safety needs as active motivators. Just as a sated man no longer feels hungry, a safe man no longer feels endangered. If we wish to see these needs directly and clearly we must turn to neurotic or near neurotic individuals, and to the economic and social underdogs. In between these extremes, we can perceive the expressions of safety needs only in such phenomena as, for instance, the common preference for a job with tenure and protection, the desire for a savings account, and for insurance of various kinds (medical, dental, unemployment, disability, old age).

Other broader aspects of the attempt to seek safety and stability in the world are seen in the very common preference for familiar rather than unfamiliar things, or for the known rather than the unknown. The tendency to have some religion or world-philosophy that organizes the universe and the men in it into some sort of satisfactory coherent, meaningful whole is also in part motivated by safety-seeking. Here too we may list science and philosophy in general as partially motivated by the safety needs (we shall see later that there are also other motivations to scientific, philosophical or religious endeavor).

Otherwise the need for safety is seen as an active and dominant mobilizer of the organism's resources only in emergencies, *e.g.*, war, disease, natural catastrophies, crime waves, societal disorganization, neurosis, brain injury, chronically bad situation.

Some neurotic adults in our society are, in many ways, like the unsafe child in their desire for safety, although in the former it takes on a somewhat special appearance. Their reaction is often to unknown, psychological dangers in a world that is perceived to be hostile, overwhelming and threatening. Such a person behaves as if a great catastrophe were almost always impending, *i.e.*, he is usually responding as if to an emergency. His safety needs often find specific expression in a search for a protector, or a stronger person on whom he may depend, or perhaps a Fuehrer.

The neurotic individual may be described in a slightly different way with some usefulness as a grown-up person who retains his childish attitudes toward the world. That is to say, a neurotic adult may be said to behave "as if" he were actually afraid of a spanking, or of his mother's disapproval, or of being abandoned by his parents, or having his food taken away from him. It is as if his childish attitudes of fear and threat reaction to a dangerous world had gone underground, and untouched by the growing up and learning processes, were now ready to be called out by any stimulus that would make a child feel endangered and threatened.[12]

The neurosis in which the search for safety takes its clearest form is in the compulsive-obsessive neurosis. Compulsive-obsessives try frantically to order and stabilize the world so that no unmanageable, unexpected or unfamiliar dangers will ever appear.[13] They hedge themselves about with all sorts of ceremonials, rules and formulas so that every possible contingency may be provided for and so that no new contingencies may appear. They are much like the brain injured cases, described by Goldstein,[14] who manage to maintain their equilibrium by avoiding everything unfamiliar and strange and by ordering their restricted world in such a neat, disciplined, orderly fashion that everything in the world can be counted upon. They try to arrange the world so that anything unexpected (dangers) cannot possibly occur. If, through no fault of their own, something unexpected does occur, they go into a panic reaction as if this unexpected occurrence constituted a grave danger. What we can see only as a none-too-strong preference in the healthy person, *e.g.,* preference for the familiar, becomes a life-and-death necessity in abnormal cases.

The love needs.—If both the physiological and the safety needs are fairly well gratified, then there will emerge the love and affection and belongingness needs, and the whole cycle already described will repeat itself with this new center. Now the person will feel keenly, as never before, the absence of friends, or a sweetheart, or a wife, or children. He will hunger for affectionate relations with people in general, namely, for a place in his group, and he will strive with great intensity to achieve this goal. He will want to attain such a place more than anything else in the world and may even forget that once, when he was hungry, he sneered at love.

In our society the thwarting of these needs is the most commonly found core in cases of maladjustment and more severe psychopathology. Love and affection, as well as their possible expression in sexuality, are generally looked upon with ambivalence and are customarily hedged about with many restrictions and inhibitions. Practically all theorists of psychopathology have stressed thwarting of the love needs as basic in the picture of maladjustment. Many clinical studies have therefore been made of this need and we know more about it perhaps than any of the other needs except the physiological ones.[15]

One thing that must be stressed at this point is that love is not synonymous with sex. Sex may be studied as a purely physiological need. Ordinarily sexual behavior is multi-determined, that is to say, determined not only by sexual but also by other needs, chief among which are the love and affection needs. Also not to be overlooked is the fact that the love needs involve both giving *and* receiving love.[16]

The esteem needs.—All people in our society (with a few pathological exceptions) have a need or desire for a stable, firmly based, (usually) high evaluation of themselves, for self-respect, or self-esteem and for the esteem of others. By firmly based self-esteem, we mean that which is soundly based upon real capacity, achievement and respect from others. These needs may be classified into two subsidiary sets. These are, first, the desire for strength, for achievement, for adequacy, for confidence in the face of the world, and for independence and freedom.[17] Secondly, we have what we may call the desire for reputation or prestige (defining it as respect or esteem from other people), recognition, attention, importance or appreciation.[18] These needs have been relatively stressed by Alfred Adler and his followers, and have been relatively neglected by Freud and the psychoanalysts. More and more today however there is appearing widespread appreciation of their central importance.

Satisfaction of the self-esteem need leads to feelings of self-confidence, worth, strength, capability and adequacy of being useful and necessary in the world. But thwarting of these needs produces feelings of inferiority, of weakness and of helplessness. These feelings in turn give rise to either basic discouragement or else compensatory or neurotic trends. An appreciation of the necessity of basic self-confidence and an understanding of how helpless people are without it, can be easily gained from a study of severe traumatic neurosis.[19,20]

The need for self-actualization.—Even if all these needs are satisfied, we may still often (if not always) expect that a new discontent and restlessness will soon develop, unless the individual is doing what he is fitted for. A musician must make music, an artist must paint, a poet must write, if he is to be ultimately happy. What man *can* be, he *must* be. This need we may call self-actualization.

This term, first coined by Kurt Goldstein, is being used in this paper in a much more specific and limited fashion. It refers to the desire for self-fulfillment, namely, to the tendency for him to become actualized in what he is potentially. This tendency might be phrased as the desire to become more and more what one is, to become everything that one is capable of becoming.

The specific form that these needs will take will of course vary greatly from person to person. In one individual it may take the form of the desire to be an ideal mother, in another it may be expressed athletically, and in still another it may be expressed in painting pictures or in inventions. It is not necessarily a creative urge although in people who have any capacities for creation it will take this form.

The clear emergence of these needs rests upon prior satisfaction of the physiological, safety, love and esteem needs. We shall call people who are satisfied in these needs, basically satisfied people, and it is from these that we may expect the fullest (and healthiest) creativeness.[21] Since, in our society, basically satisfied people are the exception, we do not know much about self-actualization, either experimentally or clinically. It remains a challenging problem for research.

The preconditions for the basic need satisfactions.—There are certain conditions which are immediate prerequisites for the basic need satisfactions. Danger to these is reacted to almost as if it were a direct danger to the basic needs themselves. Such conditions as freedom to speak, freedom to do what one wishes so long as no harm is done to others, freedom to express one's self, freedom to investigate and seek for information, freedom to defend one's self, justice, fairness, honesty, orderliness in the group are examples of such preconditions for basic need satisfactions. Thwarting in these freedoms will be reacted to with a threat or emergency response. These conditions are not ends in themselves but they are *almost* so since they are so closely related to the basic needs, which are apparently the only ends in themselves. These conditions are defended because without them the basic satisfactions are quite impossible, or at least, very severely endangered.

If we remember that the cognitive capacities (perceptual, intellectual, learning) are a set of adjustive tools, which have, among other functions, that of satisfaction of our basic needs, then it is clear that any danger to them, any deprivation or blocking of their free use, must also be indirectly threatening to the basic needs themselves. Such a statement is a partial solution of the general problems of curiosity, the search for knowledge, truth and wisdom, and the ever-persistent urge to solve the cosmic mysteries.

We must therefore introduce another hypothesis and speak of degrees of closeness to the basic needs, for we have already pointed out that *any* conscious desires (partial goals) are more or less important as they are more or less close to the basic needs. The same statement may be made for various behavior acts. An act is psychologically important if it contributes directly to satisfaction of basic needs. The less directly it so contributes, or the weaker this contribution is, the less important this act must be conceived to be from the point of view of dynamic psychology. A similar statement may be made for the various defense or coping mechanisms. Some are very directly related to the protection or attainment of the basic needs, others are only weakly and distantly related. Indeed if we wished, we could speak of more basic and less basic defense mechanisms, and then affirm that danger to the more basic defenses is more threatening than danger to less basic defenses (always remembering that this is so only because of their relationship to the basic needs).

The desires to know and to understand.—So far, we have mentioned the cognitive needs only in passing. Acquiring knowledge and systematizing the universe have been considered as, in part, techniques for the achievement of basic safety in the world, or, for the intelligent man, expressions of self-actualization. Also freedom of inquiry and expression have been discussed as preconditions of satisfactions of the basic needs. True though these formulations may be, they do not constitute definitive answers to the question as to the motivation role of curiosity, learning, philosophizing, experimenting, etc. They are, at best, no more than partial answers.

This question is especially difficult because we know so little about the facts. Curiosity, exploration, desire for the facts, desire to know may certainly be observed easily enough. The fact that they often are pursued even at great cost to the individual's safety is an earnest of the partial character of our previous discussion. In addition, the writer must admit that, though he has sufficient clinical evidence to postulate the desire to know as a very strong drive in intelligent people, no data are available for unintelligent people. It may then be largely a function of relatively high intelligence. Rather tentatively, then, and largely in the hope of stimulating discussion and research, we shall postulate a basic desire to know, to be aware of reality, to get the facts, to satisfy curiosity, or as Wertheimer phrases it, to see rather than to be blind.

This postulation, however, is not enough. Even after we know, we are impelled to know more and more minutely and microscopically on the one hand, and on the other, more and more extensively in the direction of a world philosophy, religion, etc. The facts that we acquire, if they are isolated or atomistic, inevitably get theorized about, and either analyzed or organized or both. This process has been phrased by some as the search for "meaning." We shall then postulate a desire to understand, to systematize, to organize, to analyze, to look for relations and meanings.

Once these desires are accepted for discussion, we see that they too form themselves into a small hierarchy in which the desire to know is prepotent over the desire to understand. All the characteristics of a hierarchy of prepotency that we have described above, seem to hold for this one as well.

We must guard ourselves against the too easy tendency to separate these desires from the basic needs we have discussed above, *i.e.,* to make a sharp dichotomy between "cognitive" and "conative" needs. The desire to know and to understnad are themselves conative, *i.e.,* have a striving character, and are as much personality needs as the "basic needs" we have already discussed.[22]

III. FURTHER CHARACTERISTICS OF THE BASIC NEEDS

The degree of fixity of the hierarchy of basic needs.—We have spoken so far as if this hierarchy were a fixed order but actually it is not nearly as rigid as we may have implied. It is true that most of the people with whom we have worked have seemed to have these basic needs in about the order that has been indicated. However, there have been a number of exceptions.

1) There are some people in whom, for instance, self-esteem seems to be more important than love. This most common reversal in the hierarchy is usually due to the development of the notion that the person who is most likely to be loved is a strong or powerful person, one who inspires respect or fear, and who is self confident or aggressive. Therefore such people who lack love and seek it, may try hard to put on a front of aggressive, confident behavior. But essentially they seek high self-esteem and its behavior expressions more as a means-to-an-end than for its own sake; they seek self-assertion for the sake of love rather than for self-esteem itself.

2) There are other, apparently innately creative people in whom the drive to creativeness seems to be more important than any other counter-determinant. Their creativeness might appear not as self-

actualization released by basic satisfaction, but in spite of lack of basic satisfaction.

3) In certain people the level of aspiration may be permanently deadened or lowered. That is to say, the less prepotent goals may simply be lost, and may disappear forever, so that the person who has experienced life at a very low level, *i.e.,* chronic unemployment, may continue to be satisfied for the rest of his life if only he can get enough food.

4) The so-called "psychopathic personality" is another example of permanent loss of the love needs. These are people who, according to the best data available[23] have been starved for love in the earliest months of their lives and have simply lost forever the desire and the ability to give and to receive affection (as animals lose sucking or pecking reflexes that are not exercised soon enough after birth).

5) Another cause of reversal of the hierarchy is that when a need has been satisfied for a long time, this need may be underevaluated. People who have never experienced chronic hunger are apt to underestimate its effects and to look upon food as a rather unimportant thing. If they are dominated by a higher need, this higher need will seem to be the most important of all. It then becomes possible, and indeed does actually happen, that they may, for the sake of this higher need, put themselves into the position of being deprived in a more basic need. We may expect that after a long-time deprivation of the more basic need there will be a tendency to reevaluate both needs so that the more prepotent need will actually become consciously prepotent for the individual who may have given it up very lightly. Thus, a man who has given up his job rather than lose his self-respect, and who then starves for six months or so, may be willing to take his job back even at the price of losing his self-respect.

6) Another partial explanation of *apparent* reversals is seen in the fact that we have been talking about the hierarchy of prepotency in terms of consciously felt wants or desires rather than of behavior. Looking at behavior itself may give us the wrong impression. What we have claimed is that the person will *want* the more basic of two needs when deprived in both. There is no necessary implication here that he will act upon his desires. Let us say again that there are many determinants of behavior other than the needs and desires.

7) Perhaps more important than all these exceptions are the ones that involve ideals, high social standards, high values and the like. With such values people become martyrs; they will give up everything for the sake of a particular ideal, or value. These people may be understood, at least in part, by reference to one basic concept (or hypothesis) which may be

called "increased frustration-tolerance through early gratification."
People who have been satisfied in their basic needs throughout their
lives, particularly in their earlier years, seem to develop exceptional
power to withstand present or future thwarting of these needs simply
because they have strong, healthy character structure as a result of basic
satisfaction. They are the "strong" people who can easily weather disagreement or opposition, who can swim against the stream of public
opinion and who can stand up for the truth at great personal cost. It is
just the ones who have loved and been well loved, and who have had
many deep friendships who can hold out against hatred, rejection or
persecution.

I say all this in spite of the fact that there is a certain amount of sheer
habituation which is also involved in any full discussion of frustration
tolerance. For instance, it is likely that those persons who have been accustomed to relative starvation for a long time, are partially enabled
thereby to withstand food deprivation. What sort of balance must be
made between these two tendencies, of habituation on the one hand, and
of past satisfaction breeding present frustration-tolerance on the other
hand, remains to be worked out by further research. Meanwhile we may
assume that they are both operative, side by side, since they do not
contradict each other. In respect to this phenomenon of increased
frustration tolerance, it seems probable that the most important grati-
fications come in the first two years of life. That is to say, people who
have been made secure and strong in the earliest years, tend to remain
secure and strong thereafter in the face of whatever threatens.

Degrees of relative satisfaction.—So far, our theoretical discussion
may have given the impression that these five sets of needs are somehow
in a step-wise, all-or-none relationship to each other. We have spoken in
such terms as the following: "If one need is satisfied, then another emerges." This statement might give the false impression that a need must
be satisfied 100 per cent before the next need emerges. In actual fact,
most members of our society who are normal, are partially satisfied in
all their basic needs and partially unsatisfied in all their basic needs at
the same time. A more realistic description of the hierarchy would be
in terms of decreasing percentages of satisfaction as we go up the
hierarchy of prepotency. For instance, if I may assign arbitrarily figures
for the sake of illustration, it is as if the average citizen is satisfied 85
percent in his physiological needs, 70 per cent in his safety needs, 50
per cent in his love needs, 40 per cent in self-esteem needs, and 10 per
cent in his self-actualization needs.

As for the concept of emergence of a new need after satisfaction of the prepotent need, this emergence is not a sudden, saltatory phenomenon but rather a gradual emergence by slow degrees from nothingness. For instance, if prepotent need A is satisfied only 10 per cent then need B may not be visible at all. However, as this need A becomes satisfied 25 per cent, need B may emerge 5 per cent, as need A becomes satisfied 75 per cent need B may emerge 90 per cent, and so on.

Unconscious character of needs.—These needs are neither necessarily conscious nor unconscious. On the whole, however, in the average person, they are more often unconscious rather than conscious. It is not necessary at this point to overhaul the tremendous mass of evidence which indicates the crucial importance of unconscious motivation. It would by now be expected, on a priori grounds alone, that unconscious motivations would on the whole be rather more important than the conscious motivations. What we have called the basic needs are very often largely unconscious although they may, with suitable techniques, and with sophisticated people become conscious.

Cultural specificity and generality of needs.—This classification of basic needs makes some attempt to take account of the relative unity behind the superficial differences in specific desires from one culture to another. Certainly in any particular culture an individual's conscious motivational content will usually be extremely different from the conscious motivational content of an individual in another society. However, it is the common experience of anthropologists that people, even in different societies, are much more alike than we would think from our first contact with them, and that as we know them better we seem to find more and more of this commonness. We then recognize the most startling differences to be superficial rather than basic, *e.g.,* differences in style of hairdress, clothes, tastes in food, etc. Our classification of basic needs is in part an attempt to account for this unity behind the apparent diversity from culture to culture. No claim is made that it is ultimate or universal for all cultures. The claim is made only that it is relatively *more* ultimate, more universal, more basic, than the superficial conscious desires from culture to culture, and makes a somewhat closer approach to common-human characteristics. Basic needs are *more* common-human than superficial desires or behaviors.

Multiple motivations of behavior.—These needs must be understood *not* to be *exclusive* or single determiners of certain kinds of behavior. An example may be found in any behavior that seems to be physiologically motivated, such as eating, or sexual play or the like. The clinical psychologists have long since found that any behavior may be a channel through which flow various determinants. Or to say it in another way, most behavior is multi-motivated. Within the sphere of motivational determinants any behavior tends to be determined by several or *all* of the basic needs simultaneously rather than by only one of them. The latter would be more an exception than the former. Eating may be partially for the sake of filling the stomach, and partially for the sake of comfort and amelioration of the other needs. One may make love not only for pure sexual release, but also to convince one's self of one's masculinity, or to make a conquest, to feel powerful, or to win more basic affection. As an illustration, I may point out that it would be possible (theoretically if not practically) to analyze a single act of an individual and see in it the expression of his physiological needs, his safety needs, his love needs, his esteem needs and self-actualization. This contrasts sharply with the more naive brand of trait psychology in which one trait or one motive accounts for a certain kind of act, *i.e.,* an aggressive act is traced solely to a trait of aggressiveness.

Multiple determinants of behavior.—Not all behavior is determined by the basic needs. We might even say that not all behavior is motivated. There are many determinants of behavior other than motives.[24] For instance, one other important class of determinants is the so-called "field" determinants. Theoretically, at least, behavior may be determined completely by the field, or even by specific isolated external stimuli, as in association of ideas, or certain conditioned reflexes. If in response to the stimulus word "table," I immediately perceive a memory image of a table, this response certainly has nothing to do with my basic needs.

Secondly, we may call attention again to the concept of "degree of closeness to the basic needs" or "degree of motivation." Some behavior is highly motivated, other behavior is only weakly motivated. Some is not motivated at all (but all behavior is determined).

Another important point[25] is that there is a basic difference between expressive behavior and coping behavior (functional striving, purposive goal seeking). An expressive behavior does not try to do anything; it is simply a reflection of the personality. A stupid man behaves stupidly, not because he wants to, or tries to, or is motivated to, but simply because he *is* what he is. The same is true when I speak in a bass voice rather than tenor or soprano. The random movement of a healthy child, the smile on the face of a happy man even when he is alone, the springiness of the healthy man's walk, and the erectness of his carriage are other examples of expressive, non-functional behavior. Also the *style* in which a man carries out almost all his behavior, motivated as well as unmotivated is often expressive.

We may then ask, is *all* behavior expressive or reflective of the character structure? The answer is "No." Rote, habitual, automatized, or conventional behavior may or may not be expressive. The same is true for most "stimulus-bound" behaviors.

It is finally necessary to stress that expressiveness of behavior, and goal-directedness of behavior are not mutually exclusive categories. Average behavior is usually both.

Goals as centering principle in motivation theory.—It will be observed that the basic principle in our classification has been neither the instigation nor the motivated behavior but rather the functions, effects, purposes, or goals of the behavior. It has been proven sufficiently by various people that this is the most suitable point for centering in any motivation theory.[26]

Animal- and human-centering.—This theory starts with the human being rather than any lower and presumably "simpler" animal. Too many of the findings that have been made in animals have been proven to be true for animals but not for the human being. There is no reason whatsoever why we should start with animals in order to study human motivation. The logic or rather illogic behind this general fallacy of "pseudo-simplicity" has been exposed often enough by philosophers and logicians as well as by scientists in each of the various fields. It is no more necessary to study animals before one can study man than it is to study mathematics before one can study geology or psychology or biology.

We may also reject the old, naive, behaviorism which assumed that it was somehow necessary, or at least more "scientific" to judge human beings by animal standards. One consequence of this belief was that the whole notion of purpose and goal was excluded from motivational psychology simply because one could not ask a white rat about his purposes. Tolman[27] has long since proven in animal studies themselves that this exclusion was not necessary.

Motivation and the theory of psychopathogenesis.—The conscious motivational content of everyday life has, according to the foregoing, been conceived to be relatively important or unimportant accordingly as it is more or less closely related to the basic goals. A desire for an ice cream cone might actually be an indirect expression of a desire for love. If it is, then this desire for the ice cream cone becomes extremely important motivation. If however the ice cream is simply something to cool the mouth with, or a casual appetitive reaction, then the desire is relatively unimportant. Everyday conscious desires are to be regarded as symptoms, as *surface indicators of more basic needs*. If we were to take these superficial desires at their face value we would find ourselves in a state of complete confusion which could never be resolved, since we would be dealing seriously with symptoms rather than with what lay behind the symptoms.

Thwarting of unimportant desires produces no psychopathological results; thwarting of a basically important need does produce such results. Any theory of psychopathogenesis must then be based on a sound theory of motivation. A conflict or a frustration is not necessarily pathogenic. It becomes so only when it threatens or thwarts the basic needs or partial needs that are closely related to the basic needs.[28]

The role of gratified needs.—It has been pointed out above several times that our needs usually emerge only when more prepotent needs have been gratified. Thus gratification has an important role in motivation theory. Apart from this, however, needs cease to play an active determining or organizing role as soon as they are gratified.

What this means is that, *e.g.,* a basically satisfied person no longer has the needs for esteem, love, safety, etc. The only sense in which he might be said to have them is in the almost metaphysical sense that a sated man has hunger, or a filled bottle has emptiness. If we are interested in what *actually* motivates us, and not in what has, will, or might motivate us, then a satisfied need is not a motivator. It must be considered for all practical purposes simply not to exist, to have disappeared. This point should be emphasized because it has been either overlooked or contradicted in every theory of motivation I know.[29] The perfectly healthy, normal, fortunate man has no sex needs or hunger needs, or needs for safety, or for love, or for prestige, or self-esteem, except in stray moments of quickly passing threat. If we were to say otherwise, we should also have to aver that every man had all the pathological reflexes, *e.g.,* Babinski, etc., because if his nervous system were damaged, these would appear.

It is such considerations as these that suggest the bold postulation that a man who is thwarted in any of his basic needs may fairly be envisaged simply as a sick man. This is a fair parallel to our designation as "sick" of the man who lacks vitamins or minerals. Who is to say that a lack of love is less important than a lack of vitamins? Since we know the pathogenic effects of love starvation, who is to say that we are invoking value-questions in an unscientific or illegitimate way, any more than the physician does who diagnoses and treats pellagra or scurvy? If I were permitted this usage, I should then say simply that a healthy man is primarily motivated by his needs to develop and actualize his fullest potentialities and capacities. If a man has any other basic needs in any active, chronic sense, then he is simply an unhealthy man. He is as surely sick as if he had suddenly developed a strong salt-hunger or calcium hunger.[30]

If this statement seems unusual or paradoxical the reader may be assured that this is only one among many such paradoxes that will appear as we revise our ways of looking at man's deeper motivations. When we ask what man wants of life, we deal with his very essence.

IV. SUMMARY

1) There are at least five sets of goals, which we may call basic needs. These are briefly physiological, safety, love, esteem, and self-actualization. In addition, we are motivated by the desire to achieve or maintain the various conditions upon which these basic satisfactions rest and by certain more intellectual desires.

2) These basic goals are related to each other, being arranged in a hierarchy of prepotency. This means that the most prepotent goal will monopolize consciousness and will tend of itself to organize the recruitment of the various capacities of the organism. The less prepotent needs are minimized, even forgotten or denied. But when a need is fairly well satisfied, the next prepotent ("higher") need emerges, in turn to dominate the conscious life and to serve as the center of organization of behavior, since gratified needs are not active motivators.

Thus man is a perpetually wanting animal. Ordinarily the satisfaction of these wants is not altogether mutually exclusive, but only tends to be. The average member of our society is most often partially satisfied and partially unsatisfied in all of his wants. The hierarchy principle is usually empirically observed in terms of increasing percentages of non-satisfaction as we go up the hierarchy. Reversals of the average order of the hierarchy are sometimes observed. Also it has been observed that an individual may permanently lose the higher wants in the hierarchy under special conditions. There are not only ordinarily multiple motivations for usual behavior, but in addition many determinants other than motives.

3) Any thwarting or possibility of thwarting of these basic human goals or danger to the defenses which protect them or to the conditions upon which they rest, is considered to be a psychological threat. With a few exceptions, all psychopathology may be partially traced to such

threats. A basically thwarted man may actually be defined as a "sick" man, if we wish.

4) It is such basic threats which bring about the general emergency reactions.

5) Certain other basic problems have not been dealt with because of limitations of space. Among these are (*a*) the problem of values in any definitive motivation theory, (*b*) the relation between appetites, desires, needs and what is "good" for the organism, (*c*) the etiology of the basic needs and their possible derivation in early childhood, (*d*) redefinition of motivational concepts, *i.e.,* drive, desire, wish, need, goal, (*e*) implication of our theory for hedonistic theory, (*f*) the nature of the uncompleted act, of success and failure, and of aspiration-level, *(g)* the role of association, habit and conditioning, (*h*) relation to the theory of interpersonal relations, (*i*) implications for psychotherapy, (*j*) implication for theory of society, (*k*) the theory of selfishness, (*l*) the relation between needs and cultural patterns, (*m*) the relation between this theory and Allport's theory of functional autonomy. These as well as certain other less important questions must be considered as motivation theory attempts to become definitive.

NOTES

[1] A. H. Maslow, "A Preface to Motivation Theory," *Psychosomatic Medicine,* Vol. 5, 1943, pp. 85-92.

[2] M. Wertheimer, unpublished lectures at the New School for Social Research.

[3] K. Goldstein, *The Organism* (New York: American Book Co., 1939).

[4] S. Freud, *New Introductory Lectures on Psychoanalysis* (New York: Norton, 1933).

[5] A. Adler, *Social Interest* (London: Faber & Faber, 1938).

[6] W. B. Cannon, *Wisdom of the Body* (New York: Norton, 1932).

[7] P. T. Young, "The Experimental Analysis of Appetite," *Psychological Bulletin,* Vol. 38, 1941, pp. 129-164.

[8] Maslow, *loc. cit.*

[9] As the child grows up, sheer knowledge and familiarity as well as better motor development make these "dangers" less and less dangerous and more and more manageable. Throughout life it may be said that one of the main conative functions of education is this neutralizing of apparent dangers through knowledge, *e.g.,* I am not afraid of thunder because I know something about it.

[10] M. Shirley, "Children's Adjustments to a Strange Situation," *Journal of Abnormal (Soc.) Psychology,* Vol. 37, 1942, pp. 201-217.

[11] A "test battery" for safety might be confronting the child with a small exploding firecracker, or with a bewhiskered face, having the mother leave the room, putting him upon a high ladder, a hypodermic injection, having a mouse crawl up to him, etc. Of course I cannot seriously recommend the deliberate use of such "tests" for they might very well harm the child being tested. But these and similar situations come up by the score in the child's ordinary day-to-day living and may be observed. There is no reason why these stimuli should not be used with, for example, young chimpanzees.

[12]Not all neurotic individuals feel unsafe. Neurosis may have at its core a thwarting of the affection and esteem needs in a person who is generally safe.

[13]A. H. MASLOW and B. MITTLEMANN, *Principles of Abnormal Psychology* (New York: 331-344,

[14]Goldstein, *loc. cit.*

[15]Maslow and Mittelmann, *loc. cit.*

[16]For further details see A. H. Maslow, "The Dynamics of Psychological Security-Insecurity," *Character and Personality,* Vol. 10, 1942, pp. 331-344, and J. Plant, *Personality and the Cultural Pattern* (New York: Commonwealth Fund, 1937), Ch. 5.

[17]Whether or not this particular desire is universal we do not know. The crucial question, especially important today, is "Will men who are enslaved and dominated, inevitably feel dissatisfied and rebellious?" We may assume on the basis of commonly known clinical data that a man who has known true freedom (not paid for by giving up safety and security but rather built on the basis of adequate safety and security) will not willingly or easily allow his freedom to be taken away from him. But we do not know that this is true for the person born into slavery. The events of the next decade should give us our answer. See discussion of this problem in E. Fromm, *Escape from Freedom* (New York: Farrar and Rinehart, 1941).

[18]Perhaps the desire for prestige and respect from others is subsidiary to the desire for self-esteem or confidence in oneself. Observation of children seems to indicate that this is so, but clinical data give no clear support for such a conclusion.

[19]A. Kardiner, *The Traumatic Neuroses of War* (New York: Hoeber, 1941).

[20]For more extensive discussion of normal self-esteem, as well as for reports of various researches, see A. S. Maslow, "Dominance, Personality and Social Behavior in Women," *Journal (Soc.) of Psychology,* Vol. 10, 1939, pp. 3-39.

[21]Clearly creative behavior, like painting, is like any other behavior in having multiple determinants. It may be seen in "innately creative" people whether they are satisfied or not, happy or unhappy, hungry or sated. Also it is clear that creative activity may be compensatory, ameliorative or purely economic. It is my impression (as yet unconfirmed) that it is possible to distinguish the artistic and intellectual products of basically satisfied people from those of basically unsatisfied people by inspection alone. In any case, here too we must distinguish, in a dynamic fashion, the overt behavior itself from its various motivations or purposes.

[22]M. Wertheimer, unpublished lectures at the New School for Social Research.

[23]D. M. Levy, "Primary Affect Hunger," *American Journal of Psychiatry,* Vol. 94, 1937, pp. 643-652.

[24]I am aware than many psychologists and psychoanalysts use the term "motivated" and "determined" synonymously, *e.g.,* Freud. But I consider this an obfuscating usage. Sharp distinctions are necessary for clarity of thought, and precision in experimentation.

[25]To be discussed fully in a subsequent publication.

[26]The interested reader is referred to the very excellent discussion of this point in H. A. Murray, *et al., Explorations in Personality* (New York: Oxford University Press, 1938).

[27]E. C. Tolman, *Purposive Behavior in Animals and Men* (New York: Century, 1932).

[28]A. H. Maslow, "Conflict, Frustration, and the Theory of Threat," *Journal of Abnormal (Soc.) Psychology,* Vol. 38, 1943, pp. 81-86.

[29]Note that acceptance of this theory necessitates basic revision of the Freudian theory.

[30]If we were to use the word "sick" in this way, we should then also have to face squarely the relations of man to his society. One clear implication of our definition would be that (1) since a man is to be called sick who is basically thwarted, and (2) since such basic thwarting is made possible ultimately only by forces outside the individual, then (3) sickness in the individual must come ultimately from a sickness in the society. The "good" or healthy society would then be defined as one that permitted man's highest purposes to emerge by satisfying all his prepotent basic needs.

6

Motivational Determinants
of Risk-Taking Behavior*

JOHN W. ATKINSON

There are two problems of behavior which any theory of motivation must come to grips with. They may finally reduce to one; but it will simplify the exposition which follows to maintain the distinction in this paper. The first problem is to account for an individual's selection of one path of action among a set of possible alternatives. The second problem is to account for the amplitude or vigor of the action tendency once it is initiated, and for its tendency to persist for a time in a given direction. This paper will deal with these questions in a conceptual framework suggested by research which has used thematic apperception to assess individual differences in strength of achievement motivation (Atkinson, 1954; McClelland, 1955; McClelland, Atkinson, Clark, and Lowell, 1953).

The problem of selection arises in experiments which allow the individual to choose a task among alternatives that differ in difficulty (level of aspiration). The problem of accounting for the vigor of response arises in studies which seek to relate individual differences in strength of motivation to the level of performance when response output at a particular task is the dependent variable. In treating these two

*The reader should note that in this selection references are made to other chapters in *A Theory of Achievement Motivation.* It is suggested that these may be of value and should be examined.

Reprinted by permission of the author and publisher from J. W. Atkinson, "Motivational Determinants of Risk-Taking Behavior." In *A Theory of Achievement Motivation,* by J. W. Atkinson and N. T. Feather. New York: John Wiley and Sons, © 1966. An earlier version appeared in *Psychological Review* 64 (1957): 359-72. The publisher's permission to use is acknowledged.

78

problems, the discussion will be constantly focused on the relationship of achievement motivation to risk-taking behavior, an important association uncovered by McClelland (1955, 1961) in the investigation of the role of achievement motivation in entrepreneurship and economic development.

Earlier studies have searched for a theoretical principle which would explain the relationship of strength of motive, as inferred from thematic apperception, to overt goal-directed performance. The effect of situation cues (e.g., of particular instructions) on this relationship was detected quite early (Atkinson, 1950, 1953), and subsequent experiments have suggested a theoretical formulation similar to that presented by Tolman (1955) and Rotter (1954). It has been proposed that *n* Achievement scores obtained from thematic apperception are indices of individual differences in the strength of achievement motive, conceived as a relatively stable disposition to strive for achievement or success. This motive-disposition is presumed to be latent until aroused by situation cues which indicate that some performance will be instrumental to achievement. The strength of *aroused* motivation to achieve as manifested in performance has been viewed as a function of both the strength of motive and the *expectancy* of goal-attainment aroused by situation cues. This conception has provided a fairly adequate explanation of experimental results to date, and several of its implications have been tested (Atkinson, 1954; Atkinson and Reitman, 1956).

The similarity of this conception to the expectancy principle of performance developed by Tolman, which also takes account of the effects of a third variable, *incentive,* suggested the need for experiments to isolate the effects on motivation of variations in strength of expectancy of success and variations in the incentive value of particular accomplishments. The discussion which follows was prompted by the results of several exploratory experiments. It represents an attempt to state explicitly how individual differences in the strength of achievement-related motives influence behavior in competitive achievement situations. . . .

Three variables require definition and, ultimately, independent measurement. The three variables are *motive, expectance,* and *incentive.* Two of these—expectancy and incentive—are similar to variables presented by Tolman (1955) and Rotter (1954). An expectancy is a cognitive anticipation, usually aroused by cues in a situation, that performance of some act will be followed by a particular consequence. The strength of an expectancy can be represented as the subjective probability of the consequence, given the act.

The incentive variable has been relatively ignored, or at best crudely defined, in most research. It represents the relative attractiveness of a specific goal that is offered in a situation, or the relative unattractiveness of an event that might occur as a consequence of some act. Incentives may be manipulated experimentally as, for example, when amount of food (reward) or amount of shock (punishment) is varied in research with animals.

The third variable in this triumvirate—motive—is here conceived differently than, for example, in the common conception of motivation as nondirective but energizing *drive* (Brown, 1953, 1961). A motive is conceived as a disposition to strive for a certain kind of satisfaction, as a capacity for satisfaction in the attainment of a certain class of incentives. The names given motives—such as achievement, affiliation, power—are really names of classes of incentives which produce essentially the same kind of experience of satisfaction: pride in accomplishment, or the sense of belonging and being warmly received by others, or the feeling of being in control and influential. (See Atkinson, 1958c.) McClelland (1951, pp. 341-352 and 441-458; McClelland, Atkinson, Clark, and Lowell, 1953) has presented arguments to support the conception of motives as relatively general and stable characteristics of the personality which have their origins in early childhood experience. The idea that a motive may be considered a *capacity for satisfaction* is suggested by Winterbottom's finding that children who are strong in achievement motive are rated by teachers as deriving more pleasure from success than children who are weak in achievement motive. (McClelland, Atkinson, Clark, and Lowell, 1953; Winterbottom, 1953, 1958.)

The general aim of one class of motives, usually referred to as appetites or approach tendencies, is to maximize satisfaction of some kind. The achievement motive is considered a disposition to approach success.

The aim of another class of motives is to minimize pain. These have been called aversions, or avoidant tendencies. An avoidance motive represents the individual's capacity to experience pain in connection with certain kinds of negative consequences of acts. The motive to avoid failure is considered a disposition to avoid failure and/or a capacity for experiencing shame and humiliation as a consequence of failure.

The Principle of Motivation

The strength of motivation to perform some act is assumed to be a multiplicative function of the strength of the motive, the expectancy (subjective probability) that the act will have as a consequence the attainment of an incentive, and the value of the incentive: Motivation = f (Motive × Expectancy × Incentive). This formulation corresponds to Tolman's (1955) analysis of performance except, perhaps, in the conception of a motive as a relatively stable disposition. When both motivation to approach and motivation to avoid are simultaneously aroused, the resultant motivation is the algebraic summation of approach and avoidance. The act which is performed among a set of alternatives is the act for which the resultant motivation is most positive. The magnitude of response and the persistence of behavior are functions of the strength of motivation to perform the act relative to the strength of motivation to perform competing acts.

Recent experiments (Atkinson and Reitman, 1956) have helped to clarify one problem concerning the relationship between measures of the strength of a particular motive (*n* Achievement) and performance. Performance is positively related to the strength of a particular motive only when an expectancy of satisfying that motive through performance has been aroused, and when expectancies of satisfying other motives through the same action have not been sufficiently aroused to confound the simple relationship. This is to say that when expectancies of attaining several different kinds of incentives are equally *salient* in a situation, the determination of motivation to perform an act is very complex. Performance is then overdetermined in the sense that its strength is now a function of the several different kinds of motivation which have been aroused. The *ideal situation* for showing the relationship between the strength of a particular motive and behavior is one in which the only *reason* for acting is to satisfy that motive.

The theoretical formulation which follows pertains to such an *ideal achievement-related situation,* which is at best only approximated in actual experimentation or in the normal course of everyday life. The discussion will deal only with the effects of the two motives, to achieve and to avoid failure, normally aroused whenever performance is likely to be evaluated against some standard of excellence.

Behavior Directed Toward Achievement and Away from Failure

The problem of selection is confronted in the level-of-aspiration situation where the individual must choose among tasks which differ in degree of difficulty. The problem of accounting for the vigor of perform-ance arises in the situation which will be referred to as *constrained performance*. Here there is no opportunity for the individual to choose his own task. He is simply given a task to perform. He must, of course, decide to perform the task rather than to leave the situation. There *is* a problem of selection. In referring to this situation as constrained per-formance, it is the writer's intention to deal only with those instances of behavior in which motivation for the alternative of leaving the situa-tion is less positive or more negative than for performance of the task that is presented. Hence, the individual does perform the task that is given. The level of performance is the question of interest.

Elaboration of the implications of the multiplicative combination of motive, expectancy, and incentive, as proposed to account for strength of motivation, will be instructive if we can find some reasonable basis for assigning numbers to the different variables. The strength of expec-tancy can be represented as a subjective probability ranging from 0 to 1.00. But the problem of defining the positive incentive value of a par-ticular accomplishment and the negative incentive value of a particular failure is a real stickler.

In past discussions of level of aspiration, Escalona (1940) and Festinger (1942b; see Lewin, Dembo, Festinger, and Sears, 1944) have assumed that, within limits, the attractiveness of success is a positive function of the difficulty of the task, and that the unattractiveness of failure is a negative function of difficulty, when the type of activity is held constant. The author will go a few steps farther with these ideas, and assume that degree of difficulty can be inferred from the subjective probability of success P_s. The task an individual finds difficult is one for which his subjective probability of success P_s is very low. The task an individual finds easy is one for which his subjective probability of success P_s is very high. Now we are in a position to make simple assumptions about the incentive values of success or failure at a par-ticular task. Let us assume that the incentive value of success I_s is a positive linear function of difficulty. If so, the value $1 - P_s$ can repre-sent I_s, the incentive value of success. When P_s is high (e.g., .90), an easy task, I_s is low (e.g., .10). When P_s is low (e.g., .10), a difficult task, I_s is high (e.g., .90). The negative incentive value of failure I_f can be taken as $-P_s$. When P_s is high (e.g., .90), as in confronting a very easy task, the sense of humiliation accompanying failure is also very great (e.g.,—.90). However, when P_s is low (e.g., .10), as in confront-ing a very difficult task, there is little embarrassment in failing (e.g.,

—.10). We assume, in other words, that the (negative) incentive value of failure I_f is a negative linear function of difficulty.

It is of some importance to recognize the dependence of incentive values intrinsic to achievement and failure upon the subjective probability of success. One cannot anticipate the thrill of a great accomplishment if, as a matter of fact, one faces what seems a very easy task. Nor does an individual experience only a minor sense of pride after some extraordinary feat against what seemed to him overwhelming odds. The implications of the scheme which follows rest heavily upon the assumption of such dependence.

In Table 1, values of 1 have been arbitrarily assigned to the achievement motive M_S and the motive to avoid failure M_{AF}. Table 1 contains the strength of motivation to approach success ($M_S \times P_s \times I_s$) and motivation to avoid failure ($M_{AF} \times P_f \times I_f$) through performance of nine different tasks labeled A through I. The tasks differ in degree of difficulty as inferred from the subjective probability of success (P_s). The incentive values of success and failure at each of the tasks have been calculated directly from the assumptions that incentive value of success equals $1 - P_s$ and that incentive value of failure equals $- P_s$; and P_s and P_f are assumed to add to 1.00.

TABLE 1

Aroused motivation to achieve (approach) and to avoid failure (avoidance) as a joint function of motive *(M)*, expectancy *(P)*, and incentive *(I)*, where $I_s = (1 - P_s)$ and $I_f = (-P_s)$

	Motivation to Achieve				Motivation to Avoid Failure			Resultant Motivation (Approach—Avoidance)
	$M_S \times P_s \times I_s =$			Ap-proach	$M_{AF} \times P_f \times I_f =$		Avoid-ance	
Task A	1	.10	.90	.09	1	.90	—.10	—.09	0
Task B	1	.20	.80	.16	1	.80	—.20	—.16	0
Task C	1	.30	.70	.21	1	.70	—.30	—.21	0
Task D	1	.40	.60	.24	1	.60	—.40	—.24	0
Task E	1	.50	.50	.25	1	.50	—.50	—.25	0
Task F	1	.60	.40	.24	1	.40	—.60	—.24	0
Task G	1	.70	.30	.21	1	.30	—.70	—.21	0
Task H	1	.80	.20	.16	1	.20	—.80	—.16	0
Task I	1	.90	.10	.09	1	.10	—.90	—.09	0

Table 1 may be considered an extension of ideas presented in the *resultant valence* theory of level of aspiration by Escalona and Festinger (see Lewin, Dembo, Festinger, and Sears, 1944). The present formulation goes beyond their proposals *(a)* in making specific assumptions regarding the incentive values of success and failure, and *(b)* in stating explicitly how individual differences in strength of achievement motive and motive to avoid failure influence motivation.[1]

When the Achievement Motive Is Stronger ($M_S > M_{AF}$)

The right-hand column of Table 1 shows the resultant motivation for each of the tasks in this special case where achievement motive and motive to avoid failure are equal in strength. In every case there is an approach-avoidance conflict with resultant motivation equal to 0. This means that if the achievement motive were stronger than the motive to avoid failure—for example, if we assigned M_S a value of 2—the resultant motivation would become positive for each of the tasks and its magnitude would be the same as in the column labeled *Approach*. Let us therefore consider only the strength of approach motivation for each of the tasks, to see the implications of the model for the person in whom the need for achievement is stronger than his disposition to avoid failure.

One thing is immediately apparent. Motivation to achieve is strongest when uncertainty regarding the outcome is greatest, i.e., when P_s equals .50. If the individual were confronted with all of these tasks and were free to set his own goal, he should choose Task E where P_s is .50, for this is the point of maximum approach motivation. The strength of motivation to approach decreases as P_s increases from .50 to near certainty of success ($P_s = .90$), and it also decreases as P_s decreases from .50 to near certainty of failure ($P_s = .10$).

If this person were to be confronted with a single task in what is here called the constrained performance situation, we should expect him to manifest strongest motivation in the performance of a task of intermediate difficulty where P_s equals .50. If presented either more difficult tasks or easier tasks, the strength of motivation manifested in performance should be lower. The relationship between strength of motivation as expressed in performance level and expectancy of success at the task, in other words, should be described by a bell-shaped curve.

When the Motive to Avoid Failure Is Stronger ($M_{AF} > M_S$)

Let us now ignore the strength of approach motivation and tentatively assign it a value of 0, in order to examine the implications of the model for any case in which the motive to avoid failure is the stronger motive. The resultant motivation for each task would then correspond to the values listed in the column labeled *Avoidance.*

What should we expect of the person in whom the disposition to avoid failure is stronger than the motive to achieve? It is apparent at once that the resultant motivation for every task would be negative for him. This person should want to avoid all of the tasks. Competitive achievement situations are unattractive to him. If, however, he is constrained (e.g., by social pressures) and asked to set his level of aspiration, he should *avoid* tasks of intermediate difficulty (P_s =.50) where the arousal of anxiety about failure is greatest. He should choose either the easiest (P_s =.90) or the most difficult task (P_s =.10). The strength of avoidant motivation is weakest at these two points.

In summary, the person in whom the achievement motive is stronger should set his level of aspiration in the intermediate zone where there is moderate risk. To the extent that he has any motive to avoid failure, this means that he will voluntarily choose activities that *maximize* his own anxiety about failure! On the other hand, the person in whom the motive to avoid failure is stronger should select either the easiest of the alternatives or should be extremely speculative and set his goal where there is virtually no chance for success. These are activities which *minimize* his anxiety about failure.

How does the more fearful person behave when offered only a specific task to perform? He can either perform the task or leave the field. If he chooses to leave the field, there is no problem. But if he is constrained, as he must be to remain in any competitive achievement situation, he will stay at the task and presumably work at it. But how hard will he work at it? He is motivated to avoid failure, and when constrained, there is only one path open to him to avoid failure—success at the task he is presented. So we expect him to manifest the strength of his motivation to avoid failure in performance of the task. He, too, in other words, should *try hardest*[2] when P_s is .50 and less hard when the chance of winning is either greater or less. The 50-50 alternative is the last he would choose if allowed to set his own goal, but once constrained he must try hard to avoid the failure which threatens him. Not working at all will guarantee failure of the task. Hence, the thought of not working at all should produce even stronger avoidant motivation than that aroused by the task itself.

In other words, irrespective of whether the stronger motive is to achieve or to avoid failure, the strength of motivation to perfrom a task when no alternatives are offered and when the individual is constrained should be greatest when P_s is .50. This is the condition of greatest uncertainty regarding the outcome. But when there are alternatives which differ in difficulty, the choice of level of aspiration by persons more disposed to avoid failure is diametrically opposite to that of persons more disposed to seek success. The person more motivated to achieve should prefer a moderate risk. His level of aspiration will fall at the point where his positive motivation is strongest, at the point where the odds seem to be 50-50. The fearful person, on the other hand, must select a task even though all the alternatives are threatening to him. He prefers the least threatening of the available alternatives: either the task which is so easy he cannot fail, or the task which is so difficult that failure would be no cause for self-blame and embarrassment.

(Editors' Note: The two preceding paragraphs and other sections of this 1957 statement of theory contain several grossly misleading conjectures about the effect of motivation to avoid failure on the level of performance. The misleading ideas, which clearly depart from the inherent logic of the theory as stated, were soon discovered in the course of designing some of the experiments reported in later chapters. The basic error was in supposing that motivation to avoid failure $M_{AF} \times P_f \times I_f$ might sometimes function to instigate (or excite) achievement-oriented performance. We wish to call the reader's attention to this misleading departure from what the theory actually implies. We shall anticipate, in other words, the clarification of the theory brought about by several of the studies designed to test it (see particularly Chapters 4, 5, 8).

The positive product of $M_S \times P_s \times I_s$, which is called motivation to achieve or motivation to approach success, is interpreted as a tendency to undertake an activity that is expected to lead to success. The negative product of $M_{AF} \times P_s \times I_s$, called motivation to avoid failure, must therefore be consistently interpreted as a tendency to avoid undertaking an activity that is expected to lead to failure. Motivation to avoid failure should always be conceived as inhibitory in character. It specifies what activities a person is not likely to undertake, not what activities he is likely to undertake. This avoidant tendency always opposes, resists, or dampens the influence of motivation to achieve *success and extrinsic positive motivational tendencies to undertake some task. This function is clearly apparent in the conception of Resultant Motivation as the algebraic sum of Approach and Avoidance tendencies as shown in Table 1. It is also clearly apparent when one asserts that an individual in whom $M_{AF} > M_S$ will not undertake an achievement-oriented activity at all unless constrained by some other extrinsic source of positive motivation (e.g., the need for social approval).*

Given this concept of a tendency to inhibit (i.e., to avoid) performance of actions that are expected to lead to failure, it follows that the person in whom $M_{AF} > M_S$ should always resist achievement-oriented activity and that his resistance will be greatest when P_s is .50. The theory does not imply, as was erroneously concluded in 1957 in the preceding paragraphs, that such a person would "try hardest" when P_s is .50, perhaps only to suffer a performance decrement because he is anxious; quite the contrary. The theory implies that the person in whom $M_{AF} > M_S$ should always suffer a decrement in the final strength of achievement-oriented tendencies and the greatest decrement when P_s is .50, because extrinsic motivation to undertake the task is opposed by the greatest inhibitory tendency when P_s is .50. This weakening of the total motivation to undertake an achievement-oriented activity should normally produce a decrement in the level of performance (but see Chapter 19 for a possible exception). Achievement-oriented activity should be completely depressed (i.e., not undertaken at all) when motivation to avoid failure is stronger than the positive motivation to undertake an activity. The latter is attributable to motivation to achieve plus extrinsic sources of positive motivation. This initially elusive conception of how motivation to avoid failure influences behavior is developed fully in Atkinson (1964) and in a contemporary restatement of the theory given in the concluding chapter.)

The tendency for anxious persons to set either extremely high or very low aspirations has been noted over and over again in the literature on level of aspiration (Lewin, Dembo, Festinger, and Sears, 1944). Typically, *groups* of persons for whom the inference of greater anxiety about failure seems justified on the basis of some personality assessment show a much greater variance in level of aspiration than persons whose motivation is inferred to be more normal or less anxious. When the details of behavior are examined, it turns out that they are setting their aspiration level either *defensively* high or *defensively* low.

Without further assumptions, the theory of motivation, which has been presented when applied to competitive-achievement activity, implies that the relationship of constrained performance to expectancy of goal-attainment should take the bell-shaped form shown in Figure 1, whether the predominant motive is to achieve or to avoid failure (see Editors' Note, p. 87). Further, the theory leads to the prediction of exactly opposite patterns for setting the level of aspiration when the predominant motivation is approach and when it is avoidant, as shown in Figure 2.

Both of these hypotheses have been supported in recent experiments. The writer (Atkinson, 1958b) offered female college students a modest monetary prize for good performance at two 20-minute tasks. The probability of success was varied by instructions which informed the

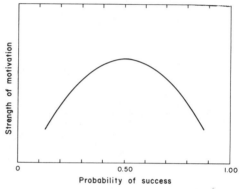

Figure 1 Strength of motivation to achieve or to avoid failure as a function of the subjective probability of success (i.e., the difficulty of the task).

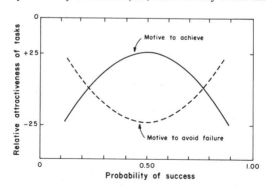

Figure 2 Relative attractiveness of tasks which differ in subjective probability of success (i.e., in difficulty). The avoidance curve has been inverted to show that very difficult and very easy tasks arouse less fear of failure and hence are less unattractive than moderately difficult tasks.

subject of the number of persons with whom she was in competition and the number of monetary prizes to be given. The stated probabilities were 1/20, 1/3, 1/2, and 3/4. The level of performance was higher at the intermediate probabilities than at the extremes for subjects having high thematic apperceptive *n* Achievement scores, and also for subjects who had low *n* Achievement scores, presumably a more fearful group.[3]

McClelland (1958b) has shown the diametrically opposite tendencies in choice of level of aspiration in studies of children in kindergarten and in the third grade. One of the original level-of-aspiration experiments, the ring-toss experiment, was repeated with five-year-olds, and a nonverbal index of the strength of achievement motive was employed. Children who were high in *n* Achievement more frequently set their level of aspiration in the intermediate range of difficulty. They took more shots from a modest distance. Children who were low in *n* Achievement showed a greater preponderance of choices at the extreme levels of difficulty. They more often stood right on top of the peg or stood so far away that success was virtually impossible. The same difference between high and low *n* Achievement groups was observed on another task with children in the third grade. McClelland views these results as consistent with his theoretical argument concerning the role of achievement motivation in entrepreneurship and economic development (1955). He has called attention to the relationship between achievement motivation and an interest in enterprise which requires moderate or calculated risks, rather than very safe or highly speculative undertakings.

In an experiment designed for another purpose, Clark, Teevan, and Ricciuti (1956) have presented results with college students comparable to those of McClelland. Immediately before a final examination in a college course, students were asked a series of questions pertaining to grade expectations, affective reactions to grades, and the grades they would *settle for* if excused from taking the exam. A number of indices were derived from responses to these questions, by which the students were classified as: *hopeful of success,* i.e., if the *settle-for* grade was near the maximum grade the student thought he could possibly achieve; *fearful of failure,* i.e., if the *settle-for* grade was near the minimum grade the student thought he might possibly drop to; and *intermediate,* i.e., if the *settle-for* grade fell somewhere between these two extremes. Previously obtained *n* Achievement scores were significantly higher for the *intermediate* group than for the two groups who set either extremely high or low levels of aspiration.

In terms of the model presented in Table 1, the two extreme patterns of aspirant behavior which were designated *hope of success* and *fear of failure* by Clark et al., are to be considered two *phenotypically* dissimilar alternatives that are *genotypically* similar. That is, they both function to avoid or reduce anxiety for the person in whom the motive to avoid failure is stronger than the motive to achieve.

A question may arise concerning the legitimacy of inferring relatively stronger motive to avoid failure from a low *n* Achievement score in thematic apperception. The inference seems justified on several counts. First, the kind of learning experience which is thought to contribute to the development of a positive motive to achieve (McClelland, 1951; Winterbottom, 1958) seems incompatible with the kind of experience which would contribute to the development of an avoidant motive. . . . Second, even if it is assumed that high and low *n* Achievement groups may be equal in the disposition to be fearful of failure, the fact that one group does not show evidence of a strong motive to achieve (the group with low *n* Achievement scores) suggests that fear of failure should be *relatively* stronger in that group than in the group which does show evidence of strong *n* Achievement (high *n* Achievement scores). Finally, Raphelson (1956) has presented evidence that *n* Achievement, as measured in thematic apperception, is *negatively* related to both scores on the Mandler-Sarason Scale of Test Anxiety and a psychogalvanic index of manifest anxiety obtained in a test situation. Test anxiety scores and the psychogalvanic index of manifest anxiety were *positively* correlated, as they should be if each is an effective measure of fear aroused in a competitive situation. . . .[4]

The details of the exploratory experiments suggest that one further assumption be made. In both experiments, the high *n* Achievement groups showed evidence of maximum motivation when the observed or stated probability of success was approximately .33. At this point, the high *n* Achievement group showed the highest level of constrained performance. And this point was most favored by the high *n* Achievement group in setting level of aspiration in the McClelland experiment. The assumption to be made seems a reasonable one: the relative strength of a motive influences the subjective probability of the consequence consistent with that motive, i.e., biases it upwards. In other words, the stronger the achievement motive relative to the motive to avoid failure, the higher the subjective probability of success, given stated odds. The stronger the motive to avoid failure relative to the achievement motive, the higher the subjective probability of failure, given stated odds or any other objective basis for inferring the strength of expectancy. Some evidence from two earlier studies is pertinent. When subjects stated the score that they *expected* to make on a test with very ambiguous or conflicting cues from past performance (Mc-Clelland, Atkinson, Clark, and Lowell, 1953, p. 247) or when faced with a novel task at which they had no experience (Pottharst, 1955), the stated level of *expectation* was positively related to *n* Achievement. The biasing effect of the motive on subjective probability should diminish with repeated learning experience in the specific situation.

When this assumption is made, the point of maximum motivation to achieve now occurs where the stated (objective) odds are somewhat *lower* than .50; and the point of maximum motivation to avoid failure occurs at a point somewhat higher than stated odds of .50, as shown in Figure 3. The implications of this assumption for constrained performance in somewhat novel situations are evident in the figure. When the achievement motive is stronger than the motive to avoid failure, there should be a tendency for stronger motivation to be expressed in performance when the objective odds are long, i.e., below .50. When the motive to avoid failure is stronger than the achievement motive, there should be greater motivation expressed when the objective odds are short, i.e., above .50 (see Editors' Note p. 87).

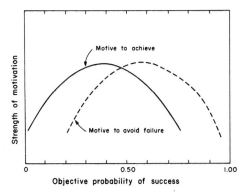

Figure 3 Strength of motivation to achieve and to avoid failure as a function of the *objective* probability of success. It is assumed that the subjective probability of the consequence consistent with the stronger motive is biased upwards.

The Effects of Success and Failure

Let us return to the model and ask, "What are the effects of success and failure on the level of motivation?" We may refer back to Table 1 to answer this question. First, let us consider the effects of success or failure on the level of motivation in a person whose motive to achieve is stronger than his motive to avoid failure. In the usual level-of-aspiration situation, he should initially set his goal where P_s equals .50. In Table 1, this is Task E. If he succeeds at the task, P_s should increase. And, assuming that the effects of success and failure generalize to similar tasks, the P_s at Task D, which was initially .40, should increase toward .50. On the next trial, P_s at Task E is now greater than .50, and P_s at Task D now approaches .50. The result of this change in P_s is diminished motivation to achieve at the old task, E, and increased motivation to achieve at Task D, *an objectively more difficult task.* The observed level of aspiration should increase in a step-like manner following success, because there has been a change in motivation.

A further implication of the change in strength of motivation produced by the experience of success is of great consequence: given a single, very difficult task (e.g., $P_s = .10$), the effect of continued success in repeated trials is first a gradual increase in motivation as P_s increases to .50, followed by a gradual decrease in motivation as P_s increases further to the point of certainty ($P_s = 1.00$). Ultimately, as P_s approaches 1.00, satiation or loss of interest should occur. The task no longer arouses any motivation at all. Why? Because the subjective probability of success is so high that the incentive value is virtually zero. Here is the clue to understanding how the achievement motive can remain insatiable while satiation can occur for a particular line of activity. The strength of motive can remain unchanged, but interest in a particular task can diminish completely. Hence, when free to choose, the person who is stronger in achievement motive should always look for new and more difficult tasks as he masters old problems. If constrained, the person with a strong achievement motive should experience a gradual loss of interest in his work. If the task is of intermediate difficulty to start with ($P_s = .50$), or is definitely easy ($P_s > .50$), his interest should begin to wane after the initial experience of success.

But what of the effect of failure on the person who is more highly motivated to achieve than to avoid failure? Once more we look at the *Approach* column of Table 1. If he has chosen Task E ($P_s = .50$) to start with and fails at it, the P_s is reduced. Continued failure will mean that soon Task F (formerly $P_s = .60$) will have a P_s near .50. He should shift his interest to this task, which was *objectively less difficult* in the initial ordering of tasks. This constitutes what has been called a lowering of the level of aspiration. He has moved to the easier task as a consequence of failure.

What is the effect of continued failure at a single task? If the initial task is one that appeared relatively easy to the subject (e.g., P_s =.80) and he fails, his motivation should increase! The P_s will drop toward .70, but the incentive value or attractiveness of the task will increase. Another failure should increase his motivation even more. This will continue until the P_s has dropped to .50. Further failure should then lead to a gradual weakening of motivation as P_s decreases further. In other words, the tendency of persons who are relatively strong in achievement motive to persist at a task in the face of failure is probably attributable to the relatively high subjective probability of success, initially. Hence, failure has the effect of increasing the strength of their motivation, at least for a time. Ultimately, however, interest in the task will diminish if there is continued failure. If the initial task is perceived by the person as very difficult to start with (P_s <.50), motivation should begin to diminish with the first failure.

Let us turn now to the effect of success and failure on the motivation of the person who is more strongly disposed to be fearful of failure. If the person in whom the motive to avoid failure is stronger has chosen a very difficult task in setting his level of aspiration (e.g., Task A where P_s =.10) and succeeds, P_s increases and his motivation *to avoid* the task is paradoxically increased! It would almost make sense for him deliberately to fail, in order to keep from being faced with a stronger threat on the second trial. If there are more difficult alternatives, he should raise his level of aspiration to avoid anxiety! Fortunately for this person, his strategy (determined by the nature of his motivation) in choosing a very difficult task to start with protects him from this possibility, because P_s is so small that he will seldom face the paradoxical problem just described. If he fails at the most difficult task, as is likely, P_s decreases further, P_f increases further, and the aroused motivation to avoid failure is reduced. By continued failure he further reduces the amount of anxiety about failure that is aroused by this most difficult task. Hence, he should continue to set his level at this point. If he plays the game long enough and fails continuously, the probability of failure increases for all levels of difficulty. Sooner or later the minimal motivation to avoid failure at the most difficult task may be indistinguishable from the motivation to avoid failure at the next most difficult task. This may ultimately allow him to change his level of aspiration to a somewhat less difficult task without acting in gross contradiction to the proposed principle of motivation.

If our fearful subject has initially chosen the easiest task (Task I where $P_s = .90$) and if he fails, P_s decreases toward .80, and his motivation to avoid the task also increases. If there is no easier task, the most difficult task should now appear least *unattractive* to him, and he should jump from the easiest to the most difficult task. In other words, continued failure at a very easy task decreases P_s toward .50; and, as Table 1 shows, a change of this sort is accompanied by increased arousal of avoidant motivation. A wild and apparently irrational jump in level of aspiration from very easy to very difficult tasks, as a consequence of failure, might be mistakenly interpreted as a possible effort on the part of the subject to gain social approval by seeming to set high goals. The present model predicts this kind of activity without appealing to some extrinsic motive. It is part of the strategy of minimizing expected pain of failure after one has failed at the easiest task.

If our fear-disposed subject is successful at the most simple task, his P_s increases, his P_f decreases, and his motivation to avoid this task decreases. The task becomes less and less unpleasant. He should continue playing the game with less anxiety.

Table 1, when taken in its entirety, deals with the special case of the person in whom the two motives are exactly equal in strength. The implications are clear. In the constrained-performance situation, he should work hardest when the probability of success is .50, because motivation to achieve and motivation to avoid failure will summate in the constrained instrumental act which is at the same time the pathway toward success and away from failure. (This summation should also occur in the cases where one motive is stronger.)[5] But in the level-of-aspiration setting where there is an opportunity for choice among alternatives, the avoidance motivation exactly cancels out the approach motivation. Hence, the resultant motivation for each of the alternatives is zero. His choice of level of aspiration cannot be predicted from variables intrinsic to the achievement-related nature of the task. If there is any orderly pattern in this conflicted person's level of aspiration, the explanation of it must be sought in extrinsic factors, e.g., *the desire to gain social approval*. Such a desire can also be conceptualized in terms of motive, expectancy, and incentive, and the total motivation for a particular task can then be attributed to both achievement-related motives and other kinds of motives engaged by the particular features of the situation.

In recent years there has been something of a rebirth of interest in the problems of level of aspiration, particularly in pathological groups.

The tendency for anxious groups to show much greater variability in level of aspiration, setting their goals either very high or very low relative to less anxious persons, was noted in early studies by P. Sears (1940), Rotter (1954), and others (Lewin, Dembo, Festinger, and Sears, 1944). Miller (1951), Himmelweit (1947), and Eysenck and Himmelweit (1946) have produced substantial evidence that persons with affective disorders (neurasthenia or dysthymia) typically set extremely high goals for themselves; hysterics, on the other hand, show a minimal level of aspiration, often setting their future goal even below the level of past performance. In all of these studies, normal control groups have fallen between these two extremes, as might be expected from the present model if *normals* are relatively more positive in their motivation in achievement-related situations.

In the work of Eysenck (1955) and his colleagues, both dysthymics and hysterics show greater *neuroticism* than normal subjects. Eysenck's interpretation of this factor as autonomic sensitivity is consistent with the implications of the present model, which attributes the setting of extremely high or low levels of aspiration to relatively strong motivation to avoid failure. A second factor, *extraversion-introversion,* discriminates the affective disorders and hysterics where the present model, dealing only with motives intrinsic to the competitive achievement situation, does not. An appeal to some other motivational difference, e.g., in strength of *n* Affiliation, might also predict the difference in pattern of level of aspiration.

PROBABILITY PREFERENCES

The present analysis is relevant to another domain of current research interest, that specifically concerned with the measurement of subjective probability and utility. Edwards (1953, 1954a), for example, has reported probability preferences among subjects offered alternative bets having the same expected value. We (Atkinson, Bastian, Earl, and Litwin, 1960) have repeated the Edwards type experiment (e.g., 6/6 of winning $.30 versus 1/6 of winning $1.80) with subjects having high and low *n* Achievement scores. The results show that persons high in *n* Achievement more often prefer intermediate probabilities (4/6, 3/6, 2/6) to extreme probabilities (6/6, 5/6, 1/6) than do persons low in *n* Achievement. What is more, the same differential preference for intermediate risk was shown by these *same* subjects when they were allowed to choose the distance from the target for their shots in a shuffleboard game. In other words, the incentive values of winning *qua* winning, and losing *qua* losing, presumably developed in achievement activities early in life, generalize to the gambling situation in which winning is really *not* contingent upon one's own skill and competence.

SOCIAL MOBILITY ASPIRATIONS

Finally, the present model may illuminate a number of interesting research possibilities having to do with social and occupational mobility. The ranking of occupations according to their prestige in Western societies clearly suggests that occupations accorded greater prestige are also more difficult to attain. A serious effort to measure the perceived probability of being able to attain certain levels on the occupational ladder should produce a high negative correlation with the usual ranking on prestige. If so, then the present model for level of aspiration, as well as its implications for persons who differ in achievement-related motives, can be applied to many of the sociological problems of mobility aspirations. A recent paper by Hyman (1953) has laid the groundwork for such an analysis.

NOTES

[1]In the resultant valence theory of level of aspiration, the resultant force (f^*) for a particular level of difficulty equals probability of success (P_s) times valence of success (Va_s) minus probability of failure (P_f) times valence of failure (Va_f). It is assumed that the valence of a goal [$Va(G)$] depends partly on the properties of the activity and specific goal (G) and partly on the state of need [$t(G)$] of the person, [$Va(G) = F(G)t(G)$] (Lewin, 1951, p. 273). In the present conception, the relative rewarding or punishing properties of specific goals (i.e., incentive) and the more general disposition of the person toward a class of incentives (i.e., his motive) are given independent status.

[2]I do not mean to exclude the possibility that the very anxious person may suffer a performance decrement due to the arousal of some "task-irrelevant" avoidant responses, as proposed in the interpretation of research which has employed the Mandler-Sarason Measure of Test Anxiety (Mandler and Sarason, 1952).

[3]New evidence has been presented by French and Lesser (1964) and Lesser, Krawitz, and Packard (1963) concerning the circumscribed conditions under which TAT *n* Achievement scores yield valid indication of the strength of motivation in female college students. The earlier assumption of the validity of the scores of the females S_S now seems unwarranted. The average level of performance of all female S_S was highest when P_s was .50. This result is consistent with the theory if it can be assumed that on the average M_S is stronger than M_{AF} in a representative sample of college women. (The Editors).

[4]More recent evidence, presented in subsequent chapters, suggests that the two motives are uncorrelated among college men. This means that resultant achievement motivation, and hence also preference for intermediate risk, will be weaker when *n* Achievement is low, even though a low *n* Achievement score may not imply that $M_{AF} > M_S$. (The Editors.)

⁵Here again is the error discussed in the Editors' Note on page 86. The summation of approach and avoidance motivation will always reduce the resultant strength of the approach tendency. When M_S and M_{AF} are equal, resultant achievement motivation is zero. (The Editors.)

7

Toward a Theory of
Task Motivation and Incentives[1]

Edwin A. Locke

In 1929, Bills and Brown introduced a report concerned with the effects of mental set as follows:

One of the most important factors determining the level of efficiency which an individual may attain in . . . work is the attitude or set with which he enters upon the task. . . . But more effort has been directed toward controlling attitude as a disturbing variable than toward studying it for its own sake. As a result little is known regarding the . . . influence of set in . . . work (p. 301).

In 1963, Ryan[2] made the following observation about recent work in human motivation:

It is impossible to perform a psychological experiment upon a human subject without manipulating and controlling his intention or task. In spite of this fact, the experimental study of tasks has been relatively neglected in modern psychology (Ch. V, p. 1).

These two statements, made nearly 35 years apart, indicate a persistent neglect in experimental psychology of the study of conscious factors

[1]The research on which many of the studies cited in this paper were based, was supported by Nour contract 4792(00) from the Office of Naval Research. Other studies were supported by grant No. MH 12103-01 from the National Institutes of Mental Health. The author would like to thank Miss Judith F. Bryan of the American Institutes for Research for her help in all phases of the research.
[2]The following mimeographed chapters by Ryan are available from the Department of Psychology, Cornell University, Ithaca, New York: Chapter I: Explaining behavior; Chapter II: Explanatory concepts; Chapter V: Experiments on intention, task and set; Chapter VI: Intentional learning; and Chapter VII: Unintentional learning.

Reprinted by permission of the author and publisher from *Organizational Behavior and Human Performance* 3 (1968):157-59.

in task performance. The cause of this neglect is a doctrine which has dominated experimental psychology for the last several decades: the doctrine of behaviorism. Its fundamental thesis is that psychology is the study of observable behavior and that (human) behavior can be understood without the use of explanatory concepts referring to states or actions of consciousness.

In recent years, however, some psychologists have become dissatisfied with the limitations placed upon research and theory by the behaviorist dogma. A growing number of investigators have begun to study the effects of conscious goals, intentions, desires, and purposes on task performance. The basic (implicit or explicit) premise of this research is that man's conscious ideas affect what he does, i.e., that one of the (biological) functions of consciousness is the regulation of action (see Branden, 1966; Rand, 1964, for a fuller discussion of the nature and functions of consciousness).[3]

It is argued here, in agreement with Ryan (1958), that:

Tasks [intentions, goals, etc.] . . . are to be treated as causal factors in behavior. By this I mean that a task is a necessary condition for most kinds of behavior. (To find and account for the exceptions is an empirical problem). . . . I shall assert that a very large proportion of behavior is initiated by tasks, and that a very large proportion of tasks lead to the behavior specified by the tasks (p. 79).

It is the purpose of this paper to draw together and integrate the existing literature on the relationship between conscious goals or intentions and task performance. For our purposes the terms goal and intention will be used in their vernacular meaning as "what the individual is consciously trying to do." (Some distinctions between these two terms will be made later in the paper.)

It should be stressed that in the last analysis the content of a particular individual's goals and intentions must be inferred from his verbal report (based on his introspection). However, there are still a number of different procedures that may be used to study the relationship between conscious goals or intentions and task performance: (1) goals can be assigned by the experimenter before performance and the subject's acceptance of these goals (i.e., his decision to actually try for them) checked later by questioning; (2) subjects can be given a limited choice

---

[3]There are important philosophical issues involved in the decision to use or not to use concepts referring to states of consciousness as explanatory terms. These issues are both epistemological, e.g., the problem of the privacy of conscious states, and metaphysical, e.g., the mind-body problem. Due to space limitations, however, the present paper is confined exclusively to a discussion of experimental findings.

of goals before task performance and asked to choose one of them; (3) subjects can be allowed to set any goals they wish on the task and then asked to indicate what their goal was after performance. In addition, these methods can be used in various combinations; for example, results obtained using method (3) can be checked using method (1), i.e., by assigning the same goals to a new group of subjects that a previous group had set themselves. In the studies to be reported here, all three methods were used and all yielded substantial relationships between goals or intentions and task performance. Thus for our purposes, the advantages and disadvantages of the different procedures are not important (though in other contexts, it might be of interest to study them).

No attempt is made in the studies reported to specify the ultimate roots or causes of the particular goals or intentions an individual develops on a task. Our interest here is only in the relationship between these goals and intentions, once established, and subsequent behavior. Thus, we are not presenting a complete theory of task performance but only some foundations for a theory.

Turning briefly to the issue of nonintentional behavior, it is obvious that no individual is aware of or consciously intends every single action or movement he makes. But it remains to be seen just how much behavior can be explained with reference to conscious intent. For instance, Ryan (1958) argues: "The concept of *determining tendency* would suggest that the effect of a task [intention] may operate over such a time-span that it may produce an effect at a time when the individual is no longer aware of the task as such" (p. 82).

It may be instructive in this context to discuss four types of "unintentional" behavior that occur frequently in everyday life in order to see to what degree these might be explained in terms of conscious intent: 1) *One category is behavior whose end is foreseen but in which each movement in the sequence that is the means to the end is not consciously initiated.* For example, in returning an opponent's shot in tennis, an experienced player is not consciously aware of his footwork, backswing, or grip, but only of the intent to approach and return the shot. In such cases as this, the action leading to the goal has become automated through extended practice; each response automatically sets off the next response in the sequence. However, it should be recognized that the behavior sequence as a whole must still be *triggered* by a conscious intent (e.g., as "to return the shot" or "win the point" in the example above). Once the initial intent is abandoned, action ceases, e.g., if the tennis player suddenly decides not to try to return a shot, the usual action sequence will not occur.

Furthermore, automated behavior of this type is *initially learned* consciously and intentionally. This is true of any series of skilled goal-directed movements or actions taken by man (though such actions will involve physiological activities of which he may never be aware introspectively; see type 4 below).

2) A second category involves *behavior in which a different end occurs than is intended due to error or lack of ability.* For instance, one could try to return a tennis shot but hit the net instead. The behavior would be consciously initiated but the outcome would be imperfectly correlated with the intended outcome due to lack of knowledge or ability. Such behavior is usually described as "accidental." Clearly concepts other than conscious intent are required to explain accidents, but it should be recognized that accidents often involve very small deviations from the intended outcome (e.g., as when a tennis shot goes out of bounds by an inch). Thus conscious intent would be *one* factor in the explanation of the action sequence as a whole.

3) A third type of nonintentional behavior is *behavior in which the end that is foreseen logically entails another end that is not foreseen as such.* For example, in a verbal "conditioning" or a free-association experiment, one might intentionally give only the names of "jewels" (rubies, emeralds, diamonds, etc.). In doing so one would also be giving "plural nouns." Plural nouns would not be consciously intended as such but would be logically entailed by the intention to list jewels. Dulany (1961, 1962) uses the term "correlated hypotheses" to describe subjects' hypotheses in verbal-conditioning experiments which are correlated with the "correct" hypothesis. One could similarly use the term "correlated behavior" to describe behavior which was not intended as such but which was logically correlated with intended behavior.

4) Finally, there is *behavior which is not and never was under direct conscious control, but may be indirectly controlled.* For instance, in the course of carrying out a voluntary act, many automatic, nonconscious physiological actions will occur (e.g., muscle contractions, neural activity, glandular secretions, etc.)—actions which one could not become aware of using the unaided senses. But by initiating certain molar actions one may indirectly control some of these molecular actions.

The key point to recognize in the above four cases is that all the actions in question were or could be *initiated* by a mental act, that they were or could be originally *set in motion* by a conscious goal or intention. In addition, the results or outcomes of the behaviors are ordinarily either the ones intended or are correlated with those intended (the size of the correlation depending upon the individual's capacity, knowledge, ability, and the situation).

The research to be reported here involves predominantly simple tasks in which learning complex new skills and making long-term plans and strategies is not necessary to achieve goals—tasks of the type in which effort and concentration are likely to have a relatively direct effect on output or choice.

The paper is divided into two parts. Part I reports research dealing with direct relationships between goals or intentions and task performance. Part II is an extension of the theory to attempt to account for the motivational effects of external incentives on task performance. *An external incentive is defined as an event or object external to the individual which can incite action.* It is argued that if goals or intentions are a necessary condition for most kinds of behavior, then incentives will affect behavior only through their effects on goals and intentions and will have no effect independent of their effects on goals and intentions. Part II reports research relevant to this deduction.

I: GOALS, INTENTIONS, AND TASK PERFORMANCE

Goal Difficulty and Level of Performance

The studies in this section are concerned with the relationship between the level or difficulty of the goal the subject is trying for and the quantitative level of his performance (amount of output, speed of reaction time, school grades, etc.). If goals regulate performance, then hard goals should produce a higher level of performance than easy goals, other things (such as ability) being equal.

Figure 1 shows the combined results of 12 studies on this topic by the present investigator and colleagues. In some of these studies goals were assigned to subjects by the experimenter and goal acceptance was checked by interviews. In other studies subjects set their own goals. In all cases goals were expressed in terms of some specific quantitative score that the subject was trying to achieve on each trial or on the task as a whole. Goal difficulty is expressed in Fig. 1 in terms of the percentage trials on which the subjects trying for a particular goal actually beat that goal. Performance level is expressed in terms of the within-study z-score for performance for the particular goal group in question.

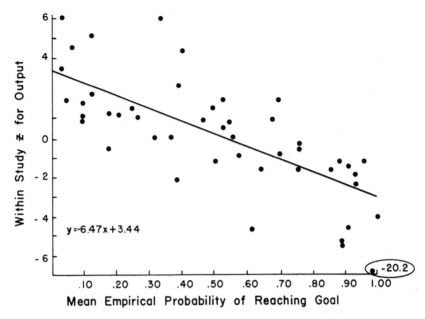

$$y = -6.47x + 3.44$$

FIGURE 1. Output as a function of goal difficulty for 12 studies combined.

Thus each point represents a particular group (a particular goal) in a particular study; it indicates the probability of the subjects in that group reaching their goal and their mean output in relation to the other goal groups in that study.

The results are unequivocal: the harder the goal the higher the level of performance. (This was also true within each study.)* Although subjects with very hard goals reached their goals far less often than subjects with very easy goals, the former consistently performed at a higher level than the latter. The rank-order correlation between goal difficulty and performance for all the points shown in Fig. 1 is .78 ($p<.01$). (The one extreme point, circled in Fig. 1, was not used, however, in calculating the slope of the function, as this would have given a misleading picture of the general relationship between the two variables.)

The nature of the experiments from which the above data were obtained utilized a variety of different tasks: brainstorming, complex computation, addition, perceptual speed, toy construction, reaction time, grade achievement in college—thus indicating the generality of the results across tasks.

---

*The studies are marked with an asterisk in the reference section.

There have been a small number of studies by other investigators of goal difficulty and performance, and the findings have been similar to those reported above. Dey and Kaur (1965) using a letter cancellation task found hard (assigned) output goals to produce a higher level of performance than easy goals. Mace (1935) in a study of psychomotor performance found that subjects who were instructed to try to improve their scores 25% per day, improved at a faster rate than those instructed to improve at a rate of 5% per day. Siegal and Fouraker (1960), using an experimental bargaining task, asked some subjects to try for a specific quantitatively high profit and others to try for a specific quantitatively low profit. The former group actually negotiated higher profits than the latter. Locke (1966b) reanalyzed some data gathered by Fryer in a study of code learning, in which some subjects set goals before each trial and some did not. Locke found that those subjects who set high goals in relation to their previous performance performed better on the task than those who set comparatively low goals. Eason and White (1961) found that subjects who were instructed to try to stay on target in a pursuit rotor task for 0, 50, and 100% of the time, respectively, actually did so. Eason and White also found that subjects tracking a smaller target showed greater muscular control (greater precision of movement) than those tracking a larger target. (This is an example of category type 3 of unintended behavior discussed above: the subjects with smaller targets were not trying explicitly for greater muscular control than those with larger targets: this outcome was a logical correlate of the former subjects trying to "stay on" a smaller target).

Stedry (1960), in a study of problem solving, demonstrated the importance of distinguishing between instructions and the subjects' personal goals. He told different groups of subjects to try to complete different numbers of problems in the time allowed. He also had subjects indicate their own personal levels of aspiration, either before or after the goals were assigned by the experimenter. He found that hard assigned goals led to a higher number of problems completed than easy goals only if the goals were assigned *before* the hard-goal subjects set their personal goals. If they set personal goals first, they tended to reject the assigned hard goals and performed quite poorly on the task.

Two previous studies have found significant relationships between students' grade goals and actual grade performance in school (controlling for scholastic ability). Uhlinger and Stephens (1960) and Battle (1966) used college freshmen and junior high school students as subjects, respectively. Unfortunately, however, the grade-goal questionnaires were administered near the end of the semester during which the grades were obtained, thus making the cause-effect relationship somewhat equivocal.

A study of "real life" goal-setting was carried out by Zander and Newcomb (1967). They studied the United Fund campaigns of 149 selected communities over a period of 4 years. It was found that communities who set monetary goals that were higher than their previous year's performance raised more money (in dollars per capita) in relation to their previous year's performance than communities who set goals that were lower than their previous year's performance. Further analyses supported the view that these goals were a cause rather than an effect of actual performance. (One exception to the former finding was that for communities with a history of failure to reach their fund goals, there was no correlation between goals and performance.)

In the industrial area, numerous investigators have observed that workers' output norms influence their level of production (e.g., Mathewson, 1931; Roethlisberger and Dickson, 1939; Smith, 1953; Whyte, 1955). The focus of interest in these field studies, however, was on the negative side of work norms and standards, on their effect in keeping *down* production. But a broader view of the issue should recognize that norms have a positive side; they also hold *up* production. A production norm is simply a work goal shared by a group of workers. . . .

Relationship of Qualitatively Different Goals
to Level of Performance

The studies in this section are concerned with the relationship of qualitatively different goals to level of performance. Most of them deal with a comparison of the assigned goal of "do your best" with specific hard goals. The former was chosen for research by the present writer because it is used, explicitly or implicitly, in virtually all psychological experiments. Yet, just what it means is not exactly clear. It was believed that such a goal did not necessarily lead to the highest performance possible. Thus it was decided to compare the output induced by a "do-best" goal with that which could be produced by specific quantitative hard goals of the type used in the studies described in the previous section.

Eight studies were conducted by the present writer and Bryan in which these two types of goals were compared.* In six of the eight

---

*These are marked with a dagger (†) in the reference section.

studies the subjects trying for specific hard goals performed at a significantly higher level than subjects trying to "do their best." Thus, a
"do best" goal does not tend to produce (under the conditions of these
studies) the highest possible level of performance.

Mace (1935) obtained a similar finding in a study of complex computation. He gave one group of subjects specific hard standards, geared to
their ability level, to aim for in each work period, whereas other subjects
were told simply to "do their best." The group with hard standards
improved much faster than the "do best" group. Mace also analyzed the
within-trial rates of the hard-goal and do-best groups and found that the
difference between the groups was due entirely to the hard-goal group
showing higher output toward the end of each 20-minute-trial period as
compared with the do-best group. Both groups worked at the same pace
early in each work period but the difference between them grew as the
work period progressed. However, in one of the studies reported above
(Locke and Bryan, 1966a) the superiority of the hard-goal groups was
equally large during each segment of the work period (although in the
latter study the periods were only 10-minutes long). On the other hand,
in two other studies reported above (Locke and Bryan, 1967a) using
single trials that lasted 1½-2 hours, Mace's finding was replicated. The
difference between the groups increased steadily during the course of
these long work periods. Clearly one reason that specific hard goals
enhance performance is that they prolong effort during the latter portions of long work sessions.

In a study of a somewhat different nature, Henderson (1963) assigned
fifth-grade children stories to read, but asked them to indicate what their
reading purposes would be before they began. He found that children
who formulated more complex, numerous, and creative purposes actually attained their purposes more fully and completely than did subjects
who formulated fewer, less complex, and less creative purposes.

Finally, an industrial study by Meyer, Kay and French (1965) examined the effects of goal-setting during appraisal interviews on subsequent
job performance. They found that of those performance items which
were translated into specific goals, 65% showed subsequent improvement, while of those performance items that did not get translated into
goals, only 27% showed subsequent improvement.

Behavioral Intentions and Choice

The designs of the studies reported in the preceding sections required
all subjects to work at the same task (do the same thing) and the focus

of interest was on how well they did it (i.e., output). The experiments to be reported in this section were designed so that subjects had a *choice* either as to the difficulty of the *task* they would work on or the particular kinds of *responses* they would give. The intention to make a certain task choice or to respond in a certain way will henceforth be called a *behavioral intention* (after Dulany, 1962).

Three studies conducted by the present writer and colleagues (Locke, Bryan, and Kendall, 1968) examined the relationship between behavioral intentions and task choice. The task in all cases was word unscrambling and subjects were allowed to choose, on each trial, the length of the word (e.g., four letters, five letters, six letters, etc.) they would try to unscramble. Subjects had 45 seconds to try to solve each word chosen. Word-length choice was the dependent variable.

In the first study there were three blocks of ten trials each and subjects filled out a 5-point behavioral-intention scale before each trial and before each block of trials. The scale asked the subject to indicate whether she intended to choose a "very hard word," a "hard word," a "moderately hard word," etc. on the next trial or block of trials. The intention ratings were quantified on a 5-point scale: 1 for the "very easy words" alternative, to 5 for the "very hard words" alternative. The mean within-subject correlation between word length choice and intentions across the 30 trials was .81 (median=.80). The mean within-block, between-individual correlation between block intention and mean word choice on that block was .60 ($p<.01$).

In the second study, the first block consisted of ten choices. Before trial 1, one third of the subjects were told to try to "succeed" as much as possible; one third were told to "get as great a sense of personal achievement as possible," and one third were told to try and "overcome the greatest possible challenges." Behavioral intentions were measured on a 5-point scale completed before the block began and were quantified on a 5-point scale as in the previous study (see above). The relationship between instructions, intentions and mean word choice is shown in Fig. 2. Clearly the "challenge" group developed the "hardest" intentions and chose the hardest (longest) words while the "success" group developed the easiest intentions and chose the easiest (shortest) words. The "achievement" group was intermediate on both variables. The correlation between instructions (quantified 5, 3, and 1 for the challenge, achievement and success groups, respectively) and mean word-length choice on the ten trials was .67 ($p<.01$), while that between intentions and mean word-length was .88 ($p<.01$).

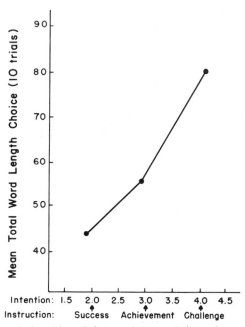

FIGURE 2. The relationship of instructions and intentions to word-length choice.

On block II, there were ten more trials but no specific instructions. The correlation between intentions and word-length choice was .81 ($p<.01$).

In the third study, subjects had five blocks of five choices each and they filled out an intention rating before each block. The within-block correlations between mean word-length choice and intentions were .78, .83, .79, .85, and .79 for the five blocks, respectively (all p's $<.01$).[4]

Let us turn now to studies in which all subjects had to work on the same task but had a choice of *responses*. These studies have all been in the "verbal-conditioning" area. Subjects are asked to free associate or to make up sentences and are "reinforced" (by the experimenter saying "good" etc.) for listing certain types of words or certain kinds of sentences. Dulany (1962) gave his subjects postexperimental interviews asking them to report their behavioral intentions and found highly significant correlations in three different studies between the subjects' behavioral intentions and the actual number of responses given in the intended category. For instance, subjects who intentionally tried to make up only sentences beginning with "I" or "We" actually made more such sentences than those who did not try to do this.

A study of a similar nature was conducted by Holmes (1966). Subjects who tried intentionally to give "I" or "We" sentences gave significantly more of them than those who did not try to do this, even when both groups were aware that "I," "We" sentences were the kind the experimenter was "reinforcing" them for giving.

Two later studies by Dulany (1968) reported correlations of .94 and .90, respectively, between behavioral intentions and responses on a task where the subject was to select, on each trial, one of two sentences presented to him.

Finally, a field study by Leventhal and Niles (1964) showed subjects films which demonstrated the danger of smoking and its relationship to lung cancer. Afterwards, they asked each subject to indicate how much *desire* he had to get a chest X-ray. The stronger the desire to get an X-ray the more likely the subject was to actually have one taken.

II. GOALS AND INTENTIONS AS MEDIATORS OF THE EFFECTS OF EXTERNAL INCENTIVES

A General Note on Instructions

In a number of the experiments reported in Part I, goals were manipulated by instructions. However, in most of the studies conducted by the author subjects' *acceptance* of their assigned goals was corroborated by interviews. Thus these studies were legitimately described as dealing with the relationship between goals and performance rather than the relationship between instructions and performance.

As every experimenter and shop foreman knows, one of the most efficient ways to get somebody to do something is to ask him, i.e., to *assign* him a goal or task. But it is important to recognize that instructions do not inevitably nor automatically affect an individual's goals or behavior. For example, in some of the studies reported in Part I, post-experimental interviews revealed that subjects did *not* accept their assigned goals. For these subjects there was no relationship between assigned goals and performance. Only when these subjects were re-classified according to the goals they actually reported working for did a relationship between goals and performance emerge (e.g., see Locke and Bryan, 1966b, 1967a).

Our theory suggests that instructions will affect behavior only if they are consciously accepted by the individual and translated into specific goals or intentions. This applies equally well to the instruction by an experimenter to "try for quality in your answers" to the instruction by a shop foreman to "produce 400 portzeebies an hour." It is not enough to know that an order or request was made; one has to know whether or not the individual heard it and understood it, how he appraised it, and what he decided to do about it before its effects on his behavior can be predicted and explained.

There have been very few studies in which the effectiveness of instructions and intentions in accounting for behavior have been actually compared. However, in the second study (Study 4 in Locke *et al.*, 1968) of word unscrambling discussed previously in Part I, subjects were instructed to choose words to unscramble which would provide either "success," "achievement," or "challenge"; instructions correlated significantly with word choice ($r = .67$, $p < .01$), but this correlation was completely vitiated when the subjects' own behavioral intentions (established after the instructions were given) were partialed out ($r_p = .08$). In other words, the instructions were correlated with choice only by virtue of their correlation with intentions and had no effect on behavior over and above their effect on intentions.

Stedry's (1960) study (discussed in Part I) should also be recalled in this context. Subjects tended to reject hard goals assigned by the experimenter if they had already set their own personal goals.

In a memory experiment Eagle (1967) instructed different subjects to use either a rehearsal strategy or an associative strategy in memorizing a list of words. Eagle found that instructions per se had no effect on amount of recall; only when subjects were reclassified according to the strategy they *actually reported using* did a difference between groups emerge (in favor of those using the associative strategy).

Although instructions are the most commonly used incentive in everyday life, most psychological research has been focused on other types of incentives such as money, knowledge of results, participation, etc. Let us turn now to evidence concerning the dependence of their effects on goals and intentions.

Goals as Mediators of the Effects of Incentives on Level of Performance

Money. In a study reported by Locke *et al.* (1968) subjects worked on a brainstorming task (giving uses for objects) for three blocks of seven trials each. Goal-setting instructions and amount of incentive offered for output were systematically manipulated. It was found that subjects who set their goals high on block III relative to block II improved their performance on block III more than those whose block III goals were not substantially higher than their block II goals. On the other hand, there was no main effect of incentive independent of goal level. Subjects who had the same output goals produced the same amount whether they were paid a bonus for reaching the goal or not. Using groups means as the units of analysis, the rank order correlation between output and goal level was .85 ($p < .01$).

In a second study reported by Locke *et al.,* 30 subjects worked for 50 minutes at a toy construction task. The subjects set output goals at the beginning and at the halfway point of the work period. Half the subjects were paid on a piece-rate system and half were paid only for participation. It was found that the mean output of the two groups did not differ significantly in either half of the work period. This finding was congruent with the fact that mean goal level of the two groups did not differ significantly in either period. On the other hand, when all subjects were combined, there was a significant relationship between second-half performance and second-half goal level.

Numerous industrial studies of the effects of monetary incentives on performance have found that the effectiveness of piece-rate incentive systems depends on the particular production quotas that workers have (e.g., Mathewson, 1931; Roethlisberger and Dickson, 1939; Whyte, 1955). If the workers feel that their long-term self-interest (either in terms of interpersonal relations, effort, or job tenure) will be threatened by trying to go "all out" for piece-rate earnings, they will restrict production to what they consider to be a "safe" level (a level that will protect their jobs and/or keep the time study man from retiming the job and setting new rates, etc.).

One effect of a well-run incentive system is that (providing the workers value money) it will encourage workers to accept tasks and set goals that they would not accept or set on their own (i.e., for the intrinsic enjoyment of the work itself). Thus, money can serve to *commit* subjects to tasks which they would not otherwise undertake. The use of incentives to insure goal acceptance was a key element in Taylor's (1911) "scientific management" system.

Knowledge of score. The studies to be reported in this section are concerned only with the effects of overall scores (KS) on a task or knowledge of score on a task where there are no right or wrong answers (e.g., reaction time). Thus, we are concerned with "motivational" knowledge as opposed to epistemic knowledge of the type that can be used to correct errors (e.g., visual feedback on a dart-throwing task).

An initial study by Locke and Bryan (1966b) compared the effect of KS vs. NoKS on a complex computation task. Some subjects were allowed to compute their scores after each trial and some were not. The subjects had six trials of 10 minutes each. No difference was found between the KS and NoKS groups in performance. However, when the subjects were reclassified according to their postexperimental goal descriptions, a significant relationship of goals to performance was found.

Two subsequent studies manipulated goal-setting and KS independently using a 2 × 2 design (Locke, 1967b; Locke and Bryan, 1967c). In both studies subjects worked on five trials of irregular duration (mean = 12 minutes) at an addition task. Periodically half the subjects (KS group) were given their scores and half (NoKS group) were not. In the first study, half the subjects were given specific hard goals to aim for on each trial, while the other half were told to "do their best." In the second study, half the subjects were given easy goals to aim for and half were given hard goals. In both studies, the subjects with hard goals performed significantly better than those with easy or do-best goals, but no difference in performance was found between the KS and NoKS groups. The results for the Locke (1967b) study are shown in Figs. 3a and b. The hard-goal group is clearly superior to the do-best group in performance whereas the KS and NoKS groups have very similar performance curves.

Another study (Locke and Bryan, 1967b) found that when KS does facilitate performance, it does so only *through* its effects on goal-setting. Subjects were given 16 5-minute trials on a complex computation task.

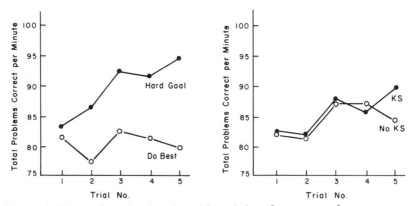

FIGURE 3. The relationship of goals and knowledge of score to performance.

One group of subjects were allowed to compute their scores after each trial and another was not. Subjects filled out goal description questionnaires before, during, and after performance. It was found that the KS subjects performed significantly better than the NoKS subjects on the last eight trials, and it was only on these trials that the KS subjects set harder goals than the NoKS subjects. When differential goal-setting was controlled by partialing, the relationship of KS condition to performance was vitiated.

The important thing about KS, then, is not merely whether it is given or not given but how a subject interprets and evaluates it, and what goals he sets in response to it. The *form* in which KS is given, of course, can influence its effectiveness. For instance, if KS is given in such a form that it cannot be used to set goals or to judge one's progress in relation to a standard (as in Locke, 1967b; Locke and Bryan, 1967c) it will not affect motivation.

If, on the other hand, KS is given in relation to standards, the level of the standard can influence goal level. Locke (1967c) gave subjects feedback on a reaction-time task in relation to different standards; some subjects were told on each trial whether or not they had beaten their *best* previous score and others whether or not they had beaten their *worst* previous score. Positive feedback was given by means of a green light which signalled that subject successfully beat the standard. In this study, subjects with the harder ("best") standards showed faster reaction times than those with easier ("worst") standards. To get green-light feedback, they had to try harder in the former case than in the latter. Thus giving knowledge in relation to the different standards in effect influenced the difficulty of the goals subjects tried for.

Time limits. Two studies by Bryan and Locke (1967b) gave subjects different amounts of time to complete an addition task. One group of individuals was given just enough time to complete the problems (the number being geared to the subject's level of ability) while another group was given twice this amount of time. It was found that the subjects given an excess amount of time took longer to complete the task than those given a minimum amount of time. The subjects given an excess amount of time also set easier goals on the task than did those given a minimum amount of time. When time limits were removed and subjects were free to work at their own pace, both experimental groups set their goals at the same level and worked at the same pace. Thus, the effect of the different time limits appeared to be a function of the differing performance subgoals which they induced. Their effects did not extend to a situation where the work was self-paced.

The foregoing studies of time limits can be viewed as belonging to a wider class of studies concerned with the effect of task difficulty on performance. The difference between these studies and those discussed above is that in the present case no goals (other than completing the problems in the time allowed) were assigned as such; the subject was simply given a task and told how much time he had to complete it. The effect of the imposed time limits was a function of the goals the subjects set in response to them.

The above studies virtually exhaust the literature on the topic of goals as mediators of the effect of incentives on performance level. Our treatment of the next three incentives: participation, competition, and praise and reproof, is therefore confined mainly to a discussion of experiments in which goal-setting was mentioned only incidentally, or to discussion at the theoretical level.

Participation. A number of investigators have argued that employee participation in the decisions that affect them motivates better job performance (e.g., Maier, 1955; Likert, 1961; Viteles, 1953; Vroom, 1964), and there is research evidence that would appear to support this claim. However, the question that concerns us here is *how* participation serves to motivate job performance when it does so. In the typical field experiment on participation, many aspects of the job are likely to be changed: e.g., job method (method of performing the task), method of payment, rate of pay, quality and quantity of training, type of supervision, commitment of the worker to his assigned quota, the level of the quota, etc. Any one of these factors could affect subsequent production, but experimental research has not systematically tested the relative importance of each.

It will suffice for our purposes to point out that goal-setting, specifically a change in the production quota, has been an explicit element in many participation studies. For example, see the following description of Bavelas' study by Viteles (1953, p. 167):

. . . in the course of . . . [participation] meetings, the experimenter . . . talked about the greater ease of working together as a team; discussed individual production levels with the group; questioned its members as to the level of production which might be obtained if they worked as a team, and *asked if they would like to set a team goal for higher production* (italics mine).

In another study of participation by Lawrence and Smith (1955), the authors write:

Members of these groups were encouraged to use their own judgement in setting goals, but were reminded that *unless they set the goal a little above their present accomplishment they would be unable to determine the effectiveness of the group when working as a team* (p. 334, italics mine).

Similarly in a study of participation at General Electric reported by Sorcher (1967): "The employees were asked . . . to set quality goals for themselves, and to discuss how they might improve their performance so as to improve the quality of their output" (p. 16). In this study substantial improvements in work quality were obtained as a result of the group meetings.

Most revealing of all is a recent field study conducted by Meyer *et al.* (1965) where the effects of participation and goal-setting were more clearly separated. The authors found that: "While subordinate participation in the goal-setting process had some effect on improved performance, *a much more powerful influence was whether goals were set at all"* (p. 126, italics mine). In other words the content of the participation sessions was more important than the fact of participation itself. (The results of goal-setting in this study were given previously in Part I.)

The above quotes should not be taken to imply that participation has no motivational effect in and of itself. For example, Macoby (quoted in Viteles, 1953) suggests that participation may help to internalize motivation—to increase a subject's *commitment* to performance standards. The point is that goal-setting has been an integral part of previous studies of participation. Considering the amount of evidence there is (see Part I) that goals regulate performance, it must be concluded that the results of at least some of these studies can be attributed largely, if not entirely, to the goal-setting which was associated with or induced by the experimental design.

Competition. It is well known, both from experimental studies and from everyday experience, that competition can serve as an incentive to increase one's effort on a task. This phenomenon is an intrinsic part of athletics and business and is not unknown in academia. In the paradigm case of competition *another person's or groups' performance is the standard by which goals are set and success and failure judged.* One reason competition in athletics is so effective is that winning requires that one surpass the performance of the *best* existing competitor. This typically results in the standard of success becoming progressively more difficult with time. Each time a record is broken, the level of performance required to win (against the record holder) is raised. Each competitor must then readjust his goal and his level of effort to the difficulty of the task. The result is progressively better performance. (Of course cognitive factors can facilitate performance improvement, i.e., discovering better methods of performing the task. But it is the individual's *goal* to win or improve that generally motivates the search for such innovations.)

The case is similar though not identical in business. (Unlike athletics, business is not a "zero-sum game," where one man's gain necessarily means another man's loss. In business, wealth is *created* and therefore everyone benefits in the long run.) Competition will encourage the development of better and better products as long as there are firms who wish to increase their share of the market. Competition may also spur firms to increase their quality or lower prices in order not to lose business.

The effect of competition, both between individuals and between groups, depends upon the particular person or persons one is competing with and one's own values. In athletics, the goal is typically to beat the best other competitor. In business this is not always the case; typically, business firms are satisfied to surpass their own best previous performances. Students, if they are competing, will ordinarily pick other students with grades or abilities similar to their own to compete with, or else will try to surpass their own best previous grade-point average.

The case of an individual trying to improve over his own previous performance on a task can be considered a special case of competition: *self-competition.*

As with participation, competition may have other effects besides inducing goal-setting. Above all, competition probably encourages individuals to remain *committed* to goals that they might otherwise abandon in the face of fatigue and difficulty. For instance, if mile runners only ran against themselves or against a stop watch, the 4-minute mile might never have been broken.

In addition, competition encourages the setting of goals that might not have been set at all in the absence of the other party. For example, if the Ford Motor Company had not developed a massed-produced low-priced automobile, General Motors might not have thought of developing a similar (competing) model (at that particular time).

Praise and reproof. A recent review of the literature on praise and reproof (Kennedy and Willcutt, 1964) concluded that the effects of both incentives were highly variable though praise was generally more effective in improving performance. Most studies have found complex interactions between praise and reproof and such variables as: age, social class, race, sex, task, and intelligence.

As with all the other incentives discussed heretofore, the present theory suggests that the effects of praise and reproof will be a function of what goals the individual sets in response to them. It is clear from introspection and from everyday experience that sometimes the reaction to criticism is to clench one's teeth and try harder; at other times, the reaction is to give up (and "sulk") or to deliberately do badly (to "get even" with the critic). Similarly, praise sometimes leads to the setting of new and higher goals and at other times it is taken as a signal to "goof-off."

A theory explaining the precise circumstances in which praise and reproof will lead to the setting of higher and/or lower goals is beyond the scope of this paper. The important point is, however, that the effects of these incentives on performance should be a function of the goals the individual's set in response to them. The highly inconsistent results obtained by previous investigators may be attributed to their failure to control for differential goal-setting by subjects in the different experimental conditions.

The importance of goal-setting was implicitly recognized in one study, whose authors Kennedy and Willcutt (1964) paraphrase as follows:

The authors concluded that when the examiner's statements led subjects to assume that a particular level of performance is expected or that his performance is less satisfactory than that of other subjects, failure increases motivation; but when the examiner's statements only comment upon the subject's performance, failure lowers motivation (p. 329).

This implies that reproof will have a facilitative effect on performance when it is given *in relation to a standard.* Our previous discussion of knowledge of score suggested the same thing; giving scores in relation to a standard is one means of implicitly manipulating or encouraging goal-setting by a subject.

Another factor that has not always been controlled in studies of praise and reproof is that of success and failure. In some studies (e.g., Anderson, White, and Wash, 1966) subjects were given fictitious test scores in relation to some (fictitious) norm and then praised (for high scores) or reproved (for low scores). Without two control groups given success and failure feedback alone, the relative contribution of praise and reproof as compared with task success and failure cannot be determined.

Let us turn now to the effects of incentives on choice.

Behavioral Intentions and Desires as Mediators of the Effects of Incentives on Choice

Money. Each of the three studies of word unscrambling described above (and reported in Locke *et al.,* 1968) involved monetary incentives. In the first study, subjects were offered: 0 cents for successfully unscrambling their chosen word on the first block of ten trials; 2 cents for each word solved correctly (regardless of length) on the second block; and 10 cents for each word solved correctly (regardless of length) on the third block. It was found that subjects tended to choose easier words as the payment for success became greater. There was a correlation across blocks between amount of incentive and mean word length choice of—.51 ($p < .05$). However, this correlation was vitiated ($r = .22$, ns) when the effects of intentions were partialed out, indicating that the money did not affect word choice independent of its effects on the subjects' intentions.

In the second study discussed above, subjects were given "success," "achievement," or "challenge" instructions on the first block of ten trials, but were offered no money for correct solutions. On the second block, subjects were given no instructions but were offered 4 cents for each word correctly solved regardless of length. The point biserial correlation, for all subjects combined, between mean word-length choice and incentive (coded 0 and 1 for blocks I and II, respectively) across blocks was —.48 ($p < .01$). However, when intentions were partialed out this r was reduced to a nonsignificant —.10. In contrast, intentions correlated .86 ($p < .01$) with word choice across blocks after incentive was partialed out.

In the third study in this series described above, subjects had five blocks of five trials each; on each block the subject was offered either 1, 2, 3, 4, or 5 cents for each word solved correctly on that block regardless of length. (The order was counterbalanced across subjects.) Again subjects tended to choose easier words when offered the higher incentive. The relationship of intentions and incentive to mean word choice is shown in Fig. 4, where word choice is plotted as a function of incentive for each of three levels of intention. (Intention level 1.0 corresponds to the "very easy words" alternative on the intention scale; 2.0 corresponds to the "fairly easy words" alternative; 3.0 corresponds to the "neither too easy nor too hard" alternative; the few subjects who checked intentions harder than this are also included in this group.) It is clear that the effect of intention on word choice was considerable but there was no effect of incentive within any given intention level. As in the previous two studies, incentive had no effect

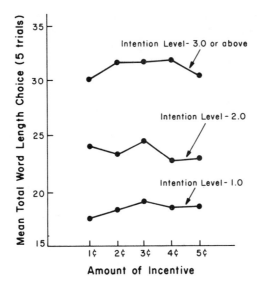

FIGURE 4. Word-length choice as a function of incentive for three levels of intention.

on word choice independent of the subjects' behavioral intentions. (There was also a no-incentive comparison group in this study. The results were the same whether or not this group was included. For the complete report, see Locke *et al.,* 1968, Study 5.) The overall correlation across blocks between intentions and word choice was .83 ($p <$ .01); this correlation remained unchanged after partialing incentive. In contrast, the correlation across blocks of incentive with word choice after partialing intentions was .04 (ns).

Verbal "reinforcement." The previously discussed findings of Dulany (1962, 1968) and Holmes (1966) regarding behavioral intentions and verbal responses were obtained in studies of "verbal conditioning." The subjects in these studies were instructed to free associate or to make up sentences beginning with one of a number of pronouns, and the experimenter reinforced some arbitrarily designated class of words (e.g., plural nouns) or pronouns (e.g., I, or We) by saying "good" or "Mmm-hmm" after each response in that class. In the above three studies it was found that such "reinforcement" had no effect on responses independent of subjects' intention to give the "correct" response.

Another series of studies in this same area examined the effects of the subjects' conscious *desires* on behavior. In these studies subjects

were asked to indicate the strength of their desire to get the reinforcement ("good," etc.) which the experimenter provided (e.g.,
DeNike, 1965; Spielberger, Berger, and Howard, 1963; Spielberger,
Bernstein, and Ratliff, 1966; Spielberger, Levin, and Shepard, 1962).
It was found that the frequency of emission of the "correct" response
class was a direct function of the strength of the subjects' desire to get
the reinforcement (provided he knew what the "correct" response
class was).

III: Discussion

There is considerable evidence to support the view that goals
and intentions are important determinants of task performance. It is
argued that these long-neglected concepts are important enough so
that any tenable theory of human motivation must take account of
them. This conclusion is based both on the fact that consciousness is
man's means of survival (Rand, 1964) and on the strong empirical
relationships that have been obtained between goals and behavior.

The experimental findings also indicate that goals and intentions
mediate the effects of incentives on behavior. It appears that a necessary condition for incentives to affect behavior is that the individual
recognize and evaluate the incentive and develop goals, and/or intentions in response to this evaluation. A careful examination of the subjects' goals and intentions in research on incentives should produce
more clear-cut results as well as providing a theoretical rationale for
explaining how incentives affect action.

A highly simplified schematic showing the hypothesized sequence
of events leading from events in the environment to action is given
below:

Environmental		Goal-setting		
Event → Cognition →	Evaluation →	Intention →	Performance
(e.g., incentive)				
(1) (2)	(3)	(4)	(5)

The present research examined only the relationships between
stages 4 and 5, and between 1, 4, and 5. Cognition and evaluation
were assumed to occur, but their contents were not specified. The
focus of interest was on the *results* of these processes (the goals or
intentions established) and subsequent action. A complete theory of
task motivation would, of course, have to deal with the processes of

cognition and evaluation (and their determinants) as well as their outcomes.

It may be useful theoretically to classify the various incentives that
were discussed in Part II. For our purposes the dimension of interest
is the degree to which the different types of incentives suggest *specific*
goals or intentions to subjects.

Instructions, of course, are the most direct means of manipulating
goals and intentions. Instructions will influence behavior providing:
(1) the individual accepts them, i.e., accepts the assignment as his
own goal or intention, and (2) he is able to do what is asked (this will
depend upon his knowledge, ability and the situation).

Giving an individual specific *time limits* is another fairly direct
means of manipulating goals, given the same qualifications as for
instructions. It was shown previously that individuals who accept
different time limits will set different subgoals as well, but these were
a result of their accepting the different time limit initially.

Two less direct means of manipulating goals are giving *knowledge
of score* and providing *competition.* These incentives do not tell the
subject directly what goal to try for, but if given in the right form,
they may *suggest* specific standards to him. For instance, giving a subject his raw scores after each trial may suggest the goal of improvement (providing the trials are all the same length so that the trial
scores are comparable). Similarly, giving KS in relation to some external standard is certain to imply a goal to the subject. Giving scores
in relation to those of another person is a common way of combining
KS and competition. Again the effects of both incentives will be dependent upon the subject choosing to use the KS to set goals or to try
to beat the other individual. These two incentives are usually quite
effective in experimental situations where the subject is actively looking for cues as to what he is supposed to do and is anxious to cooperate (Orne, 1962).

Money, praise and *reproof,* and *participation,* in contrast to the
above incentives, are quite indirect means of manipulating goals. None
of them directly suggests or implies that the subject should try for a
particular goal as such. Offering an individual money for output may
motivate him to set his goals higher than he would otherwise but this
will depend entirely upon how much money he wishes to make and
how much effort he wishes to expend to make it. It is useful in this
context to recall the well-known sociologist Max Weber's observation
that the introduction of high incentive pay may reduce output if the
worker's income aspirations remain the same as before the incentive

was introduced. Some workers would prefer to make the same money in less time than to make more money in the same amount of time. The most important role played by money is probably to get a subject to accept an assigned task or goal or to insure his commitment to a job.

Similarly participation as such will not necessarily suggest a higher output goal; this will depend on the particular *content* of the participation process (the particular nature of the decisions reached). The most direct effect of participation is probably to commit a subject to the decision reached (as with money), whatever that might be.

The effects of praise and reproof on goal-setting are also indirect. Praise and reproof per se represent only evaluations of the subject's past performance and do not imply what *he should do* in the future. A subject's reaction to these incentives will depend on such factors as whether he considers the comments just or unjust, the particular work context in which the comments were made, his liking and respect for the person making the comments, his own personality, etc.

In most real life work situations a combination of all of these incentives are employed. A worker is hired and *instructed* on what to do and *how fast* to do it; he is given or gets *knowledge of performance* either from others or from the task itself; he may *compete* with others for promotion; he is *paid* for working, he is *evaluated* by his supervisor, and sometimes he *participates* in decision making. All of these factors can be considered ways of (1) getting the subject to set or accept work goals, and (2) retaining his commitment to them and insuring persistence over time.

The issue of goal commitment has not been dealt with in any of the research discussed above, but it is no doubt an important factor in performance. The subject's degree of commitment to his goal may play an important role in determining how easily he will give up in the face of difficulty, how likely he will be to "goof-off" when not being pressured from the outside, how likely he will be to abandon hard goals, and how prone he will be to "leave the field" (i.e., job) in the face of stress.

Finally, a word is in order about the possible industrial applications of the finding that goal setting is a major determinant of task performance. There are two recent trends in industry, which, although they were not inspired by this research, are quite congruent with its implications. One is a motivational program called *Zero Defects* (American Management Association, 1965). The purpose of a zero-defects program is basically to reduce errors in workmanship (i.e., increase the quality of work) by persuading workers to adopt higher goals with regard to quality. Carrying out the program often involves the gathering of more precise quality data (knowledge of results of the epistemic type) and changing of work methods, and some programs are supplemented by the introduction of group competition and prizes for accomplishment. Huse (1966) has argued that another important aspect of zero-defects programs is the opening up of channels of communication between the workers and management.

Without carefully controlled studies, of course, it cannot be determined just what particular aspects of the zero-defects programs are most responsible for the success that they have apparently enjoyed. But changing the quality goals of individual workers and managers does seem to be the key element; not only does it affect work directly but it apparently stimulates employees to try to *discover* better methods of doing the work.

While zero-defects programs are usually focused on work at the blue collar level, the focus of a second major trend is on work at the white collar level. It is called *Management by Objectives* (see Hughes, 1965; Valentine, 1966, for details). The key element in this system is the setting of specific performance goals by executives and managers. Goals are usually set jointly by the manager and his supervisor, thus participation is involved. Goals can involve sales, growth, output, income, costs or some combination of these, depending upon the particular type of job. The process involves: the delineation of company goals and the translation of these into goals relevant to the individual's own job, setting up hierarchies of objectives, planning out the means by which each goal is to be reached, and agreeing upon the criteria to be used in evaluation. (Zero defects could be interpreted as the application of this general approach to the particular problem of work quality.) Again, many different factors are involved in management by objectives programs but the setting of specific goals is the cardinal element.

REFERENCES

AMERICAN MANAGEMENT ASSOCIATION, *Zero Defects: doing it right the first time.* Management Bulletin, **71**, 1965.

ANDERSON, H. E., WHITE, W. F., AND WASH, J. A. Generalized effects of praise and reproof. *Journal of Educational Psychology,* 1966, **57**, 169-173.

ATKINSON, J. W. Towards experimental analysis of human motivation in terms of motives, expectancies, and incentives. *In* J. W. Atkinson (Ed.), *Motives in fantasy, action and society.* New York: Van Nostrand, 1958, pp. 288-305.

124THEORIES

ATKINSON, J. W., AND FEATHER, N. T. *A theory of achievement motivation.* New York: Wiley, 1966.

BATTLE, ESTHER S. Motivational determinants of academic competence. *Journal of Personality and Social Psychology,* 1966, **4,** 634-642.

BILLS, A. G., AND BROWN, C. The quantitative set. *Journal of Experimental Psychology,* 1929, **12,** 301-323.

BRANDEN, N. The Objectivist theory of volition. *The Objectivist,* 1966, **5,** No. 1, 7-12.

†BRYAN, J. F., AND LOCKE, E. A. Goal-setting as a means of increasing motivation. *Journal of Applied Psychology,* 1967, **51,** 274-277. (a)

BRYAN, J. F., AND LOCKE, E. A. Parkinson's law as a goal-setting phenomenon. *Organizational Behavior and Human Performance,* 1967, **2,** 258-275. (b)

DENIKE, L. D. Recall of reinforcement and conative activity in verbal conditioning. *Psychological Reports,* 1965, **16,** 345-346.

DEY, M. K., AND KAUR, G. Facilitation of performance by experimentally induced ego motivation. *Journal of General Psychology,* 1965, **73,** 237-247.

DULANY, D. E., JR. Hypotheses and habits in verbal "operant conditioning." *Journal of Abnormal and Social Psychology,* 1961, **63,** 251-263.

DULANY, D. E., JR. The place of hypotheses and intentions: an analysis of verbal control in verbal conditioning. *In* C. W. Eriksen (Ed.), *Behavior and awareness.* Durham, North Carolina: Duke Univ. Press, 1962, pp. 102-129.

DULANY, D. E., JR. Awareness, rules and propositional control: a confrontation with S-R behavior theory. *In* D. Horton and T. Dixon (Eds.), *Verbal behavior and general behavior theory.* Englewood Cliffs, New Jersey: Prentice-Hall, 1968, pp. 340-387.

EAGLE, M. N. The effect of learning strategies upon free recall. *American Journal of Psychology,* 1967, **80,** 421-425.

EASON, R. G., AND WHITE, C. T. Muscular tension, effort, and tracking difficulty: studies of parameters which affect tension level and performance efficiency. *Perceptual and Motor Skills,* 1961, **12,** 331-372.

HENDERSON, E. H. A study of individually formulated purposes for reading in relation to reading achievement comprehension and purpose attainment. Unpublished Ph.D. dissertation, Univ. of Delaware, 1963.

HOLMES, D. S. Verbal conditioning or problem solving and cooperation? Midwestern Psychological Association, 1966.

HUGHES, C. L. *Goal-setting.* New York: American Management Association, 1965.

HUSE, E. F. Do zero defects programs really motivate workers? *Personnel,* 1966, **43,** 14-21.

KENNEDY, W. A., AND WILLCUTT, H. C. Praise and blame as incentives. *Psychological Bulletin,* 1964, **62,** 323-332.

LAWRENCE, L. C., AND SMITH, P. C. Group decision and employee participation. *Journal of Applied Psychology,* 1955, **39,** 334-337.

LEVENTHAL, H., AND NILES, P. A. A field experiment on fear arousal with data on the validity of questionnaire measures. *Journal of Personality,* 1964, **32,** 459-479.

LIKERT, R. *New patterns of management.* New York: McGraw-Hill, 1961.

LOCKE, E. A. The relationship of intentions to level of performance. *Journal of Applied Psychology,* 1966, **50,** 60-66. (a)

*Locke, E. A. A closer look at level of aspiration as a training procedure: A re-analysis of Fryer's data. *Journal of Applied Psychology,* 1966, **50**, 417-420. (b)

Locke, E. A. Relationship of goal level to performance level. *Psychological Reports,* 1967, **20**, 1068. (a)

†Locke, E. A. The motivational effects of knowledge of results: Knowledge or goal-setting? *Journal of Applied Psychology,* 1967, **51**, 324-329. (b)

*Locke, E. A. The effects of knowledge of results and knowledge in relation to standards on reaction time performance. American Institutes for Research (unpublished results), 1967. (c)

†Locke, E. A., and Bryan, J. F. Cognitive aspects of psychomotor performance: The effects of performance goals on level of performance. *Journal of Applied Psychology,* 1966, **50**, 286-291. (a)

† *Locke, E. A., and Bryan, J. F. The effects of goal-setting, rule-learning and knowledge of score on performance. *American Journal of Psychology,* 1966, **79**, 451-457. (b)

† *Locke, E. A., and Bryan, J. F. Performance goals as determinants of level of performance and boredom. *Journal of Applied Psychology,* 1967, **51**, 120-130. (a)

Locke, E. A., and Bryan, J. F. Goal-setting as a determinant of the effect of knowledge of score on performance. American Institutes for Research (unpublished results), 1967. (b)

*Locke, E. A., and Bryan, J. F. Knowledge of score and goal difficulty as determinants of work rate. American Institutes for Research (unpublished results), 1967. (c)

*Locke, E. A., and Bryan, J. F. Grade goals as determinants of academic performance. *Journal of General Psychology,* 1968 (in press).

*Locke, E. A., Bryan, J. F., and Kendall, L. M. Goals and intentions as mediators of the effects of monetary incentives on behavior. *Journal of Applied Psychology,* 1968 (in press).

McClelland, D. C. *The achieving society.* Princeton, New Jersey: Van Nostrand, 1961.

Mace, C. A. Incentives: Some experimental studies. Industrial Health Research Board (Great Britain), 1935, Report No. 72.

Maier, N. F. *Psychology in industry.* New York: Houghton, 1955, pp. 137-180.

Mathewson, S. B. *Restriction of output among unorganized workers.* New York: Viking Press, 1931.

Meyer, H. H., Kay, E., and French, J. R. P., Jr. Split roles in performance appraisal. *Harvard Business Review,* 1965, **43**, 123-129.

Orne, M. T. On the social psychology of the psychological experiment with particular reference to demand characteristics. *American Psychologist,* 1962, **17**, 776-783.

Rand, Ayn. The Objectivist ethics. *In* Ayn Rand (Ed.), *The virtue of selfishness,* New York: Signet, 1964, pp. 13-35.

Roethlisberger, F. J., and Dickson, W. J. *Management and the worker.* Cambridge, Massachusetts: Harvard Univ. Press, 1939.

Ryan, T. A. Drives, tasks, and the initiation of behavior. *American Journal of Psychology,* 1958, **71**, 74-93.

Siegal, S., and Fouraker, L. E. *Bargaining and group decision making.* New York: McGraw-Hill, 1960, pp. 61-70.

SMITH, P. C. The curve of output as a criterion of boredom. *Journal of Applied Psychology,* 1953, **37,** 69-74.

SORCHER, M. Motivating the hourly employee. General Electric, Behavioral Research Service, 1967.

SPIELBERGER, C. D., BERGER, A., AND HOWARD, K. Conditioning of verbal behavior as a function of awareness, need for social approval, and motivation to receive reinforcement. *Journal of Abnormal and Social Psychology,* 1963, **67,** 241-246.

SPEILBERGER, C. D., BERNSTEIN, I. H., AND RATLIFF, R. G. Information and incentive value of the reinforcing stimulus in verbal conditioning. *Journal of Experimental Psychology,* 1966, **71,** 26-31.

SPIELBERGER, C. D., LEVIN, S. M., AND SHEPARD, M. The effects of awareness and attitude toward the reinforcement on the operant conditioning of verbal behavior. *Journal of Personality,* 1962, **30,** 106-121.

STEDRY, A. C. *Budget control and cost behavior.* Englewood Cliffs, New Jersey: Prentice-Hall, 1960.

TAYLOR, F. W. *The principles of scientific management.* New York: Harper, 1911.

UHLINGER, C. A., AND STEPHENS, M. W. Relation of achievement motivation to academic achievement in students of superior ability. *Journal of Educational Psychology,* 1960, **51,** 259-266.

VALENTINE, R. F. *Performance objectives for managers.* New York: American Management Association, 1966.

VITELES, M. S. *Motivation and morale in industry.* New York: Norton, 1953.

VROOM, V. H. *Work and motivation.* New York: John Wiley, 1964.

WHYTE, W. F. *Money and motivation.* New York: John Wiley, 1955.

ZANDER, A., AND NEWCOMB, T. Group levels of aspiration in United Fund campaigns. *Journal of Personality and Social Psychology,* 1967, **6,** 157-162.

8

Expectancy Theory in
Managerial Motivation:
An Integrative Model

ROBERT J. HOUSE

AND

MAHMOUD A. WAHBA

Expectancy or instrumentality-valence theory is perhaps the most widely accepted theory of work and motivation among today's industrial and organizational psychologists. The theory is based on two familiar concepts: expectancy (subjective probability) and valence (anticipated value). The theory proposes, generally, that work-related behavior can be predicted once we know the valence people attach to certain outcomes and their expectations of the occurrence of these outcomes. According to the theory, an individual chooses the behaviors he engages in on the basis of the interaction between (1) the valences he perceives to be associated with the outcomes of the behavior under consideration and (2) his subjective estimate of the probability that his behavior will indeed result in the outcomes. It is further proposed that the resulting function is a nonlinear, monotonically increasing product of expectations and valences.

Expectancy theory has generated a great deal of research in industrial and organizational psychology. It has been suggested that the theory can provide the basis to prescribe, describe, and predict a wide variety of work-related variables. The theory has been proposed to predict the following variables: *job effort and job performance*

EDITORS' NOTE: This paper and the one appearing in Part Three entitled "Expectancy Theory in Managerial Motivation: Review of Relevant Research" were originally prepared by House and Wahba as a single work. It has been divided because of the treatment of theories and critiques in this collection.

Printed by permission of the authors. Unpublished paper, Bernard M. Baruch College of the City University of New York, 1972.

(Georgopoulos, Mahoney, and Jones, 1957; Vroom, 1964; Galbraith and Cummings, 1967; Lawler and Porter, 1967; Hackman and Porter, 1968; Graen, 1969; Gavin, 1970; Goodman, Rose, and Furcon, 1970; Mitchell and Albright, 1971; Wofford, 1971); *job satisfaction* (Vroom, 1964; Lawler and Porter, 1968; Graen, 1969; Lawler, 1970; Wofford, 1971); *organizational practices* (Evans, 1968); *managerial motivation* (Campbell, Dunnette, Weick, and Lawler, 1970); *occupational choice* (Vroom, 1964; Mitchell and Knudson, 1971); *the importance of pay and pay effectiveness* (Dunnette, 1967; Lawler, 1971); and *leadership behavior and leader effectiveness* (Evans, 1968; House, 1971). In addition, Vroom (1964) asserts that the theory could easily explain the following work-related variables: *occupational preference, morale, need achievement, group cohesiveness,* and *motivation for effective performance.*

The purpose of this paper is threefold: First, to develop a general model integrating various formulations of expectancy theory. Second, to review the overall findings of recent empirical research with reference to the major constructs of the integrative model. Third, to suggest some areas in need of further research in the theory, especially as related to managerial motivation.

It should be noted, however, that most of the following discussion is based on the findings of studies in both managerial and non-managerial populations. However, studies that deal only with managers are few indeed. This, in itself, suggests that some of the general findings reviewed here should be cross validated in managerial populations.

Expectancy Theory: A Brief Description

Expectancy theory was first proposed as an explanation of work behavior by Vroom (1964).[1] Vroom proposed three related models: a job satisfaction model, a work motivation model, and a job performance model.

The job satisfaction model states that the satisfaction or "the valence of an outcome to a person is a monotonically increasing function of the algebraic sum of the products of the valences of all

---

[1]Expectancy theory derives from economic expected utility theory and from psychological theories of choice behavior. As such, earlier versions of expectancy theory were applied to phenomena other than work motivation as early as 1738. See Wahba and House (1972) for an historical review of the development of the theory and the relationship between alternative formulations.

other outcomes, and his conceptions of the specific outcome's instrumentality for the attainment of these other outcomes" (Vroom, 1964:17). Instrumentality is defined as the degree to which the person sees the outcome in question as leading to the attainment of other outcomes and varies from –1 (certainty of negative outcome) to +1 (certainty of positive outcome). Valence is defined as an affective orientation toward an outcome.

The work motivation model states that "the force on a person to perform an act is a monotonically increasing function of the algebraic sum of the products of the valences of all outcomes and the strength of his expectancies that the act will be followed by the attainment of these outcomes" (Vroom, 1964:18). Expectancy is defined by Vroom as the subjective probability that a given act will be followed by a given outcome and varies between 0 (certain non-occurrence) and 1 (certain occurrence).

The job performance model proposes that job performance is a function of the product of multiplying ability and motivation. Specifically, Vroom (1964:203) states

Performance = f (Ability × Motivation). It follows from such a formula that, when ability has a low value, increments in motivation will result in smaller increases in performance than when ability has a high value. Furthermore, when motivation has a low value, increments in ability will result in smaller increases in performance than when motivation has a high value.

Operationally, Vroom's model implies that people choose among alternative work-related actions in a manner that optimizes their expected valences. That is, for each action, people multiply their perceived valence of each possible outcome by the perceived expectancy of their occurrence, find the algebraic sum across all outcomes, and, then, choose the action with the highest expected summation. For example, consider the case in Table 1.

Imagine an employee choosing between two actions (effective or noneffective performance) each with two alternative financial outcomes. Suppose further, that the employee's expectations of the occurrences of the outcomes are as shown in the table. According to Vroom:

(a) The force to choose effective performance is = ($100 × 0.8) + ($0 × 0.2) = $80.

(b) The force to choose noneffective performance is = ($100 × 0.2) + ($0 × 8) = $20.

Table 1

A Simple Two Actions, Two Outcomes Work Choice Situation

Possible Consequences / Alternative Actions	C_1	C_2
A_1 Effective performance	bonus (\$100) expectancy 0.8	no bonus (\$0) expectancy 0.2
A_2 Noneffective performance	bonus (\$100) expectancy 0.2	no bonus (\$0) expectancy 0.8

Assuming that the employee is optimizing his gains, he should choose effective performance over noneffective performance.

The original Vroom model has undergone four developments in the last few years: (1) the distinction between first-level and second-level outcomes; (2) identification of intrinsic sources of valence; (3) the distinction between expectancy I and expectancy II; and (4) the incorporation of additional variables in the model to explain job performance, and the equity concept to explain job satisfaction, and so forth. We will review only the first three of these developments since the fourth development did not change the general formulation of the theory.

Galbraith and Cummings (1967), Porter and Lawler (1967), and Graen (1969) distinguished between first- and second-level outcomes. The first-level outcome is the work behavior, such as job performance, and the second-level outcome is the event to which the first level outcome is expected to lead, such as a reward. A distinction was also made between the different kinds of valences associated with these outcomes. Galbraith and Cummings (1967) extended the theory by pointing out that certain intrinsic valences are associated with the work behavior itself. House (1971) distinguished between two kinds of intrinsic valences: (1) those associated with task performance, such as the development of valued skills or social satisfaction involved in interpersonal tasks, and (2) those associated with task accomplishment, such as pride in work or the satisfaction of achieving a challenging goal.

Campbell, Dunnette, Lawler, and Weick (1970) extended the model further by distinguishing between two types of expectancies: Expectancy I, concerning whether or not the individuals will actually accomplish that task goal or work role, and Expectancy 2, concerning whether or not achievement of a specified task goal will actually be instrumental in the attainment of the intrinsic first-level outcome. House (1971) asserted that the different kinds of valences are associated with these two kinds of expectancies in a differential manner.

An Integrative Model of Expectancy

The developments referred to above can be integrated in the following general model:

$$M = IV_{bi} + E_1 \left[IV_{ai} + \sum_i^n (E_{2i} V_i) \right]$$

$$i = 1, \ldots, n$$

where:

M = motivation to work;

IV_{bi} = intrinsic valences associated with task behavior or performance;

IV_{ai} = intrinsic valences associated with task accomplishment;

V_i = extrinsic valences associated with task or work goal accomplishment;

E_1 = expectancy 1, the subject's probability estimate that his effort will lead to first-level outcomes;

E_2 = expectancy 2, the subject's probability estimate that first-level outcome will lead to extrinsic rewards or punishments (second-level outcomes).

According to the formulation advanced here, the individual makes probability estimates with respect to two linking points connecting behavior with its outcomes, and subjectively places values on the outcomes. The magnitude of these probability estimates indicates the degree of instrumentality of his behavior for work-goal accomplishment and valence.

The integrative model has several theoretical and empirical advantages:

First: The empirical validity of the model can easily be tested by reference to the current research evidence on the subject. This is because most of the proposed relations between the constructs are derived from the empirical findings. As such, the model brings closer the theoretical and empirical studies in the field.

Second: The model distinguishes between two types of valences: extrinsic and intrinsic. Furthermore, the model distinguishes between two types of intrinsic valences: one associated with task performance and the second associated with task or goal accomplishment. These distinctions are empirically valid and prove useful in the discussion of the research findings in many areas of industrial and organizational psychology, as will be shown later.

Third: The model does not utilize the concept of instrumentality. The original formulation of the concept of instrumentality has been found to be ambiguous (see Wahba and House 1972 for details). Rather, Expectancy 2 is used to measure the likelihood that first-level outcomes (such as performance) will lead to the attainment of a second-level outcome (such as reward). Expectancy 1 is viewed as an action-outcome association and based on direct (or simple) probability. Expectancy 2, on the other hand, is viewed as an outcome-outcome association and is based on conditional rather than direct probability. Operationally, Expectancy 2 is a function of the product of the probability estimation of the simple action-outcome expectation multiplied by the simple outcome-outcome expectation. The substitution of Expectancy 2 for the concept of instrumentality makes it possible to utilize the statistical theory of probability for further development of the expectancy model. In addition, this makes it possible to relate the expectancy model in industrial and organizational psychology to other expectancy models in psychology and mathematical statistics.

Fourth: The model can be used to study both job satisfaction and work motivation. This is because work motivation is viewed as a function of the interaction between expectancy and valence, while job satisfaction is viewed as a function of the presence of various relevant valences.

Fifth: The model allows for the study of other related work variables, such as job performance, leadership behavior, occupational choice, and others by the incorporation of some additional variables (such as ability in the case of job performance). It should be pointed out, however, that future studies are needed to determine the nature of the variables to be incorporated in each case and the nature of interactions of these variables with both expectancy and valence.

REFERENCES

CAMPBELL J. P.; DUNNETTE, M. D.; LAWLER, E. E.; and WEICK, K. E. 1970. *Managerial behavior, performances and effectiveness.* New York: McGraw-Hill.

DUNNETTE, M. D. 1967. The role of financial compensation in managerial motivation. *Organizational Behavior and Human Performance* 2:175-216.

EVANS, M. G. 1968. The effects of supervisory behavior upon worker perception of their path-goal relationships. Ph.D. dissertation. Yale University.

GALBRAITH, J., and CUMMINGS, L. 1967. An empiric investigation of the motivational determinants of past performance: Interactive effects between instrumentality-valence, motivation, and ability. *Organizational Behavior and Human Performance* 2, no. 3:237-57.

GAVIN, J. F. 1970. Ability, effort, and role perception as antecedents of job performance. *Experimental Publication System* 5, manuscript number 190A.

GEORGOPOULOS, B. S.; MAHONEY, G. M.; and JONES, N. W. 1957. A path-goal approach to productivity. *Journal of Applied Psychology* 41:345-53.

GOODMAN, P. S.; ROSE, J. H.; and FURCON, J. E. 1970. Comparison of motivational antecedents of the work performance of scientists and engineers. *Journal of Applied Psychology* 14:491-95.

GRAEN, G. 1969. Instrumentality theory of work motivation: Some experimental results and suggested modifications. *Journal of Applied Psychology Monograph* 53, no. 2:1-25.

HACKMAN, J. R., and PORTER, L. W. 1968. Expectancy theory predictions of work effectiveness. *Organizational Behavior and Human Performance* 3:417-26.

HENEMAN, H. H., and SCHWAB, D. P. (In press.) An evaluation of research on expectancy theory predictions of employee performance. *Psychological Bulletin.*

HOUSE, R. J. 1971. A path goal theory of leader effectiveness. *Administrative Science Quarterly* 16, no. 3:321-38.

LAWLER, E. E. 1966. Ability as a moderator of the relationship between job attitudes and job performance. *Personnel Psychology* 19:153-64.

———. 1968. A correlational-causal analysis of the relationship between expectancy attitudes and job performance. *Journal of Applied Psychology* 52:462-68.

———. 1970. Job attitudes and employee motivation: Theory, research, and practice. *Personnel Psychology* 23:223-37.

———. 1971. *Pay and organizational effectiveness: A psychological perspective.* New York: John Wiley & Sons.

LAWLER, E. E., and PORTER, L. W. 1967. Antecedent attitudes of effective managerial performance. *Organizational Behavior and Human Performance* 2:122-42.

MITCHELL, T. R., and ALBRIGHT, D. (In press.) Expectancy theory predictions of job satisfaction, job effort, job performance, and retention of naval aviation officers. *Organizational Behavior and Human Performance.*

MITCHELL, T. R., and KNUDSON, B. W. 1971. Instrumentality theory predictions of students' attitudes toward business and their choice of business as an occupation. Working paper, July. University of Washington, Technical Report 71-27.

PORTER, L. W., and LAWLER, E. E. 1968. *Managerial attitudes and performance.* Homewood, Ill.: Irwin-Dorsey.

VROOM, V. H. 1964. *Work and motivation.* John Wiley & Sons.

WAHBA, M., and HOUSE, R. 1972. Expectancy theory in work and motivation: Some logical and methodological issues. Working paper, Baruch College, City University of New York.

WOFFORD, J. C. 1971. The motivational basis of job satisfaction and job performance. *Personnel Psychology* 24:501-19.

9

Inequity in Social Exchange

J. STACY ADAMS

I. INTRODUCTION

Philosophers, political scientists, politicians, jurists, and economists traditionally have been the ones concerned with the just distribution of wealth, power, goods, and services in society. Social psychologists and their brethren, with the notable exceptions of Blau (1964), Homans (1961), and Thibaut and Kelley (1959), have displayed remarkably little professional interest in this, despite the fact that the process of exchange is almost continual in human interactions. They have, of course, studied social behavior involving reciprocal, as distinguished from unilateral, transactions, but their sights have been focused on the amount and content of communications; attitudinal, affective, motivational, perceptual, and behavioral changes; changes in group structure, leadership, and so on, rather than on exchange proper. Yet, the process of exchange appears to have characteristics peculiar to itself and to generate affect, motivation, and behavior that cannot be predicted unless exchange processes are understood.

A distinguishing characteristic of exchange processes is that their resultants have the potentiality of being perceived as just or unjust. But what are the consequences of outcomes being perceived as meeting or not meeting the norms of justice? Nearly all the attention given to this question has been to establish a relationship between perceived injustice and dissatisfaction (Homans, 1950, 1953, 1961; Jaques, 1956, 1961a; Patchen, 1959, 1961; Stouffer *et al.,* 1949; Vroom,

Reprinted by permission of the author and publisher from *Advances in Experimental Psychology,* ed. L. Berkowitz, pp. 157-89. New York: Academic Press, Inc., 1965.

1964; Zaleznik *et al.,* 1958). Not surprisingly, this has been accomplished with success. Does a man treated unfairly simply express dissatisfaction? Are there not other consequences of unfair exchanges? What behavior is predictable? These questions and related ones are a principal concern of this paper.

Rather than simply present a theory from which the behavior of persons engaged in a social exchange may be deduced, the plan of this chapter is to present first in chronological order two major concepts relating to the perception of justice and injustice. First is the concept of relative deprivation and the complementary concept of relative gratification, developed by Stouffer and his associates (1949). Homans' highly elaborated concept of distributive justice (1961) will be discussed next. These will then be integrated into a theory of inequity from which it will be possible to specify the antecedents and consequences of injustice in human exchanges.

II. RELATIVE DEPRIVATION

Following World War II, the publication of the first *American Soldier* volume by Stouffer and his colleagues (1949) excited interest among sociologists and social psychologists. The effect was at least in part due to the introduction of a new concept, relative deprivation, used by the authors to explain what were seemingly paradoxical findings. According to Merton and Kitt (1950), the formal status of the concept was that of an intervening variable which explained the observed relationship between an independent variable, such as education level or rate of promotion, and a dependent variable, such as satisfaction with some aspect of Army life.

Relative deprivation was not formally defined by the authors, however, nor by Merton and Kitt (1950), who analyzed in great detail the implication of the concept for sociological theory in general and for reference group theory in particular. The essential meaning of the concept may be inferred from two illustrations of its use by the authors of *The American Soldier*. Despite the objective fact that soldiers with a high school education had better opportunities for advancement in the Army, high school graduates were not as satisfied with their status and jobs as were less educated men. This apparent paradox is explained by assuming that the better-educated men had higher levels of aspiration, partly based on what would be realistic status expectations in civilian life, and that they were, therefore, relatively deprived of status and less satisfied with the status they

achieved. It may be noted that the validity of this explanation depends
upon showing that level of aspiration is greater than status achieved
among high school graduates as contrasted to soldiers with less education. While this is not demonstrated by the authors, it appears to
be a credible assumption. It is the relative deprivation, then, that accounts for less satisfaction among better-educated men.

A second illustrative use of relative deprivation is made by the
authors of *The American Soldier* in accounting for the puzzling fact
that Army Air Corps men were less satisfied with promotion opportunities than were men in the Military Police, even though objective
opportunities for mobility were vastly greater in the Air Corps. Relative deprivation is invoked to explain the anomaly as follows: The high
promotion rate in the Air Corps induces high expectations of
mobility; lower-ranking and low-mobile men, compared to higher-
ranking and high-mobile men, feel deprived in the face of their expectations and express dissatisfaction. Among military policemen, on the
other hand, expectations of promotion are low, and the fate of most
policemen is quite similar: namely, low rank. In sum, there is a discrepancy between expectation and achievement among Air Corps en-
listed men and little or no discrepancy between expectation and
achievement among men in the Military Police. The discrepancy results in dissatisfaction with mobility. Or more precisely, the assumed
existence of a discrepancy between expectation and achievement is
held to account for the empirical observation that men were less satisfied in one branch than in the other.

Spector (1956), in an experiment directly related to these findings by Stouffer *et al.*, varied perceived probability of promotion and
fulfillment and tested the hypothesis that *"on failing to achieve
an attractive goal, an individual's morale will be higher if the probability of achieving the goal had been perceived to be low than if it
had been perceived to be high"* (p. 52). He found that the high expec-
tations-nonpromotion group had lower morale and was less satisfied
with the promotion system than was the low expectations-
nonpromotion group, thus corroborating experimentally the military
survey findings. Comparable findings have been made by Gebhard
(1949).

The effects of relative deprivation (the unfair violation of expectations) upon sociometric choices are clearly shown in an experiment
designed by Thibaut (1950) to learn about the conditions that affect
group cohesiveness. Underprivileged boys from camps and settlement
houses in the Boston area participated in the experiment in groups of

10 to 12 boys, all of whom had known, played, and lived with one another for some time. After filling out a questionnaire in which they were asked to rank the four boys they would most like to have on their team to play games if their groups were to be divided, the boys in each group were split into two teams of five or six. Thibaut formed each team so that each boy would have about an equal number of preferred and of nonpreferred partners and so that each team would be composed of approximately the same number of popular, or *central,* and less popular, or *peripheral,* boys in terms of sociometric choices received. Although there were several experimental conditions in his study, only one of them concerns us here. This is the condition in which each set of two teams played four games and one of the pairs was given consistently an inferior, menial, uninteresting, or unpleasant role during the series of games. These were the *low-status* teams (called "unsuccessful low-status" by Thibaut).

Following the last game, each boy answered a questionnaire in which he was again asked to order his preferences for teammates. A general finding was that a boy tended to shift his sociometric choices after the games to boys who had actually been teammates. Of greater interest here is the fact that low-status *central* boys were more likely to display such shifts than were low-status *peripheral* boys. The former were popular boys, presumably aware of their status among their fellows, who were forced to assume low-status roles in violation of the roles they would customarily play. The role of the low-status peripheral boys, on the other hand, were more or less a confirmation of their relatively low popularity among their friends. Compared to the peripheral boys, then, the central boys were relatively deprived, and they manifested their greater dissatisfaction with their fate by shifting to a greater extent their sociometric choices from central boys on the opposing team to boys on their own team. Thibaut also reports evidence that the low-status central boys displayed exceptional hostility to members of the opposing (high-status) teams and that all low-status boys keenly felt the injustice of their fate.

These findings are of especial interest because they cannot be accounted for simply on the hypothesis that abuse or minority group membership will result in withdrawal and increased cohesiveness. Such a hypothesis would have required that low-status peripheral and central boys show the same behavior. But, as noted, central boys were more likely to shift their sociometric choices and to display overt hostility to opponents. They were the ones who suffered the greater relative deprivation.

The studies that have been described form an interesting set. In the data from the surveys by Stouffer *et al.* (1949), there is no empirical evidence of relative deprivation. None of the soldiers or airmen were asked, for example, if specific expectations were violated or, more directly, if they felt relatively deprived with respect to status. Relative deprivation was used, ex post facto, to explain anomalous findings. The concept had no existential character; it was a hypothetical construct—rather than an intervening variable, as Merton and Kitt classified it (1950). The Spector (1956) experiment, by manipulating expectations of promotions and achievement, created a condition of relative deprivation. Thus, operationally, relative deprivation took on the status of a variable, an independent variable, variations in which were related to variations in "morale." In another laboratory experiment, Thibaut (1950) created conditions of relative deprivation, which were not any the less real for having been created unintentionally by his manipulations of group status and group success. In this respect his experiment is analogous to Spector's. But the nature of his experimental task allowed a very broad range of behavior to be displayed spontaneously. As a result there was direct evidence of feelings of injustice in reaction to the manipulation of relative deprivation, as well as of dissatisfaction, hostility, withdrawal, and changes in sociometric choices. Thus, proceeding from the military surveys to the Thibaut experiment, a useful construct emerges, receives experimental support, and its meaning becomes elaborated.

Bearing this and the survey and experimental data described earlier in mind, there emerge certain conclusions. First, it seems that manifest dissatisfaction and other behavior are responses to acutely felt injustice, rather than directly to relative deprivation. Relative deprivation is a condition occurring naturalistically or an experimental manipulation which elicits feelings of injustice. In turn, feelings of injustice trigger expressions of dissatisfaction and, in addition, the kind of behavior exhibited by Thibaut's juvenile subjects. Injustice, then, may be said to mediate the effects of relative deprivation. A second conclusion is that what is just is based upon relatively strong expectations, such as that educational achievement will be correlated with job status achievement and that one will be promoted at about the same rate as one's fellows, or that the role one plays in one situation—in laboratory games—will be in line and with the role one usually assumes—in the settlement house or camp.

Thirdly, it is clear that a comparative process is inherent in the development of expectations and the perception of injustice, as implied by the term *relative* deprivation. Well-educated men felt unfairly treated in comparison to the treatment they would have received in civilian life or in comparison to the treatment civilians did receive. Injustice was suffered by unpromoted or less-mobile airmen in relation to the general mobility of men in the Air Corps, whereas there was no such felt injustice among low-mobile military policemen when they compared their rate of promotion to the low promotion rate prevalent in the Military Police.

A particularly felicitous additional example of the process of comparison and its importance is provided by Sayles (1958). He notes that " . . . foundries are often hot spots, highly aggressive in seeking fulfillment of their demands where they are part of larger manufacturing organizations. However, when the plant is entirely devoted to the foundry operation, they are relatively weak and inactive" (p. 104). Foundry workers are highly paid to compensate for the unpleasant work conditions and the high physical exertion required and because of a short labor supply in this skill area. Other workers, however, rank foundry operators quite low and look down on them, according to Sayles. Thus, when foundry employees are present for purposes of comparison, other workers feel relatively deprived as regards earnings, and the resulting dissatisfaction may take hostile forms. Conversely, the foundry workers, being the butt of the despisement of others, may react by being unusually assertive and demanding.

Finally, it may be noted, if it is not obvious, that felt injustice is a response to a *discrepancy* between what is perceived to be and what is perceived should be. In the illustrative cases taken from *The American Soldier* and from the Spector and Thibaut experiments, it is a response to a discrepancy between an achievement and an expectation of achievement.

III. DISTRIBUTIVE JUSTICE

The existence of relative deprivation necessarily raises the question of distributive justice, or of the fair share-out of rewards; for, as noted earlier, deprivation is perceived relationally. The concept is not new, having been explored by political philosophers and others from the time of Aristotle. In the hands of Homans (1950, 1953, 1961) and of his colleagues (Zaleznik *et al.,* 1958), the concept of distributive justice has taken on the articulated character of what may be more properly called a theory. As fully developed by Homans (1961), it is a theory employing quasi-economic terms. According to him, distributive justice among men who are in an exchange relationship with one another obtains when the profits of each are proportional to their investments. Profit consists of that which is received in the exchange, less cost incurred. A cost is that which is given up in the exchange, such as foregoing the rewards obtainable in another exchange, or a burden assumed as a specific function of the exchange, such as a risk, which would include not only potential real loss but the psychological discomfort of uncertainty as well. Investments in an exchange are the relevant attributes that are brought by a party to the exchange. They include, for example, skill, effort, education, training, experience, age, sex, and ethnic background.

Schematically, for a dyad consisting of A and B, distributive justice between them is realized when:

$$\frac{\text{A's rewards less A's costs}}{\text{A's investments}} = \frac{\text{B's rewards less B's costs}}{\text{B's investments}}$$

When an inequality between the proportions exists, the participants to the exchange will experience a feeling of injustice and one or the other party will experience deprivation. The party specifically experiencing relative deprivation is the one for whom the ratio of profits to investments is the smaller.

Making explicit that it is the relation between *ratios* of profits to investments that results in felt justice or injustice is a distinct contribution that takes us beyond the concept of relative deprivation. To be sure, an individual may feel deprived, but he feels deprived not merely because his rewards or profits are less than he expected or felt was fair. Many men, when comparing their rewards to those of another, will perceive that their rewards are smaller, and yet they will not feel that this state of affairs is unjust. The reason is that persons obtaining the higher rewards are perceived as deserving them. That is, their rewards are greater because their investments are greater. Thus, for example, if being of the male sex is perceived as a higher investment than being of the female sex, a woman operator earning less than a man doing the same work will not feel unjustly treated. The proportionality of profits to investments is comparable for the woman and for the man. Similarly, a young instructor usually does not feel that his rewards, low as they may be, compare unfairly with those of an associate professor in his department. As Homans notes, "Justice is a curious mixture of equality within inequality" (1961, p. 244).

The theory of distributive justice also addresses itself to the case of two or more persons, each of whom receives his rewards from a third party: an employer, for example. In such an instance, each of the persons is in an exchange with the employer, as in the simple dyadic situation discussed; but, in addition, each man will expect that the employer will maintain a fair ratio of rewards to investments between himself and other men. This, of course, is the perennial dilemma of employers, and it almost defies a perfect solution, though it is capable of better solutions than are often developed. One difficulty with finding neat solutions is that A's perception of his rewards, costs, and investments are not necessarily identical with B's perception of A's situation. To complicate matters, two persons, though they might agree as to what their investments are, may disagree as to the weight each investment should be given. Should age count more than sex? Should education be given as much weight as job experience? The psychometrics of this have not yet received much attention.

The relationship of distributive justice to satisfaction is treated only briefly by Homans, but it is nevertheless the subject of a formal theoretical proposition. If a state of injustice exists and it is to a man's disadvantage—that is, the man experiences deprivation—he will "display the emotional behavior we call anger" (Homans, 1961, p. 75). Here Homans is overly influenced by Skinnerian rhetoric. He means, plainly, that dissatisfaction will be felt or expressed. If, on the other hand, distributive justice fails of realization and is, to an observer at least, to a man's advantage, he will feel guilty. This aspect of the proposition is more novel and is substantiated by observations by Jaques (1956, 1961a) and by laboratory experiments by Adams (1963a) that will be discussed later. Homans also implies that the thresholds for displaying dissatisfaction and guilt are different when he remarks that ". . . he (the guilty man) is less apt to make a prominent display of his guilt than of his anger" (1961, p. 76). This suggestion, also made by Adams (1963a) and deducible from observations made by Jaques (1956), implies that distributive justice must fail of realization to a greater extent when it is favorable to an individual before he reacts than when it is to his disadvantage.

Others have stated formal propositions that obviously refer to the same phenomena as encompassed by the theory of distributive justice. The propositions listed by two writers are especially noteworthy because they were expressed in terms similar to those of Homans. Sayles (1958, p. 98), discussing the manifestation of dissatisfaction in industrial work groups, surmised that factory workers "compute" the fairness of their wages as follows:

$$\frac{\text{Our importance in the plant}}{\text{Any other group's importance}} = \frac{\text{Our earnings}}{\text{Their earnings}}$$

When the equality obtains, satisfaction is experienced. An inequality between the ratios causes pressures for redress, accompanied by dissatisfaction. "Importance in the plant" may be taken as equivalent to the perceived investments of group members, including skills and type of work performed, length of service, and such. This is made explicit in his model of the "economic world of the worker in his work group." According to this analysis, men are portrayed as comparing their jobs to other jobs and asking the questions, "Are these higher paying jobs actually more skilled than our own?" and "Do we earn *enough more* than the lower rated jobs to compensate for the skill difference?" (Sayles, 1958, p. 105). The term "earnings" is, of course, comparable to Homans' rewards but is a less comprehensive term, excluding other outcomes such as intrinsic job rewards. It also subsumes less than the concept of profit or net reward, since it makes no provision for negative outcomes or costs, such as unfavorable work conditions or tyrannical supervision. Nevertheless, it is clear that Sayles conceives of justice as being a function of the perceived equality of ratios of investments and of rewards.

Using the terms of Festinger's theory of cognitive dissonance (1957), Patchen postulates that workers making wage comparisons make a cognitive relation of the following type (1961, p. 9):

$$\frac{\text{My pay}}{\text{His (their) pay}} \quad \text{compared to} \quad \frac{\text{My position on dimensions related to pay}}{\text{His (their) position on dimensions related to pay}}$$

This formulation is similar to Sayles' but more explicit, for dimensions related to pay are specified as being attributes such as skill, education, and seniority. These are clearly the same as Homans' investments. Patchen differs somewhat from Homans in his conceptualization, however, in that he also includes job interest among his "dimensions" related to pay. This is not so much an investment as it is a reward, either with positive or negative valence. When, according to Patchen, an inequality results from the comparison of the two proportions, cognitive dissonance is experienced. In turn, dissatisfaction is manifested. However, dissonance and the attendant dissatisfaction are not necessarily a bad state of affairs from the point of view of the individual. Patchen points this out in an interesting departure from dissonance theory. Although consonant comparisons may be satisfying, they provide no basis for mobility aspirations, whereas dissonant comparisons unfavorable to the person permit a man to think that he is more deserving, that he merits higher pay or status. In effect, then, Patchen suggests that the motivation to attain consonance may be dominated by achievement motivation, and that under these circumstances dissatisfaction resulting from dissonant comparisons may be tolerated. Parenthetically, it may be pointed out that the pitting of these two motivations may partially explain why researchers have been unable to replicate some experiments that offered support for dissonance predictions (see Conlon, 1965, for example).

Relative deprivation and distributive justice, as theoretical concepts, specify some of the conditions that arouse perceptions of injustice and, complementarily, the conditions that lead men to feel that their relations with others are just. But they fail to specify theoretically what are the consequences of felt injustice, other than dissatisfaction. To be sure, Sayles (1958) mentions the use of grievance procedures and strikes to force redress, Homans (1961) cites a study by Clark (1958) in which a female employee reported slowing her pace of work as a means of establishing a more just relation with a co-worker, and Patchen (1961) gives evidence of dissonance reduction when wage comparisons are dissonant. However, these are more or less anecdotal and are not an articulated part of a theory. Men do not simply become dissatisfied with conditions they perceive to be unjust. They usually do something about them. In what follows, then, a theory will be developed that will specify both the antecedents of perceived injustice and its consequences. It is not a new theory. There are already too many "little" theories in social psychology. Rather, it builds upon the work previously described, and, in addition, derives a number of major propositions from Festinger's theory of cognitive dissonance (1957).

IV. INEQUITY

In what follows it is hoped that a fairly comprehensive theory of inequity will be elaborated. The term *inequity* is used instead of *injustice* first, because the author has used this term before (Adams and Rosenbaum, 1962; Adams, 1963a,b, 1965; Adams and Jacobsen, 1964), second, to avoid the confusion of the many connotative meanings associated with the term *justice,* and third, to emphasize that the primary concern is with the causes and consequences of the absence of equity in human exchange relationships. In developing the theory, major variables affecting perceptions of inequity in an exchange will be described. A formal definition of inequity will then be proposed. From this point the effects of inequity upon behavior and cognitive processes will be discussed and research giving evidence of the effects will be presented. For heuristic purposes employee-employer exchanges will be a focus because such relations are within the experience of almost everyone and constitute a significant aspect of human intercourse. Moreover, much empirical research relating to inequity has been undertaken in business and industrial spheres or in simulated employment situations. It should be evident, however, that the theoretical notions offered are quite as relevant to any social situation in which an exchange takes place, explicitly or implicitly, whether between teammates, teacher and student, lovers, child and parent, patient and therapist, or opponents or even enemies, for between all there are expectations of what is fair exchange.

A. Antecedents of Inequity

Whenever two individuals exchange anything, there is the possibility that one or both of them will feel that the exchange was inequitable. Such is frequently the case when a man exchanges his services for pay. On the man's side of the exchange are his education, intelligence, experience, training, skill, seniority, age, sex, ethnic background, social status, and, of course, the effort he expends on the job. Under special circumstances other attributes will be relevant. These may be personal appearance or attractiveness, health, possession of certain tools, the characteristics of one's spouse, and so on. They are what a man perceives as his contributions to the exchange, for which he expects a just return. As noted earlier, these are the same as Homans' (1961) investments. A man brings them into an exchange, and henceforth they will be referred to as his *inputs*. These inputs, let us emphasize, are *as perceived by their contributor* and are not necessarily isomorphic with those perceived by the other party to the exchange. This suggests two conceptually distinct characteristics of inputs, *recognition* and *relevance*.

The possessor of an attribute, or the other party to the exchange, or both, may recognize the existence of the attribute in the possessor. If either the possessor or both members of the exchange recognize its existence, the attribute has the potentiality of being an input. If only the nonpossessor recognizes its existence, it cannot be considered psychologically an input so far as the possessor is concerned. Whether or not an attribute having the potential of being an input is in fact an input is contingent upon the possessor's perception of its relevance to the exchange. If he perceives it to be relevant, if he expects a just return for it, it is an input. Problems of inequity arise if only the possessor of the attribute considers it relevant to the exchange, or if the other party to the exchange considers it irrelevant and acts accordingly. Thus, unless prohibited from doing so by contract terms, an employer may consider seniority irrelevant in granting promotions, thinking it wiser to consider merit alone, whereas the employee may believe that seniority is highly relevant. In consequence, the employee may feel that injustice has been done. Conversely, the employer who is compelled to use seniority rather than merit as a promotion criterion may well feel that he has been forced into an inequitable exchange. In a personal communication Crozier (1960) made a relevant observation. Paris-born bank clerks worked side by side with clerks who did identical work and earned identical wages but who were born in the provinces. The Parisians were dissatisfied with their wages, for they considered that a Parisian upbringing was an input deserving recognition. The bank management, although recognizing that place of birth distinguished the two groups, did not, of course, consider birthplace relevant in the exchange of services for pay.

The principal inputs that have been listed vary in type and in their degree of relationship to one another. Some variables such as age are clearly continuous; others, such as sex and ethnicity, are not. Some are intercorrelated: seniority and age, for example. Sex, on the other hand, is largely independent of the other variables, with the possible exception of education and some kinds of effort. Although these intercorrelations, or the lack of them, exist in a state of nature, it is probable that the individual cognitively treats all input variables as independent. Thus, for example, if he were assessing the sum of his inputs, he might well "score" age and seniority separately. It is as if he thought, "I am older and have been with Acme longer than Joe," without taking account of the fact that the two attributes are correlated. This excursion into the "black box" should not imply, as Homans (1961) seems to imply, that men assess various components of an exchange on an ordinal scale. If the work of Jaques on equitable payment (1956, 1961a) is taken at face value, there is reason to believe in this respect that men employ interval and ratio scales, or that, at the very least, they are capable of making quite fine ordinal discriminations.

On the other side of an exchange are an individual's receipts. These *outcomes*, as they will be termed, include in an employee-employer exchange pay, rewards intrinsic to the job, satisfying supervision, seniority benefits, fringe benefits, job status and status symbols, and a variety of formally and informally sanctioned perquisites, such as the right of a higher-status person to park his car in a privileged location. These are examples of positively valent outcomes. But outcomes may have negative valence. Poor working conditions, monotony, fate uncertainty, and the many "dissatisfiers" listed by Herzberg *et al.* (1959) are no less "received" than, say, wages and are negatively valent. They would be avoided, rather than approached, if it were possible. As in the case of job inputs, job outcomes are often intercorrelated. For example, greater pay and higher job status are likely to go hand-in-hand.

In other than employee-employer exchanges, though they are not precluded from these exchanges, relevant positive outcomes for one or both parties may consist of affection, love, formal courtesies, expressions of friendship, fair value (as in merchandise), and reliability (as part of the purchase of a service). Insult, rudeness, and rejection are the other side of the coin. It may be noted that in a vast array of social relations reciprocity is a functional element of the relation. What is in fact referred to by reciprocity is equality of exchange. The infinitive "to reciprocate" is commonly used to denote an obligation to give someone equal, positively valent outcomes in return for outcomes received. When a housewife says, "John, we must have the Browns over, to reciprocate," she means to maintain a social relationship by reestablishing a parity in the outcomes of the two families. In this connection, it can be observed that reciprocation is usually "in kind." That is, there is a deliberate effort to match outcomes, to give equal value for value received. People who undershoot or overshoot the mark are called "cheapskates" or "uppish" and pretentious, respectively.

In a manner analogous to inputs, outcomes are *as perceived,* and, again, they should be characterized in terms of recognition and relevance. If the recipient or both the recipient and giver of an outcome in an exchange recognize its existence, it has the potentiality of being an outcome psychologically. If the recipient considers it relevant to the exchange and it has some marginal utility for him, it *is* an outcome. Not infrequently the giver may give or yield something which, though of some cost to him, is either irrelevant or of no marginal utility to the recipient. An employer may give an employee a carpet for his office in lieu, say, of a salary increment and find that the employee is dissatisfied, perhaps because in the subculture of that office a rug has no meaning, no psychological utility. Conversely, a salary increment may be inadequate, if formalized status recognition was what was wanted and what had greater utility. Or, in another context, the gift of a toy to a child may be effectively irrelevant as reciprocation for a demonstration of affection on his part is he seeks affection. Fortunately, in the process of socialization, through the reinforcing behavior of others and of the "verbal community" (Skinner, 1957), the human organism learns not only what is appropriate reciprocation, but he learns also to assess the marginal utility of a variety of outcomes to others. In the absence of this ability, interpersonal relations would be chaotic, if not impossible. An idea of the problems that would exist may be had by observing travelers in a foreign culture. Appropriate or relevant reciprocation of outcomes is difficult, even in such mundane exchanges as tipping for services.

In classifying some variables as inputs and others as outcomes, it is not implied that they are independent, except conceptually. Inputs and outcomes are, in fact, intercorrelated, but imperfectly so. Indeed, it is because they are imperfectly correlated that there need be concern with inequity. There exist normative expectations of what constitute "fair" correlations between inputs and outcomes. The expectations are formed—learned—during the process of socialization, at home, at school, at work. They are based by observation of the correlations obtaining for a reference person or group—a co-worker or a colleague, a relative or neighbor, a group of co-workers, a craft group, an industry-wide pattern. A bank clerk, for example, may determine whether her outcomes and inputs are fairly correlated, in balance so to speak, by comparing them with the ratio of the outcomes to the inputs of other female clerks in her section. The sole punch-press operator in a manufacturing plant may base his judgment on what he believes are the inputs and outcomes of other operators in the community or region. For a particular professor the relevant reference group may be professors in the same discipline and of the same academic "vintage." While it is clearly important to be able to specify theoretically the appropriate reference person or group, this will not be done here, as the task is beyond the scope of the paper and is discussed by others (e.g., Festinger, 1954; Hyman, 1942; Merton and Kitt, 1950; Patchen, 1961). For present purposes, it will be assumed that the reference person or group will be one comparable to the comparer on one or more attributes. This is usually a co-worker in industrial situations, according to Livernash (1953), but, as Sayles (1958) points out, this generalization requires verification, as plausible as it may appear.

When the normative expectations of the person making social comparisons are violated, when he finds that his outcomes and inputs are not in balance in relation to those of others, feelings of inequity result. But before a formal definition of inequity is offered, two terms of reference will be introduced to facilitate later discussion, *Person* and *Other*. *Person* is any individual for whom equity or inequity exists. *Other* is any individual with whom Person is in an exchange relationship, or with whom Person compares himself when both he and Other are in an exchange relationship with a third party, such as an employer, or with third parties who are considered by Person as being comparable, such as employers in a particular industry or geographic location. Other is usually a different individual, but may be Person in another job or in another social role. Thus, Other might be Person in a job he held previously, in which case he might compare his present and past outcomes and inputs and determine whether or not the exchange with his employer, present or past, was equitable. The terms Person and Other may also refer to groups rather than to individuals, as when a class of jobs (e.g., toolmakers) is out of line with another class (e.g., lathe operators), or when the circumstances of one ethnic group are incongruous with those of another. In such cases, it is convenient to deal with the class as a whole rather than with individual members of the class.

B. Definition of Inequity

Inequity exists for Person whenever he perceives that the ratio of his outcomes to inputs and the ratio of Other's outcomes to Other's inputs are unequal. This may happen either (a) when he and Other are in a direct exchange relationship or (b) when both are in an exchange relationship with a third party and Person compares himself to Other. The values of outcomes and inputs are, of course, as perceived by Person. Schematically, inequality is experienced when either

$$\frac{O_p}{I_p} < \frac{O_a}{I_a} \quad \text{or} \quad \frac{O_p}{I_p} > \frac{O_a}{I_a},$$

where $O = \Sigma_{oi}$, $I = \Sigma_{oi}$ and p and a are subscripts denoting Person and Other, respectively. A condition of equity exists when

$$\frac{O_p}{I_p} = \frac{O_a}{I_a} \ .$$

The outcomes and inputs in each of the ratios are conceived as being the sum of such outcomes and inputs as are perceived to be relevant to a particular exchange. Furthermore, each sum is conceived of as a weighted sum, on the assumption that individuals probably do not weight elemental outcomes or inputs equally. The work of Herzberg *et al.* (1959) on job "satisfiers" and "dissatisfiers" implies strongly that different outcomes, as they are labeled here, have widely varying utilities, negative as well as positive. It also appears reasonable to assume that inputs as diverse as seniority, skill, effort, and sex are not weighted equally. Zaleznik *et al.* (1958), in attempting to test some predictions from distributive justice theory in an industrial corporation, gave equal weight to five factors which correspond to inputs as defined here—age, seniority, education, ethnicity, and sex—but were unable to sustain their hypotheses. In retrospect, they believe (Zaleznik *et al.*, 1958) that weighting these inputs equally may have represented an inadequate assumption of the manner in which their respondents summed their inputs.

From the definition of inequity it follows that inequity results for Person not only when he is, so to speak, relatively underpaid, but also when he is relatively overpaid. Person, will, for example, feel inequity exists not only when his effort is high and his pay low, while Other's effort and pay are high, but also when his effort is low and his pay high, while Other's effort and pay are low. This proposition receives direct support from experiments by Adams and Rosenbaum (1962), Adams (1963a), and Adams and Jacobsen (1964) in which subjects were inequitably overpaid. It receives some support also from an observation by Thibaut (1950) that subjects in whose favor the experimenter discriminated displayed "guilty smirks" and "sheepishness." The magnitude of the inequity experienced will be a monotomically increasing function of the size of the discrepancy between the ratios of outcomes to inputs. The discrepancy will be zero, and equity will exist, under two circumstances: first, when Person's and Other's outcomes are equal and their inputs are equal. This would be the case, for example, when Person perceived that Other's wages, job, and working conditions were the same as his and that Other was equal to him on such relevant dimensions as sex, skill, seniority, education, age, effort expended, physical fitness, and risk incurred (risk of personal injury, of being fired for errors committed, for instance). Secondly, the ratios will be equal when Person perceives that Other's outcomes are higher (or lower) than his and that Other's inputs are correspondingly higher (or lower). A subordinate who compares himself to his supervisor or work group leader typically does not feel that he is unjustly treated by the company that employs them both, because the supervisor's greater monetary compensation, better working conditions, and more interesting, more varied job are matched on the input side of the ratio by more education, wider range of skills, greater responsibility and personal risk, more maturity and experience, and longer service.

Although there is no direct, reliable evidence on this point, it is probable, as Homans (1961) conjectured, that the thresholds for inequity are different (in absolute terms from a base of equity) in cases of under- and overreward. The threshold would be higher presumably in cases of overreward, for a certain amount of incongruity in these cases can be acceptably rationalized as "good fortune" without attendant discomfort. In his work on pay differentials, Jaques (1961b) notes that in instances of undercompensation, British workers paid 10% less than the equitable level show "an active sense of grievance, complaints or the desire to complain, and, if no redress is given, an active desire to change jobs, or to take action . . ." (p. 26). In cases of overcompensation, he observes that at the 10 to 15% level above equity "there is a strong sense of receiving preferential treatment, which may harden into bravado, with underlying feelings of unease . . ." (p. 26). He states further, "The results suggest that it is not necessarily the case that each one is simply out to get as much as he can for his work. There appear to be equally strong desires that each one should earn the right amount—a fair and reasonable amount relative to others" (p. 26).

In the preceding discussion, Person has been the focus of attention. It should be clear, however, that when Person and Other are in an exchange interaction, Other will suffer inequity if Person does, but the nature of his experience will be opposite to that of Person. If the outcome-input discrepancy is unfavorable to Person, it will be favorable to Other, and vice versa. This will hold provided Person's and Other's perceptions of outcomes and inputs are equivalent and provided that the outcome-input ratio discrepancy attains threshold level. When Person and Other are not engaged in an exchange with one another but stand in an exchange relationship with a third party,

Other may or may not experience inequity when Person does. Given the prerequisites mentioned above, he will experience inequity if he compares himself to Person with respect to the same question as induces Person to use Other as a referent (e.g., "Am I being paid fairly?").

C. Consequences of Inequity

Although there can be little doubt that inequity results in dissatisfaction, in an unpleasant emotional state, be it anger or guilt, there will be other effects. A major purpose of this paper is to specify these in terms that permit specific predictions to be made. Before turning to this task, two general postulates are presented, closely following propositions from cognitive dissonance theory (Festinger, 1957). First, the presence of inequity in Person creates tension in him. The tension is proportional to the magnitude of inequity present. Second, the tension created in Person will motivate him to eliminate or reduce it. The strength of the motivation is proportional to the tension created. In short, the presence of inequity will motivate Person to achieve equity or to reduce inequity, and the strength of motivation to do so will vary directly with the magnitude of inequity experienced. From these postulates and from the theory of cognitive dissonance (Festinger, 1957; Brehm and Cohen, 1962), means of reducing inequity will be derived and presented. As each method of reduction is discussed, evidence demonstrating usage of the method will be presented. Some of the evidence is experimental; some of it is the result of field studies, either of a survey or observational character.

1. Person Altering His Inputs

Person may vary his inputs, either increasing them or decreasing them, depending on whether the inequity is advantageous or disadvantageous. Increasing inputs will reduce felt inequity, if

$$\frac{O_p}{I_p} > \frac{O_a}{I_a}$$

conversely, decreasing inputs will be effective, if

$$\frac{O_p}{I_p} < \frac{O_a}{I_a} \ .$$

In the former instance, Person might increase either his productivity or the quality of his work, provided that it is possible, which is not always the case. In the second instance, Person might engage in "production restriction," for example. Whether Person does, or can, reduce inequity by altering his inputs is partially contingent upon whether relevant inputs are susceptible to change. Sex, age, seniority, and ethnicity are not modifiable. Education and skill are more easily altered, but changing these requires time. Varying inputs will also be a function of Person's perception of the principal "cause" of the inequity. If the discrepancy between outcome-input ratios is primarily a function of his inputs being at variance with those of Other, Person is more likely to alter them than if the discrepancy is largely a result of differences in outcomes. Additionally, it is postulated that given equal opportunity to alter inputs and outcomes, Person will be more likely to lower his inputs when

$$\frac{O_p}{I_p} < \frac{O_a}{I_a}$$

than he is to increase his inputs when

$$\frac{O_p}{I_p} > \frac{O_a}{I_a} \ .$$

This is derived from two assumptions: first, the assumption stated earlier that the threshold for the perception of inequity is higher when Person is overrewarded than when he is underrewarded; secondly, the assumption that Person is motivated to minimize his costs and to maximize his gains. By the second assumption, Person will reduce inequity, insofar as possible, in a manner that will yield him the largest outcomes.

Altering certain inputs has the corollary effect of altering the outcomes of Other. A change in the quality and amount of work performed, for instance, will usually affect the outcomes of Other. When this is the case, the effect of both changes will operate in the same direction in the service of inequity reduction. It follows, therefore, that *less* a change in inputs is required to eliminate inequity than if the change had no effect on Other's outcomes. Inputs, a change in which would have no or very little impact on Other's outcomes, are attributes such as education, age, and seniority—at least to the extent that they are uncorrelated with performance.

Several experiments have been conducted specifically to test the hypothesis that Person will reduce inequity by altering his inputs (Adams and Rosenbaum, 1962; Adams, 1963a; Adams and Jacobsen, 1964). The most recent of these will be described in detail here. In this experiment the hypothesis tested was that if Person perceives that he is overpaid in an exchange with his employer because his inputs are inadequate, he will experience inequity and attempt to reduce it by increasing relevant inputs.

Students hired to proofread galley pages were exposed to one of three conditions of inequity. In a *high inequity* condition (H), they were induced to perceive that they were unqualified to earn the standard proofreader's rate of 30 cents per page and were told that they would, nevertheless, be hired and paid that rate. Another group of subjects were in the *reduced inequity* condition (R), in which an identical perception was induced, but in which the piece rate was reduced to 20 cents by reason of the subjects' lack of qualifications. In this condition, in effect, the low inputs of subjects were matched by low outcomes. Thus, if the basic model of inequity was valid, subjects in this condition should suffer no greater feelings of inequity than subjects in the third, *low inequity* condition (L), in which persons hired were made to believe that they were fully qualified to earn the standard rate of 30 cents per page. The task consisted of correcting errors in simulated galley proof pages from a manuscript on human relations in industry. Proofreading required that each page be read, that each error detected be underlined in the text, and that a checkmark be placed in the margin at the level of the error. Each galley page contained a standard number of words, and a set number of errors were introduced systematically on each page. The errors were misspellings, grammatical mistakes, incorrect punctuation, and typographical errors, such as transpositions of letters. Productivity was measured by the number of pages proofed in one hour; work quality was measured by the mean number of errors detected per page proofed.

Since they could not alter their outcomes, it was predicted that H subjects would attempt to reduce inequity by investing high inputs, which, in this situation, they could also perceive as increasing the outcomes of the employer. More specifically, it was hypothesized that the work quality would be higher among H subjects than among R and L subjects, and that it would not vary significantly between the R and L conditions. The prediction that input differences would be on the dimension of work quality was based on the consideration that the only other relevant input subjects could vary was productivity; but since an increase in productivity would result in increased outcomes, due to the piece-rate payments, inequity could not be reduced in this manner. Doing better quality work *on each piece,* however, would effectively serve to reduce inequity. Following this reasoning, a second hypothesis could be formulated: Productivity among H subjects would be lower than among R and L subjects, since more careful work would require additional time to complete each page.

The results supported the hypothesis. Subjects in the H condition performed significantly better work, as measured by the number of introduced errors detected per page, and produced significantly less in one hour than subjects in the R and L conditions. The latter did not differ from each other with respect to either quality of work or productivity. An unexpected finding was that significantly more non-errors were classified as errors by subjects in the H condition than in the other conditions. Generally, these misclassified nonerrors were of a type that permitted minimal or no basis for being perceived as errors. For example, the word "conceive" was underlined as an error by several subjects, although it was correctly spelled. This gives some indication of the strength of motivation underlying the behavior. A somewhat analogous finding was made by Arrowood (1961). He paid his subjects in advance for three hours of work and found that those who perceived their pay as too great tended to work more than three hours.

In similar experiments (Adams and Rosenbaum, 1962; Adams, 1963a), subjects were paid by the hour. In these it was predicted that in the high inequity conditions subjects would alter their productivity inputs. The data bore this out. In one of these experiments subjects performed identical tasks under hourly and piece-rate wage conditions. Under a high inequity induction, productivity was higher with hourly pay and lower with piecework pay than under a low inequity induction. These results give support to the earlier suggestion that there exists a tendency to reduce inequity in a manner that yields the largest outcomes. Hourly paid workers could have reduced inequity by improving the quality of their work, but this would have lowered their outcomes. On the other hand, pieceworkers had no choice but to reduce inequity by increasing work quality, with consequent loss of income. Considering the fact that subjects in this experiment, as in others, needed their earnings, the results also suggested that the need to establish equity was a more potent motivation than the motivation to maximize monetary gains.

In the experiments described above, inequities potentially advantageous to Person were the focus because, if the hypotheses were sustained, the evidence would be more striking. There is, of course, also evidence that Person will reduce his inputs when he suffers the disadvantages of inequity, when the discrepancy of outcome-input ratios is unfavorable to him. This is apparent in a field study by Clark (1958), which investigated supermarket checkout counters manned by a "ringer" (cashier) and a "bundler." These two were not involved in a direct exchange with one another; rather, both were in an exchange with the employer and expected him to see to it that their outcome-input ratios were not incongruous. Under normal conditions, ringing was a higher-status, better-paid job, handled by a permanent, full-time employee. Bundling was of lower status and lower pay, and was usually done by part-time employees, frequently youngsters. Furthermore, psychologically, bundlers were perceived as working *for* ringers.

Because customer flow in supermarkets varied markedly from day to day, a preponderance of employees were part-timers. This same fact required that many employees be assigned to checkout counters during rush hours. When this occurred, many ringer-bundler teams were formed, and it is this that resulted in inequities, for employees differed considerably in a number of input variables, notably sex, age, and education. Not infrequently, a bundler would be directed to work for a ringer whose status (determined by sex, age, and education) was lower. For example, a college male 21 years of age would be ordered to work for a high school girl ringer of 17. Or a college girl would be assigned as a bundler for an older woman with only a grade school education. The resulting inequities may be described as follows in theoretical terms: A bundler with higher inputs than a ringer had lower outcomes—i.e., working *for* someone of lower status, which is assumed to be invidious and psychologically negatively valent, as well as receiving lower wages.

When interviewed by the investigator, the store employees were quite explicit about the inequities that existed. It appeared that the principal means used by the bundlers to reduce inequities were to decrease the rate at which they filled shopping bags—i.e., by reducing their inputs, which would have effectively decreased inequity since some of their other inputs were too high relative to their own outcomes and to the inputs of the ringers. One girl explicitly stated to the investigator that when she was ordered to bundle for a ringer of lower status than herself, she deliberately slowed up bundling.

Interestingly, this behavior is nicely reflected in the financial operation of the stores. A substantial part of the total labor cost of operating a supermarket is the cost of manning checkout counters. It follows, therefore, that one should be able to observe a correlation between the incidence of inequities among ringer-bundler teams and the cost of store operations, since the inequity reduction took the form of lowered productivity. This is indeed what was found. When the eight supermarkets were ranked on labor efficiency (number of man-hours per $100 of sales) and "social ease" (an index of the proportion of ringer-bundler pairs whose outcome-input ratios were discrepant), the two measures correlated almost perfectly: the greater the inequity, the greater the cost of operating the stores. To give an example, one of the two stores studied most intensively ranked high in inequity and had labor efficiency of only 3.85, whereas the other which ranked low in inequity, had a labor efficiency of 3.04. Thus, it cost approximately 27% more to operate the store in which inequities were more frequent.

A further finding of Clark's is worth reporting, for it gives one confidence that the relative inefficiency of the one store was indeed due to the presence of relatively more inequity. This store went through a period of considerable labor turnover (perhaps as a result of employees leaving the field to reduce inequity), and associated with this was an increase in labor efficiency and an increase in the "social ease" index. There is, therefore, quasi-experimental evidence that when inequities are reduced, individual productivity increases (i.e., production restriction is lowered), with the result that operating costs decrease.

2. Person Altering His Outcomes

Person may vary his outcomes, either decreasing or increasing them, depending on whether the inequity is advantageous or disadvantageous to him. Increasing outcomes will reduce inequity, if

$$\frac{O_p}{I_p} < \frac{O_a}{I_a}$$

conversely, decreasing outcomes will serve the same function, if

$$\frac{O_p}{I_p} > \frac{O_a}{I_a} \; .$$

Of these two possibilities, the second is far less likely, and there is no good evidence of the use of this means of reducing inequity, though some may be available in the clinical literature. There are, however, data bearing on attempts to increase outcomes, data other than those related to wage increase demands in union-management negotiations, probably only a part of which are directly traceable to wage inequities.

In the experiment by Thibaut (1950), to which reference was made earlier, teams of 5 or 6 boys made up of approximately equal numbers of popular and unpopular boys were assigned either high- or low-status roles in playing a series of four games. The low-status teams were unfairly treated in that, although they were comparable in their characteristics (i.e., their inputs) to the high-status teams, they were forced to adopt an inferior, unpleasant role vis-à-vis the other team. For example, in one game they formed a human chain against which the other team bucked; in another, they held the target and retrieved thrown bean bags. Thus, since their inputs were equal to, and their outcomes lower than, those of the high-status teams, they were clearly suffering the disadvantages of inequity. From Thibaut's report of the behavior of the low-status teams, it is evident that at least four means of reducing the inequity were used by them: lowering the high-status team members' outcomes by fighting with them and displaying other forms of hostility; lowering their inputs by not playing the games as required, which would also have had the effect of lowering the outcomes of the high-status team members; by leaving the field, that is, withdrawing and crying; and by trying to interchange roles with the high-status teams. The latter is the relevant one for purposes of discussion here.

Thibaut (1950) reports that about halfway through the second game the participants had come to understand the experimenter's intention, i.e., that the status differentiation was to be permanent. At this stage of the experiment low-status subjects began to express mobility aspirations, asking the experimenter that the roles of the two teams be reversed. This may be interpreted as an attempt to establish equity by increasing outcomes, since assumption of high status would have been accompanied by pleasurable activities. Interestingly, though the report is not entirely clear on this point, there is the suggestion that, when the attempt of low-status subjects to increase their outcomes was rejected by the experimenter, they desisted and, instead, engaged more in withdrawal.

Also giving evidence that increasing outcomes will serve to reduce inequity is a study of unfair wages among clerical workers by Homans (1953). Two groups of female clerical workers in a utilities company, cash posters and ledger clerks, worked in the same, large room. Cash posting consisted of recording daily the amounts customers paid on their bills, and management insisted that posting be precisely up to date. It required that cash posters pull customer cards from the many files and make appropriate entries on them. The job was highly repetitive and comparatively monotonous, and required little thought but a good deal of walking about. Ledger clerks, in contrast, performed a variety of tasks on customer accounts, such as recording address changes, making breakdowns of over- and underpayments, and supplying information on accounts to customers and others on the telephone. In addition, toward the end of the day, they were required by their supervisor to assist with "cleaning up" cash posting in order that it be current. Compared to the cash posters, ledger clerks performed a number of nonrepetitive clerical jobs requiring some thought; they had a more *responsible* job; they were considered to be of higher status, since promotion took place from cash poster to ledger clerk; and they were older and had more seniority and experience. Their weekly pay, however, was identical.

Summarizing in the terms of the inequity model, cash posters had distinctly lower inputs than ledger clerks (i.e., they were younger, and had less experience, less seniority, and less responsbilitiy). With respect to outcomes they received equal wages, but their jobs were somewhat more monotonous and less interesting. On the other hand, the ledger clerks' inputs were superior with respect to age, experience, seniority, skill, responsibility, and versatility (they were required to know and do cash posting in addition to their own jobs). Their earnings were equal to the cash posters', but they were required to "clean up" (note connotation) posting each day, an activity that would deflate self-esteem and would, therefore, be a negative outcome. In the balance, then, the net outcomes of ledger clerks and cash posters were approximately of the same magnitude, but the inputs of the clerks were definitely greater. From this it would be predicted that the ledger clerks felt unfairly treated and that they would try to increase their outcomes.

The evidence reported by Homans (1953) is that the ledger clerks felt the inequity and that they felt they ought to get a few dollars more per week to show that their jobs were more important—that their greater inputs ought to be matched by greater outcomes. On the whole, these clerks seemed not to have done much to reduce inequity, though a few complained to their union representative, with, apparently, little effect. However, the workers in this division voted to abandon their independent union for the CIO, and Homans intimates that the reason may have been the independent union's inability to force a resolution of the inequity.

The field studies of dissatisfaction with status and promotions by Stouffer *et al.* (1949) and the experiments by Spector (1956), in which expectation of promotion and morale, which were described in Section II, may also be interpreted as cases of inequity in which dissatisfactions were expressions of attempts by Persons to increase their outcomes.

3. Person Distorting His Inputs and Outcomes Cognitively

Person may cognitively distort his inputs and outcomes, the direction of the distortion being the same as if he had actually altered his inputs and outcomes, as discussed above. Since most individuals are heavily influenced by reality, substantial distortion is generally difficult. It is pretty difficult to distort to oneself, to change one's cognitions about the fact, for example, that one has a BA degree, that one has been an accountant for seven years, and that one's salary is $700 per month. However, it is possible, within limits, to alter the utility of these. For example, State College is a small backwoods school with no reputation, or, alternatively, State College has one of the best business schools in the state and the dean is an adviser to the Bureau of the Budget. Or, one can consider the fact that $700 per month will buy all of the essential things of life and a few luxuries, or, conversely, that it will never permit one to purchase a Wyeth oil painting or an Aston Martin DB5. There is ample evidence in the psychological literature, especially that related to cognitive dissonance theory, that individuals do modify or rearrange their cognitions in an effort to reduce perceived incongruities (for a review, see Brehm and Cohen, 1962). Since it has been postulated that the experience of inequity is equivalent to the experience of dissonance, it is reasonable to believe that cognitive distortion may be adopted as a means of reducing inequity. In a variety of work situations, for example in paced production line jobs, actually altering one's inputs and outcomes may be difficult; as a consequence these may be cognitively changed in relatively subtle ways.

Although not a cognitive change in inputs and outcomes per se, related methods of reducing inequity are for Person to alter the *importance* and the *relevance* of his inputs and outcomes. If, for example, age were a relevant input, its relative importance could be changed to bring about less perceived inequity. Person could convince himself that age was either more or less important than he thought originally. In terms of the statement made earlier that net inputs (and outcomes) were a weighted sum of inputs, changing the importance of inputs would be equivalent to changing the weights associated with them. Altering the relevance of inputs and outcomes is conceived of as more of an all-or-none process: Present ones are made irrelevant or new ones are made relevant. For instance, if Person perceived that the discrepancy between his and Other's outcome-input ratios were principally a result of his outcomes being too low, he might become "aware" of one or more outcomes he had not recognized as being relevant before, perhaps that his job had variety absent from Other's job. Obviously, importance and relevance of inputs and outcomes are not completely independent. An outcome suddenly perceived as being relevant automatically assumes some importance; conversely, one that is made irrelevant in the service of inequity reduction assumes an importance of zero. Nevertheless, the psychological processes appear to be different and it is useful, therefore, to keep them conceptually distinct.

Evidence of cognitive distortion to reduce inequity is not very impressive. In a study by Leventhal et al. (1964), subjects were hired to participate in an experiment to taste pleasant and unpleasant liquids. At the end of the task one-third of the subjects were told they would receive a payment of 60 cents in lieu of the promised $1.25, one-third were informed they would be paid $1.90 in lieu of $1.25, and to the remaining one-third it was stated they would be paid the promised $1.25. According to the inequity model, the first two groups presumably felt unfairly rewarded. When asked under what circumstances they felt subjects should be paid for their services, these two groups were significantly less likely to assert that they should always be paid than were subjects who were paid the full amount promised. Considering first only the underpaid subjects, this can be taken as an indication that they revised either the judgment of their inputs, by lowering it, or their estimate of fair outcomes, by lowering it. They could, in effect, have been saying, "What I did wasn't much," or "Sixty cents is about the right amount for this kind of task." Alternatively, they could have adduced a new, relevant outcome, such as satisfaction of contributing to science. An equally plausible explanation which is unrelated to the reduction of inequity is offered by Leventhal and his associates, namely, that the decreased payment induced a low expectancy set with respect to payment in experiments. The lower expectancy of the overpaid subjects does not manifest inequity reduction by cognitive distortion. More likely, as Leventhal *et al.* suggest, this indicates a desire to rectify the inequity by accepting lower payment in subsequent experiments, that is, to increase the experimenter's outcomes on a later occasion.

An experiment by Weick (1964) suggests that subjects, some of whose outcomes are unjustly low, may increase their net total outcomes by "task enhancement," that is, by distorting their evaluation of the task. Weick found that subjects working for an inconsiderate experimenter who had lured them to work for no credit, evaluated their task more highly than subjects who worked for normal course credits. Specifically, it appeared that the subjects who were short-changed by the experimenter distorted their outcomes by coming to believe that the experiment was relatively quite interesting and important.

4. Person Leaving the Field

Leaving the field may take any of several ways of severing social relationships. Quitting a job, obtaining a transfer, and absenteeism are common forms of leaving the field in an employment situation. These are fairly radical means of coping with inequity. The probability of using them is assumed to increase with magnitude of inequity and to decrease with the availability of other means.

Data substantiating the occurrence of leaving the field as a mode of reducing inequity is sparse. In the aforementioned study by Thibaut (1950), it was observed that low-status team members withdrew from the games as it became increasingly clear what their fate was and as, it must be presumed, the felt injustice mounted. In a study by Patchen (1959) it was observed that men who said their pay should be higher had more absences than men who said the pay for their jobs was fair. This relationship between perceived fairness of pay and absenteeism was independent of actual wage level. That absenteeism in this study was a form of withdrawal is strongly supported by the fact that men with high absence rates were significantly more likely than men with low rates to say that they would not go on working at their job, if they should chance to inherit enough money to live comfortably without working.

5. Person Acting on Other

In the face of injustice, Person may attempt to alter or cognitively distort Other's inputs and outcomes, or try to force Other to leave the field. These means of reducing inequity vary in the ease of their use. Getting Other to accept greater outcomes, which was a possible interpretation of some of the findings by Leventhal *et al.* (1964), would obviously be easier than the opposite. Similarly, inducing Other to lower his inputs may be easier than the reverse. For example, all other things being equal, such as work group cohesiveness and the needs and ability of an individual worker, it is probably easier to induce a "rate buster" to lower his inputs than to get a laggard to increase them. The direction of the change attempted in the inputs and outcomes of Other is the reverse of the change that Person would make in his own inputs and outcomes, whether the change be actual or cognitive. By way of illustration, if Person experienced feelings of inequity because he lacked job experience compared to Other, he could try to induce Other to decrease a relevant input instead of increasing his own inputs.

Cognitive distortion of Other's inputs and outcomes may be somewhat less difficult than distortion of one's own, since cognitions about Other are probably less well anchored than are those concerning oneself. This assumption is consistent with the finding that "where alternatives to change in central attitudes are possible, they will be selected" (Pilisuk, 1962, p. 102). Acceptable evidence that inequity, as such, is reduced by cognitive distortion of Other's inputs or outcomes is nonexistent, although there is ample evidence that cognitive dissonance may be reduced by perceptual distortion (e.g., Bramel, 1962; Brehm and Cohen, 1962; Steiner and Peters, 1958). An observation made while pretesting procedures for an unpublished study by Adams (1961) is little better than anecdotal. To test some hypotheses from inequity theory, he paired a subject and a stooge at a "partner's desk." Each performed sequentially one part of the preparation of a personnel payroll. In one condition the subject was paid $1.40 per hour and performed the relatively complex task of looking in various tables for standard and overtime rates, looking up in other tables the products of pay rates and hours worked, and recording the products on a payroll form. The stooge, whose pay was announced as being $2.10 per hour, performed the presumably much easier task of summing products on a machine and recording the totals on the form the subject passed to him across the desk. In addition, the stooge was programmed to be slightly ahead of the subject in his work, so that his task appeared fairly easy. It was hoped that these conditions would lead the subject to perceive that, compared to the stooge, he had higher inputs and lower outcomes. Nothing of the sort happened. Most subjects pretested felt that the relationship was equitable, and this appeared to result from the fact that they distorted cognitively the stooge's inputs in an upward direction. Specifically, they convinced themselves that the stooge was performing a "mathematical task." Simple *adding* on a machine became *mathematics*.

Forcing Other to leave the field, while theoretically possible, is probably difficult of realization and would, no doubt, be accompanied by anxiety about potential consequences or simply by the discomfort of having done something socially unpleasant. This aspect makes it costly to Person; it lowers his outcomes to some extent. Firing an individual in an employer-employee exchange and some divorces and separations are common examples of this means put to use. Somewhat though barely more subtle is the practice of creating an inequity by withholding expected outcomes (e.g., salary increases, promotions) to the point where an individual leaves the field "voluntarily."

6. Person Changing the Object of His Comparison

Person may change Other with whom he compares himself when he experiences inequity and he and Other stand in an exchange relationship with a third party. This mode is limited to the relationship specified; it is not applicable when Person and Other are in a direct exchange. Changing the object of comparison in the latter situation would reduce to severing the relationship.

The resolution of inequity by changing comparison object is undoubtedly difficult of accomplishment, particularly if Person has been comparing himself to Other for some time. Person would need to be able to make himself noncomparable to Other on one or more dimensions. For instance, if Other, whose outcome-input ratio was previously equal to Person's received a salary increase without any apparent increment in inputs, Person could try to reduce the resulting feeling of inequity by conceiving of Other as belonging now to a different organizational level. But this would likely meet with little success, at least in this culture. A cognitive change of this sort would be extremely unstable, unless it were accompanied by changes in the perception of Other's inputs: for instance, that Other had assumed greater responsibility when his salary was increased. But this involves a process of inequity reduction already referred to.

In the initial stages of comparison processes, as when a man first comes on the job, it probably is relatively easy to choose as comparison Others individuals who provide the most equitable comparisons. This does not necessarily entail making comparisons with men whose outcomes and inputs are the same as one's own; it is sufficient that their outcome-input ratio be equal to one's own. In a study of the choice of wage comparisons, Patchen (1961) asked oil refinery workers to name someone whose yearly earnings were *different* from theirs and then proceeded to ask them questions about the resulting wage comparisons and about their satisfaction with them. Of the workers who named someone earning *more* than they, 60% indicated satisfaction with the comparison and only 17.6% reported dissatisfaction. Among those who were satisfied, 44.6% stated they were satisfied because they had financial or other advantages, i.e., compensating outcomes, and 55.8% indicated satisfaction with the upward comparison because the person with higher earnings had more education, skill, experience, seniority and the like, i.e., higher inputs. Patchen's data may be recast and reanalyzed to make a different point. Among the men who chose comparison persons whose outcome-input ratios seemingly were equal to theirs, approximately 85% were satisfied with the comparison and only about 4% were dissatisfied. While Patchen's study does not bear directly either on what wage comparisons men actually make in their day-to-day relations with others or on changes in comparison persons when inequity arises, it gives clear evidence that comparisons are made on the basis of the equality of the outcome-input ratios of the comparer and comparison person and that such comparisons prove satisfying, i.e., are, at least, judged to be not inequitable.

7. Choice among Modes of Inequity Reduction

Although reference has been made previously to conditions that may affect the use of one or another method of reducing inequity, there is need for a general statement of conditions that will govern the adoption of one method over another. Given the existence of inequity, any of the means of reduction described earlier are potentially available to Person. He may alter or attempt to alter any of the four terms in the inequality formula or change his cognitions about any of them, or he may leave the field and change his comparison Other, but it is improbable that each of the methods are equally available to him *psychologically* (no reference is made to environmental constraints that may affect the availability of methods), as the work of Steiner and his colleagues on alternative methods of dissonance reduction suggests (Steiner, 1960; Steiner and Johnson, 1964; Steiner and Peters, 1958; Steiner and Rogers, 1963).

Set forth below are some propositions about conditions determining the choice of modes by Person. As will be noted, the propositions are not all independent of one another, and each should be prefaced by the condition, *ceteris paribus*.

(a) Person will maximize positively valent outcomes and the valence of outcomes.

(b) He will minimize increasing inputs that are effortful and costly to change.

(c) He will resist real and cognitive changes in inputs that are central to his self-concept and to his self-esteem. To the extent that any of Person's outcomes are related to his self-concept and to his self-esteem, this proposition is extended to cover his outcomes.

(d) He will be more resistant to changing cognitions about his own outcomes and inputs than to changing his cognitions about Other's outcomes and inputs.

(e) Leaving the field will be resorted to only when the magnitude of inequity experienced is high and other means of reducing it are unavailable. Partial withdrawal, such as absenteeism, will occur more frequently and under conditions of lower inequity.

(f) Person will be highly resistant to changing the object of his comparisons, Other, once it has stabilized over time and, in effect, has become an anchor.

These propositions are, admittedly, fairly crude, but they permit, nevertheless, a degree of prediction not available otherwise. In the resolution of a particular injustice, two or more of the processes proposed may be pitted one against the other. To propose which would be dominant is not possible at this stage of the development of the theory. One might propose that protection of self-esteem would dominate maximization of outcomes, but it would be conjecture in the absence of evidence.

V. Conclusion

Dissatisfaction is both so commonplace and such an irritant, particularly in industrial and other large organizations, that it has been the subject of widespread research (see Vroom, 1964, for a recent, thorough review). Despite prima facie evidence that feelings of injustice underlay a significant proportion of cases of dissatisfaction, thorough behavioral analyses of injustice were not made until recently. In the classic Hawthorne studies (Roethlisberger and Dickson, 1939), there was ample evidence that much of the dissatisfaction observed among Western Electric Company employees was precipitated by felt injustice. Describing complaints, the authors referred frequently to reports by workers that wages were not in keeping with seniority, that rates were too low, that ability was not rewarded, and the like, as distinguished from reports that, for example, equipment was not working and that the workshop was hot. They stated that "no physical or logical operations exist which can be agreed upon as defining them" (p. 259), and they sought "personal or social situations" (p. 269) that would explain the complaints parsimoniously. Yet, the notion of injustice was not advanced as an explanatory concept.

It is not contended here, of course, that all dissatisfaction and low morale are related to a person's suffering injustice in social exchanges. But it should be clear from the research described that a significant portion of cases can be usefully explained by invoking injustice as an explanatory concept. More importantly, much more than dissatisfaction may be predicted once the concept of injustice is analyzed theoretically.

In the theory of inequity that has been developed in this chapter, both the antecedents and consequences of perceived injustice have been stated in terms that permit quite specific predictions to be made about the behavior of persons entering social exchanges. On the whole, empirical support for the theory is gratifying, but it falls short of what is desirable. More research is required. This is particularly so because some of the support comes from data leading to the formulation of parts of the theory. Needed are direct tests of propositions made in theory, as well as empirical tests of novel derivations from the theory. Some research filling these needs is under way. Being tested, for example, is the hypothesis that overpaid workers for whom an increase in inputs is impossible will reduce inequity by decreasing their outcomes, specifically by developing unfavorable attitudes toward their employer, their working conditions, the pay rates, and so on.

In order for more refined predictions to be made from the theory, theoretical, methodological, and empirical work are also required in at least two areas related to it. First, additional thought must be given to social comparison processes. The works of Festinger (1954), Hyman (1942), Merton and Kitt (1950), Newcomb (1943), and Patchen (1961) are signal contributions but still do not allow sufficiently fine predictions to be made about whom Person will choose as a comparison Other when both are in an exchange relationship with a third party. For example, as a function of what variables will one man compare himself to a person on the basis of age similarities and another man compare himself on the basis of attitude similarities? Second, psychometric research is needed to determine how individuals aggregate their own outcomes and inputs and those of others. Is the assumptive model that net outcomes are the algebraic sum of elemental outcomes weighted by their importance a valid one?

The need for much additional research notwithstanding, the theoretical analyses that have been made of injustice in social exchanges should result not only in a better general understanding of the phenomenon, but should lead to a degree of social control not previously possible. The experience of injustice need not be an accepted fact of life.

REFERENCES

ADAMS, J. S. (1961). Wage inequities in a clerical task. Unpublished study. General Electric Company, New York.

ADAMS, J. S. (1963a). Toward an understanding of inequity. *J. abnorm. soc. Psychol.* **67**, 422-436.

ADAMS, J. S. (1963b). Wage inequities, productivity, and work quality. *Industr. Relat.* **3**, 9-16.

ADAMS, J. S. (1965). Etudes expérimentales en matière d'inégalités de salaires, de productivité et de qualité du travail. *Synopsis* **7**, 25-34.

ADAMS, J. S., AND JACOBSEN, PATRICIA R. (1964). Effects of wage inequities on work quality. *J. abnorm. soc. Psychol.* **69**, 19-25.

ADAMS, J. S., AND ROSENBAUM, W. B. (1962). The relationship of worker productivity to cognitive dissonance about wage inequities. *J. appl. Psychol.* **46**, 161-164.

ARROWOOD, A. J. (1961). Some effects on productivity of justified and unjustified levels of reward under public and private conditions. Unpublished doctoral dissertation (Dep. Psychol.), Univer. of Minnesota.

BLAU, P. (1964). *Exchange and power in social life.* New York: Wiley.

BRAMEL, D. (1962). A dissonance theory approach to defensive projection. *J. abnorm. soc. Psychol.* **64**, 121-129.

BREHM, J. W., AND COHEN, A. R. (1962). *Explorations in cognitive dissonance.* New York: Wiley.

CLARK, J. V. (1958). A preliminary investigation of some unconscious assumptions affecting labor efficiency in eight supermarkets. Unpublished doctoral dissertation (Grad. Sch. Business Admin.), Harvard Univer.

CONLON, ELIZABETH T. (1965). Performance as determined by expectation of success and failure. Unpublished doctoral dissertation (Dep. Social Psychol.), Columbia Univer.

CROZIER, M. (1960). Personal communication to the author.

FESTINGER, L. (1954). A theory of social comparison processes. *Hum. Relat.* **7**, 117-140.

FESTINGER, L. (1957). *A theory of cognitive dissonance.* Evanston, Ill.: Row, Peterson.

GEBHARD, MILDRED E. (1949). Changes in the attractiveness of activities: the effect of expectation preceding performance. *J. exp. Psychol.* **39**, 404-413.

HERZBERG, F., MAUSNER, B., AND SNYDERMAN, BARBARA B. (1959). *The motivation to work.* New York: Wiley.

HOMANS, G. C. (1950). *The human group.* New York: Harcourt, Brace.

HOMANS, G. C. (1963). Status among clerical workers. *Hum. Organiz.* **12**, 5-10.

HOMANS, G. C. (1961). *Social behavior: its elementary forms.* New York: Harcourt, Brace.

HYMAN, H. (1942). The psychology on status. *Arch. Psychol.* **38**, No. 269.

JAQUES, E. (1956). *Measurement of responsibility.* London: Tavistock.

JAQUES, E. (1961a). *Equitable payment.* New York: Wiley.

JAQUES E. (1961b). An objective approach to pay differentials. *Time Motion Study* **10**, 25-28.

LEVENTHAL, G., REILLY, ELLEN, AND LEHRER, P. (1964). Change in reward as a determinant of satisfaction and reward expectancy. Paper read at West. Psychol. Assoc. Portland, Ore.

LIVERNASH, E. R. (1953). Job evaluation. In W. S. Woytinsky *et al.* (Eds.), *Employment and wages in the United States.* New York: Twentieth Century Fund, pp. 427-435.

MERTON, R. K., AND KITT, ALICE S. (1950). Contributions to the theory of reference group behavior. In *Continuities in social research.* R. K. Merton and P. F. Lazarsfeld (Eds.), Glencoe, Ill.: Free Press, pp. 40-105.

NEWCOMB, T. M. (1943). *Personality and social change: attitude formation in a student community.* New York: Dryden.

PATCHEN, M. (1959). Study of work and life satisfaction, Report No. II: Absences and attitudes toward work experience. Inst. for Social Res., Ann Arbor, Mich.

PATCHEN, M. (1961). *The choice of wage comparisons.* Englewood Cliffs, N.J.: Prentice-Hall.

PILISUK, M. (1962). Cognitive balance and self-relevant attitudes. *J. abnorm. soc. Psychol.* **65**, 95-103.

ROETHLISBERGER, F. J., AND DICKSON, W. J. (1939). *Management and the worker.* Cambridge, Mass.: Harvard Univer. Press.

SAYLES, L. R. (1958). *Behavior of industrial work groups: prediction and control.* New York: Wiley.

SKINNER, B. F. (1957). *Verbal behavior.* New York: Appleton.

SPECTOR, A. J. (1956). Expectations, fulfillment, and morale. *J. abnorm. soc. Psychol.* **52**, 51-56.

STEINER, I. D. (1960). Sex differences in the resolution of A-B-X conflicts. *J. Pers.* **28**, 118-128.

STEINER, I. D., AND JOHNSON, H. H. (1964). Relationships among dissonance reducing responses. *J. abnorm. soc. Psychol.* **68**, 38-44.

STEINER, I. D., AND PETERS, S. C. (1958). Conformity and the A-B-X model. *J. Pers.* **26**, 229-242.

STEINER, I. D., AND ROGERS, E. D. (1963). Alternative responses to dissonance. *J. abnorm. soc. Psychol.* **66**, 128-136.

STOUFFER, S. A., SUCHMAN, E. A., DeVINNEY, L.C.; STARR, SHIRLEY A., AND WILLIAMS R. M., JR. (1949). *The American soldier: adjustment during army life.* Vol 1. Princeton, N. J.: Princeton Univer. Press.

THIBAUT, J. (1950). An experimental study of the cohesiveness of underprivileged groups. *Hum. Relat.* **3**, 251-278.

THIBAUT, J. W., AND KELLEY, H. H. (1959). *The social psychology of groups.* New York: Wiley.

VROOM, V. H. (1964). *Work and motivation.* New York: Wiley.

WEICK, K. E. (1964). Reduction of cognitive dissonance through task enhancement and effort expenditure. *J. abnorm. soc. Psychol.* **66**, 533-539.

ZALEZNIK, A., CHRISTENSEN, C. R., AND ROETHLISBERGER, F. J. (1958). The motivation, productivity, and satisfaction of workers. A prediction study (Grad. Sch. Business Admin.) Harvard Univer.

10

Equity in Compensation

ELLIOTT JAQUES

The work I am going to describe began in 1948 as an applied social research project financed by a government research grant, and was conducted in the factory of the Glacier Metal Company in the United Kingdom. The original work was done in collaboration with the company and a research team from the Tavistock Institute of Human Relations. In 1951, the government research grant came to an end, but the work was continued by the company, with the unanimous concurrence of its Works Council. I was responsible to the Works Council, rather than to the management of the firm, and acted on a part-time basis as a consulting social analyst. This new relationship began in January 1952, and has continued in essentially the same form up to the present time.

Some examples of the types of projects undertaken were an extensive study and analysis of all of the executive and representative organizations in the company, and the design and development of a management training program. I worked on such projects in close association with a planning group charged with that responsibility. In September 1952, I was asked by a Works Council member representing a section of the staff to work through a problem they were wrestling with concerning staff status and work level grading. This subsequently grew into an in-depth analysis of salary and wage differentials, status and grading, promotion, and selection and appointments procedures within the company as a whole. It was this work which led

Printed by permission of the author. Paper delivered at the McKinsey Seminar on Managerial Motivation and Compensation, Tarrytown, New York, 1967.

to the discovery of time-span of discretion and its apparent relationship to perceived equitable payment for work, hierarchical organization structure, and the development of human capacity to carry responsibility in work.

The basic problem that we began to explore in 1952 was how to determine the appropriate level of pay and status that should be afforded individuals for the work they do. Appropriate, as we used the term, meant a level of pay and status such that individuals would feel they were receiving an equitable and just return for the work they were doing, as well as a payment level that was sound from an economic point of view. There had been general dissatisfaction at Glacier, we were quick to discover, with the system of work and pay level classification that the company was using at the time. Suffice it to say that it was very similar to most industrial job evaluation plans with which we are all familiar. No matter how industriously individuals would work with the system, there never seemed to be any end to the differing views held by those involved as to how much weight a given factor should be given, how the factor was really involved in work content (if at all), and, more importantly, why that particular factor was related to level of work and pay, when often it seemed as though some other element of the work itself was a more descriptive yardstick than the factor or factors included in the job evaluation system. In short, the system then in use in the company seemed to be "missing something" and simply couldn't be operated with consistency to anyone's satisfaction.

It was after several months of working at this problem that we more or less stumbled onto the realization that payment is very often expressed in varying periods of time. Hourly employees have their pay calculated on an hourly basis, higher levels are calculated weekly, still higher levels on a monthly basis, and top management on an annual basis. Other relationships between time and employment began to emerge. For example, the longer the period of time in which a person's salary is expressed, the longer the period of notice he must give if he resigns. These relationships led to the observation that the higher the level of the position, the longer it took for a new incumbent to become oriented to the work and to perform it at a fully qualified level. Another familiar notion was also derived from our discussions of work, namely, that higher-level positions were thought of as having longer-term responsibilities than lower levels. The people working on the problem began to feel that they were really on to something significant here, and thought they might be able to develop a time-related measure of responsibility for work. It was this preliminary work which eventually led to the development of the time-span of discretion instrument that became central to subsequent study of payment, work, and organization levels in the company.

In the process of developing the final instrument, several insights were gained that were to become extremely useful. The recognition that all employment work has both a prescribed and a discretionary content proved to be important, because while the discretionary content of work was frequently its least apparent characteristic, it developed that the length of time a subordinate was free to exercise his own discretion in the carrying out of his work tasks without the review of his superior matched quite closely people's intuitive feeling about differential levels of responsibility when comparing various jobs with which they were familiar. Detailed analyses of several individual jobs were carried out, and it was found that this "time-span of discretion" actually could be measured. It was found in exploratory studies that the higher the level of work, in general terms, the higher the time-span of discretion. However, it was one thing to note a general relationship between time-span and executive level, but it was quite another to suggest that the maximum time-span of discretion itself was a measurement of level of work. This very possibility began to come to light, however, as more and more positions were analyzed. A regular relationship started to emerge between time-span of discretion and salary.

In conducting interviews with employees at all levels of the firm, it was not unusual for the question of their salaries to be raised. Not only did I learn the actual salaries of a large number of employees, but—what proved to be more significant—I learned the salaries that they considered to be fair payment for the work they were doing. After a sizable number of these data had been gathered, a very important relationship obtained: employees who had the same maximum time-span of discretion, regardless of their title or occupation, stated with very slight variation the same salary or "felt-fair pay" for their various positions. These results were shown to hold true at whatever level of the company I happened to be working. Work with the time-span of discretion instrument has been undertaken elsewhere in the United Kingdom as well as in Holland, France, and here in the United States, and the same general finding continues to emerge.

I have developed an Equitable Work-Payment Scale for the United Kingdom which depicts the time-span felt-fair pay relationship and is shown in Figure 1 (copy from p. 125, *Equitable Payment*). The

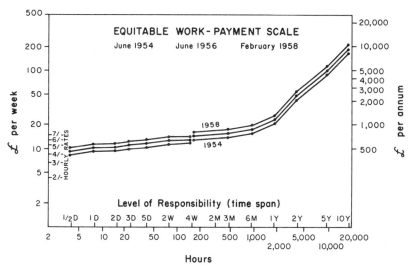

FIGURE 1.

The Equitable Work-Payment Scale

curves were made by plotting data from over 1,000 individual cases, and it should be mentioned that the deviations in felt-fair pay at any given time-span are in the order of ±5 percent, with standard deviations in the order of 2 to 3 percent. The earnings depicted represent total emoluments and are independent of the amount of income tax paid by individuals. Notice, too, that the standards of equity shift upward at a rate generally equivalent to increases in the Ministry of Labour's wages index. The discontinuity in the curves at the four-week time-span level represents the effect on the equity norms of overtime payment. At about the one-month time-span level, I have found that individuals begin to think in terms of a weekly salary and no longer seem to take overtime into account in their equitable payment perceptions. The Equitable Work-Payment Scale shows, therefore, the first of several relationships between work, pay, organization structure, and human capacity that we were to eventually develop over the years in the context of the Glacier Project. The two variables that we have explored up to this point are "level of work," as measured in terms of time-span of discretion, and "level of felt-fair pay" as perceived by incumbents of organizational positions doing employment work.

The third variable, that of organization structure (or executive strata), was explored from the base-point of some rather simple and common empirical observations. First of all, from as far back as we can go in human history, it will almost uniformly be found that when man has had to undertake a task requiring the efforts of a number of individuals, he has organized himself into an executive structure, usually pyramid shaped, and divided into a hierarchy of horizontal strata. Second, from discussions with the management people in several countries, I found a universal, intuitively held assumption of optimum manager-subordinate distance expressed in salary dollars. For example, if one were to present a simplified organization chart showing a top manager with two subordinates reporting to him, and in turn two lower subordinates reporting to each of them, and if one were to put a salary next to the top manager's position of $25,000 per annum, one would find knowledgeable businessmen generally agreeing as to what would represent an optimal salary distance between the top manager and his subordinates and each of them with their subordinates. Twenty-four thousand dollars would be felt as "too close" a salary for the top manager's direct subordinates, $5,000 "too far away," and so on. By a series of successive approximations, you would find them agreeing that "$17,000 to $19,000 would be about right." Similarly, the second level subordinates would be seen with salaries between $12,000 and $14,000 as appropriate. This universal structuring of appropriate manager-subordinate "salary distance" dovetails with time-span of discretion measurement that I have used frequently as an aid in organization analysis. In those cases where I have found positions involving full managerial authority over subordinates, they always have in their complement of work tasks some with time-spans of at least three months. To say it another way, I have yet to find a true manager-subordinate relationship where the manager did not have at least a three-month time-span of discretion in his own work role. From actual data, I have observed other "natural" hierarchical levels at six months, one-year, two-year, and five-year time-spans of discretion. On top of the five-year time-span level I have found a clearly discernible ten-year level, with the possibility of a twenty-year level beyond that. My data beyond the ten-year time-span stratum are rather meager, however, so I can only speculate from limited source information. The five-year time-span level, on the other hand, and those below it as well, are sufficiently supported by a great deal of data, giving me some confidence in these observations.

Following from these data, then, is the hypothesis of an optimal number of horizontal strata in an executive hierarchy. The breakpoints or boundaries between these levels are stated in terms of "felt-fair pay," but could just as easily be expressed in terms of their time-span of discretion correlates. Once this is done, what we have created, in effect, is a hierarchy of time-spans reflecting the increasing extent of discretion necessary to carry out management roles. These strata are shown in Table 1.

Table 1

Equitable Payment Levels

Time-Span Boundaries	Strata	U.S.A.	U.K.
20 years	Stratum 7	$200,000	£28,500
10 years	Stratum 6	$100,000	£14,500
5 years	Stratum 5	$ 50,000	£ 7,250
2 years	Stratum 4	$ 25,000	£ 3,625
1 year	Stratum 3	$ 12,000	£ 1,725
3 months	Stratum 2	$ 8,000	£ 1,200
less than 3 months	Stratum 1	less than $ 8,000	less than £ 1,200

The data in the table are based on current U. K. information, with the United States equitable payment levels reflecting my best approximations from rather limited 1967 inputs. If the relationships between U.K. and U.S. salaries retain their historical differentials, however, then my U.S. approximations should be fairly close to what one would find in an empirical investigation. This points to the need, by the way, for some good hard empirical work to test the results I have found in my social-analytic relationships at Glacier Metals and elsewhere. Some work has been done in this country, but I would like to see my speculations and hypotheses rigorously tested, since my information has essentially been gathered on a "catch-as-catch-can" basis over the years.

To return to the notion that there may be rather concise strata of time-spans in executive organization, an interesting possibility presents itself. It would appear that the largest corporation could be run with no more than seven executive strata from the shop floor to the manager's office. This idea may not be as unusual as it might first appear when we consider a couple of factors. First of all, what is one of the first recommendations that the typical management consulting firm will make at the conclusion of an organizational analysis? At least in the United Kingdom I find that they usually suggest the stripping out of executive levels. Time and time again they find, by whatever methods they use, that most organizations seem to have "too many management levels." I have found in my own work a sort of confirmation of this phenomenon, but I have approached it through the use of time-span.

My work suggests that in order for an optimum manager-subordinate relationship to exist, two conditions must be fulfilled: first, the time-spans of the two positions must be in contiguous strata as indicated in Table 1; and second, the roles must be in such a relationship that there is a "one-stratum distance" between them. This second condition requires a bit of explanation. The levels of work in two positions in a manager-subordinate relationship are "one-stratum distance" apart, as measured in time-span, in the time-span range of two adjacent executive strata. As an example, a time-span of fifteen months is just over one-stratum apart from a three-year time-span; the fifteen-month being roughly one-quarter up stratum-3, and the three-year time-span being about one-third of the way up stratum-4. This situation is depicted in Figure 2.

```
                   _____ 5 years
    Stratum-4 ------------ X ------------------------ 3 years
                   _____ 2 years
                              one-stratum distance
    Stratum-3 ------------ X ------------------------15 months
                   _____ 1 year
```

FIGURE 2

It has been my experience that when the actual difference of the level of work in the manager-subordinate relationship is less than a one-stratum distance, for example, when both of the roles are in the same executive stratum, then the subordinate will be found to "go around" his boss a great deal, and receive many of his assignments and work guidance from the "manager-once-removed" (that is, his manager's manager). Further, I have noticed that at salary review time, it is the manager-once-removed who has the major input in the determination of the subordinate's increase. Usually it will be found that it is also the manager-once-removed who selects a replacement for the subordinate, if that circumstance arises, determines the kinds of assignments that will be injected into the role, and who in almost every other significant management action is really the subordinate's boss. One hears this sort of thing: "Who's my boss? Well, I'm supposed to report to Joe (his manager), but I really work for Sam (the manager-once-removed)."

Should one find, on the other hand, that there is a greater-than one-stratum distance between the manager and the subordinate, then I have observed that another set of circumstances usually obtains. If the manager has other subordinates who are, in fact, in an adjacent executive stratum, one-stratum distance from the manager, then the subordinate who is in the stratum *below* the other subordinates is usually not considered to be in the same category or relationship to the manager as are they. A manager and his secretary may serve as an example, or a subordinate who is a personal assistant. These latter types of roles are not seen as being in a full-colleague or peer relationship to the manager's other two subordinates. The former usually will be found to serve the manager on an ad hoc basis, that is, they do not have ongoing, long-term assignments as would the manager's other subordinates, but rather serve him by gathering information for his review and decision, or conveying his wishes to other sectors of management, or performing routine tasks such as typing, filing, and the like. There are, of course, other permutations and combinations that occur, but the examples should serve to illustrate the potential for the use of time-span as an organization analysis tool. It may be possible to hypothesize, therefore, that organizational efficiency will be best realized when manager-subordinate reporting relationships are structured at a one-stratum distance from the top of an organization to the bottom. This illustrates, then, how it could be possible for large corporations to be organized and managed with optimum efficiency with only seven levels in the management hierarchy.

Before leaving the question of executive structure, I should like to draw a distinction that is often confused in the usual discussions of the relationship between organization structure and salary structure. One of the more common fallacies prevalent in organization analysis is the practice of assuming that because there may be, say, fifteen distinct salary ranges in a company, there are fifteen discrete executive levels. From my exposure to the way business enterprises carry out their affairs, nothing could be further from the truth. Yet it seems as if the assumptions of the complementarity of the two structures creep into the staffing of organizations with a perseverance that is difficult to account for. If we just look at the level of pay issue for a moment, we can sometimes account for the multiplicity of levels by examining the specific case. For example, I am sure we have all come across the case of a weak manager who, for a number of reasons, cannot be replaced. The level of work to be done in his role, however, still must be carried out. As a result, he will be "beefed up" by a strong subordinate who really does his job for him. Usually the subordinate will be paid very close to the manager's salary, and since we need to do that in order to keep the "bright young man" content, we slot his position in a salary level very close to that of the weak manager—say 10 percent lower. Then, as is all too often the case, because the bright subordinate is in his slot, those employees who work for him are moved to an appropriate position with respect to his range, and we are off on a compounding effect that in large organizations is the bane of their existence—if I can believe the inherent dissatisfaction expressed by so many company executives whenever a discussion ensues relative to the relationship between pay levels and organization levels. This is but one example of the dilemma many companies find themselves in whenever managerial levels are attached to grades and payment brackets for whatever reason. A corollary difficulty arises, however, even if we assume that all members of management are well suited to manage respective levels of work. If these managers are squeezed into the usual salary structure hierarchy, we find ourselves with the so-called pay compression problem. The distance between managers and their subordinates in terms of salary is far too small to reflect accurately the distance we intend to establish in organizational terms. Further, reporting relationships that are so established over time are usually such that subordinates are too close to their bosses in terms of their capacity to carry out work assignments. Fine delineations of human work capacity are extremely difficult to come by, but in spite of this fact, managements seem to feel constrained to follow the levels in their salary structure in establishing reporting relationships. In the case where the capacity of the manager is too close to that of the subordinate, the manager is often found to be a so-called straw boss, with the subordinate really reporting to and working for someone higher in the organization. In all of the cases referred to, and in many others we have all experienced, the end result is the same—a gross and unrealistic proliferation of management levels in the firm—and we are back where we started from. This situation can only be overcome, it seems to me, if salary brackets are kept separate and distinct from management organization levels. This may not be as difficult a problem as it may first seem. The key is the measurement of level of work, and it is here that I believe the time-span instrument may prove quite beneficial.

From the organizations within which I have worked, I have concluded that the hierarchy of reporting relationships can be structured in the seven distinct levels we have already explored in Table 1, that is, stratum-7, twenty-year time-span; stratum-6, ten-year time-span; stratum-5, five-year time-span; stratum-4, two-year time-span; stratum-3, one-year time-span; stratum-2, three-month time-span; and stratum-1, less than three-month time-span. The meaningfulness of this suggestion can be seen if we tie it into the "one-stratum distance" reporting relationship discussed above. If, as I believe, optimum organization is achieved when manager-subordinate roles are one-stratum distance apart as measured in time-span terms, then this should be the criterion used to establish proper reporting relationships, not a set of subjectively derived salary brackets. In short, I would turn the process completely around, that is, rather than establishing an organization structure essentially using salary brackets as the criterion, I would establish optimum reporting relationships first, then fit a set of salary ranges to them. Whether or not a company would elect to establish "felt-fair pay" equivalents to each time-span stratum is a matter of company compensation policy. The point is, whatever approach is used to establish "the rate for the job," a company should be certain to establish these *after*, and independent of, the establishment of an efficient organization structure. This is not to say that payment brackets are not related to the organizational level of a position. All I am saying is that salary brackets should be grouped so that they fit into the organizational structure within the boundaries of the delineated executive strata.

If a management were to establish organizational and payment structures independently, yet related to each other as I have suggested, then a relatively flexible method of organization and salary level control becomes possible. For example, if the level of work in a given management position should change, for whatever reason, a management is free to move that position from one work-level bracket to the next within any given organizational stratum without having to modify the executive structure. An appropriate salary range for the changed role can also be established without doing violence to reporting relationships that may continue to be appropriate to obtain maximum efficiency.

It is not possible at this juncture to go further in this discussion without considering the growth of individual capacity to effectively carry out employment work and the question of individual payment progression practices that appear to me to be consistent within the full perspective of the relationship between level of work, level of individual capacity, and level of individual payment.

Human capacity is a difficult construct to deal with, and I do not wish to go into it in extensive depth here. Suffice it to say that the capacity which I wish to explore is the capacity of individuals to carry given levels of responsibility in executive organization. I am not speaking, of course, about intelligence per se, although I would agree that however we might choose to define it, it would probably be a significant component of capacity, as I am using the term. I prefer to explore capacity as a construct having to do with the actual behavior of working in discharging real responsibilities. Although I realize full well the circularity of what I am about to offer as a more complete, operational definition of the term, nevertheless, I have found it useful in exploring the relationships involving man, his work, and the payment he receives for that work. The particular capacity to which I refer, I shall call "time-span capacity"—the individual's total complement of human characteristics that enable him to carry out tasks of given levels of work as measured in time-span. The higher the level of work (as measured in time-span) the individual is demonstrably capable of carrying, the higher the level of capacity I shall say he has. If we assume for a moment that time-span capacity is distributed in large populations in the same way as other characteristics tend to be distributed, we would have a Gaussian distribution with a left hand skew. This is shown in Figure 3.

There are some interesting characteristics we may note in this distribution. The dotted line cutting the distribution on the left could illustrate the level of capacity below which members of the population would probably not be able to engage in employment work in industry at all. As we move to the right in the distribution, we note that there is still a relatively large number of people who would have less capacity than the largest segment of the population. Continuing to the right, we pass through the mode of the capacity distribution—that point which I would speculate represents the capacity level characterized as the semiskilled and clerical worker. As we move still further to the right, we move to increasingly higher levels of capacity, but the number of people in the distribution at each point diminishes rather steadily. It is interesting to speculate, if this line of reasoning has any validity

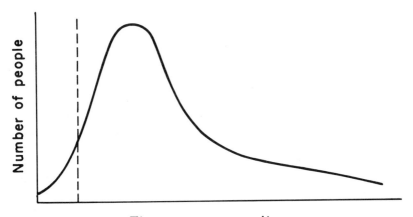

Time - span capacity

FIGURE 3

at all, that as the level of capacity in the population increases, the number of individuals capable of operating in higher levels of executive organization decreases. Along with this decrease, we note that executive organizations themselves have a smaller number of roles the higher we move up the managerial chain of command. In short, these speculations may show how the organization of executive hierarchies reflects the distribution of individual time-span capacity in the population. When we couple this notion with the observation that executive organizations seem to consistently take on the characteristic of horizontal strata in their hierarchy, we can further speculate that the function of this stratification is to achieve a situation whereby a manager at one level of the organization can assign and get work done through subordinates at a lower level and still remain accountable for the total task of getting the work done. What I am proposing here is a "division of labor," if you will, stratified upon level of time-span capacity. We know that this stratified division of labor is not always successfully achieved, but surely there must be some quality or qualities in human beings that make it possible for a superior to do something called "manage" a subordinate. I believe time-span capacity of an individual is at least as good a candidate to represent these qualities as some of the constructs used by others.

If my speculations regarding time-span capacity and the structure of organizational hierarchies have any merit at all, then in order to pursue them further, we must ask whether, in fact, there are identifiable differences in the quality of capacity of a manager and his subordinate that enable the manager to do that which we refer to as "managing his subordinate." Can different levels of capacity be described? Can these different levels be identified in real life? Does capacity increase or grow over time? Answers to these questions would be important in increasing our understanding of the workings of executive organization, and further would provide a framework within which the objective measurement of individual capacity could be enhanced.

We have already reviewed the concept of "one-stratum distance" in the reporting relationship between superior and subordinate in the context of apparent bands or strata of organizational hierarchies as measured in time-span. If these strata can be conceived of as qualitatively different in addition to the quantitative time-span differential, we would introduce the consideration that there might be changes in the inherent nature of capacity which accompany increases in the quantity. I have recently undertaken work in this area which suggests the hypothesis that executive strata may reflect qualitative differences in the levels of abstraction that must be employed in order to make it possible for managerial authority and leadership to be exercised in a meaningful way. If this hypothesis is valid, it would mean that a manager, well-established in his role at one organizational stratum as measured in time-span, would be working at a qualitatively different level of abstraction from one of his subordinates equally well-established in his role working one organizational stratum below the manager's. To look at the relationship in a different mode, that of promotion, a person would be considered close to being ready for promotion to the next higher organizational stratum when he began to be capable of demonstrating a higher level of abstraction in his work. Were the individual, in fact, promoted, there would ensue a period of adjustment that could last for a few months to a year or longer, depending upon the rate of development of the individual's capacity and the level of the role into which he had been promoted.

I believe that these changes in the content of capacity—qualitative changes in level of abstraction—are identifiable, and that individual differences in higher and lower capacity to carry out work are not simply a matter of differences in the *quantity* of capacity alone. Preliminary work at Brunel University points to the possibility of the existence of a number of discrete distributions in the population at different capacity levels rather than the more conventional single normal distribution. Initial indications reflect a multi-modal distribution of capacity indicating the distinct possibility of the qualitative differences referred to earlier. In an overall sense, the distribution has the general form of time-span capacity illustrated in Figure 3, but with the differential modes clearly in evidence. The preliminary results are shown in Figure 4.

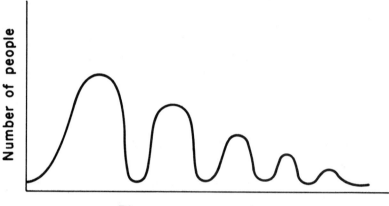

Time-span capacity
FIGURE 4

The qualitatively delineated levels of capacity I shall now briefly discuss are based entirely upon direct observations of work at the Glacier Metals Company and elsewhere. In describing these various levels of abstraction, I shall be considering the nature of the relationship between the individual and his work task. In essence, the hypothesis is that the more proximate to a work task an individual must be in the psychological sense, the lower the level of abstraction, and vice versa.

First Level of Abstraction: Perceptual-Concrete

Individuals with an apparent time-span capacity of two months must have the object of the work task physically present for the work to be done. Regardless of whether or not the work is clerical or manual, the object of the task—a piece of paper or a piece of metal stock—must be in contact with one of the senses. In the absence of this perceptual contact with the work object, the individual is unable to work. This is not to say, however, that the individual cannot be assigned work verbally or in other abstract media. It simply means he cannot perform work without the concrete presence of the work object.

Second Level of Abstraction: Imaginal-Concrete

At about the three-months' level of time-span capacity, the characteristic of being able to work with an imaginal picture of the physical object begins to emerge. The actual physical object of the work task need not be physically or perceptually present. This may explain why it is possible to manage the work of others working at the Perceptual-Concrete level of abstraction. The planning, directing, allocating, programming, and controlling of subordinate's tasks are possible because the superior's level of abstraction is sufficiently high to conceive these tasks imaginally, obviating the need to be bound to actual physical contact with them.

Third Level of Abstraction: Conceptual-Concrete

The individual's work tasks begin to take on an additional quality connected with the future at time-span capacity levels of over one year. One must deal not only on an imaginal level with current tasks, but must also develop a temporal sense of the forward load of tasks and the activities and changes requiring linkage to meet them. The individual must conceive of his work in terms of inter-related categories and functions of tasks over time that must eventually mesh into an overall result. The imaginal, temporal picture of the tasks, however, remains tied to a conception of the work in physical terms, still directly connected, that is, to the concrete.

Fourth Level of Abstraction: Abstract Modeling

As an individual approaches the two-year time-span capacity level, a quite profound change begins to take place in the quality of abstraction employed in carrying out tasks. This is the place where the concrete gives way to true abstract. This does not mean simply thinking in abstract terms, since our use of words, ideas, concepts, beliefs, and the like reflects a capability to deal with a degree of abstraction by all human beings, save the relatively few unfortunates. The fourth level of abstraction, rather, implies the usage of abstractions in a particular way. While I have a strong feeling for what is involved here, I am not yet able to formulate it clearly, but can describe the process in somewhat general terms. What is most important at this level of abstraction is the observation that those who have demonstrable capacity at this level deal with the object of their work in terms of concepts and features that are no longer "pictures" of the concrete object. Rather, the expression takes the shape of analogues of the concrete expressed in abstract terms of force fields, vectors, power, stresses, direction of movement, degrees of freedom, and the like. The individual is able to detach himself from the concrete representation of the work object and immerse himself in the manipulation and consideration of his abstractions without reference to the real object at all. Yet he seems to retain a firm grip on the real nature of his work: the requirement that he eventually translate his abstract model into something concrete which can be constructed, tested, and evaluated against the pragmatics of the physical world. In short, the individual must be able to detach himself from the reliance of the presence of the work object—whether physical, imaginal, or conceptual —yet maintain a sufficient intuitive contact with the concrete while dealing in the abstract such that the latter may be translated to the former and yield practical results.

Fifth Level of Abstraction: Theory Construction

At the beginning of the five-year time-span capacity level up to about the ten-year, I feel another change in the quality of abstraction takes place; namely, the construction and use of theory. (It is possible that this change may prove to be an even higher level of abstraction. I simply am not certain.) A characteristic of this level is the need for only one-time contact with the concrete. A manager of work at this level operates in such a way that given exposure to a theory (for example, the application of a new technology in product development) and one detailed example of its application, it is possible for him to understand what will happen in other cases similar to the example and covered by the theory. An interesting dialogue often transpires between managers at this level and their subordinates. I have seen managers, for example, urged by their subordinates to come and see the latest design of a prototype involving the application of a new process. The manager will often reply that he does not need to see another example of the application, but his subordinates continue to press him to do so. Yet, since the manager himself does not feel he has to take the time for another exposure, he often becomes impatient and ends the discourse. What may be happening here is the interaction of two different frames of reference (levels of abstraction), the higher applying the intuitive generalization realized from only passing con-

tact with the concrete. In other words, a generalization having the
characteristic of an intuitive constructed theory.

Sixth and Seventh Levels of Abstraction

Since there is some evidence from business organization that two
further levels of executive strata exist—stratum-six, beginning at a
ten-year time-span level, and stratum-seven beginning at a twenty-year
time-span—my feeling is that qualitatively different and still higher
capacity levels may exist. I have not, however, had sufficient evidence
or experience relative to the work of individuals at such levels to
make any meaningful hypotheses. With what limited experience I do
have, the quality of individual capacity operationally takes on the
nature of policy-setting with regard to financial, market, and product
matters. Clearly, theory construction seems to remain in evidence,
yet the emphasis shifts from a concern with the functional aspects of
the business (such as engineering, production, or sales) to a concentration on matters necessary to establish a synthesis of these sub-
systems, if you will, into an entity that has as its primary focus the
overall success and survival of the business enterprise as such. This
is about all I can really offer with regard to differential capacity to
successfully carry out employment work at differing levels of executive organization. The frame of reference I have outlined describes
the outward expression of capacities that appear to be operative in
individual behavior. It is recognized, of course, that the framework
tells us nothing about the mental tools themselves which are the
source of the expression. At best it represents a description of the mode
of the relationship between the individual, expressed in capacity terms,
and the tasks he is carrying out, expressed in discretionary terms.
The notion of time-span is the linking pin, which may prove to be
a variable of heuristic value in helping to show the way to a
deeper understanding of the mental processes involved in the conduct of work itself by an individual human being. The intrigue
of the apparent relationship between higher levels of capacity in
executive organization and the increase in the time-span of discretion
of these tasks remains. Indeed, time-span provides a means of objective measurement of the level of work in a task, and correlates
with both the felt-fair pay variable and our speculations regarding a
hierarchy of levels of abstraction, resulting in the obvious hypothesis
of the existence of a tightly related "work-pay-capacity" nexus.

Before exploring this formulation, however, I shall have to briefly review my data and rationale regarding the rate of development of individual work capacity.

I have had innumerable occasions in my work at Glacier to be present when heated debates were undertaken regarding the appropriate level of payment for a given individual. Now when a person (or group of persons) complains that he is not being fairly paid, he may be referring to any of three possibilities. First, he may mean that he is not being paid fairly for the work he is doing as compared with what others are being paid for similar work. Second, he may mean he is dissatisfied with his own standard of living regardless of whether or not others at a similar income level find it possible to make ends meet. The third possibility is that even if the first two conditions are met, he may still consider himself underpaid if he feels he is capable of successfully performing a higher-level job commanding a higher salary. In the later case, while I have observed that such individuals do feel underpaid, the root of the problem can be seen to be "underemployment." Such an individual, although equitably paid for the work he is doing, feels barred from the possibility of promotion into positions whose level of work, and thus pay, would be more consistent with his own self-image of his capacity. Failure to recognize the differences in the three cases of pay dissatisfaction bedevil the choice of appropriate corrective action by a manager. All too often, the manager will conclude that the individual is simply interested in more pay, and miss the relevance of underemployment. It was the realization that while extensive work had been done in developing a measurement of the level of work in a job and the equitable payment norms that related to a given level, little study has been undertaken as to which individual should be assigned to any given job. Further, once the individual has been so assigned there didn't seem to be any method of determining precisely what he should be paid at any given moment over time.

At about this stage in the Glacier Project, I had been carrying on a longitudinal study of the career progressions of individuals in different jobs using the time-span measurement. The results suggested that individuals became emotionally unsettled if their level of work was too high or too low for their capacity. The idea then developed that if individuals were not receiving perceived fair payment for the level of work they were capable of performing, then this relationship between payment (and progress in payment) and individual capacity (and progress in capacity) could be explored in its own right. The potential of such a study might lend itself to the establishment of a systematic basis for considering individual career progression in work, and perhaps the development of more effective techniques for the administration of pay.

An initial test of these assumptions was made on a small sample of individuals, and their actual pay progressions, corrected for increases due to conditions of economic inflation, were drawn for each person. In individual discussions with each of these persons, it appeared that each reacted to upward and downward movement of his earnings as if they were movements toward or away from some internalized standard of what constituted an expected or desired progress for himself. By a trial and error method, a smoothed curve could be drawn that represented dynamic equilibrium for each person over time. Deviations downward from this smoothed curve were reacted to with dissatisfaction, and deviations above the curve—the rarer of the two conditions—being reacted to with a sense of being relatively better off than one might have expected.

This experience led me to the conclusion that there might possibly be a smoothed curve of progression in earnings for each person which coincided with his development in capacity, representing, therefore, the equilibrium situation with regard to his economic and career progress. The next step was to obtain the earnings data of some 250 persons and plot them in graphic form, corrected for periodic movements in the U.K.'s wages index. The earnings data reflected total emoluments comprising salary, established bonuses, and any other forms of compensation—such as a company-provided car—that were recognized by the individual as having some personal value. The data were plotted on semi-logarithmic graph paper to facilitate plotting and to enable percentage changes in earnings to be read directly from the charts by simple arithmetic measurement. Since the study was interested in pursuing the topic of career movement, the earnings were plotted against age. The results are displayed in Figure 5.

It is worth noting that these data are considerably different from those usually plotted—the so-called maturity curves. The latter reflect the growth of the average salary of a group of individuals at each point on the abscissa, and in no way reflect the actual progression of a single individual. The use of such averaged curves in the consideration of the payment progression for a given individual is fraught with hazard, but that is a topic for another time and place.

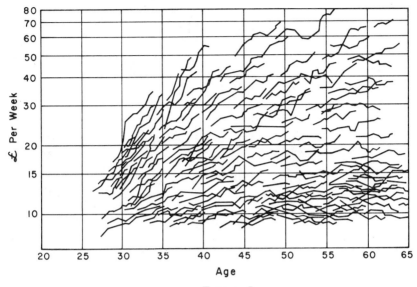

£ Per Week

Age

FIGURE 5

In examining Figure 5, a very decided pattern of the curves became apparent to me. There is a general fanning of the curves upward from the left-hand corner. The overall trend is that of a faster acceleration in the younger age group, slowing down with age, but a higher rate of progression maintained throughout, the higher the earning level. I then drew a number of smoothed continuous curves through the individual progressions in Figure 5 representing the general trend lines that were apparent to me, discounting both the nonuniformity within the individual progressions and the deviations of individual curves from the trend line. My thinking was that while there were many potential explanations for these deviations, for the moment they could be my major concern. As we shall see later, however, empirical work has been done on the question of the deviations that has significant potential as a tool in the study of the specific career growth of individuals.

The plotting of the smoothed curves over the original data is illustrated in Figure 6. These smoothed curves, which I term "Standard Earning Progressions," are illustrated in a more elaborate form in Figure 7. The pattern of the standard progression curves of Figure 7 demonstrates the possibility of drawing a set of smoothed curves, in the manner already described, which in a general way seem to reflect both the predominant trend in actual earning progressions

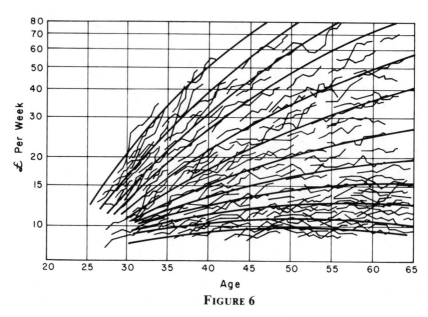

FIGURE 6

and also confirm the assumptions I had made with regard to the direction these smoothed curves were likely to follow. It remained to demonstrate, however, whether or not the progression curves were anything more than a neat, but meaningless, construction. I shall now turn to my findings from the use of these curves which have led me to conclude that they do, in fact, represent a close approximation to a description of the lines of growth of time-span capacity in individuals, and, therefore, of the lines of dynamic equilibrium for an individual with regard to his actual earning progression in terms of the current equitable payment rates for the level of work he would be performing and that would be consistent with his capacity at any age. Incidentally, while I cannot go into them in depth, data are available from several companies in the United States which indicate that the standard earning progression array applies for this country precisely as for the United Kingdom. Furthermore, some twelve thousand individual progressions have recently been plotted by the Dutch General Employer's Association, and once again the array dovetails almost perfectly with the U.K. data. This additional work, representing quite divergent economic and historical characteristics, serves to reinforce the assumption that the curves reflect a very general characteristic of human development as it relates to employment work.

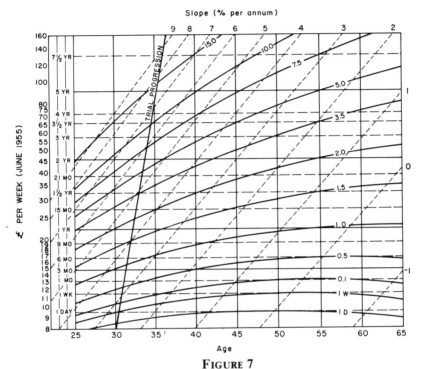

FIGURE 7

Earning Progression Data Sheet (1963 Revision)

© The Glacier Project

In looking at Figure 7, some definition and explanation is in order if we are to understand the use of the progression curves in organization study and individual payment determinations. As has been mentioned earlier, the *earnings* plotted for an individual on the Standard Earning Progression curves would be the total emoluments he received in connection with his work. The result of plotting these earnings at each age point would reflect an individual's *actual earning progression* over time, corrected back to the 1955 level of the wages index as a baseline, with subsequent movements in the index removed from an individual's payment progression at each point where the index movement is equal to or greater than 2 percent. The *potential progression* of an individual would refer to the progress in level of work he would achieve if he were continuously employed at the full level of his capacity. Since we do not as yet have an objective measure of capacity, the potential progression of an individual must rest on a managerial assessment of the level of work an individual is likely to achieve in practice. This *potential progress assessment* (PPA) can be expressed in terms of that earning progression an individual would achieve were he to receive the equitable rate of payment for his work. The curves in Figure 7 can themselves be thought of as PPA curves and labeled in terms of the time-span level at the point where a given curve cuts the vertical scale at age fifty-five. As an example, an individual age thirty, working at a time-span level of one year, and paid the equitable payment rate (in 1955 pounds) of £22 per week, could be considered by his manager to be capable of assuming future work assignments that would place him on the curve that intersects the coordinates "thirty years of age" and "£22 per week." If this' were so, then the individual would be said to have a PPA of 5.0 years in time-span terms. The 5.0 identification is simply the time-span level on the ordinate that that particular curve crosses at age fifty-five on the abscissa. This labeling of PPA curves is a convenient shorthand that will save us time as we discuss one or two individual examples of work and payment progression assessments.

Before discussing the application of the curves in conjunction with level of work measurement in time-span terms, it is necessary to lay out another hypothesis derived from the work at Glacier. If on a continuing basis over time we can assume that (a) in an abundant employment setting, that is, one in which an individual may not only find a job, but in addition find one that he considers to be "just right" for him; (b) it is true that an individual seeks a level of work consistent with his capacity; (c) it is also true that an individual seeks a level of payment which he considers equitable for such work; then the actual salary progression of an individual over time would support the conclusion that a curve drawn to that progression would reflect the pattern of the normal development of his capacity to carry out employment work. It is my speculation that the standard earning progression curves can be used as just such an indicator of capacity growth when they are coupled with a managerial potential progress assessment (PPA). To look at this derived assumption in another way—if a person's achieved progress in earnings did conform to a standard earning progression—he should show evidence either (a) of being satisfied that, whatever else might be happening, he was at least achieving a rate of financial progress that matched his rate of capacity development; or (b) of having a sense that his financial progress was maintaining a steady and unvarying level above or below satisfaction level. With regard to point (b), if his achieved earning progression deviated downward in relation to the standard progression pattern, he should experience a sense of retardation in his rate of progress in earning. If, on the other hand, his pay progression deviated upward with regard to the standard, he should experience a sense of acceleration in his rate of financial progress.

A person's primary drive with respect to his work is toward a level of that work that can absorb his capacity—toward a job in which he can use his capacity to the full. His urge or drive for money is derived from this primary goal of matching level of work with capacity, and is a drive for a rate of return or reward that is equitable and gives him a relative economic status coinciding with his capacity. The notion that individuals strive primarily to get all the money they can is, in my experience, a grossly simplistic, unnecessarily nihilistic account of human behavior. The hypothesis I have put forth assumes that a person's attitude with regard to his earnings is strongly influenced by norms of equity that are interrelated with the primary striving for a level of work consistent with his own capacity as he, himself, perceives it. The proof of such an hypothesis, however, requires a series of measuring instruments beyond our current grasp. Capacity measurement still eludes us, although, as mentioned earlier, some encouraging initial results have been found. They are far too tentative as yet; so in the absence of an objective measure, the salary progression curves coupled with managerial potential progress assessment are about as close as we can come. A description of how such a system works in practice and a brief summary of its apparent utility through the discussion of one or two case histories should illustrate the potential value I believe exists in using the instruments, crude though they may be, in helping match the right man to the right job at the right level of pay.

In practice it has not proven to be too difficult to establish a working baseline for the individual and his growth of capacity; that is, tentatively establishing an estimate of his likely progression in level of work and adjusting this estimate up or down in the light of experience with his actual performance. This datum line is what I have referred to previously as the potential progress assessment (PPA). The tentative establishment of this PPA is achieved by combining time-span analysis with the evaluation of work performance in the following way. It is usually possible to find at least one point in the career of an individual where he felt his level of work fully occupied his capacity, and his manager at that time would agree. Further, the individual may or may not have felt that his level of pay at the time was keeping pace with his progress in his work. To take an example, he may have been appointed at the age of thirty-five to a position with a range level of work of six months to one year, measured in time-span terms, placing him at a June 1955 equitable payment salary range of £775 to £1,150. The individual considered himself "just ready" for his new job, and his manager confirmed that after a break-in time of three months or so, the man was performing satisfactorily and likely to develop well. In another example, a person may have reached the top level of a job with a time-span of three to six months, and an equitable salary range of £700 to £775, again, say, at the age of thirty-five. He would know he had reached a ceiling on that particular job, because no particular opportunity for new types of work or extension of responsibility presented itself. This experience of there being no further scope and of having fully encompassed all the job has to offer can usually be confirmed by the manager who cannot see any other way to build additional challenge or discretionary latitude into the job.

In both of these two examples, I would make the assumption that each person had reached the six-month time-span level, and its co-variate £775 equitable payment level, at the age of thirty-five. Reference to the standard earning progression curves in Figure 7 would indicate a PPA of 1.2—that is, the points described are on the curve that cuts the vertical scale (at age fifty-five) at 1.2 years time-span. The greater the number of such assessments of performance level and age that can be made for a person, the farther it is possible to go toward constructing a meaningful potential progress assessment for him. Even the estimation of one such point in a person's career, however, will allow the selection of that standard earning progression curve which, according to the underlying assumptions, should conform to the normal rate of progress in the individual's performance level as indicated by time-span.

In the absence of time-span data, a rough guide to a person's potential progress assessment can be constructed if he has progressed through a job or jobs which have known salary brackets. His achieved progress, in terms of the age at which he reached various bracket limits, may be treated in much the same manner as that described for time-span brackets. The potential progress assessment thus obtained will be limited in its accuracy, however, by the accuracy of the salary brackets themselves—accuracy in the sense of how closely they conform to the equitable payment rates perceived for the range of level of work in the jobs concerned. Without some form of level of work measurement, the accuracy of this conformance between the salary brackets and the range of level of work cannot, of course, be known.

Taking my experience as a whole with the use of the time-span of discretion, the equitable work-payment scale, and the standard earning progression curves, and with due regard for the strengths and weaknesses of the data which have been described, a number of assumptions seem to me to be warranted—some of which I have already stated:

1) We each have an accurate unconscious awareness of the level of work we are capable of doing, the level of work extant in the role we occupy, and the equitable payment level for both the level of work we are carrying and the level which we are capable of carrying (should these be different).

2) We are each aware of any discrepancies which may exist between our capacity and our level of work, and between our actual payment and the payment which would be equitable for our work.

3) We each have an accurate unconscious awareness of our level of capacity for discriminating expenditure as a consumer and of our level of satisfaction consumption, and we are aware of the extent to which our actual income may deviate—either above or below—from that which would provide abundance.

4) The development of our potential capacity follows a regular course which can be described by a standard earning progression curve representing the earnings that would be equitable for work consistent with our capacity at any given age.

5) We are each attracted toward a level of work that is consistent with our capacity, and a rate of progress in our work that conforms to our rate of progress in capacity.

6) We are each concerned with receiving equitable payment for our work.

7) Each of us will be stimulated toward the maximum psychological equilibrium of which we are capable, by a level of work consistent with our capacity and equitable payment for that work within an economy of abundance.

APPLICATION

The implementation of these assumptions centers on what I shall term the "standard payment and progression method." This method uses the time-span of discretion instrument for measuring level of work, the equitable work-payment scale for assigning payment levels, and the standard earning progression curves as the baseline for administering individual progress. It is aimed toward achieving dynamic equilibrium between an individual's level of capacity (C), his level of work (W), and the amount of payment (P) for that work. It assumes that this C-W-P equilibrium nexus provides the optimum foundation for both economic efficiency and individual satisfaction.

I shall first outline the method, then consider in some detail the implications for executive organization in industry; since the implementation of the standard payment and progression method throws into sharp relief some of the shortcomings of the usual methods of control of organization and manning usually practiced in industry—especially the limitations in personnel methods and the policies governing personnel management.

The standard payment and progression method is this:

1) Determine the level-of-work bracket for each role, using the time-span of discretion instrument, and assign to it the equitable wage or salary bracket corresponding to the level of work.

2) Plot on an Earning Progression Data Sheet (the same as Figure 7) the achieved earning progression of each individual, along with the level-of-work bracket of the role he occupies.

3) Let the manager-once-removed (that is, the individual's manager's manager) determine a potential progress assessment (PPA) for each person on the basis of performance or work history, and express this as a progression curve on the Earning Progression Data Sheet. This establishes the baseline against which performance will be reviewed.

4) During the performance review period, adjust individual payment as necessary should there be upward movement in the wages index.

5) Independently of these wage index adjustments, let the immediate manager assess the individual's performance in his work during the period under review:

  a) if he judges his performance to have shown that he has worked at full capacity and at full stretch, then let his wage or salary be maintained at or brought to that level called for by his PPA;

  b) if his actual performance is judged to have fallen short of his potential, then let his wage or salary be placed at a level correspondingly lower than the level called for by his PPA.

6) If the continued performance of the individual gives evidence that his PPA has been pitched too high or too low, then let the manager-once-removed alter his assessment in accord with the more comprehensive information and experience available.

7) If at any time, in response to a call for a spurt or special individual effort, an individual works beyond his normal pace and application, then let him be paid an *ex gratia* or bonus payment over and above his wage or salary at the time the spurt is made.

8) If the level of work in the role is undergoing permanent, authorized change, then let the manager-once-removed sanction this change, record it, and alter the payment bracket accordingly.

9) If the level of capacity of an individual is too high or too low for the level of work in his role, consider whether to pay above or below the bracket, or whether it is possible to adjust the work in the role to match the individual—while still conforming to the demands of the work situation— before deciding to remove the individual from the role or to indicate to him that further progress would require a change of role.

10) In the case of a change in the PPA of an individual, or a change in the level of work in his role, the type of alteration and its implications for his progress and career future should be considered and discussed with him.

If managers are capable of doing their job of assessing the performance of their subordinates, the standard payment and progression method ensures the rewarding of those persons within a common frame of reference, yet permitting the recognition of individual differences. For example, due weight can be given to differences in age: if an older man and a younger man have demonstrated equal performance, a common tendency is to give the same size increase to each— overlooking the fact that the younger man is usually increasing his performance (and hence capacity) at a more rapid rate, and, therefore, requires a correspondingly increased rate of progress. This distinction between an achieved quantum of performance at a given point in time and the *rate* of performance improvement over time is often overlooked or simply not realized, yet the distinction must be as clearly made as between the concepts of speed and acceleration in physics.

The sensitivity of the earning progression array to age can be seen by reference to individual differences in the progression curves of persons at, say, twenty-eight and thirty-two years of age, with both working in roles at the one-year time-span level. It is essential that managers have a differentiated picture of the age and normal expected rate of development of all their subordinates; otherwise, they could easily assume that their two employees were displaying equal potential as a result of equal performances. Other things being equal, the standard payment and progression method would assume, on the other hand, that the twenty-eight year-old very likely would be the one with the greater capacity-growth potential.

As a result of the implementation of a systematic policy such as I am advocating, the use of methods of control which make use of artificial, stereotyped and irrationally generalized criteria may be avoided. Among these artificial criteria is the use of automatic annual increments that progress all individuals through a given bracket at the same predetermined rate, regardless of the age at which each particular person entered the job and his demonstrated rate of progress in performing work assignments. I would include, also, those intuitive references to "market values" or "the rate for the job" by which increases are so often justified. Also avoided is the common procedure where an individual is progressed in his salary bracket until he reaches his so-called level, and then tapered off. In my experience, this practice very often does a particular disservice to higher potential personnel. A man reaches, say, a general manager at £5,500 per annum position at the age of forty-eight. If the employing firm regards this as his "true level," he is essentially carried at that salary level with occasional increases that just keep him in pace with increases in the cost of living. The findings I have described lead to a quite different conclusion; namely, that such a person, assuming he is successfully performing the work at £5,500 per annum level, will continue to grow in capacity and performance, and that this growth should be recognized in position and salary progression. I would expect that, given normal development, such a person as I've used in the example is quite likely to progress to one further stratum in capacity and to seek promotion to work of that level.

Realistic and practical assessment and planning for the individual employee and manpower planning for the enterprise both become possible when progression is systematically considered as I have suggested. The adjectives "realistic" and "practical" are used to indicate that I am not here speaking of vocational guidance, as we usually consider the term with its emphasis on valued outcomes for the individual. Rather, career assessemnt, in the terms I have been using it, is as much a practical necessity for the employer as it is for the employee. It is the necessary foundation for the maximum return to both parties—in essence, the key to a type of manpower planning that can serve the economic needs of the enterprise and the psycho-economic needs of the individual.

There are certain minimum organizational requirements that must be met, however, before the standard payment and progression method can be used, and its goal of maximum return to the firm and the individual realized. In order to describe these requirements, I must first briefly review my observations of the structure of the executive organization concerning payment and progress that are prerequisite to the probability of achieving differentially valued outcomes to individuals and business enterprises.

The manager in charge of a role allocates work into it, but it is the manager-once-removed who authorizes such an allocation. A similar and dependent principle can be seen at work in the case of the assessment and progress of subordinates. It is the manager who assigns work to his subordinate, relies upon him to carry out the work, and who reviews the quality of his work. He is in the best position to assess the subordinate's performance and actual achievement and his potential capacity for doing the work assigned to him. The direct manager is not in a satisfactory position, however, to assess his subordinate's potential for progress to higher levels of work, since usually that higher level is the manager's own. It would be unrealistic, in general, to rely on a manager to be able to assess the potential capacity of a subordinate to do work at his own level, although no doubt there exists the rare manager capable of doing so.

If we now move up to the level of the manager-once-removed, a different type of responsibility emerges in connection with the potential progress of subordinates. While he is as directly responsible for assessing the accomplishment of his own direct subordinates as they are with theirs, with regard to the manager's subordinates at one level removed, he is much more concerned with their potential. He is the one who sets policy or limits within which "subordinates-once-removed" are appointed and progressed in order to provide for future manpower requirements within his own direct command. His direct managerial subordinates simply cannot carry that responsibility.

Against this background, then, responsibilities for rewarding current accomplishment rest with the immediate superior, while those for assessing potential rest with the manager-once-removed. The manager-once-removed is responsible for deciding the potential progress assessment (PPA) of individual subordinates "once-removed." Once established, this PPA becomes the baseline against which the subordinate's *immediate* manager constructs his evaluation of that subordinate's actual performance and suitably rewards him.

These organization notions are embedded in the standard payment and progression method outlined earlier.

The organization and manning work necessary for the application of the standard payment and progression method may seem to be highly specialized and somewhat at odds with the usual role undertaken by the personnel function in industry. It requires the conducting of level-of-work analysis and job specification based on the time-span concept; the maintenance of earning progression data and their analysis and interpretation; and assisting in the appraisal of individuals for purposes of establishing their potential progress assessment. Under this formulation the personnel function is a specialist role accountable for assisting the operational manager in maintaining an efficiently deployed, executive organization and in keeping it effectively manned. It is through intimate participation with the operational manager in the planning and coordination of the on-going work task that the organization and manning personnel specialist keeps contact with the executive organization. Therefore, when a personnel requisition reaches him, he is in possession of knowledge about the organizational situation. He has his on-going specialist assessment to call upon in deciding whether the requisition is a straight-forward matter or whether there are accumulating or forthcoming changes in the work situation which call for him to get in touch with the requisitioning manager and review with him any necessary modifications in organization.

The personnel specialist is also in a position to keep abreast of the structure of payment throughout his manager's command because of his knowledge of the current work content of roles in that command. He knows of required changes in payment because of his direct involvement in work planning and his resulting knowledge of change in the work content of roles. Payment brackets for jobs can, thus, be modified on managerial initiative whenever permanent changes in work have occurred of sufficient size to be reflected in a change in the bracket. The personnel specialist thereby assists his manager to assume genuine managerial leadership in connection with the payment structure, rather than waiting for initiative to come from below in the form of piled-up grievances and complaints.

The manning of roles follows from the deep involvement with his manager's work task, and the organization of the work system to carry out that task. In the first place, jobs are specified in terms of the targets or objectives of the work, and the discretionary and prescribed responsibilities to be carried in reaching those objectives. Such a specification points up both the formal knowledge required for the work (expressed in the prescribed content) and the kind of experience and interest needed (in order to exercise the discretion called for). Application of the standard progression method then puts the personnel specialist in possession of systematic information about the progress of individuals in their roles and the potential rate of change of personnel, and lays the basis for the development of systematic man-power plans. Any other activities of a personnel specialist grow requisitely out of these central responsibilities.

This formulation of personnel work may at first appear to have less "human relations" in it than the usual description of the function. The opposite, I would strongly hold, is in fact the case. Genuinely good human relations and individual welfare in work organizations arise from recognizing the reality of the work contract—that is to say, the reality of the fact that each individual's relation to the enterprise is founded on his contracting to do the work in exchange for payment. If the enterprise organizes requisitely, fills its jobs soundly, pays equitably, and progresses its individual members on a systematic basis and in accord with performance, then the basis is laid for serving the needs of both the enterprise and the individual. If this basis is soundly constructed, good working relationships are encouraged, and individual satisfaction may be heightened. The responsibility in the organization and manning type of personnel work referred to here gives the specialist assistance in helping keep such a state of affairs in being.

In conclusion, it may strike you as unusual that I have not used the word "motivation" at all in the presentation of my work at the Glacier Metals Company and elsewhere. Very honestly, "motivation" is a construct that I have not found to be independent of the work, capacity, and payment nexus that has been at the heart of the empirical work that has occupied the fifteen or so years of my intense involvement with employees and their superiors in the industrial work environment. My interest has not been to directly investigate motivation as such, but rather has been focused, as a social-analytic consultant, on the investigation and resolution of actual problems—not as derived from the desire to support or reject any existing theoretical construct— but rather from the point of view of those individuals directly involved in carrying out employment work. Now if we define motivation as the activation, direction, and maintenance of behavior, then I would conclude that the inter-related work, capacity, and payment formulation provides a framework within which to explore the motivational process. We have been discussing the relationship between motivation and pay, but my feeling is we have not fully recognized the role of what I have called "capacity"—the individual-difference variable of maximum importance in any consideration of the relationship between the worker and his work. Rather it is the role of pay, ceteris paribus, that has been studied most intensively. Differential capacity, however, is the weakness in the ceteris paribus assumptions. This is not to say that pay is an unimportant variable, but simply that its effects cannot be studied without the establishment of an individualistic behavioral baseline, taken in concert with the motivational content of work itself. This is particularly true in the investigation of pay as an incentive. The simplified notion that the offering of more pay ensures the expenditure of greater human work effort begs the question of whether or not a given individual has the capacity to produce more effort, even if he were wont to do so. The emphasis in the motivational literature has been on this latter point—a person's desire, with all too little work being done on the question of his capacity.

The work I have been involved with in industry leads to a somewhat different systematic formulation of the nature of incentives in work. It is simply this—we each do our best at our work when we are carrying out work which interests us, under conditions of dynamic equilibrium between our level of work, our capacity, and our payment. To use the symbols employed earlier, I am referring to a dynamic equilibrium between C = W followed by pay (P). It is the relationship between capacity and level of work that is crucial and primary; not the relationship between work and pay, with differential capacity either assumed to be equal or ignored. An optimum "incentive system" is, therefore, one in which there are mechanisms for facilitating the movement and progress of individuals in line with *both* their interests and level of capacity; for paying in accord with perceived equity in the C = W sense; and for ensuring the continuous availability and allocation of the quantity of work that is expected to be done for the success of the business enterprise.

Important to the understanding of the nature of incentives in the formulation presented, is the definition of what is meant by the term "incentive." The typical use of the term has debased its value by attaching to it the meaning of "encouragement to work at some abnormally fast pace." I am reminded of the classic admonition to anglers to "fish faster." Even though this crude conception of employees working physiologically faster and faster may not be universally held, it is nevertheless a sufficiently widespread caricature of the truth to be worth getting out of the way.

In order to get at the question of "rate of work" (or activity) in the usual sense, we must first distinguish between a person's rate of work, referring to his physiological pace and his rate of work referring to the amount of work he turns out, that is, his output. In order to avoid any possibility of confusion, I shall use the terms "physiological pace" and "quantity of output," and shall not use the phrase "rate of work" at all. Further, it is essential that we distinguish clearly and unequivocally between "physiological pace," "intensity of physical and mental concentration," and "level of capacity." Physiological pace refers to the actual rate of movement in work—for example, the distinction between walking slowly, walking quickly, and running. Intensity of physical and mental concentration refers to the degree of application to the job. It includes the continuity of thinking about it, and the continuity of physical application, with minimum interruption for thoughts about other things or through minor unnecessary absences from the job during the working day. Level of capacity, on the other hand, refers to the capability—the physiological and mental skill and ability—necessary to carry higher or lower levels of work.

All these three factors—pace, application, and capacity—combine to determine the quantity and quality of a person's work. The important thing to note, however, is that none of the factors can be readily influenced by outside conditions as may often be thought to be the case. In particular, intensive experience on the shop floor has led me to the conclusion that we each have a normal pace of work which we cannot easily depart from—either by slowing down or by speeding up—for any appreciable length of time. The level of capacity we exercise remains relatively fixed unless affected by some kind of emotional disturbance—it being impossible to exercise more than the capacity we possess, and difficult to purposely exercise continuously less.

Intensity of mental and physical application, however, is probably rather more influenced by external circumstances than is either of the other two factors. Nevertheless, it is important to note that we each appear to have a normal level of intensity of application. The effect of outside conditions is to interfere with our normal concentration —to disturb or inhibit it— rather than to spur us on to maintain an intensity of application at a level above our norm. The same inhibitory effect is true also for physiological pace.

In short, we each have our normal level of output in work, determined by our normal pace, concentration, and capacity. External
conditions may pull us down from our normal output, mainly by
disturbing our inner state of mind and interfering with our physiological pace and our intensity of physical and mental concentration
on the job. The importance of external conditions—so-called incentives—then, is to facilitate the expression of normal pace, concentration, and capacity in work and to prevent interference with that
expression.

Over and above the continuous expression of normal pace, concentration, and capacity, it is possible for individuals to achieve above-
normal rates of output in work, but only for very short periods of
time. Everyone will have experienced such spurts or bursts of special
effort, but these cannot be maintained for more than a few days at
a time—perhaps longer in exceptional circumstances—without fatigue
and slowing up. Overall, then, the notion that incentive systems can
encourage individuals to maintain such spurts continuously in the
normal course of their work is, in my mind, a fallacy.

My line of argument may seem to be contradicted by the fact
that two different individuals doing the same kind of work (let us
assume that analysis and measurement have shown the jobs to be
identical) may differ considerably in the amount of work of a given
quality that they continue to turn out. Such differences, while easily
enough demonstrated, cannot, however, be simply interpreted as
showing that one must necessarily be working harder than the
other—in the sense of putting "more effort into it" or working at a
faster physiological pace. If the difference should persist, then I
would put forward the notion that the main factor causing the difference is likely to be a difference in their levels of capacity. This follows from my model, which implies that given a level of work consistent with capacity, and equivalence of interest and experience, two
persons of the same capacity will continue to turn out the same
amount of work of given quality. In my experience, this factor of
individual differences in level of capacity must be given serious
consideration as the chief factor determining differences in output
before any conclusions can be drawn as to possible differences in
physiological pace or intensity of concentration—often referred to as
differences in "motivation." Overall, then, this formulation of the
nature of incentives in work implies that "doing our best at our
work" is the application of our normal physiological work pace, our
normal intensity of physical and mental concentration, and our

capacity—with the recognition that special effort or spurts in work output are possible from time to time in order to cope with emergencies of one kind or another that might arise. This is the approach to motivation to work that has served me well in my social-analytic work. While I have been continually sensitive to studies with differing points of view in the field of motivation, I have not found them to provide sufficient breadth nor depth to cope with individualistic human behavior such as I have witnessed, studied, and been embroiled in within industry over the past years. The model of dynamic equilibrium between level of work, capacity, and pay, on the other hand, has proven of sufficient heuristic and explanatory value for me not to be coaxed or led into the utilization of other formulations.

Finally, it is my hope that the findings I have presented and the speculations built upon these findings may contribute to a more orderly and objective way of dealing with the disordered state of industrial relations, differential payment, and the employment of individual talent. In viewing man in his work in society, it seems to me that to the employing enterprise goes the responsibility for pursuing its economic aims with realism and creative initiative. It must be requisitely organized and manned in such a manner that an effective organization may be achieved. It must know its work sufficiently well to maintain an explicit appreciation of the level-of-work brackets for its various roles by reference to level-of-work measurement of baselines. It must administer equitable payment brackets for the level-of-work brackets in those roles. Further, to the employing organization falls the responsibility for taking the initiative in progressing its members at a rate consistent with their performance and capacity, within the limits of the work it has available, recognizing that no employing organization can hope to guarantee having just the right role at just the right time to satisfy the growing capacity and interests of every one of its employees. The individual firm should be charged, however, with helping people for whom it cannot provide adequate opportunities for progress to find appropriate jobs in other firms.

It is this responsibility for payment and progress that resolves the problem of managerial leadership I touched upon earlier. It is the manager's responsibility to know his subordinates and the work allocated to them. The equitable work-payment scale then gives him the baseline referent needed for determining fair payment for work. Initiative and responsibility for ensuring fair payment and appropriate progress thus become an integral part of the leadership situation in managing subordinates. They are an essential part of establishing and maintaining an efficient organization over time.

To the individual falls the responsibility for deciding on his career and training. He must choose which work he wants to do and seek out the training relevant to that work. He must seek appropriate opportunities at change points in his career. When, for example, he reaches the limit of potential for progress in his current role, he must decide which new line to try to follow. Finally, of course, he must discharge his responsibilities in his job.

In conclusion, the nation and the enterprise should be responsible for maintaining the external conditions necessary for effective work and progress of individuals. The individual, on the other hand, must direct his own use of these conditions in following the career he chooses and deploy his capacity in fulfilling his work obligations. It is only within this meaningful interaction between the individual, his work, and his society that economic and social justice lies for all of mankind.

PART THREE

Critiques

One of the dangers that a theorist faces when he puts forth a position is the analysis of his propositions by others. As is often the case, critical analysis finds most theories lacking in something of importance.

In this section we turn to those who have presented some critical considerations of the ideas offered in the preceding section. These critiques deal with a methodology used to arrive at the formulation, as is the case with the analysis of the Hawthorne study, or with questions about the construction of concepts, such as Weick's questions on how equity ratios are computed by individuals. So, the theoretical propositions of Part Two have some limitations. In this section, it is hoped that these limitations will be made more explicit. The "classical management" linkage of incentives to performance is examined by Filley and House. Their main point, after an extensive review of research dealing with performance and incentives, is that the "classical theory . . . fails to specify some important considerations which affect motivation to work." This, of course, has been the major criticism of others and was given force by the Hawthorne research. Roethlisberger and Dickson conclude that none of their results give "the slightest substantiation to the theory that the worker is motivated primarily by economic interests." Carey, however, in an incisive analysis of the Hawthorne studies argues to the contrary. He concludes that the data rather support the "old world view about the value of monetary incentives, driving leadership, and discipline."

Filley and House, in a review of literature on needs theory, find that it is fairly consistent with the more complex motivational struc-

207

tures implied in the Hawthorne research. They suggest, however, that care should be taken in the interpretation of research using the Maslow formulation as a base due to the possible sensitivity of the results to a research bias.

Locke directs his criticism of Atkinson primarily at the manner in which Atkinson conceptualizes the relationship between "probability of success" and "incentive value." Locke argues for the need for further research to resolve this problem. Of course, Locke has his own theoretical structure, which he proposes. Dobmeyer, in his paper, deals with some of the limitations he finds in Locke's "incomplete" theory and raises questions about the conceptual nature of Locke's work. He also deals with the nature of Locke's criticism of Atkinson and how the two authors differ in the manner in which they relate the variables of goal difficulty and performance.

House and Wahba discuss the research and implications of the instrumentality approach. They point out that even with the difficulties, it appears to have some promise as a predictive approach.

Weick points to the major problems implicit in the equity theory. "It seems," he says, "sufficiently relevant that it deserves and requires more scrutiny; but it . . . may be relevant to a more limited range of problems than investigations have realized and the limiting conditions should be studied."

In considering Jaques' work on equitable payment, Gordon argues that some of the hypothesized relationships appear to be inconsistent. Nevertheless, he concludes that the work represents a "first approximation to a general program of research on pay . . . (and highlights) . . . a number of important, fundamental issues which investigators who research pay must ultimately resolve."

11

Some Empirical Evidence
About Classical Theory

ALAN C. FILLEY

AND

ROBERT J. HOUSE

Organizational members are primarily motivated by opportunities for economic gain, and therefore are induced to perform better by conditions where such gain is a direct result of increased productivity.

Taylor produced some empirical evidence in support of the classical theory (Proposition 1). For example, at the Bethlehem Steel Company, he was able to increase the average number of tons handled per man per day from 16 to 59, reducing the average cost of handling a ton from 7.2 cents to 3.3 cents—even though average daily earnings per man increased from $1.15 to $1.88. He and other members of the scientific management school cite many similar examples (Taylor, 1919).

Not all the fantastic increases in productivity that grew out of the application of Taylor's ideas were due to the financial incentive system he developed, nor did he claim they were. Much of the increase was due to improved work methods. But he did believe that the motivation provided by the extra money made it possible to get the men both to accept the new methods and to put forth their best effort.

Many managers still agree with Taylor about motivation. In 1947, the Opinion Research Corporation asked 50 manufacturing executives what they considered of importance in gaining worker productivity. Forty-four percent replied without qualification that "money alone is the answer." And a study by Mahoney (1964) of managers in three

Reprinted by permission of the authors and publisher from *Managerial Process and Organizational Behavior*, by A. C. Filley and R. J. House, pp. 368-73. Chicago, Illinois: Scott, Foresman and Company, © 1969.

different large corporations revealed an overwhelming preference for salary compensation rather than nonsalary rewards. This preference seemed relatively uniform, regardless of variations in personal characteristics, level of responsibility, or salary and income levels.

Wage Incentive Plans. A number of different types of wage incentive systems have been developed to provide the money motivator, and many of them have been used in a large number of industrial settings. Some of the major ones are:

1) *Piecework:* The worker is paid a given amount for each piece produced.
2) *Task bonus:* The worker is paid an established hourly rate, and receives a bonus if he completes a task in or under a computed standard time.
3) *Point incentive:* Tasks are rated in points based on standard time units, and the worker receives bonuses for points above a specified number accrued in a given time period.
4) *Group Incentive:* Each worker receives a bonus for increased output by his group.
5) *Scanlon plan:* Target norms are set, and the worker is paid a bonus for performance exceeding the norm.
6) *Profit sharing:* The worker receives a share of the company profits.

A number of surveys show that increases in productivity have followed the introduction of wage incentive plans.

One of the earliest field experiments on the role of money in motivating workers was made by Wyatt (1934), who studied ten 15- to 16-year-old girls employed in a chocolate manufacturing plant. The girls worked in a special experimental room, were given five repetitive tasks connected with packaging the product, and were paid according to different systems during different periods: (1) by fixed weekly wages (time rate) for 9 weeks; (2) by a competitive bonus wage (bonus rate) for 15 weeks; and (3) by a flat piece rate for 12 weeks.

Performance time was the criterion used to determine productivity; by this measure, productivity increased 46 per cent immediately on introduction of the bonus rate. When the piece-rate plan was introduced, production went up another 30 per cent. When the time rate was reintroduced, output dropped. The investigators observed that the girls themselves regarded the piece rate as the fairest compensation method; while it was in effect, the girls were less talkative, fewer instances of troublesome conduct occurred, and both frequency and duration of stoppages were reduced.

A government survey of 514 wage incentive plans in the United States revealed that production increased on the average 38.99 per cent, labor costs decreased on the average 11.58 per cent, and the workers' take-home pay increased on the average 17.58 per cent; other surveys show much the same results (Viteles, 1954; Lynton, 1949).

Viteles (1954) reviewed the evidence in detail and concluded that wage incentives do substantially improve productivity, but that industrial surveys and case studies are inadequate for determining their exact effect on motivation. Generally, the introduction of an incentive system, or a change in an existing system, is accompanied by changes in facilities, work methods, and organization. Consequently, as Viteles observes, it is difficult to separate the effect of incentive plans from other changes in the workers' environment.

There is evidence from laboratory experiments that when all other influences are held constant, individuals who are not self-motivated toward high levels of achievement (those scoring low on measures of need for achievement) will achieve higher levels of task performance when they are told they will receive financial rewards for good performance. However, the offer of increased monetary rewards contingent on task performance was found to have a detrimental effect on persons who are intrinsically motivated (those who scored high in need-for-achievement measures). For example, McClelland (1961) reports on three studies which led him to conclude that those high in need for achievement are not influenced much by monetary rewards, but rather by achievement. Those with low achievement needs tend to be more influenced by money and "can be made to work harder for money or other such external incentives."

Although there seems to be little question that incentive programs frequently result in greater productivity, the effect of both individual and group plans have been shown to vary with such factors as the attitudes and background of employees, the nature of the task performed, informal work norms, and the size of the work group.

Employe Attitudes and Background. Not all workers consider the opportunity to make financial gain to be of paramount importance. For example, Georgopoulous, *et al.* (1957) found that workers who expect productivity to result in long-run financial gain are more inclined to be high producers than those who feel that productivity is either not related to, or inhibits the attainment of money. And they also found that workers who expect increased productivity to result in greater acceptance by co-workers are more likely to be high producers than those who think productivity unrelated to, or an inhibiting factor in gaining co-worker acceptance. Some workers ranked opportunities for economic gain high in importance; others viewed social consequences as more important.

Dalton (1948) compared the personality characteristics of "restricters" and the "ratebusters." Twenty-two of the 25 restricters were Democrats. They were generally sons of unskilled industrial workers, had grown up in large cities, and had been active in boys' games. In contrast, eight of the nine ratebusters were Republicans, and had typically grown up either on farms or in urban lower-middle class families. The restricters led an active social life, both inside and outside the work situation, and were described as "living in the present," spending money freely on themselves and on others while socializing. On the other hand, the ratebusters tended to be social isolates inside and outside the work situation. They were described as shunning social activities that cost money, seeking instead to build up their savings or to invest in property of recognized market value.

Nature of Task. Depending on the nature of the work, wage incentive systems can have dysfunctional consequences. Babchuck and Goode (1951) report that an individual incentive payment system for selling in a department store caused employes to neglect stock work and display arrangements. Employe morale declined, and the group finally replaced the competitive incentive system with an informal cooperative system of pooling. Stock work was equally distributed, quotas were set, and sales were shared among group members so that each person would receive an equal paycheck at the end of the week, regardless of individual cash-register readings.

This study demonstrates that group incentive plans are more effective than individual plans when tasks are highly interdependent, and require cooperation among group members, or when it is impossible to obtain comprehensive and meaningful measures of individual performance.

Informal Work Norms. Wage incentive plans often fail because they run counter to informal work norms. Studies by Mathewson (1931), Roethlisberger and Dickson (1939), Collins, *et al.* (1946), Roy (1952), and Viteles (1954) show that wage incentive plans may actually encourage restriction of output. Frequently the members of the work group informally establish norms of individual output, which may work for or against the purposes of the organization, depending on whether or not the prevailing attitude in the group is in sympathy with organizational objectives. When a work group is cohesive, its influence is strong (Schachter, *et al.,* 1951; Seashore, 1954). This strength may be exerted for or against organizational purpose. As Roethlisberger and Dickson (1939) state: "In [one case], there was an informal organization which could be characterized better as a set of practices and beliefs which had many points working against the economic purposes of the company" (pp. 560-61).

Taylor (1919) was well aware of the influence of a work group on the outcome of wage incentive systems. He relates an instance he experienced as a supervisor at Midvale Steel Company in 1878, during which the workers in his work group told him that they did not expect him to deviate largely from the piece rates which they felt were appropriate. They threatened to throw him "over the fence" if he did.

Taylor went on to say that if anyone going against the work group had been one of the workmen, and had lived where they lived, they would have brought such social pressure to bear upon him that it would have been impossible to have stood up against them. "He would have been called 'scab' and other foul names every time he appeared on the street, his wife would have been abused, and his children would have been stoned" (p. 51).

Such incidents are not uncommon. Informal work groups can exert considerable influence on the individual employe to prevent him from producing more than the norm set by the group, even though he could easily do so and earn more money. Two important reasons given by group members for exerting pressure for a low rate of production are the fear that a high level of performance will result in a tightening of rates (Whyte, 1955; Hickson, 1961) and the fear of unemployment (Roethlisberger and Dickson, 1939; Mathewson, 1931).

Group Size. If an incentive system is based on group rather than individual performance, the size of the work group is an important consideration. Both Marriott (1949) and Campbell (1952) found that group incentives are more effective for small groups than for large groups. Marriott (1949) found that the mean level of individual performance decreases as group size increases, under both the group piece rate plan and a group bonus plan.

Campbell studied the effect of incentives in two factories. His interviews revealed that the greater the number of workers in the work group, the less the workers understood the group incentive system employed, and the less satisfied they were with the method of compensation. Also, records disclosed that members of large groups were less productive than members of small groups. Other studies of the relationship between group size and wage incentive plans are consistent with these findings (Marriott, 1951; Marriott and Denerley, 1955).

From findings relevant to the effect of individual and group wage incentive systems it seems apparent that money is an important work incentive, but that the classical theory of motivation to work fails to specify other important considerations that affect individual motivation to work.

12

The Hawthorne Studies:
A Radical Criticism

ALEX CAREY

There can be few scientific disciplines or fields of research in which a single set of studies or a single researcher and writer has exercised so great an influence as was exercised for a quarter of a century by Mayo and the Hawthorne studies. Although this influence has declined in the last ten years as a result of the widespread failure of later studies to reveal any reliable relation between the social satisfactions of industrial workers and their work performance, reputable textbooks still refer almost reverentially to the Hawthorne studies as a classic in the history of social science in industry.

One might have expected therefore that the Hawthorne studies would have been subjected to the most searching and skeptical scrutiny; that before the remarkable claims of these studies, especially about the relative unimportance of financial rewards compared with purely social rewards, became so widely influential, the quality of the evidence produced and the validity of the inferences from it would have been meticulously examined and assessed. There have been broad criticisms of Mayo's approach and assumptions, many of them cogent. They include charges of pro-management bias, clinical bias, and scientific naiveté.[1] But no one has applied systematically and in detail the method of critical doubt to the claim that there is scientific worth in the original reports of the Hawthorne investigators.

Reprinted by permission of the author and publisher from *American Sociological Review* 33 (1968):403-416.

BACKGROUND

The Hawthorne studies comprise a long series of investigations into the importance for work behavior and attitudes of a variety of physical, economic, and social variables. The principal investigations were carried out between 1927 and 1932, whereafter economic depression caused their suspension. The component studies may be distinguished as five stages:

Stage   I: The Relay Assembly Test Room Study. (New incentive system and new supervision).

Stage   II: The Second Relay Assembly Group Study. (New incentive system only).

Stage III: The Mica Splitting Test Room Study. (New supervision only).

Stage   IV: The Interviewing Program

Stage   V: The Bank-Wiring Observation Room Study.

Stages I to III constitute a series of partially controlled studies which were initially intended to explore the effects on work behavior of variations in physical conditions of work, especially variations in rest pauses and in hours of work, but also in payment system, temperature, humidity, etc.

However, after the studies had been in progress for at least twelve months the investigators came to the entirely unanticipated conclusion that social satisfactions arising out of human association in work were more important determinants of work behavior in general and output in particular than were any of the physical and economic aspects of the work situation to which their attention had originally been limited.[2] This conclusion came as "the great *éclaircissement* . . . an illumination quite different from what they had expected from the illumination studies."[3] It is the central and distinctive finding from which the fame and influence of the Hawthorne studies derive.

This "éclaircissement" about the predominant importance of social satisfactions at work occurred during Stage I of the studies. In consequence, all the later studies are in important ways subordinate to Stage I: "It was the origin from which all the subsequent phases sprang. It was also their main focal point. It gave to these other phases their significance in relation to the whole enquiry."[4]

Stages II and III were "designed to check on" (and were taken to supplement and confirm) the Stage I conclusion "that the observed production increase was a result of a change in the *social situation* . . . (and) not primarily because of wage incentives, reduced fatigue or similar factors."[5] *Stage IV* was an interviewing program undertaken to explore worker attitudes. *Stage V* was a study of informal group organization in the work situation.

The two later studies (IV and V) resulted directly from conclusions based on Stages I-III about the superior influence of social needs. Observations made in both were interpreted in the light of such prior conclusions. Hence it is clear that, as maintained by Urwick, Stage I was the key study, with Stages II and III adding more or less substantial support to it. The present paper will therefore be limited to a consideration of the evidence produced in Stages I-III for the famous Hawthorne conclusions about the superior importance for work behavior of social needs and satisfactions.

THE PREFERRED INCENTIVE SYSTEM AND OUTPUT

Stage I: Relay Assembly Test Room (new incentive and new supervision). In Stage I of the Hawthorne studies, five girls who were employed assembling telephone relays were transferred from the factory floor to a special test room. Here their output of relays was recorded for over two years during which a large number of alterations were made in their working conditions. These alterations included a much less variable assembly task,[6] shorter hours, rest pauses, freer and more friendly supervision, and a preferred incentive system.[7] These changes were introduced cumulatively and no control group was established. Nonetheless, it was originally expected that the study would yield information about the influence of one or another physical condition of work.[8]

At the end of two years, the girls' output had increased by about 30 percent.[9] By this time, the investigators were confident that the physical changes in work conditions had been of little importance, and that the observed increase was due primarily to a change in "mental attitude" of the employees resulting from changed methods of supervision.[10] This change in mental attitude was chiefly characterized by a more relaxed "relationship of confidence and friendliness . . . such . . . that practically no supervision is required."[11]

However, the standard report of the study recognizes that any of several changes introduced concurrently could, hypothetically, have caused both the observed change in mental outlook and the associated increase in output. The authors of the report list the following as pro-

viding possible "hypotheses to explain major changes" in work behavior:[12] (i) changes in the character and physical context of the work
task; (ii) reduction of fatigue and monotony consequent upon introduction of rest pauses and reduced hours of work;[13] (iii) change in the
payment system; and (iv) changes in supervision with consequent
social changes in group relations.

The remainder of this paper will critically examine the evidence and
arguments from which the investigators reached conclusions favorable
to the last of these alternative hypotheses.

First hypothesis: changes in work task and physical context. The investigators allow that "the fact that most of the girls in the test room
had to assemble fewer types of relays could not be entirely ignored.
Operator 5's performance offered a convincing example. Of all the girls
in the room she had had more different types of relays to assemble and
of all the girls her output rate had shown the least improvement."[14]
Whitehead reports that "later (1930-31) her (Operator 5's) working
conditions were in line with the rest of the group and her comparative
standing in the group definitely improved."[15]

However, it was subsequently found that statistical analysis of the
relevant data (i.e., the varying output of five girls who were subjected
to numerous cumulatively introduced experimental changes) did not
show "any *conclusive* evidence in favor of the first hypothesis." On this
ground the investigators "concluded that the change from one type of
relay to another familiar type did not sufficiently slow up output to explain the increased output of the relay test room assemblers as compared with the assemblers in the regular department."[16] This conclusion leads the investigators to dismiss from further consideration the
possibility that changes in task and conditions played any part at all in
the observed increase in output.[17]

*Second hypothesis: reduced fatigue due to rest pauses and shorter
hours.* The investigators recognize that "the rest pauses and shorter
hours (may have) provided a relief from cumulative fatigue" resulting in
higher output. They acknowledge that the fact that the rate of output of
all but the slowest worker declined once the girls were returned to
standard hours is "rather convincing evidence in favor of this
argument."[18] Yet the investigators eventually dismiss these factors on
the grounds that under the new conditions of work neither work curves
nor medical examinations provided evidence that fatigue effects were
present. Viteles has commented bluntly in this connection: "It is interesting to note that (these grounds) are exactly the same used by other

investigators in illustrating the effectiveness of rest pauses *by reason of reduced fatigue."*[19]

By these arguments, the investigators eliminated the first two of the four hypotheses originally proposed as alternative explanations of the 30 percent increase in output observed in Stage I. This left two contending "explanations," the new incentive system, and the new kind of supervision and related social factors. The problem of choosing between these explanations led directly to the next two major experiments.

Stage II: Second Relay Assembly Group (new incentive system only). "The aim of (this experiment) was to reproduce the test-room situation (i.e., Stage I) only in respect to the one factor of method of payment, using another group of operators. Since method of payment was to be the only alteration from the usual situation, it was thought that any marked changes in output could be reasonably related to this factor."[20]

Five girls who were employed on the same sort of task as the girls in Stage I under normal conditions on the factory floor were given the preferred incentive system which had been used throughout Stage I. Under this system, the earnings of each girl were based on the average output of the five. Under the regular payment system, the earnings of each girl were based on the average output of the whole department (i.e., about 100 girls).

Almost at once the Stage II girls' output increased by 12.6 percent.[21] But the experiment caused so much discontent among the rest of the girls in the department, who wanted the same payment conditions,[22] that it was discontinued after only nine weeks. The output of the five girls promptly dropped by 16 percent.[23]

As Viteles comments, "the increase in output during the period when the wage incentive was in effect, followed by a production decrease with the elimination of the wage incentive, represents evidence ordinarily interpreted as indicative of the direct and favorable influence of financial incentives upon output."[24] However, the investigators reject this interpretation and, without producing supporting evidence of any substance, conclude firmly[25] that the increase was due to intergroup rivalry resulting from the setting up of this second small group.

The change in payment system alone (Stage II) produced as much increase in output in nine weeks (possibly five weeks[26]) as was produced in about nine months by a change in payment system together with a change to genial supervision (Stage I).[27] Yet, this comparison appears not to have made any impression on the investigators' confidence about the superior importance of social factors.[28]

Stage III: Mica Splitting Test Room (new supervision but no change in payment system). In *Stage I,* numerous changes had been introduced, resulting in a 30 percent increase in output, in *Stage II,* only one of these changes (the preferred incentive system) was introduced and a rapid 12 percent increase in output resulted. In *Stage III,* "the test-room situation was to be duplicated in all respects except for the change in pay incentive. If . . . output showed a trend similar to that noted in (Stage I), it would suggest that the wage incentive was not the dominant factor in the situation."[29] Stage III, then, sought to test the combined effect on output of change to a separate room, change in hours, and the introduction of rest pauses and friendly supervision. Again a selected group of five girls was closely studied and an increase in output was recorded—15.6 percent in fourteen months[30] or, if one follows Pennock, 20 percent in twelve months.[31]

A comparison between Stage III and Stage I has little prospect of scientific usefulness since in Stage III (i) the incentive system was different from both the disliked system used at the beginning of Stage I and the preferred system introduced shortly afterwards, (ii) the type of work was quite different from Stage I, and (iii) the experimental changes were quite different.[32] However, it is this comparison which has been taken by reporters of the studies[33] and by textbook authors[34] to provide the principal experimental evidence about the relative importance of financial and social motives as influences on output. Assuming with Roethlisberger and Dickson that Stage I and Stage III have some minimum comparability, it is important to examine precisely how the investigators dealt with the evidence from these stages for the purpose of the comparison.

Comparison Between Results in Stages I, II, and III. (i) Stage III produced a claimed 15 percent increase in rate of output over fourteen months. Thereafter the group's average rate of output declined for twelve months before the study was terminated due to the depression and lay-offs. The investigators attribute this decline *entirely* to anxieties induced by the depression,[35] ignoring the possibility that the preceding increase might also have been influenced by changing general economic and employment conditions. They do this despite evidence that output among a group of 5,500 Hawthorne workers rose by 7 percent in the two years preceding the experiment.[36]

(ii) In Stage III, the output rate for each girl shows continuous and marked fluctuations over the whole two years of the study.[37] To obtain the percentage increase to be attributed to each girl the investigators chose, for each girl, a "peak" output period within the study period and measured her increase as the difference between this peak and her output rate at the outset of the study.[38] These peaks occur at different dates for different girls. To secure the 15 percent increase that is claimed, the study is, in effect, terminated at different conveniently selected dates for different girls. There is *no one period* over which the group achieved the 15 percent average increase claimed.[39]

(iii) In Stage I, two measures of the workers' performance are used: total output per week,[40] and hourly rate of output by weeks.[41] It is not clear from Roethlisberger and Dickson's report of Stage I whether the increase is in *total output* or *rate of output*. It is described only as "increase in output," and "output rose . . . roughly 30%,"[42] which would ordinarily be taken to mean an increase in *total output*. But the investigators make it clear in passing[43] that throughout the studies they used rate of output per hour as "the most common arrangement of output data" by which to "portray the general trend in efficiency of each operator and of the group." Whitehead, who produced a two-volume statistical study of Stage I as companion volumes to Roethlisberger and Dickson's standard report, is very clear on this point: "All output will be expressed in the form of a *rate* . . . as so many relays per hour."[44]

However, Whitehead employs throughout his study the description *"weekly rate of output"* when he means *rate of output per hour by weeks*.[45] This practice, coupled with his habit of not labelling the ordinates of his charts dealing with changes in output, and added to by Roethlisberger and Dickson's use of phrases such as "increase in output" to mean both *increase in rate of output per hour* and *increase in total output,* has led to widespread misinterpretation of the Hawthorne results, and textbook accounts which are seriously in error.[46]

Several points are of present importance. For Stage I, it is not clear whether the 30 percent increase in output claimed refers to *rate of output* or *total output*. It does not matter which measure is used to calculate percent increase in output in Stage I since the total hours worked per week at the end of the study period is only 4.7 percent less than at the beginning.[47] Thus, an increase of the order of 30 percent would result from either method of calculation. In Stage III, however, it makes a great deal of difference which method is used, and hourly rate of output is the only measure used. Thus, the 15 percent "increase in output"[48] claimed for Stage III is an increase in *rate of output per hour worked,* not in *total output.* Indeed, it is only by this measure that any increase *at all* in output can be shown.

If *total output per week* is used to measure performance in Stage III, the 15 percent increase claimed for Stage III reduces to less than zero because although output per hour increased by 15 percent, the weekly hours decreased by 17 percent, from 55½ to 46⅙.[49]

From Evidence to Conclusions. By subtracting the 15 percent increase in Stage III (which is an increase in *rate* of output) from the 30 percent increase in output in Stage I (which is all, or nearly all, an increase in *total* output), the investigators conclude that 15 percent remains as "the maximum amount (of increase in output) to be attributed to the change in wage incentive" introduced in Stage 1. The investigators acknowledge the wholly speculative nature of this calculation, yet go on to assert in a summary of events to date that the conclusion "seemed to be warranted from the test room studies so far . . . that it was impossible to consider (a wage incentive system) as a thing in itself having an independent effect on the individual."[50]

It is important to appreciate just how invalid are the inferences made. In Stage I, friendly supervision and a change to a preferred incentive system led to an increase in total output of about 30 percent. In Stage III, friendly supervision without a change in payment system led to no increase in total output, but to a less than compensating increase in output per hour over a period during which working hours were reduced from 55½ to 46⅙. This could be interpreted to mean that when working hours exceed about 48 per week such extra working-time may bring little or no increase in total output—a finding which had been well-established many years before.[51] This interpretation would have left the way clear to attribute 30 percent increase in Stage I entirely to the preferred incentive system. Instead, by the rather special method of analysis and argument that has been outlined, the investigators reached the conclusion that the effect of a wage incentive system is so greatly influenced by social considerations that it is impossible to consider it capable of independent effect.

A similar situation holds with regard to Stage II. As Stage II was planned, the "method of payment was to be the only alteration from the usual situation" with the express intention that "any marked changes in output" could then be "related to this factor."[52] There *was* a marked change in output—an immediate 12 percent increase. There *was* an immediate change in behavior—the other girls in the department demanded the same conditions. This would seem to require a conclusion in favor of the importance of a preferred incentive system, but no such conclusion was reached.

As a first step in the interpretation of the Stage II results, Roethlisberger and Dickson noticed, *post hoc,* that somewhere in the "daily history record" of the Stage I group was a reference to a comment by one member of that group that a "lively interest" was being taken in their output by members of the new Stage II group.[53] At this point, the investigators simply note this and hint at significance to come. Twenty-four pages later we are told that "although output had risen an average of 12% (in Stage II) it was *quite apparent* that factors other than the change in wage incentive contributed to that increase. . . . *There was some evidence* to indicate that the operators (in Stage II) had seized upon this test as an opportunity to prove to everyone that they could do as well as the (Stage I) operators. They were out to equal the latters' record. In view of this, even the most liberal estimate would put the increase in output due to the change in payment alone at somewhat less than 12%." (Italics added.) Since no additional evidence had been produced, this judgment lacks any serious foundation.

Much later (p. 577) the matter is returned to and, with no additional evidence, we are given to understand that the increase in output in Stage II was due to certain "social consequences" of the "basic social situation." This situation is simply asserted to have been one in which "rivalry (with the Stage I group) was brought to a focus" by setting up the Stage II group whose "output rose rapidly" in consequence.

Stage II was "designed to test the effect of a (change in) wage incentive" on output.[54] The preferred incentive system was introduced and output immediately rose 12 percent. It was withdrawn and output immediately dropped 17 percent. Not encouraging results for anyone who believed that wage incentives were relatively unimportant and incapable of "independent effects." Yet these awkward results were not only explained away but converted to positive support for just such conclusions, all on the basis of a single hearsay comment by one girl.

The investigators carry the day for the hypothesis that "social factors were the major circumstances limiting output." They conclude that "none of the results (in Stages I, II and III) gave the slightest substantiation to the theory that the worker is primarily motivated by economic interest. The evidence indicated that the efficacy of a wage incentive is so dependent on its relation to other factors that it is impossible to separate it out as a thing in itself having an independent effect."[55] This conclusion is a striking contrast to the objective results obtained in Stages I, II, and III as these bear on incentive systems: (i) when a preferred wage incentive system was introduced, total weekly output per worker rose (Stage I and Stage II); (ii) when the preferred incentive system was withdrawn, output promptly dropped (Stage II); (iii) when changes in supervision, hours, etc. were introduced but with *no change in incentive system,* no increase in weekly output per worker resulted (Stage III).

Viteles, an unusually perceptive critic of the Hawthorne studies, has commented caustically on Stage III: "This increase in output, representing an average rise of 15% in the first 14 months of the experiment, would ordinarily be accepted as evidence that the introduction of rest pauses and the shortening of the work day can in themselves result in increased output, even in the absence of changes in the way of enhancing the wage incentive."[56] Yet Viteles misses the important point that there was no overall increase in total weekly output in Stage III— only a less than compensating increase in output per hour when shorter hours were worked. It is clear that he supposes the 15 percent increase to be an increase in total output.[57] Viteles' patience is great, and his criticism of the Hawthorne studies restrained. But they eventually draw from him a testy general protest about "the more 'subtle'—certainly more subjective—form of analysis and interpretation which has generally characterized interpretation of the Hawthorne data by the Harvard group."[58]

It remains to consider more closely the complementary Hawthorne claim that it was friendly supervision and social factors which were the principal influences leading to the large rise in output in Stage I.

A CLOSER LOOK AT FRIENDLY SUPERVISION IN ACTION

The *whole* of the Hawthorne claim that friendly supervision and resulting work-group social relations and satisfactions are overwhelmingly important for work behavior rests on whatever evidence can be extracted from Stage I, since that is the only study in the series which exhibits even a surface association between the introduction of such factors and increased output.

Stage I began with five girls specially selected[59] for being both "thoroughly experienced" and "willing and cooperative,"[60] so there was reason to expect this group to be more than ordinarily cooperative and competent. Yet from very early in the study "the amount of talking indulged in by all the operators" had constituted a "problem," because it "involved a lack of attention to work and a preference for conversing together for considerable periods of time."[61] The first indication in the report that this might be a serious matter occurs on August 2nd, 1927, twelve weeks after the girls' installation in the test-room, when four of the five operators were brought before the foreman[62] and reprimanded for talking too much.[63] Until November, however, "no attempt had been made to do away with this privilege, although several attempts had been made by the foreman to diminish what seemed to him an excessive amount of talking." But Operators 1A and 2A in particular continued to fail to display "that 'wholehearted cooperation' desired by the investigators." "Any effort to reprimand them would bring the reply 'We thought you wanted us to work as we feel,'"[64] since that was what the supervisors had told them at the beginning of the study.[65]

By November 17th, 1927, the situation had not improved and disciplinary rules were resorted to. All of the operators were required to call out whenever they made mistakes in assembly, and they were prevented from talking. By December, "the lack of cooperation on the part of some of the operators was seriously alarming a few of the executives concerned." Supervisors were asked to give the girls a "hint" by telling them that they were not doing as well as expected of them and that if they didn't improve they would lose their free lunches.[66]

From now on the girls, but especially 1A and 2A, were "threatened with disciplinary action" and subjected to "continual reprimands." "Almost daily" 2A was "reproved" for her "low output and behavior" (sic).[67] The investigators decided 1A and 2A did not have "the 'right' mental attitude." 2A was called up before the test-room authorities "and told of her offenses of being moody and inattentive and not cooperative." She was called up again before the superintendent.[68] Throughout this period output for all five girls remained static or falling.[69] After eleven weeks of serious but ineffective disciplinary measures and eight months after the beginning of the study, 1A and 2A were dismissed from the test room for "gross insubordination" and declining or static output.[70] Or, as Whitehead puts it, they "were removed for a lack of cooperation, which would have otherwise necessitated greatly increased disciplinary measures."[71]

1A and 2A were replaced by two girls chosen by the foreman[72] "who were experienced relay assemblers and desirous of participating in the test." These two girls (designated Operators 1 and 2) were transferred to the test room on January 25th, 1928.[73] They *both* immediately produced an output much greater (in total and in rate per hour) than that achieved by *any* of the original five girls on their transfer to the test room and much above the performance *at any time* of the two girls they replaced.[74]

Operators 1 and 2 had been friends in the main shop. Operator 2 was the only Italian in the group; she was young (twenty-one) and her mother died shortly after she joined the test room;[75] after this "Operator 2 earned the larger part of the family income." "(F)rom now on the history of the test room revolves around the personality of Operator 2."[76] Operator 2 rapidly (i.e., without any delay during which she might have been affected by the new supervision) adopted and maintained a strong and effective disciplinary role with respect to the rest of the group,[77] and led the way in increased output in *every* period from her arrival till the end of the study. In this she was closely followed by the other new girl, Operator 1.[78]

At the time that Operators 1 and 2 were brought into the test room, daily hours of work were shortened by half an hour but it was decided to *pay the operators the day rate for the half hour of working time lost*. A little later, the working day was reduced by a further half hour, and again the girls were paid for the time (one hour per day) they didn't work.[79] Later still, the girls were given Saturday mornings off and again they were paid for the time not worked.[80]

Summing up experience in the test room up to *exactly* the time when the two operators were dismissed,[81] the investigators claim that "it is clear" that over this period there was "a gradual change in social inter-relations among the operators themselves, which diplayed itself in the form of new group loyalties and solidarities . . . (and) . . . a change in the relations between the operators and their supervisors. The test room authorities had taken steps to obtain the girls' cooperation and loyalty and to relieve them of anxieties and apprehensions. From this . . . arose . . . a change in human relations which came to be of great significance in the next stage of the experiment, when it became necessary to seek a new hypothesis to explain certain unexpected results of the inquiry."[82] In view of the evidence reviewed here this would seem to be a somewhat sanguine assessment of developments in the test room up to this point. It is, therefore, necessary to examine more systematically the way in which the behavior of the supervisors on the one hand and of the operators on the other (including their changing output) varied during the period under consideration.

It is already clear that whatever part satisfying social relations at work—resulting from free and friendly supervision—may have played in producing the increase in output, there were other influences likely to have been important, e.g., a period of fairly stern discipline, the dismissal of two workers, and their replacement by people of rather special personality and motivation. In order to assess these various influences on output it is necessary to consider how work performance varied during the periods when these changes were introduced. This is difficult because none of the reports of the Hawthorne studies provides actual figures covering the way in which output changed throughout Stage I. Consequently, one must work with such estimates as can be derived from the various graphs and charts of output-change that are supplied, and supplemented by occasional statements in the texts which give additional quantitative information.

AN EXAMINATION OF THE EVIDENCE: VARIATIONS IN SUPERVISORY PRACTICE AND VARIATIONS IN OUTPUT

For present purposes, Stage I may be divided into three phases: Phase I: the first three and a half months in the test room during which supervision seems to have been fairly consistently friendly, casual, and at low pressure; Phase II: a further interval of about seven months during which supervision became increasingly stern and close. This phase culminates in the dismissal of two of the five operators and their replacement by workers of rather special character and motivation; Phase III: a final long period during which output rose rapidly and there was a return to free and friendly supervision.

Supervision during Phase I. "Besides the girls who composed the group under study there was a person in the experimental room who was immediately in charge of the test." This was the test room observer whose twofold function was "to keep accurate records . . . and to create and maintain a friendly atmosphere in the test room." He "assume(d) responsibility for most of the day to day supervision" while in other matters such as accounting, rate revision, and promotion, responsibility rested with the foreman.[83]

It is quite clear from Roethlisberger and Dickson's account that during Phase I the supervisors did everything in their power to promote a free, cooperative, and non-coercive relationship.[84] At the outset of the study the girls "were asked to work along at a comfortable pace" and were assured "that no attempt would be made to force up production." They were led to expect changes in working conditions which might be "beneficial and desirable from the employees' point of view," and were told that there was no reason why "any (such) change resulting in greater satisfaction of employees" should not be maintained, and this "regardless of any change in production rate."[85] "The test room observer was chiefly concerned with creating a friendly relation with the operators which would ensure their cooperation. He was anxious to dispel any apprehensions they might have about the test and, in order to do this, he began to converse informally with them each day."[86] Some weeks after the study began, there was a friendly talk with the doctor about the physical examinations and ice cream was provided and a party planned. Also, the girls were "invited to the office of the superintendent who had talked to them, and in various other ways they had been made the object of considerable attention."[87] Although there had been from almost the beginning a good deal of talking among the girls, a fairly permissive attitude had been taken about this.[88]

Output during Phase I. There was "no appreciable change in output" on transfer to the test room,[89] but there was a "downward tendency" during the first five weeks thereafter,[90] despite facilities which "made the work slightly easier."[91]

At the end of five weeks, the new wage incentive system was introduced and output increased.[92] From the output chart[93] this increase may be estimated at 4 or 5 percent. However, this increase must be accepted with some caution, for the investigators report that the "change in method of payment necessitated a change in piece rates."[94] It was apparently judged that under the new conditions of work (which did not include all of the types of relay assembled on the shop floor, and where there was one layout operator to five assemblers instead of one to six or seven as on the shop floor) new rates were necessary. We are told that "the chief consideration in setting the new piece rates was to determine a rate for each relay type which would pay the operators the same amount of money they had received in the regular department for an equivalent amount of work."[95] But it is well-established that the unreliability of time-study ratings can be expected to yield errors of at least 5 percent between different ratings of similar tasks.[96] So no great reliance can be placed on the observed 4 or 5 percent increase in output following the introduction of the new incentive system and the associated new piece-rates. Indeed, there is perhaps some recognition of this in Roethlisberger and Dickson's introductory comment that early in the study "a change in wage payment was introduced, a necessary step before the *experiment proper* could begin."[97] Phase I ends after fifteen weeks of friendly supervision with a somewhat doubtful increase of 5 percent which occurred with the introduction of a preferred incentive system.

Supervision during Phase II. "The second phase . . . covering an interval of approximately seven months was concerned with the effects of various kinds of rest pauses."[98] The investigators emphasize that by the *beginning* of this phase not only was supervision friendly, but the relation between workers and supervisors was "free and easy."[99] Their account of actual supervisory behavior during succeeding months supports these claims. (i) On each of the four occasions when rest pauses were varied, the girls were consulted in advance, and on all but one occasion their expressed preferences were accepted. (ii) The investigators decided to pay the girls their bonuses monthly instead of weekly, but when the girls were told about this decision they objected and the plan was dropped. That the girls "felt free to express their attitudes" and that the investigators altered their plans out of regard for these attitudes is said to be "typical of the supervisory technique employed" which "proved to be a factor of utmost importance in interpreting the results of the study." (iii) Later the girls were given free lunches and were consulted about what should be served.[100]

However, the problem of excessive talking among the girls worsened. No attempt had been made to prohibit talking, although four of the girls had been "given a talk regarding their behavior."[101] Now this "lack of attention to work and preference for conversing together for considerable periods" was judged to be reaching such proportions that the "experiment was being jeopardized and something had to be done."[102] A variety of disciplinary procedures of increasing severity were applied, but with little effect. Finally, the leaders in talking (operators 1A and 2A) were dismissed from the test room "for lack of cooperation which would have otherwise necessitated greatly increased disciplinary measures."

Output during Phase II. There was no change in weekly output during this six-month period. "Total weekly output does not decline when rest pauses are introduced, but remains practically the same during all the rest period experiment."[103]

Supervision during Phase III. At the beginning of Phase III,[104] the two dismissed girls were replaced by two girls chosen by the foreman. Something has already been said about the way in which these girls at once took and maintained the lead in output and about how one of them, who had a special need for more money took over the general leadership and discipline of the rest of the group. These points will bear underlining by direct quotation:

"When Operator 2 joined the group, her home was largely dependent upon her earnings, and within a few weeks her father lost his job and became temporarily unemployed. Thus, to her natural sense of responsibility was added the factor of poverty; and Operator 2 began to urge the remainder of the group to increase their output."[105]

"Operators 1 and 2 were very definitely the fastest workers of the group in 1928, and this was freely recognized by the others."[106]

"On the whole, from January to November 1928, the Relay Test Group showed no very marked developments apart from a growing tendency for the discipline to pass from the hands of the supervisor to those of the group itself, largely as represented in the person of Operator 2."[107]

"Operator 2 became recognized as the leader of the group, both by the operators themselves and by the supervisor. It is doubtful whether any operator could have secured this position unless she had been the fastest worker, but the other qualifications possessed by Operator 2 were a high sense of the importance of the work for the group and a forceful personality."[108]

"Op. 2. 'Oh! what's the matter with those other girls. I'll kill them.' "[109] (This expostulation was provoked by the output curves showing operators 3, 4, and 5 on a downward trend.)

From then on supervision again became increasingly friendly and relaxed. This friendliness of supervision often had a very tangible character. From the arrival of the new workers in the test room, the observer "granted them (all) more and more privileges." The preferred incentive system, the rest pauses, the free lunches, and the "parties" following the regular physical examinations all continued.[110] In addition, within the next eight months the girls were first paid for half an hour per day not worked, and then for an hour a day not worked, and finally for Saturday mornings not worked. Approximately eight months after the arrival of the new girls, all these privileges except the preferred incentive system and the parties were withdrawn. The girls were warned in advance about this withdrawal of privileges and were assured that the new and heartily disliked conditions "would terminate after approximately three months." Despite this promise, the girls' work deteriorated immediately: they wasted time in various ways such as reading newspapers, eating candy, and going for drinks and the observer shortly "discovered that the girls were attempting to keep the output rate low . . . so as to make sure that rest pauses would be reinstated." The observer "again tried to stop the excessive talking" by "reprimand and threat." He told the girls that "unless excessive talking ceased it might become necessary to continue the experiment without rest pauses for a longer period."[111]

At this point, the girls had been in the test room eighteen months and had achieved nearly all the eventual 30 percent increase in output. Yet it would seem that Operator 2, the incentive system, and the other privileges, as well as "reprimand and threat" played a significant part in determining the work behavior and output of the group. It is also clear from Roethlisberger and Dickson's account that for a great part of the time following the arrival of Operators 1 and 2, the girls worked very well and happily and that while they did so, supervision was relaxed and friendly and relations continued to be satisfactory. But there would seem to be good grounds for supposing that supervision became more friendly and relaxed because output increased rather than vice versa.

Output during Phase III. Output for the whole group rose markedly during the several months after the dismissal of 1A and 2A, owing chiefly to the contributions from the new operators.[112] Thereafter, the group's total output rose more slowly for a further year (with a temporary drop when the Saturday morning shift was discontinued for a time).

SUMMARY OF EVIDENCE ABOUT SUPERVISION AND OUTPUT

(i) Apart from a doubtful 4-5 percent increase following the introduction of a preferred incentive system, there was no increase in weekly output during the first nine months in the test room, despite a great deal of preoccupation on the part of the supervisors with friendliness towards the workers, with consultation, and the provision of a variety of privileges not enjoyed on the factory floor.

(ii) From the beginning of what Roethlisberger and Dickson describe as the "experiment proper," that is, after the period in which the new incentive system was introduced, there was no increase in weekly output during the next six months. When it became apparent that free and friendly supervision was not getting results, discipline was tightened, culminating in the dismissal of two of the five girls.

(iii) The dismissed girls were replaced by two girls of a special motivation and character who *immediately* led the rest in a sustained acceleration of output. One of these girls who had a special need for extra money rapidly adopted and maintained a strong disciplinary role with respect to the rest of the group. The two new girls led the way in increased output from their arrival till the end of the study.

(iv) Total output per week showed a significant and sustained increase only after the two girls who had the lowest output[113] were dismissed and replaced by selected output leaders who account for the major part of the groups' increase, both in output rate and in total output, over the next seventeen months of the study.

(v) After the arrival of the new girls and the associated increase in output, *official* supervision became friendly and relaxed once more. The investigators, however, provide no evidence that output increased because supervision became more friendly rather than vice versa. In any case, friendly supervision took a very tangible turn by paying the girls for time not worked. The piece-rate was in effect increased.

DISCUSSION AND CONCLUSIONS

The critical examination attempted here by no means exhausts the gross error and the incompetence in the understanding and use of the scientific method which permeate the Hawthorne studies from beginning to end. Three further studies were conducted: the Bank Wiring Observation Room Study; the Interviewing Program; and the Counselling Program. These studies cannot be discussed here but I believe them to be nearly as worthless scientifically as the studies which have been discussed.[114] This should not be surprising, for they arose out of "evidence" found and conclusions reached in the earlier studies and were guided by and interpreted in the light of the strongest preconceptions based on the conclusions of the earlier studies.

There are major deficiencies in Stages I, II and III which have hardly been touched on: (i) There was no attempt to establish sample groups representative of any larger population than the groups themselves. Therefore, no generalization is legitimate. (ii) There was no attempt to employ control data from the output records of the girls who were *not* put under special experimental conditions. (iii) Even if both of these points had been met, the experiments would still have been of only minor scientific value since a group of five subjects is too small to yield statistically reliable results. Waiving all these points, it is clear that the objective evidence obtained from Stages I, II, and III does not support any of the conclusions derived by the Hawthorne investigators. The results of these studies, far from supporting the various components of the "human relations approach," are surprisingly consistent with a rather old-world view about the value of monetary incentives, driving leadership, and discipline. It is only by massive and relentless reinterpretation that the evidence is made to yield contrary conclusions. To make these points is not to claim that the Hawthorne studies can provide serious support for any such old-world view. The limitations of the Hawthorne studies clearly render them incapable of yielding serious support for any sort of generalization whatever.

If the assessment of the Hawthorne studies offered here is cogent, it raises some questions of importance for university teachers, especially for teachers concerned with courses on industrial organization and management. How is it that nearly all authors of textbooks who have drawn material from the Hawthorne studies have failed to recognize the vast discrepancy between evidence and conclusions in those studies, have frequently misdescribed the actual observations and occurrences in a way that brings the evidence into line with the conclusions, and have done this even when such authors based their whole outlook and orientation on the conclusions reached by the Hawthorne investigators? Exploration of these questions would provide salutary insight into aspects of the sociology of social scientists.

NOTES

[1] For a review of these charges and criticisms see Delbert Miller and William Form, *Industrial Sociology*, New York: Harper, 1951, pp. 74-83. For a defense see Henry A. Landsberger, *Hawthorne Revisited*, New York: Cornell, 1958. Landsberger's defense is restricted to the report of the Hawthorne studies by Fritz J. Roethlisberger and William Dickson, *Management and the Worker*, Cambridge: Harvard Univ. Press, 1939. Even this report, in Landsberger's view, has "done the field of human relations in industry an amount of harm which, in retrospect, appears to be almost irreparable." Landsberger, *op. cit.*, p. 64.

[2] George A. Pennock, "Industrial Research at Hawthorne," *Personnel Journal*, 8 (February, 1930), pp. 296-313; Mark L. Putman, "Improving Employee Relations," *Personnel Journal*, 8 (February, 1930), pp. 314-325.

[3] Fritz J. Roethlisberger, *Management and Morale*, Cambridge: Harvard University Press, 1941, p. 15.

[4] Lyndall Urwick and Edward Brech, *The Making of Scientific Management*, vol. III, London: Management Publications Trust, 1948, p. 27. See also Roethlisberger and Dickson, *op. cit.*, p. 29.

[5] Morris S. Viteles, *Motivation and Morale in Industry*, London: Staples, 1954, p. 185.

[6] Roethlisberger and Dickson, *op. cit.*, pp. 21, 26.

[7] *Ibid.*, pp. 22, 30-73.

[8] *Ibid.*, p. 129; Pennock, *op. cit.*, p. 299.

[9] Roethlisberger and Dickson, *op. cit.*, p. 160.

[10] *Ibid.*, pp. 189-190; Pennock, *op. cit.*, pp. 297-309.

[11] Pennock, *op. cit.*, p. 309.

[12] Roethlisberger and Dickson, *op. cit.* pp. 86-89.

[13] The investigators list fatigue and monotony as separate hypotheses. For brevity, these have been combined as one hypothesis. The same sort of critical objections are relevant to the arguments and evidence advanced by the investigators with respect to both.

[14] *Ibid.*, p. 87.

[15] T. North Whitehead, *The Industrial Worker*, London: Oxford Univ. Press, 1938, Vol. I, p. 65.

[16] Roethlisberger and Dickson, *op. cit.*, p. 89. (Italics added.)

[17] The scientifically illiterate procedure of dismissing non-preferred explanations on the grounds that (i) the experimenters had found no *conclusive* evidence in favor of them

and/or (ii) there was no evidence that any *one* of these explanations, considered by itself, accounted for *all* the effect observed, recurs throughout Roethlisberger and Dickson's report of the Hawthorne studies. This procedure is never applied to preferred hypotheses, which are assumed to be well-founded provided only that the evidence *against* them is less than conclusive. See, e.g., Roethlisberger and Dickson, *op. cit.,* p. 160 and pp. 96, 108, 127.

[18]*Ibid.,* p. 87.

[19]Morris S. Viteles, *Industrial Psychology,* New York: Norton, 1932, p. 476. Italics in original.

[20]Roethlisberger and Dickson, *op. cit.,* p. 129.

[21]*Ibid.,* pp. 131-132, 577; Pennock, *op. cit.,* p. 307.

[22]*Ibid.,* p. 133.

[23]According to an earlier report (Pennock, *op. cit.,* p. 307), the increase in output was 13.8 percent, the experiment was discontinued after five weeks, and output then fell by 19-24 percent.

[24]Viteles, *Motivation . . . , op. cit.,* p. 187.

[25]Roethlisberger and Dickson, *op. cit.,* pp. 133-134, 158, 577.

[26]Pennock, *op. cit.,* p. 307.

[27]That is, by the end of Experimental Period 7 in Roethlisberger and Dickson's output chart, *op. cit.,* p. 78.

[28]Roethlisberger and Dickson, *op. cit.,* pp. 160, 577.

[29]*Ibid.,* p. 129.

[30]*Ibid.,* p. 148.

[31]Pennock, *op. cit.,* p. 307.

[32]Roethlisberger and Dickson, *op. cit.,* pp. 156, 159.

[33]*Ibid.,* pp. 146-149, 159-160; Pennock, *op. cit.,* p. 307.

[34]For example, "we cannot avoid being impressed by the fact that a wage incentive alone (Stage II) increased production 12%, a change in the social situation raised output 15%, (Stage III) and a combination of the two gave an increase of 30%. This looks surprisingly like an additive effect, with the social rewards being somewhat more potent in influencing behaviour than the monetary reward." Ross Stagner, *Psychology of Industrial Conflict,* New York: Wiley, 1956, pp. 131-132. See also Milton Blum, *Industrial Psychology and Its Social Foundations,* New York: Harper, 1949, p. 26.

[35]Viteles comments on this period of declining output: "Both 'the investigators and the operators were of the opinion that the rates on the new piece parts were not high enough in comparison with the old.' Nevertheless scant consideration is given to the possibility that . . . a reduced appeal to economic motives could readily account in large part for the very severe drop in output observed during this final phase of the *Mica Splitting Room experiment.*" Viteles, *Motivation . . . , op. cit.,* p. 191.

[36]Whitehead, *op. cit.,* vol. II, Chart J-53.

[37]Roethlisberger and Dickson, *op. cit.,* p. 147.

[38]*Ibid.,* p. 148.

[39]*Ibid.,* pp. 146-148, 159-160.

[40]*Ibid.,* p. 78.

[41]*Ibid.,* p. 76.

[42]*Ibid.,* p. 160.

[43]*Ibid.,* pp. 55, 77.

[44]Whitehead, *op. cit.,* vol. I, p. 34.

[45]*Ibid.,* vol. II, Chart B4.

[46]For example, Edwin Ghiselli and Clarence Brown, *Personnel and Industrial Psychology,* New York: McGraw Hill, 1948, pp. 435-437; and James A. C. Brown, *Social Psychology of Industry,* Harmondsworth: Penguin, 1954, pp. 71-72. These authors incorrectly report an almost continuous increase in total weekly output over the first nine months of Stage I. In fact, there was no increase except in the period of eight weeks

immediately following the introduction of the preferred incentive system. There was no improvement in weekly output in either the preceding period or the four experimental periods extending over six months which followed it.

[47]Roethlisberger and Dickson, *op. cit.*, pp. 76-77.

[48]*Ibid.*, pp. 159-160.

[49]*Ibid.*, pp. 136-139.

[50]*Ibid.*, p. 160. Viteles bluntly rejects this inference as invalid, but textbook treatments of the Hawthorne studies generally accept it without demur. Viteles, *Motivation . . . , op. cit.*, p. 193.

[51]Horace M. Vernon, *Industrial Fatigue and Efficiency,* London: Dutton, 1921. Ghiselli and Brown have summarized Vernon's findings as follows: "In a munitions plant, when the working week was reduced from 66 to 48.6 hours (a reduction of 26%) hourly output was increased by 68% and total output for the week by 15%. This instance could be multiplied many times." Ghiselli and Brown, *op. cit.*, p. 242.

[52]Roethlisberger and Dickson, *op. cit.*, p. 129.

[53]*Ibid.*, p. 134.

[54]*Ibid.*, p. 576.

[55]*Ibid.*, pp. 575-576.

[56]Viteles, *Motivation . . . , op. cit.*, p. 190.

[57]*Ibid.*, p. 5.

[58]*Ibid.*, p. 256.

[59]Note, however, that while the five girls were "all chosen from among those with a considerable experience in the assembly of this kind of relay" . . . "the actual method of selection was quite informal and somewhat obscure; it appears to have been determined by the girls themselves in conjunction with their shop foreman." Whitehead, *op. cit.*, vol. I, p. 14.

[60]Roethlisberger and Dickson, *op. cit.*, p. 21.

[61]*Ibid.*, p. 53.

[62]Foremen were on a par with departmental chiefs and four ranks above operatives. *Ibid.*, p. 11.

[63]*Ibid.*, p. 38.

[64]*Ibid.*, p. 53.

[65]*Ibid.*, p. 21; Whitehead, *op. cit.*, vol. I, p. 26.

[66]Whitehead, *op. cit.*, vol. I, p. 16.

[67]*Ibid.*, pp. 116-118.

[68]Roethlisberger and Dickson, *op. cit.*, p. 55. Superintendents controlled a branch of the works and were seven ranks above operators. *Ibid.*, p. 11.

[69]*Ibid.*, p. 78. See Experimental Period 7 in Figure 7.

[70]*Ibid.*, pp. 53-57.

[71]Whitehead, *op. cit.*, vol. I, p. 118. In Mayo's accounts it is first said that these two operators "dropped out" (Elton Mayo, *The Human Problems of an Industrial Civilization,* Boston: Harvard Business School, 1946, p. 56) and later that they "retired." (Elton Mayo, *The Social Problems of an Industrial Civilization,* London: Routledge and Kegan Paul, 1949, p. 62.) It is also interesting to compare the above account of events in the test room and drawn from the standard reports with Mayo's picture of the test room. According to Mayo's account, success was achieved "largely because the experimental room was in charge of an interested and sympathetic chief observer. He understood clearly from the first that any hint of the 'supervisor' in his methods might be fatal to the interests of the inquiry . . . He helped the group to feel that its duty was to set its own conditions of work, he helped the workers to find the 'freedom' of which they so frequently speak . . . At no time in the (whole period of the study) did the girls feel that they were working under pressure" (Mayo, *The Human Problems . . . , op. cit.*, pp. 68-69).

[72]Roethlisberger and Dickson, *op. cit.*, p. 60.

[73]*Ibid.*, pp. 55, 56, 60.

[74]*Ibid.*, Figure 6, p. 76 and Figure 7, p. 78. Compare output curves during the first seven Experimental Periods with output from the second week of Experimental Period 8.

[75]*Ibid.*, pp. 61-62.

[76]Whitehead, *op. cit.*, vol. I, p. 120.

[77]*Ibid.*, pp. 120-129; Roethlisberger and Dickson, *op. cit.*, pp. 63, 74, 86, 156, 167.

[78]Roethlisberger and Dickson, *op. cit.*, p. 162.

[79]Whitehead, *op. cit.*, vol. I, pp. 121-122. Roethlisberger and Dickson (*op. cit.*, pp. 60, 62) give no indication that the operators were paid for these hours not worked. Indeed, their account clearly implies that they were not so paid (*ibid.*, pp. 63-64). But Whitehead is quite explicit on this point.

[80]Roethlisberger and Dickson do report (*op. cit.*, p. 68) that the girls were paid for the half day on Saturdays which was not worked. They acknowledge that this "added a new factor to the situation which cannot be disregarded and which has to be taken into account in comparing this period with any other" (*ibid.*, p. 69). They take no further account of it, however, just as they take no further account of the unworked hours paid for on the occasions when the work day was shortened.

[81]That is, up to the end of Experimental Period 7 in Roethlisberger and Dickson's terminology.

[82]Roethlisberger and Dickson, *op. cit.* pp. 58-59.

[83]*Ibid.*, pp. 22, 37.

[84]*Ibid.*, pp. 32-39.

[85]*Ibid.*, p. 33.

[86]*Ibid.*, p. 37.

[87]*Ibid.*, pp. 34, 39.

[88]*Ibid.*, p. 53.

[89]Pennock, *op. cit.*, pp. 301, 304.

[90]Roethlisberger and Dickson, *op. cit.*, p. 58.

[91]*Ibid.*, pp. 33-34, 39.

[92]*Ibid.*, p. 58.

[93]*Ibid.*, p. 56.

[94]*Ibid.*, p. 34.

[95]*Ibid.*, p. 35.

[96]Viteles, *Motivation . . ., op. cit.*, pp. 30-38.

[97]Roethlisberger and Dickson, *op. cit.*, p. 29, italics added.

[98]*Ibid.*, p. 40. This phase actually extends from Aug. 8, 1927 to January 21, 1928, a period of twenty-four weeks.

[99]*Ibid.*, pp. 45-46.

[100]*Ibid.*, pp. 48-9, 51.

[101]*Ibid.*, p. 38.

[102]*Ibid.*, pp. 53-54.

[103]*Ibid.*, p. 79.

[104]Actually on January 25, 1928, two days after the beginning of Phase III. Thus, the resulting sharp rise in output does not show fully on Roethlisberger and Dickson's weekly output charts (*op. cit.*, pp. 76, 78) until the second week of their Experimental Period 8.

[105]Whitehead, *op. cit.*, vol. I, pp. 122-123.

[106]*Ibid.*, p. 126.

[107]*Ibid.*, p. 124.

[108]*Ibid., p. 129.*

[409]*Ibid.*, p. 127.

[110]Roethlisberger and Dickson, *op. cit.*, pp. 71, 72, 77.

[111]*Ibid.*, pp. 70-72.

[112]*Ibid.*, Figure 7, p. 78.

[113]*Ibid.*, p. 162.

[114]For substantiation of this judgment with respect to the Bank Wiring Observation Room Study see A. J. Sykes, "Economic Interest and the Hawthorne Researches: A Comment," *Human Relations,* 18 (August, 1965), pp. 253-263.

13

Some Empirical Evidence
About Needs Theory

ALAN C. FILLEY

AND

ROBERT J. HOUSE

Under all but exceptional circumstances, an individual strives to satisfy a predictable sequence of needs, beginning with efforts to fulfill physiological needs, followed by efforts to fulfill safety, social, ego, and self-realization needs.

Survey research by Haire and Gottsdanker (1951) supports Maslow's need theory (Proposition 2). In a morale survey of grocery employes, they found a hierarchy of job elements listed in an order compatible with Maslow's theory. They concluded from this that "less important factors became real demands only after previously more basic ones have been satisfied."

Porter (1961; 1962; 1964) attempted a somewhat "projective" study whereby he hoped to get responses not biased by the wording of the questions. On one part of the two-part study, respondents marked a 13-item questionnaire relating to need-fulfillment concepts. The questionnaire was marked first according to how much of the characteristic was currently present in the respondent's management position; a second time according to how much of the characteristic should have been present; and a third time according to the importance of the characteristic to the respondent. The three responses were analyzed to see what discrepancies emerged in present satisfaction, amount of deficiency, and value.

The second phase of the study involved an approach using seven-

Reprinted by permission of the authors and publisher from *Managerial Process and Organizational Behavior*, by A. C. Filley and R. J. House, pp. 374-78. Chicago, Illinois: Scott, Foresman and Company, © 1969.

point semantic-differential scales, intended to obtain an objective estimate of job attitude by allowing respondents to describe their management position in terms of a series of dichotomized variables, such as "varied-routine," "complex-simple," "challenging-not-challenging." Previous research with this method has shown it to be effective in masking out the psychological bias of managers who feel their responses might reveal disloyalty to their company.

Porter found higher level jobs described in clearly more favorable terms than lower level jobs. The higher level jobs were seen as demanding a greater degree of independent judgment and individual self reliance, but the payoff in psychological rewards were seen as worth the extra effort. Security and social needs were apparently better satisfied at the higher levels. Also, the higher the level in the hierarchy, the greater the expectation for self-realization and autonomy. But the increase in this expectation was found to be greater than the satisfaction, except at the top. These results are consistent with Maslow's assertion that industrial and business organizations do a better job of satisfying security and social needs than satisfying self-fulfillment needs. And, as Maslow's theory would predict, higher order needs were usually activated and satisfied after lower order needs were fulfilled.

However, with respect to the kind of methodology used with the Haire and Gottsdanker and Porter studies, Hall and Nougaim (1968) state that "one problem from inferring the existence of a need hierarchy from a study of deprived satisfied groups is that selection and situational or cultural factors, not personality processes may be affecting the result." To combat this problem, Hall and Nougaim designed and conducted a rather elaborate longitudinal study of 49 managers in American telephone and telegraph companies.

Hall and Nougaim found that after five years their respondents were more concerned with affiliation, achievement, esteem, and self-actualization—and less concerned with safety—than when they first began employment with the company. These findings are in accord with relationships between need strength and job level reported by other researchers (Davis, 1946; Pellegrin and Coates, 1957; Porter, 1962, 1963; Centers, 1948; Morse and Weiss, 1955; Lyman, 1955; Veroff, *et. al.*, 1960). Hall and Nougaim point out that these previous studies are cited in support of the need hierarchy, but that none of them, with the exception of Porter (1962; 1963), directly measured both need strength and satisfaction; therefore they had to rely on inference to measure these variables.

Hall and Nougaim collapsed the higher level needs—affiliation, achievement, esteem, and self-actualization—into one category, and computed a correlation between it and the safety need (in effect, a test of a two-level hierarchical theory of needs and motivation). They hypothesized that satisfaction of the safety need would positively correlate strongly with higher level need strength. As before, the results did not support a hierarchy.

Hall and Nougaim finally concluded that the changes they had found could only be explained in terms of developing career concerns rather than prepotent need gratification. According to their theory, an individual is primarily concerned with safety at the beginning of his career, followed by concern for promotion and achievement. At this intermediate stage, he is not so concerned with fitting into an organization as with moving upward in it and mastering it.

The last period represents a terminal plateau. The individual has cues that he is nearing the limit of his advancement, his career starts to level off, and his need or opportunity for competition decreases. He has achieved his own particular level of success, and he now must find some other means of gratification. If he feels he has been successful, he may become interested in helping younger men, in order to strengthen the organization and perpetuate his work. Even if he feels he has been unsuccessful, he may still help the younger men, or he may use his power to block their progress.

Hall and Nougaim's data support this interpretation, as do other studies they cite which indicate that the early stages of a career are characterized by concern with security—gaining recognition and getting established in a profession or an organization. During the first to eighth years of employment, however, the concern shifts to achievement and autonomy.

Hall and Nougaim then hypothesized a "success syndrome," which is suggested by their data:

1) For all managers, the need for achievement and esteem increases over the years that they are with a company.

2) Managers who have met high standards of performance will be rewarded with promotions and pay increases, or, in overall terms, with success.

3) Successful managers achieve a great deal and are given increased managerial responsibility. Therefore, by their fifth year, their achievement and esteem satisfaction becomes significantly greater than that of their less successful colleagues.

4) Possibly as a result of greater achievement and esteem satisfaction, successful managers become more involved in their jobs. By their fifth year, work is significantly more essential to their overall need satisfaction than it is for the less successful group.

5) With increased job involvement, managers are more likely to be successful in future assignments. Thus they are caught in an upward spiral of success.

The converse of the success syndrome does not seem to occur for less successful managers; although their satisfaction with achievement and esteem decreases, their average work centrality score does increase slightly. If this score had decreased, we could say that these people were becoming alienated and withdrawing emotionally from their work. But they seem to remain at about the same level of work centrality, with their other higher need strengths increasing at about the same rates as the successful group, but with their higher order satisfaction *not* increasing.

Three conclusions may be drawn from our review of studies concerned with Maslow's theory. First, survey research evidence suggests that the theory is valid with respect to the sequential emergence of needs. However, in the light of more complete data collected longitudinally, this first proposition (hierarchical prepotence of needs) does not appear to be valid—which leads to our second conclusion, concerning the choice of appropriate methodology. Our review of studies illustrates the potential pitfalls of relying exclusively on survey research data collected at a single point in time, and underscores the need to test theoretical propositions by experimental or longitudinal studies. Such studies provide a basis for determining whether or not purported causal variables actually precede in time the variables they are predicted to cause.

The third conclusion that can be drawn concerns the career stages and the success syndrome hypothesized by Hall and Nougaim. Since these hypotheses are consistent with previous research and with Hall and Nougaim's own data, they deserve to be considered along with existing theory. Since they help to explain what attracts and motivates a manager at various stages in his career, they provide direction for continued research in important problem areas. If these hypotheses are supported by further research, they might provide the basis for designing effective management recruiting, motivation, and development programs, which could significantly contribute to increased organizational effectiveness.

14

A Comment on Atkinson's "Motivational Determinants of Risk-Taking Behavior"

EDWIN A. LOCKE

Since the experimental studies mentioned* above were unanimous in finding that hard goals produced a higher level of performance than easy goals, a word is in order regarding a theory of task performance which would not have predicted these findings. Atkinson and Feather (1966) regard level of performance to be a function of the product of the probability of reaching the goal (task difficulty) and the incentive (satisfaction) value of reaching it. They assume that probability of success (PS) and incentive value (I) are inversely and linearly related, so that a high-PS task yields low satisfaction with success (I) whereas a low-PS task yields high satisfaction with success. Thus the highest product of these two scores and, thence, the highest output, should occur when both have a value of .50, which means when probability of success is .50[1] (see Atkinson, 1958). The curve relating probability of success to output should be bell-shaped, with extreme values of PS producing low output, and moderate values producing high output.

*The studies here refer to those described in Part Two, E. A. Locke, "Toward a Theory of Task Motivation." All references herein may be found there also.

[1]Atkinson's complete theory also incorporates the influence of need for achievement and fear of failure on performance. For purposes of this discussion it is assumed that the motive to approach success is greater than the motive to avoid failure. However, even if this were not true of the subjects used in the studies cited, there is no way that Atkinson's theory, as it now stands, could be made to predict a linear relationship between task difficulty and performance level.

Reprinted by permission of the author and publisher from E. A. Locke, "Toward a Theory of Task Motivation and Incentives." In *Organizational Behavior and Human Performance* 3 (1968):167-68.

It is clear that the results of studies cited above* flatly contradict the theory. The source of the contradiction involves the subjects with hard goals. The above cited studies found that subjects with hard goals worked harder, not less hard, than subjects with moderate goals. In other words, the *S*s adjusted their effort to the difficulty of the goal or task undertaken (see Bryan and Locke, 1967b). If the task was hard, they worked hard; if it was easy they worked less hard. And, in fact, it would have been irrational for them to act otherwise. If an individual genuinely has a difficult goal, it would be self-contradictory for him not to work hard to achieve it. If he did not do so, we would question whether he really had such a goal at all.

The issue here is one brought up by Stedry (1960) and discussed above:* it concerns the difference between goal or task *assignment* and goal *acceptance*. It is true that many people reject difficult tasks which are assigned to them and probably more people reject very hard tasks than reject moderately hard tasks. But the point is that once a hard task *is* accepted, the only logical thing to do is to try one's hardest until one decides to lower or abandon the goal. It is argued that people who do stop trying when confronted by a hard task are people who have decided the goal is impossible to reach and *who no longer are trying for that goal.* In the above studies,* most subjects assigned hard goals or tasks evidently accepted them (for some exceptions, see Locke and Bryan, 1967a).

Atkinson (1958), however, conducted one study which seemed to support his theory; subjects were given two tasks and were told that either ½₀, ⅓, ½ or ¾'s of the subjects in the group they were in would win a monetary prize, the winners being those who showed the highest output on the two tasks. The highest output was achieved by the ⅓ and ½ probability-of-success groups with the two extreme groups showing the lowest output. In this study it is likely that many of the subjects in the ½₀ group *did not try to win,* because they thought their chances were poor. The *actual goals* of the subjects in the different groups were not determined. Furthermore, an attempted replication of this study by McClelland (1961, p. 216) obtained a (negative) *linear* relationship between PS and output—a finding which supports the present theory.

---

*See note p. 242.

15

A Critique of Edwin Locke's Theory of
Task Motivation and Incentives

THOMAS W. DOBMEYER

Edwin Locke's "Theory of Task Motivation and Incentives" has resulted from an extensive series of laboratory studies (Locke 1968). These studies have been designed to empirically investigate the nature of the relationship between conscious goals and task performance. Locke also attempts to determine experimentally how incentives influence performance.

An individual's conscious goals, or intentions, occupy the role of a pivotal variable in Locke's theory. Conscious goals are viewed both as a dependent and an independent variable. As the latter, goals can range along such dimensions as "easy—hard" or "specific—nonspecific." A great deal of research has been conducted in which goals have served as dependent variables. The entire level of aspiration literature can be considered in this light. Goals also can be considered dependent variables when they are choices resulting from decision making.

Locke (1968) has assigned yet another general function to goals when he states that they mediate the effects of incentives on behavior. That is, incentives can affect behavior when the individual changes his intentions (conscious goals) as a result of being offered or receiving an incentive.

Much of what Locke says is intuitively appealing. Many anecdotes are available depicting the way in which individuals have achieved new heights because of self-set goals. Beyond the intuitive level,

Printed by permission of the author. Unpublished paper, University of Minnesota, 1970.

the notion of goal-directed behavior has been theoretically incorporated into the domain of motivation. At least, goal setting has been paid lip service in the vernacular of motivation theory. Once the *direction* of behavior has been established through choice of a goal, the *amplitude* of behavior tends to be proportional to the level of goal difficulty. Goals are also used as explanatory devices to account for the *persistence* of behavior. Suffice it to say that goal setting as a phenomenon is worthy of study.

One must be aware, however, of the possible pitfalls of using goal setting or intentionality as an explanatory device. It seems especially important when dealing with mentalistic concepts, such as intentionality or conscious goals as variables in a theoretical sense, to avoid teleological arguments.

LOCKE'S THEORY

A critique of Locke's (1968) theory is somewhat difficult because, as he admits, it is not complete. His formulation has been induced from a series of related laboratory studies. A close reading of his work allows the identification of several key variables and concepts around which the results of his numerous studies can be organized. For purposes of clarity, several ideas central to the theory are defined here.

Intentions or Conscious Goals. The terms *intentions* and *conscious goals* are synonymous; they are defined as "what the individual is consciously trying to do" (Locke 1968, p. 159).

Task Goal. A task goal is a performance standard. Locke does not make a sharp distinction between a conscious goal and a task goal. The former results when an individual accepts the latter and redefines the task in terms of the goal (Bryan and Locke 1967). The task goals or performance standards in Locke's studies usually have been defined in quantitative terms, and little attention has been paid to qualitative performance standards.

Goal Acceptance. Locke makes a distinction between goal acceptance and goal commitment. Goal acceptance refers to whether or not an individual assumes or takes up a task goal or performance standard. Goal commitment refers to how long an individual expends effort in attempting to achieve a performance standard. Goal commitment, then, seems equivalent to the persistence of behavior. Unfortunately, Locke (1968) has not yet included the concept of goal commitment in his theory:

The issue of goal commitment has not been dealt with . . . but it is no doubt an important factor in performance. The subject's degree of commitment to his goal may play an important role in determining how easily he will give up in the face of difficulty (pp. 185-86).

Incentive. An incentive is defined by Locke (1968, p. 161) *"as an event or object external to the individual which can incite action."*[1] This is a broad definition of incentive, and Locke, in effect, assigns several functions to it. One of these functions is to suggest specific performance standards.

Task. Locke does not explicitly define task, nor does he systematically vary the nature of the tasks used in his laboratory studies. Although he maintains that his results hold up over a wide variety of tasks, most of those used have been of a relatively rote variety requiring little complex ability.

Locke's major theoretical proposition is that conscious goals or intentions influence task performance. Conscious goals are also believed to mediate the influence of incentives on behavior. That is, incentives may lead an individual to set goals or to accept performance standards assigned by someone else.

The domain of Locke's (1968) theoretical formulations is made more explicit when one considers his following statement:

No attempt is made . . . to specify the ultimate roots or causes of the particular [conscious] goals or intentions an individual develops on a task. Our interest . . . is only in the relationship between these goals and intentions, once established, and subsequent behavior. Thus, we are not presenting a complete theory of task performance but only some foundations for a theory (p. 159).

A sample of Locke's research is presented below with some of his major conclusions.

THE RELATIONSHIP OF GOALS TO PERFORMANCE

Locke argues that variation in performance can be better understood if the individual's conscious goals prior to performance are taken into account. He has attempted to demonstrate that goal difficulty directly influences level of performance. Generally speaking, hard-to-attain goals assigned to subjects in a laboratory setting lead to higher quantitative levels of task performance than do easier goals.

---

[1]Italics Locke's.

In three initial experiments (Locke 1966) "easy," "medium," and "hard" goals were assigned to college students serving as subjects. The experimental tasks involved listing words describable by adjectives such as "heavy," or thinking of several different uses for common objects. Subjects assigned hard goals gave significantly more responses during each of the fifteen one-minute trials than did medium or easy goal groups. The medium goal group gave significantly more responses per trial than the easy goal group. Locke concluded that a linear relationship exists between intended level of achievement and level of performance. The harder the goal, the higher the performance level. He states that this rule applies even though the subject's subjective probability of success of reaching hard goals was less than .10.

Perhaps Locke's conclusions should be qualified to state "given a high degree of goal commitment, hard goals lead to higher quantitative levels of task performance than do easy goals." The way in which he insures a high degree of goal commitment somewhat limits the generalizability of his results. Locke, in effect, uses the demand characteristics (Orne 1962) of the laboratory setting to insure that his subjects are highly committed to the goals assigned them.

Locke could argue that it does not matter how goal commitment is achieved as long as it is held constant, and perhaps he would be justified in making such a case. One still could demonstrate the effect of conscious goals on performance level. What is being questioned here, however, is Locke's generalization (1968, p. 162) that a linear relationship exists between performance (output) and goal difficulty level. Perhaps such a relationship exists for high levels of goal commitment achievable only in laboratory-like situations. Because Locke has not systematically varied goal commitment, no inference can be made about the relationship between conscious goals and performance at other than high levels of goal commitment.

Locke (1968, pp. 167-68) further points out that his results contradict the theory of Atkinson and Feather (1966). In their theory, the probability of success (PS) and satisfaction (or incentive, I) combine to determine level of performance. Since they are inversely and linearly related, maximum performance is said to occur when PS and I are equal to .50. "The curve relating probability of success to output should be bell-shaped, with extreme values of PS producing low output, and moderate values producing high output" (Locke 1968, p. 167).

Thus Locke's theory makes a prediction contrary to that of Atkinson and Feather. The subjects to whom Locke had assigned hard goals had higher performance levels than did subjects with moderate goals (see Figure 1).

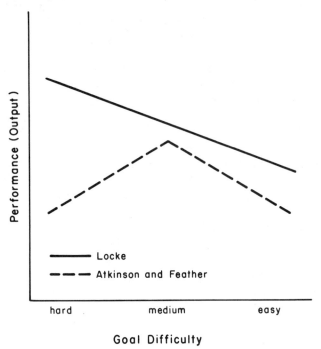

Goal Difficulty

FIGURE 1. Performance as a Function of Goal Difficulty for Locke (1968) and Atkinson and Feather (1966)

Locke explains this difference in terms of goal acceptance. If an individual really accepts a hard goal, then he will work to achieve it. Locke (1968) continues:

It is true that many people reject difficult tasks which are assigned to them and probably more people reject very hard tasks than reject moderately hard tasks. But the point is that once a hard task is accepted, the only logical thing to do is to try one's hardest until one decides to lower or abandon the goal. It is argued that people who do stop trying when confronted by a hard task are people who have decided the goal is impossible to reach and *who are no longer trying for that goal* (p. 168).[2]

---

[2]Italics Locke's.

Locke seems to imply that once a hard goal is accepted one will work to achieve it as long as he is *committed* to achieving that goal. Locke cannot justifiably use goal commitment as an explanatory device because he has not systematically varied goal commitment.

Perhaps goal acceptance could be used as an explanatory concept. However, to say that the subjects of Atkinson and Feather with the lowest probability of success did not perform at a high level because they did not *accept* hard goals leaves one with the task of explaining the actual acceptance of hard goals. Locke does not do so because, as he was quoted earlier, "No attempt is made to specify the ultimate roots or causes of the particular goals or intentions an individual develops on a task" (Locke 1968, p. 159). It appears that Locke's arguments are circular. He has attempted to explain a difference between two sets of empirical results by merely naming a possible explanatory variable—goal acceptance. Simply saying that subjects in low probability of success conditions vary in performance because of their differential acceptance of hard goals places a burden on one to try to explain the differential acceptance of hard goals. The theory of Atkinson and Feather contains manipulable variables which are said to influence task performance. Locke's variable of goal acceptance really does little to offer any systematic differential predictions. An individual accepts a hard goal or he does not. What influences an individual to accept a hard goal?

Specific versus Non-specific Goals

Locke offers a good deal of evidence indicating that specific quantitative hard goals lead to higher levels of performance than do goals of "do your best." Locke and Bryan (1966) compared the effectiveness of difficult specific goals with "do your best" goals. The task in this study required two groups of subjects to perform a matching procedure on a complex psychomotor task. Half the subjects (individually run) were given specific hard goals to reach on each of the twelve ten-minute trials. These goals were based on their performance on each immediately preceding trial. The other half of the subjects were told to "do their best." Post-experimental debriefing indicated that subjects in the hard goal group were actually trying to beat the standard set by the experimenter. Results of this study indicate that the performance level of both groups improved continuously over the twelve trials. The hard goal subjects, however, made more matches on all trials and increased their number of matches at a higher rate.

Two additional experiments (Locke and Bryan 1967) lend support to the view that specific hard goals lead to higher performance levels than do "do best" goals. A number cancellation task was used in the first of these experiments. Subjects in the hard goal group were offered a monetary incentive for reaching their assigned goals after the ninety-minute experimental period. Another group of subjects was told to "do its best." Once again, the hard goal group performed at a higher level. In the second experiment, a hard goal group solved a significantly greater number of addition problems than did a do best group. Each S (run individually) worked on the task for two hours. A third experimental group was given specific subgoals to reach at fifteen-minute intervals. This group performed at a level intermediate to the levels of performance of the hard goal and do best groups.

To summarize, it appears that setting specific goals does affect performance levels. In a laboratory setting specific hard goals produce higher quantitative levels of performance than do easy goals or goals of "do your best."

Apparently people told to do their best really do not. Thus, when trying to insure maximum effort expenditure from laboratory subjects, one may be wise to instruct subjects to strive to reach specific hard performance standards. Such a principle may be extended to situations beyond the laboratory. Kay, Meyer, and French (1965), for example, studied goal setting in an industrial setting. They found that setting specific goals during appraisal interviews led to better performance than not setting them. Goal setting in this case may have led to a clarification of performance duties so that effort expenditure was more efficient.

INCENTIVES

We will now turn our discussion to the role of incentives in Locke's theory. As previously defined, an incentive is an external object or event which incites action in the individual. Locke argues that an incentive does not affect behavior automatically but, rather, that the influences of incentives on behavior are the results of their effects on goals and intentions. Locke implies that incentives are effective in terms of the degree to which they "suggest specific goals or intentions to subjects" (Locke 1968, p. 184).

Locke actually attributes five functions to incentives: (1) they can incite action in the individual; (2) they somehow can affect an individual's ongoing goals and intentions; (3) to varying degrees, they can suggest specific goals or intentions to subjects; (4) they can get people to accept work goals; and (5) they can help insure an individual's commitment to goals over time. These five functions are not mutually exclusive, but it is difficult to come up with a common dimension pervading all of the functions Locke has specified.

Perhaps Locke's inclusiveness as to what an incentive is renders the task of arriving at a unique function difficult. The things he lists as incentives are: instructions, time limits, knowledge of score, competition, money, praise and reproof, and participation. Each of these incentives no doubt has differential effects on behavior both between and within individuals. At its current stage of development, Locke's theory is not concerned with differential evaluation of incentives.

Locke and his associates have conducted research on two of the previously mentioned incentives: knowledge of results and money. Several of their studies are discussed here.

Knowledge of Results

Of the five possible functions of incentives, the first three could describe the incentive nature of knowledge of results (KR). According to Locke, KR serves as an incentive when it suggests specific goals or performance standards. This motivational or incentive function is to be distinguished from the cue properties of KR. Both Ammons (1956) and Vroom (1964) note the difficulty of distinguishing between the motivational effects of KR and its cue function. The cue function provides one with information as to how to perform a task. The motivational function of KR has been demonstrated in studies such as that performed by Arps (1920). Subjects performed a weight lifting task which required little learning and cues were unnecessary. A group given KR performed the task at a faster rate and for a longer period of time than a group given no KR. Such results are believed to indicate that KR serves as a motivator in a general sense.

Two studies were carried out in an attempt to demonstrate empirically that the effect of KR is dependent on an individual's tendency to set goals when given KR (Locke 1967; Locke and Bryan 1969). Using a 2 x 2 analysis of variance, Locke (1967) attempted to separate the effects of KR from the effects of goal setting. The variables used were KR versus no KR and hard goals versus "do best" goals. The task consisted of adding a series of three two-digit numbers. Trial lengths were of either ten or fifteen minutes so that a subject could not easily keep track of the number of problems he attempted. In the KR condition subjects were told the number of problems they had correctly solved at the end of each trial. Subjects given no KR were given no such information. Hard goal subjects were given goals 10 percent higher than matched "do best" subjects. Results indicated a significant goal effect but no significant KR effect and no interaction. Locke concluded that KR has no automatic effect on performance level. One also must know whether an individual uses KR to set performance goals.

In the second study to be considered here (Locke and Bryan 1969), a similar 2 x 2 design was used. In this experiment subjects were given specific easy goals rather than "do best" goals. Greater care also was taken to insure that subjects in the no KR condition received no information they could use in setting performance goals. This was accomplished by putting the addition problems on paper tape and exposing them on a drum to the subject. Subjects in the hard and easy goal conditions were informed of their progress toward these goals, but supposedly not in a way conducive to the establishment of performance standards.[3] Once again, hard goal subjects performed at a higher level on the addition task than easy goal subjects. There was no significant KR effect and no interaction.

To reiterate Locke's point of view, KR will serve to increase performance levels only when the KR can be used to establish goals. If KR is given in such a way that an individual cannot easily establish performance standards, KR will not lead to increased performance.

The mere presence of KR does not always lead to goal setting. In a real-world study devoid of demand characteristics, Chapanis (1964) found that subjects given KR tended not to increase their

---

[3]As a matter of fact, the experimenter paced the subjects' work rate by signaling to them with a series of lights. That is, subjects were informed of their progress toward a goal. This procedure is somewhat suspect, because for KR (knowledge of total problems attempted) to have had an effect, subjects would have had to work at a faster rate than suggested by the lights controlled by the experimenter.

performance level. Locke (1968, p. 185) notes that KR is usually effective as an incentive in a laboratory setting because "the subject is actively looking for cues as to what he is supposed to do and is anxious to cooperate."

Money

The incentive function of money is considered to be somewhat different from that of KR. Knowledge of results may suggest goals or it may allow the individual to evaluate progress toward a goal. Locke (1968, p. 185) states that "the most important role played by money is probably to get a subject to accept an assigned task or goal or to insure his commitment to a job."

In an attempt to substantiate their hypothesis of how money acts as an incentive, Locke, Bryan, and Kendall (1968) performed a rather complex series of experiments. In the first of these, subjects performed a laboratory task under various goal and incentive conditions. The task consisted of one-minute trials during which subjects were to think of uses for common objects such as a cardboard box. Following two practice trials, and prior to each of two blocks of seven experimental trials, each of the experimental conditions was introduced. The effects of four experimental conditions were tested in a 2 x 2 analysis-of-variance design. The two levels of the goal dimension consisted of (1) goals being assigned by the experimenter, and (2) goals being self-set by the subject. The incentive dimension consisted of the presence of a monetary incentive versus no monetary incentive.

The performance level of subjects in each cell of the 2 x 2 table increased from the first block of seven trials to the second block of seven trials. This increase in performance corresponded to higher goals set by the experimenter in the assigned goal group as well as higher goals self-set by subjects in the non-assigned goal condition. With performance improvement scores from the first block of seven trials to the second block of seven trials taken as the dependent variable, a significant goal effect was obtained. The assigned goal groups demonstrated greater performance improvement than did the self-set goal group. There was no incentive or interaction effect. There was no difference in the performance levels of the two groups given assigned goals even though one received incentive and the other did not. Similarly, the self-set goal groups did not differ in performance level as a result of incentives.

Locke et al. take these results as supportive of their basic assumption that incentives affect behavior only through their effect on an individual's intentions. The authors argue that "the same goal level produced the same level of performance regardless of whether incentives were offered for goal attainment or not" (Locke, Bryan, and Kendall 1968, p. 110). Here it seems that the authors are essentially accepting the null hypothesis as support for their viewpoint. There was no significant incentive effect, therefore, incentives have no effect. To lend direct support to the notion that incentives influence performance through their effect on goals it would have to be demonstrated that incentives made an individual more committed to a goal or that he was able to reach a goal more often than someone not receiving an incentive. In this experiment, non-incentive subjects were apparently just as committed as subjects receiving an incentive.

Two additional groups were run in this first experiment. The same task was used, but goals were set so high that subjects in group I reached them 37 percent of the time on block I trials, and group II subjects reached them 32 percent of the time on block I. These percentages of success changed to 10 and 18 percent respectively for block II trials. Both groups were assigned these specific hard goals. Group I was given all or none incentive; group II was given no incentive. There were no significant performance differences between the two groups for either block of trials. Again the authors take this as support for their view that "incentive differences will not produce performance differences if the goal levels are the same" (Locke, Bryan, and Kendall 1968, p. 109). Both of these groups were probably performing at such a high level that an incentive effect could not occur.

In another experiment (Locke, Bryan, and Kendall 1968) the authors studied the effect of intentions and incentives as independent variables on the dependent variable, task choice. There were three blocks of ten one-minute experimental trials during which each subject was to unscramble words. Subjects had a choice as to the length of word they chose to unscramble (three to eleven letters) on each trial. The subjects were given no incentive for words unscrambled on block I trials, two cents for each word unscrambled on block II trials and ten cents for each word unscrambled on block III trials. The intention measure consisted of the subject's making a rating before each block of trials (B-intention) and each individual trial (T-intention) as to whether he would choose easy words or hard words to unscramble. Thus the dependent variable was the choice of the length of the word to be unscrambled. Incentives led to significantly easier word choices. To quote the authors, the results also indicated

that both B-intentions and T-intentions were significantly correlated with word choice both before and after amount of incentive was partialled out. In contrast, while amount of incentive was related significantly to word choice before partialling, the relationship was vitiated when T-intentions were partialled out, or when both B-intentions and T-intentions were partialled out (Locke, Bryan, and Kendall 1968, p. 113).

The results of this experiment really are not very compelling. T-intentions correlate very highly with word choice (r = .84). When the effects of incentive are partialled out the correlation decreases very little (r = .79). Incentive, on the other hand, correlates -.51 with word choice; the higher the incentive the shorter the word chosen to unscramble. When T-intentions are partialled out incentive correlates .21 with word choice. The logic here becomes somewhat clouded. It can be argued that one of the experimental cues that leads subjects to "intend" to choose short words in the first place is the presence of an incentive condition. Incentive in this case does not function so much as a traditional motivational concept as it does a cue telling a subject how he is to perform. To then partial out the effect of incentive from the effect of intention really is somewhat meaningless since the incentive caused the intentions the subjects had. In summary, the effects of intentions are associated with the effects of incentives since the incentive conditions in this experiment made up the vehicle by which intentions were instigated.

In the fourth experiment, intentions and incentive were again related to the dependent variable—length of word choice. Using partial correlation techniques, the authors concluded that intention was the primary factor influencing word choice. Incentives and the experimental instructions had a lesser effect. Intentions of subjects were determined by means of ratings after they had been instructed to either (1) achieve success, (2) achieve personal achievement, or to try to overcome the greatest possible challenges. These instructions were rated 1, 3, and 5 respectively in order of difficulty. When instructions were partialled out, the correlation of intentions with word choice dropped from .88 to .76. The logic of partialling out instructions designed to establish intentions is again of questionable value. To cause intentions by means of instructions and then

partial out instructions to demonstrate the potency of intentions
seems somewhat meaningless.

The authors conclude by claiming that the results of these studies
support their views. That is,

if goal or intention level was partialled out, there was no effect of
incentive on behavior. This was demonstrated in the studies of performance
level by showing that the same goal level produced the same performance
level regardless of whether incentives were offered by performance or not.
The same fact was demonstrated in the studies of choice by showing that
when behavioral intention level was partialled out, the initial effects of
incentives on choice were vitiated. Finally, [the authors conclude] the three
studies of choice demonstrated that when incentives did affect behavior,
these behavior differences were associated with equivalent differences in
behavioral intentions (Locke, Bryan, and Kendall 1968, p. 119).

It seems important to reiterate a fact to consider when one is
attempting to demonstrate that incentive influences choice. It is important that the "incentive variable" not serve as a cue prescribing
the socially desirable choice for a laboratory subject to make. If
incentive does act as such a cue (demand) in the laboratory, then
it would seem essential to include those salient characteristics of the
laboratory setting influencing the effect of incentive on behavior into
a theory dealing with the role of incentives on behavior. Of course,
this is not usually done. The value of laboratory experimentation
exists because facts established in the laboratory are generalizable to
the real world.

To summarize this discussion of the role of incentives in Locke's
theory, he generally views goals and intentions as helpful in explaining the effects of incentives on behavior. Locke (1968, p. 184) has
schematicized elements of his theory as follows:

Environmental   Goal
Event   Setting
e.g., Incentive → Cognition → Evaluation → Intention → Performance
      1   2   3   4   5

In Locke's words, he deals with the connections between events
4 and 5, and 1, 4, and 5. A complete theory of task motivation,
he says, also would have to deal with events 2 and 3. He does
state that the sequence of events in the schematic is highly simplified. As depicted, an incentive somehow gives rise to cognition,
evaluation, goal setting, and finally all of this somehow influences
performance. The effects of incentives are probably more complex.

They do not merely suggest performance goals. A laboratory setting is the place where incentives are probably most suggestive of specific performance standards; this is true because subjects are actively looking for stimuli to guide their behavior.

Lest this critique seem too critical, this paper is not meant to slight the importance of such topics as intentionality, goal setting, and task variables in general. There also has been no intent to slight Locke's productive research efforts. He has presented some rather compelling evidence indicating that an individual's conscious goals do influence his performance. Suffice it to say that goal setting may be an effective way of inducing increased effort over an extended period of time if the goals are realistically set and goal attainment is rewarded. Goal setting also may be facilitative if the act of goal setting clarifies requirements of the task to be performed. Perhaps Locke's most substantive contribution is related to this latter point. He has demonstrated that specific hard goals lead to higher quantitative levels of performance than less specific "do your best" goals.

At this point it might prove enlightening to place Locke's research in further perspective. Where do his results fit into the motivation literature?

When studying a phenomenon such as the effect of conscious goals on performance, one has the option of studying it in the laboratory or in the real world. There are advantages and disadvantages inherent in both settings. While real world studies may produce more generalizable results, laboratory studies may offer the opportunity to isolate a phenomenon and to study the phenomenon independent of extraneous variables. Locke has been able to isolate the facilitative effects of conscious performance goals in the laboratory. He has also been successful in demonstrating the effect of incentives in the laboratory. The major question arising from Locke's laboratory results is one of generalizability. Will conscious performance goals and incentives exert such powerful influences in non-laboratory settings where goal commitment is low and incentives are less of a cue prescribing socially expected behavior?

Some current research trends indicate that we eventually may find out more about the effects of goal setting and incentives. Current hybrid models of motivation (Porter and Lawler 1968; Campbell, Dunnette, Lawler, and Weick 1970) seem to envelop some of Locke's research and theoretical formulations. The Campbell et al. model points specifically to needed areas of research.

We need to know how an individual's subjective probability of goal accomplishment influences his effort expenditure. Campbell et al. (1970) suggest that in a real world setting the primary determiner of such probabilities, or expectancies, may be the individual's perception of his own abilities to achieve the goal. One would expect these perceptions to be somewhat more salient or influential in tasks or work requiring complex ability.

Individual preferences for goals of varying difficulty also should be investigated. Perhaps some individuals actually will expend more effort if they strive to reach easy goals and are under less pressure. We also should be cognizant of the direction of effort expenditure in relation to goal difficulty. If task requirements are more demanding of performance quality than performance quantity, for example, what kinds of goals (if any) should be assigned?

With regard to incentives, we need to know how an individual's expectancy of reward, given goal accomplishment, influences his striving toward that goal. Do monetary incentives assure maximum effort expenditure if the individual does not perceive them to be contingent on goal accomplishment? How are individual preferences for different kinds of incentives related to effort expenditure and goal commitment? Certainly these are not new questions, and we are beginning to accumulate some answers. The questions are raised here because they are related to Locke's research.

REFERENCES

AMMONS, R. B. 1956. Effects of knowledge of performance: A survey and tentative theoretical formulation. *Journal of General Psychology* 54: 279-99.

ARPS, G. F. 1920. Work and knowledge of results versus work without knowledge of results. *Psychological Review Monograph Supplement* 28 (3, Whole No. 125).

ATKINSON, J. W., AND FEATHER, N. T. 1966. *A theory of achievement motivation.* New York: Wiley.

BRYAN, J. F., AND LOCKE, E. A. 1967. Parkinson's law as a goal setting phenomenon. *Organizational Behavior and Human Performance* 2: 258-75.

CAMPBELL, J. P. et al. 1970. *Managerial effectiveness: Current knowledge and research needs.* New York: McGraw-Hill.

CHAPANIS, A. 1964. Knowledge of performance as an incentive in repetitive monotonous tasks. *Journal of Applied Psychology* 48: 263-67.

KAY, E.; MEYER, H. H.; AND FRENCH, J. R. P., JR. 1965. Split roles in performance appraisal. *Harvard Business Review* 43:123-29.

LOCKE, E. A. 1966. The relationship of intentions to level of performance. *Journal of Applied Psychology* 50: 60-66.

——— . 1967. The motivational effects of knowledge of results: Knowledge or goal setting? *Journal of Applied Psychology* 51: 324-29.

——— . 1968. Toward a theory of task motivation and incentives. *Organizational Behavior and Human Performance* 3: 157-89.

LOCKE, E. A., AND BRYAN, J. F. 1967. Performance goals as determinants of level of performance and boredom. *Journal of Applied Psychology* 51: 120-30.
——— . 1969. Knowledge of score and goal level as determinants of work rate. *Journal of Applied Psychology* 53: 59-65.
LOCKE, E. A.; BRYAN, J. F.; AND KENDALL, L. M. 1968. Goals and intentions as mediators of effects of monetary incentives on behavior. *Journal of Applied Psychology* 52: 104-21.
ORNE, M. T. 1962. On the social psychology of the psychological experiment with particular reference to demand characteristics. *American Psychologist* 17: 776-83.
PORTER, W., AND LAWLER, E. E. 1968. *Managerial attitudes and performance.* Homewood, Illinois: Irwin.
VROOM, V. H. 1964. *Work and motivation.* New York: Wiley.

16

Expectancy Theory in Managerial Motivation:
Review of Relevant Research

ROBERT J. HOUSE

AND

MAHMOUD A. WAHBA

Recently, three reviews of empirical research based on expectancy theory have been published. Mitchell and Biglan (1971) reviewed the concept of expectancy in three areas of psychology: verbal conditioning, attitude, and industrial psychology. In the area of industrial psychology they reviewed six studies. Heneman and Schwab (in press) reviewed the research design and measurement issues connected with nine field studies. Wahba and House (1972) summarized fourteen empirical studies (including five studies dealing specifically with managers). They also compared fifteen alternative models of expectancy derived from psychology and economics.

These reviews show that the predictions of expectancy theory are generally supported. However, it is also evident that the magnitude of the support for the theory is inconsistent from study to study. It is discomforting to note that the levels of the concurrent or predictive validity coefficients (usually in the form of multiple regression coefficients) range from .72 for predictions of satisfaction to as low as .11 for predictions of performance. The coefficient of satisfaction is generally about .50 and the coefficient of performance rating is generally about .30 in the majority of the studies. Also, it was concluded by Heneman and Schwab (in press) that the research on the theory has been inadequate in three respects: the number of independent variables studied, the measurement of these variables, and the statistical analysis performed. It was additionally concluded that there is an obvious discrepancy between the theoretical and the

Printed by permission of the authors. Unpublished paper, Bernard M. Baruch College of the City University of New York, 1972.

operational definitions of the relevant variables. Mitchell and Biglan (1971) noted that the uses of expectancy theory in industrial and organizational psychology have been less successful than its uses in the areas of verbal conditioning and attitude formulation.

In an earlier paper, the present authors (Wahba and House 1972) attributed these and other problems to some unresolved logical and methodological issues basic to the theory. It was pointed out that the essence of expectancy theory in work and motivation is *choice behavior*. As such, it was shown that the present formulation of the theory, and consequently the empirical research based on it, ignores the rationality assumptions underlying choice behavior.[1] It was also pointed out that the major concepts of the theory (namely, expectancy and valence) lack the necessary theoretical clarification. Furthermore, it was shown that the typical formulation of the theory is based on optimization choice criteria (most writers imply gain maximizations, few propose satisficing instead of maximizing). The empirical validity of these criteria was questioned in light of recent findings in other studies of choice behavior in general. Alternative criteria were proposed.[2]

Whereas the papers by Mitchell and Biglan (1971) and Heneman and Schwab (in press) reviewed some studies in detail, the present paper will attempt to review the overall findings of fourteen studies with regard to the parameters of the integrative model proposed by the writers elsewhere.

Expectancy I and II

Despite the clarification added to the theory by the distinction between Expectancy 1 and Expectancy 2 (E_1 and E_2), there are only two studies which indicate that this distinction is empirically (as opposed to conceptually) useful (Georgopolous et. al. 1957; Graen 1969). Georgopolous et. al. operationalized E_1 by obtaining subject self-ratings of their freedom to vary their level of performance. This inferred (as opposed to direct) measure of E_1 was found to be

---

[1]The rationality assumptions discussed in the earlier paper include preference and indifference among alternatives, transitivity of preferences and indifferences, dominance, independence of irrelevant outcomes, continuity, and independence of expectancy and valence.

[2]Some of these alternative criteria include variance preference, probability preference, the sure-thing principle, the regret matrix, and potential surprise criterion.

positively related to self-reports of performance and to moderate the relationship between E_2 and performance in a manner consistent with the theory (i.e., subjects with high E_1 had significantly greater relationships between E_2 and performance).

Graen (1969) operationalized E_1 by a single question to his experimental subjects. He found that this measure correlated .32 with performance. When weighted by E_1, the correlation between the valence of outcomes and performance ranged from .18 to .46, indicating that E_1 alone generally predicted as well as outcomes multiplied by E_1. As in most other studies, the correlations between the outcomes alone and performance were not computed, and thus the interacting effect of E_1 and extrinsic valence (V) could not be compared with the effect of V alone.

Other attempts to operationalize E_1 have all been based on a small number of questionnaire items and have either failed to add significantly to the amount of performance or effort variance accounted for in regressions (Mitchell and Albright 1971), or have been found to be very highly correlated with E_2 (Lawler 1966; Lawler and Porter 1967; Lawler 1968; Porter and Lawler 1968). These studies suggest that E_1 and E_2, when operationalized by questions with similar format [e.g., "If I work hard my performance will improve" (E_1), or "If my performance improves I will receive more pay" (E_2)] share common method variance. E_1 might be better measured indirectly by asking respondents to indicate how much they personally control their own performance, or how free they are to vary their level of effort.

E_1 and E_2 have been combined into a single measure ($E_1 + E_2$) in studies by Lawler (1965), Lawler (1966), Lawler and Porter (1967), Porter and Lawler (1968). In all of these studies this scale has been positively related to self and supervisory ratings of the subjects' performance and effort. Lawler (1966) also found this scale to interact with the subject's ability in a manner consistent with Vroom's theory.

The independent effects of E_2 have been measured by Georgopolous et. al. (1957) and Galbraith and Cummings (1967). Georgopolous found E_2 to be positively related to self-ratings of performance. Galbraith and Cummings found it not to be a significant predictor alone, but to interact significantly with: (a) subjects' ability *and* valence of supervisory supportiveness and pay, and (b) with E_1 and valence of pay.

These studies suggest that new measures of E_1 are needed, and that its independent effects and its independence from the other variables of the theory remain to be determined. They also suggest that E_2 is both a consistent predictor alone and in combination with other independent variables.

The Distinction Between Various Types of Valences

The distinction between (*a*) intrinsic and extrinsic valence and (*b*) intrinsic valence of behavior (IV_b) and intrinsic valence of accomplishment (IV_a) appears to be conceptually useful. For example, these distinctions permitted House (1971) to fit prior leadership findings together into a meaningful and consistent pattern that could be explained by viewing the findings from the perspective of the leader's effect on the intrinsic and extrinsic valence and on E_1 and E_2 of the subordinate.

House argued that prior conflicting findings regarding leader consideration and initiating structure could be reconciled by considering the amount of intrinsic valence inherent in the subject's required task behavior (IV_b) and goal attainment (IV_a).

Similarly, Lawler (1970) argued that prior findings showing job enlargement to be generally more related to quality than quantity of performance could be explained in terms of intrinsic valence increases which accompany job enlargement. Specifically, he argued that such increases in valence should, according to the theory, result in increases in vigilance and pride of product rather than higher expenditures of physical effort. Vigilance and pride of product should, in turn, be more related to quality than quantity of work performed. These two applications of the intrinsic-extrinsic distinction illustrate its potential theoretical usefulness. Unfortunately, there have been only three studies that have operationalized these distinctions. These will be reviewed here.

The intrinsic valences. Galbraith and Cummings (1967) were the first to distinguish between intrinsic and extrinsic valence and the first to operationalize the distinction. They operationalized intrinsic valence by use of a self-report ego-involvement questionnaire, which appears to be primarily a measure of involvement in the task, or IV_b. Galbraith and Cummings tested various combinations of V and ability by use of stepwise regression analyses. They found ego involvement to be moderated positively by the subject's ability and the expectancy that work leads to peer acceptance. Alone, IV_b was not found to have a significant effect on performance. Graen (1969) and Mitchell and Albright (1971) compared the relative power of intrinsic and extrinsic valences as predictors of performance and satisfaction. In both studies it was found that effort and performance were more strongly related to valence of intrinsic rewards, such as work pride, self-esteem, personal development, and experience of important achievement (IV_a) than to valence of extrinsic rewards, such as pay, promotion or recognition (V). The implications of this finding are important and will be discussed in the concluding section.

The extrinsic valences. Surprisingly, the effect of the valence of specific extrinsic rewards alone on performance has been compared only a few times with the effect of extrinsic rewards with valence in interaction with other variables. The major exception to this statement concerns pay. Two of the three studies in which such a comparison was made indicate that the valence of monetary rewards bears a significant positive relationship to performance for non-managers (Georgopolous et. al. 1959) and for both government and industrial managers from seven different organizations (Porter and Lawler 1968). Cummings and Galbraith (1967) also made such comparisons and found no independent effect of the valence of money, group acceptance, fringe benefits, promotions, or supervisory supportiveness. They did find th.t valence of group acceptance and pay is significant when moderated by E_2 and that valence of pay and supervisory supportiveness, in joint interaction with ability and E_2, was also significant.

When multiplied by their respective second-level expectancies, extrinsic valences have been consistently predictive. The valence of such widely varied extrinsic rewards as working conditions, company practices, superior recognition, pay, peer acceptance, and fringe benefits, when multiplied by E_2, has been shown to be related to satisfaction (Mitchell and Albright 1971) and performance (Hackman and Porter 1968; Lawler 1968; Lawler and Porter 1967; Lawler 1966). These correlations range widely (from .11 to .72) and are highly inconsistent from study to study.

Several other studies have shown that the sum of the products of *several* (as opposed to one) extrinsic valences multiplied by respective second-level expectancies have had moderate (.30 to .60) relationships to satisfaction (Graen 1969) and performance (Goodman et. al. 1970; Lawler 1966; Graen 1969; Lawler and Porter 1967; Porter and Lawler 1968; Hackman and Porter 1967; Lawler 1968). Although these studies did not test for the significance of valence alone, they are consistent with the predictions of the theory.

Summary and Conclusions

When viewed collectively, the studies reviewed above provide the basis for several important conclusions.

First, it appears that the distinctions between E_1 and E_2 give promise of increasing the predictive power of the theory. However, methods of operationalizing E_1 so as not to confound it with E_2 are yet to be developed, and additional studies designed to test its predictive power are required.

Second, E_2 and intrinsic valence have been shown to be important, if not indispensable, constructs. In some studies E_2 and IV_b or IV_a were significant independent predictors. In other studies, extrinsic valences were not predictive alone, but when multipled by E_2 were predictive. In all studies except one (Galbraith and Cummings 1967) in which intrinsic valence was measured separately, it was a significant predictor of performance.

Third, valence of intrinsic rewards is shown to be a more powerful predictor than the valences of all extrinsic rewards. This finding is significant because it suggests that management practices directed at providing intrinsic satisfactions are more powerful than the conventionally used extrinsic rewards. The fact that the finding is demonstrated with young (fifteen- to eighteen-year-old) part-time female employees (Graen 1969) as well as a higher occupational level group (Mitchell and Albright 1971) makes it even more significant, since young females would intuitively be expected to be motivated more by supplemental income than by intrinsic job factors.

It is likely that intrinsic rewards are more motivational not only because they are more highly valued but also because the receiver does not have to depend on others for them. Rather, they are obtained directly from job accomplishment. Consequently, the corresponding expectancy of attaining intrinsic rewards as a result of working hard is also more likely than the expectancy of attaining extrinsic rewards.

Fourth, the only extrinsic valence which is found to be consistently predictive is that associated with pay. Pay has been shown to be predictive alone and also when weighted by E_2. All other extrinsic valences have been shown to be unrelated to performance unless multiplied by E_2. These findings concerning intrinsic rewards, pay, and other extrinsic rewards are consistent with Graen's (1969) assertion that unless the relationships between effort-accomplishment and rewards is concretely and unambiguously established, the theory will not hold. Since intrinsic rewards follow directly from effort or goal accomplishment, their linkage to performance is both clear and highly probable. Pay is generally the most tangible and concrete of the extrinsic rewards and most likely to be linked, in the perception of the subject, to goal attainment in an unambiguous and concrete manner. Other extrinsic rewards, not necessarily following directly from performance and being less tangible than pay, are less likely to be perceived as contingent on performance unless management makes a visible effort to establish such a linkage. When the research explicitly considers the subject's E_2, we consistently find extrinsic rewards significantly correlated with performance.

Thus the evidence to date indicates that, generally, the valence of extrinsic rewards has little effect on performance or satisfaction unless multipled by E_2, and then the effect varies widely but is generally quite low. The major exception to this statement concerns valence of pay, which has been shown to have a motivating effect on non-management and government and industrial managers in seven different organizations.

Fifth, the above review clearly suggests that more complete tests of the theory are in order. A greater effort should be directed toward testing the overall prediction of the theory. Most of the previous studies tested only limited parts of the theory. Consequently, the overall predictive validity of the theory is virtually unknown. This complete test of the theory should be performed for managers and non-managers.

Only the studies by Graen (1969) and Mitchell and Albright (1971) included measures of E_1, E_2, performance and satisfaction, and V. Not surprisingly, these two studies yielded more information than any of the other studies singly and perhaps in combinations.

Finally, the overall state of empiric knowledge can be summarized as follows:

$$M = IV_b, E_1, [IV_a + \sum_{i=1}^{n} (E_2 \times V)].$$

That is, the predictive power of IV alone is well established as is the power of extrinsic rewards (V) when multiplied by E_2. The predictive power of E_1 and IV_b is suggested by some studies, but the manner by which they should be combined with the IV_a, E_2, and V is still to be determined.

REFERENCES

CAMPBELL, J. P.; DUNNETTE, M. D.; LAWLER, E. E.; and WEICK, K. E. 1970. *Managerial behavior, performances and effectiveness.* New York: McGraw-Hill.

DUNNETTE, M. D. 1967. The role of financial compensation in managerial motivation. *Organizational Behavior and Human Performance* 2:175-216.

EVANS, M. G. 1968. The effects of supervisory behavior upon worker perception of their path-goal relationship. Ph.D. dissertation. Yale University.

GALBRAITH, J., and CUMMINGS, L. 1967. An empiric investigation of the motivational determinants of past performance: Interactive effects between instrumentality-valence, motivation, and ability. *Organizational Behavior and Human Performance* 2, no. 3:237-57.

GAVIN, J. F. 1970. Ability, effort, and role perception as antecedents of job performance. *Experimental Publication System* 5: manuscript number 190A.

GEORGOPOULOS, B. S.; MAHONEY, G. M.; and JONES, N. W. 1957. A path-goal approach to productivity. *Journal of Applied Psychology* 41:345-53.

GOODMAN, P. S.; ROSE, J. H.; and FURCON, J. E. 1970. Comparison of motivational antecedents of the work performance of scientists and engineers. *Journal of Applied Psychology* 14:491-95.

GRAEN, G. 1969. Instrumentality theory of work motivation: Some experimental results and suggested modifications. *Journal of Applied Psychology Monograph* 53, no. 2:1-25.

HACKMAN, J. R., and PORTER, L. W. 1968. Expectancy theory predictions of work effectiveness. *Organizational Behavior and Human Performance* 3:417-26.

HENEMAN, H. H., and SCHWAB, D. P. (In press.) An evaluation of research on expectancy theory predictions of employee performance.

HOUSE, R. J. 1971. A path goal theory of leader effectiveness. *Administrative Science Quarterly* 16, no. 3:321-38.

LAWLER, E. E. 1966. Ability as a moderator of the relationship between job attitudes and job performance. *Personnel Psychology* 19:153-64.

———. 1968. A correlational-causal analysis of the relationship between expectancy attitudes and job performance. *Journal of Applied Psychology* 52:462-68.

———. 1970. Job attitudes and employee motivation: Theory, research, and practice. *Personnel Psychology* 23:223-37.

———. 1971. *Pay and organizational effectiveness: A psychological perspective.* New York: John Wiley & Sons.

———, and PORTER, L. W. 1967. Antecedent attitudes of effective managerial performance. *Organizational Behavior and Human Performance* 2:122-42.

MITCHELL, T. R., and ALBRIGHT, D. (In press.) Expectancy theory predictions of job satisfaction, job effort, job performance, and retention of naval aviation officers. *Organizational Behavior and Human Performance.*

MITCHELL, T. R., and KNUDSON, B. W. 1971. Instrumentality theory predictions of students' attitudes toward business and their choice of business as an occupation. Working paper, July. University of Washington, Technical Report 71-27.

PORTER, L. W., and LAWLER, E. E. 1968. *Managerial attitudes and performance.* Homewood, Ill.: Irwin-Dorsey.

VROOM, V. H. 1964. *Work and motivation.* John Wiley & Sons.

WAHBA, M., and HOUSE, R. 1972. Expectancy theory in work and motivation: Some logical and methodical issues. Working paper, Baruch College, City University of New York.

WOFFORD, J. C. 1971. The motivational basis of job satisfaction and job performance. *Personnel Psychology* 24:501-19.

17

The Concept of Equity
in the Perception of Pay

KARL E. WEICK

Anyone who tries to develop systematic notions about the effects of pay has to contend with some puzzling behaviors. He has to explain, for example, why assembly line workers who are overpaid dislike their job and their supervisor more than assembly line workers who are paid less money.[1] He has to explain why overpayment on an hourly basis leads to high productivity whereas overpayment on a piece-rate basis leads to restriction of output.[2] He has to explain why a person might try to convince a coworker to expend more effort, even when this would decrease his own financial outcomes and might anger the coworker.

It is very difficult to explain these behaviors. Obviously these findings are not consistent with a model of economic man[3]; neither do they fit neatly into an instrumental model,[4] or an achievement model.[5] In the absence of satisfactory models to explain the effects of incentives, investigators have usually resorted to specific and limited explanations. When an increase in incentive is not accompanied by an increase in effort, it is suggested that more effort would disrupt group affiliations,[6] or that other needs are being satisfied, such as taking it easy.[7] Although plausible, these explanations lack predictive power and are not fruitful in generating hypotheses.

A recent theoretical wedge into problems of compensation has been provided by equity theory,[8] which is one of several recent theories that exploit an exchange model of interaction.[9] Gamson,

Reprinted by permission of the author and publisher from *Administrative Science Quarterly* 11 (December 1966):413-19.

for example, has shown that more accurate predictions can be made of coalition formation, if one assumes that the participants who band together are influenced by a parity norm when they divide their winnings.[10] Jones has demonstrated that illegitimate social influence (ingratiation) can be explained by concepts of exchange.[11] Equity theory focuses on the fact that the outcomes of any process of exchange can be perceived as just or unjust, equitable or inequitable. The theory then is concerned with antecedents of inequity and the actions that an individual takes to restore equity. Although equity theory has implications for numerous settings besides industry, this paper centers on the implications of equity for financial compensation.[12]

IMPORTANT THEMES

A definition and an example best illustrate equity theory. Adams defines inequity as follows: "Inequity exists for Person whenever he perceives that the ratio of his outcomes to inputs and the ratio of Other's outcomes to Other's inputs are unequal, either (a) when he and Other are in a direct exchange or (b) when both are in an exchange relationship with a third party and Person compares himself to Other."[13] This definition is quite different from the earlier definition that guided equity research.[14] The chief differences are: *(1)* the definition now refers to an unequal relationship between the two persons, whereas earlier, reference was made to an obverse relationship; *(2)* the definition explicitly refers to a ratio of outcomes to inputs, whereas the earlier version had no reference to the idea of ratio; and *(3)* "Other" can be either the object of an exchange or a coworker, whereas the earlier definition covered only relationships with a coworker.

If some liberties are taken with Milgram's obedience paradigm, it is possible to illustrate some features of a situation of inequity.[15] Three subjects are supervised by an experimenter who urges the subjects throughout their task to continue to follow the rules, regardless of the consequences. One subject reads a list of paired associates to a victim who is to learn them, another subject records whether learning takes place, and the third worker—the only naive subject in the experiment—sets a shock intensity dial and administers *increasing* amounts of electric shock whenever the victim fails a learning trial. All three workers seemingly have similar outcomes,

which are fairly high: they are each paid $4.50, they have the satis-
faction of helping science, and so on. But there are striking differences in inputs. Both the worker who reads the list and the worker
who records the errors perform effortless, trivial tasks; however, the
person who selects the shock levels and administers painful shock
(the "victim" screams and pleads for relief at high-intensity shock
levels), not only has more costly inputs (for example, he worries more
about what each charge does, and is more deliberate and hesitant
in changing the setting), but his outcomes may be lowered by guilt
and anxiety about what he has done to the victim. Assuming that
the person who administers shock feels the inequity of having higher
inputs than either of his two coworkers for the same and possibly
lower outcomes, he can react in one of several ways: (1) he can
lower his inputs by using lower shock levels or minimizing his role
in the task; (2) he can persuade the other workers to raise their inputs or deceive himself into thinking they are making high inputs;
(3) he can try to convince the coworkers that they should accept
lower outcomes for their inputs (for example, give back part of the
$4.50 that they are paid); or (4) he can leave the situation. Any
one of these actions should reduce the tension associated with his
feeling of inequity.

This obedience paradigm is not intended to convey a model of
industrial work behavior, but it does convey the principal concepts
of equity theory. Equity, first of all involves a ratio of outcomes
to inputs as *perceived* by the person. Inputs can include such items
as age, beauty, education, and effort—anything that a person regards
as relevant in the exchange and for which he expects a just return.
Outcomes involve pay, intrinsic job satisfaction, rewarding supervision, a parking place, and so on. These several inputs and outcomes are summed to determine the ratio and weighted according
to importance.

Questions of equity arise when a person compares his ratio with
coworkers, supervisors, groups, or even with one's own ratio. Equity
exists when the ratio of inputs and outcomes are identical between
two people (for example, both exert high effort for little money)
or when *both* the inputs and outcomes of the other person are higher
or lower than *both* the inputs and outcomes of the person. Dissatisfaction occurs when ratios are unequal, and it is assumed that
the greater the discrepancy between ratios, the greater the inequity
and the pressures to reduce it. Thus, a person will feel inequity if
he expends high effort for low outcomes (high/low) while his co-

worker gets high outcomes for the same amounts of effort (high/high); but, he will be even more bothered if the coworker obtains his high outcomes with low inputs (low/high). It is also assumed that the threshold for feelings of inequity is higher when a person is overrewarded than when his rewards are inadequate.[16] Overrewards can be perceived as "good fortune" or as secretly deserved. Jones's studies of ingratiation have shown that vanity is a crucial variable in social interaction.[17]

Inequity can be reduced in several ways: (*1*) by actually altering either inputs or outcomes, (*2*) by perceptually distorting inputs or outcomes, (*3*) by leaving the field, (*4*) by getting the comparison person to change, or (*5*) by changing to another comparison person. Although there are few explicit principles about choice of resolution, it is assumed that persons strive for maximally positive outcomes, that they adopt the least effortful resolution, and that they act so as to preserve self-esteem.[18] Equity theory is especially appropriate for the study of compensation, because effort is assumed to be one of the most tractable inputs; and wages, especially piece-rate, are unambiguous yet tractable outcomes. Most of the data obtained so far by Adams involve situations of overpayment; the worker has low inputs (he is unskilled), yet he receives wages normally given only to those who are highly skilled.[19] Overpayment on a piece-rate basis leads to greater concern with quality.[20] It is presumed that a person who tries to resolve inequitable piece-rate overpayment by producing more units may increase inequity with respect to a comparison worker, whereas being quality conscious enables him to keep his financial outcomes down while increasing his inputs. Adams reports data from a field study by Clark,[21] which show that persons who have higher inputs than their coworkers (because of more education), yet receive identical wages, will reduce inputs such as effort expenditure. With this brief review of the theory, some conceptual and empirical issues raised by equity theory can be examined more closely.

CONCEPTUAL AND EMPIRICAL PROBLEMS

Ambiguity of Input and Outcome

The content of most existing experiments in equity theory has drawn attention away from the simple but important problem that it is often difficult to determine whether a given behavior is an input or an outcome. In the laboratory settings, subjects usually focus on their own effort as the salient input and on their own salary as the salient outcome. But in everyday work situations many more behaviors can be recognized and weighted in determining the input-outcome ratio, and many of these can be assigned to *either* side of the ratio. This compounds the problem of making accurate predictions, because if the behavior is perceived as an outcome, the result may be inequity, but if it is viewed as an input, equity will occur.

For example, suppose a worker observes that his comparison person sweats profusely while he works. He could view this behavior either as an indication that the comparison person works hard and invests much effort in his job (i.e., he has high inputs) or as an indication that his coworker receives considerable physical discomfort from the job (i.e., he has low outcomes). If the observer himself has low inputs and low outcomes, he will experience inequity if he sees sweating as an input, but he will *not* experience inequity if he sees it as an outcome. Perhaps, then, persons perceive ambiguous work behaviors in whatever form will create equity. In the example of sweating, the observer might be expected to regard this behavior as an outcome and not an input, since this would create equity and reduce tension.

Other examples of potentially ambiguous behaviors could be cited. If a comparison person persistently gets to work late, the observer might view this either as a low input (he contributes less time to his job) or as a high outcome (he has shorter hours and more time to himself). If a comparison person spends much time talking with people around him, the observer could see this either as a low input (he spends less time and energy on his job) or as a high outcome (not only does he get the same salary, but he has friends and a more varied work day). If a comparison person trains a new worker, this could be seen as a high input (he has to work *and* train for no extra pay), or as a high outcome (he has higher status and a more interesting job).

Although ambiguous work behaviors make it more difficult to predict when inequity will be perceived, they provide a means of predicting how inequity might be resolved once it does occur. The example of sweating illustrates how insight into resolutions might be gained. Suppose the observer has high inputs and receives relatively low outcomes (high/low). If his sweating coworker is a low/low worker, the observer might be expected to view sweating as an input, which would make the coworker's inputs change from low to high, so that equity would be established. If the coworker is high/ high, sweating would be viewed as an outcome, since this enables the observer to recast the coworker into a high/low situation. If the sweating coworker is low/high (a situation of maximum inequity for the observer might see sweating as *both* an input and an outcome: a high input, which raises one side of the ratio, and also as a low outcome which lowers the other side of the ratio. If the coworker, like the observer, is in a high/low situation, assignment of sweating to both sides enables the observer to confirm an equitable relationship.

The preceding line of argument has several implications for equity theory. First, the assignment of work behaviors to inputs or outcomes might be an effective means of reducing inequity or maintaining equity. Second, in a work situation in which there are several ambiguous work behaviors, it might be difficult for large inequities to develop. Possible inequity could be met by frequent reinterpretation of ambiguous work behaviors so as to preserve equity. Third, it suggests that the resolution of inequity by changing to a new comparison person would rarely occur,[22] because once a person chose a comparison worker, there would be considerable latitude for the interpretation of his behavior. A fourth implication is that comparison persons probably will be chosen for reasons other than their similarity in input-outcome ratios. Once a person has selected someone with whom to compare himself, for whatever reason, he should have considerable freedom to perceive the work behaviors of the other person in an equitable manner. Adams notes that "cognitive distortion of Other's inputs and outcomes may be somewhat less difficult than distortion of one's own, since cognitions about Other are probably less well anchored than are those concerning oneself."[23] However, equity theory as it is currently formulated does not seem to exploit this possibility sufficiently.

Interdependence of Input and Outcome

Even when inputs and outcomes can be distinguished, they are often intercorrelated. Adams observes that "in classifying some variables as inputs and others as outcomes, it is not implied that they are independent, except conceptually. Inputs and outcomes are, in fact, intercorrelated but imperfectly so."[24] Intercorrelation is cited both to point up the importance of perceptual variables and to indicate that it is precisely because of imperfect correlations that problems of equity arise. If inputs and outcomes are interrelated, however, then it could be difficult to reduce inequity even if the interrelation is only moderate. The difficulty arises because an attempt to adjust one side of one's ratio to align it with a comparison person's ratio might also unintentionally change the *other* side of one's ratio, creating a new source of inequity.

Consider a person making low inputs to his job and receiving low outcomes (low/low), while his comparison person receives high outcomes for the same low inputs (low/high). The person must raise his outcomes to establish equity. Suppose that he decides to raise his outcomes by making his job more attractive. He might institute an informal job rotation arrangement with coworkers. Rotation systems may be difficult to start as well as maintain, and they probably require considerable surveillance, especially if company policy frowns on rotation. If the person succeeds in creating a rotation system, he probably will raise his outcomes; but if his efforts to establish the system are also salient, then his inputs to the job have also increased. Once the system operates, the person could be in a situation of high inputs and high outcomes (high/high) which might be inherently attractive, *but* which is still inequitable in relation to his low/high partner.[25]

A similar overshooting of the point of equity would occur if the subject used a less social means to make his job attractive, and looked closely for attractive features of his own job.[26] Having found these, he would then have higher outcomes. But, task enhancement typically results in an increase in the level of effort expended; for the task becomes worthy of involvement. If effort expenditure increases, equity is not resolved. The person has successfully aligned his outcome with those of his comparison person (both now have high outcomes), but he has now thrown their inputs out of alignment: the person makes high inputs while his comparison makes low inputs.

The preceding analysis suggests that equity can be difficult to resolve and that oscillation might occur. The person tries to resolve inequity in one portion of the ratio only to create inequity in another portion, and then in trying to resolve the new equity, destroys the equity which had been established by the initial resolution. This suggests that cognitive realignments probably will accompany most resolutions. Thus, in the example of job rotation, it would be expected that once the plan started, the person would try to convince himself that the plan was a cooperative venture (by reducing his responsibility for the plan, he maintains his inputs at a relatively low level); he probably would avoid close monitoring of the plan to keep his efforts low; or he might try to convince himself that the others worked just as hard as he did to get the plan started, an interpretation which would imply that both he and his comparison person are in a situation of high inputs and high outcomes.

Probably the most important implication of the problem of the interdependence of elements is that a more detailed picture is needed of cognitive changes that accompany resolutions to suggest more clearly what changes in perception are necessary to restrict the resolution to the desired portion of the input-outcome ratio. Knowledge of these cognitive changes should help the investigator to understand puzzling behaviors that often accompany resolutions. Since the ratio of inputs to outcomes is assumed to consist of several behaviors that are summed and weighted, the problem of compensating changes in inputs is a real one. Only if the cognitive accompaniments of equity resolutions are understood will the full implications of a resolution be realized.

Alteration of Outcomes

Equity theory pays little attention to the fact that persons can also control their outcomes to reduce inequity. Undoubtedly the preoccupation with money as an outcome, coupled with the fact that it is usually hard for a person to change his wages unless he is on piece-rate work, has contributed to a neglect of other alterations of outcomes, such as an increased attraction to the task or to the behavior that it elicits.

Equity theory seems to have considerable difficulty explaining the resolutions in the dilemma of the high/low person. If such a person compares himself to a low/low worker he can either increase his outcomes—an action to be expected on the grounds that people prefer positive outcomes—or he can lower his inputs—an equally plausible solution, since persons apparently prefer to manipulate inputs. This results in predicting two different resolutions of the same dilemma and uncertainty as to whether positive outcomes or least effort would predominate in the resolution. It is tempting to assume that this dilemma is usually solved by lowering inputs, but a potentially more attractive alternative to the person—that of task enhancement to heighten outcomes—has usually been overlooked.

Empirical studies have shown that persons who contribute their skills, time, and effort in return for insufficient monetary rewards, do not restrict their efforts. Instead they gain increased satisfaction from performing the task itself, exhibit high productivity, realistic goal-setting that ensures success, and alter their beliefs about the importance of rewards.[27]

It is argued that not only is it relatively easy to raise outcomes by task enhancement, but that such a resolution enhances self-esteem and is fairly permanent. Furthermore, it does *not* alienate the coworker, no matter what coworker's ratio of inputs to outcomes, because a high/low person who raises these outcomes by task enhancement, is in an equitable relationship with both the high/high, and low/low coworker. In addition, since task enhancement may be an essentially private matter—the subject can enjoy the task without this outcome being visible to his coworker—he can achieve a ratio much like a person in a high/low situation. Task enhancement does not permit the person to achieve total equity with a coworker who is low/high, but it at least enables him to reduce the inequity, for instead of both inputs and outputs being discrepant, only the inputs would now be discrepant. It is possible that outcomes increased by task enhancement are not enough comparable with those of a coworker, that inequity would develop. The outcomes are different enough that neither person feels pressures to make very extensive comparisons.

Mobility and Equity

Inequity can occur either in an exchange relationship (e.g., a person provides services useful to an employer from whom he receives compensation) or in a coacting relationship (e.g., the person and a comparison worker provide similar inputs and both are in an exchange relationship with a third party, the employer). The second relationship is exceedingly complex when viewed in terms of equity theory, because of the nature of an exchange relationship. "When Person and Other are in an exchange interaction, Other will suffer inequity if Person does, but the nature of his experience will be opposite to that of Person. If the outcome-input ratio discrepancy is unfavorable to Person, it will be favorable to Other and vice versa. This will hold provided Person's and Other's perceptions of outcomes and inputs are equivalent and provided that the outcome-input ratio discrepancy attains threshold."[28]

In an exchange relationship, the resolution should occur more rapidly and require less change, because the persons are interdependent. As the person raises his inputs, he also lowers the inputs of the other person or vice versa; the same relationship holds when outcomes are altered. Consider a person and his comparison worker, who perform similar tasks on which each expends considerable effort for little pay (high/low). The two workers have equitable relationships with respect to each other, but there is inequity between their input-outcome ratio and that of their employer, which is the mirror image of theirs; that is, he expends little effort (low inputs) because the employees work hard, but he has considerable income (high outcomes), since he pays low wages. The interesting question is which of these two persons, the coworker or the employer, does the person align his ratio with?

The answer is undoubtedly affected by the person's interest in being promoted and his mobility in the organization. If it is the employer who determines promotion, the employer's input-outcome ratio should be more salient for the aspiring person than the ratio of the comparison worker, because of "anticipatory socialization."[29] The essence of this concept is that persons who aspire to a group of which they are not a member adopt the values of that group and reject the values of their own group. Anticipatory socialization is functional in helping the person gain membership in the new group (he exhibits appropriate values) and in easing his adjustment once he is promoted.[30] Positive orientations to groups of which one is not a member can be costly, however. "Since the assumption that its members will be loyal is found in every group, else it would have no group character, no dependability of action, transfer of loyalty to another group . . . is regarded primarily in affective terms of sentiment rather than in detached terms of analysis. The renegade or traitor or climber—whatever the folk-phrase may be—more often becomes an object of vilification than an object of sociological study."[31] It seems clear that once the person behaves like someone in the other group, relations within his own work group will deteriorate, which should produce even more positive sentiments toward the group to which he aspires.

Anticipatory socialization could affect equity in several ways. First, a person who aspires to a higher position probably will pay more attention to the ratios of persons in the desired group than to those of his own group, and therefore will be more interested in establishing equity with supervisors than with coworkers. But the precise form of these relationships is not clear; i.e., precisely what it means in this instance to "adopt the values of an employer." This could mean that the person will identify with the employer and act toward his coworker as if they are in an *exchange* relationship rather than a relationship of coaction. Then a situation in which both the person and coworker have high inputs and low outcomes (a situation of seeming equity) would in fact be viewed as a situation of *inequity*; because the coworker is high/low, but the person, if he adopts the position of the manager, is in a low/high relationship to the coworker, and has equity with the manager. If the person treats his relationship with a coworker as if it were an exchange, it seems likely that negative sentiments would be produced. He would see his own situation as one of low inputs and high outcomes, the mirror image of the coworker, and would try to change the coworker to establish equity. But the coworker sees little reason for these adjustments since presumably an equitable relationship already exists. Thus to establish equity, the person has to raise his inputs and lower his outcomes. But, if he sees himself in an exchange relationship with the employer, then he has to make just the opposite changes to establish equity. He has to lower his inputs and raise his outcomes. It would appear that resolutions under these conditions permit little compromise. As the person aligns his ratio with one person, he makes it more discrepant with the other one.

A person's interest in promotion might be sufficiently intense that the rather intricate resolutions mentioned would simply not take place. Instead, the person would try to determine the pattern of behavior most conducive to promotion and engage in this pattern regardless of the attendant inequities. If promotion is rather rapid within the firm, the person would have to tolerate the discomfort of coworker inequity for a relatively short time. As more time is required for promotion, one would expect the person to confront some of the inequity dilemmas discussed above and decide who the relevant comparison person was—the coworker or the employer.

It seems clear that workers aspiring to promotion will take the employer into account in confronting issues of inequity, and that mobility will be relevant to such decisions, therefore mobility should be incorporated into a theory "from which it will be possible to specify the antecedents and consequences of injustice in human exchanges."[32]

Equity in the Social Isolate

One of the strengths of equity theory is that it includes inter-personal processes, namely social comparison,[33] as well as refer-ence groups,[34] but these bases often neglect the possibility that under some conditions a person evaluates his outcomes as equi-table or inequitable in terms of some composite internal standard, which is not tied to a group or person. If internal standards are used in place of social standards, then a person should experience equity when his inputs are in alignment with his outcomes, re-gardless of whether both are low or high. When inputs and out-comes are unequal, as in the case where a person works hard, yet is paid very little, tension would be expected, *even if the person's comparison person also had high inputs and low outcomes.* The fact that someone shares his plight would not be sufficient for him to experience equity.

Consider a person who expends little effort to write a paper, composes it in a relaxed, possibly frivolous mood, sends it to a contest, and then wins $1,000. Here inputs are low but outcomes are high. When the writer confronts the fact that if his inputs alone are considered, they do not warrant the prize, an expectancy is controverted.

If a relevant comparison person has had a similar experience, that is, has also received high outcomes for slight inputs, this would not ease guilt, nor would it change the fact that expectancies were controverted. If the person discussed the situation with his com-parison person, he would be expected to talk *not* about the fact that the paper was easily written and that the prize was attractive, but rather that such papers were difficult to write and that these prizes, after all, were insignificant indications of accomplishment. If he could not gain support from his comparison person on this point, he could be expected to seek out some person who was similar, but who saw the prize situation as an occasion where in-puts and outcomes were more equitable.

Other cognitive alterations would be likely, alterations in which either the perceived inputs would be raised (e.g., "the paper was worrying me all year"; "I have worked on and off on the ideas for some time"; "the preparation was sizable"; "several other persons also made inputs to the project"; etc.) or the perceived outcomes would be lowered (e.g., "there probably weren't many entrants"; "anyone could have done this"; "the judges weren't very perceptive";

"the prize doesn't mean anything"; "the sponsoring organization benefited more than I did"; etc.).

Obviously, these predictions must be subjected to test. Several interesting questions might be explored. It would be predicted that persons who have a ratio with equal inputs and outcomes (e.g., high/high), would engage in less social comparison than persons with unequal ratios. If a person could select among a series of comparison persons, he would prefer that comparison whose inputs and outcomes were in alignment, even if this meant that initially there would be some inequality between their ratios. For example, a high/low person might be expected to prefer the person with the low/low even though this meant that for some time the ratios of the two persons would be unequal, because the low/low comparison offered the person some promise of resolving his lingering imbalance between inputs and outcomes.

It is possible to sharpen the prediction about choice of comparison person if the variable of situational uncertainty is added.[35] In Festinger's original statement of comparison theory, he mentioned that persons can evaluate their abilities and attitudes either by using objective data (physical reality) or social consensus (social reality).[36] It was hypothesized that persons prefer objective standards and turn to social comparisons only when objective data are ambiguous. This would imply that persons would rely on comparison persons and try to adjust their ratios toward equality with them largely when it is difficult to gauge task accomplishment. When concrete measures of accomplishment were available, persons would have less recourse to social standards. Thus, if a person had high inputs and low outcomes (high/low) he would prefer the (high/low) partner when standards were not clear; but when the standards were clear, he would avoid comparison with the partner and resolve the inequity toward either a high/high or low/low resolution.

Suppose that a person has a situation of maximum inequity, he works hard and gets little (high/low), while his partner expends little effort and receives higher rewards (low/high). To establish equity two changes are needed. The person must lower his inputs but he also must raise his outcomes if he is to reduce tension. If it is assumed that he adjusts both sides of the ratio separately, he passes a point where his own inputs and outcomes are momentarily aligned. If, in the first stage of his resolution he lowers his inputs, he is at a point of low/low, which is still unequal with reference to his partner but *is* balanced with respect to an internal reference point. If the propositions suggested here have any plausibility, the person's resolution should stop at this point, especially if the situation was unambiguous.

The issue of internalized inequities has been slighted in equity theory, but addition of these variables does not seem inconsistent with current research with balance models. There is evidence that persons strive to align discrepancies, even when they are alone or comparison persons are not around. Furthermore, dissonance theory, a major stimulant to the development of equity theory, is a theory of violated implications, and a violation of input-outcome relationships within a person would seem to be no less disturbing than a violation localized in some other person.[37]

Expanded Work Settings

A neglected but important set of inputs to be considered in any application of equity theory are job-related behaviors *outside* the actual work setting. Persons not uncommonly engage in work even when not at their place of employment. Work is taken home, time is spent recruiting (or discouraging) potential workers, extolling (or downgrading) company virtues, supporting (or subverting) company-sponsored projects such as public service, and so on. These external behaviors could be processed in the input-outcome ratio. Thus, by expanding or compressing the work situation, the person might encounter new sources of inequity or find new ways to resolve inequity.

The important question then arises as to what relation these additional inequities have to those that occur in the immediate work situation. Workers may maintain separate ratios, one for external job behavior and one for internal job behavior; but it is also possible that behaviors inside and outside the organization may be seen as interchangable. If this last possibility approximates everyday life, then it becomes more difficult to localize inequity and observe resolutions. Work relationships within the firm may appear to be inequitable, but persons do nothing about them. Such an observation would not necessarily controvert equity theory, because persons might be including their inputs and outcomes *outside* the organization in their ratios. Or the reverse is possible.

Still a third possibility exists. A person may use the external setting, not to resolve an inequity that originated within the organization, but to confirm that an inequity does in fact exist. One might wonder why a worker would try to *increase* the level of inequity by finding new indications of it in another setting.

Much of the emphasis in this paper is that work situations possess considerable ambiguity. Given these ambiguities, inequities could exist but the details of the inequity not be clear. With content vague, resolutions would be difficult, therefore efforts might be made to *increase* inequity in order to produce a situation where action was demanded and in which details of a potential resolution would have become more explicit.

Two assumptions in equity theory suggest this behavior. First, inequity is perceived only when the difference between two ratios exceeds some hypothetical threshold. Second, pressures to reduce inequity increase directly as inequity increases. A person might, therefore, find himself with lingering, ill-defined discomfort produced by subthreshold inequity. Appropriate corrective actions to reduce discomfort would not be clear and the lack of clarity could persist even when the threshold was moderately exceeded. Presumably, appropriate actions would become more apparent if the worker paid more attention to the dilemma, and attentiveness should increase as discomfort increases. Attending to the inequity should facilitate action. An expedient resolution of inequity would be changing to a new comparison person. It probably is difficult to undertake and justify a change unless there is *strong* evidence that the comparison person is inappropriate. If a person experiences inequities with a comparison person both inside and outside of the organization, it should be easier for him to justify to himself that a new person or group is needed.

Increasing inequity becomes more plausible if external job-related behaviors are considered. Assessing the extent to which external job behaviors are treated as if they were internal, and then determining the interrelationship that exists between inequities that arise in each setting would make predictions more accurate, although the assessment of external behaviors would increase the difficulty of equity research. Furthermore, considering the internal-external dimension might make it possible to reinterpret studies which do not seem to confirm the theory.

Temporal Dimensions of Inequity

Contacts between a worker and his comparison person typically extend over long periods of time, but the temporal factor has not yet been incorporated into equity theory, although it may alter both the antecedents and resolutions of inequity.

Does the prospect of prolonged contact with a coworker hasten or retard the resolution of inequity? Prolonged contact could hasten the resolution process because the person receives more frequent "reminders" that ratios are imbalanced and tensions could cumulate or at least be continually salient. Since inequity also carries evaluative overtones—a person is viewed as a "rate-buster," lazy, exploiting others, "uppity," and so forth—there should be considerable pressure to rid prolonged relationships of these negative evaluations. Furthermore, once an evaluative label is attached to the other person, subsequent interactions might be characterized by attempts to support the initial evaluation. Newcomb's discussion of "autistic hostility" suggests that once the person forms a negative evaluation of someone else, he avoids him and, therefore, receives little new information to force a revision of the negative assessment.[38] In such a setting, the person might feel under considerable pressure to realign ratios whenever they begin to appear unequal.

Long-term relationships could have quite the opposite effect, however; for if inequity is not reduced as soon as it occurs, there will be continuing circumstances, possibly more advantageous than the present one, in which ratios can be aligned. With prolonged contact, it is also possible that the person would be able to tolerate greater inequity without taking any action. If the person delays his resolution, he may be able to learn more about the comparison or his work behaviors, and this new information could be used to re-establish equity.

An important moderator variable that could affect the immediacy with which a resolution is initiated is the time perspective of the person. Goodman's recent investigations of the congruency between individual time preferences and the time demands of jobs suggest that time perspective does make a difference in organizational life. He distinguished between time extension, a cognitive dimension, which "refers to the average temporal distance of the farthest salient cues in a variety of representative decisions," and time value orientation, an evaluative dimension and defined as "the value a person gives to living for the future relative to the present."[39] It seems clear that both would affect the urgency with which a person tried to reduce inequity. As the individual is disposed to conceptualize longer periods of future time (time extension) and as he lives more for the future than for the present (time value orientation), it would be predicted that less inequity would be perceived, and that when inequity did occur, there would be less felt pressure to reduce it. Significant moderator variables have often been difficult to find in equity research, but time perspective appears to be promising, especially given the recent interest in the time-span requirements of jobs.[10]

In equity theory it is assumed that when tension arises, persons take immediate action to reduce it. This assumption, however, ignores important individual differences as well as temporal properties of organizations, which influence the degree of tension. Individuals probably do not have a single preference about optimal time span, but a range of preferred values. A person could then lengthen or shorten his time perspective as another means of resolving inequity. For example, when inequity occurs, a person could *maintain* the unequal ratio with the coworker and still reduce the attendant discomfort, if he could lengthen his perspective and become convinced that the condition was only temporary, that it was insignificant when placed in the context of an extended, relatively clear future. Conversely, if time perspective is shortened, inequity should be heightened, which, as already noted, could facilitate the resolution process.

Populations to which equity theory is generalized typically maintain interpersonal contacts of considerable duration, and there may be less (or more) necessity for immediate resolutions in actual organizations than in the laboratory. Temporal dimensions intrude into equity processes both in the form of individual difference variables and situational variables, therefore consideration of these variables should increase the predictive value of equity theory.

Social Constraints on Resolution Processes

In the discussion of the social isolate, it was argued that equity theory neglected the possibility that individual standards often are quite compelling; here it is argued that equity theory does not take account of a sufficient number of social pressures. In the concern with reference group pressures, equity theory seems to ignore other social variables. This restricted view of social processes is not altogether surprising, since in most equity experiments conducted so far, the comparison person is fictitious. The subject therefore has no opportunity to choose his comparison worker. As already noted, equity theory has significant gaps about the bases on which a comparison person is chosen and how these choices are justified. Also with a fictitious coworker, it should be easy for the subject to distort ideas about the coworker. Since the subject has only the investigator's description of the coworker to constrain his thinking, he would have some latitude to alter his views of the comparison person to reduce inequity. Equity theory argues that a person is more likely to distort the ratio of a comparison person than his own ratio.[41] But cognitions about the comparison person may be just as resistant to change as are cognitions about the self, and the presumed fluidity of cognitions about the other is due to overlooking the problem of choice and also the use of fictitious others in experiments.

Similarity of Comparison Person. Comparison persons are usually chosen because they are "comparable to the comparer on one or more attributes,"[42] a fact that has clear implications for the argument that it is easy to resolve inequity by misperceiving the comparison person.[43] As more and more points of similarity exist between a person and his comparison worker, distortion of the other person becomes more difficult. As actual similarities increase, persons typically assume that the comparison person is also similar in unknown characteristics. This suggests that impressions of the comparison person may be as firmly anchored as are impressions of the self, and that it is not much easier (or harder) to distort the other than it is to distort the self.

A strong relationship between a person and his comparison implies that whatever constraints (e.g., self-esteem, desire for positively valent outcomes) limit the person's own resolutions, the same constraints may limit how he will construe the comparison person. Thus, if the person feels that it is mature to be flexible and to be capable of change, and if he maintains several points of similarity with his comparison, then he would assume that the comparison person has a similar view of change. Having ascribed this characteristie to the comparison person, the person would be willing to undergo some change, but he would also expect the other person to change. Also if ambiguous work behaviors can be reinterpreted to reduce inequity, a comparison person will probably not be chosen solely because he supplies the most equitable comparison.[44] Instead he will be chosen on the basis of more enduring and possibly more central dimensions on which similarity exists.[45] This suggests that equity resolutions could serve to justify relationships that originate for reasons other than equity. In other words, a person chooses a comparison person on the basis of similarities and then resolves whatever inequities occur in ways that maintain the relationship. This argues that an important datum in equity investigations is the interaction between the number and types of dimensions on which persons are similar and how these constrain the form of a resolution. For example, if a person compares himself with another who is similar only in the amount of education, will educational inputs be the only salient means by which inequity will be resolved, or will everything *except* education be included in the resolution?

As similarity increases, liking should also increase. This could mean that inequity is tolerated and/or avoided when similarity is high, but if inequity did penetrate such a relationship the discomfort might be expected to be quite high. Furthermore, resolutions adopted might be expected to preserve the relationship, even if this meant that the person might receive a net loss through the resolution.

Notice that each of the expectations mentioned is dependent on the number of similarities that exist between the person and his comparison person. Equity theory does not take account of the fact that the number of points of similarity will affect resolution processes, and it is the contention here that this variable needs to be considered.

Comparison Person as Model. Visibility is another social variable that influences equity. Coworkers are usually physically visible to the person. Thus, a person of higher status who experiences inequity because he sacks groceries and works for a lower status cashier, can actually see the cashier.[46] Or cash posters and ledger clerks in a utilities company, who receive similar salaries, can see that the attractiveness of their respective jobs varies considerably.[47] This means that additional social processes may be engaged because persons are behaving in the presence of one another. For example, Bandura[48] and Zajonc[49] have recently shown several conditions under which imitation (primary cues of learner are responses of leader) or vicarious learning (cues for leader are available as cues for learner) occurs. In some situations of inequity, especially those which are ambiguous in which the comparison person seems to receive valued rewards such as pay, the person may adopt the comparison person's pattern of behavior, not to reduce inequity, but because he also wants to obtain rewards. Since comparison persons are often chosen for their similarities, it seems clear that they can be rewarding persons and that the person might wish to model his actions after those of an attractive person.

Comparison Person as Spectator

Visibility may also result in social facilitation processes, which may influence resolutions of inequity. From a recent review of evidence on social facilitation Zajonc stated that "the presence of others, as spectators or as co-actors, enhances the emission of dominant responses."[50] The presence of coactors is assumed to serve an arousal function, and whatever a person's dominant responses are, they have a higher probability of being emitted if other persons are present. Arousal also raises more responses above threshold, however, so there may be a greater number of potentially competing responses when others are present; the critical variable is the strength of the dominant response relative to the other potentially competing responses.

Since inequity can be resolved in many ways and each situation of inequity has some unique properties, it would appear that transfer of learning from one situation of inequity to the next one might be limited, that several competing responses relatively equal in strength may appear in response to inequity, and that resolutions could be difficult to establish. If a resolution requires the acquisition of new responses, it would be expected that the larger the number of coworkers, the greater the interference with the resolution process. Support for this expectation derives from the fact that a resolution often involves some relearning for the person, and analysis of existing data suggests that "the emission of well-learned responses is facilitated by the presence of spectators, while the acquisition of new responses is impaired."[51]

The preceding discussion of social variables indicates that comparison persons do more than simply provide standards against which the person can judge the equity of his work situation. They also serve as persons with whom the observer might wish to affiliate, models for appropriate work behavior, and sources of arousal that affect learning and performance.

Discussion

It is clear that the preceding arguments are laden with apparent contradictions. At one point it is argued that it should be difficult to establish inequity, while at another point it is argued that inequity might be even more intense than would be expected. At some points it is argued that some dilemmas are impossible to resolve, while at other points the argument is that there are even more ways to resolve inequity than investigators have realized. Although these points appear contradictory, most of the contradictions arise because the limiting conditions of equity phenomena have not been made explicit.

Much of the problem in working with equity theory seems to arise from the notion that equity is defined by a ratio of inputs and outcomes. The notion of a ratio seems to blur several issues. For example, it is argued that persons have equity if their ratios are equal in numerical value, but the ratios need not be similar in actual content.[52] This means that when a person experiences inequity he should be free to make whatever change he wants as long as it affects the ratio. This compounds the problem of specifying a resolution. If a worker expends low effort and receives low wages, but his comparison person expends high effort for the same low wages, it is not clear whether the person could resolve this dilemma only by increasing his input of effort or whether he could avoid a change in effort and instead substitute an increase in some other input such as getting more training, coming to work earlier, buying costly new tools, increasing his personal attractiveness, working for the company in his off-hours, etc. Although the notion of a ratio simplifies the problem of conceptualizing equity, when the content of the ratio is examined more closely, content does make a difference. Thus, in the discussion of various problems that might be associated with predictions of resolutions, the discussion has been in terms of adjustments to the input and outcome side. In most instances, the content of the inequity, the precise way in which the ratio was imbalanced, did make a difference in the expected resolution. Equity research itself seems to ignore the idea of the ratio and instead is tied much more closely to the specific content of situations. It would appear that greater attention to the details of equity dilemma might aid in the identification of critical mediating variables.

Finally, much of the preceding argument suggests that insufficient attention has been paid to properties of organizations that might influence equity processes. For example, it would appear that inequity would be most likely to occur when work-related behavior outside the actual work setting is at a minimum, outcomes are fixed, work groups have high cohesion, persons and comparison workers perform identical tasks, workers have limited aspirations towards promotion, both the workers and the job demands are characterized by relatively short time perspectives, and where there is little secrecy concerning outcomes. Viewed in this way, equity theory may be applicable to a more limited set of working conditions. But this is clearly an empirical question. The intent of this paper has been to suggest some questions that seem relevant.

It should be emphasized that the questions raised do not in any way imply that equity theory is unimportant. Indeed, the theory seems to be sufficiently relevant that it deserves and requires close scrutiny; but it is suggested that equity theory may be relevant to a more limited range of problems than investigators have realized and that the limiting conditions should be studied. Equity theory appears to be among the more useful middle-range theories of organizational behavior. It clearly has guided organizational researchers into problem areas that were unfamiliar but highly relevant, and it has generated experiments, the outcomes of which any responsible theorist must cope with. A theory that can produce such outcomes in such a short time warrants increased inputs from investigators.

NOTES

[1] J. S. Adams, "Inequity in Social Exchange," in L. Berkowitz (ed.), *Advances in Experimental Social Psychology* (New York: Academic Press, 1965), Vol. 2, pp. 267-299.

[2] J. S. Adams and Patricia R. Jacobsen, Effects of Wage Inequities on Work Quality, *Journal of Abnormal Social Psychology,* 69 (1964), 19-25.

[3] J. G. March and H. A. Simon, *Organizations* (New York: Wiley, 1958).

[4] V. H. Vroom, *Work and Motivation* (New York: Wiley, 1964).

[5] D. C. McClelland, "Business Drive and National Achievement," in H. J. Leavitt and L. R. Pondy (eds.), *Readings in Managerial Psychology* (Chicago: University of Chicago, 1964), pp. 122-146.

[6] S. Schacter, N. Ellerston, Dorothy McBride, and Doris Gregory, An Experimental Study of Cohesiveness and Productivity, *Human Relations,* 4 (1951), 229-238.

[7] H. J. Leavitt, *Managerial Psychology* (Rev. ed., Chicago: University of Chicago, 1964.)

[8] Adams, *op. cit.* and J. S. Adams, Toward an Understanding of Inequity, *Journal of Abnormal Psychology,* 67 (1963), 422-436.

[9] P. Blau, *Exchange and Power in Social Life* (New York: Wiley, 1964), and G. C. Homans, *Social Behavior: Its Elementary Forms* (New York: Harcourt Brace, and World, 1961).

[10] W. A. Gamson, "Experimental Studies of Coalition Formation," in L. Berkowitz (ed.), *Advances in Experimental Studies of Coalition Formation* (New York: Academic Press, 1964), Vol. 1, pp.81-110.

[11] E. E. Jones, *Ingratiation* (New York: Appleton-Century, 1964).

[12] This is a revised version of a paper presented at the symposium of the Midwestern Psychological Association, April 30, 1965, entitled "The Role of Financial Compensation in Managerial Motivation." Preparation of this paper was facilitated by National Science Foundation Grants GS-356 and GS-955.

[13]Adams, *op. cit.* (1965).

[14]Adams, *op. cit.* (1963), 424.

[15]S. Milgram, Liberating Effects of Group Pressure, *Journal of Personality and Social Psychology,* 1 (1965), 127-134.

[16]Adams, *op. cit.* (1965), p. 274.

[17]E. E. Jones, *op. cit.*

[18]Adams, *op. cit.* (1965), pp. 295-296.

[19]Adams and Jacobsen, *op. cit.*

[20]*Ibid.*

[21]J. V. Clark, "A Preliminary Investigation of Some Unconscious Assumptions Affecting Labor Efficiency in Eight Supermarkets" (Unpublished doctoral dissertation, Harvard Graduate School of Business Administration, Harvard University, 1958).

[22]Adams, *op. cit.* (1965), p. 284.

[23]*Ibid.,* p. 293.

[24]*Ibid.,* p. 279.

[25]*Ibid.,* p. 295.

[26]K. E. Weick, Reduction of Cognitive Dissonance Through Task Enhancement and Effort Expenditure, *Journal of Abnormal Psychology,* 68 (1964), 533-539.

[27]*Ibid.*

[28]Adams, *op. cit.* (1965), p. 282.

[29]R. K. Merton, *Social Theory and Social Structure* (New York: Free Press, 1957), pp. 265-271.

[30]*Ibid.,* p. 265.

[31]*Ibid.,* p. 269.

[32]Adams, *op. cit.* (1965), p. 268.

[33]L. Festinger, A Theory of Social Comparison Processes, *Human Relations,* 7 (1954), 117-140.

[34]Merton, *op. cit.*

[35]M. Sherif and Carolyn W. Sherif, *An Outline of Social Psychology* (Rev. ed., New York: Harper, 1956).

[36]Festinger, *op. cit.* (1954).

[37]L. Festinger, *A Theory of Cognitive Dissonance* (Evanston, Ill: Row-Peterson, 1957).

[38](1947), 69-86.

[39]P. S. Goodman, "An Empirical Examination of Elliott Jaques' Concept of Time Span" (Unpublished manuscript, University of Chicago, 1966).

[40]E. Jaques, *Measurement of Responsibility* (London: Tavistock, 1956).

[41]Adams, *op. cit.* (1965), pp. 293, 296.

[42]*Ibid.,* p. 280.

[43]*Ibid.,* p. 294.

[44]*Ibid.*

[45]T. M. Newcomb, *The Acquaintance Process* (New York: Holt, Rinehart, and Winston, 1961).

[46]Clark, *op. cit.*

[47]G. C. Homans, The Cash Posters, *American Sociological Review,* 19 (1954), 724-733.

[48]A. Bandura, "Vicarious Processes: A Case of No-Trial Learning," in L. Berkowitz, *op. cit.*

[49]R. B. Zajonc, *Social Psychology: An Experimental Approach* (Belmont, California: Wadsworth, 1966).

[50]R. B. Zajonc, Social Facilitation, *Science,* 149 (1965), 269-274.

[51]*Ibid.,* 173.

[52]*Ibid.,* 270.

18

An Evaluation of Jaques' Studies of Pay in the Light of Current Compensation Research[1]

MICHAEL E. GORDON

Summary

ELLIOTT Jaques' work in the area of compensation is evaluated for two major reasons: first, to ascertain its methodological fitness and meaningfulness; and, second, to discuss the impact of his work on the course of psychological research on pay. It is concluded that, although Jaques is the first psychologist to have attempted to bind theoretically a number of vaguely related concepts such as job analysis, equity, level of work, and pay curves, his pay technology has not achieved its goal due to a poor methodological foundation. Replication of Jaques' studies is virtually impossible because his instruments and concepts are poorly defined. Furthermore, some of the hypothesized relationships among the constructs contained within the model appear inconsistent. However, Jaques' work is valuable because it has served as a first approximation to a general program of research on pay. Furthermore, his work has highlighted a number of important, fundamental issues which investigators who research pay must ultimately resolve. Several of these issues are discussed.

[1]The author would like to thank Professors Mason Haire and Lyman Porter for their comments on the preliminary drafts of this paper.

Reprinted by permission of the author and publisher from *Personnel Psychology* 22 (1962):369-89.

Introduction

Although the significance of pay has varied for students of industrial problems, undeniably wages always have played a major role in industry in the Western World. It is unusual, therefore, that by the late 1960's psychologists possess only sparse knowledge and understanding of the characteristics of pay and its effects on human behavior. Haire, Ghiselli, and Porter (1963) have characterized the status of current salary administration as dominated by tradition and fixed by past practices. A similar evaluation has been provided by Lawler (1966) who has investigated the "mythology" in current compensation programs which has prevailed due to the absence of sound psychological research on pay.

Articles such as those mentioned above have made psychologists aware of their meager understanding of pay, and a number of investigations have been initiated to ameliorate the situation. Current research on compensation has become focused upon the behavior of pay itself over time (Hilton & Dill, 1962; Brenner & Lockwood, 1965; Haire, Ghiselli & Gordon, 1967). Recently, another cluster of studies has been focused upon pay preferences (Hickson, 1963; Nealey, 1963; Mahoney, 1964; Nealey & Goodale, 1967). Finally, equity theory has received a great deal of attention in recent years (Homans, 1961; Adams, 1963; Andrews, 1967; Lawler & O'Gara, 1967).

Of utmost importance, however, is the fact that research on compensation no longer is undertaken with the *a priori* assumptions derived from the philosophies of scientific management and neo-human relations that pay must be placed at the exact center or outermost periphery of the worker's life space. Instead, the importance of pay has been examined empirically in a number of studies on workers in a variety of job situations.

Elliott Jaques' work on pay evolved from an interest in job analysis. Nevertheless, many of his ideas are characteristic of contemporary research in the field of compensation. Although he started with different premises and techniques, Jaques' research has provided evidence which directly relates to other current psychological work on compensation. In addition, Jaques has developed a fairly intricate theory to provide a framework for his results and to suggest further research in areas related to pay.

Initial reaction to *Equitable Payment,* Jaques' (1961) major treatise on compensation, has been mainly one of disparagement (Beal, 1963; Vroom, 1964), although there are a few authors who have displayed some degree of interest in Jaques' work (Smith, 1962). Opsahl and Dunnette (1966) consider the results of Jaques' work "highly tentative," and report that his conclusions "must be regarded with caution." While the critics have very astutely recognized some of the serious methodological shortcomings in Jaques' work, they have simultaneously omitted reference to a number of the important and provocative aspects of it.

Interest in Jaques' work is justified for several reasons in spite of some startling defects and inconsistencies. First, *Equitable Payment* represents one of a very limited number of psychological texts devoted to the area of pay. Second, because of its scope, Jaques' work provides both data and theory on a great many issues connected with the topic of pay. No other presentation on pay encompasses as wide a variety of issues related to compensation research and practice. For example, Jaques has drawn together the concepts of equity and pay curves in his theory. Third, critical examination of Jaques' theory may force psychologists and businessmen alike to think about the requirements and issues which must be encompassed by a theory of pay and sound compensation practice.

The purpose of this paper is to discuss the investigations and theory of Elliott Jaques, both as a representative of current research on pay and as a unique contribution to the field.[2] A definition and evaluation of his work will be presented. The evaluation of the theory will entail methodological considerations and discussion of how the content of the theory relates to other research in the area. Finally, Jaques' ideas will be evaluated in an attempt to measure their importance for future psychological research on pay.

The Theory

According to Jaques, the reason that crude argumentative techniques must be employed to settle labor-management negotiations over wages is the absence of an adequate criterion for measuring and quantifying the levels of work in different individual jobs. Jaques has dismissed the traditional standards of comparison such as actual work

---

[2]Several authors have already published remarks concerning other aspects of Jaques' work. For example, Beal (1963) has discussed the comparative merits of Jaques' measurement of level of work and traditional methods of job analysis. Goodman (1967) has examined the adequacy of Jaques' hypotheses regarding the interrelationships of individual capacity, job satisfaction, and level of work.

procedures, worker qualifications, and productivity as unrealistic premises upon which to negotiate. In an effort to remedy the "chronic cankers upon our social life" caused by industrial disputes over wages, Jaques has applied himself to an intensive examination of a large variety of jobs in the attempt to find an underlying, measurable dimension of work which could be utilized as a basis for comparing all levels of employment. To this end, Jaques has studied a wide variety of jobs and has formulated a new conceptualization of work.

Of utmost importance is his distinction between the *prescribed* and *discretionary* content of work. The prescribed content of a job consists of "those elements of the work about which the member was left no authorized choice" (Jaques, 1961, p. 33). The discretionary content of work "has to do with deciding what steps to take to achieve the results prescribed—how best to do the job allocated within the resources provided, company policies and regulations, set methods, administrative procedures and routines, and other prescribed limits" (Jaques, 1961, p. 51).

Jaques' investigations, which were conducted primarily by means of "social-analytic" interviews, resulted in the discovery that the prescribed content of a job was not sensed as work; rather, the exercise of discretion was principally connected with the sensation of the amount of responsibility or level of work in a job. In order to quantify the level of work in terms of the magnitude of discretionary content, Jaques developed a measure called the time-span of discretion (henceforth referred to as TSD) which indicates "the period of time during which marginally substandard discretion could be exercised in a role before information about the accumulating substandard work would become available to the manager in charge of the work" (Jaques, 1961, p. 99). TSD is an index which supposedly can be used to measure and compare the level of work in all forms of "psychological-economic-contractual employment" regardless of content.

Jaques' interviews also focused on what individuals considered fair pay for a particular level of work. Data for this investigation were gathered from respondents on over one thousand jobs in several companies. "The results suggest the existence of an unrecognized system of norms of fair payment for any given level of work, unconscious knowledge of these norms being shared among the population engaged in employment work" (Jaques, 1961, p. 124). Jaques goes on to describe these norms by stating, "These norms of equity, because their existence has not been consciously known, have suffused our money relationships with each other, imparting a vague sense of what ought to be, but without our being able to quite put our finger on what ought to be done to ensure all-around justice" (Brown & Jaques, 1965, p. 249). The totality of these norms constitutes a pattern of equitable differential payment for differentials in level of work, called the Equitable Work-Payment Scale.

Jaques also claims that the analysis of career development in workers reveals that "each individual is endowed with a given potential capacity for work, this potential capacity showing a characteristic pattern of growth and decline with age" (Jaques, 1961, p. 11). Jaques has called these growth patterns Standard Earning Progression curves (henceforward to be referred to as SEP) and has interpreted them as being representative of the growth of time-span capacity. Because equitable payment was found to be highly correlated with time-span, the SEP curves also approximate the lines of equilibrium for actual earning progressions in terms of the current equitable rates for levels of work consistent with an individual's capacity.

"Each individual is unconsciously aware of his own current potential capacity for work, the level of work in the role in which he is employed, and the equitable payment level for his role . . . . Each individual is therefore unconsciously aware of the extent to which his actual payment conforms to equity or deviates from it . . ." (Jaques, 1961, pp. 17-18).

Whether an individual's pay and/or level of employment does not correspond to the level which is appropriate, as determined from the SEP curves, a feeling of disequilibrium ensues. The magnitude of disequilibrium, as measured by the intensity of response during the "social-analytic" interview, is a function of the degree to which actual pay or position deviates from the level of equity.

The Definition

What does Jaques' work represent? Because of its obvious relevance to a great deal of behavioral research, pay has frequently been incorporated into general psychological theories of motivation, especially in connection with discussions of acquired drives. This general psychological approach usually treats compensation as one of a number of human motivators and provides some formulation of the basis of pay's motivating powers. For example, Brown (1961) has hypothesized that, by means of higher-order conditioning, the absence of money evokes a state of anxiety. The anxiety is reduced only after the individual has acquired money. Vroom's (1964) cognitive theory of motivation stresses pay's instrumentality in the attainment of goals through the acquisition of money.

The above theories attempt to fit pay into a cogent explanatory scheme of motivation in which the need for pay is treated merely as one type from among many forms of motivation. Furthermore, the methods by which all motivators affect behavior is subsumed under a set of related fundamental principles within each theory. Although these general theories differentiate among various motivations in terms of their antecedent conditions, no distinction is made in terms of their postulated energizing effect on behavior.

With these properties of general motivational theories in mind, it becomes evident that Jaques' work does not belong within this category of scientific endeavor. His work does not contain any references to the relationship of the characteristics of pay to those of other motivators, nor does Jaques discuss the means by which pay acquires its motivating properties. Rather, Jaques' work represents a technology of presenting rewards which, by one means or another, possess the capacity to influence behavior. Economic motivation is depicted as a function of the congruence or consonance between actual and "felt-fair" pay. And, given that a state of incongruence or "disequilibrium" has motivating or energizing properties, Jaques attacks the problem of how to modify the administration of pay to establish among the workers a feeling of being paid fairly for a day's work.

Jaques has rejected the need for qualitative differences or variety in pay. In his system, special needs of the worker normally satisfied by fringe benefits are placed within the domain of responsibility of the national government. Instead, Jaques has constructed a compensation technology which seeks to maximize the worker's feeling of equity by varying only the amount of pay. In psychological parlance, Jaques' technology of wage and salary administration seems to be based solely upon one of the parameters of reinforcement: the magnitude of reward.[3]

In summary, Jaques' work does not represent a general psychological theory of motivation but rather a psychological theory of how much to pay. Whereas the former represents explanations of pay's function as a motivator in energizing behavior and the method by which pay acquires motivational properties, the latter begins with the

---

[3]Rothe (1960) has examined a number of compensation policies from the standpoint of the dimensions of reinforcement. The presentation of reward under each remunerative program is examined in terms of its probable response-strengthening capacity.

fact that the need for pay is a motivator and proceeds to develop a technology of wage administration based upon man's response to changes in a single dimension of pay.

The Evaluation

Operationism

The description of the results of his interviews with workers concerning levels of "felt-fair" pay and individual capacity are stated by Jaques in such a manner as to demand further inquiry into his process of data collection. "Unrecognized system of norms," "unconscious awareness," and "unconscious knowledge" are examples of the phrases Jaques used to specify the nature of the concepts studied. Presumably, measurement of these internalized standards was achieved by Jaques' adroitness as a psychoanalytic interviewer. The impression created is that we cannot merely accept the straightforward verbal responses of a worker. Rather, the employee's initial conscious estimates must be modified in some respect through interaction with the interviewer in order to determine the interviewee's "true," unconscious compensation expectations.

As yet, Jaques has not published adequate instructions for other investigators on the method of recognizing when the level of "unconscious awareness" has been reached during the interview. Despite a concerted effort to define his concepts operationally (Jaques, 1964), his definitions leave a great deal to be desired.[4] This represents the major deficiency in Jaques' work; i.e., intersubjective testability is impossible unless *all* interviewers *always* utilize the same criteria to recognize manifestations of the unconscious, a possibility which seems very remote based upon the diversity of opinion in the writings of a number of personality theorists. Furthermore, the absence of clearly established criteria for perceiving an interviewee's "system of unrecognized norms" would appear to magnify the potential error due to interviewer bias in eliciting and interpreting responses.

---

[4]For example, Jaques' definition of equitable payment contains a number of ambiguous terms. "Equitable payment: the common norms of payment which have been discovered to be held by individuals in roles of the same time-span, when asked under confidential conditions to state what they would consider to be fair pay" (Jaques, 1964, p. 7). Any attempt to use this construct in further research would be hindered because its definition leaves unanswered certain crucial questions such as: What are confidential conditions? How do you establish conditions which facilitate candid discussion of compensation matters? How do you know when you have actually gained the confidence of the worker?

Some readers might consider the preceding comments captious sniping at the clinical approach, which derives its uniqueness and value from these individualized in-depth techniques. However, a clinical orientation towards research does not obviate the need for operationalizing basic constructs. There have been more than a few successful attempts to operationalize theoretical constructs dealing with personality dynamics (see Munsterberg & Mussen, 1953; Murray & Berkun, 1955 as examples of methods for operationalizing various Freudian concepts).

Therefore, the hypothesized relationships incorporated in the theory appear to be unverifiable because the theoretical constructs which they embrace lack unambiguous operational definitions. In order to become functional, Jaques' system must be redefined in such a manner that the empirical constructs can be measured unambiguously and become amenable to intersubjective testability. Crossman (1965) has taken a step in this direction by transposing Jaques' concepts so that they may be reinterpreted as fundamental measures of "subsystem performance relevant to the problem of hierarchical control and division of labor (p. 1)." Goodman (1967) has conceptualized time span capacity in terms of two concepts—time extension (TE) and time value orientation (TVO). TE refers to "the length of future time which is conceptualized by the individual," while TVO refers to the "value a person gives to living for the future relative to the present."

The work of Lawler and Porter (1963) has substantiated part of Jaques' findings by using responses to a questionnaire item as a measure of "felt-fair" pay. Although the questionnaire technique contains a number of sources of error, at least a lack of operationism is not among them. Moreover, a valid interpretation of the results is possible because the researcher usually can recognize or measure these sources of error and compensate for them. The methodology in this study constitutes another alternative approach to the measurement of concepts which appear not unlike those of Jaques.

Further Examination of Jaques' Methodology

Jaques' work provides evidence in three major areas of recent interest in the psychological study of pay: the behavior of pay over time, equity theory, and the relationship of pay and productivity. This portion of the paper contains remarks about the methodology and logic of Jaques' work in these three areas as well as a comparison of his research findings with those of other men in the field.

SEP curves. Jaques' series of SEP curves purport to describe the relationship between equitable pay and the growth of individual capacity. Jaques' research hypothesis was that employee satisfaction is a function of the equilibrium which exists between a person's level of work as measured by TSD and his individual capacity for performing that work. The logic underlying his investigation appears to be as follows. TSD has been shown to be related to equitable pay. Therefore, if TSD is related to individual capacity, then measures of individual capacity and equitable pay should also be related.

In order to implement this research proposal, Jaques has assumed that the development of individual capacity is similar to other forms of biological growth; i.e., it may be represented by a sigmoidal-shaped function. One could imply that TSD and individual capacity were related by demonstrating that a plot of the TSD for work carried out over the years was also describable by a sigmoidal-shaped growth function. To test this, Jaques gathered longitudinal data on pay for 250 employees as a representation of TSD and plotted pay vs. age.

"It also seemed likely to me, since this (growth of capacity) was concerned with an aspect of human development, that these individual equilibrium curves (SEP) might order themselves into a continuous family of curves according to a common underlying pattern of biological growth. . . . In order to check these notions, and to see whether I could construct some kind of approximation to an orderly pattern of equilibrium progression, I decided to plot the actual earnings over time of a number of individuals" (Jaques, 1961, p. 177, information in parentheses mine).

At first blush, the series of SEP curves presented by Jaques provide a very compelling argument for his notion of the relationship between TSD and biological growth. This family of curves is purported to "represent a close approximation to a description of the lines of growth of time-span capacity in individuals and, therefore, of the lines of equilibrium for actual earning progressions for those individuals in terms of current equitable rates of work consistent with their capacity" (Jaques, 1961, p. 184).

Jaques concludes: "The pattern of these standard progressions, *drawn by the method I have described,* follows the sigmoidal progression characteristic of biological growth, although this fact does not in itself prove that we are dealing with a biologically determined general pattern" (Jaques, 1961, p. 184, italics mine).

There are several reasons for questioning the cogency of Jaques' major conclusion that the SEP curves represent a family of sigmoidal

functions. After devoting a great deal of effort to distinguishing between actual and felt-fair pay, and relating TSD to felt-fair pay, Jaques
proceeded to use actual earnings to test his hypothesis about the relation of TSD to individual capacity. Jaques has provided neither empirical nor logical evidence to justify the use of actual pay as a
measure of felt-fair pay in his attempt to plot the growth of TSD. This
seems to be a serious oversight and contradiction. It is an indication
that the derivation of the SEP curves is logically inconsistent.

Aside from what appears to be an unfortunate use of measures
in the development of the curves, the statistical procedures used to
construct the SEP curves also should be questioned. The curves are
abstractions from bits of data collected over short periods of time
from a number of different workers. It was Jaques' contention that
general trends would reveal themselves if all the bits of data were
plotted on the same graph "like a visually observable, regular pattern
in which iron filings array themselves in response to a magnetic field
of force" (Jaques, 1961, p. 178). It is clear that Jaques linked the
earnings histories of different people taken at different periods in their
respective careers for the purpose of tracing the growth of individual
capacity. This is not a completely acceptable procedure because Jaques
has provided no assurance that the people who are grouped together
to form one SEP curve actually represent a single level of individual
capacity in its various stages of development. Any possibility of classifying people in this manner seems remote because Jaques admits that
an independent, objective measure of individual capacity does not exist.

Forgetting for the moment Jaques' intention to plot the growth of
individual capacity, the actual pay data are interesting in and of themselves. It is possible to ask whether salary growth can be described
by a sigmoidal function.

Jaques' use of semilogarithmic graph paper to plot the curves has
obscured to some extent the form of the original data, and the shape
of the progressions are the most crucial feature of his evidence. When
the SEP curves are plotted with equal interval scales on *both* the
ordinate and abscissa, many of the curves which have been described
as "sigmoidal progressions" are actually positively accelerated functions
for *the entire span of time* investigated. However, if these positively
accelerated curves were extrapolated and the function plotted as the
time variable was allowed to assume larger values, it is then possible
that these curves would display a negatively accelerated portion and
hence assume a sigmoidal shape.

The flaw in Jaques' logic is that he seems to have overlooked the fact that unlike time, there is a physiological and oftentimes a legal limit on the number of years a man is able to work. Therefore, extrapolation of mathematical functions beyond 35 years or so is totally unrealistic when the independent variable represents the span of employment. Curves which are still in the positively accelerated phase after forty years cannot be interpreted as sigmoidal because we are able to predict mathematically that a negatively accelerated phase will follow. Rather, we must interpret this type of curve as describing a group of workers whose history of earnings is characterized by steadily increasing increments each year throughout their working lifetime. It appears, therefore, that Jaques has inappropriately interpreted his data. Jaques has used all of his curves in an inferential manner when the problem and the appropriate treatment of the analysis are actually descriptive.

It is interesting that longitudinal studies of the pay of executives have also discovered a positively accelerated function relating pay and time. Haire, Ghiselli, and Gordon (1967) found pay to be a positively increasing function of age throughout the careers of their subjects which extended in many instances over 25 years. This would seem to indicate that the growth of salary is not isomorphic with a sigmoidal biological growth function for at least some groups of employees.

There are additional reasons for doubting that a sigmoidal function actually represents salary growth for all types of workers. Weissinger (1958) and Patton (1961) have published salary-experience curves based upon the earnings of technically-trained employees, such as engineers and chemists.[5] All the salary-experience curves reported are negatively accelerated increasing functions.

Furthermore, Haire, Ghiselli, and Gordon (1967) have provided the rationale for a variety of pay curves. For example, a negatively accelerated pay curve would be the result of progressively decreasing increments in salary each year of employment. This type of compensation would be the reflection of management's assumption that a worker will be reluctant to seek employment elsewhere early in his career if he receives generous rewards. The longer the worker stays on with the firm, the more of a personal and financial invest-

---

[5]Salary-experience or maturity curves are graphs of pay as a function of time elapsed since the employee received his first professional degree. Maturity curves are based upon cross-sectional data; i.e., the average pay for different groups of people with different numbers of years of employment with the company is used to plot each point on the curve. This procedural variation may account for the difference in the shapes of the SEP and maturity curves.

ment he has in his job and, therefore, he will be more likely to remain with the organization despite the trend toward smaller raises.

Equity theory. Jaques has emphasized that equitable pay is pay which reflects differences between jobs and the capacity of the individual to perform jobs with different levels of responsibility. Consequently, he states that the magnitude of pay in itself is not what is important; rather, its importance is dependent upon the amount of compensation other people receive. This conclusion has been verified by Herzberg (1954) in a survey of over one thousand supervisors. His study indicated, "Where morale surveys have differentiated between dissatisfaction with the amount of salary as opposed to the equity of salary, the latter looms as the more important source of dissatisfaction" (Herzberg, Mausner & Snyderman, 1959, p. 116).

Jaques has employed a model of equilibrium as an explanatory device to account for different degrees of satisfaction with pay, i.e., feelings of equity. This mechanism is similar to the dissonance theories utilized by Adams (1963) and Patchen (1961) in their studies of pay. Both the dissonance theories and Jaques' equilibrium model predict that feelings of inequity will result from too much as well as too little pay. Data collected both by Jaques (1961) and Adams and Rosenbaum (1962) confirm this prediction. According to Adams (1963), the magnitude of dissonance will be equivalent in comparable over- and underpayment circumstances, while the data from Jaques' interviews have revealed the added distinction that there are qualitative differences between the dissonance experienced in the two situations. Whereas too little pay produces unrest and dissatisfaction with both the job and management, Jaques reports that "overequity payment brings about disequilibrium in the form of an insecure non-reliance upon the continuation of the earnings," and "provokes fear of rivalry in others who are not favoured" (Jaques, 1961, pp. 142-143).

There are, however, differences between Jaques' theory and the dissonance models, the most notable being that Jaques presents a simplified picture of equity involving only one dimension, pay, and only one person, the interviewee. Whereas the components in Jaques' system are only actual and felt-fair pay, both Adams and Patchen have included a dimension related to pay and a specific social referent, i.e., a person with whom the individual compares himself on the basis of pay and a pay-related dimension. Jaques implies that felt-fair pay encompasses these other dimensions because he has developed the construct of equity as a concept which reflects "differentials." However, the definition, identity, and importance of the social referent and the pay-related dimension are not presented explicitly in Jaques' theory of equity.

The more elaborate cognitive models have provided the theoretical foundation for a number of studies which have attempted to refine the notion of equity by discovering the variables with which it is associated. For example, Patchen (1961) found that feelings of equity among individuals within the same level of the organization are a function of the opportunity for promotion and the position of the comparison person. Andrews and Henry (1963) investigated satisfaction with pay in a sample of 228 managers from five companies. They found that the choice of the social referent was a function of amount of formal education and that the social referent frequently occupied a position outside the employee's own organization. Finally, Andrews (1967) was able to demonstrate a relationship between the effects of underpayment and previous wage experience.

It would seem reasonable to believe that Jaques' measure of equitable compensation also would reflect the involvement of these other cognitions even though he does not specifically attempt to estimate their effects. This influence would be manifested in the form of a sizable variance of the distribution of judgments of felt-fair pay of the occupants of similar jobs at a given level of the organization. That is, because occupants of a given job probably differ in terms of the variety of people implicitly selected with whom they compare their pay, their levels of aspiration, and the range of previous wage experience, the judgment of felt-fair pay also should vary considerably. This situation would be reflected by a measurable variance around the mean felt-fair pay for a given job. Again, because he does not have other variables in his model to account for this variance, it would be treated as error variance. But, based upon the findings of other investigators, one would strongly suspect that some variance would be found.

Unfortunately, Jaques does not report variances or any other measures of dispersion for the distribution of judgments. He merely indicates that the unconscious of his interviewees yielded estimates of equitable pay which displayed only slight variation. "Regardless of the actual wage or salary they might have been earning, regardless of type of occupation . . ., regardless of position . . ., and regardless of income tax paid, individuals in jobs whose range of level of work as measured by time-span was the same, privately stated a *very similar* wage or salary bracket for the work they were doing" (Jaques, 1961, p. 123, italics mine).

One must assume that Jaques' interview technique was responsible for the narrow range of felt-fair pay at each job level. It would be most interesting to determine how this interview technique operates and whether it is structured in any way to account, for, or adjust to, the different levels of the many extraneous variables which have been shown to be related to equity.

Finally, Jaques' report of the existence of an equitable salary norm for each level of work has received partial support from the results of a study by Lawler and Porter (1963). In this study, managers at different organizational levels were asked to rate the amount of salary that should be paid in their present position, this question being part of a series of items designed to measure satisfaction with pay. Within each group of managers at a given level, the pay considered appropriate for the job was almost precisely the same, regardless of the current actual salary of the respondents. Thus, there seemed to exist a stable norm for employees within each specific level of the organization.

Lawler and Porter also reported that managers' expectations about the pay they should receive were related to management level, this result being entirely consistent with Jaques' finding that different norms of equitable pay would exist corresponding to different levels of work. Lawler and Porter base their conclusion upon a very slight observable downward trend in the plots of "should-be" pay from top management down to lower management. No statistics were presented by the authors to support this conclusion.

Pay and productivity. Jaques' description of the impact of individual incentive plans on productivity is very similar to the effects noted by Whyte (1955). Jaques has expressed the belief that additional payments in the form of incentive wages are an ineffective device for creating long-range increases in productivity by inducing employees to work harder. He has denounced the commonly-expressed notion that the effect of piecework is to encourage greater effort in the sense of maintaining a faster pace of work. With the exception of short-lived spurts of intensive activity for which *ex gratia* payments should be awarded, Jaques considers it ridiculous to attempt to link pay and productivity because the latter is a function of the physiological and psychological capacity of the worker. "They (incentive plans) are more likely to turn out to be schemes whose real action is to reduce the inhibition and bottling up of application and resourcefulness, rather than schemes which somehow get more than normal work out of employees" (Jaques, 1961, p. 230, information in parentheses mine).

This conclusion about the motivational effect of incentive plans is similar to the results reported by Whyte (1955) based upon impressions gathered in case studies. Whyte reports that when piecework is utilized "there seems to be general agreement that the workers are not working exceptionally hard. The pace of factory work seems rather relaxed. On the other hand, there is a general agreement that there is much less 'goofing off' than there used to be" (Whyte, 1955, p. 133-134).

Although the evidence from case studies conducted in on-going organizations indicates that pay has little effect on productivity, this finding contradicts the results of the equity studies conducted in experimental environments (Adams & Rosenbaum, 1962; Andrews, 1967; Lawler & O'Gara, 1967). These experimental studies have demonstrated clear relationships between both the quality and quantity of production and the conditions of payment. One such reliable finding from the equity studies is that workers who feel overpaid on a piecerate basis reduce their disequilibrium by restricting production and increasing the quality of their work.

The mere fact that the different findings are associated with different research designs suggests a variety of sources of measurement variance which could account for the conflicting results. One probable explanation is the difference in the time periods during which the impact of pay was studied. The experimental studies are based upon the productivity of workers over only a few hours, whereas the case studies were based upon data collected on a more-or-less regular basis over a much longer period (Jaques has been intensively studying the Glacier Metal Company since 1948). Hence, pay may have a short-run effect on productivity as Jaques suggests but little effect over the long run. Alternatively, time may allow the worker to adjust his perceptions of his inputs and outcomes on the job, thereby changing his motivation to work harder or more carefully.

Other methods of resolving the differences in results associated with differences in research design are to attribute them to differences in subjects (experimental studies used college students while case studies used actual workers), differences in the nature of the motivation in the two situations, and differences in the perceived reality of the two environments (new and artificial for the experimental studies, routine and very real for the case studies).

General Remarks About
Theory and Research on Pay

Analysis of Jaques' writings illustrates both the need for, and complexity of, developing theoretical guidelines for future research on compensation. For while psychologists are rapidly accumulating empirical evidence on pay, there is an ever-widening gap between the number of facts and the number of valid constructs which form cohesive bonds among the isolated bits of knowledge from separate spheres of research. As mentioned earlier, Jaques is one of the few theorists who has attempted to draw together and place in meaningful juxtaposition the essential elements from several diverse areas of compensation research. The final portion of this paper will be devoted to a discussion of a few guidelines for future research and theory construction on pay.

To what theoretical constructs is pay related? What are we trying to predict ultimately? As a result of its traditional role in the systems of scientific management and human relations, pay has typically been connected with productivity and job satisfaction. Although research has been directed toward ascertaining the functional relationships among these constructs, there is no general agreement on the effects of pay on each of these variables. For example, as previously mentioned, the evidence of Jaques and Whyte is diametrically opposed to the results of Adams' equity studies on the matter of pay's relation to productivity.

Undoubtedly, there are a number of additional factors which complicate the conditions under which pay affects satisfaction and productivity. For example, Campbell (1952) found that satisfaction with an incentive plan was a function of the size of the work group. Nealey (1963) and Mahoney (1964) have shown that preference for different forms of compensation is a function of various demographic variables such as age and number of dependents, while Meyer and Walker (1961) have provided evidence that persons who display high need achievement as measured by risk preferences react more favorably to a compensation policy based on merit increases rather than scheduled increases.

It would appear profitable to continue to investigate these interactive effects which reveal the complexity of the underlying relationships among pay, satisfaction, and productivity. Jaques' renunciation of so many variables dealing with the parameters of pay and the characteristics of the work environment in the development of his rather narrowly-circumscribed technology leaves little room for this type of investigation within the framework of his existing theory. Whatever the nature of the thoery or theories selected to assist the advance of understanding in the area of pay, the empirical evidence up to the present indicates the necessity of incorporating a wide variety of variables into the explanatory scheme.

How is pay perceived? There seems to be widespread agreement concerning the importance of the workers' perception of pay on its motivational properties. Ultimately, it is the way pay is perceived which represents the effective stimulus or experienced basis of pay's reinforcing properties. Haire (1965, pp. 13-17) has stressed the importance of translating the objective, dollar value of the external stimulus into a subjectively-experienced scale of perceived value. This type of psychological project would result in a relationship somewhat akin to the economist's utility function.

Whereas Haire's article is exceptional in its effort to plot a psychophysical function for money, the notion of working with the perceived value of pay enters into psychological research under a variety of guises. Jaques' entire approach is structured around the notion of ascertaining equity of perceived value of money in terms of a unit of work. Similarly, Vroom's (1964) model deals with the expected utility of money as a means for realizing specific ends. And finally, Gellermen (1963) has stated that money can only be described in terms of the values it represents for each individual: "The important point is that money derives its compelling power to motivate . . . from the fact that it has no intrinsic meaning of its own. It can therefore absorb whatever meaning people want to find in their lives (p. 168).

The evidence which has accumulated up to now points to the necessity of defining constructs in terms of the way pay is experienced in any theoretical treatment of compensation.

What is the value in varying the quality of reward? Can all workers be paid by the same method of compensation? Jaques' technology is unique among the research reported on pay in that he stressed the need for uniform methods of compensation for all workers. That is, Jaques has prescribed a policy under which all workers would receive straight cash in return for their services. The effect of this prescription would be the complete dissolution of the old dichotomy of compensation practices for hourly-paid and salaried workers. For example, the prerogative to purchase company stock traditionally has been restricted to only a few members of the organization, usually the upper echelons of management. With his insistence on discontinuing the use of fringe benefits, stock options, and other forms of compensation, Jaques has completely eliminated the differences in remunerative policies which distinguish the methods of payment of white- and blue-collar employees.

This is an interesting notion. One can only speculate about the possible motivational effects of such a policy, especially for lower and middle managers. Paul (1958) has discussed the way managers utilize the wider variety of compensation benefits usually offered to them to rationalize the steadily decreasing differential in earnings between their salaries and the wages paid to their subordinates who occupy manufacturing jobs.

Looking toward the future. While Jaques' work is limited by a number of serious methodological shortcomings, he has obviously given some thought to the kinds of issues and areas of research which must be incorporated in a theory of pay. Jaques' most important contribution has been the structure he has provided for relating diverse areas of pay research. An analysis of his work makes it easier to visualize the details and understand the direction of future work on pay. The following recommendations for research are in large measure directed toward achieving a valid theoretical system of pay which is similar in both content and scope to the work of Jaques.

First of all, it is clear that we ought to know more about the behavior of pay over time. Industry's traditional reluctance to make salary data available for study may cause a problem here. However, effort should be made to get a large longitudinal sample together for study. Such a sample should not be selected on the basis of a terminal criterion which would limit the generality of the results.

Second, a statistical model of pay (Haire, Ghiselli & Gordon, 1967) should be used to analyze the behavior of pay in this sample. This model has the distinct advantage of making our conceptualization of pay both concrete and specific; that is, vaguely-defined aspects of the topic of pay have been clearly operationalized and structured in terms of mathematical relationships among statistical concepts.

And third, speculation has abounded concerning the relationship of pay to the constructs within the realm of other areas of psychology. The need is apparent for a great deal of additional work on the relationship of the parameters of pay to variables like morale, productivity, job satisfaction, etc. For example, work should be done on the relative effectiveness of different compensation programs using a variety of criteria. Also, Jaques' lead of relating equity and pay curves should be followed up. Finally, empirical evidence should be gathered to determine whether or not changes in compensation policy are actually perceived by the workers affected by the changes. Much of the salary administrator's effectiveness is based upon the assumption that workers will be sensitive to variations in remunerative policy.[6] Note that in each of these areas of research the statistical model of Haire *et al.* (1967) would be very useful in operationalizing those aspects or parameters of pay which would serve as experimental variables.

REFERENCES

ADAMS, J. S. AND ROSENBAUM, W. B. "The Relationship of Worker Productivity to *Social Psychology,* LXVII (1963), 422-436.

ADAMS, J. S. AND ROSENBAUM, W. B. "The Relationship of Worker Productivity to Cognitive Dissonance about Wage Inequities." *Journal of Applied Psychology.* XLVI (1962), 161-164.

ANDREWS, I. R. "Wage Inequity and Job Performance: An Experimental Study." *Journal of Applied Psychology,* LI (1967), 39-45.

ANDREWS, I. R. AND HENRY, M. M. "Management Attitudes toward Pay." *Industrial Relations,* III (1963), 29-39.

BEAL, E. F. "In Praise of Job Evaluation." *California Management Review,* V (1963), 9-16.

BRENNER, M. H. AND LOCKWOOD, H. C. "Salary as a Predictor of Salary: A 20-Year Study." *Journal of Applied Psychology,* XLIX (1965), 295-298.

BROWN, J. S. *The Motivation of Behavior.* New York: McGraw-Hill Book Company, 1961.

BROWN, W. AND JAQUES, E. *Glacier Project Papers.* London: Heinemann Educational Books, Ltd., 1965.

CAMPBELL, H. "Group Incentive Pay Schemes." *Occupational Psychology,* XXVI (1952), 15-21.

CROSSMAN, E. R. F. W. "Time-Span of Discretion, Span of Control, and Hierarchical Command-Control Organization." *HFT Group Research Note,* University of California, 1955.

GELLERMAN S. W. *Motivation and Productivity.* New York: American Management Association, Inc., 1963.

GOODMAN, P. S. "An Empirical Examination of Elliott Jaques' Concept of Time Span." *Human Relations,* XX (1967), 155-170.

HAIRE, M. "The Incentive Character of Pay." In I. R. Andrews (Editor), *Managerial Compensation.* Ann Arbor, Michigan: Foundation for Research on Human Behavior, 1965.

HAIRE, M., GHISELLI, E. E. AND GORDON, M. E. "A Psychological Study of Pay." *Journal of Applied Psychology Monograph,* LI (1967). Whole No. 636.

---

[6]Shimmin (1959) has presented negative evidence on the assumption that workers are sensitive to the characteristics of the compensation program by which they are paid. Her studies revealed that little correlation exists between workers' understanding of the formal aspects of an incentive plan and their ability to judge the amount of their own earnings.

HAIRE, M., GHISELLI, E. E. AND PORTER, L. W. "Psychological Research on Pay: An Overview." *Industrial Relations,* III (1963), 3-8.

HERZBERG, F. "An Analysis of Morale Survey Comments." *Personnel Psychology,* VII (1954), 267-275.

HERZBERG, F., MAUSNER, B. AND SNYDERMAN, B. *The Motivation to Work* (Second Edition). New York: John Wiley & SONS, 1959.

HICKSON, D. J. "Worker Choice of Payment System." *Occupational Psychology,* XXXVII (1963), 93-100.

HILTON, T. L. AND DILL, W. R. "Salary Growth as a Criterion of Career Growth." *Journal of Applied Psychology,* XLVI (1962), 153-158.

HOMANS, G. C. *Social Behavior: Its Elementary Forms.* New York: Harcourt, Brace & World, 1961.

JAQUES, E. *Equitable Payment.* New York: John Wiley & Sons, 1961.

JAQUES, E. *Time-span Handbook.* London: Heinemann Educational Books, Ltd., 1964.

KAHN, R. L. AND KATZ, D. "Leadership Practices in Relation to Productivity and Morale." In Cartwright, D. and Zander, A. (Editors), *Group Dynamics* (Second Edition). Evanston, Ill.: Row, Peterson, 1960, 554-570.

LAWLER, E. E. "The Mythology of Management Compensation." *California Management Review,* IX (1966), 11-22.

LAWLER, E. E. AND O'GARA, P. W. "Effects of Inequity Produced by Underpayment on Work Output, Work Quality, and Attitudes toward the Work." *Journal of Applied Psychology,* LI (1967), 403-410.

LAWLER, E. E. AND PORTER, L. W. "Perception Regarding Management Compensation." *Industrial Relations,* III (1963), 41-49.

MAHONEY, T. A. "Compensation Preference of Managers." *Industrial Relations,* III (1964), 135-144.

MEYER, H. H. AND WALKER, W. B. "Need for Achievement and Risk Preference as They Relate to Attitudes toward Reward Systems and Performance Appraisal in an Industrial Setting." *Journal of Applied Psychology,* XLV (1961), 251-256.

MUNSTERBERG, E. AND MUSSEN, P. H. "Personality Structures of Art Students." *Journal of Personality,* XXI (1953), 457-466.

MURRAY, E. J. AND BERKUN, M. M. "Displacement as a Function of Conflict." *Journal of Abnormal and Social Psychology,* LI (1955), 47-56.

NEALEY, S. M. "Pay and Benefit Preference." *Industrial Relations,* III (1963), 17-28.

NEALEY, S. M. AND GOODALE, J. G. "Worker Preferences among Time-Off Benefits and Pay." *Journal of Applied Psychology,* LI (1967), 357-361.

OPSAHL, R. I., AND DUNNETTE, M. D. "The Role of Financial Compensation in Industrial Motivation." *Psychological Bulletin,* LXVI (1966), 94-118.

PATCHEN, M. *The Choice of Wage Comparisons.* Englewood Cliffs, N.J.: Prentice-Hall, 1961.

PATTON, A. *Men, Money, and Motivation.* New York: McGraw-Hill, 1961.

PAUL, E. F. "Equitable Salary Structures for Managers and Executives." In "Assuring Economic Satisfaction (Round Table)." *Management Record,* XX (1958), 158-162.

ROTHE, H. F. "Does Higher Pay Bring Higher Productivity?" *Personnel,* XXXVII (1960), 20-27.

SHIMMIN, S. *Payment by Result: A Psychological Investigation.* London: Staples Press, 1959.

SMITH, P. C. "Rewards for Responsibility." *Contemporary Psychology,* VII (1962), 330-332.

VROOM, V. H. *Work and Motivation.* New York: John Wiley & Sons, 1964.

WEISSINGER, T. E. "Equitable Salary Structures for Professionals." In "Assuring Economic Satisfaction (Round Table)." *Management Record,* XX (1958), 162-165.

WHYTE, W. F. *Money and Motivation.* New York: Harper and Brothers, 1955.

PART FOUR

Some Research on Compensation

There is, of course, an abundance of research literature on the subject of compensation. It is not the intent in this section to present an exhaustive review of this material since this has been done elsewhere (see Opsahl and Dunnette's paper on "The Role of Financial Compensation in Industrial Motivation"). Rather, in this section, a range of topics related to compensation is presented.

Mahoney, for instance, in an earlier study on preferences for compensation systems concluded that managers' preferences for alternative forms of compensation are relatively uniform, regardless of variations in personal characteristics, levels of responsibility, and salary and income levels.

Beer and Gery, however, in their later research, after additional theoretical development had occurred, found that preferences for systems did vary; that different systems would more likely serve different functions for individuals with various need structures.

The remaining research papers have a foundation of some sort in equity theory. One of Andrews and Henry's conclusions was that an equitable pay comparison "between oneself and one's subordinate appeared to be of critical importance to satisfaction with pay." Lawler, in his paper on "Pay Perceptions," concluded that there was a tendency for managers to consistently overestimate the pay of their subordinates.

Andrews' second paper deals with the results of wage inequity on performance. Clearly the concern with equitable perceptions of the distribution of compensation not only must focus on what factors are related to perceptions of inequity, but also on the effects on both attitudes and performance.

Finally, the study by Ryterband and Thiagarajan examines the relationship of cultural and economic differences in the way managers perceive pay and its relationship to performance. They suggest that cultural factors may well affect the manner in which equity is evaluated.

Under any circumstances, it is clear that Opsahl and Dunnette's point made in the first paper in this book is well taken: the "principal research problem is to discover the way in which money motivates employees and how this, in turn, affects their behavior.

19

Compensation Preferences of Managers

THOMAS A. MAHONEY

The last fifteen years have seen the development of widely varying forms of compensation.[1] Almost total reliance on wages and salaries as the means for rewarding employees has given way to compensation packages wherein fringe benefits and other nonsalary items account for upwards of 25 per cent of total employee cost. The changes have been most striking at the managerial level, although they have been somewhat less well documented and analyzed than those at non-managerial levels. Rapidly changing patterns of managerial compensation have led to charges of faddism and gimmickry, as well as to attempts to defend each new form of benefit.[2] Practice has out-stripped theory; we have only begun to develop the kinds of study and analysis necessary to evaluate company policies adequately.

A recent symposium in INDUSTRIAL RELATIONS directed attention to the need for more knowledge about the impact of compensation

---

[1]The study reported here was conducted by the Management Development Laboratory of the University of Minnesota Industrial Relations Center. It was supported in part through a grant from the University of Minnesota Graduate School and companies contributing to the Laboratory. The following people participated in research activities: Thomas H. Jerdee, Stephen Carroll, Glenn Schleede, John Franke, and Wayne Sorenson.

[2]For example, see Arch Patton, "Executive Compensation: Are 'Gimmicks' Necessary?" *The Management Review* (April, 1954), pp. 258-259; Perrin Stryker, "How Much Is An Executive Worth?" *Fortune* LI (April, 1955), 108-111, 226-234; and Charles C. Abbott, J. D. Forbes, and Lorin A. Thompson, *The Executive Function and Its Compensation,* prepared by the Graduate School of Business Administration of the University of Virginia for General Dynamics Corporation, 1957.

Reprinted by permission of the author and publisher from *Industrial Relations* 3 (1964): 135-44.

practices on the individual employee.[3] Before we develop a theory we must learn how managers perceive and evaluate alternative forms of compensation. Many companies make implicit assumptions about these preferences, but as yet we have little accurate information about what managers really want. This article reports a study of managerial preferences for alternative forms of compensation and provides preliminary evidence concerning the validity of the assumptions on which compensation is based.

DESIGN OF THE STUDY

While numerous studies of employee needs and preferences (e.g., those which compare compensation with job security and supervisory practices) have been reported, there has been relatively little study of employee preferences for alternative forms of compensation. One of the few that has been done was reported in the symposium mentioned above.[4] That study investigated relative preferences of nonmanagerial employees.

Our study involved a sample of 150 to 190 managers in each of three large corporations (N = 459). The corporations produce different kinds of products; all compete in national and international markets. Compensation practices and levels of compensation vary among the three. The sample of managers in each company was stratified by organization level and selected randomly within organization levels from the president through the supervisor. Mailed questionnaires were used to collect the data; the percentage of returns varied from 76 per cent in one firm to 96 per cent in another. The average respondent was about 41 years old; he had three dependents and his youngest child was nine. Depending on his firm, his seniority with his present company varied from 7½ to 13 years. The median of annual salaries among the three companies ranged from $9,720 to $11,290 and family income from $11,000 to $14,412.

Preferences for the following general types of compensation were measured and analyzed:

1) individual salary compensation;

2) current individual-incentive compensation, such as a semiannual bonus for exceeding sales quota or cost-cutting;

---

[3]"A Symposium: Psychological Research on Pay," *Industrial Relations,* III (October, 1963), 3-50.

[4]Stanley M. Nealey, "Pay and Benefit Preference, " *Industrial Relations,* III (October, 1963), 17-28.

3) deferred individual-incentive compensation, such as semiannual or annual bonus deposited in an account to be paid upon retirement or separation;

4) current group-incentive compensation, such as profit-sharing, where the total fund is allocated annually in individual payments fixed as a proportion of salary;

5) deferred group-incentive compensation, such as profit-sharing in proportion to annual salary where payments are deposited in a fund which can be withdrawn only upon retirement or separation;

6) pension contributions;

7) company-paid insurance, including life, medical, hospitalization, and other;

8) vacation;

9) other benefits, such as company-paid memberships, free medical examination and treatment, scholarships for children, and the like.

Thus, we have included most of the forms of compensation found in current practice. Stock options were omitted because of the difficulty of measuring their current value to the individual manager. Expense accounts were not considered because of corporate policies concerning their administration. And nonmonetary forms of compensation, such as professional and social memberships, tuition refunds, and status symbols, were excluded because it was so hard to estimate their value. The breakdown of types of compensation listed above permits grouping for the comparison of preferences for incentive versus nonincentive compensation, individual versus group-determined compensation, current versus deferred compensation, and taxable versus tax-free compensation.

Participating managers were asked initially for their perceptions of the amount paid them during the preceding year in each of the forms listed; actual measures of the amounts paid were obtained from the firms as a check upon the accuracy of managerial perceptions. Three different measures of preferences for the alternative forms of compensation then were obtained.

1) Managers were asked to indicate their preferred allocation of total compensation among the different forms. An expressed preference for an increase in one form of compensation required a balancing reduction in other forms since the managers were only permitted to reallocate their compensation, not increase the total received.

2) Managers were asked to rank the listed forms of compensation in preferred order for receipt of a small increase in total compensation.

3) A measure of strength of preference was obtained by asking man-

agers to indicate the single form most preferred for each of three successive increases in total compensation.

Age, number of dependents, age of youngest child, tenure, salary level, family income, net worth, and job type have been suggested as determinants of managerial preferences for alternative forms of compensation. These variables and accuracy of managerial perceptions of current compensation practice were measured and analyzed for relationships with compensation preferences.

How Accurate Are Estimates?

The accuracy of managers' estimates of their compensation was investigated as a possible explanation of preferences, e.g., a manager who underestimates pension contributions might be expected to want a greater proportion of compensation in the form of pension contributions. At the same time, the accuracy of perceptions provides a means of evaluating a firm's communication program; if perceptions are inaccurate, perhaps the firm's compensation practice is not being communicated effectively.

On the average, estimates of monetary compensation were relatively accurate in all three companies. With the exceptions noted below, the median percentages of error in estimation of salary and all forms of incentive compensation were zero. The median percentages of error in estimation of insurance and pension contributions were larger, although the absolute error in dollar terms was considerably smaller. In general, managers tended to overestimate the company's payments for insurance and to underestimate their contributions for pensions.

Managers in two firms made errors in estimating their incentive payments. In one firm the managers gave relatively accurate estimates of their *total* group-incentive payments, but erred in their estimates of how these payments were split between current and deferred compensation. Their confusion was understandable since this firm used a relatively complex formula to divide group-incentive payments between the two forms. A more serious error was made by managers in another firm who estimated accurately the amount paid in incentive compensation, but who perceived this compensation as group incentive payments, although the firm intended them as individual incentive payments. These perceptions may accurately reflect compensation practice at variance with policy, or may be misperceptions of actual practice. In either case, the wrong compensation criterion was communicated to these managers.

WHAT FORMS OF COMPENSATION DO MANAGERS PREFER?

Anticipating that managers would find it difficult to compare alternative forms of compensation, we tried out several measures of preference. For example, we anticipated that, while a manager might want a larger pension, he probably would not be willing to give up much money for it. As noted above, one measure of preferences focused on the proportion of total compensation desired in each form; a second measure obtained rank order of preference among alternate forms of increased compensation; and a third measure obtained nominations of the single form most desired for each of three successive increases. Ranked preferences obtained in the second and third measures were correlated r = .66, so only results of the first and second measures are discussed here.

As expected, managers wanted the largest proportion of their compensation to be in the form of salary. Table 1 presents the percentage distribution of managers in each company who prefer various proportions of compensation as salary. The preferences in the three companies were grouped around the medians of 76 per cent, 82 per cent, and 83 per cent, respectively.

TABLE 1
Managers' Preferences for Salary as a Proportion
of Total Compensation

Compensation desired as salary (Percentage)	Managers		
	Company A (N = 147)	Company B (N = 125) (Percentage)	Company C (N = 124)
100	. . .	1	. . .
95-100	1	17	17
90-95	2	15	10
85-90	15	13	17
80-85	30	19	16
75-80	36	13	17
70-75	11	10	5
65-70	2	8	3
60-65	2	2	9
55-60	1	1	. . .
50-55	. . .	1	4
45-50	. . .	. . .	1
40-45	. . .	. . .	. . .
35-40	. . .	. . .	1

The proportion of compensation desired as incentives ranged from zero to 60-65 per cent, with an average of zero in two companies and about 8.5 per cent in the third company. A large majority of managers in Company A distinguish between individual and group incentives and reject individual incentives. The average manager in this company desires about 8.5 per cent in current group incentives, and 6 per cent in deferred group incentives. Managers in Company C, on the other hand, distinguish between current and deferred incentives; about 94 per cent reject deferred incentives, regardless of the group or individual basis of payment, while only about 65 per cent reject current incentives. Managers in Company B fail to distinguish between incentives on either the basis of payment or the timing of payment; about 70 per cent of these managers reject any form of incentive payment. Finally, the average manager in all three companies wanted only a very small proportion of his compensation in the form of insurance (2 per cent) and pension (4 per cent).

Median preference ranks assigned to the various forms of a compensation increase tend to support our other findings. As might be expected, in all three companies salaries received first choice. Managers in Company A rank group incentives higher than individual incentives, and then rank current incentives higher than deferred incentives. Managers in Companies B and C, however, distinguish first between current incentives and deferred incentives in that order, and only then rank individual incentives and deferred incentives. Nonmonetary forms of compensation (pension, insurance, vacation) generally are ranked below all forms of monetary compensation. Few managers wanted further increase in nonmonetary compensation. A longer vacation was generally ranked as the least desirable form of increased compensation, except by lower-level supervisors.

The general picture which these measures give us is that managers have an overwhelming desire to receive their compensation in the form of salary and want only minimal protection in the form of insurance and pensions. Preferences for various forms of incentive compensation varied from one company to another and appeared to reflect differences in company practice. All the managers in Company A, for example, were paid group incentives, both current and deferred, and they preferred group incentives over individual incentives. Only selected managers in Companies B and C were eligible for incentive compensation and this compensation usually took the form of current individual incentives. The preference of managers in these two companies for current incentive payments appears to reflect the general desire of all

TABLE 2
Managers' Preferences for Form of Increase in Total Compensation

Form of Compensation	Median preference rank		
	Company A	Company B	Company C
Salary	1	1	1
Current individual incentives	4	2	2
Current group incentives	2	3	3
Deferred individual incentives	7	4	6
Deferred group incentives	3	5	7
Pension	5	6	4
Insurance	5	7	5
Vacation	6	8	8

managers to receive their compensation in cash, and the secondary choice for individual rather than group incentives appears to reflect the practice in their own companies. None of the three companies studied offered other forms of compensation, such as stock options, club memberships, and the like, to any noticeable extent and the managers generally indicated little desire for these benefits.

Managerial preferences expressed in this study differ from the nonmanagerial preferences reported by Nealey. Nealey's blue-collar employees preferred fringe items such as sick leave and added vacation to pay increases. The only employees in his study who ranked pay as first choice were those judged as expressing "unfavorable" attitudes toward the company; preferences for pay increases declined as employee income increased. It would appear that managers and nonmanagers view compensation quite differently and it would be quite risky to generalize from one group to the other.

INFLUENCE OF PERSONAL AND FAMILY CHARACTERISTICS

An interesting hypothesis relates managers' preferences for alternative forms of compensation to personal characteristics and family circumstances. The General Dynamics Corporation, for example, reasons that younger managers with larger numbers of young dependents and relatively smaller incomes and net worth will prefer insurance and salary, while older managers with fewer young dependents and with relatively larger incomes and net worth will prefer forms of deferred compensation. The preferred allocations of total compensation discussed above generally were grouped around the median, although a few managers expressed relatively extreme preferences for each form of compensation. Managers with extreme preferences were identified separately within each company. Thus, for example, managers expressing extreme preferences for salary in Company A were those managers desiring more than 86 per cent or less than 73 per cent of compensation in this form. Approximately 15 to 20 managers in each company were identified in this manner. Since the median proportion desired in each of the other forms of compensation was approximately zero, only those managers desiring unusually large proportions in nonsalary forms of compensation were identified as having relatively extreme preferences. Within each company, personal characteristics of managers expressing relatively extreme preferences for a form of compensation were compared with the personal characteristics of the remaining managers. A chi-square test of significance at the 10 per cent level was applied as a method of identifying relevant differences in personal characteristics. Only differences which were found significant in at least two of the companies are reported below.

Salary preferences. Managers desiring a relatively large proportion of compensation in the form of salary payments tended to receive below average salaries and reported below average family income. Nealey observed a similar relationship among nonmanagerial preferences, suggesting that the relationship is general within employee groups. The managers preferring large proportions of compensation in the form of salary also tended to be younger and had less tenure with the employing company. On the other hand, managers expressing preferences for relatively small proportions of compensation in the form of salary received above average salaries, reported above average family income and net worth, were older than average, had above average tenure, and reported older children than average. The variables, age, tenure, salary, income, and dependents, tend to be interrelated, so the findings are consistent with the hypothesis that salary preferences are determined by need as well as the hypothesis that salary preferences are determined by income tax considerations. However, there is no evidence that managers with a large number of children want an unusually high percentage of their compensation as salary. Therefore, we incline toward the explanation in terms of tax considerations.

Incentive preferences. Those few managers who desired to have more than 10 per cent of their compensation in the form of incentives were considered to be "extreme." These managers reported above average salary, family income, or net worth and so apparently could afford the risk of a fluctuating income.

Additional characteristics were found related to preferences for specific forms of incentives. For example, managers who preferred current incentive payments (individual or group) were younger than average, as were the managers who preferred individual incentives (current or deferred). Managers who preferred deferred incentives (individual or group) and managers who preferred group incentives (current or deferred) tended to be older than average and their children were older than average.

It appears that managers desiring to gamble on incentives tend to be relatively more secure financially than other managers, and that age is inversely related to desire to gamble upon one's personal performance and is directly related to desire to postpone receipt of income.

Pension contributions. As expected, managers who preferred relatively high pension contributions were older than average, reported above average net worth, had relatively longer tenure with their organizations, and reported children above average in age.

Vacation. Managers who preferred increases in vacation rather than in other forms of compensation tended to earn below average salaries and were low in the management hierarchy.

One other factor was found present in each group of managers expressing relatively extreme preferences for a form of compensation; these managers consistently erred in their estimates of the proportions of total compensation received and estimated compensation received in any form tended to vary directly with the proportion desired in that form. The causal relationship, if any, between these two variables might flow in either direction and be consistent with other findings of the study. We incline toward the explanation that preferences reflect current practice as perceived by the individual manager.

These variations in managerial preferences are generally consistent with popular beliefs. Younger, less established, and less financially secure managers with large family responsibilities prefer current payments, while older, more financially secure managers with fewer family responsibilities are more inclined toward pensions and deferred compensation. Interestingly, only younger managers appear inclined toward individual incentives, while older managers prefer group incentives. This relationship probably reflects in part the greater predominance of older managers at higher levels of the hierarchy where it is more difficult to measure individual contribution, but age is more closely related to this preference difference than is organizational rank. Of more significance, however, is the fact that while relatively extreme preferences can be explained in terms of personal characteristics, the influence of personal characteristics is far from uniform. While managers preferring relatively large proportions of compensation in salary payments are younger than average, young managers as a group are not more inclined toward salary compensation than are older managers. In short, preferences appear to be related to a combination of circumstances rather than to variation on a single dimension.

SUMMARY

We studied only three corporations and so our findings cannot be generalized for other organizations. Our findings are valuable because they help us test current hypotheses concerning managers' preferences and because more definitive findings are not available.

This study suggests that managers' preferences for alternative forms of compensation are relatively uniform, regardless of variations in personal characteristics, level of responsibility, and salary and income levels. Managers in all three companies expressed an overwhelming preference for salary compensation with minimal protective compensation in the form of insurance and pension. Compensation preferences which differed among the three companies tended to parallel differences in company practice, thus suggesting relative satisfaction with existing practices. Little support is provided for suggestions that wide differences exist among managers' preferences which are not recognized in current compensation practices. Rather, results of this study suggest that there is limited desire for the many newly developed forms of nonsalary compensation. While these new benefits may be justified in terms of relative cost, they do not appear to attract significant managerial attention. Finally, the relatively close parallel between managerial preferences and perceptions of current compensation practice, even when these perceptions are in error, raises the suspicion that managers have no strong preference for alternative forms of compensation as long as protective compensation is perceived as adequate and the major portion of compensation is provided in the form of salary. In short, fine distinctions among alternative forms of compensation probably are considerably less important in managerial motivation than is often suggested.

20

Individual and Organizational Correlates of Pay System Preferences

MICHAEL BEER

AND

GLORIA J. GERY

An organization's pay system is one of the key forces available for influencing the behavior of its members. Little systematic data are available about the effects of different types of pay systems on behavior or attitudes. Pay systems evolve over time, and often administrative considerations and tradition override the more important considerations of behavioral outcomes in determining the shape of the system and its administration.

The research reported in this paper was an attempt to gain a fuller understanding of employe attitudes toward and potential behavioral outcomes of the introduction of a new pay system. Such changes often are planned and executed on the basis of untested assumptions and incomplete understanding. Aside from the contributions to the fields of industrial psychology and personnel administration, we hope that the following discussion of the research study will serve as an illustration of how successful research can be designed and carried out in an organizational setting to help in understanding how individual variables and managerial climate variables interact with pay systems. This should help in predicting the effects of a change in pay systems.

A study of nonexempt* salaried employes was conducted at a medium-sized manufacturing organization (23,000 employes, $444

---

* Includes employes who are not exempt from the Federal Wage and Hours Laws requiring payment of overtime rates for over forty hours' work per week. In this company these employes are primarily clerical and technical in nature.

Printed by permission of the authors. Unpublished paper prepared especially for this volume. Corning, New York, 1970.

million sales) in 1967 to determine: (1) this group's preference for various types of salary systems, and (2) correlates of these preferences. The study was conducted at a time when the company was considering a change in the salary system, and a major purpose of the study was to attempt to predict potential acceptance of such a change. The proposed shift was from a salary system composed of a guaranteed increase and a single-step merit increase for satisfactory performance to a two-step merit system which would provide increases for satisfactory and outstanding performance and eliminate the provision for a guaranteed annual increase.

Nealey and Goodale (1967) have conducted research on the preference of blue-collar workers for six proposals for additonal paid time off the job and a comparable fringe and wage increase. Using a paired comparison technique, they were able to quantify the relative preference of employes for each of these alternatives. The value of these data for bargaining strategies is obvious, but they do not provide information about preference for various pay systems. Meyer and Walker (1961) have conducted research on the relationship of "need achievement" levels to preference for a salary plan based on "pay for performance" philosophy and found that managers high in "need achievement" preferred a merit system more than those who were low in need achievement. This relationship did not hold for nonmanagers. There has been no research on the relative preference of white-collar employes for pay systems that differ in provisions for recognizing merit. Such data were obtained in this study on four different pay systems ranging from a guaranteed increase system to a full merit system as a means of predicting acceptance of change.

A second major purpose of the study was to identify various individual and environmental correlates (administrative conditions and managerial practices) of pay system preference. This was done to predict which subgroups of employes (plants, salary levels, age groups, need levels, types, and so forth) would be most receptive to the new pay system, and which subgroups of employes would be least receptive. Furthermore, correlations between various managerial and/or salary administration practices and pay system preference would provide useful information about the optimum condition for acceptance of change. Since such practices are within the control of management, it was felt that they could be "tuned up" in anticipation of the change, increasing the probability of acceptance of and satisfaction with the new system.

In addition, correlates of pay system preferences were of interest as a means of predicting the potential motivational value of a merit system. While the effects of a pay system change on effort or motivation can be measured directly only after the change has been implemented, correlation of psychological needs with pay system preference provides some insight into the effects of a merit system on motivation.

The relative strength of a series of needs was measured, and the correlation of need strength and pay system preference was examined to draw some conclusion about the instrumentality of four pay systems to need satisfaction and their potential motivational effects. After the study was conducted, a recommendation was made to change the corporate salary system to a merit salary system. Although this change was not made immediately, for a number of significant reasons which are unrelated to our purposes here, as of this writing it is being planned for the near future. Hence, the effects of a change cannot be reported here. However, preferences for pay systems and their correlates have many practical and theoretical implications, which will be discussed.

RESEARCH DESIGN AND ANALYSIS

The first phase of the research consisted of eighteen in-depth interviews with a randomly selected representative group of male and female, nonexempt, salaried, clerical, and technical personnel at the company's corporate headquarters. Each interview took approximately one and a quarter hours and followed a general protocol relating to the employe's feelings about and experience with the present salary system, his preferences for various types of salary systems, attitudes toward employe benefits, and his feelings about and experience with performance reviews. The interviews were open-ended and served to provide a framework or structure for the second research phase, the questionnaire survey.

A ninety-five item questionnaire was developed to measure the basic questions and concerns explored in the interview phase of the study. The questionnaire consisted of Likert-type and paired-comparison items and was pretested on another representative group of thirty nonexempt clerical and technical employes. In addition to pay system preference, a number of a priori factors measured by one or more items were included based on their hypothesized relationship to pay system preference. They are as follows:

1) The relative importance of eight psychological needs
2) Knowledge of the present corporate pay system
3) Background factors, such as age, type of work, and the like
4) Performance feedback experience

5) Quality of superior/subordinate relationship
6) Individual's perception of his performance
7) Satisfaction with pay
8) Payroll identification
9) Past experience with pay
10) The perceived relationship between pay and performance

The questionnaire was administered to a stratified random sample consisting of 580 clerical employes and technicians at twenty-eight manufacturing plants, corporate office headquarters, and corporate research and development headquarters. It was composed of approximately 50 percent male and 50 percent female respondents and was representative of all lengths of company service (over six months), salary grades, education, and type of work.

The questionnaire was administered at group meetings by personnel supervisors in various branch plants, corporate offices, and corporate research and development facilities throughout the United States and was anonymously completed and returned to the research group at corporate headquarters.

Descriptive statistical analysis yielded frequencies, mean scores, and standard deviations for each Likert-type item. Paired comparisons of pay system preferences and the importance of work-related needs were reduced to preference indexes for each pay system and for each need. Finally, t tests or Chi Square (x^2) tests were used to test for the significance of relationship between preference for each system and items representing the various a priori factors listed above. No items were combined to arrive at total scores for the factors since these were a priori factors. A Chi Square analysis seemed appropriate in most instances as a measure of relationship because many of the variables consisted of discrete categories or did not meet the assumptions for a parametric test.

SUMMARY AND CONCLUSIONS

We will now summarize our major findings and discuss our conclusions concerning the problems associated with changing a pay system and the overall issue of pay and motivation. The most important data supporting these conclusions are presented in Table 1. The first part

---

EDITORS' NOTE: *The data section of this report has been omitted. The relevant tables have been included in the summary section.*

of this section will attempt to communicate to the manager the implications of this research for practical application. The second part will deal with theoretical implications.

The study has shown that while-collar, nonexempt employes prefer a two-step differential merit system (5 percent and 10 percent increases) to a general increase system; partial merit system; and a high-risk, one-step merit system (Table 1). This finding confirms that nonexempt, salaried, clerical, and technical employes should not be thought of as significantly different from the managerial and professional work force, and that there is ample possibility for integrating these two groups with respect to pay practices. Management of this group has not always been based on correct assumptions. It is hoped that studies of this type will bring into focus correct assumptions and relevant managerial practices. However, the reader must be cautious about these findings in one important respect. The data on pay system preferences were gathered in the summer of 1967, a period of relatively little inflation. Since that time inflation has significantly increased. It is possible that the broad economic environment affects pay system preferences. In a time of inflation employes may be less willing to work under a merit system that does not provide for annual guaranteed economic adjustment and gives the supervisor complete control over the amount and timing of increases. That is, security and monetary needs may become more important during these periods and, as our study showed, pay systems that provide for some annual increase may be preferred under these conditions. No data are available at the moment to shed light on this matter.

TABLE 1
Rank Order of Pay System Preference and Risk

System	Mean Preference (Maximum Points = 3.00)	Rank of Risk Involved
System B (differential merit system)	2.20	2
System C (combined merit and general system)	1.95	3
System D (above average merit raise only)	1.03	1
System A (all general increase system)	.82	4

While the overall findings concerning pay system preferences for the white-collar, nonexempt employe are encouraging with respect to the potential integration of pay practices for this group and the exempt, professional and managerial work force, the correlates of pay system preferences indicate that preference is a function of many variables. A strong correlation was found between eight of ten a priori factors. The ten factors and their relationship to pay system preference have been condensed into five major categories and will be discussed and summarized within this broader framework.

Individual Needs

Individual needs for advancement, responsibility, interesting and challenging work, security, vacations, and money were all found to be related to pay system preference (Tables 2 and 3). Individuals high in the first three needs, referred to by Herzberg (1959) as "motivator" needs, were found to favor a merit system more than those low in these needs. Individuals high in the last three needs, referred to by Herzberg as "hygiene" needs, were found to favor a general increase system (no provision for merit increases) more than individuals low in these needs. A person high in the first three needs would appear to be high in the need for achievement and have a life style that places work in a relatively central position. A person high in the last three needs is probably more security oriented and places less value on achievement and work. Thus, not surprisingly, the basic orientation of the individual toward work, achievement, and risk has much to do with the pay system he prefers. The most interesting implications of these findings are that the form of payout, rather than money in and of itself, is the key to the potential motivational value of a pay system and that pay in the form of a merit system could satisfy achievement-oriented needs. Therefore, a merit system can probably be utilized effectively by management in motivating employes. This concept has been in disfavor recently, but our findings indicate that more might be done with money in motivating people, particularly those who are work and achievement oriented in the first place.

While a merit system would seem to be less need satisfying to the security-oriented individual and, therefore, potentially less motivating, there is probably a net gain in installing a merit system. Those who are high in achievement-oriented needs will be stimulated by such a system to greater heights of performance, while those who are high in security-oriented needs will become more dissatsified and, it is hoped, will leave.

TABLE 2
Relationship Between Motivator Need Strength and Salary System Preference

Need	System A		System B		System C		System D	
	Low Need	High Need	Low Need	High Need	Low Need	High Need	Low Need	High Need
Advancement opportunity	.97	.66*	2.05	2.34**	1.98	1.95	1.00	1.05
Responsibility	.97	.66**	2.08	2.32**	2.01	1.93	.95	1.09
Interesting and challenging work	.91	.72*	2.17	2.24	1.94	1.99	.98	1.05
Recognition	.82	.79	2.20	2.21	2.00	1.94	.98	1.06

* t Test significant at p = .10
** t Test significant at p = .01

System A—7% general economic increase
System B—5% and 10% merit system
System C—3% general economic increase and 5% merit increase for satisfactory performance
System D—10% merit increase for above average performance only

TABLE 3
Relationship Between Strength of Hygiene Needs and Salary System Preference

Need	System A		System B		System C		System D	
	Low Need	High Need	Low Need	High Need	Low Need	High Need	Low Need	High Need
Job security	.76	.86*	2.30	2.09**	1.94	2.00	1.00	1.05
Vacations	.69	.94**	2.28	2.12*	1.96	1.98	1.07	.96
Supervisory practices	.74	.88	2.23	2.17	2.01	1.92	1.02	1.03
Money	.67	.92**	2.21	2.20	2.02	1.93	1.10	.96**

* t Test significant at p = .10
** t Test significant at p = .01

System A—7% general economic increase
System B—5% and 10% merit system
System C—3% general economic increase and 5% merit increase for satisfactory performance
System D—10% merit increase for above average performance only

In other words, the human resources available will be better utilized by means of a merit system, and the mix of the work force may change in a favorable direction with turnover of those who do not find such a merit system satisfying. At the same time, it is hoped that greater attraction of new recruits who share concern for achievement and work will occur. The direct effect on individual needs of a merit system is unknown, but it is possible that under a merit system the security-oriented individual may learn to have higher work- and achievement-oriented needs.

Clearly no individual is purely work- and achievement-oriented or purely security-oriented. Since both sets of needs and orientations reside within individuals in different mixes, it would appear that an ideal pay system may include both a general increase and merit provisions. The general increase provision would provide satisfaction of security and equity needs, while the merit part would provide the motivation or incentive to perform. Our study shows that the merit part of the system would have to include several merit steps. Many pay systems in American industry attempt to satisfy both sets of needs with one system, usually a merit system. The management administering such a system must utilize it for the dual purpose of rewarding performance and providing equitable pay and security. The result is that employes do not see a clear relationship between pay and performance which in turn reduces the motivational qualities of the system.

Several background factors were also found to be significantly related to pay system preference, but these were largely interpreted as being indicative of groups which share similar values and needs. The finding that older and longer-service employes have a higher preference for the highest-risk merit system may indicate that economic security, which is probably more assured for this group, is important if a merit system is to be accepted and is to motivate. This would reinforce the idea that a system combining a general economic adjustment and several merit steps would be optimum. Thus a feeling of security may be helpful in making a merit system an effective motivator and acceptable.

The effects of background factors and needs on pay system preference indicate a strong individual component in the question of what pay system is preferred and which pay system might motivate and satisfy. Perhaps the idea of a cafeteria of pay systems and fringe benefits may hold some promise.

Individual Expectations

An estimate of the individual's expectations under a merit system is available from three of the factors measured:
1) The individual's perception of his own performance
2) His perception of the relationship between pay and performance
3) His past experience with pay

TABLE 4
Relationship Between Self-Rating of Performance and
Salary System Preference

Self-Rating of Performance	Salary System				
	A*	B	C	D	N
Top 10%	.78	2.23	1.90	1.10	319
Top 10-20%	.89	2.24	1.95	.91	123
Top 20-30%	.78	2.11	2.11	1.00	37
Top 30-40%	.90	1.97	2.29	.84	31
Upper 40-50%	1.11	2.04	1.96	.89	28
Lower 25-50%	.75	2.25	2.00	1.00	4
Lower 25%	1.25	2.00	2.00	.75	4

* X^2 significant at p = .10

TABLE 5
Relationship Between Number of Times Asked Supervisor for a Salary
Increase and Salary System Preference

Number of Times Asked Supervisor for Salary Increase	Salary System				
	A	B*	C	D	N
None	.80	2.20	1.95	1.04	372
1 - 3	.97	2.19	1.90	.94	108
4 - 5	.81	2.10	2.12	.98	42
6 - 8	.62	2.08	1.69	1.62	13
9 - 12	.57	2.86	1.71	.86	7
13 - 30	.50	2.00	2.25	1.25	4

* X^2 significant at p = .10

TABLE 6
**Relationship Between Perception of Frequency of Asking for a Salary
Increase and Salary System Preference**

Perception of Frequency	Salary System				
	A	B	C	D	N
Always	.84	2.14	1.96	1.05	56
Frequently	.93	2.00	2.11	.96	45
Sometimes	.70	2.35	1.86	1.09	107
Rarely	.87	2.35	1.88	.90	60
Never	.84	2.15	1.96	1.05	279

Past experience with pay and self-perception of performance were clearly related to pay system preference. The more competent an individual perceives himself to be, the more he prefers a merit system and the less he prefers a security system (Table 4). The better the individual's past experience with pay (he has not had to ask for increases and has always been told why he has received an increase) the more he prefers a merit system and the less he prefers a general increase system (Tables 5 and 6).

Clearly the individual's past experience and perceptions lead him to develop expectations of what it would be like under a given pay system, and this helps determine his preference. While differences in expectations may be difficult to deal with by management in planning a pay system change, they can have influence on the practices that lead to these expectations. It would appear that practices which assure the individual that he will not be forgotten by the system enhance preference for a merit system. This finding was strongly supported by the interviews. Perhaps a change to a merit system should be preceded by a period of strenuous effort to administer pay in such a way that it will lead to favorable expectations on the part of the individual employe. Thus effective utilization of the present system may be a prerequisite for the effective change and implementation of new systems.

Leadership Climate

Quality of superior/subordinate relationship and amount and quality of performance feedback were found to be related to pay system preference. The more the individual feels his supervisor understands him and the more freedom he feels to discuss his personal goals with his supervisor, the greater the preference for a merit system and the

TABLE 7
Relationship Between How Well People Feel Their Supervisor Understands Them and Salary System Preference

Supervisor's Understanding	Salary System				
	A*	B**	C	D	N
Complete understanding	.72	2.01	1.88	1.39	67
Considerable understanding	.71	2.33	1.91	1.04	233
Some understanding	.97	2.13	2.01	.90	167
Little understanding	.86	2.21	1.95	.97	66
No understanding	1.15	1.73	2.15	.96	26

* X^2 significant at p = .02
** X^2 significant at p = .05

TABLE 8
Relationship Between Perceived Freedom to Discuss Personal Goals with Supervisor and Salary System Preference

Perceived Freedom	Salary System				
	A	B	C*	D*	N
Always feel free	.75	2.19	1.89	1.16	226
Usually feel free	.80	2.27	1.95	.99	137
Sometimes feel free	.88	2.22	1.95	.95	95
Rarely feel free	.98	2.00	2.24	.77	66
Never feel free	1.06	2.15	1.76	1.03	34

* X^2 significant at p = .05

lower the preference for a general increase system (Tables 7 and 8). The more frequent the formal and informal reviews of performance and the more the individual is told about reasons for an increase (that is, the more frequent and better the feedback), the greater his preference for a merit increase and the lower his preference for a security system (Tables 9 and 10).

These findings lead us to the strong conclusion that the supervisor is a key link in the preference for pay systems and probably in the satisfaction and motivation of the individual under a given pay system. If preferences are affected by the type of supervision, surely

TABLE 9
Relationship Between Frequency of Informal Performance Feedback
and Salary System Preference

Frequency	A*	B*	C	D*	N
		Salary System			
Almost never or never	1.04	2.02	2.02	.92	179
Yearly	.86	2.12	2.12	.90	97
Every few months or monthly	.73	2.33	1.85	1.09	181
Weekly or several times monthly	.56	2.32	1.84	1.27	99

* X^2 significant at p = .05
These frequency categories are combinations of more discrete alternatives in the original questionnaire. Significance was obtained for the original question breakdown.

the type of supervision moderates the impact of the pay system on the individual's satisfaction and motivation. This hypothesis has been harbored by many for a long time, and now there appears to be some evidence for it.

Since the perception and intended effects of a pay system probably vary widely, depending on the supervisor, the most carefully designed pay system may be for naught in the hands of a close supervisor who provides little performance feedback. The implications for the acceptance of change to a merit-based system from some more security-based system are clear. Effective supervisory training in performance feedback and effective human relations at the minimum will be essential for the acceptance and potential satisfaction of the employes under such a merit plan. Thus, supervisory training and development should be as much the concern of salary administration departments as any other group in the corporation.

Organizational Culture

Organizational culture is a broad term which has been widely used and variously interpreted. It seemed to us that several of the items in our questionnaire could be viewed as measures of organizational culture. Two items ascertained the payrolls (management and professional salaried, technical and clerical salaried, or blue-collar) with which the individual has had the most contact. One item asked if the individual had been on another payroll before his present job, and which one. A second item asked with which payroll the individual associated most on the job. It seems to us that data from these items are some indication of the values and norms that prevail in the individual's group relative to pay, and the basis for pay.

TABLE 10
Relationship Between Quality of Performance Feedback at Last Merit Increase and Salary System Preference

	Salary System				
Amount of Feedback	A	B*	C	D	N
Reasons behind increase					
were disucssed in full	.74	2.28	1.89	1.09	315
Simply informed of increase;					
reasons not discussed	.95	2.11	1.99	.95	149
Received increase without					
being informed by supervisor	.77	1.85	2.19	1.19	26
No increases	.97	2.17	2.02	.84	58

*X^2significant at p= .01

Several items measured the degree to which individuals had knowledge about the pay system (pay range, their position in it, and so forth). This would seem to measure the openness of the culture, or at least the degree to which a normally taboo topic, such as pay, is openly discussed.

While the items just described are not all-inclusive measures of organizational culture, they do fall into this category. Therefore, the data generated by these items would seem to be some indication of the potential effects of culture on pay system preferences and perhaps satisfaction and motivation under various pay systems.

Our findings are that organizational culture as described above does relate to pay system preference. The more knowledge about pay the individual has, the greater the preference for a merit system and the lower the preference for a security system (Table 11). The more the individual reports previous or present association with a professional or managerial group, the higher the preference for a merit system and the lower the preference for a security-based pay system (Tables 12 and 13).

That culture should have an influence on pay system preference is of interest; that it might have effects on satisfaction and motivation

TABLE 11

Knowledge of Present Salary and Salary System Preference

	Salary System							
	A		B		C		D	
Area of Knowledge	Knowledge	No Knowledge	Knowledge	No Knowledge	Knowledge	No Knowledge	Knowledge	No Knowledge
1. His salary grade classification	.72	.92*	2.34	2.07**	1.91	1.98	1.03	1.03
2. His salary range minimum	.78	.91*	2.25	2.11*	1.92	2.00	1.06	.99
3. His salary range maximum	.77	.94*	2.24	2.10*	1.93	1.99	1.06	.97
4. Type of increases presently available	.82	.93	2.23	2.02	1.93	2.09	1.01	.95
5. Size of merit increases presently available	.69	.88*	2.37	2.12**	1.82	2.00*	1.11	1.00
6. Frequency of eligibility for merit increases	.79	.89	2.28	2.05**	1.89	2.05*	1.04	1.01

* t Test significant at p = .10
** t Test significant at p = .01

TABLE 12
Relationship Between Payroll History and
Salary System Preference

	Salary System				
Payroll History	A	B	C	D	N
Exempt salaried	.50	2.42	1.83	1.25	12
No other payroll	.81	2.23	1.96	1.00	347
Both hourly (production) and exempt	.82	2.18	2.00	1.00	17
Hourly (blue-collar production)	.90	2.10	1.93	1.07	182

TABLE 13
Relationship Between Payroll Association and
Salary System Preference

	Salary System				
Payroll Association	A	B*	C	D	N
Hourly	1.17	1.72	1.94	1.17	18
Hourly-weekly	.84	2.08	1.72	1.36	25
Hourly-monthly	.90	2.10	1.95	1.05	20
Hourly-weekly-monthly	.88	2.18	1.92	1.02	170
Weekly	.91	1.96	2.09	1.04	55
Weekly-monthly	.79	2.27	1.99	.96	210
Monthly	.64	2.38	1.89	1.10	61

*X^2 significant at p = .10

under a given pay system is crucially important. The implications are that planned changes in organizational culture to more openness about pay, greater work involvement, and greater emphasis on reward for performance only (professional and managerial values) may be necessary preconditions for acceptance of new pay systems. The implication is that more motivation and satisfaction may be elicited under merit systems if they are accompanied by complementing cultures. In short, changes in pay systems need to be preceded by or accompanied by cultural changes. The optimization of an existing pay system may also depend on the establishment of an appropriate matching culture. The implication for the salary administrator is that he must be concerned about the culture of his organization and its influence on groups of individuals before designing pay systems. It may also mean that in large multi-divisional or multi-plant corporations, differences in cultures that exist between organizational components will mean that differences in pay systems may have to exist for optimum satisfaction and motivation. Since this usually presents difficulties for a corporation that transfers people across these units, it may be desirable for an organization to develop a uniform culture.

Satisfaction with Pay

Satisfaction with pay was measured by several items which ascertained the individual's general attitude toward pay. These items showed that there is a relationship (although not always statistically significant) between degree of satisfaction with the present system and preference for various types of pay systems (Tables 14, 15, and 16). The most consistent finding is that preference for a multiple-step merit system (System B) increases as satisfaction with pay decreases. The relationships between satisfaction with pay and preferences for the security system (System A), partial system (System C), and the high risk, one-step merit system (System D) were generally complex and difficult to interpret. In our opinion, these complexities can be explained in two ways. First, preference for pay systems was measured by a paired comparison system, resulting in lack of independence between preference indexes. Second, the overall measure of satisfaction with pay reflects a multitude of reasons for satisfaction or dissatisfaction. Thus two individuals with the same degree of satisfaction might have different preferences for pay systems because of their reasons for satisfaction or dissatisfaction.

Perhaps the clearest example of this came from the item that asked individuals to check the nature of their complaints about the present system. When those who complained about the lack of incentive in the system were compared with those who had complaints unrelated to lack of incentive, we found a significant difference in pay system preference (Table 17). Those who complained about the lack of incentive in the system had a higher preference for the multiple-step merit system (System B), and the single-step, high-risk merit system (System D), and a lower preference for the partial security system (System C).

The finding that satisfaction with pay is inversely related to preference for a merit system was counter to our hypothesis. We assumed that dissatisfaction with pay would result in distrust, a lack of desire for change in the pay system, and, therefore, greater preference for the existing partial security system than for the multiple-step merit system. In retrospect, however, our findings make sense. Those who are dissatisfied with pay are expressing as much dissatisfaction with the mode of payment as with the amount. Since a large percentage of the sample complained about the lack of incentive in the existing partial security system, satisfaction was found to be inversely related to preference for a merit system. Too often dissatisfaction with pay is assumed to mean dissatisfaction with amount. Our findings suggest that a change to a merit system with no increase in amount payed out by the company will increase satisfaction.

Situational variables can also be expected to influence an individual's pay system preference, although we did not analyze our data in a way that would allow us to test this hypothesis directly. For example, the individual's expectation about how he would fare under each alternative system based on his past experience with pay, his relationship with his boss, and organizational culture could moderate the relationship between satisfaction with pay and pay system preference.

A Model for Understanding
Pay System Preference

The discussion above has been an attempt to summarize the findings of this study in terms of a few broad categories which are conceptually distinct and theoretically meaningful. How do they relate to each other and interact in their effects on pay system preference and potential acceptance of a given pay system?

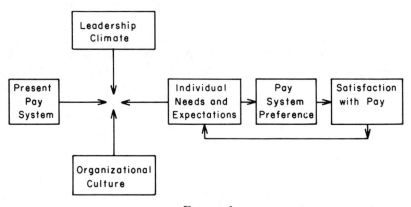

FIGURE 1

The model represented in Figure 1 is our estimate of how pay system preferences develop. The existing pay system has only an indirect effect on individual attitudes toward and preferences for various pay systems. More than likely an individual's pay system preferences are heavily moderated by the culture in which the pay system is embedded (the openness of the culture about pay, for example), the particular manner in which the individual's pay is administered, and the way he is supervised by his boss. The individual's experience with and subsequent feelings about the present system as filtered through these environmental factors affects his expectations about what would happen under various types of systems in the future and to some degree may affect his basic needs as well. Then his needs and expectations interact in a multiplicative manner (Vroom, 1964) and result in some pattern of pay system preferences. Satisfaction is shown as a final outcome. It is likely to be determined in part by the degree of discrepancy between the existing system and the preferred system. As the data on satisfaction showed, dissatisfaction was associated with stronger preference for systems other than the existing system. Of course, satisfaction is also determined through a comparison by the individual of the amount actually payed with the amount expected, but this seems to be only part of it. Finally, the model shows a feedback effect on individual needs and expectations resulting from degree of need satisfaction.

The validity of this model cannot be totally determined from the data presented in this paper, since the data analysis was only of the relationship of each factor with pay system preference. The model

TABLE 14
Relationship Between Satisfaction with Present Pay
and Salary System Preference

	Salary System				
Satisfaction	A*	B	C	D	N
Completely satisfied	.88	2.00	1.88	1.23	26
Quite well satisfied	.82	2.12	2.00	1.05	120
Fairly satisfied	.80	2.19	1.95	1.05	239
Somewhat dissatisfied	.81	2.28	1.94	.96	138
Very dissatisfied	1.03	2.23	1.89	.86	35

* X^2 significant at p = .01

TABLE 15
Relationship Between Perception of Salary Treatment
and Salary System Preference

	Salary System				
Treatment	A	B	C	D*	N
Very unfairly	.71	2.00	2.08	1.21	24
Somewhat unfairly	.98	2.28	1.94	.80	99
Fairly	.79	2.24	1.95	1.02	196
Somewhat fairly	.77	2.14	1.95	1.15	124
Very fairly	.86	2.12	1.96	1.06	113

* X^2 significant at p = .10

TABLE 16
Relationship Between Frequency of Thoughts of Leaving the Company Due
to Salary Dissatisfaction and Salary System Preference

	Salary System				
Considered Leaving	A*	B	C	D	N
Many times	.76	2.33	1.81	1.10	42
Several times	.92	2.32	1.83	.92	65
Once or twice	.63	2.38	1.90	1.09	100
Yes, but never seriously	.84	2.20	1.96	.99	134
Never	.90	2.04	2.00	1.06	211

* X^2 significant at p = .05

represents our estimate of the interaction of the various factors based on past research and theory and our knowledge gained from interviews and observation. For example, it is unlikely that pay system preferences are directly affected by the existing pay system itself. We found in our interviews that supervisory style and cultural factors modify the perception the individual has of the existing pay system. Two people may have radically different feelings about the system because of their experience with it. The experience is largely a function of their organizational setting or culture and their boss. With respect to satisfaction, current theories view it as an outcome variable rather than an independent variable (Porter and Lawler, 1968), and this would seem to make sense here. Furthermore, both our interviews and the data presented

TABLE 17
Relationship Between Whether Complaints About the Present Salary System Refer to the Lack of Merit or Incentive and Salary System Preference

| | Mean Salary System Preference | | |
Salary System	Complaints About Lack of Merit or Incentive[a]	Complaints Not Related to Merit Qualities of Present Pay System[b]	Significance of Difference*
A	.72	1.21	NS
B	2.47	1.93	.05
C	1.58	2.14	.02
D	1.23	.71	.10

*Significance was determined by means of a t Test.

[a] Present System Complaints
1. Provides little incentive for better performance
2. Amounts available are too small
3. Above average performance is not rewarded more than average performance

[b] Present System Complaints
1. Eligibility periods are too infrequent
2. Not enough information is given to people
3. Other (open comments)

above suggest that dissatisfaction is strongly associated with and probably caused by preference for a system which will provide more incentive and which would satisfy achievement needs. Finally, the multiplicative interaction of needs and expectations is hypothesized based on Vroom's work (1964).

If this model is accurate, and we feel more research is necessary to determine this, it has implications for a salary administrator contemplating a pay system change. It is clear that preference for a system and, therefore, potential acceptance of it can be strongly influenced by a number of factors within the control of management. The model and our data strongly suggest that the development of an open culture with respect to pay and the training and development of supervisors in performance feedback and salary administration can materially affect the individual's expectations about what will happen under a merit system and may even affect his needs. Even in the event that needs remain unaffected, the multiplicative interaction of expectations with needs can have a strong effect on final pay system preference and potential acceptance. The conclusion is clear. Plans for a change from a security pay system to a merit system require prior supervisory and organizational development. At the very least, it requires such steps concurrently with pay system introduction to assure acceptance of the pay system. A merit system will not be accepted and may not have the intended motivational effects if supervisors do not actively administer a performance appraisal system, practice good human relations, explain the reasons for increases, and ensure that employes are not forgotten when eligibility dates come and go. The organization must provide an open climate with respect to pay and a culture where work and effort are valued.

The salary administrator rarely concerns himself with the assessment of these managerial and organizational factors or with their development in advance of a pay system change. This study shows that these factors are as critical as the design of the system itself.

Theoretical Implications

While the research reported in this chapter deals primarily with the question of pay system preference and the problems of change, the data also bear on a number of theoretical issues which are summarized below.

The data show that merit systems are perceived as instrumental to the satisfaction of what Herzberg (1959) has called "motivator" needs (responsibility, challenging and interesting work, and advancement), and the security systems are instrumental to the satisfaction of what he calls "hygiene" needs (security, money, vacations). The role of money in motivation has been deemphasized in recent years. Perhaps research findings and current conclusions concerning pay are a function of the fact that most pay systems do not, in fact, reward for performance. Thus Herzberg's findings concerning pay may be a function, not of people's potential response to money, but merely to the form in which it is currently distributed. Our finding that preference for a merit system increases as satisfaction decreases also supports the notion that mode of payment is an important variable in satisfaction. The finding that those who complain about the lack of incentive in the existing pay system prefer a merit system further substantiates that pay systems can be instrumental to the satisfaction of motivator needs and will probably motivate under those circumstances.

The fact that security systems (complete or partial guaranteed annual increases) are perceived as instrumental to the satisfaction of security needs implies that no one system can serve all needs. Since individuals have a whole range of needs, an optimum system may be a combination of a security system and a true merit system. In this system equity would be provided by a general adjustment tied to market changes, and variable increases would be tied to performance only.

The relationships of self-perception of performance and past pay experience with pay system preference confirm that expectations play a key role in pay system preference and probably in motivation. The concept of expectations has a long history in psychology, but most recently has been discussed in connection with motivation at work by Vroom (1964) and Porter and Lawler (1968). Our data tend to support the continued importance of this concept in any theory of motivation.

In their recent book, Porter and Lawler (1968) indicate that satisfaction with pay is an outcome in a model of motivation and individual performance with subsequent feedback effects on individual needs and expectations. While the evidence in this study is barely sufficient, our data would support this notion. Higher levels of dissatisfaction were associated with preferences for a different system than now exists, indicating that perhaps needs, but certainly goals, are restructured and rearranged as a result of dissatisfaction. The relationship found between type of dissatisfaction (complaints about the lack of incentive in the system) and preference for a merit system would further support this conclusion.

The finding that the more information the individual had about the pay system, the more he preferred a merit system is reminiscent of Lawler's (1967) findings and conclusions about the effects of secrecy on satisfaction and motivation. While preference for a merit system cannot be equated with potential motivation under it, the gap is not so great as to prevent our findings from reinforcing Lawler's. The openness measured by our items implies that merely communication about the nature of the system, as opposed to full disclosure of salaries, may have a positive effect.

The data concerning the effects of supervisory behavior and practices on pay system preference provide the first data known to us concerning the moderating effect of this organizational variable on perception of the pay system and probably its motivational and behavioral outcomes. The evidence is not direct since motivation and behavior were not measured, but the relationship between leadership climate and pay system preference is at least a strong indication that this important variable moderates the effect of the pay system on effort and performance.

We have strongly suggested throughout this discussion that this research has implications for a model of pay and motivation even though the outcome measured by this research is preference for differ-

ent pay systems. The assumption is that an individual's preference indicates something about his perception of the instrumentality of a
pay system to the satisfaction of his needs (our data show this) and,
as such, the potential effort he will exert to obtain incentives offered
by the system. If this assumption is correct, the data presented in
this paper provide some insights into the moderating effects of organizational and individual variables on the relationship between the pay
system (the administrative entity) and resultant motivation or effort.
We have summarized our view of the interaction between the pay system and the moderating variables in Figure 2. This model suggests
that the individual's perception of the pay system and its effects on him
(the probability of reward for effort) is probably heavily moderated by
how his boss uses the system, supervises him (openness of relationship),
and reviews his performance. It is also moderated by the culture, its
openness with respect to pay and the value placed on achievement and
effort. The supervisor and culture are also likely to affect the relative
strengths of the individual's needs and expectations, although needs
may be a little more fixed due to early development and learning.
Satisfaction will relate to effort but only indirectly through its feedback
on needs and expectations. Again, satisfaction is viewed as a dependent
variable. Our view of the effects of pay on motivation does not
differ from that of Porter and Lawler (1968), but we have added our
view of the organizational variables that will strongly influence perception of the system and consequently its effects on effort.

Finally, the findings of this research show that we cannot think
of changing organizational systems, in this case, a pay system, without considering steps for managerial and cultural changes. Organi-

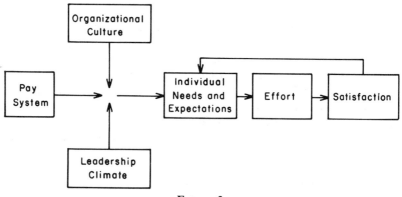

FIGURE 2

zational systems and organizational culture are intertwined and must be changed simultaneously or in some planned sequence for dramatic and permanent changes in organizational effectiveness to occur. This dual consideration, as we are finding in other research (Beer, 1969) is important whether the starting point is culture or systems. One without the other does not carry the full intended effects of change.

In general, the findings of this study are encouraging from the point of view of organizational change. The indication is clear that individual attitudes and potential acceptance of new systems (whether pay or other systems) are as much a function of organizational process within the control of management as they are a function of fundamental individual difference.

21

Management Attitudes
Toward Pay

I. R. Andrews

AND

Mildred M. Henry

Previous research has indicated that many members of lower and lower-middle management feel that their pay is inadequate, and that managers rank adequate pay as high among their needs.[1] Yet, with one exception,[2] there has been little research to date on the factors which influence how managers view their pay. The present study was undertaken as a preliminary study of several variables which might be related to managerial attitudes toward pay.[3] Among the questions we will consider are the following:

1) Do management groups systematically differ in terms of the groups with which they compare their pay? Is there a relationship between this type of comparison and satisfaction with pay?

2) Are there systematic relationships between demographic variables (such as age, education, management level, and whether a man is staff or line) and satisfaction with pay?

3) Who is most content with his pay, the man who anticipates a large pay increase over the next five years, or the man who anticipates only a small pay increase?

4) Are there systematic differences between groups in terms of their relative preferences as between fringe benefits and take-home pay?

RESEARCH METHODOLOGY

The data were obtained from a questionnaire which was sent to

Reprinted by permission of the authors and publisher from *Industrial Relations* 3 (October 1963); reprinted in *Psychological Research on Pay,* Reprint No. 220 (1964); 29, 31-39.

490 managers in five San Francisco area firms (see selected questions in appendix to this article). Of the 490 questionnaires, 299 were returned, giving a response rate of 61 per cent. The rate of return was approximately equal for the five companies. Among the 299 questionnaires returned, three were unusable and 68 were from research personnel not clearly a part of management, leaving a usable sample of 228.

About half the sample classified themselves as having line positions, and the remainder were distributed fairly evenly between "staff" and "combined line and staff" jobs. The median age was 42.5 years. The median monthly salary, in a salary range beginning at $390 and going beyond $2,000, was $745. Assignment of each subject, on the basis of salary and job title, to one of three management job levels produced a distribution with 58 per cent falling into lower management (people whose subordinates are nonmanagement persons), 34 per cent in lower-middle management (people whose subordinates are in lower management), and 8 per cent in middle management (people at the top of a small operating unit, plus people at or near the top of a medium-size operation). Since only 8 per cent, or 18 persons, were classified as middle management, the size of this group precluded its division into the smaller subgroups which would have been required under various control conditions. Therefore, aside from the major comparisons involving management level as the independent variable, only two levels of management, lower and lower-middle, were involved. Because of this restriction in number of management levels, the effects of this variable may have been underestimated.

We classified the answers to our questions initially by our four demographic variables: management level, education, age, and position (line, staff, combined line-staff). Each of the four demographic variables was then retested under separately applied control conditions for the other three demographic variables.[4]

RESULTS AND DISCUSSION

Reference groups for pay comparisons. As pointed out by Patchen, how a person feels about his salary depends not only on its absolute size but also on how it stacks up against those of other people with whom he compares himself.[5] In other words, if the differences between his salary and that received by the person with whom he compares himself seem to be appropriate in terms of other differences between them—differences such as age, education, skill, etc.—then the comparison increases his satisfaction. On the other hand, if the pay differential exceeds the perceived difference in pay-related attributes, then, for the person on the short end of the comparison, pay satisfaction is diminished. Therefore, for the administrator who seeks to establish salary levels which will appear to be equitable in salary comparisons, it becomes important to know which persons tend to be chosen for salary comparisons.

TABLE 1
Choice of Reference Group as a Function of Management Level
(Per cent of first choice)

	Choice of reference group				
	Within company			Outside company	
	Higher level	Same level	Lower level	All outside choices	N
Middle management	12	12	41	35	(17)
Lower-middle management	17	20	10	53	(70)
Lower management	16	34	15	35	(134)

As Table 1 suggests, lower-middle management was more likely to make external comparisons with groups outside the company than were middle and lower management.[6] Middle management tended to compare its pay with those on a lower level, while members of lower management were more concerned with keeping up with their peers. (Recall here that what we call "middle management" includes local top management in branch plants. Had they been drawn instead from middle positions in larger operating units, the emphasis upon "lower level" comparisons might not have appeared.)

The greater a man's education, the more likely he was (1) to compare his pay with persons outside the company ($x^2 > .025$), and (2) *not* to compare himself with his peers within the company (Table 2). The first trend persisted in three of three age groups and in two of two management-level groups. The second trend held for all comparisons under all control conditions. The choice of "same level" also diminished at higher management levels (Table 1), producing a trend which persisted in all groups under controls for age and for position and in two of three groups under a control for education.

Age seemed to affect the comparison process very little, except for a consistent tendency for the youngest age group to choose outside reference groups with particular frequency. Within this youngest age group, the greatest emphasis upon outside reference choices was found in the college degree and postgraduate samples.

Dissatisfied members of lower and lower-middle management were more likely to compare themselves with "lower-level" positions than individuals who indicated average or above-average pay satisfaction. Similarly, managers were more likely to be unhappy over too *small* a differential between the pay of themselves and their subordinates than over a too *large* differential between themselves and their boss. Of those persons who checked "below average" on over-all pay satisfaction, only 39 per cent said that upward pay differential was too large, whereas 87 per cent said that downward differential was too small.

TABLE 2
Choice of Reference Group as a Function of Education
(Per cent of first choice)

	Choice of reference group				
	Within company			Outside company	
	Higher level	Same level	Lower level	All outside choices	N
Some high school	29	43	21	7	(14)
High school degree	5	45	21	29	(38)
Some college	18	31	14	37	(49)
Business college	15	35	5	45	(20)
College degree	19	21	12	48	(58)
Postgraduate	12	12	20	56	(41)

The importance of outside pay comparisons was indicated by the finding that over-all pay satisfaction was predicted better by relative pay position within the total sample of all companies than by relative pay position within the employee's own company. Moreover, persons with a relatively good pay level (and position) in a low-paying company reported less satisfaction with pay than did persons whose pay (and position) was about average in a high-paying firm. In other words, a good relative pay position within a company did not compensate for an inadequate pay level taken within a broader context.

Summarizing, the data suggest that higher levels of management and those with more education are less likely to compare their pay with individuals on the same level in their company; indeed the frequency of out-of-company comparison tends to increase sharply with education. Thus, the data suggest that *both* external and internal comparisons are important.

Degree of satisfaction with pay. Degree of satisfaction with pay showed no *clear* trend as a function of education except that those with postgraduate training were least satisfied of all. There was no consistent trend for pay satisfaction to vary as a function of age or as a function of line or staff position.

As might be expected from the fact that higher levels of management are better paid, the degree of pay satisfaction increased steadily with increase in management level ($x^2 > .001$), although the differences were clearer among staff than line personnel. The only exception was in one of the five companies where pay differences between lower and lower-middle management were in fact quite small.

TABLE 3
Over-all Pay Satisfaction as a Function of Amount of Pay
(Per cent values)

Monthly salary	Decrease in below average	Below average	Average	Above average	Increase in above average	Total change	N
$390-539		50	44	6			(18)
	-16				+5	21	
$540-689		34	55	11			(65)
	-9				+11	20	
$690-839		25	53	22			(68)
	-10				+9	19	
$840-989		15	54	31			(26)
	-4				+17	21	
$990-1,289		11	40	48			(27)
	-0				+15	15	
$1,290-over $2,000		11	22	67			(18)

As is obvious in Table 3, the indicated degree of pay satisfaction increased steadily with increase in salary. Note, however, that beyond the salary level of $840-989 a month, almost all the total improvement came from an increase in persons checking "above average" on the pay satisfaction question (Question 1 [b] in appendix). In terms of the per cent checking "below average," there was virtually no difference between the top three salary groups. A coincidental finding from another question (11 [a] in appendix) showed that the $840-989 salary range was also the point beyond which there was no further reduction in the percentage of persons who checked "payment of debts" or "payment of mortgage" as their first choice, among 12 possible choices, for the disposition of a hypothetical 20 per cent pay increase.

These last two findings can be considered in the light of Herzberg's conclusion from interview data that even though inadequate pay can engender *negative* job feelings, a surplus of money beyond the fulfillment of deficiency needs is not, in itself, an important contributor to *positive* job feelings.[7] In terms of the present data, Herzberg's conclusion would suggest that the improvements in pay attitude which accompanied salary increases up to the $840-989 range were of greater consequence to the enhancement of over-all feelings about the job than the improvements in pay attitudes after the $840-989 range, since the former involved correction of a deficiency, while the latter involved a surplus beyond the correction of a deficiency.[8]

Pay satisfaction as a function of anticipated pay increase. As shown in Table 4, those who anticipate a large increase in pay over the next five years reported *less* satisfaction with present pay than those who anticipate only a small increase in pay ($x^2 > .05$). This trend held for six of six different salary levels ranging from around $400 a month to well over $2,000 a month, and held in two of three age groups and in two of four education groups.

TABLE 4
Over-all Pay Satisfaction as a Function of Amount of Pay
Increase Anticipated Over the Next Five Years

Anticipated increase in monthly salary	Below average	Average	Above average	N
$ 0-100	11	50	39	(36)
$200-500	26	49	25	(156)
$600-800	40	47	13	(30)

A clearly fundamental difference between persons expecting a large pay increase and those expecting a small pay increase was indicated by answers to a question (Question 12 in appendix) about the strongest motivation for outstanding job performance: "promotion" was chosen more often by the former, whereas "doing a good job for its own sake" was chosen by the latter ($x^2 > .001$). Consistent with this pattern was the tendency for persons expecting a large increment, as compared to those expecting a small increment, to be: stronger in their emphasis on merit as opposed to seniority (trend); much more willing to take a cut in security to gain an increase in pay ($x^2 > .01$); more apt to use "higher level" as a reference group when comparing their pay against the pay of others (trend); more inclined to view the "top managers'" pay as being too small ($x^2 > .025$).

A demographic breakdown revealed a consistent trend for the anticipation of larger pay increments to be associated with higher education level, younger age, and a *higher* level of present pay. It should be noted that high-expectation persons reported less satisfaction with present pay in spite of the strong trend reported above for higher pay to be associated with a higher degree of satisfaction with pay.

From the foregoing description of the high-anticipation group, it appears that many of these persons have already experienced a fairly rapid rise in their companies. And since pay is at least partially determined by the time in the job and in the company, it is plausible to suspect that such individuals are receiving salaries which are toward the bottom end of the salary range for their jobs. In such a circumstance, younger men who have advanced rapidly sometimes find that their salaries are but little higher than those paid to subordinates who carry less responsibility, but have greater seniority. Within the present sample, for example, the only person who checked "very low" on pay satisfaction was a young man in middle management whose pay was $50 a month less than that of his chief subordinate.

Another explanation for the pay dissatisfaction expressed by the high-anticipation group might be based on a more direct hypothesis: namely, that for individuals with a high degree of upward mobility, present pay is evaluated at least partially in reference to an aspired-to position and pay level, rather than strictly in terms of the appropriateness of pay for the present position. Patchen found that nonmanagement refinery workers with the best chances for upward mobility outside the refinery were, "more likely than others to choose *presently* dissonant comparisons and more likely to be presently dissatisfied with comparisons."[9] In terms of further research along this line, it seems safe to conclude that it would be helpful to distinguish carefully between the perceived fairness of pay evaluated within the framework of a self-estimate of personal worth and the perceived appropriateness of the pay for the job itself.

Merit vs. seniority, pay vs. security, pay vs. benefits. A similarity of response patterns permits the grouping of the following questions (respectively, Questions 6, 10[b], and 11[c] in appendix): (1) In determining the amount of pay an individual should receive, what relative importance should be attached to merit as opposed to seniority? (2) Which is preferable, a cut in pay to obtain increased security, or a decrease in security to get an increase in pay? (3) Which is preferable, an increase in pay or an increase in benefits (i.e., such things as pension plan, sick leave, etc).

With increased amounts of formal education there was a very strong trend for greater emphasis on merit as opposed to seniority ($x^2 > .001$), a very strong trend to be more willing to take a decrease in company-provided security to obtain an increase in pay ($x^2 > .001$), and a very strong trend for the choice of increased pay in preference to increased benefits ($x^2 > .001$) (Table 5). With increase in age, however, the reverse emerged, i.e., a slight trend toward less emphasis on merit ($x^2 > .10$), a strong trend toward greater willingness to take a pay cut to gain an increase in company-provided security ($x^2 > .01$), and a very strong trend toward the selection of increased benefits instead of increased pay ($x^2 > .001$).

TABLE 5
Responses to Pay and Benefit Choices, by Education

Formal education	Merit vs. seniority in pay setting			Security vs. pay			Choice of increased pay or benefits		
	Per cent choosing			Per cent choosing			Per cent choosing		
	More merit	O.K. as is	Less merit	More pay, less security	More security, less pay	Prefer pay	Half pay, half benefits	Prefer benefits	N
Some high school	14	86	0	36	64	47	33	21	(15)
High school degree	46	44	10	39	61	36	41	23	(39)
Business college	20	65	15	38	62	50	40	10	(20)
Some college	45	47	8	64	36	55	25	20	(50)
College degree	70	28	2	72	18	78	13	8	(61)
Postgraduate	67	26	7	97	3	81	17	2	(42)

From the above, it appears that persons in management vary systematically by age and education in what they want from the company in terms of pay and benefits.[10] At the two extremes, the young, well-educated person prefers pay to security and other benefits, whereas the older, less-educated person is relatively less interested in pay and is relatively more concerned about security and other benefits. It does not seem likely, then, that the same pay-benefit package would have the same motivational appeal for these two groups. It seems more likely that a pay-benefit package weighted differentially for the two groups would provide much greater motivational appeal. Or, going just one step farther, the motivational appeal might be maximized in a situation where each person had some say in how a given amount of salary was to be distributed between pay and the various possible benefits. Before the development of cost accounting and the perfection of large, multi-purpose computers, such a practice was feasible only for top-level executives. But now that the technological problems can be solved, it would seem that individualized pay-benefit packages could be offered to all levels of management. As a preliminary step in such a direction, the attitude of management individuals toward such a possibility should be explored. Then, if results were favorable, the idea might be extended to an experimental introduction of an individualized pay-benefit program.

SUMMARY

A questionnaire distributed to all members of management in five companies was returned by 228 persons. Analysis of questionnaire responses led to the following results:

1. The subjects' choice of reference persons for purposes of pay comparison varied as a function of management level and amount of formal education. An equitable pay comparison between oneself and one's subordinate appeared to be of critical importance to satisfaction with pay. Outside pay comparisons seemed to play an important role in the process of individual pay evaluation.

2. Management level was the only demographic variable which was consistently related to degree of satisfaction with pay.

3. Satisfaction with present pay tended to be inversely related to the amount of pay increase anticipated over the next five years.

4. Because of the systematic variations by age and education in what was wanted from the company in terms of pay and benefits, experimentation with individualized pay-benefit packages was suggested.

APPENDIX: *Selected questions from management-incentive questionnaire*

1. (a) Approximately what is your monthly pay, i.e., income from your position
   before taxes and other deductions?

   $_____month

   (b) Which of the following phrases best describes your feeling of satisfaction
   or dissatisfaction with the *pay* for your present position? *Circle one.*

very low	below average	average	above average	very high
satisfaction	satisfaction	satisfaction	satisfaction	satisfaction

2. Your feeling of satisfaction or dissatisfaction with your pay is very likely to
   be influenced by the amount of pay received by others around you. What
   persons are you most likely to use for comparison in regard to pay? Indicate
   your first three choices, using numbers 1, 2, and 3.

   _____people in your company at *higher* level positions
   _____people in your company at the *same* level positions
   _____people in your company at *lower* level positions
   _____personal friends (not in company)
   _____relatives
   _____people in other companies in jobs similar to yours
   _____people in other occupations (e.g., tradesman, professional, etc.)
   _____other (please specify) _____
   _____other (please specify) _____

6. The amount of pay given an individual is usually influenced by both seniority
   and merit considerations. In your estimation:

   (a) What relative importance is *currently* attached to these factors? *Check one.*

   _____ 0% merit, 100% seniority
   _____ 20% merit, 80% seniority
   _____ 40% merit, 60% seniority
   _____ 60% merit, 40% seniority
   _____ 80% merit, 20% seniority
   _____100% merit,   0% seniority

   (b) What relative importance do you think *should be* attached to these factors? *Check one.*

   _____ 0% merit, 100% seniority
   _____ 20% merit, 80% seniority
   _____ 40% merit, 60% seniority
   _____ 60% merit, 40% seniority
   _____ 80% merit, 20% seniority
   _____100% merit,   0% seniority

10. (b) Which of the following jobs would you choose? *Check one.*

Monthly Pay		Security provided by the company
—Job E. 20% *increase* in pay	- with -	40% *decrease* in amount of above
—Job F. 10% *increase* in pay	"	20% *decrease* in amount of above
—Job G. 10% *decrease* in pay	"	20% *increase* in amount of above
—Job H. 20% *decrease* in pay	"	40% *increase* in amount of above

   (d) Which of the following jobs would you choose? *Check one.*

Monthly Pay		*Feeling of worthwhile accomplishment*
—Job M. 20% *increase* in pay	- with -	40% *decrease* in amount of above
—Job N. 10% *increase* in pay	"	20% *decrease* in amount of above
—Job O. 10% *decrease* in pay	"	20% *increase* in amount of above
—Job P. 20% *decrease* in pay	"	40% *increase* in amount of above

11. (a) Assume that the cost of living index remains the same and you are given a 20% increase in monthly PAY. Indicate how you would spend the money by *noting your first three choices* (1, 2, and 3) among the areas listed below.

_____savings and investments
_____life insurance
_____home improvements
_____down payment on a new house
_____travel
_____new automobile
_____education of children

_____payment of debts (other than mortgage)
_____payment of mortgage on house
_____clothes
_____furnishings and appliances
_____entertainment and hobbies
_____other (please specify)_____
_____other (please specify)_____

(c) Indicate how you would want a 20% increase to be divided between pay and benefits. *Circle one.*

20% pay	15% pay	10% pay	5% pay	0% pay
0% benefits	5% benefits	10% benefits	15% benefits	20% benefits

12. In your position, which of the following provides the strongest motivation for outstanding job performance? *Check one.*

_____possibility of incentive bonus (any pay other than basic salary)
_____possibility of raise in pay (other than automatic increases or cost of living increases)
_____possibility of promotion
_____doing a good job for its own sake
_____other (please specify) _____
_____(In my position, there are no strong motivations for outstanding job performance.)

13. Approximately how much increase in monthly pay do you anticipate receiving in the next five years? (Assume that there is no general cost of living increase in wages.) *Circle one.*

None $50 $100 $200 $300 $400 $500 $600 $700 $800 or more

Notes

[1] L. W. Porter, "A Study of Perceived Need Satisfactions in Bottom and Middle Management Jobs," *Journal of Applied Psychology* XVL (February, 1961), 1-10.

[2]F. Herzberg, B. Mausner, and Barbara B. Snyderman, *The Motivation to Work* (New York: Wiley, 1959).

[3]The authors wish to express their thanks to L. W. Porter of the University of California and R. S. Peck of the IBM Company for their indispensable contributions to the analysis and interpretation of the data.

[4]Results were considered to be significant in those cases where demographic differences were large enough to produce a chi square significant at the .05 level or better without application of control and where the same trend persisted in the majority of comparisons under each control condition. For example, management-level differences with respect to satisfaction with amount of pay differential between self and subordinate were considered significant when chi square without controls was significant at the .025 level and the same trend persisted in two of three education subgroups, two out of three age subgroups, and in two of three line-staff subgroups.

[5]M. Patchen, *The Choice of Wage Comparisons* (Englewood Cliffs, N.J.: Prentice-Hall, 1961).

[6]This tendency ($x^2 > .025$) for lower-middle management to choose reference groups outside the company more frequently than did lower management held for two of three line-staff groupings, two of three age groups, and for two of three education groups.

[7]Herzberg, Mausner, and Snyderman, *op. cit.*

[8]In the same vein as Herzberg's hypothesis, but focused more directly on job motivation, is Rothe's hypothesis that surplus payments are motivating only when they tie into higher need fulfillment. H. F. Rothe, "How Much Incentive in Incentive Pay?" *Supervisory Management,* V (August, 1960), 11-15. McDermid suggests that surplus payments are less motivating than job reorganizations which permit a more direct fulfillment of higher needs. C. D. McDermid, "How Money Motivates Men," *Business Horizons,* III (Winter, 1960), 93-100. This notion was supported in the present study by the finding that 67 per cent of the management sample said (see Question 10[d] in appendix) that they would take a pay *decrease* to obtain an increase in feelings of worthwhile accomplishment.

[9]Patchen, *op. cit.*

[10]R. P. Meiklejohn, "Financial Incentives Beyond Base Pay," *Management Record,* XX (May, 1958), 165-170.

22

Managers' Perceptions of Their Subordinates' Pay and of Their Superiors' Pay[1]

EDWARD E. LAWLER III

There has long been a recognition in the social sciences that an individual's perception of his environment is shaped by his social frame of reference. Stouffer, *et al.* (1949) in their first American soldier volume clearly showed that the attitudes of the soldiers could best be understood by knowing their reference groups. More recently, studies by Patchen (1961) and Andrews and Henry (1963) have used the reference group and social comparison concepts to explain employees' attitudes toward their pay. Results have shown that employees evaluate their pay not only in terms of what other people at their level receive but also in terms of what other employees above them and below them receive. In addition, such factors as age, education, and potential for upward mobility have been shown to determine which reference group an individual will choose.

However, the understanding of an individual's attitudes and perceptions with regard to his pay requires more than just information about where he looks for his reference group and the actual characteristics of the group he views. It is equally important to know what the individual sees when he views the pay of his reference group or groups since an individual responds to his environment in terms of his perception of it and not in terms of its objective characteristics. A thousand dollar pay difference between the pay of a superior and his subor-

---

[1]The author would like to thank L. W. Porter and D. W. Taylor for their helpful comments on an earlier version of this paper.

Reprinted by permission of the author and publisher from *Personnel Psychology* 18 (1965): 413-22.

dinate may objectively be large, but the superior who sees his job as much more difficult than that of his subordinate may see the difference as very small. In addition, it is not known if the secrecy policies that most organizations maintain toward management compensation rates have any effect on the accuracy with which managers perceive the pay rates of their comparison groups.

To explore managers' perceptions of other managers' pay, the following specific questions were investigated:

1) Is there a tendency for managers to feel that there is too large or too small a difference between their pay and that of their subordinates? Between their pay and that of their superiors?

2) Is a manager's satisfaction with the size of the difference between his pay and that of his superior or subordinate related to his satisfaction with his overall pay level?

3) Do managers have an accurate picture of the pay of other managers?

METHOD

Research Sites

The present study was carried out in seven organizations. Three of the organizations were divisions of state governments and were subject to civil service policies. The managers studied from these government organizations were engaged in a variety of activities. One group managed a retail liquor store, another managed unemployment offices, and the third worked for a conservation department. The other four organizations were privately-owned companies. These four organizations varied widely in their activities. One was a food processor, another was a chemical manufacturer, the third was in the aerospace industry, and the fourth was a public utility.

Pay Programs of the Organizations

The three government organizations studied were all under civil service compensation systems and thus were subject to similar compensation programs. In these organizations, pay ranges were established for each job. Information concerning the ranges for all jobs was made public, but none was available concerning the average or median salary for any job.

In the four privately-owned organizations, each job had a pay range also. However, there was little additional similarity between the pay programs of the private and government organizations. The four private organizations maintained policies of strict secrecy with regard to both individuals' pay and the pay ranges for management jobs. Further, all the organizations had control points in their range systems that prevented all but a few of the managers in the organization from reaching the top of the pay range for a given job. The purpose of this control point was to make merit an important factor in determining individual managers' pay.

Because of the many similarities among the pay policies within the two types of organizations, the three government organizations were combined and analyzed as a single government sample and the four private industries were combined and analyzed as a single private industry sample.

Sample

The percentage of questionnaires returned was high for all of the seven organizations participating in the study. The response rate for the private industry sample was 86.5 percent while the response for the government sample was 91.5 percent. The overall response was 88.7

TABLE 1
Characteristics of the Sample by Type of Organization

	Type of Organization		
	Government	Private	Total
N Lower Management [a]	112	162	274
N Middle Management [b]	125	164	289
Mean Age (Years)	46.0	44.3	45.0
Mean Seniority (Years)	16.0	18.1	17.2
Mean Time in Position (Years)	4.5	4.1	4.3
Education Level:			
% Having Beyond High School Degree	78.1	65.0	70.5
Average Annual Salary (Dollars)	10,535	11,900	11,325

[a] Lower management is defined as those managers who are on the lowest level of management in the organization and who generally were first-line supervisors, although not typically blue-collar foremen in the case of the present sample.

[b] Middle management is defined as consisting of those positions above the first level of supervision but below the vice-presidential, company, officer, or major departmental head level.

percent, with 563 of the 635 questionnaires distributed being returned. Table 1 presents information on the demographic characteristics of the government and private industry samples. The two samples are quite similar with regard to all the characteristics considered except education. Because our sample is not a random sample of managers in general, our conclusions must, strictly speaking, be restricted to the organizations studied. However, there is a great deal of similarity between the characteristics of both of the present samples and the characteristics of a previous broad sample of lower and middle level managers (Porter, 1961). This suggests that the present sample may represent a fairly "typical" cross-section of lower and middle level managers. The fact that the present sample was drawn from a variety of organizations and the fact that a high response rate was obtained also suggest that the sample may represent a good cross-section of management. Thus, the findings of the present study may well be applicable to other organizations.

Questionnaire

The questionnaire used contained two parts which are relevant for the present study. Part I asked the managers to rate each of three characteristics associated with their pay. The printed instructions for this part of the questionnaire stated:

In the section below are listed three characteristics connected with the pay for your management position. For each such characteristic you will be asked to give two ratings.
a. How much of the characteristic is there now?
b. How much of the characteristic do you think there should be?

For each of the three items, the subjects were asked to answer the above two questions by circling a number on a rating scale from 1 (minimum) to 7 (maximum).
The specific items for which the ratings were given are as follows:

1. The pay for my management position.
2. The difference between the pay for my management position and the pay of my subordinates at a level just below me.
3. The difference between the pay for my management position and the pay of my superiors at a level just above me.

For each of the three items, satisfaction was measured by comparing the manager's answer to part (a) with his answer to part (b). When (a) and (b) were the same, it was considered that the manager was satisfied. When (b) exceeded (a), it was considered that the manager felt there was too little of the characteristic and when (a) exceeded (b), it was considered that the manager felt there was too much of the characteristic. The advantages and rationale for using these questions and measures are discussed in a previous article (Porter, 1961).

Part II of the questionnaire asked the managers to answer the following questions to the best of their knowledge about their organizations:

1) Approximately what do you believe is the average yearly salary of managers who are at *your present level?*

2) Approximately what do you believe is the average yearly salary of managers who are *one level above you?*

3) Approximately what do you believe is the average yearly salary of managers who are *one level below you?*

Factual answers to these questions were obtained by consulting with the organizations' personnel officers and by checking the companies' records.

The questionnaires were distributed individually (either by company mail or by United States mail) to the members of management in each organization. Each questionnaire was accompanied by a letter from the chief officer of the plant or division studied. In the letter, the company officer urged the manager to complete the questionnaire. However, it was pointed out that participation was completely voluntary. The questionnaires were numbered in order to identify the respondents, but each manager was assured that his responses would be completely confidential. Along with the questionnaire and the letter, each respondent received a stamped, self-addressed envelope in which to return his completed questionnaire directly to the University.

RESULTS AND DISCUSSION

Table 2 and Table 3 present the data concerning the answers of the managers to the three questions about satisfaction with pay and pay differences. The data clearly show that in addition to feeling that their own pay is too low, these managers feel that the pay of both their subordinates and their superiors is too close to their own pay. These managers apparently feel that the pay scales in their organizations are too compact and that, as a result, not enough separation exists between the salaries at different management levels. Thus, regardless of whether a manager looks upward or downward for his pay comparisons, it is likely that he will be dissatisfied with what he sees. However, the results do indicate that upward differences are less likely to be seen as too small than are downward differences (65.8% vs. 48.5% for government and 55.0% vs. 38.0% for private industry, both differences being significant beyond the .01 level). This finding may help explain why Andrews and Henry (1963) found that managers who looked downward for their pay comparisons were more likely to be dissatisfied with their pay than were managers who looked upward for their pay comparisons.

It is interesting to note from Table 2 and Table 3 the small percentage of managers who reported that they are overpaid (.8% of government managers and 4.3% of private industry managers). Overpayment has recently been studied as one type of inequity that may be present

TABLE 2

Responses of the Government Sample to the Three Questions Concerned with Satisfaction with Pay

(The number of cases is given in parentheses below each per cent.)

Questionnaire Items	% Too Much	% Satisfied	% Too Little
1. Pay for Own Position	.8 (2)	13.1 (31)	86.0 (203)
2. Difference between Own and Subordinate	5.1 (12)	29.1 (69)	65.8 (156)
3. Difference between Own and Superior	17.0 (40)	34.5 (81)	48.5 (114)

TABLE 3

Responses of the Private Industry Sample to the Three Questions Concerned with Satisfaction with Pay

(The number of cases is given in parentheses below each per cent.)

Questionnaire Items	% Too Much	% Satisfied	% Too Little
1. Pay for own position	4.3 (14)	28.4 (92)	67.3 (218)
2. Difference between Own and Subordinate	9.5 (31)	35.5 (116)	55.0 (180)
3. Difference between Own and Superior	20.1 (62)	41.9 (131)	38.0 (119)

(Adams, 1963). However, Vroom (1964) has suggested that feelings of inequity due to overpayment are not stable and as such may not be prevalent in American industry. Feelings of overpayment are felt to be unstable because managers can easily reduce these feelings by raising the value which they attach to their work and abilities. The data from the present study support Vroom's point.

Table 4 presents the Pearson product-moment correlation coefficients between the managers' responses to the two items concerned with the upward and downward pay differences and their satisfaction with their pay. In both the government and the private industry sample there is a significant trend for those managers who feel there is too small a difference between their own pay and that of their subordinates to be dissatisfied with the overall level of their pay. It is impossible from the present study to determine if the perception of too small a difference between their own and their subordinates' pay caused the managers to be more dissatisfied with the level of their pay. However, based upon the concept that one evaluates his own pay in terms of others' pay, it does seem reasonable to assume that these differences do influence managers' satisfaction with their pay. Table 4 also shows that there is some tendency for the perception of too small a difference between a manager's own pay and that of his superior to be associated with dissatisfaction with pay. However, these correlations (.06 for government and .25 for private industry) are both significantly lower ($P < .05$) than were those between satisfaction with the downward

TABLE 4

Correlations between Satisfaction with Own Pay and Satisfaction with the Differences between Own and Subordinates' Pay and between Own and Superiors' Pay

Questionnaire Item	Pay for position $(b-a)$†	
	Government Sample	Private Industry Sample
2. Difference between Own and Subordinate $(b-a)$†	.40**	.49**
3. Difference between Own and Superior $(b-a)$†	.25**	.06

**$P < .01$.

† Basic figures for correlation were obtained by subtracting rating (1-7) assigned for question (a) from rating assigned for question (b) (see text).

differences and satisfaction with pay. Apparently, downward comparisons have the greatest impact in determining a manager's satisfaction with his pay.

TABLE 5
Accuracy of the Government Sample in Estimating the Pay of Other Managers
(The number of cases is given in parentheses below each per cent.)

Questionnaire Item	% Under-Estimate	% Correct[a]	% Over-Estimate	Level of Significance[b]	Average Error
One Level Below	17.8 (40)	23.1 (52)	59.1 (133)	.01	+$340
Same Level	19.0 (44)	37.5 (87)	43.5 (101)	.01	+$161
One Level Above	26.0 (56)	37.7 (81)	36.3 (78)	NS	+$24

[a] An estimate was considered correct if it was within $200 of the actual average salary.
[b] The statistical significance of the managers' tendencies to over- or underestimate other managers' pay were tested by the sign test. Correct estimates were not considered and the number of overestimates was compared with the number of underestimates to see if there was a significant tendency for managers to over- or underestimate.

TABLE 6
Accuracy of the Private Industry Sample in Estimating the Pay of Other Managers
(The number of cases is given in parentheses below each per cent.)

Questionnaire Item	% Under-Estimate	% Correct[a]	% Over-Estimate	Level of Significance[b]	Average Error
One Level Below	28.8 (80)	11.5 (32)	59.7 (166)	.01	+$475
Same Level	37.5 (112)	17.4 (52)	45.1 (135)	NS	+$60
One Level Above	62.4 (181)	10.3 (30)	27.2 (79)	.01	+$425

[a] Within $200 of actual salary.
[b] Computed by sign test.

Table 5 and Table 6 present the data from the questions designed to determine the accuracy of the managers' perceptions of the amount of pay other managers receive. The managers from both the government and the private industry sample show a consistent tendency to overestimate the pay of their subordinates. Similarly, there was some tendency for the managers in both samples to overestimate the pay of managers at their own level. The managers from the private industry sample showed a strong tendency to underestimate the pay of their superiors; however, the data from the government sample did not show a similar trend.

The data on accuracy of perceptions clearly point to the importance of determining what a person sees as well as the objective characteristics of the object he looks to in making his social comparisons. The data show that managers have considerably distorted perceptions of what the pay rates of their comparison groups are like. Upon the basis of previous evidence, it was logical to assume that one of the sources of the managers' dissatisfaction with their pay is that the actual differences between their pay and that of their subordinates is too small. The present data suggest that it may not be the actual size of this difference but the perceptually distorted size of this difference that is too small. It is quite possible that if the managers had an accurate picture of the pay of their subordinates, they would be better satisfied with their own pay. Some evidence to support such a conclusion is provided by the fact that those managers who accurately perceived their subordinates' pay were better satisfied with the downward pay difference than were those managers who did not accurately perceive their subordinates' pay. The correlations were .39 ($P < .01$) for the private industry sample and .20 ($P < .01$) for the government sample.

Undoubtedly, one of the sources of these distortions is the policy of extreme secrecy that surrounds the pay rates for management jobs. When managers try to determine the relative standing of their pay, they are faced with an ambiguous stimulus to interpret, and apparently they interpret in a way which leads to dissatisfaction with their own pay relative to other managers' pay. Whether this situation could be improved by providing more complete information on pay rates cannot be established from these data. However, it is interesting to note that the managers in the government sample were more accurate in their estimates of the other managers' pay and, as pointed out earlier, the government managers did have more information about the pay rates in their organizations. Thus, it seems likely that secrecy policies with regard to pay may be contributing to dissatisfaction rather than reducing it, as is frequently claimed.

SUMMARY

This study investigated by means of a questionnaire the attitudes and perceptions of 563 managers toward the pay of their subordinates and of their superiors. The results indicated that managers felt there was too small a difference between their own pay and that of both their superiors and their subordinates. A significant relationship was found between the feeling by a manager that there was too small a difference between his subordinates' pay and his own pay and the feeling that his own pay was too low. The results also showed that managers tended to consistently overestimate the pay of their subordinates. It was suggested that some of the dissatisfaction of the managers with the difference between their own pay and that of their subordinates might be due to this tendency to overestimate the subordinates' pay.

REFERENCES

ADAMS, J. S. "Toward an Understanding of Inequity." *Journal of Abnormal and Social Psychology,* LXVII (1963), 422-436.

ANDREWS, I. R. AND HENRY, MILDRED M. "Management Attitudes Toward Pay." *Industrial Relations,* III (1963), 29-39.

PATCHEN, M. *The Choice of Wage Comparisons.* Englewood Cliffs, N. J.: Prentice-Hall, 1961.

PORTER, L. W. "A Study of Perceived Need Satisfaction in Bottom and Middle Management Jobs." *Journal of Applied Psychology,* XLV (1961), 1-10.

STOUFFER, S. A., SUCHMAN, E. A., DeVINNEY, L. C., STAR, SHIRLEY A. AND WILLIAMS, R. M. *The American Soldier: Adjustment During Army Life,* Volume 1. Princeton: Princeton University, 1949.

VROOM, V. H. *Work and Motivation.* New York: John Wiley & Sons, 1964.

23

Wage Inequity and Job Performance:
An Experimental Study

I. R. ANDREWS

This study provides a further test of Adams' (1963a) theory of inequity, as applied to the special case of wage inequity. Inequity is said to exist when "inputs" (such as age, education, effort expended, etc.) are not in the expected balance with "outcomes" (such as pay received, job status, etc.). A perceived inequity is said to motivate the worker to correct the imbalance through the adjustment of inputs or outcomes, either in actual fact or through psychological distortion. (For a more precise statement of the theory, see Adams, 1963a, 1965.)

Experimental data (Adams, 1963b; Adams & Jacobsen, 1964; Adams & Rosenbaum, 1962; Arrowood, 1961) tend to support the theory, but are limited in the following ways: only college students have been studied; work periods have been very short; workers were isolated from all co-workers; only two work tasks have been used, and there has been no comparison across these two tasks; wage-inequity dissonance has been induced only through a manipulation of perceived inputs, specifically, the degree to which the worker was said to be qualified for the job; there may have been some confounding by the possibility that overpaid workers were striving harder to protect their jobs; only the over-payment side of inequity has been studied. Though also limited by the first three points above—college-student sample, short work period, and worker isolation—the present study attempted to go beyond earlier studies in the following respects:

Reprinted by permission of the author and publisher from the *Journal of Applied Psychology* 51, no. 1 (1967):39-45.

1) Inequity dissonance was induced through a manipulation of outcomes instead of through a manipulation of perceived inputs.

2) Since all workers shared the expectation that their job would last for only 2 hours, there was no confounding by the possibility that some workers worked harder because they were trying to protect their job.

3) The effects of underpay inequity were examined. More specifically, the experiment attempted to compare a small amount of underpay inequity against a larger amount of overpay inequity.

4) The possibility of a task difference in the effects of wage inequity was tested.

5) Also studied was the effect of previous wage experience on a worker's reaction to his present wage.

In earlier studies, perceived job inputs (qualifications for the job) were varied by the experimenter (E) while wage rate was held constant. In the present study, wage rate was varied by E while perceived job inputs were held constant by random assignment of workers to different wage groups. This modification served three purposes: first, it tested the theory through a different kind of experimental manipulation; second, it eliminated the possibility of confounding due to differences in feelings of job security; and third, it permitted a more precise manipulation of underpay and overpay inequity.

As in Adams' later studies, this study employed a piecework pay system. This choice was dictated in part by the fact that underpayment on an hourly pay basis would have led to a self-selection of subjects (Ss), thus producing a biased sample.

Under the piecework pay system, if a worker perceives himself as underpaid, he can improve his outcomes through increased quantity of production, even though added speed may lead to a loss in work quality. Conversely, if he perceives himself as overpaid, he can reduce his outcomes by reducing production quantity, which gives him time to improve work quality. Therefore, under a piecework pay system, Hypothesis 1a can be stated as follows: As compared to workers assigned to an equitable piece rate, workers assigned to a lower piece rate will tend to produce more pieces of work but of lower quality, whereas workers assigned to a higher piece rate will tend to produce fewer pieces of work but of higher quality.

Stated in the above form, the hypothesis does not allow for individual differences in how a given pay rate is *perceived*. Yet, it seems reasonable to suspect that a worker's perception of his present pay rate will be influenced by the pay rates he has experienced on previous jobs. Therefore, as a corollary to Hypothesis 1a, Hypothesis 1b predicted differences *within* experimental groups as a function of previous wage experience: Within experimental groups, the more that present wage potential exceeds previous high wage, the lower the work quantity and the higher the work quality; the more that present wage potential is less than previous high wage, the higher the work quantity and the lower the work quality.

As defined by Adams, outcomes include not only pay received, but also such factors as intrinsic job interest, job status, etc. Moreover, outcomes are assumed to be additive and interchangeable, so that a partial absence of one outcome can be balanced by the presence of another outcome. For example, a partial absence of pay can be balanced by high intrinsic job interest. From this line of thought can be derived Hypothesis 2: Wage inequity will have more of an effect upon job performance and job attitudes when the task is dull than when the task is inherently interesting.

Adams states that it is probable that the thresholds for inequity are different in cases of under- and overcompensation. Like Jaques (1961), Adams believes that workers are more sensitive to undercompensation than to overcompensation. This idea was reflected in Hypothesis 3: A small underpay inequity will affect job performance as much as or more than a larger overpay inequity.

METHOD

There were 96 university students, hired through the student placement office, who were assigned randomly to one of six conditions of two tasks:

(a) Interviewing: Low pay rate, 15¢ per piece (n = 16); Equitable rate, 20¢ per piece (n = 16); High pay rate, 30¢ per piece (n = 16).

(b) Data Checking: Low pay rate, 15¢ per piece (n = 16); Equitable rate, 20¢ per piece (n = 16); High pay rate, 30¢ per piece (n = 16).

A comparison of these six groups on such factors as age, year in school, and previous wages earned showed no significant differences.

Procedure

Through pretesting, both tasks were adjusted to an average production of nine pieces per hour. Then, by dividing the nine pieces of work into the average hourly pay rates recommended by pretest Ss ($1.78 for interviewing and $1.79 for data checking), the equitable pay rate was set at 20¢ per piece. The overpay rate was set arbitrarily at 30¢ per piece and the underpay rate was set arbitrarily at 15¢ per piece. This asymmetric change from the 20¢ equitable rate was in keeping with the third hypothesis which stated that a small under-pay inequity would have an effect equal to, or greater than, a larger overpay inequity.

That these differences in wage potential were perceived as intended was confirmed by differences in the size of the discrepancy between "worker recommendations for an appropriate hourly pay rate" and "the amount of money which had already been earned." On the average, the recommended hourly pay rate exceeded pay already earned by $0.13 an hour in the case of the 15¢ piece-rate group, as compared to $0.05 an hour in the case of the 20¢ piece-rate group. For the 30¢ piece-rate group, the recommended hourly pay rate was $0.69 an hour *less* than the pay already earned.

Over and above the between-group differences predicted by Hypothesis 1a, Hypothesis 1b predicted within-group differences as a function of previous wage experience. For the total sample, the 25 highest paid persons earned $2.25 or more per hour while the 25 lowest paid persons earned $1.55 or less per hour, leaving a middle group which ranged from $1.60 to $2.20 per hour. These three previous wage categories were used to divide workers within each of the piece-rate groups as required by Hypothesis 1b.

As required by the second hypothesis, one task had to be of greater inherent interest than the other task. For this purpose, interviewing students on campus was selected as the interesting task while checking transcribed numbers was selected as the dull task. As evaluated by both pretest and experimental Ss, the interviewing job received an average rating of about 6 on a 7-point scale, while the data-checking job received an average rating of less than 3. This difference was highly significant.

Aside from this difference in the degree of inherent job interest, the two tasks were made as similar as possible: each employee worked for only 2 hours and had no expectation for employment beyond the two hours; each employee was given 30 pieces of work with the instruction ". . . to work on these for only 2 hours"; by pretesting and adjusting as required, the two tasks were equilibrated for the average number of pieces completed within a specified time; in pretesting and in the experimental data, the performance variance was about equal for the two tasks; piece rates paid for the jobs were identical; specific instructions about work quantity and quality were omitted deliberately; only male employees were hired; each employee worked in isolation from other employees; both tasks were presented in the guise of legitimate jobs.

For each of the two tasks there were two dependent variables, work quantity and work quality. Work-quantity data were entered in raw score form, that is, the actual number of work pieces completed in 2 hours. This was possible because the two tasks were comparable in average rate of production, production variance, and in the shape of the frequency distribution (symmetric and somewhat platykurtic).

Work-quality data, on the other hand, were completely different for the two tasks and, therefore, had to be converted to standard score form for statistical comparisons. Interviewer work quality was defined as the average number of words recorded per interview—a measure which correlated over .80 with the average number of ideas recorded per interview. The higher the average number of words recorded, the higher the work quality. For the data checkers, work quality was defined as the number of transcription errors *missed* divided by the total number of errors which had been planted in those pages which the worker said he had checked. The smaller the proportion of errors missed, the higher the work quality.

RESULTS

As predicted by Hypothesis 1a and Hypothesis 1b, quantity of output was negatively related to assigned piece rate and positively related to previous high wage per hour (Table 1). The mean difference between the 15¢ and 30¢ piece-rate groups was significant at the .02 level ($t = 2.56$), while the mean difference between the $2.25-or-more and the $1.55-or-less groups was significant at the .01 level ($t = 2.91$).

Also as predicted, quality of work was positively related to assigned piece rate and negatively related to previous high wage per hour (Table 2). The mean difference between the 15¢ and 30¢ piece-rate groups produced a t value of 1.83, not significant with a two-tailed test. If one accepts a one-tailed test on the grounds that direction of effect was predicted, then this t value was significant at the .05 level. The mean difference between the $2.25-or-more and the $1.55-or-less groups was significant at the .05 level ($t = 2.33$).

When work quality and quantity are considered simultaneously, persons who feel overpaid should produce fewer pieces of higher quality work—while those who feel underpaid should produce more pieces of lower quality work. The proportion of workers who fell in the former category—work quantity below the total sample median and work

TABLE 1
Quantity of Work as a Function of Assigned Piece Rate and Previous Wage Experience

Previous high wage per hour	15¢ per piece (n = 32)	20¢ per piece (n = 32)	30¢ per piece (n = 32)	Row average
$2.25 or more ($n$ = 25)	23.7	18.2	19.6	21.0
$1.60 to $2.20 ($n$ = 46)	22.2	20.3	17.0	20.0
$1.55 or less ($n$ = 25)	16.7	15.9	15.1	16.0
Column average	21.1	18.9	17.7	19.2

TABLE 2
Quality of Work as a Function of Assigned Piece
Rate and Previous Wage Experience

Previous high wage per hour	15¢ per piece (*n* = 32)	20¢ per piece (*n* = 32)	30¢ per piece (*n* = 32)	Row average
$2.25 or more (*n* = 25)	-0.29	-0.71	+0.18	-0.19
$1.60 to $2.20 (*n* = 46)	-0.15	-0.32	+0.20	-0.12
$1.55 or less (*n* = 25)	-0.01	+0.57	+0.62	+0.38
Column average	-0.16	-0.16	+0.30	0.00

quality above the total sample median—is shown in Table 3. The proportion of workers who fell in the latter category—work quantity above the total sample median and work quality below the total sample median—is shown in Table 4. In both tables the influence of piece rate and the influence of previous high wage are readily apparent. For example, if a worker's previous high wage was $1.55 or less and his present piece rate was 30¢, then there was a 75% chance that he would turn in fewer pieces of higher quality work and a 13% chance that he would do the reverse. The probabilities were strikingly different for a person whose previous high wage was $2.25 or more and whose present piece rate was 15¢; for such a worker there was a 10% chance that he would turn in fewer pieces of high quality work and a 60% chance that he would turn in many pieces of lower quality work.

According to the second hypothesis, the effects of wage inequity should have been greater on the dull task (data checking) than on the interesting task (interviewing). As measured by mean differences in work quantity and work quality, the data did not support the hypothesis. On the other hand, two pieces of evidence did provide some encouragement for the task-difference hypothesis. First, the correlation between "work quantity" and "the size of the discrepancy between present wage potential (9.5 times the assigned piece rate) and previous high wage per hour" was -.54 for the data checkers but only -.32 for the interviewers. The comparable correlations for work quality were .35 for the data checkers but only .20 for the interviewers. Though not reaching statistical significance, these differences in correlation size were both in the direction predicted. A second kind of support for the hypothesis stems from the way job-attitude scores (on a postwork questionnaire) varied as a function of assigned piece rate. Among the data checkers there was a systematic change across piece-rate groups—the higher the piece rate, the more favorable the job attitude on five out of six scales. In contrast, job attitudes among interviewers remained fairly constant from one piece-rate group to another. Among interviewers, for example, the mean difference between the 15¢ and 30¢ piece-rate groups on the underpaid/overpaid scale was *not* significant at the .05 level; among data checkers, on the other hand, this difference was significant at the .001 level.

TABLE 3
Chance in 100 that Work Quantity Was Kept Low
While Work Quality Was Increased

Previous high wage per hour	Assigned piece rate	Chance in 100
$2.25 or more ($n$ = 25)	15¢	10
	20¢	0
	30¢	40
$1.60-$2.20 (n = 46)	15¢	8
	20¢	21
	30¢	36
$1.55 or less (n = 25)	15¢	44
	20¢	75
	30¢	75

According to the third hypothesis, job-performance differences between the 15¢ and 20¢ groups should be equal to or greater than the performance differences between 20¢ and 30¢ groups. As shown by the column averages in Table 1, work-quantity data were consistent with this hypothesis; the mean difference for the 15¢/20¢ comparison was slightly larger than the mean difference for the 20¢/30¢ comparison, 2.2 as compared to 1.2 pieces of work. Work-quality data, on the other hand, were not consistent with the third hypothesis; the mean difference for the 15¢/20¢ comparison was 0.00 as compared to a mean difference of 0.46 for the 20¢/30¢ comparison. Though not reaching statistical significance until the .10 level, the direction of this difference in mean differences was inconsistent with the hypothesis.

DISCUSSION

The above results are consistent with earlier studies which showed that dissonance from overpayment (on a piecework pay system) can lead to a reduction in work quantity and an increase in work quality. The above results add to previous studies in the following ways:

1) Unlike earlier studies which produced inequity by the manipulation of perceived job inputs (qualifications for the job) the present study produced inequity by the manipulation of assigned piece rate. It was assumed that workers would check periodically to see how much money they were earning; those who perceived their earning rate as low would be tempted to increase their rate of production even though work quality had to be sacrificed and vice versa for those who found they were earning too much. Some support for this interpretation follows from the fact that 30¢-per-piece workers tended to do fewer pieces of work in their second hour, while 15¢-per-piece workers tended to do more pieces of work in their second hour.

Postwork discussions with workers revealed that another fairly common approach to the job was the establishment of a production quota before work was begun. For example, if a worker had a high previous wage of $2.00 per hour, then assignment to a 20¢-per-piece rate would lead to a work quota of 10 pieces per hour. That same worker assigned to a 30¢-per-piece rate would set a quota of about 7 pieces per hour, once again hoping to earn at a rate consistent with his previous wage experience. To the extent that such a worker could maintain his self-imposed rate of production, dissonance could have been avoided. For these workers, it could be argued that Adams' dissonance model was less appropriate than a cognitive consistency model which does not postulate dissonance, for example, Sampson's (1963) expectancy congruence model. This change in explanation, however, does not negate Adams' basic point, namely, that workers adapt their productive effort to maximize equity rather than total earnings.

In both of the above reaction patterns there was an adjustment in rate of output which reduced or prevented wage inequity. But not all persons responded to a perceived inequity by adjusting rate of output. For example, one 15¢-per-page data checker said that he just could not believe that it was real—that he must have misheard the instructions. He also said that at times he felt like going through the pages and changing many of the numbers. In spite of these misgivings, he turned in good quality work. Several of the underpaid workers rationalized their low earning rate by saying that they just were not well suited to the job. On the opposite side of the equity ledger, some of the overpaid workers rationalized their high earnings by saying that they were unusually skillful at this kind of work. Of these workers, several cited previous job experience which, as they saw it, developed the required skills.

Not included in any of the above reaction patterns (or in the results data) were three 15¢-per-piece workers who quit the job after 30 or 40 minutes, stating that this just was not their kind of work. No workers left their jobs in the 20¢- and 30¢-per-piece groups.

Also not included in the above reaction patterns were three 30¢-per-piece data checkers who tried to reduce overpay inequity by reporting fewer pages completed than they had actually done. Lastly, there were some workers who claimed that they were unaware of how much money they were earning. They said that they just did their jobs and did not watch the clock or count the pieces of work completed.

2) Whereas earlier studies considered only the overpayment side of inequity, the present study also examined the effects of underpayment dissonance. As expected, the average work quantity was greater for the 15¢-per-piece workers (21.1) than for the 20¢-per-piece workers (18.9). However, the expected trend did not hold for work quality where there was no difference between the 15¢- and 20¢-per-piece groups. Several explanations for this lack of difference are possible: first, the 5¢-per-piece differential between the 15¢ and 20¢ groups was too small; second, increased speed on the monotonous data-checking task kept workers more alert with the result that work quality did not suffer from a slight underpayment; third, possible confounding by a change in personnel in the student placement office—an interpretation fostered by the fact that the expected trend was very much intact *before* the addition of the last 16 Ss, workers who were hired after the personnel change at the placement office. In brief, E believes that the inconsistency of work-quality data should not be taken as evidence against the hypothesis. A subsequent study, using 10¢ per piece as the unfairly low wage and 25¢ per piece as the equitable rate, found that the underpaid Ss not only produced more pieces of work (interviews), but did so by a statistically significant reduction in work quality (Lawler & O'Gara, 1966).

3) Perhaps the most interesting result in the present study was the effect of previous wage experience. As reported in Tables 1 and 2, the within-group differences (rows) were as large as the differences between piece-rate groups (columns). This finding emphasizes Adams' position that inputs and outcomes must be evaluated in terms of the worker's

perception of them, rather than in terms of objective reality.

Worth noting in the reported row differences is the fact that the performance of the $2.25-or-more group was only slightly different from the performance of the $1.60-$2.20 group—while the performance of the $1.55-or-less group was markedly different. This fact might mean that there was a ceiling on worker pay expectations for a campus job, and once a worker's previous wage experience was high enough to bring him up to that limit, further increases in previous high wage had no additional effect.

From an applied viewpoint the within-piece-rate-group differences suggest that previous wage history should be considered in hiring new employees. Other things equal, an applicant whose previous high wage was less than the wage for the present job might be a better risk than an applicant whose previous high wage exceeded the wage for the present job.

Limitations in Generality

As always there are several considerations which limit the generality of this study and the related studies cited in this report. First, there is the time factor: that which is true for a 2-hour work period might not be true for longer work periods. Second, that which is true for a college-student population is not necessarily true for other populations. Among unskilled workers, for example, social class differences in belief value systems might lead to a different response to overpay inequity. Or, in a management population, dedication to achievement for its own sake might counteract the effects of underpay inequity. Third, in all the studies reported, each worker was isolated from all other workers. This fact is a handicap when you try to generalize to the more typical work situation where workers are involved in one or more groups. Until such time as the above considerations have been tested by additional research, caution must be exercised in drawing inferences for industrial practice. The experimental data tell only that a perceived wage inequity does influence the job performance of college students who are hired for short-term jobs which allow them to work in isolation from other workers.

REFERENCES

ADAMS, J. S. Toward an understanding of inequity. *Journal of Abnormal and Social Psychology,* 1963, **67,** 422-436. (a)

382 RESEARCH ON COMPENSATION

ADAMS, J. S. Wage inequities productivity and work quality. *Industrial Relations,* 1963, **3,** 9-16. (b)

ADAMS, J. S. Injustice in social exchange. In L. Berkowitz (Ed.), *Advances in experimental social psychology.* Vol. 2. New York: Academic Press, 1965. Pp. 267-297.

ADAMS, J. S., & JACOBSEN, P. R. Effects of wage inequities on work quality. *Journal of Abnormal and Social Psychology,* 1964, **69,** 19-25.

ADAMS, J. S., & ROSENBAUM, W. E. The relationship of worker productivity to cognitive dissonance about inequities. *Journal of Applied Psychology,* 1962, **46,** 161-164.

ARROWOOD, A. J. Some effects on productivity of justified and unjustified levels of reward under public and private conditions. Unpublished doctoral dissertation, University of Minnesota, 1961.

JAQUES, E. *Equitable payment.* New York: Wiley, 1961.

LAWLER, E. E., & O'GARA, P. W. The effects of inequity produced by underpayment on work output, work quality and attitudes toward the work. Paper read at American Psychological Association, New York, September 1966.

SAMPSON, E. E. Status congruence and cognitive consistency. *Sociometry,* 1963, **26,** 146-162.

24

Managerial Attitudes Toward Salaries as a Function of Social and Economic Development[1]

E. C. RYTERBAND

AND

K. M. THIAGARAJAN

Recently renewed interest seems to have been aroused in the systematic appraisal of psychological issues associated with wages in industry (Dunnette 1967; Opsahl 1967). For quite awhile the professional literature concentrated on studying other sources of job satisfaction, such as security, esteem, and the like, whose importance were once less obvious than money itself (Vroom 1964, 1965). From this more recent flowering of interest in money, certain key issues have emerged. A number of studies have examined or discussed the potency of money as a motivator (Bass 1968; Lawler 1967). Other studies also have examined the effects of intra- and interpersonal variables on workers' perceptions of money. Adams (1964, 1965) has established that an individual's perceptions of equity may be affected extensively by the efforts expended and rewards accrued by fellow workers with whom he compares himself. In addition, Ryterband (1966) and Weick (1966, 1967) both have found that a worker's beliefs about the intrinsic value of this task can alter his perception of equitable wages. Moreover, Haire (1965) viewed these beliefs and the needs they imply as central to defining the form of monetary compensation offered to various individuals at work.

The studies cited above are notable advances; there remains, however, much to learn. A majority of investigations to date have been restricted to examining the attitudes and reactions of line employees and students toward wages. It is equally, if not more, important for

---

Reprinted by permission of the authors. Technical Report 24. Contract NONR 624(14), University of Rochester, Rochester, New York, 1968.

us to know something about concepts of wages held by managers, who, after all, have a hand in determining wages and wage policies. An even more important limitation of the work done to date is that it has been restricted to industrially advanced countries in the West, especially the United States. This limitation ignores two major sources of variation that may affect attitudes and behavior concerning wages: the level of economic development, and sociocultural influences of the milieu in which wage decisions are being made.

One of the key questions that has not been asked of managers in different cultures concerns the personal criteria managers use in determining wage differentials. In one study done only in the United States, managers perceived greater performance or job responsibility as prerequisites for higher pay (Lawler 1966). More such efforts are needed in answering this question, since it is these and possibly other characteristics defining the worker, his job, and his performance which managers use as criteria in making wage decisions. Moreover, it seems especially important to examine these characteristics on a cross-cultural basis since these decisions reflect more basic values of managers (and organizations) and these values may vary extensively and surprisingly between one nation and another. Do managers in all countries use wage differentials in a similar fashion? Are these differentials always principally based on performance considerations, that is, does a manager first and foremost use wages as a means to reward or inspire high performance, or does he use them also (or instead) as compensation for certain special conditions such as a lack of security or hazardous working conditions associated with a particular job? If there are these "other" nonperformance considerations, what are they, and how important are they; that is, how sensitive to them are managers in various cultures?

It is being hypothesized in this study that cultural and economic differences between countries will reveal variations in the conditions that determine what is regarded as a fair wage. The present study was conceived as a means of exploring this very broad, unadventurous but hitherto untested hypothesis. It seems most important at this very early stage in cross-cultural studies of organizational behavior to first establish the extent of differences in attitudes toward wages associated with these economic and cultural variables, and then let the pattern of differences, if any, suggest more specific hypotheses that would be tested subsequently.

In testing the basic hypothesis, the authors realized certain intrinsic problems. It was recognized that it would be difficult to isolate the effects of sociocultural influences and separate them from the effects of level of economic development. The works by Harbison and Myers (1959) and Haire, Ghiselli, and Porter (1966) illustrate the interactive effects of these two sources. Although the major thesis of the Harbison and Myers study is that the level of industrialization influences managerial behavior, often they resort to explanations based on sociocultural variables. In turn, the Haire et al. study found that while many countries clustered into sociocultural groupings irrespective of level of industrialization, the developing nations examined in their study— India, Chile, and Argentina, at approximately the same level of industrialization— formed an attitude cluster irrespective of their geographic and cultural separation. This would indicate that both the above factors interact and are of considerable importance.

The present study attempts to explore the interaction of these two factors, culture and economic development, and their influences on managers' behavior and attitudes regarding wage decisions. Specifically, the investigation concerns the decisions and the criteria for salary increases used by managers in countries differing in culture and level of industrialization.

METHOD

Subjects

Four matched samples of middle managers representing different countries were studied from the United States (n = 38), Scandinavia (n = 20), India (n = 32) and Colombia (n = 24). The samples of managers from these countries were similar in terms of age, experience, and level in their companies. The United States and Scandinavia were considered industrially advanced and India and Colombia as still developing countries.[2] The data utilized in the study were all obtained while the managers were in management-development workshops in their home countries, using their native languages.[3]

Procedure

The data were gathered from responses of managers to a small-group-management-development exercise focusing on compensation practices. EXERCISE COMPENSATION is a part of a Program of Exercises (Bass 1965) simulating key management activities created for training managers. The Program of Exercises is currently translated into fourteen languages. Data are generated for this exercise while managers are taking part in a training activity. Copies of manager-trainees' responses to the exercise, which comprise those data, are automatically reproduced using non-carbon reproducing sheets in the exercise. In addition to exercise responses, personal data, descriptions of training, and the job situations of each manager are collected and used as the basis for matching samples in different countries.

Trainers, who had had previous experience with the exercise, who were natives of the country in which it was run, and who were all fluent in the language used, were principally responsible for conducting the exercise in the various locations in which it was administered.

Task

EXERCISE COMPENSATION asks participant managers to make salary recommendations for ten engineers being considered for an annual raise. Three of the ten engineers differ in merit, while the other seven are average in performance but different in their job conditions.

In a small group discussion, each participant was asked to individually assign salary increases (in percentage of present salary) to the ten hypothetical engineers with two goals in mind: equity and retention of the engineers in the company. After completing their individual decisions the participants in a study group joined in a discussion leading to recommending salary increases as a group.

Brief descriptions of the ten engineers are as follows:

Merit-differences

 1) Al—average performance, average job
 2) Bill—high performance (top 10 percent), average job
 3) Charlie—low performance (near the bottom 10 percent), average job

Socioenvironmental differences

 4) Dan—average performance, no security in job
 5) Ed—average performance, no opportunity for advancement
 6) Frank—average performance, bad working conditions
 7) Garry—average performance, low prestige job
 8) Henry—average performance, unfriendly co-workers
 9) Irwin—average performance, boring and monotonous job
 10) Jim—average performance, has a competitive job offer

Analyses

The analyses examined economic and sociocultural variables by separating the four samples into two groups of two. In the first group, managers from the United States and Scandinavia were included, representing countries of more advanced economic development. In the second group, Indian and Colombian managers were included, representing countries of less advanced economic development. Differences between the two groups were then assessed along with differences between the two samples within a group. For example, differences might be found between the combined group from the more advanced countries and the combined group from the less advanced countries. They might indicate differences due to level of economic development if in subsequent comparisons no differences were found between the culturally different but economically similar Indian and Colombian samples (and/or between the U. S. and Scandinavian samples). Thus, analyses compared combined United States and Scandinavia vs. combined India and Colombia groups, and then similar tests separately compared the United States to Scandinavia and India to Colombia.

RESULTS

Table 1 presents the mean recommended raises (in percentages). The absolute mean increase given to all ten engineers by managers from the United States and Scandinavia is 8.8 and 8.9 respectively, whereas it is 13.7 and 12.5 for Indian and Colombian managers respectively.

Analyses of these mean percentage increases revealed significant differences only between the developed and developing countries. The mean increase awarded by managers from both India and Colombia was 13.2 percent while the mean increase awarded by managers from the United States and Scandinavia was 8.8 percent. Similar differences between managers from the developing and developed countries were found when the mean of each of the ten engineers was examined. Managers from the developing countries gave all engineers higher increases than managers from the developed countries ($p \leqslant .01$). No differences on any of these means were found between managers from India and Colombia or between managers from the United States and Scandinavia. These results can easily be accounted for by the current (1967-68) differential rates of inflation in the developed and developing countries. Indices of average annual inflation are as follows:

TABLE 1
Mean Recommended Salary Increases in Percentages

Description of Engineers	U.S. (N = 38)	Scandinavia (N = 20)	India (N = 32)	Colombia (N = 24)	Developed vs. Developing (U.S.-Scand) vs. (I-C)	Developed (U.S.) vs. (Scand)	Developing (I) vs. (C)
Merit:							
Al (average)	8.0	8.3	11.7	10.8	**		
Bill (high merit)	12.5	13.8	17.3	17.6	**		
Charlie (low merit)	5.4	5.8	12.8	10.0	**		
Mean	8.6	9.3	13.9	12.8	**		
Job conditions:							
Dan (no security)	8.7	8.1	12.5	10.1	**		
Ed (no opportunity)	8.0	7.8	12.3	11.5	**		
Frank (bad working conditions)	9.4	9.9	14.3	15.4	**		
Garry (low prestige)	8.8	8.6	12.9	12.2	**		
Henry (unfriendly co-workers)	9.2	8.9	14.4	13.0	***		
Irwin (boring job)	9.4	9.6	14.7	13.7	**		
Jim (competitive offer)	9.0	8.7	14.1	11.7	**		
Mean	8.9	8.8	13.6	12.4	**		
Overall mean	8.8	8.9	13.7	12.5	**		

* Difference is significant at the .05 level (two-tailed test).
** Difference is significant at the .01 level (two-tailed test).

United States, 1.7 percent; Scandinavia, 3.7 percent; India, 10.2 percent; and Colombia, 6.0 percent.

But our interest is in wage differentials as they vary from one country to another. The inflationary effect was eliminated by relating all decisions made by each manager to that made for Al, the average engineer. If we look at the mean salary increases in relation to Al, who is average in all respects, then we can avoid the problems of inflation and differences in base salary. These relative increases are summarized in Table 2. We find in Table 2 that differences between countries appear in terms of the mean relative increase for all ten engineers. The one difference observed indicates that managers from the developing countries gave a mean relative increase of 1.17, while the managers from the developed countries gave a mean relative increase of 1.08. The difference examined by a t-test is significant at the .05 level. The increases for each individual engineer relative to the average man, however, reveal further differences of consequence.

TABLE 2
Mean Ratios of Increases Relative to Al, the Average Man

Item	Overall Mean
U.S. (N=38)	1.10
Scandinavia (N=20)	1.06
India (N=32)	1.17
Colombia (N=24)	1.16
Developed vs. Developing	
(U.S.-Scand) vs. (I-C)	*
Developed	
(U.S.) vs. (Scand)	
Developing	
(I) vs. (C)	

*Difference is significant at the .05 level (two-tailed test).

Influence of Merit in Performance on Equitable Salary Increases

Table 3 presents the mean relative salary increases given to the first three engineers who differ in performance only. The entries in the table examine the range of increases given to the three engineers of varying merit in performance. The first compares increases given the best versus the average performer, the second compares the poorest and average, the third compares the best and poorest.

TABLE 3
The Influence of Performance on Relative Salary Increases

Country	Best: Average	Poorest: Average	Best: Poorest
U.S. (N=38)	1.57	.68	2.38
Scandinavia (N=20)	1.64	.68	2.41
India (N=32)	1.49	1.10	1.35
Colombia (N=24)	1.63	.93	1.59
Developed (U.S. -Scand) vs Developing (I-C)		**	**
Developed (U.S. vs. Scand)			
Developing (I vs. C)			*

* p ≤ .05 (two-tailed test).
** p ≤ .01 (two-tailed test).

All the groups rewarded the best performer equally: about one-half times more than the average performer. They differed, however, in their behavior toward the poor performer. As t-tests revealed, differences only appeared when comparing managers from the developing countries to managers from the developed countries ($p \leq .01$). No statistically reliable differences were revealed between managers from the developed countries or between managers from the developing countries. Managers from the developed countries are similar in that they give the poor performer less than the average man (0.68 or 32 percent less), while managers from both the developing countries treat him about the same as they treat the average man. Further t-tests also were performed to compare the ratio of increments given the best and poorest performers in the four cultures. The developed countries pooled together differed significantly from the developing countries in the range of salary increases awarded to the best and poorest performer ($p \leq .01$). The managers from developed countries awarded the best performer 2.42 times the increase awarded the poorest performers, while the salary increase awarded the best performer was 1.45 times the increase awarded the poorest performer by managers from developing countries.

The result also showed that there was no significant difference within levels between U.S. and Scandinavian managers, while there were significant differences between Indian and Colombian managers ($p \leq .01$).

The managers from developed countries awarded the best performer 2.42 times the increase awarded the poorest performers, while the salary increase awarded the best performer was 1.45 times the increase awarded the poorest performer by managers from developing countries. The result also showed that there was no significant difference within levels between U.S. and Scandinavian managers, while there were significant differences between Indian and Colombian managers ($p \leqslant .05$). Colombian managers revealed a ratio of 1.59 between best and poorest managers; from India, a ratio of 1.35.

The Influence of Job Conditions on Wages

Mean relative increases given to the remaining seven engineers may be examined in Table 4. The data in that table show that all four groups considered job conditions in making their salary decisions, that is, each of the engineers described received pay increases different from the average man. The average relative wage increment given to all seven engineers is shown in the bottom row of Table 4. Those data indicate that managers from the United States gave the seven engineers an average of 12 percent above Al's increase; the managers from Scandinavia gave them an average of 6 percent above Al; managers from Colombia gave them an average of 16 percent above Al, and the managers from India gave them an average of 15 percent above Al. Comparisons of these averages revealed differences between managers from developed and developing countries ($p \leqslant .05$). Managers from the developed countries gave an average increment of 10 percent greater than Al, while managers from the developing countries gave an average increment of 16 percent greater than Al. Differences were also observed between managers from the two developed countries, the United States and Scandinavia ($p \leqslant .05$).

The data representing the influence of each of the job conditions are shown in the remainder of Table 4.

Two additional analyses were completed on these data. The first analysis compared the differences in salary increases recommended for *each* of the seven engineers in order to understand the importance attached to the seven conditions across the four countries studied. Examining the seven job conditions revealed some similarities among managers from all four countries in the apparent relevance they see in wage increases as a response to various job conditions. As a whole, the four groups gave salary increments which were considerably above average to engineers who had a "boring job," "bad working

TABLE 4
Influence of Socioenvironmental Conditions
on Salary Recommendations—Ratios Relative to Al the Average Man

Description of Engineers	U.S. (N=38)	Scandinavia (N=20)	India (N=32)	Colombia (N=24)	Developed vs. Developing (U.S.-Scand) vs. (I-C)	Developed (U.S.) vs. (Scand)	Developing (I) vs. (C)
Dan (no security)	1.09+	.98	1.07	.89			
Ed (no opportunity)	1.01	.94	1.05	1.07	*		
Frank (bad working conditions)	1.18	1.19	1.23	1.43	*		
Garry (low prestige)	1.11	1.04	1.11	1.14			
Henry (unfriendly co-workers)	1.16	1.08	1.23	1.20			
Irwin (boring job)	1.18	1.16	1.26	1.27	*		
Jim (competitive offer)	1.13	1.05	1.21	1.09	*		*
Mean	1.12	1.06	1.16	1.15	*		

+ 1.09 means 1.09 times the salary increment given to the average performer or 9 percent more than was given to Al.

* $p \leq .05$ (two-tailed test).

conditions," and "unfriendly co-workers." Conversely, engineers who "lacked opportunity for advancement" or had little "job security" were given smaller average salary increments. There were moderately above-average salary increments given by managers to engineers in the "low prestige" job condition.

The results also showed a number of differences among the management groups. The managers from the developing countries awarded significantly different raises to the engineer with "no opportunities" for advancement when compared to managers from developed countries ($p \leqslant .05$). U.S. and Scandinavian managers offered him 3 percent below the average man's increase, Indian and Colombian managers 6 percent above average. Differences between managers from developed and developing countries also appeared for the engineers in hazardous (Frank) and boring (Irwin) jobs ($p \leqslant .05$). Managers from the developed countries gave Frank 18 percent and Irwin 17 percent more salary increase than Al, while managers from the developing countries gave the same engineers 31 percent and 26 percent more than Al. For the engineer who had a competitive offer, there were significant differences between India and Colombia. Indian managers awarded him 21 percent above average increases, Colombian managers 9 percent above average.

The second analysis involved tests to compare the differences among relative salary increases awarded to the seven engineers who differed in their job conditions. The purpose of these tests was to see how much managers from each country discriminated between job conditions in awarding salary increases; that is, to compare the variability of salary increases offered for different job conditions. One way of doing this was to compare how often managers from each country did *not* give special consideration in salary decisions to engineers working under exceptional job conditions, that is, gave engineers holding these jobs the identical increase they gave Al, who had no outstanding problems with his job conditions. Chi square tests comparing those frequencies revealed that managers from the developed countries gave these last seven engineers the same salary increase they gave the average engineer, Al, more often than did managers from the developing countries ($p \leqslant .05$). No comparable differences were observed between the samples from the two developing countries. The percentages on which chi squares are based are summarized in Table 5, row 1.

A second means of comparing the amount of discrimination among job conditions was to utilize a direct measure of variability. The standard deviation of salary increments offered by each manager to the seven engineers was calculated and used as the measure of variability among the seven job conditions. Mean standard deviations for the managers from each country were then compared. These mean standard deviations are summarized in Table 5, row 2. The t-tests on the standard deviations in the relative salary increases awarded to the seven engineers showed that there were highly significant differences between the developed and developing countries ($p \leqslant .001$). While managers from developed countries tended to treat all the job conditions more uniformly, as indicated by standard deviations of .86 for the United States and 1.25 for Scandinavia, managers from developing countries made larger distinctions between the various conditions as reflected in standard deviations of 1.86 for India and 2.60 for Colombia. The difference between India and Colombia was also significant ($p \leqslant .05$).

DISCUSSION

The differences found supported the general hypothesis that both the level of economic development and sociocultural factors influence managerial judgments concerning wages. Though both economic and sociocultural factors contributed to the differences observed, the former appeared of greater consequence. It was found that managers from developing countries differed from managers from developed countries in that the former gave higher absolute and relative wage increases to all ten engineers. In addition, managers from the developing countries were less concerned with differences in merit (especially regarding below-average performers) in making wage differentials. On the other hand, they gave higher relative increases and were more sensitive to differences among employees in extenuating job conditions.

In turn, differences, though less pronounced, were found between managers from cultures at the same level of economic development concerning employee merit and working conditions as factors in determining wage increases. For example, while Indian and Colombian managers both made far fewer distinctions than U.S. or Scandinavian managers for employees of varying merit, the range of salary increases given by Indians was still somewhat smaller than that given by Colombians.

Similarities also were evident. Managers from all four countries gave the top performer the highest salary increase (about 1.5 times the average man's raise). In addition, all managers gave some added increase to employees in exceptional working conditions (though the

TABLE 5

Discrimination in Relative Salary Increments Awarded to Engineers in Different Job Conditions

(Samples)

	U.S. (N=38)	Scandinavia (N=20)	India (N=32)	Colombia (N=24)	Developed vs. Developing (U.S. -Scand) vs. (I-C)	Developed (U.S.) vs. (Scand)	Developing (I) vs. (C)
Percentage of times engineers were given the same as AI	54	58	27	36	*		
Standard deviation of salary increments	.86	1.25	1.86	2.60	***		*

1) The higher the percentage, the more often salary increments offered to engineers in the 7 special job conditions were identical to AI's.

2) The higher the standard deviation, the more salary increments varied between different job conditions.

*$p \leqslant 05$ (two-tailed test).
*** $p \leqslant 001$ (two-tailed test).

Scandinavian managers seemed most reluctant to do so). In all
samples, jobs involving hazardous and boring conditions were given the
highest consideration; while lacking opportunities for advancement,
low prestige and unfriendly co-workers did not seem to require as
much special monetary compensation.

When discussing conditions that affected wage decisions, it is
clear that implications are being made about the values of the managers
from the four countries sampled. That is, the authors hoped to un-
cover something about the values which underlie managers' decisions
about wages by examining various job factors to see which issues affect
a manager making such decisions. We argued that how much a manager
is sensitive to money and feels it is a useful response is indicated by
the extent to which he awards above- or below-average wage increments to an employee as a consequence of some particular character-
istic(s) of that employee and/or his job. The design in the present
study was simplified so that a variety of characteristics could each be
studied in isolation, since each of the hypothetical employees described
stood out in only one characteristic.

Managers from developed countries seemed to value merit more
highly in that they revealed 70 percent greater range of wage increases
to good performers, that is, they more directly related wages to merit
in job performance. Their counterparts from developing countries
tended similarly to reward superior performance but did not penalize
poor performance. Given this type of salary administration behavior
in developing countries where performance is not viewed as a bi-polar
dimension, the usefulness of pay as a reward for performance can be
questioned seriously. It is possible that, in giving such a high pay increase to an inadequate performer, managers from the developing
countries are conceiving pay as an incentive for improved future performance rather than as a reward for previously established and satisfactory performance. That is, they attempt to inspire or maintain high
levels of performance rather than to reward good and punish poor
performance. Hence their reactions to high and low performers are
not polarized as are those of managers from the developed countries.

All four groups of managers took job and working conditions into
consideration in determining salary increases for their employees and
compensated for lack of desirable job conditions with additional
(monetary) remuneration. Managers from developing countries,
however, seemed to feel more strongly that these job conditions could
be compensated for with more substantial wage increases. Moreover,
managers from the developing countries made greater distinctions be-

tween the various job conditions than did managers from developed countries. This may indicate that in developing countries money is more often viewed as a substitute for lack of certain desirable job conditions than in developed countries. The above inferences, if true, can have serious implications in terms of motivating (rew..rding) employees in developing countries. On the one hand, pay may not be adequately used as a tool in determining and rewarding (or punishing the lack of) performance. Instead, it may be seen as a substitute for (un)-desirable conditions.

The results in total seem to suggest that merit and job conditions tend to become separate as two distinct influences on wage decisions. Managers from the developed countries seem to respond to differences among the performance levels of their employees but not much to differences in their working conditions. On the other hand, managers from developing countries take greater pains to recognize differences among employees' working conditions but do not respond as much to differences in employee performance.

These differences between wealthy and poor nations, over and above sociocultural differences, form a pattern which suggests further hypotheses that might lead to more specific predictions. One could search for and test the influence of a variety of factors that might be associated with, or causative of, both a nation's wealth and subsequent decisions of its managers, such as those being studied here. These factors would possibly explain the response of U.S. and Scandinavian managers principally to merit, and Indian and Colombian managers principally to job conditions. The value differences implied here might be related to a number of "objective" conditions such as the level of unemployment prevailing in the culture studied. For example, needs for skilled labor could be higher in the developing countries, thus necessitating companies to hold on to and be more generous with engineers they employ. In turn, the higher wages offered as revealed in the present study by managers from Colombia and India, especially to average performers in exceptional job conditions, could be explained by the enhanced value of engineers in those countries. Sawyer (1967) provides a comprehensive description of the role of 282 such objective conditions that can be used in understanding and dimensionalizing differences between nations and the behavior of managers in them.

On the other hand, a more deductive approach might find one predicting these present value differences by varying a particular antecedent, such as McClelland's ubiquitous *n* Achievement.

McClelland (1961) already has demonstrated that cultures with high *n* Achievement are the more economically advanced cultures. In turn, managers from such countries might be expected to express their own higher need for achievement by valuing individual merit higher and are thus more responsive to levels of performance achieved in others.

A final critical comment needs to be made on the design of the present study. Sociocultural and economic variables were examined simultaneously but, as was previously noted, they were sampled in a way that would not lead to any final statements about the independent effects of these two variables. The present study, as the authors conceive it, is an intermediate step in a long-range study. The sampling here was based on countries from which managers' responses were currently available. It is expected that other samples from countries more independently representing these two variables will be available in the future. Until that time, the findings of the present study seem to reveal important suggestions about the combined influence of sociocultural and economic data on wage decisions.

NOTES

[1]The current findings were made available through the use of the International Research Groups on Management (IRGOM) Data Bank and the cooperation of IRGOM regional associations; in Europe (the European Research Groups on Management); in Asia (the Management Institute for Training and Research in Asia); in South America (El Comite para Investigaciones Sobre Ejecutivos Latino Americanos); and in North America (the North American Research Group on Management). Bill Whittaker assisted in the analyses of the current data, while the entire staff of the Management Research Center contributed editorially to the refinement of the present manuscript.

[2]To the extent that level of economic development and sociocultural variables are not mutually exclusive [see Weber (1930); Ayal (1963); Dasgupta (1964)], it becomes necessary to introduce external controls in order to delineate the separate influences of the two factors. In the present design, any similarities between India and Colombia, and differences between this cluster and the United States and Scandinavia are assumed to be attributed to the differences in economic development. Ideally, one would like cultures where one subset is homogeneous in terms of sociocultural backgrounds and heterogeneous in level of economic development, while the situation is reversed in another subset. For example, samples from Korea, Japan, Venezuela, and Ecuador might be ideal; Japan-Korea and Venezuela-Ecuador being culturally homogeneous, economically heterogeneous pairs, while Japan-Venezuela and Korea-Ecuador are economically homogeneous, culturally heterogeneous pairs. Thus differences could be more unequivocally attributed to culture, wealth, or the interaction of the two.

The total Gross National Product and GNP per capita for the four countries in the present sample are as follows:

	U.S.	*Scandinavia*	*Colombia*	*India*
Item		(1966)		
Gross National Product (in millions U.S. $)	756,400	40,000	6,300	4,907
Per capita GNP	3,842	2,439	319	84

(Source: *U.N. Annual Statistical Year Book, 1967*)

[3]The managers from Colombia responded to the Spanish version of the exercise, those from Scandinavia to Danish, Norwegian, and Swedish versions, while the other two groups responded in English. The managers from India are well versed in English and transact most of their regular activities in English, which in India is the *lingua franca* of business.

REFERENCES

ADAMS, J. S. 1963. Toward an understanding of inequity. *Journal of Abnormal and Social Psychology,* 67, 422-36.

———. 1965. Inequity in social exchange. In *Advances in experimental social psychology,* ed. L. Berkowitz, vol. 2, pp 267-99. New York: Academic Press.

AYAL, E. B. 1963. Value systems and economic development in Thailand and Japan. *Journal of Social Issues,* 19 (1): 35-51.

BASS, B. M. 1965. *A program of exercises for management and organizational psychology,* Management Development Associates, Pittsburgh.

———. 1968. Abilities, values and concepts of equitable salary increases in EXERCISE COMPENSATION. *Journal of Applied Psychology,* 52: 299-304.

DASGUPTA, AJIT. 1964. India's cultural values and economic development. *Economic Development and Cultural Change,* 13 (1), October.

DUNNETTE, M. D. 1967. The motives of industrial managers. *Organizational Behavior and Human Performance,* 2: 176-82.

HAIRE, M. 1965. The use of motivational techniques in increasing productivity in the business firm. In *Business schools and economic growth,* ed. Floyd A. Bond, pp. 31-43. Ann Arbor, Michigan, Bureau of Business Research.

HARBISON, F., AND MYERS, C. 1959. eds. *Management in the industrial world.* New York: McGraw Hill.

LAWLER, E. E. III. 1966. Managers' attitudes toward how their pay is and should be determined. *Journal of Applied Psychology,* 50: 273-79.

———. 1967. Secrecy about management compensation: Are there hidden costs? *Organizational Behavior and Human Performance,* 2: 182-89.

McClelland, D. 1961. *The achieving society.* Philadelphia: D. van Nostrand.

OPSAHL, R. L. 1967. Managerial compensation: Needed research. *Organizational Behavior and Human Performance,* 2: 208-16.

RYTERBAND, E. C., AND KING, D. C. 1966. An investigation of the effects of cognitive dissonance on resistance to change. *Organizational Behavior and Human Performance,* 1: 151-68.

SAWYER, J. 1967. Dimensions of nations: Size, wealth and politics. *American Journal of Sociology,* 73: (2): 145-72.

VROOM, V. H. 1964. *Work and Motivation.* New York: Wiley.

———. 1965. *Motivation in management.* New York: American Foundation for Management Research.

WEBER, M. 1930. *The protestant ethic and the spirit of capitalism.* Trans. Talcott Parsons, London: Allen and Unwin.

WEICK, K. E. 1967. Dissonance and task enhancement: A problem for compensation theory. *Organizational Behavior and Human Performance,* 2: 189-208.

PART FIVE

Performance Appraisal:

The Link Between Performance and Compensation?

One of the important problems for the manager in the use of compensation as a motivator is to devise an appraisal and evaluation method which allows a reasonably accurate assessment of performance. The papers in this section are aimed primarily at the problem of performance evaluation.

Ridgway, in a widely known article, makes clear the nature of the impact that measurement used for evaluative purposes can have on behavior. He points out that performance measures, intended to be indicators, are "probably interpreted as definitions of the important aspects of the job" and thus might lead to distortion of behavior.

Miner reviews appraisal practices as reported in the research literature. His suggestions for managers are well reasoned from the review of relevant research on the many facets of the appraisal process, ranging from the nature of the instrument itself to the types of characteristics upon which managers should be rated.

Appraisal systems of all types are fraught with problems. Tosi and Carroll review some of the recent research on management-by-objectives, reporting that it has produced some positive results, but there may be some side effects to be considered. They attempt to highlight some of the significant problems of implementation, especially regarding the linkage between performance and compensation.

Meyer and Walker's study pinpoints a critical area treated earlier by most writers on the subject. The relationship between the appraiser and the rated individual is one of prime importance. They note that the skill with which appraisal is handled can be substantial in its impact on the attitude and perceptions of the appraised individual.

The point of importance here is that problems with compensation systems in general are confounded considerably by problems of evaluation. Appraisal problems may be complicated by intensive functional interdependence and evaluations must often be made when the results of decisions or activities may not be known for many years. This can only increase the difficulty of effectively relating compensation to performance.

25

Dysfunctional Consequences of Performance Measurements

V. F. RIDGWAY

There is today a strong tendency to state numerically as many as possible of the variables with which management must deal. The mounting interest in and application of tools such as operations research, linear programming, and statistical decision making, all of which require quantifiable variables, foster the idea that if progress toward goals can be measured, efforts and resources can be more rationally managed. This has led to the development of quantitative performance measurements for all levels within organizations, up to and including measurements of the performance of a division manager with profit responsibility in a decentralized company. Measurements at lower levels in the organization may be in terms of amount of work, quality of work, time required, and so on.

Quantitative measures of performance are tools, and are undoubtedly useful. But research indicates that indiscriminate use and undue confidence and reliance in them result from insufficient knowledge of the full effects and consequences. Judicious use of a tool requires awareness of possible side effects and reactions. Otherwise, indiscriminate use may result in side effects and reactions outweighing the benefits, as was the case when penicillin was first hailed as a wonder drug. The cure is sometimes worse than the disease.

It seems worth while to review the current scattered knowledge of the dysfunctional consequences resulting from the imposition of a system of performance measurements. For the purpose of analyz-

Reprinted by permission of the author and publisher from *Administrative Science Quarterly* 1, no. 2 (September 1956):240-47.

ing the impact of performance measurements upon job performance, we can consider separately single, multiple, and composite criteria. Single criteria occur when only one quantity is measured and observed, such as total output or profit. Multiple criteria occur when several quantities are measured simultaneously, such as output, quality, cost, safety, waste, and so forth. Composite criteria occur when the separate quantities are weighted in some fashion and then added or averaged.

Single Criteria

A single criterion of performance was in use in a public employment agency studied by Peter M. Blau.[1] The agency's responsibility was "to serve workers seeking employment and employers seeking workers." Employment interviewers were appraised by the number of interviews they conducted. Thus the interviewer was motivated to complete as many interviews as he could, but not to spend adequate time in locating jobs for the clients. The organization's goal of placing clients in jobs was not given primary consideration because the measurement device applied to only one aspect of the activity.

Blau reports another case in a federal law enforcement agency which investigated business establishments. Here he found that work schedules were distorted by the imposition of a quota of eight cases per month for each investigator. Toward the end of the month an investigator who found himself short of the eight cases would pick easy, fast cases to finish that month and save the lengthier cases till the following month. Priority of the cases for investigation was based on length of the case rather than urgency, as standards of impartiality would require. This is one of many instances in which the existence of an "accounting period" adversely affects the over-all goal accomplishment of the organization.

Chris Argyris also reports this tendency to use easy jobs as fillers toward the end of a period in order to meet a quota.[2] In this case, a factory supervisor reported that they "feed the machines all the easy orders" toward the end of the month, rather than finish them in the sequence in which they were received. Such a practice may lead to undue delay of the delivery of some customers' orders, perhaps the most profitable orders.

David Granick's study of Soviet management reveals how the attention and glory that accrues to a plant manager when he can set a new monthly production record in one month leads to the neglect of repairs and maintenance, so that in ensuing months there will be a distinct drop in production.[3] Similarly, the output of an entire plant may be allowed to fall off in order to create conditions under which one worker can make a production record, when the importance of such a record is considered greater than over-all plant production.

Joseph S. Berliner's report on Soviet business administration points out sharply how the accounting period has an adverse effect upon management decisions.[4] The use of monthly production quotas causes "storming" at the end of the month to reach the quota. Repairs and maintenance are postponed until the following month, so that production lags in the early part of the month, and storming must again be resorted to in the following month. This has impact upon the rate of production for suppliers and customers who are forced into a fluctuating rate of operations with its attendant losses and wastes.

Standard costs as a criterion of performance is a frequent source of dissatisfaction in manufacturing plants.[5] The "lumpiness" of indirect charges that are allocated to the plants or divisions (indirect charges being unequal from month to month), variations in quality and cost of raw materials, or other factors beyond the control of the operating manager, coupled with inaccuracies and errors in the apportionment of indirect charges, causes distrust of the standards. A typical reaction of operating executives in such cases seems to be to seek explanations and justifications. Consequently, considerable time and energy is expended in discussion and debate about the correctness of charges. Only "wooden money" savings accrue when charges are shifted to other accounts and there is no increase in company profits. It should be pointed out, however, that having charges applied to the proper departments may have the advantage of more correctly directing attention to problem areas.

Granick discusses two measures of the success of the Soviet firm which have been considered and rejected as over-all measures by Soviet industrial leaders and economists.[6] The first, cost-reduction per unit of product, is considered inadequate because it does not provide a basis for evaluating new products. Further, variations in amount of production affect the cost-reduction index because of the finer division of overhead costs, quality changes, and assortment. The second over-all measure of a firm's performance, profitability, has been rejected as the basic criterion on the grounds that it is affected in the short run by factors outside the control of management, such as shortages of supplies. Profitability as a measure of success led to a reduction in experimental work and de-emphasized the importance of production quantity, quality, and assortment. Neither cost-reduction nor profitability was acceptable alone; each was only a partial index. The Soviets had concluded by 1940 that no single measure of success of a firm is adequate in itself and that there is no substitute for genuine analysis of all the elements entering into a firm's work.

Difficulties with single criteria have been observed in operations research, where one of the principal sources of difficulty is considered to be the choice of proper criteria for performance measurement.[7] The difficulty of translating the several alternatives into their full effect upon the organization's goal forces the operations researcher to settle for a criterion more manageable than profit maximization, but less appropriate. The efficiency of a subgroup of the organization may be improved in terms of some plausible test, yet the organization's efficiency in terms of its major goal may be decreased.

In all the studies mentioned above, the inadequacy of a single measure of performance is evident. Whether this is a measure of an employee at the working level, or a measure of management, attention is directed away from the over-all goal. The existence of a measure of performance motivates individuals to effort, but the effort may be wasted, as in seeking "wooden money" savings, or may be detrimental to the organization's goal, as in rushing through interviews, delaying repairs, and rejecting profitable opportunities.

MULTIPLE MEASUREMENTS

Recognition of the inadequacies of a single measure of success or performance leads organizations to develop several criteria. It is felt then that all aspects of the job will receive adequate attention and emphasis so that efforts of individuals will not be distorted.

A realization in the employment office studied by Blau that job referrals and placements were also important led eventually to their inclusion in measuring the performance of the interviewers.[8] Merely counting the number of referrals and placements had led to wholesale indiscriminate referrals, which did not accomplish the employment agency's screening function. Therefore, to stress the qualitative aspects of the interviewer's job, several ratios (of referrals to interviews, placements to interviews, and placements to referrals) were devised. Altogether there were eight quantities that were counted or calculated for each interviewer. This increase in quantity and complexity of performance measurements was felt necessary to give emphasis to all aspects of the interviewer's job.

Granick relates that no single criterion was universally adopted in appraising Soviet management.[9] Some managers were acclaimed for satisfying production quotas while violating labor laws. Others were removed from office for violating quality and assortment plans while fulfilling production quotas. Apparently there is a ranking of importance of these multiple criteria. In a typical interfirm competition the judges were provided with a long list of indexes. These included production of finished goods in the planned assortment, an even flow of production as between ten-day periods and as between months, planned mastery of new types of products, improvement in product quality and reduction in waste, economy of materials through improved design and changing of technological processes, fulfillment of labor productivity tasks and lowering of unit cost, keeping within the established wage fund, and increase in the number of worker suggestions for improvements in work methods and conditions and their adoption into operation. But no indication of how these indexes should be weighted was given. The pre-eminence of such indexes as quantity, quality, assortment of production, and remaining within the firm's allotment of materials and fuels brought some order into the otherwise chaotic picture. The presence of "campaigns" and "priorities" stressing one or more factors also has aided Soviet management in deciding which elements of its work are at the moment most important.

Without a single over-all composite measure of success, however, there is no way of determining whether the temporarily increased effort on the "campaign" criteria of the month represents new effort or merely effort shifted from other criteria. And the intangibility of some of these indexes makes it impossible to judge whether there has been decreased effort on other aspects. Hence even in a campaign period the relative emphases may become so unbalanced as to mitigate or defeat the purpose of the campaign.

The Soviet manager is working then under several measurements, and the relative influence or emphasis attached to any one measurement varies from firm to firm and from month to month. Profits and production are used, among other measurements, and these two may lead to contradictory managerial decisions. Granick hypothesizes that some managers have refused complicated orders that were difficult to produce because it would mean failure to produce the planned quantities. Acceptance of these orders would have been very profitable, but of the two criteria, production quantity took precedence.

Numerous American writers in the field of management have stressed the importance of multiple criteria in evaluating perform-ance of management. Peter Drucker, for example, lists market stand-ing, innovation, productivity, physical and financial resources, profitability, manager performance and development, worker per-formance and attitude, and public responsibility.[10] This list includes many of the same items as the list used by Soviet management.

The consensus at a round-table discussion of business and pro-fessional men[11] was that although return on investment is important, additional criteria are essential for an adequate appraisal of operating departments. These other criteria are fairly well summed up in Drucker's list above.

Thus we see that the need for multiple criteria is recognized and that they are employed at different levels of the organization—lower levels as in the employment agency, higher levels as considered by Granick and Drucker. At all levels these multiple measurements or criteria are intended to focus attention on the many facets of a par-ticular job.

The use of multiple criteria assumes that the individual will commit his or the organization's efforts, attention, and resources in greater measure to those activities which promise to contribute the greatest improvement to over-all performance. There must then exist a theoret-ical condition under which an additional unit of effort or resources would yield equally desirable results in over-all performance, whether applied to production, quality, research, safety, public relations, or any of the other suggested areas. This would be the condition of "balanced stress on objectives" to which Drucker refers.

Without a single over-all composite measure of performance, the individual is forced to rely upon his judgment as to whether increased effort on one criterion improves over-all performance, or whether there may be a reduction in performance on some other criterion which will outweigh the increase in the first. This is quite possible, for in any immediate situation many of these objectives may be contradictory to each other.

COMPOSITES

To adequately balance the stress on the contradictory objectives or criteria by which performance of a particular individual or organi-zation is appraised, there must be an implied or explicit weighting of these criteria. When such a weighting system is available, it is an easy task to combine the measures of the various subgoals into a composite score for over-all performance.

Such a composite is used by the American Institute of Management in evaluating and ranking the managements of corporations, hospitals, and other organizations.[12] These ratings are accomplished by attaching a numerical grade to each of several criteria such as economic function, corporate structure, production efficiency, and the like. Each criterion has an optimum rating and the score on each for any particular organization is added to obtain a total score. Although there may be disagreement on the validity of the weighting system employed, the rating given on any particular category, the categories themselves, or the methods of estimating scores in the A.I.M. management audit, this system is an example of the type of over-all performance measurement which might be developed. Were such a system of ratings employed by an organization and found acceptable by management, it presumably would serve as a guide to obtaining a balanced stress on objectives.

A composite measure of performance was employed in Air Force wings as reported by K. C. Wagner.[13] A complex rating scheme covering a wide range of activities was used. When the organizations were put under pressure to raise their composite score without proportionate increases in the organization's means of achieving them, there were observable unanticipated consequences in the squadrons. Under a system of multiple criteria, pressure to increase performance on one criterion might be relieved by a slackening of effort toward other criteria. But with a composite criterion this does not seem as likely to occur. In Wagner's report individuals were subjected to tension, role and value conflicts, and reduced morale; air crews suffered from intercrew antagonism, apathy, and reduced morale; organization and power structures underwent changes; communications distortions and blockages occurred; integration decreased; culture patterns changed; and norms were violated. Some of these consequences may be desirable, some undesirable. The net result, however, might easily be less effective over-all performance.

These consequences were observable in a situation where goals were increased without a corresponding increase in means, which seems to be a common situation. Berliner refers to the "ratchet principle" wherein an increase in performance becomes the new standard, and the standard is thus continually raised. Recognition of the operation of the "ratchet principle" by workers was documented by F. J. Roethlisberger and William J. Dickson.[14] There was a tacit agreement among the workers not to exceed the quota, for fear that the job would then be rerated. Deliberate restriction of output is not an uncommon occurrence.

Although the experiences reported with the use of composite measures of performance are rather skimpy, there is still a clear indication that their use may have adverse consequences for the over-all performance of the organization.

CONCLUSION

Quantitative performance measurements—whether single, multiple, or composite—are seen to have undesirable consequences for over-all organizational performance. The complexity of large organizations requires better knowledge of organizational behavior for managers to make best use of the personnel available to them. Even where performance measures are instituted purely for purposes of information, they are probably interpreted as definitions of the important aspects of job or activity and hence have important implications for the motivation of behavior. The motivational and behavioral consequences of performance measurements are inadequately understood. Further research in this area is necessary for a better understanding of how behavior may be oriented toward optimum accomplishment of the organization's goals.

NOTES

[1]Peter M. Blau, *The Dynamics of Bureaucracy* (Chicago, Ill., 1955).

[2]Chris Argyris, *The Impact of Budgets on People* (New York, 1952).

[3]David Granick, *Management of the Industrial Firm in the U.S.S.R.* (New York, 1954).

[4]Joseph S. Berliner, "A Problem in Soviet Business Management," *Administrative Science Quarterly,* Vol. I, 1956, pp. 86-101.

[5]H. A. Simon, H. Guetzkow, G. Kozmetsky, and G. Tyndall, *Centralization vs. Decentralization in Organizing the Controller's Department* (New York, 1954).

[6]Granick, *op. cit.*

[7]Charles Hitch and Roland McKean, "Suboptimization in Operations Problems," in J. F. McCloskey and Flora F. Trefethen (Eds.), *Operations Research for Management* (Baltimore, Md., 1954).

[8]Blau, *op. cit.*

[9]Granick, *op. cit.*

[10]Peter M. Drucker, *The Practice of Management* (New York, 1954).

[11]William H. Newman and James P. Logan, *Management of Expanding Enterprises* (New York, 1955).

[12]*Manual of Excellent Managements* (New York, 1955).

[13]Kenneth C. Wagner, "Latent Functions of an Executive Control: A Sociological Analysis of a Social System under Stress," *Research Previews,* Vol. II (Chapel Hill, N.C.: Institute for Research in Social Science, March, 1954), mimeo.

[14]F. J. Roethlisberger and William J. Dickson, *Management and the Worker* (Cambridge, Mass., 1939).

26

Management Appraisal:
A Review of Procedures and Practices

JOHN B. MINER

Does the supervisor appraise your performance? Is this appraisal written, formal, and permanent? Does it affect your performance? Are you a manager who must appraise subordinates and write up these appraisals? Has the company recently instituted a system of appraisal and development by objectives? The chances are that you answered "yes" to many or all of these questions, for approximately 80 percent of all U. S. companies have a formal management appraisal system (10). I stress management, for the shift is away from appraisal of the rank and file (42).

Many of these companies, and most of the managers being appraised, are unsatisfied with their formal appraisal system. This is a fair conclusion, for the whole concept is in a state of flux—new approaches, new plans, and new methods. With this constant change, where is a manager to turn for guidance?

For most of us, management appraisal is extraordinarily difficult. It is hard to pass judgment on a fellow man, especially if that judgment will become a permanent part of his company record, affecting his future. The procedure is further complicated by the absence of many needed facts and of widely accepted theories. Yet the attainment of any organization's goals requires that the performance of our managers be measured, compared, and recorded. Growth requires that potential be evaluated. These requirements can best be met by

Printed by permission of the author. A condensed version of this paper, entitled "Management Appraisal: A Capsule Review and Current References," appeared in *Business Horizons,* October 1968. Their permission to use the material is acknowledged.

a thoughtfully adopted formal appraisal system, one that best conforms to current knowledge and theory.

The purposes of this article are to provide this knowledge and theory in capsule form, and to offer a handy reference to current work. I have done this by asking—and answering—questions, those most frequently asked about the evaluation of executives. (The numbers in parentheses refer to the references at the end of this article.)

What Are the Relative Merits of Appraisals Made by Superiors, Peers, Subordinates, and the Man Himself?

Appraisals made by superiors, peers, subordinates, or the man himself all have merit, but for different qualities.

About 98 percent of all evaluation forms are designed to be completed by the immediate superior. Furthermore, this approach appears to have widespread acceptance. Subordinates characteristically prefer to have their work evaluated in this manner (21).

There is ample evidence that ratings made by peers differ considerably from those made by superiors. The results of a study conducted at North American Aviation (39) indicate that two levels of supervision agree reasonably well; superiors and co-workers do not. Co-workers apparently consider somewhat different factors and additionally, on the average, give higher ratings.

Similar discrepancies occur when self-ratings are compared with those of superiors. While various levels of supervision tend to agree, superior and self-ratings rarely do (34). Self-ratings emphasize getting along with others as important for success, while superiors stress initiative and work knowledge (21). Furthermore, self-ratings are usually inflated: the self-ratings consistently run higher (32).

There is reason to believe that self-interest can exert considerable influence on peer, subordinate, and self-ratings to the point where the evaluations may lack organizational relevance. Where favorable results have been reported with these techniques, it has been almost exclusively in an artificial research setting. It seems likely that their use as the *primary* element of a regular on-going appraisal system would produce somewhat different results, and that mutual- and/or self-protection could well become a more important consideration in the ratings than the profitability of the company (2).

Although the above statements argue strongly for appraisal by superiors, certain additional facts limit this conclusion. For one, many companies use a management-by-objectives approach, which has a considerable participative component. Managers have a say in setting their own objectives and in determining whether their objectives have been met. This is actually self-rating. Experimental evidence from studies done at General Electric indicates that such participation in the appraisal situation can contribute to more effective performance (12). Thus, at least for purposes of management development, self-rating of a kind has some value.

Peer rating also has received significant support from recent research. A study utilizing middle-level managers at IBM indicates quite clearly that those men rated high by other managers at the same level were more likely to be promoted subsequently (36). It seems entirely possible that at the middle and upper levels of management, where organizational commitment is often high, objective peer evaluations that are relatively free of protective bias can be obtained. Such evaluations may well prove particularly valuable in the identification of leadership potential, just as self-evaluations appear to be most useful for developmental purposes. The Air Force currently is experimenting rather extensively with peer ratings, operating on the theory that they are particularly significant in the measurement of potential.

A recent proposal favors a combination appraisal process utilizing superior, peer, and self-ratings (19). The advantages are sizable. The knowledge that superior ratings also are being obtained reduces bias in the peer and self-ratings. At the same time, the latter two techniques capitalize on unique observational opportunities. The match, or correlation, between the different types of ratings provides a measure of integrated perception among different people in the company, and thus of the capacity to concentrate effort behind goals (29). To the extent that peer and self-ratings support superior ratings, acceptance is likely to be at a high level, and personnel actions, such as promotion and firing, can be carried out without resistance. To the extent they do not, resistance is likely to emerge. Furthermore, self-ratings and peer ratings are available for purposes of development and the identification of potential. Finally, special attention can be focused on those individuals whose ratings diverge sharply. An appraisal involving high superior and self-ratings combined with very low peer ratings is clearly not the same as one with high ratings from all three sources. Yet, if only superior evaluations are obtained, significant aspects of the situation may go undetected.

The major advantage of the tripartite approach is that it provides a wealth of information about the individual and the organization. This approach also pulls together a number of schools of thought on appraisals. All in all, it appears to be *the* approach to management appraisal of the future. Development of such complex programs and effective utilization of the information made available, however, will require expertise beyond that currently available in many companies.

Are There Advantages in
Using More Than One Rater?

Research consistently shows that using more than one rater is advantageous. The best evidence comes from studies conducted by the U.S. Army (4), which indicate a clear superiority for the average of ratings made by several individuals over those made by only one person. The rationale behind averaging ratings from the same type of source—either superiors, peers, or subordinates—is that an average tends to reduce the impact of any single biased rating. The larger the number of raters, the more diluted the effects of individual bias. In one study, for example, managers who were found to be particularly considerate and kind to their subordinates also gave them very high ratings (17). When averaged with the evaluations of more production-oriented managers, such overly lenient ratings have less impact on the final appraisal. Alone, their impact is complete.

However, the availability of raters with access to a sufficiently large sample of work behaviors can set a limit on the number of raters that should be used. Increasing the size of the rating group by adding people who are not really qualified to evaluate and who, therefore, will give erroneous data defeats the value of the averaging process. One of the potential values of peer and subordinate appraisals is the availability of a large number of individuals who can qualify as raters because of their particularly good opportunities for observation.

What Is the Value of Rating Reviews
by a Hierarchical Superior of the Rater?

Various provisions for reviews by the direct-line superior of a rater are a common feature of appraisal systems (21). In the U.S. Army procedure, there are in essence two reviews—one by the indorser, who also makes his own rating, and one by the reviewer, who merely indicates that a review has been made. Thus the original rater has his evaluations scrutinized twice, the indorser once (7). A review procedure may operate in a number of ways. One approach requires the rater to present his evaluations orally to a review board of superiors (37). In other cases, as with the military, only the written forms are reviewed at higher levels. A reviewer may have the authority to change evaluations directly without any consultation, to personally require the rater to make changes, to advise on changes, or merely to indicate disagreement on the rating form.

Under appropriate circumstances, such review does appear to contribute to evaluation quality (2). Ideally, adequate knowledge of a manager's performance exists at several hierarchical levels above him. Given this requirement, the best approach is to pass the appraisals upward so each manager can make his evaluation either independently, as in the case of the immediate superior, or with knowledge only of what those below him think. This chain of evaluation should stop when it reaches a level in the hierarchy where adequate knowledge of performance does not exist. There is little point in including at the top of the chain a reviewer who does not also evaluate. If such an individual does not have any basis for evaluating a man, then there is nothing gained by adding his signature to a form. If he does have such a basis, then his ratings should be averaged with the others.

This rater-indorser chain approach has the advantage that each manager, except the one at the top, knows that his evaluations will be scrutinized. The approach also provides for multiple ratings under conditions that protect against undue influence from a superior who may have the least adequate basis for appraisal. The information flow is upward from what can be presumed to be the most knowledgeable individual to the least, rather than the reverse. The use of such an approach assumes that a superior will not change or influence his subordinate's ratings in any way. Evidence indicates that, when actual changes at higher levels are permitted, they do nothing to improve the evaluation process. However, the superior can disagree in his own ratings and thus mitigate the effects of what he feels is an error.

Should Management Appraisals Be Made at the Same Time As Salary Recommendations?

The real problem is not whether management appraisals and salary recommendations should be done together, although traditionally this is the case, but rather, to find some method of avoiding the common tendency to decide on salary first and then adjust the performance ratings to fit. Because salary, in practice, is influenced by many factors other than merit, the ratings frequently are distorted. I cannot locate any research that bears directly on the question. Nonetheless, studies at General Electric clearly indicate that feeding back information on salary actions concomitantly with management appraisal data is not desirable insofar as motivational and developmental goals are concerned (24). Criticism tied directly to pay action produces so much defensiveness that there is little prospect of learning occurring. Energies focus primarily on self-protection rather than self-improvement (33).

Separating appraisals and salary actions in time is one way of reducing distortion. Yet many managers unquestionably do prefer to couple them, which well may lead to biased appraisals. An approach that would overcome bias and still permit a simultaneous dual decision clearly would be helpful. A means of changing perceptions—of both the salary administration and appraisal processes—seems called for. Although evidence is lacking, I believe this change could be achieved through a training program, provided the content of the program truly represented top-management philosophies. The training would consider various factors that inevitably influence salary actions, including the labor market, previous salary history, budgetary limitations, equity considerations, and rate ranges as well as merit. The training also would consider sources of bias in appraisal. With such an approach, pay and performance possibly could be separated in the manager's mind just as, or perhaps more, effectively as through the interposition of time.

What Are the Pros and Cons of Feedback from the Rater to the Man Being Rated?

Usually, the results of appraisals are given to the man who has been evaluated; this may be done in a number of different ways and with varying amounts of detail (21). The question is whether it should be done at all. An adequate answer requires two kinds of information stemming from two sub-questions: (1) how does the feedback requirement affect the ratings, and (2) how does the feedback requirement affect the man who has been rated?

Feedback and Ratings

A Lockheed Aircraft study (40) provides the best example of how the feedback requirement may influence ratings. The regular evaluations, which were not revealed to subordinates, were followed at a two-week interval by a second appraisal, which included discussions of the ratings with thᵉ men. The mean score for the 485 men involved rose dramatica↗y, from an initial 60 to 84, out of a possible 100. Apparently, wʰᵉn faced with the prospect of making face-to-face negative comrₙents, many managers avoided the problem by inflating their ratings. Thus almost everyone was placed toward the top of the scale.

This problem of inflation when the man rated has access to the results has plagued the armed forces for years (7). Although direct feedback by the superior is not required by law, the legal structure does indicate that an officer may inspect the evaluations in his file and that under certain conditions he may appeal. Anticipating that efficiency reports might be inspected, raters tend to make favorable statements. A variety of techniques, including forced choice, forced distribution, and critical incidents, have been introduced with little success over the years to deal with this inflation of ratings, which remains the major problem of the armed forces appraisal systems today.

Thus, where valid ratings are necessary for salary administration, promotion, transfer, discharge, and evaluation of selection procedures, feedback is not desirable. It is particularly important to avoid optional feedback, in which a manager does as he pleases. Under such circumstances, managers who plan to discuss their evaluations with subordinates will inflate them; those who do not plan to do so will not inflate them. As a result, the two types of ratings actually will be on different scales. Assuming the existence of a single scale under these circumstances not only will result in injustice to the individual, but also will produce decisions detrimental to the organization as well.

Feedback and the Man Rated

The major source of information on the motivational or developmental effects of feedback is a series of studies conducted at General Electric (12, 16, 24). The findings of this research on the dynamics of the feedback interview are summarized as follows:

1) Criticism tends to have a negative impact on achievement of goals.

2) Praise has little effect, either positive or negative.

3) Performance tends to improve when specific objectives are established.

4) Defensiveness as a consequence of criticism results in inferior performance.

5) Coaching is best done on a day-to-day basis and in direct association with specific acts, not once a year.

6) Mutual goal setting by superior and subordinate yields positive results.

7) Interviews intended primarily to improve performance should not deal with salary and promotion at the same time.

8) Participation by the subordinate in establishing his own performance goals yields favorable results.

9) Separate performance evaluations are required for different purposes.

On the whole, the results of the General Electric research seem to provide appropriate guides for action. Nonetheless, subsequent research has raised some doubts about the value of goal setting as it actually is done within the context of the management-by-objectives approach (22).

Feedback can be an effective motivational and developmental tool, but often it is not. Whether systematic appraisal interviews should be attempted depends on the approach taken and the skill of the interviewer. Feedback very clearly can do more harm than good.

Ideally, a feedback interview should be goal-oriented and should take a problem-solving approach to make a positive contribution, but this is not easy to do. Getting a manager to agree on a set of objectives and standards is one thing; getting him to recognize where and why he has fallen short in his performance is quite another (25). However, the requisite skill can be developed in many managers through training (23, 31).

Based on the evidence currently available, the appropriate conclusion seems to be that only those ratings made specifically for motivational or developmental purposes should ever be fed back, and then only by a fully trained and skilled interviewer. Feedback has tremendous potential for harm as well as good. It can be a major source of managerial turnover.

On What Types of Characteristics
Should Managers Be Rated?

In selecting the types of characteristics on which to rate a manager, it is most important to include only those characteristics which manifest themselves in the work situation. The rating factors should be firmly anchored in behavior manifestations that characteristically occur on the job and that influence performance (10). There is a tendency to include a variety of traits that do not meet these requirements. Often rating scales deal with aspects of "good" and "bad" people that cannot be adequately judged from job contact alone, or that matter little, if at all, in effective performance. In this connection, it is well to note that it is not always the "good" people who do well. One study found that an intense sense of honesty and ethics almost guaranteed failure in a particular type of sales job (26).

Ratings also should deal with characteristics that can be described clearly so that all raters will have the same kinds of behavior in mind (2). Considerable evidence indicates that certain personality traits, such as character and aggressiveness, are viewed so nebulously that agreement on whether people possess them is almost impossible. Such traits should not be included unless qualified in considerable detail. Generally, the closer the factors are to job behavior and results, the more raters will agree in their evaluations of a person.

How Can Ratings Be Spread Out
Along a Scale Most Successfully?

One approach to spreading ratings out is the forced distribution technique, which is a variant of ranking. However, rather than having as many categories as there are managers to be rated, the number of categories is predetermined, as is the percentage of the men to be placed in each category. In theory, the technique, like ranking, has considerable appeal. In practice, however, it presents so many difficulties that, at least for *management* appraisal, it cannot be recommended. One problem is that the percentages are meaningless unless the group to be rated by a single manager is large. Where spans of control are limited, this condition is not met. Furthermore, there is the difficulty of combining groups. Is the lower 10 percent of one group likely to be at the same performance level as the lower 10 percent of another? This same problem of combining groups occurs, of course, with ranking also. Furthermore, raters tend to resist the forced distribution (42). The result is a continuing conflict between those responsible for administering the appraisal system and the managers doing the rating. In the end, either the ratings are adjusted to fit the required percentage distribution, with great potential for error (17), or the forced distribution technique is abandoned entirely.

Given the conclusion that forced distribution techniques are not satisfactory for management appraisal, what other procedures are available to produce a meaningful spread of ratings along a scale? The armed services have faced this problem continually over the years. As indicated previously, since the man rated has ready access to the Armed Service Efficiency Reports, scores tend to pile up at the high end of the scales. In the late 1940s and early 1950s, two rather complex procedures were developed to deal with this problem. The forced choice approach was introduced by the Army and then adopted by the Air Force, which subsequently developed the critical incident technique to replace it. Neither approach proved successful (9). Forced choice failed because rating officers resisted a procedure that made it difficult, if not impossible, for them to determine how they actually had rated a man; in addition, leniency was not entirely overcome. The critical incident approach proved too complicated, too time-consuming, resulted in too much concern with the final score, and did not really solve the leniency problem. In both cases, resistance from rating officers in the field eventually was sufficient to terminate use of the technique. Research evidence indicates that graphic rating scales are actually just as valid as these more complex procedures (4).

All this does not mean that steps cannot be taken to produce a satisfactory spread of ratings. The following procedures used in business organizations have proved successful in extending this range:

1) Maintain security so evaluations are not available to the men rated or fed back to them (40).

2) Avoid ambiguous descriptions of the characteristics to be rated and of steps on the scale; the rater must have a clear understanding of exactly what job behavior he is to consider (3).

3) Carry out training aimed at providing an understanding of the desirability of a wide range of scores (20). Particular stress should be placed on getting overly considerate managers, who want more than anything else to help their men, to spread their ratings out. These are the raters who typically have the smallest ranges (17).

If these three conditions are met, and an adequate number of steps or levels exist in the scale, the usual graphic rating scale should yield a satisfactory spread of scores and should prove the most generally useful (2).

Does Stress on Recent
Events Bias Ratings?

Studies do indicate, as many have hypothesized, that specific instances of effective or ineffective behavior occurring shortly before evaluations unduly affect the ratings (10). Apparently, raters remember recent events more vividly and, therefore, weigh them more heavily. This situation suggests the need for relatively frequent ratings—at least every three to six months. Averaging such evaluations to yield a running appraisal score will minimize the effects of any specific recency bias. Another antidote involves keeping managers aware of the recency problem. Some managers might be induced to keep notes on performance throughout the rating period and then to review these at appraisal time. Even without this technique, however, sensitivity to the fact that recent events can have an excessive effect should make it easier to counteract the tendency. All of this, of course, represents another training area.

Is There a Method That
Will Ensure Consistency of Application?

Evidence on the value of introducing an educational process as an integral part of a total appraisal system is consistently positive. Normally, this educational process is based on the spoken word, but, on occasion, it may utilize written materials as well. Some uses of these procedures already have been noted, but additional features of the communication problem should be mentioned. Studies indicate that training can serve to increase the agreement between different raters, reduce bias (40), increase accuracy generally, prevent inflation of scores (5), and spread out the rating distribution (20). The evidence in support of training in the skills required to conduct an effective feedback interview already has been noted. In general, training sessions should be conducted by a person qualified as an expert on management appraisal and familiar with the details of the particular system in use. There should be an opportunity for considerable discussion and some practice with the rating forms. Various sources of error and bias, as well as factors that will make the ratings most useful, need primary attention (41).

In spite of the consistently favorable evidence, a great many companies do not build training procedures into their appraisal systems. In fact, a lack of adequate training is the major problem of most programs (21). In addition, there is reason to believe that many programs that have succumbed to widespread managerial resistance could have survived had they been introduced with adequate training. Although group sessions usually are used, these may be supplemented with some individual assistance at the time the ratings are made. Manuals containing information similar to the training program also have proved useful (5).

What Can Be Done to Overcome the Resistance That Hampers Many Appraisal Systems?

Many people look on the whole process of evaluating performance quite negatively. This feeling appears related to fears of receiving low ratings if an appraisal system is instituted and survives, and to a strong belief in the seniority principle (30). Evidence shows that less effective managers tend to be the ones most opposed to performance appraisal (14). Furthermore, many managers, in addition to rank-and-file employees, strongly believe seniority is the best guide for making personnel decisions. As a result of these factors, and perhaps others, any management appraisal system will encounter some resistance. This resistance may block the initiation of a program entirely, but it is particularly likely to manifest itself once a program is instituted and there is something to shoot at. Resistance will vary, depending on the values predominant in the company, and it may relate rather specifically to certain kinds of approaches.

Obviously, the greater the resistance the more those instituting the program will have to concentrate on those who will do the rating, and the more the management group as a whole will have to be involved in developing the system. These approaches demonstrate the willingness of those who will be using the data to do part of the work to ensure a successful program. The alternative procedure involves inducing the raters to come to the users of the data. This procedure is entirely satisfactory where acceptance is high, but where it is not merely mailing out forms along with directives and follow-up memorandums will only increase negative feeling. In addition to going to the raters, having large numbers of managers participate in the construction of the system itself is another successful approach (2). This can be done extensively if managers are used both as a source for developing items and as judges of proposed items (38).

The need for special procedures to help overcome resistance will vary, depending on the nature of the program. Many managers tend to resist feeding back appraisal results, for instance. Thus, acceptance problems may be anticipated when this is required. Many managers strongly dislike peer and subordinate ratings (2). Thus the use of a tripartite system along the lines noted previously may require special attention. Forced choice and forced distribution procedures are known to be sources of resistance and, accordingly, require more than the usual efforts to develop favorable attitudes.

How Can Potential Be Evaluated
and What Factors Are Predictive of Potential?

To determine a method for evaluating potential and the characteristics that are predictive of potential, research must show that some measure did in fact predict success in management over a considerable period of time after the original measurement. The following discussion is restricted entirely to studies of this kind. Predictions made by managers are considered first, then predictions by psychologists.

Managerial Prediction

In connection with managerial appraisal programs, ratings of potential for advancement frequently are obtained. The difficulty with using ratings of this kind for research is that they are available and known and quite obviously can influence a man's career entirely apart from his actual competence. Even with this bias included, results with these potential ratings by superiors are not impressive. Clearly a great many individuals identified in this manner as having high potential do not advance very far (11). In one study, departments within a single company varied considerably in the extent to which potential ratings were even predictive of the first promotion after appraisal (29). Results like these have led some writers to conclude that the evaluation of potential is beyond the scope of the usual management appraisal system and that the matter should be left to specialists in the field (35). Many ratings of potential are believed to be merely the inverse of the manager's age and thus convey little new information.

The armed forces have carried out most of the research on the predictive value of ratings by superiors, usually with relatively short intervals between the initial predictions and the subsequent measurement of success (18). The correlations obtained are not impressive. These findings contrast sharply with those for peer ratings; in the latter case much better predictions of potential are obtained. Why this difference between superior and peer predictions exists is a matter of conjecture at the present time.

Psychological Prediction

A considerable amount of predictive research has used psychological techniques. Some studies utilize separate measures, such as psychological tests or biographical inventories; others use the overall evaluations of psychologists derived from a combination of sources, including interviews, observation of behavior, and tests. In general, tests of intelligence and mental abilities do seem to be predictive of success. However, in many highly selected managerial groups, intelligence tests are not very helpful in identifying potential because all the managers score at such a high level. At the foreman level, intelligence tests are more effective as indicators of subsequent performance (18).

Consistently positive results have been obtained with the Miner Sentence Completion Scale in a series of predictive studies (27). This measure was designed specifically for predicting success in management. Although the test discriminates most effectively at the graduate level, it can identify individuals with managerial potential as early as the third year of college (28).

Psychological tests in the personality area have produced uneven results when used individually. In a number of cases, they have not proved very useful (18). Yet, enough exceptions suggest that some personality tests can yield good potential estimates. In general, measures of characteristics such as dominance, self-confidence, and persuasiveness are most useful (10). A considerable amount of research has used biographical inventories containing questions similar to those found in application blanks. This research has produced sufficiently positive results to recommend the approach (10, 18). However, companies tend to keep the specific results of these studies secret so managerial candidates do not learn the "right" answers. Thus studies aimed at establishing those factors that are predictive in a given company must be carried out individually. Nonetheless, published research does show that a prior pattern of success is likely to be predictive of subsequent success.

Results with comprehensive evaluations by psychologists using a variety of source data also are encouraging. Studies using this approach have predicted success over a period as long as seven years (1, 8). Yet there have been some significant failures also.

A related approach, even more comprehensive in that managers are studied over a period of days with a whole host of techniques, is the assessment center. AT&T has conducted much of the research with this technique under the title of The Management Progress Study. Staff assessments of potential for advancement derived from these assessment situations have consistently proved predictive of promotion and salary progress over periods up to eight years (6). These assessments were not made available to those making promotion and compensation decisions. Research indicates that those who have moved up most rapidly are more intelligent, more active, control their feelings more, are more nonconforming, exhibit a greater work orientation (6), are more independent, desire more of a leadership role, and have stronger achievement motivation (13). Although this type of approach is extremely expensive relative to the usual psychological evaluation (15), it appears to yield even higher correlations with later success in management jobs.

There is reason to believe that any psychological approach is likely to be effective only to the extent it is attuned to the value and reward structures of the particular organization (29). Thus the development of psychological predictors to identify potential within a given company must involve a complex interaction between analysis of the individual and analysis of the organization. Such an interaction involving both individual assessment and social psychological research seems to provide the best guide for management appraisal systems of the future.

REFERENCES

(1) ALBRECHT, P. A.; GLASER, E. M.; AND MARKS, J. 1964. Validation of a multiple-assessment procedure for managerial personnel. *Journal of Applied Psychology* 48:351-60.

(2) BARRETT, R. S. 1966. *Performance rating.* Chicago: Science Research Associates.

(3) ——— et al. 1958. Rating scale content, I: Scale information and supervisory ratings. *Personnel Psychology* II:333-46.

(4) BAYROFF, A. G.; HAGGERTY, H. R.; AND RUNDQUIST, E. A. 1954. Validity of ratings as related to rating techniques and conditions. *Personnel Psychology* 7:93-113.

(5) BITTNER, R. 1948. Developing an industrial merit rating procedure. *Personnel Psychology* 1:403-32.

(6) BRAY, D. W., AND GRANT, D. L. 1966. The assessment center in the measurement of potential for business management. *Psychological Monographs* 80:1-27.

(7) BROOKS, W. W. 1966. An analysis and evaluation of the officer performance appraisal system in the United States army. M. S. thesis, George Washington University.

(8) DICKEN, C. F., AND BLACK, J. D. 1965. Predictive validity of psychometric evaluations of supervisors. *Journal of Applied Psychology* 49:34-47.

(9) DRUIT, C. A. 1964. An analysis of military officer evaluation systems using principles presently advanced by authorities in this field. M. A. thesis, The Ohio State University.

(10) DUNNETTE, M. D. et al. 1966. Identification and enhancement of managerial effectiveness. Richardson Foundation Survey Report.

(11) FERGUSON, L. L. 1966. Better management of managers' careers. *Harvard Business Review* 44:139-52.

(12) FRENCH, J. R. P.; KAY, E.; AND MEYER, H. H. 1966. Participation and the appraisal system. *Human Relations* 19:3-20.

(13) ———; KATKOVSKY, W.; AND BRAY, D. W. 1967. Contributions of projective techniques to assessment of managerial potential. *Journal of Applied Psychology* 51:226-32.

(14) GRUENFELD, L. W., AND WEISSENBERG, P. 1966. Supervisory characteristics and attitudes toward performance appraisals. *Personnel Psychology* 19:143-51.

(15) HARDESTY, D. L., AND JONES, W. S. 1968. Characteristics of judged high-potential management personnel — The operations of an industrial assessment center. *Personnel Psychology* 21:85-98.

(16) KAY, E.; MEYER, H. H.; AND FRENCH, J. R. P. 1965. Effects of threat in a performance appraisal interview. *Journal of Applied Psychology* 49:311-17.

(17) KLORES, M. S. 1966. Rater bias in forced-distribution performance ratings. *Personnel Psychology* 19:411-21.

(18) KORMAN, A. K. 1968. The prediction of managerial performance: A review. *Personnel Psychology* 21:295-322.

(19) LAWLER III, E. E. 1967. The multitrait-multirater approach to measuring managerial job performance. *Journal of Applied Psychology* 51:369-81.

(20) LEVINE, J., AND BUTLER, J. 1952. Lecture vs. group decision in changing behavior. *Journal of Applied Psychology* 36:29-33.

(21) LOPEZ, F. M. In press. *Evaluating employee performance.* Chicago: Public Personnel Association.

(22) MENDLESON, J. L. 1967. Manager goal setting: An exploration into its meaning and measurement. D. B. A. thesis, Michigan State University.

(23) MEYER, H. H., AND WALKER, W. B. 1961. A study of factors relating to the effectiveness of a performance appraisal program. *Personnel Psychology* 14:291-98.

(24) MEYER, H. H.; KAY, E.; AND FRENCH, J. R. P. 1965. Split roles in performance appraisal. *Harvard Business Review* 43:123-29.

(25) MICHAEL, J. M. 1965. Problem situations in performance counselling. *Personnel* 42:16-22.

(26) MINER, J. B. 1962. Personality and ability factors in sales performance. *Journal of Applied Psychology* 46:6-13.

(27) ———. 1965. *Studies in management education.* New York: Springer.

(28) ———. 1968. The early identification of managerial talent. *The Personnel and Guidance Journal* 46:586-91.

(29) ———. 1968. Bridging the gulf in organizational performance. *Harvard Business Review* 46:102-10.

(30) ———. 1969. *Personnel and industrial relations — A managerial approach.* New York: Macmillan.

(31) MOON, C. G., AND HARITON, T. 1958. Evaluating an appraisal and feedback training program. *Personnel* 35:36-41.

(32) PARKER, J. W. et al. 1959. Rating scale content: III. Relationships between supervisory and self-ratings. *Personnel Psychology* 12:49-63.

(33) PATTON, A. 1968. Executive motivation: How it is changing. *Management Review* 57:4-20.

(34) PRIEN, E. P., AND LISKE, R. E. 1962. Assessments of higher level personnel: III. Rating criteria: A comparative analysis of supervisor ratings and incumbent self-ratings of job performance. *Personnel Psychology* 15:187-94.

(35) RICHARDS, K. E. 1959. A new concept of performance appraisal. *Journal of Business* 32:229-43.

(36) ROADMAN, H. E. 1964. An industrial use of peer ratings. *Journal of Applied Psychology* 48:211-14.

(37) ROWLAND, V. K. 1951. Management inventory and development. *Personnel* 28:12-22.

(38) SMITH, P. C., AND KENDALL, L. M. 1963. Retranslation of expectations: An approach to the construction of unambiguous anchors for rating scales. *Journal of Applied Psychology* 47:149-55.

(39) SPRINGER, D. 1953. Ratings of candidates for promotion by co-workers and supervisors. *Journal of Applied Psychology* 37:347-51.

(40) STOCKFORD, L., AND BISSELL, H. W. 1949. Factors involved in establishing a merit-rating scale. *Personnel* 26:94-116.

(41) TIFFIN, J., AND MCCORMICK, E. J. 1965. *Industrial Psychology.* 5th ed. Englewood Cliffs, N. J.: Prentice-Hall.

(42) WHISLER, T. L., AND HARPER, S. F. 1962. *Performance appraisal.* New York: Holt, Rinehart and Winston.

27

Management-by-Objectives:
Its Implications for Motivation and Compensation

HENRY L. TOSI

AND

STEPHEN CARROLL

Since Drucker (1954) and McGregor (1960) made their popular statements about management-by-objectives in the 1950s, the method has had increasing use by organizations of all types. The early proponents of management-by-objectives treated it primarily as an approach that would lead to more objective criteria for better evaluation of performance. Subordinate managers would not be evaluated by such ambiguous characteristics as loyalty or agressiveness. Feedback could be more specific. The manager could be told more precisely where he stood. With specific objectives and action plans, the manager could give the subordinate better assistance and direction on how to improve his performance. If participation and goal setting led to higher levels of ego involvement, increased motivation and better performance could obtain. Better performance also might result from increased planning behavior, which would be reinforced. For the superior, an awareness of the objectives of subordinates might facilitate the coordination of their many activities.

In order to obtain these benefits, goals would be used as the basis for evaluation. The process through which these would be developed has been defined as a general process in which

the superior and the subordinate managers of an organization jointly define its common goals, define each individual's major areas of responsibility in terms of the results expected of him and use these measures as guides for

Printed by permission of the authors. A portion of this paper appeared in *Personnel Administration* 33 (July-August 1970):44-49. The publisher's permission to use is acknowledged.

operating the unit and assessing the contribution of each of its members (Odiorne 1965).

The logic of the objectives approach is, indeed, attractive. Yet there are some questions which seem to have been treated less than satisfactorily in the extensive writings about it. While there is an inherent attractiveness to an approach that motivates performance and enhances measurement and at the same time increases the participation of subordinates, there has been relatively little treatment of the empirical support for such a process and only a slight discussion of the problems of incorporating it into the structural system of the organization.

This paper attempts to treat these questions. First, we will review relevant research, both general and specific, dealing with the objectives approach. Some studies have examined the approach as it is used within organizations; others have examined particular elements of the process, namely, goal setting, participation and involvement, and feedback and performance evaluation.

Second, we will present some suggestions for integrating the objectives process with the organization's structural system and discuss some related problems. If compatibility can be obtained, then MBO can achieve its motivational potential. Other systemic factors will reinforce the manager's use of goal setting and feedback. Not only does a manager use the objectives approach, but reward and sanction distribution is based upon it. In this paper we will focus on integrating "objectives" with only one element of the organization structure— compensation.

We would like to stress an important *caveat*. A good case can be made that, to some degree, all managers make their subordinates somewhat aware of what is expected of them. Some managers are able to intuitively specify goals and effectively interact with subordinates, while others are less able to do so. The "objectives" approach does not necessarily mean that there be a formal program as part of the company policy and procedural structure. Most research which examines the objectives approach focuses on situations in which it is a part of a formal policy structure. Yet it may be much more relevant to look at the individual manager and the manner in which he sets goals with the subordinates. Whether or not this is part of a formal policy structure may be much less important. However, there seems to be some evidence that it is advantageous to have a formal policy of management-by-objectives.

REVIEW OF THE LITERATURE

As indicated in the previous section, the basic elements of the objectives process are goal setting, participation, and feedback and evaluation. The research dealing with these elements is reviewed here.

Goal Setting. Much of the research in the area of goal setting treats the level of aspiration. These studies examine the discrepancies between a previous level of performance and a desired level of performance (level of aspiration) as a function of previous success and failure. Subjects initially tend to set new performance goals at levels higher than previous performance levels and tend to maintain them under most conditions. Presumably, these goals would require higher levels of performance. However, if the subjects are unsuccessful in achieving goals, their aspiration levels and, consequently, goal levels are lowered (Lewin et al. 1944). The level of the current goal, therefore, is dependent upon the degree of success in achieving previous goals. The greater the success, the higher the new performance goal. These findings have been supported in studies by Gardner (1940), Klugman (1948), Child and Whitney (1949), Jucknat (1937), Festinger (1942), Anderson and Brandt (1939), and McGehee (1940).

A number of studies indicate that the degree of performance improvement depends upon past combinations of successes and failures in meeting goals (Lockette 1956; Yacorsynski 1941; and Horwitz, et al. 1953). Fryer (1963) found that when a task was difficult, forcing subjects to set goals increased the level of performance most. He also found goal setting had a greater effect on subjects' performance when they were not fed back knowledge of results.

Recently a series of studies on the effects of goals on behavior were reported by Locke and Bryan. It was found that the higher the intended level of achievement, the higher the level of performance (Locke 1966a). A specific goal (as should be developed in the objectives approach) resulted in higher levels of performance than when subjects were simply told to do their best (Locke and Bryan 1966; Locke and Bryan 1967; Locke 1967). Locke (1966b) found that high goals resulted in higher performances than low goals and that on boring tasks setting goals increased interest (Bryan and Locke 1967). Locke (1967) also found, as did Fryer, that goal setting itself increases performance more than feedback alone. Finally, and perhaps most importantly, Bryan and Locke (1967) found that an initially "low motivation" group caught up to an initially "high motivation" group when given specific goals to accomplish rather than when simply being told to do their best.

Participation. Participation, or the amount of opportunity an individual has to influence decisions which concern him, can affect his performance level, job satisfaction, and acceptance of decisions. In a field study by Lawrence and Smith (1955) two groups of workers who set their own production goals and standards had higher production than in the past. Their output also increased relative to two control groups where goals were not set by the workers but were merely discussed by them. Positive effects of participation on the production of rank and file workers were also demonstrated in studies by Coch and French (1948), Bavelas (reported in French 1950), and Bass and Leavitt (1963). Likert (1967) reports on two organizations which, when shifted over to a more participative approach, achieved substantial productivity increases in one case and substantial cost savings in the other. A number of studies, however, showed no relationship between degree of participation and increased productivity (Lewin et al. 1939; Morse and Reimer 1956).

Participation seems to result in greater subordinate acceptance of decisions (Maier 1963) and with proper leadership can result in decisions of high quality (Maier 1950; Maier and Hoffman 1960). In addition, participation can increase the amount of agreement between the individuals involved in the discussion (Hare 1953; McKeachie 1954; Bass 1957). This mutual understanding is likely to continue beyond the discussion period (Bovard 1948; Cohen 1965).

Participation also is related to job satisfaction. Vroom (1960) found those who reported high levels of psychological participation also had a more favorable attitude toward their jobs. Tosi (1968) also found the same relationship between participation and job satisfaction.

Feedback. The evidence is quite clear that feedback, or knowledge of results, improves performance and affects attitudes. Pryer and Bass (1950) gave feedback on results to thirteen of twenty-six problem-solving groups. The groups receiving feedback solved their problems more accurately and became more highly motivated to solve future problems than the other thirteen control groups. Feedback about both individual and group performance increased the performance of individual members in another study (Zajonc 1961). Smith and Knight (1959) found personal feedback from one member to another improved the efficiency of all. Training programs involving extensive feedback, such as programmed instruction, are generally more effective than conventional training programs without as much feedback (Schramm 1964).

The effect of feedback on performance has been examined in the actual job setting. A study by Weitz, Antoinett, and Wallace (1954) of life insurance salesmen revealed that those who received periodic production bulletins and personal letters commmenting on their performance improved their average performance. The average performance of a group of agents receiving no feedback actually decreased from a base performance period. In a series of studies at General Electric, Miller (1965) found that increasing the amount of feedback from foremen to workers improved their performance. He also found the effects of feedback were related to its quality. The more specific, relevant, and timely the feedback, the greater the positive effect on performance. French (1956) found that feedback was most effective when it was task-relevant.

Feedback affects attitudes. Leavitt and Mueller (1951) found that zero feedback was accompanied by low confidence and hostility, while free feedback was accompanied by high confidence and friendliness. Hamblin and Wiggins (1959) found that as ambiguity decreased with better information, innovative behavior increased and ritualism decreased. Smith (1957) found that increasing the clarity of role expectations was related to higher levels of group performance and satisfaction.

Studies of feedback in an organizational setting indicate effects on attitudes and behavior. Mahler (1957) found that formally appraised managers were more likely to regard their superiors as exercising the right kind of supervision. These managers also regarded their superiors as being more frank in telling the subordinates what they thought of the performance. Meyer and Walker (1961) found that positive actions were taken by subordinates when the appraiser exhibited supportive attitudes and behavior. Feedback could also result in defensive attitudes. Kay et al. (1962) found that under the conditions in which the appraisee expected a favorable rating, critical appraisal had a negative effect on attitudes.

Research on Management-by-Objectives

It is important to note that the research cited above treats the components of the objectives process. Research on the objectives process in organizations is quite limited, but we report here five studies which examine the process in that setting. One set of recent studies was conducted by Raia (1965, 1966). A large firm implemented "goal setting and self control"; a year later productivity increased, managers were more aware of the firm's goals, and goals were set in more areas than previously. Prior to the implementation of the program, productivity was decreasing at the rate of .4 percent per month; after implementation, the trend reversed and productivity was increasing at .3 percent per month. Raia concluded that

a contribution of the program in the area of performance appraisal has been quite significant. There was unanimous agreement among the line managers of the department, particularly plant managers, that *goals and controls* had simplified the evaluation of the individual's performance. The statement by the manager who, while being interviewed, remarked that he was now judged by his job performance and not "by the way I comb my hair" is quite meaningful.

Among other advantages were better planning of resources, pinpointing problem areas, and improved communications and mutual understanding.

The follow-up study of the same program (Raia 1966) sheds additional light on the organizational problems of the objectives approach. The study generally supported the findings of the first, but revealed significant improvements in the second year in areas related directly to production. The level of goal attainment increased, productivity continued to increase, and managerial planning and control improved. However, the goal setting process *did not filter down to lower levels of managers.* These lower levels did not participate as fully as higher levels in the process of setting goals or in the evaluation of performance. In the second year some new problems arose. Many managers began to feel that the program was "easy to beat." There was an overemphasis on production, or *measurable goals.* Some of the participants re-evaluated their initial feeling about appraisal and felt that the program did not provide adequate incentives to improve performance. They asked "What does it mean to the individual when he fails to meet certain goals?"

The nature of this field study raises some questions. No one really observed changes in goal setting behavior. It can only be assumed that the managers in the organization followed the policy dictum and used the objectives approach. Given these assumptions, what seems to emerge from this research is a strong inference that the performance of this company improved. It changed from relatively poor to relatively good. However, these improved operating results may be only temporary, and the long-term effects on the organization and its performance need to be examined. Internal as well as external factors may have had more important effects on increasing productivity levels, and Raia does not overlook these. He notes that "for a number of reasons, decision making had been highly centralized in the firm. . . . The advent of the computer . . . made it more feasible to delegate more authority to lower levels in management. Coupled with a somewhat better supply of capital and managers, these factors set the stage for a managerial philosophy of growth—the growth of individuals as well as the company."

Meyer, Kay, and French (1965) describe the results of General Electric's Work Planning and Review Program. One group of managers operated under this system, while another group operated with traditional performance appraisal methods. Those under the old method did not show any change in areas measured.

The WPR group, by contrast, expressed significantly more favorable attitudes on almost all questionnaire items. Specifically their attitudes changed in a favorable direction over the year that they participated in the WPR program with regard to:

1) the amount of help the manager was giving them in improving performance on the job and the degree to which the manager was receptive to new ideas and suggestions,
2) the ability of the manager to plan,
3) the extent to which the manager made use of their abilities and experience,
4) the degree to which they felt the goals they were shooting for were what they *should be*,
5) the extent to which they received help from the manager in planning for future job opportunities, and
6) the value of the performance discussion they had with their managers.

In addition to these changes in attitudes, evidence was also found which indicated that the members of the WPR group were much more likely to have taken specific actions to improve performance than those who were continuing to operate under traditional performance appraisal methods.

A study by Mendleson (1967) of the goal setting process attempted to measure the degree of goal setting between a superior and his subordinate. He found that while there was no significant relationship between the extent of goal setting within a superior/subordinate pair of managers and the superior's rating of his subordinate's present performance, there was, however, a positive relationship between goal setting and the superior's rating of his subordinate's promotability. The study by Mendleson is important. Contrasted with the earlier work of Raia and Meyer et al., he attempts to focus on the dyadic interaction between a superior and a subordinate in the goal setting process. Obviously the objectives approach occurs in a dyadic setting. The manager must set goals, or must be involved in some way with his subordinates. In fact, it may be this relationship which is crucial to the effectiveness of the program. There are some procedural and methodological difficulties which must be resolved. The instrument is long, and while it is composed of statements on which experts agree, there are some difficulties which may be encountered in using it as an operational measure. Regardless, it seems that the focus on the dyad is important.

Tosi and Carroll (1968), in a study of the reactions of managers to management-by-objectives, found that the acceptance of the program and satisfaction with it is related to managers' perceptions of top management support, the specificity and relevance of goals, and the frequency of feedback. The researchers noted that the major problem cited by managers was the perceived lack of feedback about performance.

Implementing the Objectives Approach

What does all this research tell us about the objectives process? From those studies treating its various elements, one can conclude the following: there can be little doubt that participation increases job satisfaction; it also affects the degree to which subordinates accept decisions reached in problems in which they are involved. There does seem to be a basis for questioning whether or not participation increases productivity. It may well be that this increase in productivity may only obtain in situations where the participation is *legitimate involvement and influence* in the development of goals and goal setting. Participation must be considered as influence. Changing the levels of participation, as might be the case with management-by-objectives, means a redistribution of influence. When it does not occur, then participation may involve nothing more than the mere act of a superior meeting with a subordinate. It is doubtful that this will have any positive effects.

The nature of the goals is important in the process. There is a tendency to set higher goals as time goes on, and higher goals lead to better performance. But this may be a function of the success or failure in achieving goals. If goals are achieved, higher goals may be

set later; if not, lower goals may be set with resulting lower performance levels. Goals also seem to be more important than feedback
alone in improving performance. It is likely that the existence of a
goal provides a reference point against which an individual himself
can check and provide "personal feedback."

The specificity of the goals seems to be important. Specific goals
not only result in higher levels of performance, but also have a
positive effect on the performance of groups that are "less
motivated." As the specificity of goals increases, so does the degree
of certainty of both the superior's and subordinate's expectations.
There is likely to be less concern about misinterpretation of expected
accomplishment levels and how they should be sought. There are
probably fewer alternatives to be evaluated since some will have
been eliminated by more precise goal definition. Therefore, the
individual may spend less time on tasks and activities which are not
goal directed and be more certain about them, which, in turn, may
reinforce goal-directed behavior, and raise performance levels.

Studies of the objectives process in organizations strongly suggest
that changes in performance and attitude, which seem positive and
desirable, appear to be associated with the formal implementation
of the technique. However, there are some signals of caution which
must be noted. The implementation of an objectives approach alters
the expectations of organization members about performance
appraisal and evaluation. These expectations, if not met, may affect
the degree to which the objectives approach is accepted (Tosi and
Carroll 1968). This problem may be resolved to some degree through
proper setting of objectives and use of the process. In the section
that follows, we specify what we believe to be the minimal conditions
that must prevail if the system is to have any motivational effect.

Goal Clarity and Relevance. No manager would quarrel with the
notion that organizational goals should be made known to the members. Individual perceptions of the goals are important here. Tosi
and Carroll (1968) have suggested some dimensions of goals which
need to be communicated to members. Goals should represent the
unit's needs, the members must be aware of the importance of the
goals, and the development of relatively objective criteria increases
the perception of goal clarity. If goals have these properties, they are
more likely to have a positive motivational effect.

Managerial Use and Support. Top management support is important for the success of any program. The best evidence of this
support is the use of the technique by the manager himself. Formu-

lating goals, discussing them with subordinates, and providing feedback based on these goals will have a substantially greater effect on a subordinate than simply saying "this has the support of top management."

Yet many managers feel that verbalization of support for a policy is adequate, and they send a memo to subordinates stating that top management wishes a program to be implemented. This, obviously, does not insure compliance. "Do as I say, not as I do" will not work. Verbalized policy support must be reinforced by the individual's perception of the superior's action and behavior in using an objectives approach. It is of little or no use to philosophically and orally support management-by-objectives and not use it.

The Need for Feedback. While a number of studies have concluded that goals have a greater impact on performance than feedback alone, we do not believe it is an either/or situation. Feedback about well-developed goals seems a fundamental requirement for behavior change. It may be that the subordinate's perception of the specificity, objectivity, and frequency of feedback is interpreted as a measure of the superior's support of an objectives approach.

Some Other Cautions. There are other significant points which must be noted here that cut across those made above. There are personal, organizational, and structural constraints which must be taken into consideration in the development and setting of goals. The organizational unit and the organization level affect the nature of the goals which can, and will, be set. Goals at lower levels may be more precisely set and probably more objectively measured. The goals of one area, engineering for instance, may be much more general than those that could be set in another, such as the marketing department.

Management-by-Objectives
and the Compensation Process

Let us now turn to the vexing question: how can the objectives approach be of any use in a compensation system? We have said earlier that the objectives approach may not be formalized. However, to link it to compensation, there must be some formal means for the development and documentation of objectives and the assessment of performance.

We should note here an important point. It may be that the objectives approach can supplant, or at least supplement, the motivational capability of compensation if financial incentives lose their effectiveness as a motivator. McClelland (1961) suggests that individuals high in need achievement (as most top managers are) will expend effort to reach challenging goals irrespective of external rewards associated with goal accomplishment. Thus the objectives approach may be used to effectively motivate those who are not motivated by money. Managers for whom money is a relatively less effective motivation would include those at the highest levels of management where the compensation is already quite high.

However, it seems to us both possible and desirable to tie management-by-objectives into the financial reward system. It is for this reason that we suggest how the two elements can be related and information obtained from MBO used in making improved compensation decisions while at the same time obtaining the reinforcing benefits of both.

Management-by-objectives may not be particularly useful in setting basic compensation levels for particular positions because this requires more information than could be obtained using the objectives approach. External market considerations, such as salaries for similar jobs in other organizations, or the scarcity of individuals with particular skills, must come into play when determining salary levels and ranges. However, internal wage administration may be facilitated by the objectives approach. It may be of assistance in developing salary differentials within a particular job class. By assessing the level of difficulty and contribution of the goals for a particular job and comparing them with similar jobs in that class, or that type, some determination of the appropriateness of basic compensation differentials can be made.

Management-by-objectives may be useful in providing information about changes in job requirements which may necessitate re-evaluation and adjustment of compensation levels for different positions. By observing changes in objectives over time, changes in job requirements may be detected which could lead to revisions in compensation schedules.

The objectives approach can aid in determining supplementary compensation levels, such as stock options, bonus plans, and administration of profit-sharing plans. This type of compensation is usually given when performance exceeds the normal position requirements. A properly developed objectives approach will take into account both normal job duties as well as goals and activities which extend beyond them. The extent to which an incumbent is able to achieve these non-routine objectives should be one, but perhaps not the only, factor in ranking unit members in order of their additional contribution to unit effectiveness. It will provide a sound basis for determining what the level of supplemental compensation should be. Needless to say, these goals beyond normal job requirements should contribute importantly to organizational success.

A problem needs to be noted, however. Goals may be set which go substantially beyond the current job requirements. These may be due to an individual's initiative and aggressiveness. If this happens, the appropriate strategy may be to change the position of the individual, not to redefine the job and change compensation. A method must be developed which takes this possibility into consideration, as well as the fact that different managers will have different goals. This does not seem to be the appropriate place to detail such a device. It simply might be suggested that a weighting approach which considers the capability of the manager, the difficulty of the goal, and its importance to the unit might resolve the problem.

If goals are developed properly, achievement may be more readily associated with the individual in order to give appropriate rewards. The *goal statement* is the heart of the "objectives approach." It is a description of the boss' expectancies which will be used in the feedback and evaluation process. It is a communicative artifact which spells out, for both the boss and the subordinate, the objectives *and* the manner in which they will be obtained. It should contain two elements: the desired *goal level* and the *activities* required to achieve that level of performance. This permits not only a comparison of performance against some criteria, but also allows determination of whether or not events, which are presumed to lead to a goal, have taken place if appropriate criteria are not available.

Making such a distinction has important implications for the problems of assessment, evaluation, and compensation. Some goals may be neither measurable nor adequately verifiable, yet intuitively we know what must be done to achieve them. If this case exists, and we have distinguished between goals and activities, we at least can determine whether activities which are presumed to lead to desired ends have taken place.

It is important to recognize the difference between measuring the achievement of a goal level and determining whether or not the event has occurred. If we are unable to quantify or specify a goal level in a meaningful way, then we simply assume that the desired level will be achieved if a particular event, or set of activities, has taken place. For example, it is very difficult to find any measurable criteria to assess a manager's capability in developing subordinates, yet we can determine if he has provided them with development opportunities. If they have participated in seminars, attended meetings, or gone to school, it may be *assumed* that the development activities are properly conducted.

SUMMARY

By its very nature, one underlying purpose of management-by-objectives is to link **performance** to the evaluation process and the reward system. Tosi and Carroll (1968) found that managers who perceived themselves as receiving more objective feedback also saw their advancement and promotion dependent upon performance. Those who saw advancement dependent upon performance also tended to report higher levels of satisfaction with pay. Porter and Lawler (1968) found that the most motivated managers saw their pay as dependent upon job performance. It appears that higher performance and motivation is most likely when there is a link between performance and the reward system. Possibly this can be achieved through the process of feedback regarding goal achievement and the association of rewards or sanctions with goal achievement. Achievement of goals should be organizationally reinforced, and the reinforcement should vary for different individuals as a function of attainment.

The use of an objectives approach in conjunction with a compensation program also may result in less dissatisfaction with the allocation of pay increases that are made. Certainly there is virtually universal agreement among managers that rewards should go for actual accomplishments rather than for irrelevant personal characteristics or for political or social standing. Herzberg (1959) and other researchers have clearly shown that perceived unfairness of the compensation system can be a major source of dissatisfaction and a negative motivator among managers and other higher-level personnel.

Yet there are problems that might arise from the use of MBO and emphasis on goals and goal achievement. Many organizations have adopted the objectives approach because it seems to be a better appraisal device, and they have used it primarily in this vein. An appraisal system should furnish information needed to make other personnel decisions, such as those about promotion and transfer. Information furnished by the objectives approach may or may not be adequate for this purpose. Accomplishment of goals at a lower-level job may be a good indicator of capability in the current job and/or level of motivation, but not of the individual's abilities to perform at higher levels of responsibility, especially if the requirements on the higher-level job are much different from the current position. (Conversely, goals accomplishment at a lower-level job may be indicative of promotability to a particular higher-level job if there is high goal congruence between the two jobs.) At any rate, there is certainly no reason to rely strictly upon the objectives approach. It can be used along with other criteria, such as assessment of traits, when this is deemed an important dimension by the decision makers.

Another potential difficulty should be pointed out. If the objectives approach becomes the basic vehicle for the determination of compensation increases, then managers will quickly learn to "beat the system." They may set objectives which have high probabilities of achievement, refraining from setting moderately high risk goals. When the system becomes too formalized, managers learn how to beat it; it is the sole basis on which appraisal and compensation decisions are made, and even those functioning with it become more concerned with simply meeting the formal requirements. Eventually, the benefits for both superior and subordinate are probably no different from earlier, more traditional, methods of appraisal.

The objectives approach is congruent with what behavior science research suggests is a practical approach for the motivation of managers. But it is not an easy path to follow. It requires a considerable amount of the time and energy of *all* managers in addition to extensive organizational support to make it work. Research demonstrates that, properly used, management-by-objectives can affect the performance and motivation of individuals. There remains the important problem of implementation. Management-by-objectives somehow loses some of its mystique, value, importance, and significance when it must be translated into a formal policy requirement. It is easy to consider a formal management-by-objectives program as another thorn in the manager's side, with no positive gains for implementing it. The program must be relevant, applicable, and helpful, and receive organization support and reinforcement. One way in which this can be done is to link it to other elements of the structural system that reinforce behavior.

REFERENCES

ANDERSON, H. H., AND BRANDT, H. F. 1939. Study of motivation involving self-announced goals of 5th-grade children and the concept of level of aspiration. *J. Soc. Psychol.* 10:209-32.

BASS, B. M. 1957. *Behavior in groups.* Third Annual Report, Contract N70NR 35609. Louisiana State University, Baton Rouge.

BASS, B. M., AND LEAVITT, H. J. 1963. Some experiments in planning and operating. *Management Science* 9:574-85.

BOVARD, E. W., JR. 1948. Social norms and the individual. *J. Abnorm. Soc. Psychol.* 43:62-69.

BRYAN, J. F., AND LOCKE, E. A. 1967. Goal setting as a means of increasing motivation. *J. Appl. Psychol.* 51:274-77.

CHILD, I. L., AND WHITNEY, J. W. 1949. Determinants of level of aspiration and evidence from everyday life. *J. Abnorm. Soc. Psychol.* 44:303-14.

COCH, L., AND FRENCH, J. R. P. 1948. Overcoming resistance to change. *Human Relations* 1:512-32.

COHEN, E. 1956. Stimulus conditions as factors in social change. *Amer. Psychol.* 11:407 (abstract).

DRUCKER, P. 1954. *The practice of management.* New York: Harper and Brothers.

FESTINGER, L. 1942. Wish expectation, and group standards as factors influencing level of aspiration. *J. Abnorm. Soc. Psychol.* 37:184-200.

FRENCH, E. G. 1956. Effects of the interaction of feedback and motivation on task performance. *Amer. Psychol.* 11:395 (abstract).

FRENCH, J. R. P., JR. 1950. Field experiments: Changing group productivity. In *Experiments in social process: A symposium on social psychology,* ed. J. G. Miller. New York: McGraw Hill.

FRYER, F. W. 1963. An evaluation of level of aspiration as a training procedure. Ph. D. dissertation, University of Maryland.

GARDNER, J. W. 1940. The use of the term "level of aspiration." *Psychol. Rev.* 47:59-68.

HAMBLIN, R. L., AND WIGGINS, J. A. 1959. Ambiguity and the rate of social adaptation. *Tech. Rept. 1,* Contract on 811 (161). St. Louis: Washington Univ.

HARE, A. P. 1954. Small group discussions with participatory and supervisory leadership. *J. Abnorm. Soc. Psychol.* 48:73-275.

HERZBERG, F.; MAUSNER, B.; AND SNYDERMAN, B. 1959. *The motivation to work.* New York: John Wiley and Sons, Inc.

HORWITZ, M. et al. 1953. *Motivational effects of alternative decision-making processes in groups.* Bureau of Educational Research, University of Illinois, 1953.

JUCKNAT, M. 1937. Performance and level of aspiration. *Psychol. Forsch.* 22:89-177.

KAY, E.; FRENCH, J. R. P. JR.; AND MEYER, H. H. 1962. *A study of the performance appraisal interview.* New York: Behavioral Research Service, General Electric Company.

KLUGMAN, S. F. 1948. Emotional stability and level of aspiration. *J. Gen. Psychol.* 38:101-18.

LAWRENCE, L. C., AND SMITH, P. C. 1955. Group decision and employee participation. *J. Appl. Psychol.* 39:334-37.

LEAVITT, H. J., AND MUELLER, A. H. 1951. Some effects of feedback on communications. *Human Relations* 4:401-10.

LEWIN, K. et al. 1944. Level of aspiration. In *Personality and the behavior disorders,* ed. J. Mc. V. Hunt, pp. 333-78. New York: Ronald Press, vol. I.

LEWIN, L.; LIPPITT, R.; AND WHITE, R. K. 1939. Patterns of aggressive behavior in experimentally created social climates. *J. Soc. Psychol.* 10:271-99.

LIKERT, R. 1967. *The human organization.* New York: McGraw Hill.

LOCKE, E. A. 1966. A closer look at level of aspiration as a training procedure. *J. Appl. Psychol.* 50:417-20.

———. 1966a. The relationship of intentions to level of performance. *J. Appl. Psychol.* 50:60-66.

———. 1967. Motivational effects of knowledge of results: Knowledge or goal setting? *J. Appl. Psychol.* 51:324-29.

LOCKE, E. A., AND BRYAN, J. F. 1966. Cognitive aspects of psychomotor performance. *J. Appl. Psychol.* 50:286-91.

———. 1967. Performance goals as determinants of level of performance and boredom. *J. Appl. Psychol.* 51:120-30.

LOCKETTE, R. R. 1956. The effect of level of aspiration upon the learning of skills. Ph. D. dissertation, University of Illinois.

MCCLELLAND, D. C. 1961. *The achieving society.* Princeton: Van Nostrand.

MCGEHEE, W. 1940. Judgment and level of aspiration. *J. Gen. Psychol.* 22:3-15.

MCGREGOR, D. 1960. *The human side of enterprise.* New York: McGraw-Hill.

MCKEACHIE, W. J. 1954. Individual conformity to attitudes of classroom groups. *J. Abnorm. Soc. Psychol.* 49:282-89.

MAHLER, W. R. 1957. Bringing about change in individual performance. *Improving managerial performance.* General Management Series, No. 186, The American Management Association.

MAIER, N. R. F. 1953. An experimental test of the effect. of training on discussion leadership. *Human Relations* 6:161-73.

———. 1963. *Problem-solving discussions and conferences.* New York: McGraw-Hill.

———. 1950. The quality of group decisions as influenced by the discussion leader. *Human Relations* 3:155-74.

MAIER, N. R. F., AND HOFFMAN, L. R. 1960. Using trained "developmental" discussion leaders to improve further the quality of group decisions. *J. Appl. Psychol.* 44:247-51.

MEYER, H. H.; KAY, E.; AND FRENCH, J. R. P. 1964. Split roles in performance appraisal. *Harvard Business Review* 43:123-29.

MEYER, H. H., AND WALKER, W. B. 1961. A study of factors relating to the effectiveness of a performance appraisal program. *Personnel Psychology* 14:291-98.

MILLER, L. 1965. *The use of knowledge of results in improving the performance of hourly operators.* General Electric Company, Behavioral Research Service.

MORSE, N. C., AND REIMER, E. 1956. The experimental change of a major organizational variable. *J. Abnorm. Soc. Psychol.* 52:120-29.

ODIORNE, G. 1965. *Management by objectives.* New York: Pitman.

PORTER, L., AND LAWLER, E. 1968. *Managerial attitudes and performance.* Homewood, Illinois: R. D. Irwin.

PRYER, M. W., AND BASS, B. M. 1950. *Some effects of feedback on behavior in groups.* Technical Report 13, Contract N70NR 35609. Louisiana State University, Baton Rouge, La.

RAIA, A. 1965. Goal setting and self control. *Journal of Management Studies,* II-I (February):34-53.

————. 1966. A second look at goals and controls. *California Management Review* (Summer):49-58.

SCHRAMM, W. 1964. *The research on programmed instruction: An annotated bibliography.* Washington, D. C.: U. S. Dept. of HEW, G. P. O., pp. 4-5.

SMITH, E. E. 1957. The effects of clear and unclear role expectations on group productivity and defensiveness. *J. Abnorm. Soc. Psychol.* 55:213-17.

SMITH, E. E., AND KNIGHT, S. S. 1959. Effects of feedback on insight and problem solving efficiency in training groups. *J. Appl. Psychol.* 43:209-11.

TOSI, H. Organizational stress as a moderator of the relationship between participation and job satisfaction, job anxiety, and productivity. Paper delivered at XV International Meetings, The Institute of Management Science, September 1968.

TOSI, H., AND CARROLL, S. 1968. Managerial reactions to management by objectives. *Academy of Management Journal.* 11:415-26.

VROOM, V. H. 1960. *Some personality determinants of the effects of participation.* Englewood Cliffs: Prentice-Hall.

WEITZ, J. A.; ANTOINETTI, J.; AND WALLACE, S. R. 1954. The effect of home office contact on sales performance. *Personnel Psychology* 7:381-84.

WHYTE, W. F. 1955. *Money and motivation: An analysis of incentives in industry.* New York: Harper.

YACORSYNSKI, G. K. 1941. Degree of effort. III. Relationship to the level of aspiration. *J. Exp. Psychol.* 30:407-13.

ZAJONC, R. B. 1961. The effects of feedback and group task difficulty on individual and group performance. *Tech. Rept. No. 15.* Contract NONR 1224(34). Ann Arbor: University of Michigan.

28

A Study of Factors Relating to the Effectiveness of a Performance Appraisal Program

HERBERT H. MEYER

AND

WILLIAM B. WALKER

INTRODUCTION

Performance appraisal is a widely practiced personnel activity which has seldom been subjected to systematic study. The premise on which the application of a formal appraisal program is based—namely, that to know where one stands with his boss and to be apprised of his shortcomings will help him to improve his performance—seems to have so much obvious validity that personnel people are apt to feel it is unnecessary to conduct formal studies of the effectiveness of this program. While some writers have recently questioned the value of formal appraisal programs, or at least of certain approaches to appraisal, few research studies have been focused on the conditions associated with the success or failure of the program.

In the course of gathering data for another study, an opportunity was provided to obtain data relating to reactions of "middle management" employees in a large manufacturing company to the performance appraisal program. While this side exploration does not by any means provide a definitive answer to the question of what factors contribute to the effectiveness of the performance appraisal program, it does throw some light on the subject.

Reprinted by permission of the authors and publisher from *Personnel Psychology* (Autumn 1961): 219-29.

DESIGN OF THE STUDY

The major study (Meyer & Walker, 1961) of which this investigation was a part was aimed at identifying some of the correlates of certain measures of achievement motivation. One of the hypotheses investigated was that high achievement motivation would be associated with positive reactions to the performance appraisal program. The subjects for testing this hypothesis consisted of 31 managers in several manufacturing components of the General Electric Company and 31 specialists whose status (position levels) in the organizations was approximately the same as the managers. These 62 men were given a thematic apperceptive measure designed to be scored for "need for achievement" and a Risk Preference Questionnaire which presented situations involving risk and required the subject to choose between low, intermediate, and high risk options. The use of this risk questionnaire as an index of achievement motivation was based on the theoretical model presented by Atkinson (1957), in which he demonstrated that the person with high achievement motivation will prefer intermediate risks (approximately 50/50 odds) whereas the person with high fear of failure motivation will prefer either safer odds or higher risk odds where failure is excusable.

All the Company components included in the study had formal performance appraisal programs. One of the primary purposes of these programs was to provide the measure of "merit" for determining pay level under a merit-pay type of salary plan. Appraisals were generally based on the responsibilities assigned to each individual as described in his "Position Guide." The appraisal forms used also included sections for identifying development needs and for suggesting remedial actions.

During the interviews conducted as a part of this research study, each subject was questioned about his experience with the performance appraisal program and was asked to give an especially detailed description of the last performance appraisal discussion he had had with his manager. Based on each subject's report, the interviewer rated the following items:

> (Note that this was the interviewer's evaluation, based on the subject's description of the discussion, not the subject's evaluation of the discussion his boss had held with him.)

1) How faithfully did the manager follow the performance appraisal procedure?

2) How skillfully did the manager handle the feed-back discussion?
3) How favorable was the respondent's attitude toward the performance appraisal program?
4) How favorable was the respondent's attitude toward the "merit-pay" plan?
5) Did the man being interviewed report that he had taken some specific action to improve his performance based on the performance appraisal discussion?

The last item was categorized simply on a "yes-no" basis by the interviewer. The man's response was coded "yes" if he could cite some specific action he had taken based on items discussed or suggestions made during the interview. He might have indicated, for example, that he had enrolled in a "Human Relations" training course at the suggestion of his supervisor, or that he had reorganized his method for keeping scrap records so that he could get an earlier indication of needed corrections, or that he had made a special effort to get reports in on time since this was mentioned by the manager as an item which needed improvement.

This latter variable, the respondent's report of whether or not he had taken constructive action to improve performance based on his last performance appraisal discussion, was used as the criterion of the success of the performance appraisal program for purposes of this study. The analysis of data was carried out by computing correlations between this criterion variable and other measures obtained in the investigation.

RESULTS

Of the 62 men interviewed in this study, 49 (23 of the managers and 26 of the specialists) reported that they had had performance appraisal discussions with their managers within the last year or two, which they could describe in some detail. Of the 49, 21 (12 managers and 9 specialists) reported that they had taken some specific constructive action to improve performance, based on suggestions made or topics discussed in the feed-back interview.

Table 1 presents correlations between the dependent variable, "constructive action taken based on last performance appraisal discussion," and the independent variables obtained in the study. It can be seen that the best predictor of whether or not the subject took constructive action based on his performance appraisal was how well his manager had handled the appraisal feed-back discussion. Of the measures designed to assess motivation, the thematic apperceptive measure of "need for achievement" showed only a low correlation, not statistically significant, with the criterion variable, while preference for intermediate level risks as an index of achievement motivation was found to be highly correlated with the criterion.

TABLE 1

Correlates of the Variable "Constructive Action Taken Based on Last Performance Appraisal Discussion"

	Managers	Specialists	Total
	(N = 23)	(N = 26)	(N = 49)
1. How well manager handled appraisal discussion	75**	55**	63**
2. Thematic apperceptive measure of "need for achievement"	04	32	21
3. Preference for intermediate level risks	48*	68**	63**
4. Attitude toward Merit Pay plan	35	60*	50*
5. Attitude toward Performance Appraisal program	05	38	30
6. Age	—46*	—48*	—48*
7. Education	—18	—38	—26

Significant at 5% level of confidence.
**Significant at 1% level of confidence.*

It is interesting to note that attitude toward the merit-pay salary plan is significantly correlated with the report of taking constructive action, whereas attitude toward the performance appraisal program itself does not correlate with the same variable at a significant level. Age shows negative correlations, as might be expected, indicating that the younger men were more likely to take constructive action to improve performance than were the older men. Education also shows negative correlations with the criterion, although these correlations are not significant. These negative correlations would indicate, however, that in this sample there was some tendency for the less well educated men to be more likely to take constructive action than was true for the better educated men.

Additional analysis, not reported in the table, showed that the first variable, "How well the discussion was handled," was significantly correlated with the participants' attitudes toward the merit-pay salary plan (.45). As an interesting sidelight, it was also noted that the interviewers' ratings of the participants' "level of understanding of the salary plan philosophy" was significantly correlated (.42) with attitudes toward the merit-pay system. In other words, those who demonstrated a better understanding of the philosophy on which the salary plan is based expressed more favorable attitudes toward the plan. (It is important to keep in mind, of course, that both of these ratings were made by the same interviewer, and therefore it is possible that the interviewer's rating of one variable could have biased his rating of the other.)

A multiple correlation for predicting action based on the appraisal discussion, from the three variables in Table 1 which show the highest correlations, would indicate that theoretically this prediction should be perfect. Figure 1 illustrates the results of combining these three variables in a crude manner to predict action based on the appraisal. It will be noted, for example, that seven out of eight of the men who were (1) below the average age for the group, (2) expressed preference for intermediate risks, and (3) whose managers had done an above-average job in handling the appraisal discussion, took some constructive action to improve performance on the basis of the discussion. At the other end of the scale, it will be noted that none of the men who scored below average on these three variables took constructive action based on their appraisal discussions. This prediction would be equally good if the multiple correlation were computed for either one of the groups and then "cross-validated" on the other group. Needless to say, this kind of check at this stage of the data analysis cannot be accepted as a legitimate cross-validation of the findings.

DISCUSSION

The results of this study suggest that the skill with which a supervisor handles the appraisal feed-back discussion with his subordinates is a key factor in determining whether or not the performance appraisal program is effective in motivating behavioral changes. It would also appear that the skill with which the supervisor handles the appraisal discussion might have an important influence on the degree to which a subordinate understands the philosophy on which

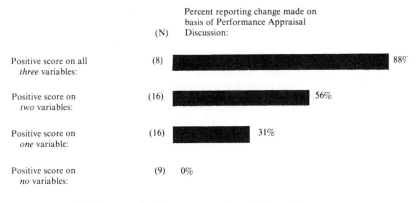

FIGURE 1
Predicting Constructive Action Based on Performance Appraisal from Scores on Three Variables

Positive scores = 1. Above average rating on *"How well manager handled appraisal discussion"*

2. Expressed *preference for intermediate risks* on Risk Preference Questionnaire

3. *Below median age* for the group

the pay-for-performance salary plan is based, and this in turn might influence his attitude toward the plan. Moreover, a favorable attitude toward the salary plan was found to be significantly correlated with whether or not the individual took constructive action based on performance appraisal. (This latter correlation could also be accounted for by the fact that both variables involved were highly correlated with "how well the appraisal discussion was handled.")

The high correlation found between preference for intermediate level risks and the subjects' reports of whether or not they took constructive action based on the performance appraisal discussion provides evidence to support the hypothesis that this measure is assessing some aspect of achievement motivation (Atkinson, 1957). It is not necessary, however, to interpret this result as indicating only that the aspect of motivation measured is a positive, success-oriented type. While this measure was scored by comparing the number of intermediate level risk choices to choices for extreme risks, whether high or low, a more detailed analysis of the results showed that preference for *low risk* alternatives actually generated the correlations found between this measure and the criterion. In other words, if preference for high level risks was lumped together with preference for intermediate level risks, and these compared with preference for low risks, the correlations found between this measure and the criterion were not affected. Thus, the preference for safe bets, or the avoidance of risk, appears to be the critical behavior tapped by this measure. This may indicate a negative, fear-of-failure type of motivation.

According to the motivation theory model presented by Atkinson (1957), one might predict that the men who show preference for safe bets would also be less likely to take constructive action based on the performance appraisal. The fact that an individual took action based on the appraisal feedback discussion must have meant that the manager discussed an area of needed improvement. This might be interpreted by the individual as a *failure* on his part in some aspect of job performance. Atkinson demonstrates that the effect of failure on the person with a high level of anxiety about failing is to decrease his motivation and cause him to avoid the situation. He also cites research evidence to support his theory (Atkinson, 1957).

The findings of this study with the most immediate practical implications are probably those relating to the skill with which appraisal feed-back discussions were handled. The fact that this variable was found to be highly correlated, not only with the tendency to take constructive action based on a performance appraisal discussion, but also with attitudes toward the salary plan and performance appraisal would indicate that any steps taken to upgrade the quality of these appraisal interviews would have a decided impact on the success of the merit-pay salary plan, and especially on the performance appraisal program as an integral part of the plan.

REFERENCES

ATKINSON, J. W. "Motivational Determinants of Risk-Taking Behavior." *Psychological Review,* LXIV (1957), 359-372.
MEYER, H. H. AND WALKER, W. B. "Need for Achievement and Risk Preferences as They Relate to Attitudes toward Reward Systems and Performance Appraisal in an Industrial Setting." *Journal of Applied Psychology,* in press, 1961.

PART SIX

Some Unresolved Issues

What do we know about managerial compensation and motivation? To this point we have examined and criticized theory, presented findings from research based on some of the theories, and read about methods and techniques used in performance appraisal. Each paper has recognized, usually very explicitly, the limitations inherent in it.

It is hoped that this last section pulls together in a more systematic way many of the suggestions presented earlier. What are the general areas where theory and research need to be sharpened? What are some methodological difficulties which may have clouded research and theory in the past? What problems must be examined by the practitioner? Lawler, in a paper presented at the McKinsey seminar, examines the implications of generally making more information available about pay levels. He points out that open pay information is a two-edged sword: it could produce anxiety for lower-paid managers and pose serious difficulties,. in terms of justification of pay differentials for people in similar positions.

Weick describes the possible effects of low pay. Recognizing the general consensus that lower pay is related to lower satisfaction levels, he directs his paper to other possible explanations, but cautions the reader about extrapolating the findings of the reviewed literature to the real world.

Korman proposes a set of research questions which could guide systematic efforts into an examination of the manner in which compensation levels are determined and their effect.

Patton notes the difficulty of formulating remuneration policies that apply to "fast track" personnel. He proposes that the compensation mechanism, especially the incentive component, must be inextricably interwoven with the processes of organizational realignment to solve the problems.

McClelland, in his seminar paper, while emphasizing the research on need achievement, makes the strong point that in considering motivation and incentives we should change orientations. The problem, he says, is managing motivation. Incentive plans "must not be seen as a primary way of accomplishing this." He suggests a larger framework in which there is consideration of the individual, the task, the manager, and the organizational climate.

In summary, one leaves this section with the general conviction that there are indeed many unresolved issues which pose significant problems for both theory and practice. It is hoped that some of the ideas in this section provide future researchers with fruitful directions for their investigation.

29

Secrecy and the Need to Know

22

EDWARD E. LAWLER III

Secrecy about management compensation is a common practice in our major corporations. Certainly one of the best accepted axioms of good personnel practice is the one which dictates that information about management compensation practices and rates is best kept secret. In a recent survey (Lawler 1966*b*), 77 percent of the managers sampled stated that pay rates should be kept secret. A conservative estimate based upon my own experience would be that in a majority of the major corporations in this country, managers are not told how their pay actually is determined nor are they told what the ranges and average salaries are for their own and other jobs in the company.

Perhaps the most interesting facet of this widespread existence of secrecy is that it appears to run counter to the general needs in people to know and understand themselves and their environment. There is, for example, a large body of literature that specifically hypothesizes that people tend to seek information about their own attitudes, abilities, performance, and outcomes by comparing them with those of other persons. Taken together, this literature suggests the basic premise upon which this paper rests. The premise is that managers need and want to determine how their pay compares to that of other managers.

The focus of this paper will be upon the effects of secrecy when it exists simultaneously with this need for pay comparisons. Initially, some consideration will be given to the evidence and theories that

Printed by permission of the author. Paper delivered at the McKinsey Seminar on Managerial Motivation and Compensation, Tarrytown, New York, 1967.

455

are relevant to the pay comparison process. Specifically, social comparison theory, relative deprivation theory, and equity theory will be considered in order to illustrate the kind of thinking that underlies the contention that managers need to make pay comparisons. Then the relationship between these theories and how a manager reacts to the amount of his pay will be considered. Finally, data will be presented from a series of studies that have considered the impact of secrecy on the kinds of comparisons managers make with respect to their pay and the effects of these comparisons on their feelings about their pay.

THEORETICAL BACKGROUND

Festinger (1954) has hypothesized that "there exists, in the human organism, a drive to evaluate his opinions and his abilities" and that "to the extent that objective, nonsocial means are not available, people evaluate their opinions and abilities by comparison respectively with the opinions and abilities of others." Recently, social comparison theory has received considerable attention; Latané (1966) has edited a monograph that contains a series of studies designed to test its various aspects. Significantly, the results of most of.these studies are congruent with the predictions of the theory.

Wheeler (1966) found strong support for the assumption that, when given the choice, people will choose to compare with someone similar to themselves. Gordon (1966) and Hakmiller (1966) both have presented data which suggest that once the comparison drive is satiated, the desire to compare with others disappears. This finding is important because it supports Festinger's original point that people have a need for comparing their abilities and opinions with those of other persons when no objective basis is available for evaluation. Thus, although the research data are limited they are in general agreement with the basic hypothesis stated by Festinger in his 1954 article. As will become clear later, the fact that these hypotheses seem to be valid has important implications for how managers evaluate their performance. Performance is relevant to social comparison because Festinger stresses that an ability is evaluated by persons considering that performance which is presumed to depend upon the ability.

Stouffer and his colleagues (1949) created a substantial stir among social scientists with the publication of the first *American Soldier* volume. Part of this excitement was due to their introduction of the concept of relative deprivation. It was used to explain the somewhat paradoxical finding that despite the fact that the Air Corps had greater opportunities for promotion than did the Military Police, they were less satisfied with their promotion opportunities. This finding was explained by the fact that the Air Corps men had much higher expectations of promotion and were therefore more dissatisfied even though greater actual opportunity for promotion existed. The obvious point in this and the other early work on relative deprivation is that a person's satisfaction with his situation is not a simple function of his actual standing or situation. Rather, it appears to be directly related to his expectations about what constitutes a fair situation.

The existence of relative deprivation leads naturally to a consideration of distributive justice. Since deprivation is perceived rationally, it has meaning only in terms of what is perceived to be a fair disbursement of goods among people. Homans (1961) has developed a theory of distributive justice which emphasizes that feelings of fairness are directly based upon a person's perception of his own rewards relative to other person's rewards. For Homans, the feeling of equity or justice will result when an individual feels there is a fair balance between his rewards and investments relative to other persons' rewards and investments. The important point for our purposes that is made both by Homans and Stouffer is that people do not evaluate the fairness of the situation in an absolute manner. Rather, they evaluate it relative to what others receive; hence it is the perceived relative value of their rewards that is important. It should be noted that this point is very similar to the one made by social comparison theory since it also stresses the importance of a relative value and a relative value that depends upon a comparison with how others are perceived.

RELATIVE VALUE OF PAY

The research on social comparisons and relative deprivation is relevant for the understanding of how people react to their pay because pay has both a relative and an absolute value. Pay has an absolute value because x amount of pay will buy a given product or commodity. However, in a competitive society such as ours where people are receiving pay that is greater than that needed for subsistence, it also has a relative value that is based upon what others receive. It is precisely because pay has a relative value that people do need to compare their pay with other peoples' pay. Hoffman, Festinger, and Lawrence (1954) make this point in one of the initial studies of the social comparison process. According to them,

discrepancies in points or other symbols come to have relative rather than absolute value. They tend to be interpreted primarily as indicators of the individual's status with respect to the other members rather than as something of direct utilitarian value. This is especially true when the points gained represent intellectual, athletic, or social ability, but it is also probably true to a large extent when they represent money or commodities.

Thus, knowing that a person receives a salary of $16,000 tells quite a bit about his purchasing power, but it does not tell anything about the relative value of his pay and how he feels about his pay. The relative value of his pay is, of course, determined by what other relevant people around him earn. In two situations a $16,000 salary might be reacted to quite differently even though its absolute value remains constant. Lawler and Porter (1963), for example, have found that managers react quite differently to a given salary depending upon their management level. They found that a foreman who earns between $12,000 and $14,000 a year is better satisfied with his pay than is a company president who earns less than $49,000. In this case, the same absolute salary is being perceived quite differently by managers at different organization levels. This means that the crucial determinant of a person's reaction to his pay is based not simply upon how much it will buy (its absolute value) but rather upon its size relative to the size of others' pay. In other words, the crucial factor is the person's perception of how his pay compares with other peoples' pay because a person's expectations about what pay he should receive are based upon what he perceives others earn.

A person's perception of the relative value of his pay undoubtedly has an influence upon a number of his other attitudes toward his pay. Lawler (1967), for example, has pointed out that how a person perceives that his earnings compare with others' probably influences both the importance he attaches to the amount he receives and his beliefs about how his pay is determined. However, in this paper the focus will be upon only two of the attitudes that may be influenced by the perceived relative value of a person's earnings. First, consideration will be given to the relationship between a person's perception of the relative value of this pay and feelings of satisfaction and equity with respect to his pay. Second, consideration will be given to the relationship between a person's perception of the relative value of his salary and his feelings about how well he is performing.

Equity Theory

The research on relative deprivation and distributive justice would appear to be directly relevant for the issue of how salary level affects satisfaction with pay. In fact, Adams (1965), in developing his theory of pay inequity, has drawn directly upon the earlier work on distributive justice and relative deprivation. In his work, Adams has developed an input-outcome model of satisfaction that makes clear predictions about the determinants of satisfaction with pay. It makes an argument that is in many ways quite similar to the earlier arguments made by Stouffer et al. in explaining the dissatisfaction of soldiers and those made by Homans (1961) in his treatment of distributive justice.

Adams emphasizes that persons' expectations are based upon the comparisons they make between themselves and others. He points out that where expectations are out of line with reality, relative deprivation appears which causes feelings of inequity; these in turn, cause dissatisfaction. According to Adams, feelings of inequity occur when a person "perceives that the ratio of his outcomes to inputs and the ratio of others' outcomes to others' inputs are unequal." Among inputs are such things as skill level, experience, and effort while among outcomes are pay, fringe benefits, and work interest. If we assume for a moment that other inputs and outcomes are constant, then a person's satisfaction with his pay should be determined by the relation of his pay to his inputs as compared with the relation between the pay and inputs for someone to whom he compares himself. Patchen (1961) has stated this somewhat differently, but again note the similar emphasis:

$$\frac{\text{My pay}}{\text{His (their) pay}} \quad \text{compared to} \quad \frac{\text{My position on dimensions related to pay}}{\text{His (their) position on dimensions related to pay}}$$

A considerable amount of research evidence exists to support the point that satisfaction with pay is indeed a function of how favorably a person's earnings compare with other persons'. Sayles (1958), for example, found that the high dissatisfaction found among employees in plants where foundry work exists could be explained by noting the high wages of the relatively unskilled foundry workers. Apparently when other workers compared themselves to the foundry workers they felt relatively underpaid because they had a less favorable input-outcome balance. Lawler and Porter (1966) found a general tendency for the higher paid managers at each management level to be the most satisfied employees. Apparently they perceived that their pay compared favorably with that of other managers with similar inputs. Andrews and Henry (1963) and Patchen (1961) also have provided data that generally tend to support the type of thinking represented in the work of Adams, Homans, and Stouffer. Thus it seems that the data support the point that satisfaction with pay is influenced by the degree to which a person's earnings compare favorably with other similar persons' salaries.

However, none of these previous studies of pay comparisons have been concerned with how accurately managers perceive other managers' earnings when they make comparisons. Andrews and Henry (1963) simply took managers' actual salaries relative to other managers' actual salaries in order to compute their relative salary standing and used this to predict their pay satisfaction. Thus they used actual relative salary rather than perceived relative salary, which is optimal only if managers have accurate pictures of what others earn. But with the existence of secrecy this may not be a legitimate assumption. Thus the key question at this point concerns the impact of secrecy on the kinds of comparisons managers make with respect to their pay and with its impact on how satisfying these comparisons are likely to be. It is the very existence of secrecy that makes the pay comparison area such an important topic for research. It provides an opportunity to focus upon what happens to the comparison process when accurate comparison information is not available. The previous work on comparisons has typically focused on situations where distortion of comparison information is not likely, and as a result the whole issue of how people react when they are confronted with ambiguous comparison objects has received little study.

SECRECY AND PAY SATISFACTION

Questions about the impact of secrecy on pay satisfaction are of particular interest because one of the most commonly stated reasons for keeping pay secret is that secrecy helps to reduce unfavorable pay comparisons. The reasoning is that if a manager does not have accurate information about what others are earning he will not make unfavorable comparisons between what he earns and what others are earning. It seems highly unlikely that secrecy prevents managers from making comparisons. In fact, Andrews and Henry (1963) found that managers did, indeed, make such comparisons. But secrecy undoubtedly makes it much more likely that managers must rely on indirect and often fallible information when they do so. One manager illustrated this point quite well when he stated in an interview, "I don't like to do it, but I can't help but look at other managers' houses, cars, and things and wonder if they are making more money than I do."

Two previous studies (Lawler, 1965; Lawler, 1967) have attempted to measure the effects of secrecy by focusing on how accurately managers preceive other managers' pay. In the first study, managers in four private companies and in three government agencies were asked in a questionnaire to estimate the average salary of managers in their organizations who were at their own level, one level above them, and one level below them. The results showed that, as expected, the managers did not have an accurate picture of what other managers were earning. However, the interesting facet of the data was the direction of the erroneous estimates of the managers. There was a general tendency for the managers to overestimate the pay of managers at their own level and at one level below them, while they tended to underestimate the pay of managers one level above them. In the government agencies where more information about pay was available, these tendencies were substantially reduced.

A second part of the questionnaire asked the managers how satisfied they were with their pay and how satisfied they were with the difference between their salaries and those of both their superiors and their subordinates. In general, the managers responded that the pay of both their superiors and their subordinates was too close to their own. The results also showed that those managers who felt their superiors' and subordinates' pay was too close to their own were the most dissatisfied with the level of their pay. The highest correlation existed when the downward difference was considered, with the greatest dissatisfaction occurring when the subordinates' earnings were felt to be too close. This finding is congruent with the work on equity theory, since when a manager perceives that his subordinate's pay is too close to his own it should make his input-outcome balance look unfair relative to that of one of his comparison groups. On the other hand, the perception that his superior's pay is too close to his own would not be expected to make a manager's own input-outcome balance look unfavorable. In fact, it should make it look more favorable.

The inaccurate perceptions of the managers in this initial study clearly point to the importance of determining what a person sees as well as the objective characteristics of the object he looks at in making his comparisons. The data show that managers have considerably distorted perceptions of the pay rates of their comparison groups. Without this distortion, it might be logical to assume that one of the sources of the managers' dissatisfaction was that the actual differences between their pay and that of their subordinates was too small. These data suggest that it may not be the actual size of this difference but the perceptually distorted size of this difference that was too small. In this instance, therefore, secrecy seems to have been contributing to dissatisfaction rather than reducing it. Given an ambiguous stimulus to interpret because of secrecy, these managers in effect were interpreting in a way that made their pay look worse by comparison to that of other managers. It is quite possible that if the managers had an accurate picture of the pay of their subordinates, they would be better satisfied with their own. Some evidence to support such a conclusion is provided by the fact that those managers who accurately perceived their subordinates' pay were better satisfied with the downward pay difference than were those managers who did not accurately perceive their subordinates' pay.

The data gathered in the initial study thus raised a number of questions about the possible negative impact of secrecy on the pay satisfaction of the members of organizations which enforce it. This concern about the possible hidden costs of secrecy prompted the second study, which was designed to replicate the basic findings of the initial study and to test empirically some of the speculation about the possible impact of secrecy that arose from the results of that study. Questionnaires were completed by 110 managers ranging in management level from supervisors to vice-presidents. The company studied was a manufacturing concern of about 3,000, and it had a policy of strict secrecy.

As in the previous study, the managers were asked to estimate the average annual salary of managers one level below them, at their own level, and one level above them. In addition, they were asked to estimate the salary of managers two levels below them and two levels above them. The data from this study showed the same strong trends which appeared in the previous one. There was a consistent tendency for the managers to underestimate their superiors' pay and to overestimate their subordinates' and peers' pay. It is interesting to note that both the trend to overestimate a subordinate's earnings and the trend to underestimate a superior's appeared even more strongly where the managers looked two levels instead of one level away from themselves. Apparently, it was not just the pay of their immediate superiors and subordinates that was misperceived by these managers, but the pay structure of the bulk of the organization. Thus any tendency for managers to feel dissatisfied with their own pay, because it was too low relative to that of their subordinates, was likely to be reinforced if the manager looked two levels below himself for a further comparison.

A question also included in the study was designed to measure the managers' satisfaction with the amount of their pay. It was expected, on the basis of the previous study, that those managers who overestimated the salaries of managers at their own level and at levels below themselves would be the most dissatisfied. It was not expected that incorrect estimation of the superiors' pay would be related to dissatisfaction, since the previous study had found little relationship between a manager's dissatisfaction with the difference between his pay and his superior's pay, and his satisfaction with the amount of his own. The results partially supported this expectation. When actual pay was held constant, overestimation by a manager of the pay of others at the same level was associated with his pay satisfaction. The more he overestimated the less satisfied he was with his salary. This finding is congruent with the belief that the relative value of pay is important in determining satisfaction, since overestimation of peers' earnings has the effect of making a manager's outcomes look smaller relative to those of one of his relevant comparison groups. However, incorrect estimation of superiors' and subordinates' pay was not found to be related to pay satisfaction. The most likely explanation for the failure to find a relationship between dissatisfaction with pay and the tendency to overestimate subordinates' pay is that in this situation lower level managers did not constitute a significant reference group for these managers; apparently their own management level in their company and perhaps managers outside their company constituted the most relevant comparison groups. This interpretation is congruent with the finding of Andrews and Henry (1963) that for one group of managers these were indeed the two most frequently chosen reference groups.

Further data of the effects of secrecy on pay comparison were gathered recently from seventy-five managers in a small company where secrecy prevailed. As in the previous studies, data were collected on the managers' estimates of what other managers around them in the organization earned as well as on the managers' satisfaction with their pay. In addition, a measure of the reference groups of the managers was included.

The same kind of errors of estimation that appeared in the previous studies also were found in this recent study. Managers tended consistently to overestimate the pay of their peers and of managers one and two levels below them while they tended to underestimate the pay of managers one and two levels above them. The average manager in this sample overestimated the salaries of his peers by almost five hundred dollars a year, an appreciable amount in a sample where the average salary is $13,600. They underestimated their superiors' pay by $1,700, also an appreciable amount. As in the original study, the managers reported that their own pay was too close to that of their subordinates. However, little dissatisfaction existed with the size of the difference between their salaries and those of their superiors. Dissatisfaction with the size of the difference between their own pay and that of their subordinates related to overall pay satisfaction. This finding was expected since the managers indicated that although they first looked to managers at their own levels in order to evaluate their earnings they considered their subordinates to be relevant for pay comparison purposes.

Based upon their effect on the degree to which an individual would see an equitable relationship between his inputs and outcomes, it was expected that the more the managers overestimated their subordinates' and peers' pay, the more dissatisfied they would be with their own. This prediction was consistently supported by the data; for example, overestimation of subordinates' earnings correlated .49 with pay dissatisfaction while overestimation of peers' pay correlated .25. High correlations also existed between the pay satisfaction of the managers and the absolute accuracy with which these managers estimated the pay of their subordinates, peers, and superiors. The greater the inaccuracy the lower the satisfaction. These data would appear to furnish strong evidence that the perceptual inaccuracies brought about by secrecy can lead to increased dissatisfaction.

It is not hard to see why this might happen. Most organizations try to structure their pay programs so that a fair relationship exists among the jobs. To the extent that organizations succeed in this, the more perceptual errors that occur in viewing the system, the more the system will appear to deviate from being fair. Hence, with errors a fair system will be perceived as an unfair one and dissatisfaction with pay will occur. It follows from this reasoning that it is the fair pay system that has the most to lose by practicing secrecy because errors inevitably will make the system look worse than it actually is.

Some additional data from this study served to emphasize the importance of distinguishing between the actual relative value of an individual's pay and his perception of its relative value. There was a significant relationship between a manager's pay satisfaction and how his salary compared with the actual average salary of a manager at his level. As expected, the more favorably a manager's salary compared with that of others doing the same job, the more satisfied he was. However, a stronger relationship existed when the difference between what he made and what he thought others made was computed and correlated with his satisfaction. In other words, his perceived relative standing predicted satisfaction better than did his actual relative standing. It is not surprising that much of the previous work on equity theory and relative deprivation has failed to emphasize the distinction between actual and perceived relative standing, since most previous studies have not considered a situation where secrecy about outcomes exists. In a situation where openness exists this distinction may indeed be academic, but where ambiguity exists it appears to have a considerable amount of explanatory power. It is quite possible that in day-to-day events ambiguity about others' outcomes is the rule rather than the exception.

It is difficult to see why managers should perceive the world in a manner that makes their own position worse than it is. Equity theory states that people seek to reduce feelings of inequity; yet these managers are perceiving the world in a manner that leads to high feelings of inequity. Thus the data do not appear to be predictable from equity theory. There are, however, some reasonable explanations for why these errors appear. The perception that their superior's pay is lower than it actually is can perhaps be interpreted as an attempt on the managers' part to feel closer to their superior and to create the feeling that they can obtain their boss's position. The overestimation of peers' and subordinates' pay may represent a fairly good reflection of the kind of information they receive about others' pay.

It is quite possible that a filter operates in organizations such that only information about good or high salaries gets put on the organization grapevine. This might occur because of a general hesitancy of managers to admit it if their salary is low. Higher paid managers, on the other hand, might be more likely to drop little hints about the size of their salaries. Regardless of its actual level, it does seem that the typical manager who gives out hints about his salary is more likely to give hints that will lead to high rather than to low interpretations by others. This would be expected because admission of low salary is, in our society at least, a partial admission of failure.

Overestimation of peers' and subordinates' pay also may be explained as a defensive reaction that protects the managers from future disappointments since in effect things are already so bad they can only get better. At this point, these explanations for the erroneous estimates are admittedly pure speculation on my part. It is hoped that in the near future some research will be directed toward what appears to be an important issue.

Taken together, the data from these three studies provide a considerable amount of evidence with respect to the impact of pay comparisons on satisfaction in situations where secrecy exists. Based upon the data, the following conclusions seem to be warranted.

First, managers evaluate their pay in terms of what other managers earn. Further, it is the relative value of pay rather than its absolute value that determines a manager's satisfaction with his own. Specifically, the data suggest that managers typically evaluate the adequacy of their pay by comparing it with the pay of other managers holding similar jobs. The importance of comparison with similar persons is suggested by Festinger's emphasis on this point in his theory of social comparisons. However, the data also point out that in some instances managers may also evaluate adequacy by comparing it with their superior's and subordinates' pay. The studies also generally suggest that the comparison with the subordinate's pay is more important in determining satisfaction than is the comparison with the superior's.

Second, the data point out that managers often erroneously perceive their relative pay standing. Thus, in understanding a manager's reactions to his pay, it is necessary to consider both his actual and his perceived relative pay standing. This conclusion is strongly suggested by the fact that perceived relative standing on pay predicted satisfaction better than did actual relative standing. It also is suggested by the fact that the size and direction of perceptual errors are consistently related to managers' satisfaction with their earnings. Equity and other theories that have been concerned with pay comparisons have tended not to emphasize the difference between the actual and perceived characteristics of the comparison object. The data on pay comparisons certainly suggest that it is important to consider both, particularly where a degree of ambiguity exists about the characteristics of the comparison object.

Finally, the data suggest that in making their pay comparisons, managers make systematic errors in estimating others' earnings and it seems that these errors lead to unfavorable comparisons. It is ironical that all the errors that managers make in estimating other managers' pay are in the direction that seems to lead to these comparisons being seen as more unfavorable than they actually are. In short, the kind of errors managers make seem to be perfectly designed to increase their pay dissatisfaction. Thus, secrecy about pay seems to contribute to rather than to reduce dissatisfaction, because it indirectly leads to pay comparisons being perceived as more unfavorable than they actually are.

SOCIAL COMPARISON THEORY AND PERFORMANCE FEEDBACK

The work on social comparison theory would appear to be directly relevant to the issue of how the size of a person's pay influences his attitudes toward the quality of his performance. Performance in most management jobs does not lend itself to absolute measurement. There are seldom any objective means against which managers can evaluate their performance. According to social comparison theory, this should lead managers to try to evaluate their performance by comparing it with the performance of others. When managers seek to compare their performance with others in order to evaluate it, money inevitably must come into play. In a society such as ours, a person's relative pay standing is one indicator of the value that others place upon his performance. Hence, it is one type of feedback to a manager about the quality of his performance.

The manager who receives low pay presumably is getting a message that his performance is poor, while the manager who is getting high pay presumably is being told that his performance is good. In this case, as in others, high and low pay, of course, refer to the relative standing of the person's pay. Thus, one prediction based upon social comparison theory would be that managers will need to evaluate their performance, and that one way they will evaluate it is by comparing the rewards they get (most notably pay) with the rewards similar others get for their performance. This proposition is, of course, based upon the view that money is for most a kind of score that reflects their proficiency in playing the game. Stated another way, it assumes that pay has meaning to managers somewhat similar to the meaning a review has for a playwright, or a tenth of a second for the runner in a hundred-yard dash. That is, it represents his score in the game.

Except for the basic research cited earlier, there is little evidence to support the contention that managers do evaluate their performance based upon how their pay compares to that of other managers. It does seem clear, however, that pay level does communicate to managers something about how well their boss considers them to be performing. Lawler (1966a) has found, for example, that managers do say that their rated job performance is one of the most important determinants of their pay. It stands to reason from this that the amount of pay a manager receives does indicate to him something about how his performance is evaluated by others. Whether it also has the effect of changing his evaluation of his performance is less clear, but it would seem likely that it frequently could. Since there are no absolute standards against which a manager can compare his performance, it would seem that his self-evaluation must at least partially reflect others' views of his performance. Still, there are situations where managers receive relatively low pay and yet still maintain that their performance is good. According to equity theory, one consequence of this would, of course, be feelings of dissatisfaction and also a need to correct this situation. One way to correct it is for the manager to lower his evaluation of his performance but, as equity theory points out, there are others. Little is known about under what condition a manager would be expected to lower his perceptions of his performance and when he would be expected to use one of the other methods of inequity reduction suggested by equity theory.

An interesting dilemma arises for the researcher considering both equity theory and social comparison theory when the object of concern is both an outcome that is being evaluated for fairness and an indication of performance. Social comparison theory appears to indicate that from performance indicators like pay individuals develop their perception of their performance and appropriately revise it. Equity theory stresses that the evaluation of the outcome will be based upon the person's estimate of his performance and that disagreement between pay level and perceived performance level may not lead to re-evaluations of perceived performance level. Obviously, there is a different emphasis in the two theories. Still, it seems likely that a person's perception of the relative size of his pay may influence his perceptions of his performance level and, perhaps more importantly for our purposes, that it does indicate to him how his superior evaluates his performance.

SECRECY AND PERFORMANCE FEEDBACK

The data reported on the kinds of errors people make in estimating how their salaries compare with other managers' salaries raise a number of interesting questions concerned with the kind of feedback managers receive about their own performance from the pay comparison process. If, as suggested by social comparison theory, managers look to the comparison between their pay and that of other managers at their own level for feedback about their performance, then the typical manager should receive negative feedback. This would come about because the overestimation of the pay of peers makes his own look worse in comparison to other managers' than it actually is. Hence, the typical manager may well feel that his performance is not being evaluated highly by his boss. At the very least, the manager is likely to get the impression that his boss is not evaluating his performance as highly as he does. How much of this negative feedback will affect his own conception of his performance is an open question. This type of feedback is only one of the pieces of information that a manager gets about his performance and certainly it is not likely to be the sole determinant of how he evaluates his own performance. However, even if this erroneous feedback does not change a manager's feelings about the adequacy of his performance, it may have other negative effects, the most likely of which would be to destroy the motivational aspects of the pay raise for the manager, and to confuse him about how his performance is evaluated.

No previous research exists that has focused upon the effect of secrecy on performance feedback. Thus, in order to attempt to measure more directly the relationship between pay perception errors and managers' reactions to how their performance is evaluated, questionnaire data were collected from 120 managers in two organizations. The decision was made to focus upon these managers' perceptions of their recent raises. Raises were dealt with rather than total salary because they represented the most recent feedback the managers received about their performance.

In one company, it was widely known that raises were given on an annual basis, but it was not known how large the raises were. In the other organization, just the opposite situation existed since everyone knew that the standard raise was 10 percent but secrecy was maintained with respect to how often they were typically given. In both companies there was general acceptance both by top managers and the managers studied of the fact that pay raises normally were based upon merit. Thus, in both organizations, the relative size and frequency of a manager's raises should be interpreted by a manager as an indication of how his performance is being evaluated. For these managers, therefore, their raises or lack of raises represent a kind of feedback about their performance from their superiors.

The data on how accurate these managers are in perceiving the average size of raises in the organization and how frequently they are given appear to be very comparable to those gathered for total salary. In the company where secrecy existed about the sizes of the raises given, managers overestimated the average size of the raise given to their peers. In the company where secrecy existed about the timing of raises, managers overestimated the frequency with which raises were given. Thus, in both cases, the managers were interpreting the ambiguous part of the raise-giving system in a way that made their own raise look worse than in reality it was. This seems to be directly analogous to the situation with total salary where other managers' total salaries were overestimated. In both cases, the consequence was that the managers saw their situation as being worse than it was. This would mean that the typical manager who compares his own raises with others might get the impression that his superior evaluated his performance more negatively than in fact was true. Some evidence that this happend in the present sample is provided by the fact that most managers rate their own performance more highly than they feel their superiors rate it. There is, of course, a strong relationship between how they evaluate their performance and how they feel their superiors rate it, but the typical manager feels his superior evaluates it significantly lower than he himself does. This might be expected from the negative feedback he is getting from his raises about his boss's evaluation.

The tendencies of managers to perceive their raises as relatively worse than they actually are is relevant to a point raised by Latané (1966). He points out that there are two possible motives for the comparison process. In addition to the self-evaluation motive, there may be a self-enhancement motive operating. He interprets Festinger's statement that in the case of abilities there is an undirectional drive upward to mean that social comparisons may serve as an ego-enhancing function. If this self-enhancement motive was crucial here, it is difficult to see why these managers would create a situation where their own raises look worse than in fact they are.

It may be that even though most managers get slightly more negative feedback about their performance from their raises than is intended, they still may be getting fairly accurate performance feedback from their raises about their relative standing. For example, in a situation where managers get a 4 percent raise when the actual average raise is 7 percent, the small raise still can have its intended effect of communicating to them that they are not performing well even though they assume the average raise is 9 percent. Admittedly, the overestimation will cause those managers who get 4 percent raises to feel their raise is relatively smaller than it actually is, but the clear message that performance is not satisfactory still may be communicated. Also, the high performer who overestimates the average raises of others may still feel that his large raise is a reward for good performance if he does not overestimate the size of other managers' raises by too much.

However, the negative effects of overestimation will be minimized only if most managers consistently tend to slightly overestimate the amount of other managers' raises and slightly underestimate the frequency with which raises are given. In any situation, there will be, of course, some variance in the managers' estimates. However, the crucial point concerns the size of the variance and whether it is related to the actual raises the managers receive. The greater the variance in these estimates the more raises will be misinterpreted because this will lead to large comparison errors being made. But more importantly, the closer the relationship between the variance in the errors and the actual size and frequency of the raises given the greater will be the misinterpretation of the raises. If, for example, the size of a manager's actual raise is closely related to his estimate of the average raise given, then the differential motivational and feedback effects of the raises will be almost entirely lost. A high correlation will lead to a situation where most managers will see their raises as having the same relative value. That is, every manager will feel that his raise is very similar to the average raise given in the organization. Thus, any motivational or feedback effects of giving different size raises will be obliterated because, on a comparison basis, the large raise will not look large to the recipient nor will the small raise look small.

The evidence from the two companies suggests that the differential feedback effects of the pay raise may have been obliterated in just this manner. In the second company where the crucial variance was in how often the raises were given, there was a correlation of .79 between the length of time the managers experienced between their last two raises and their estimates of the average length of time between raises. In the other organization, there was a correlation of .45 between the size of the managers' last raise and the degree to which they overestimated the size of the average raise given in the organization.

There is good reason to believe that, as expected, in both of the organizations the effect of these correlations was to eradicate the impact of the differential rewards. For example, in both organizations the managers typically reported that their last raise was an indication that their performance was acceptable. Very few managers stated that their last raise was an indication that their performance was poor despite the fact that a number of the managers received raises of as low as 2 percent. Interestingly, in neither organization was there a relationship between the size or frequency of a manager's raises and his feelings about how he evaluated his own performance, how he felt his superior evaluated his performance, or what he felt his last raise indicated about his superior's evaluation of his performance. This, of course, would be expected if the differential feedback effect of the raises had been wiped out by the inaccurate perceptions upon which the social comparison process was based.

Despite the fact that accurate comparisons are not easily made, it is possible to determine if social comparisons are still being made based upon the erroneous perceptions that exist. If this is occurring, then the managers' reactions to their raises should be based upon their perceived relative value rather than their absolute value. To test this point, the manager's perception of the frequency with which raises were given was compared with the time between their last two raises. In addition, the differences between the size of the managers' last raises and their perception of the average raise given was computed. In contrast to the actual frequency and size of the raises, the perceived relative value and frequency of the raises correlated significantly with some of the managers' attitudes toward their raises.

In the first organization, the perceived relative size of the raises correlated significantly with the managers' views of how favorably their superiors evaluated their performance, with whether they thought the raises were large enough, and with the degree to which the raises were perceived to be an indication of good performance. In the second organization, the perceived relative frequency of the managers' raises correlated significantly with their views of how favorably their superiors evaluated their performance, with whether their last raise was given soon enough, and with the degree to which their last raise was considered to be an indication of good performance. The fact that these relationships exist argues that managers do interpret their raises in terms of their perceived relationship to other managers' raises.

In neither company was there a very substantial relationship between the manager's evaluation of his performance and his past pay raise history. The perceived relative size and frequency of his raises showed only a slight relationship to his personal evaluation of his performance. Thus, it seems that although raise characteristics influence a manager's evaluation of how his superior evaluates his performance, it does not strongly influence his self-evaluation. This is not entirely unexpected since perceived superior's evaluation is only one of the factors that influences an individual's self-evaluation, and raise size presumably has to act through superior's evaluation in order to affect self-evaluation.

The correlation between a person's experiences with raises and his view of organization practice is not surprising. The typical manager operates in a vacuum as far as accurate information is concerned, with the only dependable input being his own experiences with the pay system. Thus, since his own history undoubtedly represents the basis for the typical manager's view of how the system operates, it would be expected that his history would influence his views on the subject. This still does not explain why there exists a general tendency for managers to see their own raises as relatively worse than they actually are. Possibly factors of the same kind that may lead to over-estimation of others' total salary operate here. That is, all the typical manager hears are references to the large salary increases other people get or the early raises others receive. In short, he may hear through the grapevine more information about the good raises than about the bad.

It seems very likely that one of the effects of the perceptual errors that exist among managers is to eliminate any positive motivational effects of the raises. Vroom (1964) has pointed out that accurate feedback about performance can be an effective motivator of good performance. Clearly, in this situation the raises are not giving accurate feedback to the managers about their performance. Differential raises, of course, are primarily given to managers in the hope of establishing the perception among them that in the organization performance is rewarded. This perception is expected to motivate them to perform effectively. Given the secrecy and confusion about what actually constitutes a large raise and the difficulty of knowing who is getting large raises, it is hard to believe that the raises are having their desired effect. Thus, it seems that the secrecy surrounding the raises given in these organizations may result in eliminating many of the potentially good effects intended by giving different-size raises based upon performance.

Taken together, the data on managers' perceptions of their raises suggest three conclusions.

First, managers appear to evaluate their pay raises in terms of their perceptions of other managers' raises. Specifically, the extent to which a manager perceives his raises as favorably comparable with those given other managers appears to influence his view of how his superiors appraise his performance. However, the absolute size and frequency of the raises seem to have little direct impact on the manager's reactions to his raises.

Second, the secrecy that exists leads managers to have rather inaccurate information about how their raises compare with other managers' raises. Specifically, the managers seem to overestimate the size of raise given to others and the frequency with which they are given.

Finally, the inaccurate social comparisons that are made as a result of the secrecy lead to managers receiving inaccurate feedback about other people's evaluation of their performance. Specifically, there seems to be a great leveling effect that creates a situation where most are getting feedback that indicates their performance is at best adequate. The degree to which this has an impact on their self-evaluation of their abilities and performance is much less clear. The net effect of the confusion would seem to be to eliminate any motivational effects that might be derived from the practice of giving differential rewards.

IMPLICATIONS FOR PRACTICE

The evidence with respect to the effects of secrecy both on satisfaction with pay and on the impact of raises suggests that secrecy causes a number of problems in the area of pay administration. Specifically, the data suggest that secrecy leads to high dissatisfaction with pay and to a situation where pay cannot be a motivator of good performance. Yet secrecy is widespread and there is no reason to believe that there is any great trend in organizations toward abandoning it and making pay information public. The reason for this reluctance is quite simply that the typical member of most organizations simply believes that secrecy is preferable to openness about salaries. Across a number of organizations, the data indicate that a good two-thirds of the members of management believe salary secrecy is best. However, it should be added that the suggestion that general information about salary ranges and midpoints be made public meets with considerably less opposition than does the suggestion that individual salaries be made public. Part of this concern about making pay public is undoubtedly warranted since there is no evidence to suggest that openness is an unmixed blessing. Although the data presented previously suggest openness might produce greater satisfaction and make pay a more effective motivator, there could be many problems created simultaneously.

One such problem is suggested by the fact that in the two companies studied above the greatest opposition to openness came from the lowest paid managers at each level. Clearly, for them openness would be very threatening since they suddenly would be identified as the lowest paid and perhaps the least valued manager at their level, which probably would be quite hard to tolerate. Openness about salaries also undoubtedly would alert some managers to the fact that they are underpaid, whereas previously they had been satisfied with their pay. This would seem to be particularly likely in organizations where salaries have been poorly administered in the past. Also, if earnings are made public, then managers who overestimate other managers' pay might feel that the company is simply a low paying organization where, although they are fairly paid relative to others, there is little chance for higher pay. Thus, many companies may have gotten themselves into a situation where their pay secrecy is causing feelings of internal inequity but where openness will lead to feelings that the company is poor-paying and externally inequitable.

Ironically, those firms that probably need openness the most are the ones where it would have the most trouble being accepted and where its implementation would cause the most problems. Firms that over the years have hidden their pay policies by secrecy typically have developed large inequities and inconsistencies in their system. Openness certainly would encourage them to correct these problems and perhaps prevent them from reoccurring, but, on the other hand, these are exactly the organizations that cannot tolerate openness because they realize they could not defend their policies.

In summary, the move to greater openness obviously would involve some gains and losses, but at this point the potential gains would appear to outweigh the losses. Perhaps the most important gain that can be expected from greater openness is that it will allow pay to be an incentive in the organization although it certainly will not automatically make it an incentive. With secrecy, however, it is difficult to see how the conditions can be created that are necessary if pay is going to operate as an incentive. Secrecy and incentive pay simply are not compatible.

REFERENCES

ADAMS, J. S. 1965. Injustice in social exchange. In *Advances in experimental social psychology,* ed. L. Berkowitz, vol. 2, pp. 267-99. New York: Academic Press.

ANDREWS, I. R., AND HENRY, M. M. 1963. Management attitudes toward pay. *Industrial Relations* 3:29-39.

FESTINGER, L. 1954. A theory of social comparison processes. *Human Relations* 7:117-40.

GORDON, B. F. 1966. Influence and social comparison as motives for affiliation. *Journal of Experimental Social Psychology,* Supplement 1, pp. 55-65.

HAKMILLER, K. 1966. Need for self-evaluation, perceived similarity and comparison choice. *Journal of Experimental Social Psychology,* Supplement 1, pp. 49-54.

HOFFMAN, P. J.; FESTINGER, L.; AND LAWRENCE, D. H. 1954. Tendencies toward group comparability in competitive bargaining. *Human Relations* 7:141-59.

HOMANS, G. C. 1961. *Social behavior: Its elementary forms.* New York: Harper & Rowe.

LATANÉ, B. 1966. Studies in social comparison—Introduction and overview. *Journal of Experimental Social Psychology,* Supplement 1, pp. 1-5.

LAWLER, E. E. III. 1965. Managers' perceptions of their subordinates' pay and of their superiors' pay. *Personnel Psychology* 18:413-22.

———. 1966. The mythology of management compensation. *California Management Review* 9:11-22*b*.

———. 1966. Managers' attitudes toward how their pay is and should be determined. *Journal of Applied Psychology* 50:273-79*a*.

———. 1967. Secrecy about management compensation: Are there hidden costs? *Organizational Behavior and Human Performance* 2.

LAWLER, E. E. III, AND PORTER, L. W. 1963. Perceptions regarding management compensation. *Industrial Relations* 3: 41-49.

———. 1966. Predicting managers' pay and their satisfaction with their pay. *Personnel Psychology* 19:363-73.

PATCHEN, M. 1961. *The choice of wage comparisons.* Englewood Cliffs, N. J.: Prentice-Hall.

SAYLES, L. R. 1958. *Behavior of industrial work groups: Prediction and control.* New York: John Wiley & Sons.

STOUFFER, S. A. et al. 1949. *The American soldier: Adjustment during army life,* vol. 1. Princeton, N. J.: Princeton University Press.

VROOM, V. H. 1964. *Work and motivation.* New York: John Wiley & Sons.

WHEELER, L. 1966. Motivation as a determinant of upward comparison. *Journal of Experimental Social Psychology,* Supplement 1, pp. 27-31.

30

Dissonance and Task Enhancement:
A Problem for CompensationTheory?[1]

KARL E. WEICK

A prominent expectation in compensation theory is that low pay leads to dissatisfaction. Many have tried to explain this relation, but surprisingly little has been done to learn what the worker does besides express dissatisfaction. The present paper examines the growing body of experimental literature suggesting that persons often respond to insufficient rewards with *increased* behavioral intensity; at times, even with heightened (instead of lessened) evaluations of their job assignments.

The common property in such experiments is that they contain discrepant cognitions salient to the task being performed. The discrepancies involve violated implications (Festinger, 1957), i.e., some of the salient cognitive elements may imply that other salient elements should either not be there or that they should be different. Task performance itself may be either central or peripheral to the violated implication. Central task involvement would occur if a worker agrees to spend a long time working at a clearly trivial task (e.g., copying nonsense syllables for eight hours). Peripheral task involvement would occur if a worker agrees to work on an ill-defined task for an inconsiderate supervisor paying him (the worker) less than the prevailing wage. The supervisor's manner and the underpayment would seem to imply that the worker should refuse the job; his acceptance of the

[1]Preparation of this paper was facilitated by Grant GS 1042 from the National Science Foundation.

Reprinted by permission of the author and publisher from *Organizational Behavior and Human Performance* 2, no. 2 (May 1967):189-208.

task violates the implication, and it is likely he will perform the job to reduce discomfort associated with the violation.

Given these two ways for task performance to yield discrepant cognitions, it is useful to detail a typical sequence of events in experiments designed to "lure" subjects into such dilemmas. Initially, negative properties of the work situation are made apparent to the subject. These may be embedded in the task by portraying it as worthless, insignificant or tedious; in the task-setter's behavior by being inconsiderate, brusque, belittling, cold; in the expected rewards by withholding them or by altering the relationship between work requirements and the quality or quantity of reward; or, in the behavior of a person's co-worker (he is more adept and belittles the subject, he ignores the subject, performs the easy, attractive portions of a joint task leaving the subject with the "dirty work," etc.). After the subject is clearly aware of the negative properties, he is made to believe that he can choose either to proceed with the assignment or not; and, after choosing to stay, he feels some responsibility for the decision. After all this, he performs the task; his quality and quantity of output are measured, or observations made of his goal-setting behavior and his persistence at essentially insolvable problems. When finished, the subject is asked to evaluate the task, his performance, and the task-setter.

Certain internal states are assumed to be created by the preceding events. As the negative properties become more apparent to the subject, he should feel tempted to leave, especially if he has an attractive competing activity. His usual reasons for not leaving are that he is somewhat uncertain what is ahead, he feels some embarassment about walking out on the experimenter, it may be difficult to "salvage" the hour with some other activity, etc. When given the choice to stay or leave, the subject reluctantly decides to stay, *but* his justification for this decision is minimal. If the subject were asked at this point, "why did you stay" the most common answer would be, "well, I thought this might be interesting," a common response even when the task itself has caused the discrepancy. Belief that a task might be interesting apparently affords a strong source of justification for an otherwise poor decision. But, task enhancement may be insufficient, especially since the subject must actually perform the task. Since persons are understandably concerned with the "correctness" of their beliefs (e.g., Festinger, 1954), we would expect that the subject would buttress this evaluation with actions showing that the task actually is worthwhile. In most cases, tasks become more interesting as persons expend more effort to accomplish them. Not only does intense effort increase the likelihood of task accomplishment, it also makes possible greater personal satisfaction from the performance (e.g., "I gave it all I had") and can, therefore, turn a potentially discomforting experience into a pleasurable one. Thus, performance associated with discrepant cognitions should be more intense than performance associated with consonant cognitions, and depending on the task requirements, higher productivity should be observed.

While the above reconstruction sketches only in the most gross fashion the hypothetical events that occur in conjunction with a task acceptance dilemma (Weick, 1966), it does help to show the varied ways in which this phenomenon has been investigated. The following section describes representative studies converging on this problem. The studies differ in several ways, but they all involve subjects performing some task other than simple evaluation for a time *after* they have been confronted with discrepant cognitions relating to task performance.

A SAMPLING OF RELEVANT EVIDENCE

Discrepant cognitions in work situations have been introduced in assigning the task, as a part of the task itself, or in relation to expected rewards for participating in the task. Most investigations have used a combination of these sources. While combining several sources of discrepancy makes interpretation difficult, such combination is justified conceptually because it is assumed that cognitive elements are additive and interchangeable and that it is the *ratio* of dissonant to consonant cognitions which determines the amount of discomfort associated with a discrepancy.

Localization of dissonance in the *assignment process* is shown in investigations by Weick (1964), Cohen, Greenbaum, and Mansson (1963), Zimbardo, Weisenberg, Firestone, and Levy (1965), and Freedman (1965). Weick's study (Weick, 1964) is most directly relevant to our present discussion. Male subjects agreed to work for a rude, inconsiderate experimenter who used deceit to lure them to the experiment, had spurious credentials as a psychologist, and who withheld credit for participating in the experiment that the subjects had expected to receive. In a concept attainment task, this group solved problems faster, made fewer errors, set more realistic levels of aspiration, retained more information, persisted longer at an insolvable problem, found the task more interesting, and said it was less important to receive credit for participating than a group working for a considerate experimenter. Procedural checks showed that subjects felt they could leave, that the experimenter indeed had been negative, and that persons who chose to leave (only 4 of 54) did not differ from those remaining. Cohen *et al.* (1963), in an elaborate experiment, found that subjects who were paid a slight amount ($1.00) to endure an additional period of social deprivation after they already had experienced considerable deprivation, showed less verbal conditioning than did subjects who were paid $5.00 to endure the additional deprivation. Zimbardo *et al.* (1965) confronted subjects with either a positive or negative communicator who tried to induce them to eat fried grasshoppers. The valence of the communicator did *not* affect the amount of overt compliance, but those complying with the negative communicator increased their liking for the grasshoppers significantly more than the subjects complying with the positive communicator. Apparently, the questionable action of complying with an unattractive communicator was "justified" by saying more nice things about the grasshoppers. Finally, Freedman (1965) showed that children given *mild* instead of *intense* threats to avoid playing with a very attractive toy avoided the toy and continued to avoid it in an unrelated experiment several weeks later.

The preceding studies though differing in procedures, subject populations, etc., all suggest that an experimenter's actions when assigning a task can produce discrepancies which are aligned when the person actually becomes engaged in the task. In each case, performance was compatible with the idea that it constituted additional justification to help resolve the discrepancy.

Studies closer to work settings and compensation questions have localized dissonance *in the task* instead of in the assignment process. Pallak (1966) gave subjects either high choice (high dissonance) or low choice (low dissonance) to spend an hour copying nonsense syllables. These choices produced dissonance not only because the task was trivial, but also because the subjects were told that they had satisfied their obligation merely by showing up and they could get credit and leave immediately. Pallak found that the high choice subjects recalled significantly more syllables after the task than the low choice subjects. The groups did not differ in their evaluation of the task although both found the task slightly more pleasant than a control group who merely performed it with none of the attendant discrepancies. Ryterband and King (1967) found that subjects choosing to perform the more bland and useless of two tasks (crossing out the letter E in pages of randomly ordered words) made significantly fewer errors than subjects given no choice. These investigators found no differences in quantity of output or liking for the task, but they did find that the "choice" subjects were more satisfied with their performance. Cohn (1964) embedded dissonance in a dyadic task by convincing the subject that the work partner whom he had chosen, and who would design tasks for him, was unattractive. Subjects with an unattractive partner initially solved concept attainment problems more slowly than persons paired with a more attractive partner, but after a "rigged" failure, dissonant subjects were significantly more productive and also were more reluctant to quit when faced with an insolvable problem. Weick and Penner (1966b) found that when a person was given the choice to work with an unattractive or attractive group, and was "guided" toward choosing the unattractive group, he cooperated with the unattractive members significantly more on a tracking task than did persons who were assigned to the unattractive group. The only study involving dissonance localized in the task not showing differences in productivity is Freedman's (1963) study. He told subjects to generate tables of random numbers for either an important or trivial project. Subjects perceiving the task as insignificant liked it more than those who saw it as important, but they did not differ in quantity generated.

The final prominent source of discrepancy is *rewards for performance*. When subjects arrive to perform the task they may find that they will earn more than they expected (e.g., Adams and Jacobsen, 1964; Weick and Penner, 1966a) or less than they expected (e.g., Ferdinand, 1965; Lawler and O'Gara, 1967; Weick and Penner, 1966a). Regardless of the direction in which the actual rewards diverge from the expected rewards, behavior is altered in ways that can be regarded as resolving the discrepancy. Lawler and O'Gara (1967) found that subjects underpaid on a piece-rate basis for obtaining interviews, collected more interviews of lower quality (measured by number of words per interview) than subjects equitably paid. The underpaid subjects saw the task as more interesting (thereby raising their otherwise inadequate outcomes) but they also saw it as simple, unchallenging, and unimportant (beliefs that aid in the reduction of inputs). Similar results are reported by Weick and Penner (1966a) and by Ferdinand (1965) using a tracking task and nonsense syllable learning respectively.

Comparing these studies yields some interesting trends. Differences in task performance were found in all studies except that of

Freedman (1963), these differences being least pronounced in Cohn's (1964) investigation and most apparent in Weick's (1964). Thus, there is support for the expectation that discrepancies are accompanied by changes in effort expenditure. But, the presumed cognitive mediation of effort expenditure by increased valuation of the task is on less stable ground. The majority of studies assessing task interest fail to show differences between high- and low-dissonance persons. While there are several ways in which the lack of linkages between beliefs and behavior might be explained (see Weick, 1966 for a discussion of this problem), it seems that a more fruitful direction might be to determine why one might expect to see differences in task behavior without any accompanying changes in beliefs about the task.

The remainder of this paper is directed toward describing a number of recurring properties of experimental situations that take on added importance when one tries to make sense out of the emerging pattern of findings. These properties suggest that it may not be necessary to postulate task enhancement to explain the effects of inconsistency on performance.

CONCEPTUAL AND PROCEDURAL AMBIGUITIES IN TASK ENHANCEMENT RESEARCH

The Hovering Experimenter

In every study—with the exception of those by Lawler and O'Gara (1967) and Freedman (1965)—the task setter was present the entire time of the subject's performance. This is important because the dilemmas discussed here are all performance-related. The experimenter is linked with the task and whatever additional aversive properties are present (i.e., a unit relationship exists, Heider, 1958). He assigns the negative task, or withholds rewards or acts in an offensive manner and thus he is responsible for the subject's plight. If he is present while the subject performs the task, his presence should serve to maintain dissonance or at least to remind the subject that he is working under less than optimal conditions. Continued presence of the experimenter should make it necessary for the subject to adopt a substantial resolution since the existence of a discrepancy is continually brought to his attention.

But the fact of the hovering experimenter creates additional problems of interpretation. The first of these concerns possible attempts by the subject to influence the experimenter's evaluation of him. Subjects may feel that the experimenter's actions imply that he has judged the subject to be unworthy or incompetent and that the rewards for performance were reduced accordingly. The subject can show the experimenter to be wrong by producing at a high level. The subject might also believe that if he works hard, the experimenter will reconsider his decision and give the subject full compensation for his efforts.

The argument so far has been that the experimenter may be perceived as someone who can be influenced. It is also conceivable that many of the manipulations used in the enhancement studies arouse sympathy rather than dislike for the experimenter. If an experimenter points to negative features of the experiment before the subject ever gets involved in it, this could imply that even though the experimenter may be inconsiderate, he at least is honest. If the experimenter then gives the subject the choice to stay in or leave the negative situation, he could become a rather attractive person, a person for whom the subject would be willing to work regardless of the consequences.

One final effect which the experimenter could have on performance—assuming now that he remains essentially a negative person—is that this could serve to relax the subject. Many persons (e.g., Riecken, 1962; Rosenberg, 1965) have noted that subjects are wary about the evaluations which experimenters make of their behavior. If an experimenter acts in a brusque, rude manner, the subject may be relieved of any concern about how the experimenter evaluates him. Once the subject becomes less concerned about being assessed, he may be able to devote more attention to the task.

Even though the experimenter is a prominent fixture in most experiments, his presence in studies of enhancement takes on added importance because he is so closely tied to the content of the dilemma. This close tie makes it more likely that he will be involved more fully in subjects' attempted resolutions. Investigators should either reduce the opportunity for the experimenter's behavior to afford avenues of resolution or systematically assess how the subject modifies his views of the experimenter.

The Locus of Choice

The status of choice in enhancement studies is not at all clear. In some studies subjects are not given a choice before they perform (e.g., Adams and Jacobsen, 1964; Freedman, 1963; Lawler and

O'Gara, 1967), whereas in other studies a choice is given in very close temporal proximity to actual performance (e.g., Pallak, 1966; Ryterband and King, 1967; Weick, 1964). Since choice has varied status in studies with roughly similar results, we might conclude that we can ignore choice as a crucial variable. This is premature, however, because "no choice" studies may still contain relevant choices. For example, both Lawler and O'Gara (1967) and Adams and Rosenbaum (1962) hired subjects to work on projects. When the subjects arrived for work, they found that conditions of pay were more or less attractive than they anticipated, but they had no opportunity to leave gracefully after discovering this. Should the initial decision to apply for the job be treated as a choice equivalent to a choice made at the time of task performance, should it be treated as a choice but different in kind, or should it be regarded simply as a situation of low choice? A subject's choice to volunteer for an experiment or to apply for a job may be the crucial one. If the experimenter overlays this choice with a second choice, "do you wish to stay or leave," the impact of the second choice may be slight.

It should also be noted that in many studies of enhancement effects, experimenters hedge the choice manipulation. Fearful that too many subjects will leave, they give a choice but also try to exert gentle pressure so that the "right" decision is made. Such procedural timidity makes it difficult to determine whether choice is or is not a significant variable. Fortunately, experimenters are becoming more bold in their manipulations of choice. Pallak (1966), for example, had confederates present at the time the experimenter read the initial instructions to the subjects. When the experimenter stated that the subjects could leave or stay, the confederates got up and left, thereby making it easier for the other subjects to leave if they wanted to. Even under these conditions the rate of leaving was not sizeable and those who left did not differ on measured characteristics from those who remained.

The Elusiveness of Negative Tasks

Negative tasks are a more elusive source of dissonance than many investigators have realized. It is difficult to create a task devoid of meaning for subjects. One way to make a task onerous is to say that a subject's data are useless (Freedman, 1963) or that his data will be discarded (Weick and Penner, 1966a). This type of manipulation might relax the subject and benefit his performance. Since the data are going to be ignored anyway, the subject has nothing to lose if he becomes involved in the task. Even if he should fail, no one will pay much attention to the failure. It is common for experimenters to avoid giving subjects much information about their performance; thus, there may be little difference between producing "useless" data and producing data with no feedback. Finally, the precise wording of the statement may make a difference in performance. The experimenter says the *data* are useless, not that the *task* is useless. This is left vague and it should still be possible for the subject to value the task independently of any of his results.

A surprising fact in many studies involving negative tasks is that the subjects really do not know that the task is negative when they make their choice. It is not uncommon in negative task manipulations to find that the subject is given only a brief, cursory, uninformative description of the supposedly negative task and is then given the choice to stay or leave. If this occurs, the choice should arouse minimal dissonance even though the eventual discovery of negativeness may be bothersome. But, if the subject finds out that the task is negative some time after the choice is made, it is difficult to know whether the situation should be analyzed as one in which dissonance was created by a *fait accompli* (Brehm, 1959) or whether several other processes might now explain the results.

The fact of task ambiguity at the choice point assumes additional importance because of a rather puzzling finding that occurs in many enhancement studies. Frequently, a subject is made uncomfortable precisely because he agrees to perform the task knowing full well that it is unattractive. If this occurs, the task should be relatively immune from evaluation change—the initial irreversible negativity created the dilemma—and other evaluative changes would be required to restore consonance. And yet, it is often reported that the subject reverses himself in his evaluation. Even though he supposedly was made uncomfortable because the task was negative, he states at the conclusion of the experiment that the task actually was quite enjoyable. Our argument is that the task was sufficiently vague at the start of the experiment that it never was an intense source of discomfort, the subject had only the most elementary ideas concerning its content and demands, and therefore, when he actually performed the task, he had considerable latitude to alter his evaluations and performance of it. Unless the experimenter permits the subject to have several practice trials with the task *before* a choice is made (e.g., Pallak, 1966), the evidence is equivocal that the subject knew the task was negative.

It is possible that task enhancement and effort expenditure occur jointly largely when the work situation is ambiguous and permits considerable cognitive realignment. If this is true, it puts an important limiting condition on the phenomenon but it does not argue that the phenomenon is any less important.

Equivocal Control Groups

As was evident from the earlier review of enhancement research, situations for studying this phenomenon are complex. Numerous cognitive elements confront the subject, many involving contradictory implications for action. It is sometimes difficult to be certain what is happening, especially in control groups. Control groups typically are established by reducing the magnitude of the discrepancy relative to that created in the experimental group. The means of reduction is either to force subjects to perform under negative working conditions (the more coercion, the less need there is to justify a situation) or to make their working conditions less aversive than those of the experimental groups.

If one examines the behavior of control groups the difficulty of knowing what is happening to them becomes even more apparent. Cohn (1964) reports that his subjects who were given the choice to work with a neutral partner were the least motivated of all groups. Weick and Penner (1966a) report that their control group (paid $1.50 for one hour of work on a task of moderate importance) was the least productive of any group and also expressed the most dislike for the task. Pallak (1966), as noted earlier, found that both his experimental and control group engaged in some task enhancement. The point of these illustrations, is that as yet, it is not clear whether choice increases productivity or whether the withholding of choice suppresses productivity. In short, appropriate, meaningful baseline data are seldom available.

Closer attention should be paid to the problem of appropriate baselines, but other alternatives might be explored. The use of subjects as their own controls, while admittedly a precarious venture in this type of research, might be considered as a possible solution. The postponement of dissonance induction until some time after the person has become accustomed to the task would permit more accurate before-after measurements. The alteration of reward conditions midway through the exercise (e.g., Crespi, 1942; Zeaman, 1949) would permit a more definitive appraisal of the content of resolutions.

Coercion or the withholding of choice seems capable of eliciting several responses other than reduced dissonance, and in the face of this possibility it becomes more crucial to establish stable baselines to determine more accurately the precise efforts of inconsistency on performance.

Remote Behaviors as Dependent Variables

Problems in interpreting task enhancement studies are sometimes compounded because task behaviors quite far removed from the dilemma itself are used to assess the effects of inconsistency. When this occurs, the subject may already have resolved the discrepancy by the time he gets to the task of interest to the experimenter. Moreover, some behaviors used to assess the effects of enhancement are so global and incidental, that it is hard to tell exactly how inconsistency may affect their performance.

Lawler and O'Gara's (1967) use of an interviewing task illustrates this problem. Underpaid subjects were expected to collect more interviews of lower quality in a two-hour period than persons paid the standard wage. Several measures relevant to this hypothesis were not collected even though they might have provided more explicit confirmation of it. Quality was assessed by number of words recorded and by a brief content analysis of the interview protocols. A more direct measure of quality might be the area in which the interviewers chose to obtain their data. It seems clear that some areas would have small numbers of highly informed respondents and others would have larger numbers of relatively uninformed respondents. Subjects concerned with quality would be more likely to seek respondents who could contribute significant opinions. Quality measures could also have been estimated by noting how often interviewers prodded taciturn respondents or squelched overly talkative ones. The relative neatness of the interview records could provide additional data. Our point is simply that global measures may mask subtle ways in which the inequity is resolved and if the inequity is resolved in these more subtle ways, predicted differences may fail to appear in global dependent variables even though the hypothesis actually is correct. The problem of knowing in advance which behaviors will reflect attempts to resolve inconsistency is sizeable. We are not trying to minimize this problem. Instead, we are simply urging that greater attention be paid to behaviors close in time and space to the dilemma and that investigators not rely solely on massive actions to the exclusion of subtle, discrete, actions.

Arousal and Behavioral Vigor

So far it has been argued that differences in effort sans differences in evaluation might occur because of attempts to influence the experimenter, felt sympathy for the experimenter, relaxation in the face of lessened concern about evaluation, superfluous choices, latitude for redefinition of negative tasks, suppression of productivity in control groups, and remote indices of performance. While this may appear to be an imposing (and possibly overwhelming) array of alternative interpretations, an additional set of explanations tied more closely to general behavior theory remain to be explored. Their potential relevance should become clear in the following discussion.

Persons who work with inconsistency models have often been chided (e.g., Cofer and Appley, 1964, p. 798) because they do not anchor their findings in some of the more venerable areas of psychology. In the case of enhancement studies, the situations parallel those examined in more traditional areas of inquiry, consequently, there are several potential mechanisms which might account for the results.

Emotion and cue utilization. Easterbrook (1959) has proposed the following provocative generalization: " . . . emotional arousal acts consistently to reduce the range of cues that an organism uses, and . . . the reduction in range of cue utilization influences action in ways that are either organizing or disorganizing, depending on the behavior concerned" (p. 183). The essence of Easterbrook's argument is that as drive increases, the number of cues which the subject observes, orients to, or associates with responses, declines. Furthermore, as the shrinkage of cues occurs, peripheral (task-irrelevant) cues are excluded before central (task relevant) cues are. This means that as drive level increases, peripheral responses are impaired whereas central responses are augmented. Thus the following relationship between drive and proficiency is predicted. If it is assumed that the simultaneous use of task-irrelevant and task-relevant cues reduces the efficiency of a response, then as drive level increases, the range of cue utilization will decrease and irrelevant cues will be the first ones to be ignored. Thus initially performance should be enhanced as the subject concentrates more fully on task-relevant cues. However, when all of the irrelevant cues have been excluded, then relevant cues will begin to be excluded and when this occurs, proficiency should decline.

Tasks obviously vary in the complexity of responses demanded. As tasks become more complex, as more task-relevant cues are required for performance, and as there is "less surplus capacity available for response to irrelevant cues," arousal and restriction of cue utilization should produce a decrease in performance because relevant cues are immediately affected. However, as tasks become less complex, both relevant and irrelevant cues are attended to. When drive is increased on a simple task, performance should improve since it is the irrelevant cues that drop out first. Easterbrook cites continuous tracking as an example of a simple task in which increased drive should facilitate performance. Examples of complex tasks in which increased drive should impair performance, include Porteus mazes (1956), mirror tracing, or memory span for digits.

The relevance of notions of emotional arousal and cue utilization to the present discussion of task enhancement should be obvious. First, it is clear that most situations of discrepancy have emotional accompaniments. Adams (1965) notes that inequity can produce either anger or guilt, and a cursory inspection of other manipulations described earlier suggests that irritation, embarrassment, hostility, etc. are often evoked. Furthermore, discrepancies have noxious properties which subjects try to avoid; they contain elements of uncertainty or disconfirmed expectancies that heighten arousal, and they elicit immediate and concerted attempts at tension reduction. If the fact of arousal is coupled with the notion of variations in cue utilization, it is possible to argue that what happens in a task acceptance dilemma is that variations in the amount of discrepancy produce variations in arousal, and that these in turn lead to greater or lesser intrusion into performance of task-irrelevant cues. Exploration of this possibility could occur if peripheral tasks were added to enhancement studies. If the cue utilization hypothesis is correct, we would expect that as dissonance increases, the central task would be performed more efficiently and the peripheral task less efficiently, whereas the opposite should occur for low dissonance subjects (see Bahrick, Fitts, and Ranken, 1952 for a prototype of this experiment). If these results were obtained, they would be difficult to derive from a strict application of dissonance theory. Furthermore, it is unnecessary to postulate an evaluative mediation of the process if these results are obtained.

Frustration. One of the more venerable findings in the extensive literature concerning frustration is that responses which occur shortly after frustration are more intense than they were prior to frustration (e.g., Brown, 1961; Lawson, 1965). While few agree whether this behavioral increment is motivational (due to an increase in drive level) or associative (learned responses to frustration are elicited), there is agreement that the effect occurs. There are interesting similarities between operations designed to create frustration and those designed to produce task-related discrepancies.

It could be argued that we are doing no great service to enhancement research by subsuming it under a concept, frustration, that is almost as complex and diverse in its meanings as is cognitive dissonance. However, evaluation of enhancement studies in light of concepts derived from frustration theory seems warranted because of methodological parallels and because frustration theory has more to say about determinants of performance. At an informal level of definition, Cofer and Appley (1964, p. 412) observe that frustration occurs when an expected outcome or consequence fails to materialize. Stated more formally, frustration is "that point in a response-shifting series which follows the failure (or anticipated failure) of available responses to attain the desired goal. In other words, only when normal coping behavior fails (or its likelihood of failure is anticipated) does the new process come into play" (p. 416). It is probable that the following are included among the "desired goals" of persons engaged in task performance: being treated as a worthy, competent person; having sizeable discretion over work activities; working for sympathetic, helpful supervisors; performing meaningful, interesting tasks; receiving equitable compensation for effort expended; etc. In most of the manipulations used to create discrepancy, one or more of these goals is thwarted. The thwarting occurs either because stimuli which maintain a behavioral sequence are removed (e.g., expected wages are reduced, approval from the supervisor for work is withheld) or because incompatible responses are elicited (e.g., the worker is tempted both to stay and perform the task and to leave for a possibly more attractive alternative activity).

Possible behavioral effects of frustration are suggested in a relatively neglected series of papers by Child and Waterhouse (1952, 1953; Waterhouse and Child, 1953). They focus attention on conditions where frustration can produce an *increment* in the quality of performance. They argue that frustration produces *both* response interference and a change in drive level. The effects of these dual changes on performance depend on the past history of the individual and the present situation. Two types of situations are distinguished depending on whether one or two activities are being performed. In the two activity situation, the first activity is frustrated and it affects the quality of performance in the second activity whereas in the one activity setting frustration and changes in quality occur in the same activity. It is unclear whether enhancement studies involve one or two activities. It could be argued that a single activity is involved, namely, participating in an experiment. On the other hand it could be argued that the studies involve two activities, spending a finite period of time in return for some reward and performing a task. Support for the view that experiments involve two activities is found in recent formulations which distinguish between the decision to participate and the decision to produce (e.g., March and Simon, 1958; Thibaut and Kelley, 1959). While it will be necessary to define more explicitly which category is more appropriate for enhancement experiments, it is interesting to review briefly the reasons in both situations why frustration might increase the quality of performance.

When two activities are involved and frustration occurs in the first one, performance of the second activity may be facilitated because (1) the second activity serves as a substitute for the first one, (2) the second activity permits the subject to escape from reminders of the initial frustration, and (3) the second activity would have normally been performed at a low level of intensity. It is the latter possibility which is of particular interest here because it is often argued that persons who participate in experiments seldom become involved in the assigned task. Child and Waterhouse (1953) describe the possibility of motivational enhancement in the following way: frustration in one activity may increase the quality of performance in a second activity "when the person was previously especially unmotivated with respect to the second activity, for it is then supposed that quality of performance may be favorably influenced by increased drive more than it is unfavorably influenced by interference" (p. 129). Thus if a subject was indifferent about performing well on the assigned task, the fact that the basis for participation was thwarted could heighten task performance.

If participation in a task enhancement study is conceived as a single activity, there are additional reasons why frustration might increase the quality of performance. These reasons derive from Hull's (1934) notion of a "habit family hierarchy." It is hypothesized that when frustration occurs, the habit strength of the most prepotent response is reduced (initial response is *not* reinforced) and that as the strength of the prepotent response declines, other responses in the hierarchy appear. Whether the quality of performance will decrease or increase under these conditions depends upon the response sequences that are lower in the hierarchy. Suppose that we take seriously the argument that subjects tend to be cautious in experiments because of apprehension about how they will be evaluated. Assume that the tendency to be cautious, to produce an average performance, is the strongest tendency when subjects arrive at an experiment. Now suppose that the activity of participating in an experiment is frustrated when expected rewards for participation fail to materialize. The rewards which maintain the response sequence of cautious performance are removed, consequently, the strength of this response is lessened. Now, if the next response in the habit family heirarchy is more achievement and task oriented, then the initial tendency toward caution should be replaced by behavior which is more task relevant and productive. Admittedly there are a host of "ifs" in this hypothetical situation, but portions of the analysis seem plausible if we pool the several notions about subject behavior that have been advanced. Furthermore, the possibility that an achievement orientation could supplant caution when response tendencies are thwarted is at least consistent with the findings that persons with high dissonance exhibit an achievement-oriented pattern of goal-setting (Weick, 1963), and that persons with dissonance persist significantly longer in the face of insolvable problems than do persons with lesser dissonance (e.g., Cohn, 1964; Weick, 1964).

While numerous additional relationships between frustration and performance could be cited, the preceding should suggest ways in which this body of research extends our thinking about mechanisms for performance enhancement. However, we should be explicit concerning how these extensions are helpful and the stature they assume. Extrapolations from frustration theory should be made with caution since many of these concepts derive from research with infra-human species. While it is not the intent of the present discussion to debate the usefulness of such data, this limitation should be recognized. While the preceding explanations may appear cumbersome and the fit between properties of enhancement studies and frustration studies strained, it should be noted that some of this ill fit is due to the complexity of the enhancement studies and some is due to the rather labored summaries we have made of this literature. There appears to be more parsimony in concepts associated with frustration theory than our discussion might suggest.

Perhaps the most important outcome of examining the relevance of frustration theory for enhancement research, is that it directs attention to several concrete questions. For example, individual difference variables assume much greater importance. It becomes more essential to know habitual modes of responding to frustration (e.g., does the person tend to persist or withdraw in the face of frustration). What is the prevailing level of motivation when persons perform tasks and are not encumbered by the trappings of evaluation associated with laboratory experimentation? What is the likelihood that when a person's usual coping responses to frustration are exhausted, he will produce novel responses that facilitate or hinder task performance? What is the meaningful unit of analysis in studying participation in experiments as a set of activities? How many activities are engaged when subjects participate in experiments and what is the interrelationship among these activities? Finally, it becomes important to determine the specific demands associated with different experimental tasks. In some tasks, frustration produced response interference could be more crucial than energizing effects whereas in other tasks, the opposite could occur.

It should be clear that these questions can be answered, but it is unlikely that they will be answered by a few elaborate studies. Instead, systematic inquiry based on more limited questions will probably be necessary. While several additional areas within traditional psychology could be tapped for further leads to explain the effects of discrepancy on performance, the preceding sample is sufficient to illustrate the fruitfulness of such probing. Clearly, many of the conjectures we have advanced are wrong or inadequate to explain the obtained results. The point is that if research on enhancement is tied more explicitly to previous research, earlier findings can be built upon, direction can be given to inquiry, and venerable problems can be confronted with relevant new data.

CONCLUSION

By now it may seem that we are quite far afield from problems of compensation. Actually we are not. Solutions to questions about compensation can only come after systematic inquiry has clarified the ambiguities that have been pointed out. Certainly, studies of task enhancement can add important knowledge to help in understanding the dynamics of wage compensation. Such studies pose a view of wage issues differing sharply from many of the constructs of the prevailing instrumental model (e.g., Vroom, 1964). Yet, tempting as it may be to extrapolate task-enhancement results to real world settings, it is clear that this is not yet warranted because of the many puzzles still to be worked out.

In fact, we may well ask whether or not a consistent body of findings has even been shown to exist. Research summarized in this paper is, after all, extremely heterogeneous. But this is partly a function of the purpose we stated at the outset; that is, to pull together studies focusing on the behavioral consequences of inconsistency. To be sure, different interests are represented in the studies, but they *all* yield implications related to inconsistency and performance, and by comparing their outcomes, we have been able to suggest certain properties that may account for the emerging pattern of results. Now, we can see more clearly where research is needed to complete the picture.

Conceptually, the occurrence of changes in performance in the absence of task enhancement is most interesting. This pattern is so frequent that it is likely that the phenomenon of task enhancement is mislabeled. Instead of enhancement occurring and leading to increased effort, it appears that just the opposite sequence occurs, namely behavioral change is followed by occasional attempts to summarize the experience evaluatively. It is conceivable that properties of task acceptance dilemmas produce invigoration of behavior leading to outcomes which subjects *perceive* as either successful (they like the tasks) or as failing (they dislike the tasks). Coupling notions taken from theories of frustration and cue utilization with concepts from level of aspiration research (Lewin, Dembo, Festinger, and Sears, 1944) leads to a possible *post hoc* explanation for findings summarized earlier. This analysis does not reduce its relevance for cognitive dissonance theory. It does suggest, as Gerard (1965) has recently argued, that more attention should be given to studies in which the initial operation of a dissonance resolution involves behavior change and this in turn produces changed evaluations.

Procedurally, the implication of the present paper is that enhancement should be studied both in simpler and in more complex settings than have been used to date. Simpler settings afford more definitive study of processes mediating discrepancy and performance. For example, Weick and Prestholdt (1966) recently adapted Findley's (1962) "switching procedure" to study whether persons who choose to work when underpaid revise their valuations of the importance of money. Their procedure measures the preferences of subjects for working for money or for feedback information. Preliminary results suggest that as dissonance increases, subjects tend more often to *avoid* reinforcement schedules involving monetary return.

The value of studying enhancement in more complex, natural settings is that pressures from evaluation apprehension are reduced;

workers have more diffuse interests than laboratory subjects; and the occurrence of discrepancies is a more common fact of life in organizations. These conditions should make it more difficult to demonstrate enhancement effects. But if they *do* occur in more natural settings, they should be taken seriously. Numerous formats for such naturalistic studies could be proposed. Introducing automated work procedures furnishes a good example. Suppose there are two groups of workers, Group A performing an interesting task and Group B performing a boring task. Suppose further that the firm decides to automate both jobs and that the workers have some feeling of participating in the decision. The automated procedure should decrease the attractiveness of work for Group A and increase it for Group B. The question is, which group will like the automated job more and be more conscientious concerning its implementation and maintenance? From the preceding analyses we would suggest that Group A will show more liking for and productivity with the automated procedure than Group B. Group A has less justification for their decision, and to heighten justification, they will become more absorbed in the new job. Outlandish as this prediction may appear, it is consistent with much of the research cited in this paper, and has sufficient relevance to contemporary issues that it would seem worthy of investigation.

The title of this paper posed the question, is task enhancement a problem for compensation theory? The most realistic answer seems to be, not yet. But given a concerted attempt to remove many of the ambiguities in this research, a very different answer can be in the offing.

REFERENCES

ADAMS, J. S. Inequity in social exchange. In L. Berkowitz (Ed.), *Advances in experimental social psychology.* Vol. 2. New York: Academic Press, 1965. Pp. 267-299.

ADAMS, J. S., AND JACOBSEN, PATRICIA R. Effects of wage inequities on work quality. *Journal of Abnormal and Social Psychology,* 1964, **69,** 19-25.

ADAMS, J. S., AND ROSENBAUM, W. B. The relationship of worker productivity to cognitive dissonance about wage inequities. *Journal of Applied Psychology,* 1962, **46,** 161-164.

BAHRICK, H. P., FITTS, P. M., AND RANKEN, R. E. Effect of incentives upon reactions to peripheral stimuli. *Journal of Experimental Psychology,* 1952, **44,** 400-406.

BREHM, J. W. Increasing cognitive dissonance by a fait-accompli. *Journal of Abnormal and Social Psychology,* 1959, **58,** 379-382.

BROWN, J. S. *The motivation of behavior.* New York: McGraw-Hill, 1961.

CHILD, I. L., AND WATERHOUSE, I. K. Frustration and the quality of performance: I. A critique of the Barker, Dembo and Lewin experiment. *Psychological Review,* 1952, **59,** 351-362.

CHILD, I. L., AND WATERHOUSE, I. K. Frustration and the quality of performance: II. A theoretical statement. *Psychological Review,* 1953, **60,** 127-139.

COFER, C. N., AND APPLEY, M. H. *Motivation: theory and research.* New York: Wiley, 1964.

COHEN, A. R., GREENBAUM, C. W., AND MANSSON, H. H. Commitment to social deprivation and verbal conditioning. *Journal of Abnormal and Social Psychology,* 1963, **67,** 410-421.

COHN, A. Behavior with and attractiveness of a partner as functions of choice and negative information. Hofstra Univ., Unpublished manuscript, 1964.

CRESPI, L. P. Quantitative variation of incentive and performance in the white rat. *American Journal of Psychology,* 1942, **55,** 467-517.

EASTERBROOK, J. A. The effect of emotion on cue utilization and the organization of behavior. *Psychological Review,* 1959, **66,** 183-201.

FERDINAND, P. R. The effect of forced compliance on recognition. Paper presented at Midwestern Psychological Association, 1965.

FESTINGER, L. A theory of social comparison processes. *Human Relations,* 1954, 7, 117-140.

FESTINGER, L. *A theory of cognitive dissonance.* Evanston, Ill.: Row, Peterson, 1957.

FINDLEY, J. D. An experimental outline for building and exploring multioperant behavior repertoires. *Journal of the Experimental Analysis of Behavior,* 1962, **5,** 113-168.

FREEDMAN, J. L. Attitudinal effects of inadequate justification. *Journal of Personality,* 1963, **31,** 371-385.

FREEDMAN, J. L. Long-term cognitive dissonance. *Journal of Experimental and Social Psychology,* 1965, **1,** 145-155.

GERARD, H. B. Deviation, conformity, and commitment. In I. D. Steiner and M. Fishbein (Eds.), *Current studies in social psychology.* New York: Holt, Rinehart, and Winston, 1965. Pp. 263-277.

HEIDER, F. *The psychology of interpersonal relations.* New York: Wiley, 1958.

HULL, C. L. The concept of the habit-family hierarchy and maze learning. *Psychological Review,* 1934, **41,** 33-52, and 134-152.

LAWLER, E. E., III., AND O'GARA, P. The effects of inequity produced by underpayment on work output, work quality, and attitudes toward work. *Journal of Applied Psychology,* 1967. In press.

LAWSON, R. *Frustration: The development of a specific concept.* New York: Macmillan, 1965.

LEWIN, K., DEMBO, TAMARA. FESTINGER, L., AND SEARS, PAULINE S. Level of aspiration. In J. Mc. V. Hunt (Ed.), *Personality and behavior disorders.* Vol. 1, New York: Ronald, 1944. Pp. 333-378.

MARCH, J. G., AND SIMON, H. A. *Organizations.* New York: Wiley, 1958.

PALLAK, M. S. Task performance and dissonance reduction processes. Yale Univ., Unpublished manuscript, 1966.

PORTEUS, S. D. Porteus maze developments. *Perceptual and Motor Skills,* 1956, **6,** 135-142.

RIECKEN, H. A program for research on experiments in social psychology. In N. F. Washburne (Ed.), *Decisions, values, and groups.* Vol. 2. New York: Pergamon, 1962. 25-41.

ROSENBERG, M. J. When dissonance fails: On eliminating evaluation apprehension from attitude measurement. *Journal of Personality and Social Psychology,* 1965, **1,** 28-42.

RYTERBAND, E. C., AND KING, D. C. An investigation of the effects of cognitive dissonance on resistance to change. *Organizational Behavior and Human Performance,* 1967. In press.

THIBAUT, J. W., AND KELLEY, H. H. *The social psychology of groups.* New York: Wiley, 1959.

VROOM, V. H. *Work and motivation.* New York: Wiley, 1964.

WATERHOUSE, I. K., AND CHILD, I. Frustration and the quality of performance. *Journal of Personality,* 1953, **21,** 298-311.

WEICK, K. E. The effect of cognitive dissonance on level of aspiration. Paper presented at Midwestern Psychological Association, May 4, 1963.

WEICK, K. E. Reduction of cognitive dissonance through task enhancement and effort expenditure. *Journal of Abnormal and Social Psychology,* 1964, **68,** 533-539.

WEICK, K. E. Task acceptance dilemmas: a site for research on cognition. In S. Feldman (Ed.), *Cognitive consistency.* New York: Academic Press, 1966. Pp. 225-255.

WEICK, K. E., AND PENNER, D. D. Justification and productivity, Univ. of Minn., Unpublished manuscript, 1966a.

WEICK, K. E., AND PENNER, D. D. The effect of discrepant group membership on cooperation. Univ. of Minn., Unpublished manuscript, 1966b.

WEICK, K. E., AND PRESTHOLDT, P. Dissonance and the realignment of reinforcement value. Univ. of Minn., Unpublished manuscript, 1966.

ZEAMAN, D. Response latency as a function of the amount of reinforcement. *Journal of Experimental Psychology,* 1949, **39,** 466-483.

ZIMBARDO, P. G., WEISENBERG, M., FIRESTONE, I., AND LEVY, B. Communicator effectiveness in producing public conformity and private attitude change. *Journal of Personality,* 1965, **33,** 233-255.

31

Some Unanswered Problems
About Management Compensation

This paper has two major goals. First, to clarify some of the major persisting problems in management compensation by indicating why they became problems originally and why they remain so today. Second, to suggest some new lines of thinking about these questions, approaches which we believe have some promise of leading to better theory and, consequently, better practice in the area.

How Can Money Be Used as a
Stimulant to Better Performance?

The use of money as a stimulant to better performance is probably the most important question management can ask from the viewpoint of the organization. It also is probably the question which has been discussed more, and about which more has been written, than any other single question in this area. Despite such concern, few would doubt that we are not much closer to answering this question today than we were at the dawn of organizational life. Why the lack of productivity?

Doubtless there are many reasons, but one in particular will be explored here since (*a*) it strikes at the very core of our traditional conceptions about the nature of money and the nature of people; (*b*) it is based on a great deal of research evidence, experimental and otherwise; and (*c*) it suggests a new way to view compensation procedures in industry, a way which is radically different from the

---

Printed by permission of the author. Unpublished paper, New York University, 1969.

traditional modes of thinking but which might be considerably more effective if our goal is to have such practices serve as stimulants to performance. Traditionally, compensation has been used as a stimulant to performance by making its attainment contingent upon performance, with the level of income to be attained being determined by the person's level of performance. The basic model for this, of course, at the sub-managerial level is known as "piece-rate" pay, but the logic is the same at the higher levels when we talk of "incentives" and, less frequently, more esoteric "performance contingency" rewards. In its most basic sense, the procedure consists simply of telling a person that if he works harder he will make more money, and if he does not he will make less.

We shall not bother reviewing the hoary arguments as to the advantages and disadvantages of incentives. The list is long and well-known. Suffice it to say that neither side has ever convinced the other, for whenever one side comes up with one "telling point" or "crucial study," the reply is usually quick and devastating from the other side. All that can be said at this point is that while sometimes incentives work, sometimes they do not (Opsahl and Dunnette 1967), and we still do not have a very good answer to the question with which we began this section; that is, if we remain glued to the incentive approach.

We would hypothesize that the best way of resolving this dilemma stems from an increasing convergence of research findings which question the very philosophical assumption upon which incentive theory is based and which argue instead for a radically different view of man. Such a view has the double advantage of both reconciling some of the puzzling, paradoxical findings in the research literature and providing an explicit guide as to how management may use compensation to stimulate performance. Although many questions remain, the relatively firm empirical grounding of this newer view provides some basis for optimism that compensation policies eventually may be considered stimulants to performance with better than chance expectancy of success.

This newer view of man differs from the more traditional view in that it argues man does not seek better outcomes and more desirable outcomes than those he is used to and thinks he deserves. It is suggested that this optimistic view, which is inherent in incentive theory, does not jibe with the increasing trend of evidence which says that man seeks not better but "consistent," "just" outcomes, that is, those outcomes which he sees as being in balance and congruent for an individual such as himself in that given situation. In other words, according to this point of view, if we wish to understand the outcomes which a person is motivated to achieve in any given job situation, we must understand what he thinks would be a "just" or "congruent" outcome for a person such as himself in that given situation, *since it is these outcomes which he seeks to attain.* Hence, if he is offered certain outcomes which meet this criterion of congruency or balance, he will seek to attain it, but if they do not, whether they are too low or too high, the outcomes will not serve as a motivating variable and performance will not be adjusted to achieve it. Furthermore, such behavior seems to occur independently of the kinds of outcomes we are talking of, money or otherwise, as Table 1 indicates. In this table we have summarized some of the studies which seem to support this point of view.

This point of view seems to suggest that the opportunity to make more money, a motivational variable assumed to be highly important and convenient across the major, if not all, segments of the working population, will not operate as an incentive to performance at all if the person does not feel that the additional income is deserved by him and is "in balance" with his capabilities for the situation. In this very important sense, then, as Table 1 indicates, the mainsprings to work motivation come not from the chance to make more money but rather from the opinions of self vis-à-vis the work situation and one's own self-perceived competence concerning the tasks to be performed. If these are high and if the individual believes himself to be extremely able in the situation, then the high rates of money to be earned by high performance will be sought because such high income denotes high performance, which is in balance with the person's high opinion of himself concerning the job. On the other hand, a person with a low opinion of himself will not seek the high rates of income since these rates indicate high performance; an outcome not in balance with the person's low opinion of his qualifications. Hence, the effectiveness of an incentive plan might be an indirect measure of how high work motivation already is in the organization, rather than being a cause of it.

Does this mean that management cannot use money to increase performance? The answer is that they can, but perhaps in a different way than previously thought. Consider our statement that a person is motivated to perform at those levels which are consistent with his self-perceived competence for the job. Where does such self-perceived competence come from? Obviously, it is a function of a person's life

Table 1

Major Findings	Investigator
1) Women of high self-esteem are more likely to engage in behavior designed to achieve stated goals than those of low self-esteem	Denmark and Guttentag (1967)
2) Individuals of high self-esteem are more likely to choose occupations where they think they have abilities than those of low self-esteem	Korman (1967, 1966)
3) Negro performance is positively correlated with expectancy of success in the given situation	Katz (1964)
4) Individuals of low self-esteem are less likely to achieve difficult self-set goals than high self-esteem individuals setting the same goals	Korman (1968a)
5) Individuals whose self-perceived competence for a task has been experimentally manipulated will decrease performance in order to match these self-conceptions	Aronson and Carlsmith (1963)
6) When rewards on a piece-rate basis are higher than an individual expects to get on the basis of previous performance, he adjusts his behavior downward and decreases his performance	Adams and Rosenbaum (1962); Andrews (1967)
7) Individuals of low self-evaluation seek less reward for a given task than those of high self-evaluation	Pepitone (1964)
8) Individuals in psychological laboratories and clinical situations seek levels of reward which are appropriate and congruent with the level that they are used to, i.e., which meet their Social Reinforcement Standard (S.R.S.)	Baron (1966)
9) Experimentally manipulated self-perceived ability on tasks is correlated with later performance on those tasks, with this holding true both for laboratory and field situations	Feather and Saville (1967); Kaufman (1962); Friedman and Goodman (1967)
10) High self-esteem sales career choice individuals see themselves as having greater initiative, interaction orientation, and need for job freedom than high self-esteem accounting career choices but these differences do not exist for low self-esteem sales and accounting career choice individuals	Korman (1966)
11) High self-esteem individuals see less discrepancy between self-perceived needs and the needs to be satisfied by their career choice than do low self-esteem individuals	Oppenheimer (1965); Korman (1966)
12) There is a correlation between need-fulfillment discrepancy and (a) job satisfaction and (b) turnover for high self-esteem individuals, but not for low	Korman (1968c)
13) There is a high positive correlation between task success and task liking for high self-esteem individuals, but not for low. This is particularly true if the task has some desirability attached to it	Korman (1968b)
14) Attraction toward an evaluator of one's ability depends on the degree to which the evaluator agrees with his (the evaluatee's) own conception of his ability, whether positive or negative	Deutsch and Solomon (1959); Howard and Berkowitz (1958); Wilson (1965)

experiences and the social interaction he has with others. Elsewhere (Korman 1968a) we have suggested that a person's self-perceived competence for a particular job or task may be divided conceptually into three aspects (although these may be, and probably are, related empirically):

a) *Chronic self-perceived competence* is a person's general overall feeling of self-esteem and belief in the quality of his abilities; this has some tendency to generalize over different situations.

b) *Task-specific self-perceived competence* stems from a person's specific learning experiences and from the recognition that no matter how generally high or low he is, there are almost always some tasks he is better in than others.

c) *Socially-influenced self-perceived competence* results from the fact that our opinions about ourselves and other social objects are very much influenced by the people around us and their opinions. To a considerable extent (never completely), what they come to value the individual values, and what they come to dislike he comes to dislike. Such tendencies toward uniformity stem from the need to avoid anxiety by developing a "real and accurate" picture of the world, a need satisfied by physical experience for physical objects, but which is determined by the guidelines offered by other people when the object of evaluation is some social object.

It is in this latter aspect that we can see the primary mechanism for utilizing compensation policies as influences on performance when such policies are weekly (or monthly or annual) assessments of value. Such assessments are *evaluations of social value,* that is, they constitute a measure of the organization's opinion of the person's value, competence, and the like. Such opinions are then internalized by the individual, becoming part of his self-perceived competence, and he becomes motivated to act in a way which is consistent with this picture of himself vis-à-vis the job. To the extent, then, that such compensation policies result in a more favorable self-evaluation on the part of the individual, to that extent we should predict a higher level of performance (including a greater receptivity to incentives if these were, for some reason, introduced). To the extent that the reverse were the case, then, of course, we would predict a lower level of performance.

The basic model would be: increase the person's self-evaluation through compensation policies and thus increase the motivation to perform. How would this be done in the actual operating situation? A quick glance indicates, not surprisingly, that much of the evidence for this approach, while sound empirically, is based on experiments that have little similarity to the actual operating questions faced in day-to-day compensation administration. Thus the translation of this approach into the realities of the business organization and how it may best be accomplished is still a matter for further research and much questioning. To indicate some of the problems involved, it might be useful to suggest some questions concerning the conditions under which the predictions about the model might be most likely to be effective. However, while each of the following questions, when tested, probably will have significant practical benefits, it is clear that these are only a few of the questions to be resolved before a final assessment can be made of the value of this model for increasing performance.

Question One: With total amount of money held constant, will an increase in compensation in high-status areas (such as stock-purchase plans) have a greater positive effect on performance than an increase in compensation in low-status areas (such as health insurance plans)?

Question Two: With total amount of money held constant, will an increase in compensation based solely on the judgment of the superior have more of an effect on performance than an increase in compensation based at least partially on threats on the part of the subordinate?

Question Three: All other things being equal, will a higher salary lead to higher self-perceived competence, and higher performance? (It should be noted here that all other things are rarely equal and that, not infrequently, an organization may use high salaries as a way of compensating for other gross environmental deficiencies which detract from performance.)

Question Four: With total amount of money held constant, will an increase in compensation which has visible, public effects and which will be seen by the recipient's peers have greater performance effects than an increase which does not have such visibility? (Such differential effectiveness may be hypothesized to come mainly from the changed social evaluation which the person will receive from his peers.)

What Are the Factors That Determine the Extent to Which We Will Compensate and/or Reward Others?

The problem we now will deal with stems from the simple observation that the assigning of rewards to others, most obviously in the form of compensation, is, despite the constraints of market wage comparisons, wage evaluation schemes, and the like, very much an arbitrary subjective decision. Furthermore, this essential element of subjectivity is much more the case at the managerial level than at the worker level, since, in the former situation, there are rarely, if ever, "hard" pieces of physical output to guide such rewards and evaluations. In other words, the assigning of rewards to others and the factors that influence them are, to a great extent and even within the constraints of overall policy, essentially subjective, psychological processes and, hence, subject to the same types of analyses undertaken for other psychological processes.

The only problem is that we have almost no information on this question. While there have been a few studies (cf. Bass 1968), these have been quite minor in nature and have such methodological flaws as unrealistic settings, simple problems, and so on. Hence, we still know almost nothing at all about such questions as:

1) Are some people more likely to reward others? If so, what are they like and what are their characteristics?

2) Is the tendency to reward others general over different kinds of reward situations? Are those who are most likely to give money also those who are most likely to promote?

3) Are some organizations more concerned with rewarding their members than others? If so, what are their characteristics? Does this relate to organizational performance?

4) What are the effects of such variables as "liking" and "similarity" between the reward-giver and the recipient on the amount and kind of reward which is given?

What Makes a Person Satisfied with His Pay?

There are two reasons why the question of pay satisfaction is of major importance from the viewpoint of the organization. First, people who are satisfied behave differently from those who are not satisfied; they are absent less frequently, they are less likely to leave, and, under some conditions, they are likely to perform better. Second, from the viewpoint of the broader community which exercises a constraint on the operations of the organization, it is better to have satisfied than dissatisfied employees.

What makes a person satisfied with his pay? Probably the only way to answer this question would be to have a good theoretical framework as to why people are satisfied with their jobs in general. For a time it appeared the Herzberg notions were going to provide such a framework, but it seems clear by now that this is not to be the case. The findings of Herzberg and his students are much too contaminated by methodological flaws and sheer illogical reasoning (Whitsett and Winston 1967) for this theory to remain a serious contender for attention.

There are, however, some good hypotheses being given increasing attention as theories of job satisfaction, and perhaps it is among these we might find the framework we need. These newer hypotheses come from the work of several investigators, but, in essence, they probably can be summarized as two kinds of theories:

 a) Need-fulfillment theories. These theories predict that people find satisfaction to the extent that jobs fulfill personal needs; in the area of pay, such a theory would predict that pay would be positively evaluated to the extent that it leads to personal need fulfillment and negatively evaluated to the extent that it does not.
 b) Reference-group theories. This group of theories predicts that people will evaluate the pay of a job positively to the extent that it meets the requirements of the social groups the individual looks to for guidance in defining "social reality"; it will be evaluated negatively to the extent that it does not meet those requirements.

While both of these theories have received considerable empirical support, many questions remain to be answered before we can make accurate predictions about pay satisfactions.

 Probably the most important of these questions is how to integrate the two approaches so that in cases of conflict between the two we can predict which will be more salient. More simply, the question is when will a person pay attention to his own desires when evaluating his outcomes (e.g., pay) rather than to the group? Korman (1968*b*) has suggested that a person with high self-esteem will pay attention to both himself and the group, whereas an individual of low self-esteem will pay attention only to the group. The low self-esteem person, in the interests of achieving a "balanced" outcome, learns to ignore his own desires since achievement of these would be incongruous with low self-esteem. However, the evidence for Korman's hypothesis is not as yet very impressive, although there has been a recent independent replication of this work (Berger 1968).

 A second problem is that given the importance of the reference-group for guidance in evaluating one's outcomes, how does one choose a reference-group? Which groups does a person choose to guide him in evaluation? Does he change his reference groups, and if so, how? How do such choices vary as a function of personal characteristics and/or environmental characteristics? While we have much evidence that reference-groups exist and are of crucial importance in determining social evaluation, we do not have evidence on how they are chosen. Consider an executive, forty-two years old, who earns $30,000 a year and lives in a $45,000 house in a suburb of New

York City. Whom does he utilize as a guide in helping him evaluate his salary—the $25,000-a-year executive in the next office, his $20,000-a-year assistant, the $40,000-a-year neighbor, or his $15,000-a-year brother who lives in the next, slightly less affluent suburb? What is the influence of general societal changes in affluence on his evaluation of his salary? Which of these comparisons does he choose? Can we make any systematic statements about such choice and the ways in which such choice might change over time? These and other similar questions are not answerable at this time, although Lawler (1965) has provided some beginnings toward answering them.

Do people who are satisfied with their pay act differently than those who are satisfied with other aspects of their job? In this last major question we are posing the following situation:

Ratings of Satisfaction with:

	Pay	Supervisor	Company	Coworker
Individual A	6.0	8.0	8.0	8.0
Individual B	8.0	6.0	8.0	8.0

The question is, given that B is more satisfied with his pay than A, less satisfied with his supervisor, and they are equal in other aspects, will he behave any differently? Is it more important in terms of implications for job behavior to be more satisfied with certain aspects of a job than with others?

So far as we know this question has never been put to empirical test, although it seems apparent that some meaningful differential predictions could be made, which, if supported, would pose important practical implications. For example, what would be some of the implications of a high and personally satisfying salary? Would the following be a reasonable hypothesis?

Could the same chart of implications be drawn for Individual A? Probably not, and certainly not one which would predict as clear external visibility of satisfaction with its possible feedback into on-the-job behavior.

It would appear that this type of question seems well worth investigating. While it is clear that general overall feelings about job satisfaction are very important, these feelings can be differentiated according to specific job components with possible differing consequences for behavior.

REFERENCES

ADAMS, J. C., AND ROSENBAUM, W. B. 1962. The relationship of worker productivity to cognitive dissonance about wage inequities. *Journal of Applied Psychology* 46: 161-64.

ANDREWS, I. R. 1967. Wage inequity and job performance: An experimental study. *Journal of Applied Psychology* 51:39-45.

ARONSON. E., AND CARLSMITH, J. M. 1962. Performance expectancy as a determinant of actual performance, *Journal of Abnormal and Social Psychology* 65: 178-82.

BARON, R. M. 1965. Social reinforcement effects as a function of social reinforcement history. *Psychological Review* 73: 527-39.

BASS, B. 1968. Ability, values, and concepts of equitable salary increase in exercise compensation. *Journal of Applied Psychology* 52: 299-303.

DENMARK, F., AND GUTTENTAG, M. 1967. Dissonance in the self-concepts and educational concepts of college and non-college oriented women. *Journal of Counseling Psychology* 14:113-15.

DEUTSCH, M., AND SOLOMAN, L. 1959. Reactions to evaluations of others as influenced by self-evaluation. *Sociometry* 22: 93-112.

FEATHER, N., AND SAVILLE, R. 1967. Effects of amount of prior success and failure on expectations of success and subsequent task performance. *Journal of Personality and Social Psychology* 5: 226-32.

FRIEDMAN, A., AND GOODMAN, P. 1967. Wage inequity, self-qualifications, and productivity. *Organizational Behavior and Human Performance* 2: 406-17.

HOWARD, I., AND BERKOWITZ, L. 1959. Reactions to the evaluators of one's performance. *Journal of Personality* 26: 494-507.

KATZ, I. 1964. Review of evidence relating to effects of desegregation on the intellectual performance of Negroes. *American Psychologist* 19: 381-99.

KAUFMAN, H. 1963. Task performance and responses to failure as functions of imbalance in the self-concept. *Psychological Monographs* 77: Whole No. 569.

KORMAN, A. K. 1966. Self-esteem variable in vocational choice. *Journal of Applied Psychology* 50: 479-86.

———. 1967a. Self-esteem as a moderator of the relationship between self-perceived abilities and vocational choice. *Journal of Applied Psychology* 51: 65-67.

———. 1967b. Ethical judgments, self-perceptions and vocational choice. Paper presented at the 1967 meeting of the American Psychological Association, Washington, D. C.

————. 1967. Relevance of personal need satisfaction for over-all satisfaction as a function of self-esteem. *Journal of Applied Psychology* 51: 533-38.

————. 1968a. Self-esteem, social influence and task performance. Paper presented at the 1968 meeting of the American Psychological Association, San Francisco, California.

————. In press b.Task success, task popularity and self-esteem as influences on task liking. *Journal of Applied Psychology.*

OPPENHEIMER, E. 1965. A self-concept approach to predicting occupational preferences. *American Psychologist* 20: 475-76.

OPSAHL, R., AND DUNNETTE, M. 1966. The role of financial compensation in industrial motivation. *Psychological Bulletin* 63: 94-118.

PEPITONE, A. 1964. *Attraction and hostility.* New York: Atherton Press, Inc.

WHITSETT AND WINSLOW. 1967. An analysis of studies critical of the motivation-hygiene theory. *Personnel Psychology* 20: 391-416.

WILSON, D. 1965. Ability evaluation, post-decision dissonance and co-worker attractiveness. *Journal of Personality and Social Psychology* 1: 486-89.

32

Manager Motivation and Money

ARCH PATTON

At a recent meeting with a major corporate client, one of my partners reviewed the pros and cons of several solutions to a particularly complex problem involving a long-established executive incentive plan. The next day at lunch, the client president remarked to me, "You know, Arch, we had considered most of the points your associate made about our incentive program, but his presentation yesterday was what clinched the decision for me. I was particularly impressed by the way he nailed down every one of his arguments for or against the various alternatives with a pertinent example from a client situation. I suppose you could call it the instinctive practicability of experience."

Having only a vicarious—and limited—exposure to the theories underlying executive motivation developed by behavioral scientists, it is this "practicability of experience" that I propose to draw on for my remarks. In nearly two decades spent in helping to resolve the executive compensation problems of some 250 companies, I have observed that some approaches to management motivation seem to work, while others do not. The theory to which I am most firmly committed is that my clients should do more of the one and less of the other.

To sharpen the focus of these comments, perhaps some background would be useful. Between now and 1974, the number of men in the thirty-five to forty-five age group will decline by eight percent. This means that one million fewer potential executives in a critically

Printed by permission of the author. Paper delivered at the McKinsey Seminar on Managerial Motivation and Compensation, Tarrytown, New York, 1967.

important age bracket will be available in the mid-1970s than there are today to provide the energy and dynamism needed in an increasingly competitive and complex business environment.

At the same time, industry's requirements for qualified men in this key age group promise to expand at an unusually rapid rate. Quite apart from the demand generated by sheer economic growth, business organizations are becoming increasingly complex. The proliferation of staff functions, such as computer systems groups, is one manifestation of this. As more and more people are being involved in decisions—more and more people are needed; as the quantitative demand increases, so do the quality requirements. We need only look at the market for staff specialists with advanced degrees in technical subjects to see that talent scarcity already is "the name of the game."

This is only the business side of the picture. When we look at the demand from nonbusiness sources for executive types in the thirty-five to forty-five age group, we find it growing even more rapidly than industry's needs. With their increasing appetite for executive manpower, governmental units—federal, state, and local—as well as educational institutions, hospitals, and other service-type organizations of all kinds will be competing strenuously with industry for a diminishing pool of critical human resources. I have come to believe that the *single* most important management problem of the 1970s will be this shortage of leadership talent. To my mind, it foreshadows many significant changes that must occur in managerial habits during the years ahead.

It is my usual practice in writing on problems of executive compensation administration to assume the role of a reporter observing the practices of leading corporations. For example, my article in the *Harvard Business Review* reports on some current measures companies are taking to cope with future executive manpower shortages. In this article, however, I will give you some pure Patton, my own assessment of the key factors that will be shaping executive motivation efforts in the early 1970s. My projections necessarily are based on the "practicability of experience" as reflected in my personal observations of the state of the motivational art today. Hopefully, these will provide a reasonable framework for considering the administrative approaches that will be needed in some future tomorrow.

ENVIRONMENT

The *New York Times* recently reported that NASA had transferred to Washington, as something called "deputy associate administrator," the executive directly in charge of the tragic Apollo launch test in which three astronauts lost their lives. Does such action signify penalty or reward? Does it tell all concerned in the NASA hierarchy that mistakes will be penalized? Or does it say that a comfortable berth will be found for poor performers?

The directors of New York's Consolidated Edison recently reached into the government to find a new chief executive for the company. The retiring chairman's sole public justification for this course of action was that he and the president were only a year or so apart in age. What effect did the fact that directors permitted this to happen have on executive morale? Is this why no inside candidate was available?

A young man I know, fresh from one of our leading graduate business schools, recently turned down a job offer from the financial vice-president of a billion-dollar company. Later he told me: "That vice-president's office was really a shock to me. It was actually less attractive than the one I had last year on a summer job with a medium-sized chemical concern. If that's the kind of working environment they provide for their senior executives, I figure that people can't rank very high as a corporate asset in top management's scheme of things." Could this young man have put his finger on one of the reasons this company's market share has dropped from 27 to 20 percent in less than six years?

The point of these vignettes is to demonstrate that environment—physical and psychological—can be a crucial factor in the success of an enterprise. If our young man had turned his nose up at the scraggly living quarters of a small, struggling company, he could be accused of reacting to the wrong evidence. Xerox, I'm sure, once had scraggly quarters. The best companies, like the best people, take pride in their homes.

The space salesmen of *Time* magazine, widely regarded as the best in their industry, are paid well above the market. The reason for this was explained to me by a top *Time* executive. He said, "We look on it as insurance—insurance that our people won't worry about small extra expenses or time commitments that help close a sale." In my experience, the leading companies in most industries follow a similar philosophy. They project, perhaps unconsciously, an image of success, and their employees absorb the élan that comes from being associated with success.

I have focused on environment at the outset because I am convinced that the effectiveness of efforts to sharpen executive motivation is *largely* determined by environmental factors. Environment, of course, is the product of a wide range of management actions: the types of people recruited into the organization, the skill with which salary and bonus are administered, the promotion process, the dynamism of the company's growth process, and the personality of the chief executive, among others. I also am fairly well convinced that the importance of environment as a factor in executive motivation frequently is overlooked because it is obscured by the history of events affecting the enterprise, the accident of top management succession, and the myopic executive viewpoint that results from organizational inbreeding. Environment is the sum total of all the elements that make up an organization's way of life. It is a forest that is often hard to recognize because of the multitude of administrative trees that it contains.

Furthermore, environment is important because it is so hard to change. Ten years ago I worked with a large, international company that had an advanced case of "civil service-itis." A new chief executive came on the scene determined to build a more competitive environment. A decade later, the company climate clearly has been changed for the better, but the chief executive is frustrated to find that the gains made by his company are about on a par with those of competitors. The fact is that his leadership effort has been inadequate to do more than keep pace with a moving target. Real environmental change, such as Harold Geneen has achieved at ITT, requires a willingness to uproot comfortable habit patterns.

More importantly, perhaps, environmental change usually necessitates alterations in many interdependent activities within an organization. What frequently is called "resistance to change" often is little more than inadequate execution: having authorized a change in one area, management fails to take steps to change habit patterns in interdependent areas. For example, a major chain decided to upgrade its image from "price-type" outlet to "fashion-type" retailer. Unfortunately, although they upgraded the merchandise in the stores and their advertising, management neglected such equally important related steps as improving store appearance, upgrading the quality of help in the stores, providing better customer service, and the like. Needless to say, there was great resistance to change, in this case on the part of customers!

Environment in the average company reflects not only the competitive needs of the industry but the cumulative impact of the leadership characteristics of its recent chief executives. Environment only rarely has been consciously developed to meet a need. In my view, the growing executive shortage will necessitate a more conscious effort by companies to exploit the subtle, but considerable, strengths to be found in environment.

RECRUITING

Any effort to influence environment certainly starts with recruiting. It makes little sense to hire creative individualists into a routine business, or to bring low-achievers into an organization that requires high-achievers for success. Nevertheless, industry's recruiting habits are expensively hit-or-miss. A company executive will tell you that it costs $10,000 to recruit and train each college man he hires, yet this same executive has no idea what to do about the fact that more than half of these recruits leave in a year or two, and the better half at that. It would not be so serious if the company simply were eliminating the poorest recruits; but, more typically, the best men are deciding to leave for better jobs elsewhere.

Relatively few companies have a consciously thought-out recruiting program that is expected to provide the management skills it will need even five years ahead. The average company simply looks for people who meet today's needs as it conceives of them, which, usually, are yesterday's needs. Many well-run companies fall far short of meeting today's demands. It is not at all unusual for a company which normally recruits 200 college and business school graduates each year to stop recruiting entirely during a period of low profits. Rather than use such a period to weed out a few score misfits hired earlier, the company penalizes the future by retaining these marginal people and cutting off the flow of potentially above-average management candidates. Many a company finds itself obliged to recruit a senior executive from outside today because of such a ridiculous hiring policy fifteen or twenty years ago.

In my view, the next few years will see real progress in recruiting. For example, as a company's long-range planning activity improves, it will be increasingly possible to identify and quantify the skills needed in the future. A mathematical model of a company's manpower and skills requirements can be built, allowing for such factors as turnover, death, and retirement. In addition, it will be more practicable than it is today to identify the mix of personal attributes, such as aggressiveness, creativity, discipline, and so on, that will produce optimum performance in particular organizations. Most companies today regard such qualities as "personal chemistry" and make little effort to isolate and evaluate them in the college recruiting effort. Yet, in the final analysis, these attributes make the difference between success and failure for the individual.

The hiring of outside executive talent is becoming less and less a satisfactory alternative to inadequate college recruiting. In the first place, the wolves are beginning to outnumber the sheep in this struggle, which means the wolves run the risk of getting hurt too! Furthermore, the quality of available executive talent is declining, for the best men usually have been skimmed off the top by earlier recruiters. Perhaps the most critical disadvantage of the outside recruiting route is its inordinately high (and rising) cost. One reason for this expense, of course, is that the premium offered the newly hired executive tends to increase the entire executive pay structure. As my later comments on executive compensation will indicate, the developing "fast-track" approach for top performing executives' pay levels will make most outside hiring prohibitively expensive. In other words, the top-quality executive will command an unrealistically high price, in view of the effect of his pay on the total compensation structure.

COMPENSATION

Having reviewed the executive compensation programs of a good many large companies, I can only conclude that very few yield outstanding motivational leverage. The problem invariably lies in administration. The average top management rarely understands the real, operational differences between good and bad compensation administration, and, as a result, conservatism is the byword.

For example, it is common to find a 10 percent merit increase awarded an outstanding performer, compared with a median merit award of 7 percent and perhaps 5½ percent for the relatively poor performer. The compression stemming from such a course of action over a period of time is often compounded by giving the outstanding man a relatively small, merit-sized promotional increase. Carried far enough, this latter practice has been known to put rapidly promoted men in jobs valued at 25-30 percent below the market, while lesser men at the same responsibility level, receiving no promotions, but frequent merit increases, end up being paid above the relative market value of their jobs.

Even bonus payments often tend to reflect this same shortsighted conservatism! Reward usually is tempered ("We don't want to push him *too* high"), and penalty receives even less critical attention ("We might as well fire him as eliminate his bonus"). It is almost as though management did not appreciate the incentive value involved in having the executive understand that outstanding performance will be rewarded accordingly, and poor performance will be penalized. (Unless penalty is involved, of course, reward loses much of its incentive value.) It is fair to say that this conservatism in compensation administration is at least partly due to management's dissatisfaction with its own ability to accurately appraise the performance of executives. Enough progress has recently been made in this area, however, to relieve much of this uncertainty and significantly improve administration.

In my opinion, the talent shortage is certain to force some major changes in compensation administration. One of the most important changes I foresee bears on the early identification of what might be called the "fast-track" man. For years, companies have sought to develop an early-warning system to identify tomorrow's top executives, but until quite recently few have recognized the need for a substantially better-than-average pay pattern geared to this high talent. The emerging "fast-track" concept clearly is to be reckoned with in executive compensation administration in the very near future. An example will explain the rationale for this belief. The compensation record of three classes of a well-known business school, graduating about five years apart, shows identical 100 percent increases in median pay during the first five years out of school. Pay doubled again during the second five-year period. In the first decade out of school, the average man in each of these three classes quadrupled his compensation.

Doubling of pay in five years is equivalent to a compound increase rate of 15 percent, a very steep rate indeed compared with the 4-5 percent upward drift of hourly and top-management pay. If this rate of gain were limited to this single group of men, we might regard it as a freak, but I have checked the rate of gain indicated for the top decile—the "fast-track boys"—in several good companies and found approximately the same increase rate of 15 percent, compounded annually. Admittedly, the facts to date underlying the figures noted here are fragmentary, but I doubt that they are misleading. There is other evidence to support the "fast-track" thesis that outstanding men advance at about 15 percent annually up to age thirty-five.

A study made by my firm last year, for example, indicated that among
the top executives in the average company, that is, the top-paid 0.5
percent of all employees, the best performing 20 percent are promoted approximately once every two years. At a lower organizational
level, of course, the promotion rate should be even more rapid. Taking
this promotion rate and normal merit increases into account, the
generalization of a compounded 15 percent gain rate for the "fast-
track" becomes increasingly persuasive.

Let us look, for example, at a twenty-five-year-old from one of the
graduate schools who starts today at $10,000. If he is on the fast track,
his pay progress will be as follows:

1st year	10 percent merit	$11,000
2nd year	10 percent merit 15 percent promotion	$13,750
3rd year	no merit no promotion	$13,750
4th year	10 percent merit 20 percent promotion	$17,875
5th year	10 percent merit	$19,662

Having doubled his pay in the first five years, this man will advance
to the $40,000 level by his thirty-fifth birthday. Present evidence
points to a slowing down in the advance during the third five-year
period, as individuals begin to "plateau out" and the S curve begins
to flatten the compensation pattern.

The mere fact that a $40,000 pay level is attained by age thirty-five
cannot help but create serious compensation problems all along the
line. For example, the starting level for graduate school students in
recent years has been rising about twice as fast as the average company's compensation structure. As a result, considerable compression
of salary levels is found in the average company among those five
to ten years out of school. Furthermore, $40,000 at age thirty-five will
be approaching the pay level of executives with much greater experience who are doing adequate, perhaps even excellent, work. Since
the age-pay relationship at the executive level normally increases at
a compound annual rate of 5 to 7 percent, the pressure that the fast-
track man exerts on the total compensation structure can hardly fail to

force top management to far greater discrimination in administering its executive payroll. The very substantial cost differential between the 5-7 percent "normal track," and the 15 percent "fast track" will surely sharpen management's awareness of the risk involved in poor administration. If top men are paid too far below the "fast track," they are likely to be hired away; if the "normal track," which involves a much larger total payroll than the "fast track," is permitted to float up toward the latter, a very major expense increase will result with little to show for it.

In my view, an increasing recognition of the fast-track concept will have several important side effects. It will compel top management to concentrate more attention on the outstanding performer, and it will provide a better yardstick to determine what such performance is worth. This will greatly aid the discrimination process by giving management a top-side compensation bench mark that heretofore has been lacking. Most top executives have been unduly conservative because they did not have a reasonable yardstick for putting dollar values on their judgments of individual performance. In the future we can anticipate a more confident value discrimination among performers, and a consequent widening of the spread between outstanding and average.

The shortage of executives surely will drive up the price management is willing to pay for top talent. At the same time, it will put high priority on the development of a sounder basis for evaluating executive quality. As all of us know, present executive compensation survey methods leave a good deal to be desired. They focus on the average and ignore the extremes, which reflect someone's judgment of executive quality. They give more weight to job title than to the incumbent's ability to influence top-management action.

One of the silliest, and most expensive, surveys in my recent experience was one designed, in effect, to keep the pay of a field organization 10 percent above its competition. Somewhere along the line, someone in the personnel department decided that if a 10 percent margin over competition was good, perhaps 15 percent was better, and maybe 20 percent would be better yet. Once having arrived at this conclusion, little effort was required to decide that low-pay competitors should be dropped from the survey, and regional areas expanded to ensure the inclusion of the highest paid competitors. As a result of their myopic survey approach, this company's field organization was being paid 19 percent above its actual competition, a figure involving several million wasted dollars.

The penalties for sloppy executive pricing are multiplying rapidly, and I believe that better yardsticks are entirely possible. Future surveys will be obliged to take age, experience, and work quality into account. It seems a little ridiculous to eliminate from the pricing of an executive's value his most important contribution, influence over critical corporate decisions, simply because it is difficult to judge, yet this is the rationale upon which today's pricing is done. It goes without saying, I suppose, that someone's judgment will be a critical ingredient in the surveys of the future, but I submit we no longer can afford to leave these judgments to the vagaries of simple arithmetic.

Increasing awareness of the "fast track" for outstanding men in industry will have the effect, I think, of stimulating the use of executive bonus plans. Theoretically, it is easier to discriminate among performers through bonus payments than through salary, for bonus reductions are more acceptable than salary cuts. If a bonus plan is to be effective, of course, an upgrading of the performance appraisal process usually is necessary to provide a credible basis for discriminating among executives.

Promotion

It will be noted in the example cited above that promotion was a sizable component in the upward thrust of our "fast-track" man, accounting for about half of his pay increase over five years. In a very real sense, the ability of an employer to promote his top talent will affect his ability to attract and retain this increasingly scarce commodity in the years ahead. Promotion is, by all odds, the primary incentive at the disposal of management. The company that has more of this motivational adrenaline available than its competitor has a consequent advantage. A comparative study my firm recently made of two companies in the same industry, one notably more aggressive and profitable than the other, showed that the first of these companies promoted its middle-management executives on an average of once every twenty-three months, while promotions in the second company averaged one in every forty-seven months. Clearly, more than coincidence was involved in this correlation.

The potency of promotion as an executive motivator argues strongly for conscious management action designed to make a company grow, thereby offering more promotional opportunities to its executives. I think it is fair to conclude that internal growth provides more promotion opportunities than would normally be expected of growth by acquisition, except when the acquiring company is in a mature industry and the acquisition is in a growth industry. Sheer organizational changes may provide promotional opportunities similar to those created by growth. I am not referring here to the insertion of group executives between the president and the division heads, or to having the treasurer and controller report to a newly designated financial vice-president. This does make more top jobs available, adding to the promotion potential of the company, and, in some cases, it probably is necessary. However, as I will point out later, the talent shortage of the future is going to make top management think twice about creating new executive positions simply to provide promotional opportunity.

The organizational change I am referring to is of a different sort. One of the main motivational values in a new job, aside from status and money, is the challenge and excitement of doing something new. A number of companies I have worked with are constantly reorganizing their activities, which means that individual executives are moving into new jobs with some frequency. The new job may not be in a higher grade, but a salary increase goes with the move and the internal value system regards it as a promotion. The fact that it is so regarded by the executive group is what makes it a real promotion in the eyes of the reassigned executive. This continuous realignment of executive responsibilities generates the same kind of internal excitement that we find in many growth companies. When well handled, it seems to say to the individual executive, "Things are happening here!" And people like to be where the action is.

The lateral promotion is quite different, but has two advantages that I believe will be more widely recognized in the future. The first is that a lateral move, when it is a normal part of a company's way of life, has some of the built-in excitement value noted in organization shifts. The man has a new job to master; if he is like most of us, he finds this exciting in itself. But the lateral promotion has another important value as a training and developmental device. As the talent shortage worsens, companies increasingly are realizing how important it is to consciously manage the careers of their employees. This requires not only a knowledge of the skills needed to handle functional positions, but an understanding of the demonstrated aptitudes and interests of individuals. In this matching of job requirements and the individual's skills, the lateral promotion helps to provide needed experience to enable an individual to advance to greater responsibility.

ORGANIZATION

While promotion is the most powerful motivation in management's arsenal, there is another that I believe will grow in importance as the executive shortage intensifies. I am referring to the incentive each of us finds in having a demanding job to do for which we are individually responsible.

After World War II, two occurrences seriously undermined this motivation. The one with which we are most familiar is the proliferation of staff jobs, spawned by industry's growing complexity. One by one, these new staff functions whittled away at the established decision-making process of the line organizations. This internecine power struggle usually reached a stalemate in which responsibility increasingly was shared, and the accountability of the individual blurred correspondingly. Inevitably, the effect was to reduce the individual's sense of responsibility for any particular action. The second postwar phenomenon that choked off job-based motivation was the unusually high level of business activity, which resulted in the attempt by many companies to stockpile people. As could have been anticipated, this action led to a further reduction in individual responsibilities when management sought to spread the work in an overstaffed organization.

In more recent years, individual companies, finding their profits squeezed, have taken steps to tidy up their organizations. The petroleum industry, for instance, went through a major shake-out in 1958 when both its growth rate and price structure slumped. However, industry generally has been in a major boom for a long time, and it is very likely that considerable fat exists in the average organization structure. In my view, the talent shortage inevitably will lead to major changes in the way most companies are organized. By and large, such reorganization is long overdue: the average company of today actually is structured to meet the conditions of five or ten years ago. This situation simply reflects the fact that organizational changes are among the most difficult of all to effect, because the individuals involved fear that any change, however innocuous, may hurt them personally.

There are two more important reasons why reorganization will be the order of the day for most companies well into the 1970s. First, a reduction of the number of executives needed for the key money-making functions of the business would offset the talent shortage; second, enlargement and clarification of individual executive performance responsibilities would enhance job motivation.

Obviously, I am not suggesting that companies are about to reorganize capable executives out of their jobs today in order to be ready for the talent shortage of tomorrow. Going on a crash diet is hardly a sensible way to prepare for a famine. What I am suggesting is that in the course of time, as executive job slots are opened up by retirement and turnover, management increasingly will see the wisdom of closing certain slots by restructuring responsibilities rather than seeking to fill them with new bodies from a dwindling pool of increasingly costly executive talent. Such restructuring, of course, automatically will enlarge the remaining jobs, broadening their scope, increasing their importance, and enhancing the motivation and job satisfaction of the individual executives who perform them.

Roy Ash, the president of Litton Industries, recently expressed his concern about current organizational approaches in these terms:

We like our executives to stand exposed to their prospective success or failure individually, rather than as an indistinguishable part of a functionalized crowd. For as a company grows more functionalized, everybody holds everybody else up, so you can't tell when one fellow is held up entirely by the crowd around him.

I think that is a statement all managers, and consultants, for that matter, well might hang in large type over their desks. In too many companies today, too many people are being held up by the crowd around them. It goes without saying that the more important any decision is to the company's economic well-being, the bigger the crowds. The bigger the crowd, the more nebulous is the responsibility of the individual and, in many instances, the less effective the decision. This is one more major reason why I believe that an era of organizational restructuring is long overdue.

Top management, I predict, eventually will come to realize that organization review must start with the basics. How does the company make money in the business it is in? What are the leverage points? And by whom should the money-making decisions be made? The company's activities need to be taken apart and examined in terms of the decisions to be made, and the actions required, to make a profit. Think how rarely the concerns you know best have so analyzed their activities in recent years.

Having examined the decision-making process in detail, it then is possible not only to organize the key activities to make more money today, but also to take a realistic reading on the relative value of the various kinds of decisions that must be made in the business. Too often, the value of responsibilities for decision influence has been permitted to float up to the level of decision making. I will venture a second prediction at this point: Such an organization study should remove the fuzz that now envelops so many executive jobs. When job responsibilities are clarified, two things are likely to happen. First, considerable overlapping of responsibilities will become apparent, making it possible either to add responsibilities or to reduce bodies. Second, whichever step is taken, the remaining executives will have clear-cut and enlarged job responsibilities, and, as a result, greater job interest.

My final prediction is more of a hope. I believe the shortage of top-notch talent will be sufficiently onerous to disenchant top management with some of the so-called principles of organization that restrict the value of the individual to his company. There are, of course, some valid reasons for the nice, tidy little boxes on our organization charts. However, individuals are different, and simply because one treasurer had the credit function in his portfolio is no reason the next one should, or vice versa. Similarly, one sales manager may have a talent for picking district sales managers, whereas the next one may not, or, again, vice versa. The point I am making is that with the growth of the "functionalized crowds," approaches to organization have become increasingly stylized. My hope is that the reorganization process I foresee will come full circle to the old-time verities; namely, the recognition of the individual as the critical factor in how activities are organized.

33

The Role of Money in Managing Motivation

DAVID C. McCLELLAND

For forty-five years, industrial psychologists have been demonstrating that money isn't nearly as potent a motivating force as theory and common sense suggest it should be. Elton Mayo's 1922 study of work output in a Philadelphia textile mill set the tone of what was to follow. Management had found that incentive payment schemes had not succeeded in increasing work or decreasing turnover in a department where the jobs were particularly monotonous and fatiguing. Mayo found, on the other hand, that allowing the men to schedule the work for themselves brought dramatic increases in productivity. Where money incentives had not proven effective, psychic rewards worked (cf. Gellerman, 1963). Over and over again later students of industrial psychology were to emphasize the same point: Money isn't everything; it won't even buy everything that is in first place. Likert and his Michigan colleagues (1959) argued that the needs of employees must be taken into account. Foremen who are employee-centered are more successful in maintaining high work output than foreman who are production-centered. All supervisory practices, including incentive schemes, should be shaped to fit the needs of particular men working under particular conditions. Herzberg (1959), too, emphasized the importance to workers of such psychic factors as having control over their work and relegated money to the position of a possible source of dissatisfaction rather than of real satisfaction. That is, money could motivate only by its absence. Whyte (1955)

Printed by permission of the author. Paper delivered at the McKinsey Seminar on Managerial Motivation and Compensation, Tarrytown, New York, 1967.

reported that very few workers were, in fact, really motivated by incentive schemes, that is, motivated enough to become "rate busters." On the contrary, most workers were more interested in the opinions of others and in having a safe, tolerable job than they were in the immediate short-run gains to be derived from working harder to get a particular money pay-off. McGregor (1960) argued persuasively that even thinking about attempting to control other people's behavior by financial lures represents "Theory X," an approach which regards human beings essentially as puppets to be manipulated. In contrast, he stressed the virtues of "Theory Y," the basis for a management system which takes everyone's needs into account along with the requirements of a production schedule.

All of these theorists seem to be making much the same point in different ways: it is scientifically useless to isolate money as if it were an important or even a key variable in motivating people to work. The meaning of money is in the eye of the beholder. The context in which incentive plans are offered makes all the difference. Psychological factors in the situation are more important than the money itself, or, to put it another way, the money functions only as a symbol representing psychological realities. Yet, after reviewing all these studies, Gellerman concludes, "Myths die hard. It is quite clear that money's reputation as the ultimate motivator is going to be a long time a-dying" (1963, p. 64).

Why, in spite of all this evidence and argument, do people still take money seriously as a motivator? Even Gellerman, after reviewing all the evidence, concludes that "obviously" money is very important, and Opsahl and Dunnette note "that money has been and continues to be the primary means of rewarding and modifying human behavior in industry" (1966, p. 94). There is, of course, a strong basis in reality for this continuing interest: work, unless it is volunteer or "play," involves a contract between two parties guaranteed by the payment of money. The pay may symbolize the psychological realities of the contract imperfectly, which is all the psychologists may be saying. That is, talking about money as a motivator represents a kind of misplaced concreteness. The employee may think he is working for it, and the manager may think he is using it to get the employee to work, but both are only partly right. If one is to understand the situation better, particularly if he wishes to manage motivation or behavior, he must penetrate beyond the money itself to what it really represents to employer and employee. The money payment may be regarded as a convenient symbol to both parties so long as they do not mistake it for all of the reality it represents.

But it is not just man's tendency to reify symbols that leads him to talk as if money were an end in itself. There are at least three other reasons why he does so. In the first place, psychologists have not helped matters any by speaking of money as if it were a secondary or substitute reward. They refer proudly to an experimental demonstration by Wolfe over thirty years ago (1936) that chimpanzees can be taught to use poker chips to get things they want, that is, just as if the poker chips were money. In fact, there is nothing particularly startling about this part of the experiment because chimps will also use sticks to get things that they want, but sticks don't look like money. So the use of poker chips gained more public attention for this part of the demonstration than it really deserved theoretically. However, some of the chimps would work hard to get the poker chips just the way they would work to get a grape or an orange. From this psychologists have concluded that the chips had "substitute reward" value of their own. They could be used to motivate behavior directly, albeit not very well.

From here it was an easy step to assume that the chimpanzee's smarter relative, *homo sapiens,* would be even more capable of detaching such symbolic rewards from what they represented so that in time man would come to work for money for its own sake. There is some sleight of hand in the reasoning here which is easy to expose. It is safe to infer that no chimpanzee ever considered a poker chip a subsititue for a grape for the very simple reason that he could not eat it. All that can be concluded from such experiments is that the poker chips got woven into a means-ends associative chain in the chimp's mind which led to satisfaction. This puts looking for poker chips in the same category for a chimpanzee as expending effort to work at disentangling a mechanical puzzle (Harlow 1953). Both are learned activities linked with pleasure or with getting the chimp's attention. Neither is a substitute reward, properly speaking. One seems to be because it involves manipulating small, round (but inedible) objects.

But old theories die hard. The real villain in the piece is the notion that in the end all learning is based on a few simple material rewards. No idea is more deeply entrenched in contemporary American psychology. I suspect that practically all top managers today learned as a basic fact in Psychology I in college that there are so-called primary material rewards, such as food and water, and that all other rewards are "secondary," getting their "motivating value" from learned associations with the primaries, just as the poker chips got associated with the grapes. Money obviously falls into the category of a secondary reward. This notion, like most preliminary scientific generalizations, involves some major misconceptions, but it has persisted because the alternatives to it are hard to formulate so simplistically.

Let me state flatly that there is no reason at all why men interested in managing motivation should continue to have their thinking shaped by this misconception. Alternatives to this could be outlined, but they would take us far afield. A quick analogy will have to serve to illustrate an alternative, because if I do not provide one, the poker chip model of how money gets its reward value will undermine what I have to say later on. Think of what goes on in a man's mind as if it were a computer print-out of a lot of miscellaneous material. In common sense terms, a number of thoughts buzz through a man's head at any given period in time. As anyone knows who has tried to do content analysis of computer print-outs, the periods or other punctuation marks are of key importance. That is, if you are to search and simplify what is otherwise a bewildering mass of material, it is necessary first to break it up into units within which co-occurrences can be noted. In real life, rewards or incentives are like punctuation marks. They break up sequences or call attention to them. They are attention-getting, set-forming, effect-producing mechanisms (rather than substitutes for something else). As such they obviously are tremendously important in producing organization or order in thought and action, but note that they are only one possible type of attention-getting mechanism. Bright lights and colors, changes in rest periods, reorganizations of work flow—all sorts of things—can also get attention and therefore belong in the same theoretical class as money. Obviously these ideas would have to be spelled out much further to make solid theoretical sense, but my purpose will have been accomplished if I have broken the set of assuming that money is some kind of a substitute for simpler material rewards. It is rather more like *one* of a class of attention getters, and, like other members of its class, it can lose its power to get attention with repetition (see Kagan 1967).

There is a second reason why managers continue to think that money is a prime motivator which has nothing to do with reading about chimps using poker chips in an undergraduate psychology course. Most managers are high in n Achievement (see McClelland 1961) and we know that for men with high n Ach, money rewards have a special significance. They believe in greater financial rewards for increasing accomplishment. Of course, everyone believes that there should be more pay for more difficult work, but for those with high n Ach the rate of increase in reward proposed for harder work is steeper than for those with low n Ach (study by Litwin, see McClelland 1961, p. 236). The reason is that men with high n Ach are particularly interested in some concrete measure that will sensitively reflect how well they have done. However, it is easy and natural for them to mistake this idea for a related one—namely, that the more money you offer, the harder someone will work. Certainly, as Opsahl and Dunnette point out (1966, p. 105), many studies have shown that managers rank pay as a more important incentive factor than workers do.

There is an obvious fallacy in this reasoning which is not only logical but also psychological. Believing in more pay for more work is simply not the same as saying that more pay will *lead* to more work. Other evidence shows clearly, if somewhat paradoxically, that men with high *n* Ach are not spurred on to greater efforts when offered money incentives (see Atkinson and Reitman 1956, or Smith 1966). While they think money is more important than other incentives, it does not motivate them to work harder! The explanation apparently is that money rewards give them the knowledge of how well they are doing and are not sought for their own sake. As Gellerman points out, the incentive value of top executive salaries must lie primarily in their merit badge quality, since high taxes result in rather minor differences in take-home pay at this level of compensation. So managers believe money is important in motivating others because they mistakenly think it motivates themselves. While it *is* more important to them as a measure of accomplishment, it does not motivate them, properly speaking, and it does not motivate others either, except indirectly, as workers and others are ready to point out whenever they are asked.

The final reason why managers regard money as a way of motivating people is because at the practical level it is the one thing they can manipulate rather easily. After all, it is part of their role responsibility to *do* something to motivate the people working for them, to get more work out of people, or, at the very least, to make sure that people are not loafing. The higher their achievement motivation, the more they will want to show an improvement in the quality or quantity of the work done under their general responsibility. They may listen patiently to the psychologists and sociologists who convince them that money is not important for its own sake, but what can they do to change those other psychological factors that supposedly are more important? Payment plans are real and manipulable; plans for dealing with psychological factors often seem not to be. Is it true that all these theorists are concluding that the nature of incentive plans makes *no* difference? It is one thing to say that psychological factors will modify how incentive plans work; it is quite another to conclude that variations in the nature of incentive plans do not make any difference.

What is needed is a change in orientation. The problem is managing motivation, not managing work but the desire of men to work. Incentive plans must be seen not as the primary way of accomplishing this end but as a particular means of accomplishing particular objectives within a larger framework. Therefore we must start with this larger framework and put payment plans in their place within it. Following Litwin and Stringer (1967), we note that a work situation involves four sets of variables which must be accurately diagnosed before a prescription can be written for improvement: (a) the motives and needs of the persons working at the task, (b) the motivational requirements of the task they have to perform, (c) the motives (or strengths and limitations) of the manager, and (d) the organizational climate.

For someone interested in managing motivation in a particular situation, it is first necessary to determine his position on all four sets of variables. Litwin and Stringer have developed measurement techniques for them. Once a manager knows where he stands on these variables, he is in a position to do various things. For example, if he finds that most of his workers are high in *n* Ach and yet the tasks to be performed are assembly line tasks which do not require *n* Ach, he has an obvious mismatch. He can hire a different type of worker or change the nature of the task. Either method should produce better performance by getting people into a situation in which the task requires what they are interested in. But our focus here is a narrower one: specifically it is on how payment plans, as one of management's tools, can be used to help motivate men, given different settings on these four types of variables. All we can do is give illustrations, since it is obvious that there can be no simple, sovereign payment system that will work best for all people under all conditions.

Variations in motives of the "to be managed." Whether workers or managers are high or low in *n* Ach makes a real difference in the effectiveness of financial incentives. Several studies have shown (Atkinson and Reitman 1956; Atkinson 1958; and Smith 1966) that offering additional financial rewards for doing a task does not make people with high *n* Ach work harder or better. On the other hand, it does elicit more work from people with low *n* Ach. For salesmen with high *n* Ach, for example, it is important to recognize that offering them bonuses for extra effort is not what produces the extra effort; yet they would be angry if their extra effort were not recognized with a much greater reward. This may seem like a psychological difference that makes no difference, but the interpretation of the meaning of the bonus plan genuinely affects performance, as an example to be given below will show.

While it is true that people with low n Ach will work harder for increased financial rewards, it is important to note that it is not the task itself that interests them, as in the case of the person with high n Ach. Rather, the money which doing the task brings them has other values for them. Two consequences flow from this simple fact: first, if there is any way to get the reward without doing the work, they will naturally tend to look for it. This means that management which relies primarily on money to activate people with low n Ach will have a much harder job of policing the work situation than if the work satisfied other motives which they do have. Such a conclusion is certainly not news to managers who have struggled with employee incentive plans over the past generation. The second implication is that the employee will have to want something that the money can buy. Obviously, there are lots of important things that money cannot buy, such as tolerable working conditions, friendship, and job security. As a number of studies have shown, even the material possessions that most middle-class managers assume everyone wants, such as a home of one's own, are, in fact, not wanted by many of the people they are trying to motivate. It follows that if a manager must deal largely in financial incentives for people with low n Ach, he will have to give some thought to creating "psychological wants" that money will satisfy—such as more education for children, a happier retirement, a more exciting (and expensive) vacation, and the like.

Money can also be important to people with high n Affiliation or high n Power. Atkinson and Reitman (1958) found, somewhat to their surprise, in their multi-incentive condition that when money prizes for work were offered, the girls with high n Affiliation actually did more work than girls with low n Affiliation, whereas there had been no difference between the two types of girls when the extra incentives were not offered. They concluded that the money was part of creating a general expectancy on the part of the subjects that they should work hard to please the experimenter. The moral again is simple: if a manager finds that his working force is high in n Affiliation, incentive plans should be offered in the context of working to please others or working together for the common good, not, as managers with high n Ach nearly always assume, working for one's own gain.

Finally, Winter (1967) has found that college students with high n Power spend more money on prestige supplies, that is, on more expensive liquor, college insignia, powerful motorcycles or cars, and so forth; in other words, on things which will make them feel or seem big, strong, powerful, and respected. If a manager finds his staff is high in *n* Power, he then should administer his financial incentives in different ways, perhaps even presenting some of them in the form of prestige supplies—such as a trip to Europe or a new Cadillac—for an especially outstanding performance. If there is one simple lesson to be learned from all these studies, it is that the motivational characteristics of the staff make a lot of difference. What will motivate a person with high or low *n* Ach will not necessarily motivate a person with high *n* Power or high *n* Aff. Even though the cost of an incentive is identical, its form and meaning have to be shaped to fit the needs of the people it is supposed to influence.

Variations in the motivational requirements of tasks. Litwin and Stringer (1967) have suggested some simple measuring devices for the motivational requirements of different tasks. For instance, they show how the job of an assembly-line worker has more affiliation than achievement elements because workers must interact with each other; successful task accomplishment depends on the cooperation of co-workers, stable working relationships over time are required, and so forth. How can incentive plans help if this is the case? Actually they can mostly hinder, because most incentive plans are based on the assumption that all tasks primarily involve achievement. Thus, as Whyte and others have complained, such plans in fact usually make less than 10 percent of the people into "rate-busters" and make the rest of the work force angry because the extra incentives reinforce behavior which is in direct opposition to the affiliation requirements of the task. Such "gung-ho" achievers often disrupt normal working patterns and lower average productivity in the long run. Management has made the simple mistake of assuming that all tasks are best thought of exclusively in achievement terms.

Even at the sales level this can be true. While, generally speaking, successful salesmen are high in *n* Ach, relatively low in *n* Aff, and high in *n* Power, Litwin and Timmons (1966) have identified at least one sales situation in which the very best salesmen are only moderately high in *n* Ach, quite a bit higher than normal in *n* Aff for salesmen, and lower in *n* Power. A job analysis explained the reason. These particular salesmen were involved in a task which required "a much greater emphasis on coordinating the efforts of the sales and service function, and on building long-term, close customer relationships involving a high degree of trust, than on entrepreneurial selling." Here an incentive plan based on simple gains in sales could easily attract the wrong men (those with high *n* Ach) into sales or influence existing salesmen to neglect the long-term customer relationships which experience shows are necessary for success in this job. Money payments have to fit not only the characteristics of the people in a work force but also the nature of the jobs they have to perform.

Variations in the motives of the manager. Much of what has been said stresses the importance to the manager of understanding his own motives. Otherwise he may project onto others what *he* wants. It is all too easy for a manager, in making plans for other people, to assume they are like himself. If he knows what he wants, he may be able to avoid falling into the trap. He may even be able to recognize that his own incentive plan may lead him to propose new ideas that have little promise of success. I have sometimes wondered how many personnel managers think up new incentive plans in order to convince *their* superiors that they are high achievers, deserving of a special bonus. Actually, a personnel man should be specially rewarded for picking and keeping outstanding men, but such day-to-day performance may be less promptly noticeable and rewardable than a brand new incentive plan. Here again, the pay system may not take into account sufficiently the fact that the personnel job cannot be transformed into, and rewarded as, a straightforward achievement proposition without distorting what the personnel manager should be spending his time trying to do.

Beyond such considerations, a manager must understand himself well enough to know what he can or should do, given the diagnosis of the organizational situation arrived at above. Thus he may discover that while his staff is heavily affiliation-oriented and therefore wants and needs many signs of approval and friendship, he himself is rather aloof, priding himself that he got where he is today by not wasting time with "the boys." Understanding himself should help him create the kind of climate that will make the incentive system work given the conditions under which it is operating.

Variations in climate. Litwin and Stringer (1967) have identified some nine different dimensions on which organizational climates can vary. Each of these variables is hypothesized to have different effects on the motivations of people working in the organization. For example, the degree of *structure* (rules, regulations, going through channels) should reduce *n* Ach and *n* Aff, but increase *n* Power. That is, since the organization emphasizes power and control, it should make its employees more power-oriented. Similarly, the degree of risk or challenge of the tasks to be performed should arouse *n* Ach, but have little or no effect on n Aff and n Power. Let us first consider a case which shows the effects of these climatic factors when the incentive system is held constant. Litwin and Timmons (1966) contrasted four outstanding sales offices with four average sales offices, not only in terms of climate differences as perceived by the salesmen, but also in terms of actual observations of how managers interacted with their men during the day. The incentive system in all offices was the same and men in the outstanding and the average offices were equally satisfied with it.

Yet other climate variables apparently made for very different performance averages, as Table 1 shows. The outstanding offices were perceived as having more structure, as evoking more identity and loyalty, and as being warmer and friendlier. The salesmen from these outstanding offices also felt that higher standards were being set, and that they were more often rewarded by the manager for their efforts rather than criticised for non-performance. Their views were substantiated by observation of managers in the two types of offices. Those from the outstanding offices gave almost double the amount of non-monetary reward as the managers from the average offices:

For example, the outstanding manager makes it a habit to compliment a man sincerely on a job well done; a personal thank you is always given over the phone and in person. He might also drop the man a note of congratulations and thanks for a successful sale. He also typically thanks the customer in the same manner and makes a real effort to visit the new installation with the salesman and compliments the salesman's efforts before the customer. In contrast, the average manager's attitude is that 'these men are on very large commissions and that's what makes them hustle. They know they can go out on any day of the week and get a raise just by selling another piece of equipment. Oh, I *might* buy them a drink, but it's money that motivates these guys' (Litwin and Timmons 1966, p. 13).

So once again we have confirmation of the fact that non-financial climatic factors are important, but with a difference. At least Litwin and Stringer have begun to spell out *in detail* the kinds of things managers *can* do (other than change payment plans) that will make a difference in performance. Furthermore, we have a nice illustration of how too exclusive a concern for money can distract a manager's attention from the other psychological climate variables that he should be taking into account.

Nevertheless, these are not the key questions under consideration. What is needed are studies in which climate factors are controlled and incentive plans are varied. It is no use repeating over and over that it

Table 1

Summary of Perceived Climate Differences in Outstanding and Average Sales Offices

Climate Scale	Percentile Scores			p Value (t tests, N=T 59)
	Outstanding	Average	Difference	
Structure	54	28	26	.01
Identity and loyalty	61	19	42	.005
Warmth and friendliness	53	22	31	.05
High standards	42	16	26	.01
Risk and challenge	54	30	24	--
Responsibility	63	48	15	--
Reward vs. punishment	49	24	25	.005
Support and encouragement	49	30	19	.10
Acceptance of conflict	63	50	13	--

(From Litwin and Timmons 1966)

all depends on the way in which financial plans are perceived. The only way one can find out if variations in the incentive plan really make any difference is to hold the perception of them constant by controlling climate variables and then checking to see if variations in them make a difference. Unfortunately, to my knowledge, no such studies have been made. Earlier studies of incentive variations have almost certainly varied climate variables at the same time, since it is only recently that we have begun to understand how to measure climate variables and have therefore been in a position to hold them constant. So what follows is speculation. It is based on some theory and laboratory research, but controlled field studies of these variables obviously need to be made before one can be very confident about the generalizations made. What are the variables to be taken into account in the incentive plan itself, assuming climatic variables are held constant?

Probability of success. Atkinson has argued extensively (1958, 1966) both for theoretical and empirical reasons that moderate probabilities of success produce better performance than either very low or very high probabilities of success. In general, he has shown that a person who has one chance in two of getting a reward will work harder than if he has a lower or higher probability of getting it, regardless of the level of his achievement motivation or the size of the money incentive (Atkinson 1958, p. 296). In a large sample consisting of boys from Brazil, Japan, and Germany, McClelland (1961, p. 218) confirmed the fact that students will work harder when the odds are lower than $3/4$ although the exact odds which produced maximum effort varied from country to country. Animal studies also show that greater effort is forthcoming if the certainty of getting a reward is less than 100 percent. The generalization seems very likely to hold for financial incentive plans, although the optimum probability for winning a special reward obviously would need to be worked out for each particular situation. Atkinson's estimate that it is somewhere around the one chance in two level is not a bad place to start.

Two further facts are known about this phenomenon. First, individuals with high n Ach work harder under somewhat longer odds (Atkinson 1958; McClelland 1961). Generally speaking, they work best when the odds for winning are as slim as one in three, or even longer. Thus, obviously a skillful manager should have one set of odds of winning for an incentive plan involving salesmen with high n Ach and another set of odds, perhaps, for a group of clerical workers who are low in n Ach. Second, it is known that the perceived probability of success changes with experience. In fact, this is the explanation commonly given as the reason why people with high n Ach work better under somewhat longer odds than the average person. They know from past experience, presumably, that they tend to be more successful than the average person in tasks they undertake. Therefore, what to the outside observer is a one-in-three chance of winning for an average worker is correctly perceived by a person with high n Ach as a one-in-two chance for him.

Many of the difficulties inherent in incentive plans flow from the fact that experience changes the perceived probability of success. Suppose a salesman or a worker exposed to a new incentive plan works extra hard and gets a special bonus. What does he do in the next time period? He may notice that many other people have made it, and, if he makes it again, he may fear that management will increase the normal work quota. Management, on its side, may wonder how it can keep the perceived probability of success at the optimal level without raising standards as individuals get better at their jobs. Theory suggests that because experience changes perceived probability of success, plans would have to be changed regularly in order to keep expectancies of winning at an optimal level for producing performance. Yet most managers are unhappy if incentive plans eventually stop working. It may be sounder for them to develop the expectancy that the plans will have to keep changing in order to stand still, motivationally speaking.

Size of incentive. When Atkinson offered his college students $2.50 for the best performance, they solved more arithmetic problems than when he offered them only $1.25, again regardless of their level of achievement motivation or the odds under which they were attempting to win the prize (1958, p. 293). Obviously size of reward makes a difference. Just as obviously *size* is a relative term—relative, that is, to one's own starting point and to what other people are getting. Five hundred dollars is much more of an incentive to a man who earns $5,000 annually than to a man who earns $50,000 annually. Almost certainly some psychological function is involved such that the increment in money necessary to create a "just noticeable incentive" is some kind of constant fraction of the base, but to my knowledge the function has never been worked out for field situations. It probably would be easier to work out in the context of recruiting people for jobs because in that case the effect of additional pay incentives is more obvious than when they are offered to a man for increased work in a given setting. Laboratory studies of the utility of money (cf. Mosteller and Nogee 1951) probably are a poor guide to the psychophysical function involved because the amounts of money dealt with are so small and the work situations so trivial or unrelated to life performance.

As Opsahl and Dunnette point out (1966), many authors recently have turned their attention to how large a man perceives an incentive to be in comparison not with his own starting level, but with what other people like him are getting. Here, oddly enough, the yardstick seems to be more absolute than relative. That is, $500 may not seem like much of an incentive to a man earning $50,000 relative to his past earnings, but it could become an important incentive if it puts him clearly ahead of another person against whom he sees himself competing. The research questions to be answered here are obvious: "just noticeable incentives" should be worked out for different levels of hourly, monthly, and annual pay scales as a function of own starting level and the level of others with whom the person compares himself.

One other finding relates to size of incentive. In two studies, notably one reported in *The Achieving Society* (1961, p. 269), executives receiving middle level compensation are higher in *n* Ach than those receiving very low compensation or very high compensation. The data are hard to interpret with any certainty but they are suggestive. One can infer that the executives with relatively low compensation (here less then $20,000 a year) are those who in this age range (35-50) just haven't "made it." They are less successful, lower in *n* Ach and less rewarded. But how can we explain the fact that those who received high compensation (here $25,000 a year and up) also have lower n Ach? What is intriguing of course is the suggestion that too much financial reward may lower motivation to achieve.

It is true that older men (who may also get higher salaries) tend to slack off in n Ach, but in this study age was controlled. It may also be, of course, that other motives are necessary for performing really well once one has reached the very top. High n Ach may be more necessary just to get to the top. At any rate, the same curvilinear relationship is found in society. It is those in the middle class "on the way up" who have the highest average n Ach, whereas those from lower and upper class backgrounds have less n Ach (Rosen 1959). This result might be interpreted as meaning that very large financial rewards decrease n Ach on the average, perhaps not because they satisfy so many needs in the traditional sense, but because they are powerful distractors that lead people to get interested in other things. The possibility that very large rewards decrease motivation deserves further investigation.

Nature of the response-reward tie-in. There are a multitude of relatively uninvestigated variables relating to the response-reward tie-in. Presumably a financial reward is offered or given for some behavior or change in behavior. Even in seniority systems where a man gets more pay as he grows older, the tacit assumption is that with greater experience on the job he is wiser and doing the job better, even though it would be impractical to try to measure in exactly what ways he is performing better. This suggests the first variable in the situation—the specified degree of definiteness of the response for which the reward is to be given. In general, the supposition is that the more the expected response is specified, the greater the incentive value of the reward offered for the simple reason that if a person does not know what he is supposed to do to earn the reward, he is obviously going to be less able to do it. In some jobs specificity is relatively easy to define (for example, selling); in others it is quite difficult, as in the case of the personnel manager mentioned earlier. Even in sales, questions can arise as to whether individuals have been fairly assigned to particular territories. Does everyone feel he has started from the same opportunity baseline? Nevertheless, most successful incentive plans would seem to involve quite specific goal setting worked out in advance by manager and staff member with as much specificity as possible about how he will know he is achieving his goal.

In specifying the response for which the reward is offered mistakes can easily be made; two types are most common. In one the manager assumes that the task primarily involves work output and specifies the responses expected in those terms. Yet a careful job analysis would show that other factors are important in success. A case in point are the sales offices mentioned above studied by Litwin and Timmons in which too heavy an emphasis on selling interfered with service functions and actually produced lower performance. In the second type of error, the manager may believe, because it is part of his business ideology, that he is rewarding better performance from his staff when in fact he is giving rewards primarily for other characteristics such as loyalty to him or "not being a troublemaker." Andrews (1967) has reported an interesting comparative study of two large business organizations in Mexico. In Company A, where rewards were clearly given for better performance, he found that men with high *n* Ach got significantly more raises over a three-year period than men with low *n* Ach. However, in Company P, where men were highly regarded if they were loyal to the boss and stayed in line, those with high *n* Power were more often promoted. Company A was growing much more rapidly than Company P, yet when asked, the president of Company P said that he certainly was interested in better performance in his top executives and in fact wondered why his company was not growing faster. He did not realize, although his subordinates did readily enough, that he was in fact dispensing financial rewards primarily for their loyalty to him.

Another important characteristic of the response for which the reward is offered is whether it is to be a group or individual response. Should incentives be pro-rated on the basis of group performance, as in profit sharing plans, or given for individual performance? No easy generalization is as yet available in this area, although everyone agrees that each work situation should be carefully analyzed to see which type of performance is most appropriate to reward in a given case. Obviously, for example, when the staff is high in *n* Aff and the job requires much interpersonal cooperation, some kind of group incentive plan would be more appropriate than one rewarding individual excellence.

It is necessary not only to define the response but to decide on the delay between the response and reward. Should the tie-in be immediate? Most studies of lower animals in simple learning situations suggest that the shorter the delay the greater the incentive value of the reward. This could lead to "atomizing" of expected improved responses so that a person could accumulate points every time he showed a better response, the points to be totalled and cashed in for money at regular intervals. How often should bonus review be held—monthly, semiannually, or annually? The ease or difficulty of making the measurements necessary to decide on whether a reward has been earned will almost certainly decide how often and how immediately such rewards can be given. Generally speaking, variations in timing of this sort are probably of less importance than other variables already mentioned, since most adults, and certainly managers, are able to work for rewards deferred at least a month and often a year or longer.

In summary, then, money is just one tool among many for managing motivation. It is a dangerous tool because it is so misleadingly concrete that it seduces many managers into neglecting the climate variables that really affect productivity. In the near future there will be less and less excuse for neglecting climate variables as the behavioral sciences begin to define them and to explain how they can be manipulated in ways which in time should prove as easy as changing a financial compensation plan. In their proper perspective as part of the overall management framework, incentive plans will continue to play an important role. But first the manager must diagnose the needs of his staff, the motivational requirements of their jobs, his own motives, and the climate of the present organizational set-up. Then he can plan rationally how to improve productivity by improving the climate, by developing certain motives in key people, by making a better match between the needs of the people and the needs of the job, or, finally, by incentive plans that are specifically geared to the diagnosis of the organizational situation. Such a view is consistent with newer theories of psychological incentives which consider them as part of attention-getting cognitive structures rather than as substitutes for material rewards.

REFERENCES

ANDREWS, J. D. W. In press. The achievement motive in two types of organizations. *Journal of Personality and Social Psychology.*

ATKINSON J. W. 1958. Towards experimental analysis of human motivation in terms of motives, expectancies, and incentives. In *Motives in fantasy, action and society,* ed. J. W. Atkinson, pp. 288-305. Princeton, N. J.: Van Nostrand.

———, ed. 1958. *Motives in fantasy, action and society.* Princeton, N. J.: Van Nostrand.

ATKINSON, J. W., AND FEATHER, N. T., eds. 1966. *A theory of achievement motivation.* New York: Wiley.

ATKINSON, J. W., AND REITMAN, W. R. 1956. Performance as a function of motive strength. *Journal of Abnormal and Social Psychology* 53: 361-66.

GELLERMAN, S. W. 1963. *Motivation and productivity.* New York: American Management Association.

HARLOW, H. 1953. Mice, monkeys, men and motives. *Psychological Review* 60: 23-32.

HERZBERG, F.; MAUSNER, B; AND SNYDERMAN, B. 1959. *The motivation to work.* 2d ed. New York: Wiley.

KAGAN, J. 1967. On the need for relativism. *American Psychologist* 22: 131-42.

LIKERT, R. 1959. A motivational approach to a modified theory of organization and management. In *Modern organization theory,* ed. M. Haire. New York: Wiley.

LITWIN, G. H., AND STRINGER, R. A. In press. *Motivation and organization climate.* Cambridge, Mass.: Harvard University Press.

LITWIN, G. H., AND TIMMONS, J. A. 1966. *Motivation and organization climate: A study of outstanding and average sales offices.* Boston, Mass.: Behavioral Sciences Center.

MCCLELLAND, D. C. 1961. *The achieving society.* Princeton, N. J.: Van Nostrand.

MCGREGOR, D. 1960. *The human side of enterprise.* New York: McGraw-Hill.

MOSTELLER, F., AND NOGEE, P. 1951. An experimental measurement of utility. *Journal of Political Economy* 59: 371-404.

OPSAHL, R. L., AND DUNNETTE, M. D. 1966. The role of financial compensation in industrial motivation. *Psychological Bulletin* 66: 94-118.

ROSEN, B. C. 1959. Race, ethnicity, and the achievement syndrome. *American Sociological Review* 24: 47-60.